Transfer of Undertakings

Employment Law Handbook

Previous edition 2007

Incomes Data Services Ltd
Finsbury Tower, 103-105 Bunhill Row, London EC1Y 8LZ
Tel: 0845 077 2911 Fax: 020 7393 8081
Website: www.incomesdata.co.uk

ISBN 978 0 414 02983 5

IDS Employment Law Handbook, 'Transfer of Undertakings', is published by Incomes Data Services Limited (Registered in England & Wales, Company No 913794. Registered Office and address for service: 100 Avenue Road, London NW3 3PF).

The information contained in this journal in not intended to be a substitute for specific legal advice and readers should obtain advice from a qualified adviser in relation to individual transactions or matters.

No natural forests were destroyed to make this product: only farmed timber was used and re-planted.

A CIP catalogue record for this book is available from the British Library.

Typeset by DC Graphic Design, Swanley Village, Kent BR8 7PA
Printed by St Austell Printing Co, 41 Truro Road, St Austell, Cornwall PL25 5JE

Transfer of Undertakings

Employment Law Handbook

MARCH 2011

IDS

Contents

4 Unfair dismissal

Abbreviations

Courts

ECJ	European Court of Justice
ECHR	European Court of Human Rights
PC	Privy Council
HL	House of Lords
CA	Court of Appeal
Ct Sess	Court of Session
NICA	Northern Ireland Court of Appeal
QBD	Queen's Bench Division
Div Ct	(Queen's Bench) Divisional Court
KBD	King's Bench Division
ChD	Chancery Division
NIRC	National Industrial Relations Court
EAT	Employment Appeal Tribunal
ET	Employment Tribunal

Case references

AC	Law Reports, Appeal Cases
All ER	All England Law Reports
Ch	Law Reports, Chancery Division
CMLR	Common Market Law Reports
COET	Employment Tribunal folio number
EAT	Employment Appeal Tribunal unreported case number
ECR	European Case Reports
ET	Employment Tribunal unreported case number
EWCA	Court of Appeal unreported case number
ICR	Industrial Cases Reports
IRLR	Industrial Relations Law Reports
ITR	Industrial Tribunal Reports
KB	Law Reports, King's Bench Division
QB	Law Reports, Queen's Bench Division
SCOET	Scottish Employment Tribunal folio number
TLR	Times Law Reports
WLR	Weekly Law Reports

Legislation

DDA	Disability Discrimination Act 1995
EA	Employment Act 2002
EqA	Equality Act 2010
EqA 2006	Equality Act 2006
EqPA	Equal Pay Act 1970
ERA	Employment Rights Act 1996
ETA	Employment Tribunals Act 1996
RRA	Race Relations Act 1976
SDA	Sex Discrimination Act 1975
TULR(C)A	Trade Union and Labour Relations (Consolidation) Act 1992

Statutory references, unless otherwise stated, are to the Transfer of Undertakings (Protection of Employment) Regulations 2006 SI 2006/246.

Many cases in this Handbook were decided under the Transfer of Undertakings (Protection of Employment) Regulations 1981 SI 1981/1794, which preceded the 2006 Regulations. However, wherever possible, reference is made to the corresponding provision in the later Regulations and not to their antecedents in the repealed legislation.

Introduction

When a business is sold by one employer to another, or the responsibility for providing a service transfers from one employer to another, the question arises as to what happens to the dedicated workforce. Do the employees concerned have the right to work for the new employer? And, if so, do they retain the contractual and other employment rights that they enjoyed prior to the transfer? These are the main issues with which the Transfer of Undertakings (Protection of Employment) Regulations 2006 SI 2006/246 (the 2006 Regulations) – the focus of this Handbook – are concerned.

Below, we explain the context in which the 2006 Regulations appeared, highlight the main differences between the Regulations and their previous incarnation, and provide a chapter-by-chapter breakdown of what this Handbook covers.

Background

In 1977 rules appeared at European level requiring the United Kingdom to legislate to protect employees affected by business transfers. These were set out in EC Council Directive No.77/187 'on the approximation of the laws of the Member States relating to the safeguarding of employees' rights in the event of transfers of undertakings, businesses or parts of businesses', which, following amendments, was reissued in its entirety as EC Council Directive No.2001/23. In essence, the two main objectives of the Acquired Rights Directive (as it is commonly known) are to ensure that when a relevant transfer of a business takes place:

- the contracts of employment of the employees assigned to the business transfer automatically from the 'transferor' (the old employer) to the 'transferee' (the new employer), with their terms and conditions intact

- both the transferor and the transferee inform and consult with representatives of those of their respective employees who might be affected by the transfer.

In order to implement the Directive, the UK Government introduced the Transfer of Undertakings (Protection of Employment) Regulations 1981 SI 1981/1794 (the 1981 Regulations). Unfortunately, these Regulations (which became widely known as TUPE) proved extremely difficult to interpret. Indeed, for many years now the question of what might amount to a 'relevant transfer' covered by TUPE has been one of the most perplexing in the employment law arena. Some of the problems in this regard have flowed from the need for the Regulations to be interpreted in the light of the Directive, the scope of which has been obscured somewhat by the European Court of Justice in a series of confusing (and in some instances confused) judgments.

i

The requirement to update TUPE to implement the 2001 version of the Acquired Rights Directive, together with a power contained in S.38 of the Employment Relations Act 1999 to provide increased TUPE protection, presented the Government with an opportunity to bring some clarity to this complex area of law. However, this was not an opportunity that gave rise to any great urgency on the Government's part. After an extremely drawn-out process, the Transfer of Undertakings (Protection of Employment) Regulations 2006 finally came into force on 6 April 2006, nearly five years after the deadline for implementing the new Directive passed.

Changes brought about by the 2006 Regulations

The 2006 Regulations contain a number of changes from the previous TUPE regime, which are explored at length in the main body of this Handbook. Those familiar with the old rules should note the following significant developments:

- Regulation 3 goes beyond the Directive's requirements to bring the vast majority of service provision changes (that is, changes of service provider resulting from outsourcing, insourcing and re-tendering exercises) within TUPE's scope. In redefining the concept of 'relevant transfer' for TUPE purposes, Reg 3 is aimed at achieving the Government's ideal, as expressed in the consultation document published in March 2005, that everyone involved in a service provision change 'should know where they stand... so that employers can plan effectively in a climate of fair competition and affected employees are protected as a matter of course'

- Regulation 4 clarifies the general circumstances in which a transferee employer is entitled to agree a variation to a transferred employee's terms and conditions of employment to the employee's detriment. These are where the variation in question is (i) unconnected with the transfer, or (ii) for a reason connected with the transfer that is an 'economic, technical or organisational reason entailing changes in the workforce'

- Regulations 8 and 9 attempt, by taking advantage of two methods set out in the Directive, to promote a 'rescue culture' by making it easier for insolvent businesses to be transferred to new employers. The first method prevents the insolvent transferor's pre-existing debts towards the affected employees from passing to the transferee. The second enables employers and employee representatives to agree changes to terms and conditions of employment if this is done with a view to ensuring the survival of the business and the preservation of jobs

- Regulation 11 introduces a requirement on the transferor to supply information about transferring employees to the transferee. In doing so, it takes advantage of an option contained in the Directive 'to ensure that the transferor notifies the transferee of all the rights and obligations which will be transferred to the transferee... so far as those rights and obligations are or ought to have been known to the transferor at the time of the transfer'.

Scheme of the Handbook

The scheme of this Handbook is as follows:

- Chapter 1 addresses that most complicated of employment law questions: what is a 'relevant transfer'? It explores the two types of transfer – the standard business transfer and the service provision change – to which the 2006 Regulations will apply

- Chapter 2 considers the matter of who will transfer from the transferor to the transferee. In doing so, it sets out the definition of 'employee' for the purposes of the Regulations; looks at when such an employee will be 'assigned' to the transferring undertaking; and discusses the assigned employees' ability to object to the transfer of their employment

- Chapter 3 details the rights, powers, duties, liabilities, acts and omissions that transfer under TUPE from the transferor to the transferee

- Chapter 4 looks at when a dismissal will be rendered automatically unfair owing to its connection with a relevant transfer, and at when an employer might be able to avoid an automatically unfair dismissal finding by pointing to an 'economic, technical or organisational reason' for dismissal

- Chapter 5 highlights the types of change to terms and conditions that are expressly permitted and expressly prohibited under the 2006 Regulations

- Chapter 6 examines the rules with regard to the transfer of insolvent businesses. In particular, it looks at the specific limitations regarding the transfer of employee debts and liabilities to the transferee where the transferor is subject to certain insolvency proceedings, and the special provision permitting employees' terms and conditions of employment to be varied where the transferor is subject to certain insolvency proceedings

- Chapter 7 discusses the impact of a TUPE transfer on an employee's continuity of employment

- Chapter 8 covers the specific rules in the 2006 Regulations with regard to information and consultation. It looks at both the new duty on the transferor to provide information to the transferee about the employees who are to transfer, and the established duty on both the transferor and the transferee to inform and consult appropriate representatives of employees who may be affected by a relevant transfer

- Chapter 9 considers whether the 2006 Regulations can apply to a transfer from or to the United Kingdom and, if they can, what this might mean in practice. It also broaches the subject of what protection the Regulations might bestow on overseas employees

- Chapter 10 explores some of the practical matters – such as due diligence, warranties and indemnities – that should be considered by those involved in a relevant transfer.

The law is stated as at 1 January 2011. This Handbook completely replaces IDS Employment Law Handbook, 'Transfer of Undertakings' (2007), which should now be discarded.

This publication aims to provide accurate, authoritative, information and comment on the subjects it covers. It is offered to subscribers on the understanding that the publisher is not in business as a lawyer or consultant.

1 Identifying a 'relevant transfer'

Standard transfers

Service provision changes

Insolvency

The public sector

When does the transfer occur?

The Transfer of Undertakings (Protection of Employment) Regulations 2006 **1.1**
SI 2006/246 (TUPE) lay down complex rules dealing with enhanced unfair
dismissal rights, the preservation of transferring employees' terms and
conditions, and the provision of information and consultation. However, none
of these rules will take effect unless a 'relevant transfer' under Reg 3 of the
2006 Regulations occurs.

For many years, the identification of a 'relevant transfer' for TUPE purposes
has been one of the most perplexing matters in the employment law arena.
With regard to service provision changes (SPCs) following outsourcing,
insourcing or re-tendering exercises, the shifting sands of European case law
concerning the application of the EU Acquired Rights Directive (No.77/187)
and its successor (No.2001/23) (the Directive), which TUPE implements in
the United Kingdom, muddied the waters severely. Thankfully, however –
albeit after a long and agonising wait – the UK Government attempted to
end the pervading confusion by making special provision for SPCs in the
2006 Regulations.

While the definition of 'relevant transfer' in Reg 3(1)(a) of the 2006 Regulations **1.2**
simply reflects that of a 'transfer of an undertaking' contained in the Directive
– and hence applies only where the Directive applies – Reg 3(1)(b) goes beyond
the Directive's requirements to bring the vast majority of SPCs within TUPE's
scope. Reg 3(1)(b) is aimed at achieving the Government's ideal, as expressed
in the 2005 Consultation Document, that everyone involved in an SPC 'should
know where they stand... so that employers can plan effectively in a climate of
fair competition and affected employees are protected as a matter of course'.
The upshot is that there are now two different (although not mutually exclusive)
routes by which a 'relevant transfer' covered by TUPE can occur: first, where
the Directive-driven definition, contained in Reg 3(1)(a), is satisfied; and
secondly, where a 'service provision change' as defined by new Reg 3(1)(b)
takes place.

1

In this chapter we examine both these definitions in detail. We then go on to consider, more specifically, when TUPE might apply in insolvency situations and to transfers within the public sector. Finally, we touch on the matter of *when* exactly a relevant transfer can be said to take place – an issue of particular concern where a transfer comprises a series of transactions.

1.3 Standard transfers

Regulation 3(1)(a) provides that the 2006 Regulations apply where there is a 'transfer of an undertaking, business or part of an undertaking or business situated immediately before the transfer in the United Kingdom to another person where there is a transfer of an economic entity which retains its identity'. This wording, which describes what we shall term a 'standard transfer', will be familiar to TUPE aficionados. It reflects the definition of a transfer of an undertaking contained in the EU Acquired Rights Directive, which in turn is based on the extensive case law from the European Court of Justice (ECJ) as to when the transfer rules should take effect.

Breaking Reg 3(1)(a) down, four questions must be answered in the affirmative in order to identify a 'relevant transfer' under that provision:

- was there a transfer 'to another person'?
- did an 'economic entity' transfer?
- did the economic entity 'retain its identity' after the transfer? and
- was that entity 'situated immediately before the transfer in the United Kingdom'?

We examine these questions in turn below.

1.4 Note that, as stated in the introduction to this chapter, outsourcing, insourcing and re-tendering exercises falling outside the traditional Reg 3(1)(a) definition of a relevant transfer will nevertheless be covered by the 2006 Regulations provided they satisfy the new 'service provision change' test set out in Reg 3(1)(b) – see 'Service provision changes' below.

1.5 **Transfer 'to another person'**

With regard to the *method* of transfer, Article 1.1(a) of the Directive states: 'This Directive shall apply to any transfer of an undertaking... *to another employer as a result of a legal transfer or merger*' (our emphasis). Attempting to clarify the Directive in this regard, the 1981 Regulations provided, at Reg 3(2), that 'these Regulations so apply whether the transfer is effected by sale or by some other disposition or by operation of law'. After the 1981 Regulations took effect, however, the ECJ added a considerable amount of meat to the bones of Article 1.1(a), rendering the Reg 3(2) wording otiose. Hence, that

2

wording was not retained in the 2006 Regulations. New Reg 3(1)(a) has nothing to say on the matter other than that TUPE will apply to a 'transfer of an undertaking, business or part of an undertaking or business... *to another person*' (our emphasis).

It has always been accepted that the transfer rules apply to the ordinary sale of a business, conducted between a vendor and a purchaser. However, as we shall see, this is not the only method by which a standard transfer can occur. In fact, keen to promote the purpose of the Directive – which is to safeguard employees' rights upon a change of employer – the ECJ has held that the transfer rules can cover an extremely wide range of events, including the termination of a lease and a change of service provider.

Below, we consider the principles to be applied to determine whether a method of transfer is capable of attracting the application of the Directive, and hence Reg 3(1)(a) of the 2006 Regulations.

Share sales not generally covered. We noted above that Article 1.1(a) of the Directive expressly applies 'to any transfer of an undertaking... *to another employer*' (our emphasis). Although the wording of Reg 3(1)(a) of the 2006 Regulations differs from that of Article 1.1(a), stating as it does that a transfer must be 'to another person' rather than 'to another employer', the DTI's 'Employment rights on the transfer of an undertaking: a guide to the 2006 TUPE Regulations for employees, employers and representatives' (the DTI Guide) clarifies that 'the identity of the employer must change' if a relevant transfer under Reg 3(1)(a) is to take place. **1.6**

It would seem to follow that neither the Directive nor the 2006 Regulations apply, in the normal course of events, to the sale of a company's shares. This is because where a share sale takes place, the identity of the 'employer' – that is, the company that has been sold – remains the same. The change in the *ownership* of the employer brought about by the share sale has no impact in itself on the contractual relations between the employer and its employees. That share sales usually fall outside the scope of TUPE was confirmed by the EAT in Brookes and ors v Borough Care Services Ltd and anor 1998 ICR 1198, EAT. In fact, the Appeal Tribunal in that case went so far as to say that TUPE will not apply to a share sale even where the transaction is designed primarily as a means of avoiding liability under the Regulations.

However, the recent case of Print Factory (London) 1991 Ltd v Millam 2007 ICR 1331, CA, has complicated matters somewhat. The claimant in that case, M, had worked for FP Ltd from 1994. In 1999 FP Ltd was sold under a share sale agreement to MC Ltd, which thus became its holding company. In 2005 both companies went into separate administrations, and M was dismissed. On the following day, TPF Ltd purchased MC Ltd from the administrators. M brought a number of claims relating to his dismissal to an employment tribunal, **1.7** and sought to establish as a preliminary issue that there had been a transfer of his employment in 1999 from FP Ltd to MC Ltd. In the tribunal's view, there had been more than a simple share sale in this case. MC Ltd had taken over the day-to-day running of FP Ltd's business, taking the key management decisions and doing 'far more than a simple shareholder would have done following a simple sale, or… a parent company of a subsidiary would have done in similar circumstances'. Thus, the tribunal stated, although *in theory* M had still been employed by FP Ltd following that company's sale, he had *effectively* been employed by MC Ltd. These findings led the tribunal to conclude that this share transfer was covered by TUPE.

On appeal, the EAT overturned the tribunal's decision. In its view, the transaction in question could not be covered by TUPE since, as a matter of law, the subsidiary company, FP Ltd, remained the employer of the employees in question following the share sale. The tribunal had erred in 'piercing the corporate veil' – that is, in looking behind the legal form and concluding that the undertaking in question 'was not in the hands of the legal entity in whose name it was ostensibly run'. The EAT held that 'as a matter of law, it is the corporate entity that runs the business and absent any sham, the courts are entitled to look no further'. Mr Justice Elias, President of the EAT, commented that 'it may be difficult to justify the different treatment of a transfer of a business and sales of shares regimes, but that distinction is firmly rooted in the law and recent amendments to TUPE have not taken the opportunity to bring the two regimes together'. M appealed to the Court of Appeal.

1.8 The Court of Appeal rejected the EAT's reasoning and reinstated the tribunal's decision that TUPE had applied. Lord Justice Buxton found that, contrary to the findings of the EAT, the tribunal had not 'pierced the corporate veil' in this case. In his view, a piercing of the corporate veil only arises 'when it is established that activity x is carried on by company A, but for policy reasons it is sought to show that in reality the activity is the responsibility of the owner of company A, company B'. That scenario did not pertain here. Rather, the tribunal found that the running of FP Ltd's business (activity x) had *actually* been carried out by MC Ltd (company B) rather than FP Ltd (company A). The EAT had given insufficient weight to this finding, and had instead concentrated on the legal structure of the two companies concerned. Buxton LJ concluded: 'The legal structure is of course important, but it cannot be conclusive in deciding the issue of whether, within that legal structure, control of the business has been transferred as a matter of fact. That was the conclusion of the employment tribunal, and the EAT demonstrated no proper basis for displacing that conclusion.' Lord Justice Moses agreed, adding that where, following a transfer of shares, a subsidiary is 100 per cent owned by a parent, the question of whether the business has been transferred for the purposes of TUPE is one of fact which must be resolved deploying the experience and expertise of the employment tribunal. He acknowledged that 'the mere fact of control, which

4

will follow from the relationship between parent and subsidiary, will not be sufficient to establish the transfer of the business from subsidiary to parent'. However, in this case the tribunal had 'identified a number of evidential indications, which, in combination, established that control of the business, in the sense of how its day-to-day activities were run, had passed from [FP Ltd] to [MC Ltd]'. It had been entitled to rely on these in concluding that there had been a TUPE transfer in this case.

The Court of Appeal's decision in Millam has certainly put the cat among the pigeons. The essential circumstances of the Millam case – where the purchasing company effectively took over the running of the purchased company – are not particularly unusual. So it *might* be that a significant number of share sales will now fall within TUPE's auspices. It remains to be seen how tribunals will react to the Millam decision, and how many share sales will be covered, but purchasing companies should no longer assume that the 2006 Regulations will not apply.

Nevertheless, it remains fair to say that there will be many share sales to which **1.9** TUPE will not apply. Thus, it will usually be easier from an employer's perspective if a share transfer rather than a business transfer takes place. This is because the special obligations under the 2006 Regulations with regard to unfair dismissal (see Chapter 4), varying terms and conditions of employment (see Chapter 5) and information and consultation (see Chapter 10) will not generally arise in such circumstances. Of course, the affected employees will still be protected to an extent by standard unfair dismissal and contract law.

Transfer of undertaking's ownership not required. It is well established that **1.10** the Directive and TUPE can apply even where the absolute ownership of the undertaking in question does not change hands. In fact, Reg 3(6)(b) of the 2006 Regulations expressly states that there may be a relevant transfer whether or not any property is transferred from the transferor to the transferee.

The ECJ's decision in Landsorganisationen i Danmark Ny Mølle Kro 1989 ICR 330, ECJ, illustrates this point well. The events leading to this case began in 1980 when H, the owner of a tavern business, leased one of its taverns to L. Later that year, L, which had begun to run the tavern, concluded a membership agreement with the Association of Hotel and Restaurant Employees, under which it was required to comply with collective agreements entered into by the Association. In January 1981 H rescinded L's lease owing to L's breaching its terms, and took over the management of the business once more. An employee argued that the reversion of the lease to H constituted a transfer of an undertaking and that, consequently, L's obligations to comply with the terms of collective agreements negotiated with the Association passed to H. The Danish Labour Court referred the matter to the ECJ, in order for that court to consider whether the words 'transfer... to another employer, as a result of a legal transfer or merger' contained in Article 1.1(a) of the Directive could cover a situation where the owner of an undertaking that has been leased takes back the running of the undertaking as a result of the breach of the lease by the managing lessee.

1.11   The ECJ emphasised that the purpose of the Directive is to safeguard, as far as possible, the rights of workers in the event of a change of employer, by allowing them to remain in employment on the same conditions as those agreed with the transferor. With this in mind, the Court felt that the Directive should apply whenever as a result of a legal transfer or merger there is a change in the natural or legal person responsible for the running of the undertaking and who because of this enters into contractual obligations as an employer towards the employees working in the undertaking. This is so, the ECJ continued, regardless of whether ownership of the undertaking has been transferred. In reaching this decision, it noted that the employees of an undertaking which changes its employers without a transfer of ownership are in a comparable situation to that of the employees of an undertaking which has been sold and therefore need equivalent protection. In the instant case, the managing lessee, L, acquired under the lease the capacity of employer, meaning that the transfer of the lease constituted a transfer of an undertaking falling within Article 1.1(a) of the Directive. When the owner of the undertaking, H, took back the running of the undertaking, that resumption also constituted a transfer, in so far as L lost the capacity of employer and that capacity was reacquired by H.

It follows from this reasoning that the Directive, and hence the 2006 Regulations, can apply to the granting, terminating, surrendering or assigning of a lease of land or property, where a business is intrinsically linked to such land or property and where, as a result of the transaction, the business changes hands and continues to be run as essentially the same business. So, if the tenant of, say, a petrol station, pub, farm or factory is replaced by the landlord (or indeed, as we shall see below, by another tenant) following the transfer of the leasehold premises, those employed in the undertaking will be able to claim the protection of the 2006 Regulations. This is subject to the usual rule that the undertaking in question retained its identity following the transfer – see 'When does an economic entity retain its identity?' below.

1.12   Similarly, the Directive and the 2006 Regulations can apply to the conferring of a franchise, licence or concession. Where, for example, a licensee enters into a contractual arrangement to carry out a business activity, the fact that certain key tangible and intangible assets of the business (e.g. intellectual property, premises and goodwill) continue to be owned by the person conferring the licence will not necessarily prevent the operation of the transfer rules.

1.13   **A series of transactions can amount to a relevant transfer.** Regulation 3(6)(a) of the 2006 Regulations provides that a relevant transfer may be effected by a series of two or more transactions. This reflects a number of decisions of the ECJ, such as that in Foreningen af Arbejdsledere i Danmark v Daddy's Dance Hall A/S 1988 IRLR 315, ECJ.

6

In that case T was employed as a manager by IC, which had taken out a non-transferable lease of a restaurant/bar belonging to another company, PT. When IC learned that its lease was to be terminated, it gave its employees notice of dismissal. A new lease was concluded between PT and DDH, as a result of which the latter immediately re-employed the ex-IC staff (including T), albeit on different terms and conditions. Shortly afterwards, T was dismissed. He brought a claim arguing that the transfer rules had applied to transfer his employment from IC to DDH, meaning that he had been entitled to a greater period of notice than that which DDH had given him. The Danish Supreme Court referred the matter to the ECJ, asking whether the Directive applies where a non-transferable lease is terminated and thereafter the owner, without interruption in the activities of the business, leases it to a new lessee who re-employs the staff of the former lessee.

The ECJ concluded that the Directive did apply in such circumstances. First, it **1.14** repeated the reasoning from the Ny Mølle Kro case (see above), stating that the Directive 'applies as soon as there is a change... of the natural or legal person responsible for operating the undertaking who, consequently, enters into obligations as an employer towards the employees working in the undertaking, and it is of no importance to know whether the ownership of the undertaking has been transferred'. But it also went one step further. In the ECJ's view, 'the fact that... the transfer takes place in two phases, in the sense that as a first step the undertaking is transferred back from the original lessee to the owner who then transfers it to the new lessee, does not exclude the applicability of the Directive as long as the economic unit retains its identity'. This view was affirmed by the ECJ in the later case of P Bork International A/S (in liquidation) v Foreningen af Arbejdsledere i Danmark and ors 1989 IRLR 41, ECJ.

Regulation 3(6)(a) – which, to recap, reflects the above ECJ case law in providing that a relevant transfer may be effected by a series of transactions – is potentially wide-ranging. For instance, it can bring the transfer of a business by way of a number of apparently discrete though connected sales – a possible TUPE-avoidance tactic – within the auspices of the 2006 Regulations. In Longden and anor v Ferrari Ltd and anor 1994 ICR 443, EAT, Mr Justice Mummery, as he then was, made the point that Reg 3(6)(a) aims to ensure that TUPE applies where 'the parties... arrange for the transfer to be effected in a series of two or more transactions... for no sensible commercial purpose, other than to avoid the consequence of the application of Regulations enacted for the protection of employees'.

Note that although it is clear that a relevant transfer can be effected by a series **1.15** of transactions, the ECJ recently established, in Celtec Ltd v Astley and ors 2005 ICR 1409, ECJ, that it is necessary to identify one specific *transfer date*. Later in this chapter, in 'When does the transfer occur?', we discuss some of the difficulties that the Celtec decision has given rise to in this regard.

1.16 **No contract required between transferor and transferee.** On their face, the words 'legal transfer or merger' in Article 1.1(a) of the Directive seem to suggest that a direct relationship between the transferor (the original employer) and the transferee (the new employer) is required in order for the Directive to apply. Case law, however, has shown that this is not so. Take Daddy's Dance Hall (above) as an example. There, IC's lease of a restaurant/bar came to an end and the landlord concluded a new lease with DDH. As a result, DDH took over the business previously run by IC. The ECJ held that those employed by IC at the restaurant/bar transferred under the Directive to DDH, rendering IC the 'transferor' and DDH the 'transferee', even though there was no direct relationship between them.

The concept of 'legal transfer' was considered further by the ECJ in Dr Sophie Redmond Stichting v Bartol and ors 1992 IRLR 366, ECJ. The transferor in that case was the Dr Sophie Redmond Foundation, which was funded by a local authority to provide assistance to drug addicts in the Netherlands. The local authority decided to terminate this funding and switch it to the Sigma Foundation (the transferee), which did similar work. Again, although there was no direct relationship between the Dr Sophie Redmond Foundation, which lost the funding, and the Sigma Foundation, which continued the work, the ECJ decided that the Directive applied, meaning that the employees working on the project transferred from one to the other. Having examined the previous case law, such as Daddy's Dance Hall and Bork (above), the Court accepted that the concept of a 'legal transfer' in Article 1.1 of the Directive must be broadly interpreted. It concluded that a legal transfer can be said to occur where 'a public body decides to terminate a subsidy paid to one legal person, as a result of which the activities of that legal person are fully and definitively terminated, and to transfer it to another legal person with similar aims', so long as the undertaking in question retains its identity. This is so whether the decision leading to the transfer was taken unilaterally by the public body or with agreement of the body subsidised. The Court noted that 'there is equally a unilateral decision where an owner decides to change a lessee, a situation which the Court has held may fall within the scope of the Directive'.

1.17 **Service provision changes.** As the 1980s progressed, more and more bodies began to outsource services such as cleaning and catering. The question soon arose as to whether the 'transfer' of such activities to an external service provider could attract the application of the Directive. Unsurprisingly – given the principles set out in the cases outlined above – the ECJ in Rask and anor v ISS Kantineservice A/S 1993 IRLR 133, ECJ, answered this question in the affirmative. The Court decided that the Directive can apply to outsourcing where the owner of an undertaking entrusts to another, by means of contract, the responsibility for providing a service. This was so regardless of the fact that the activity transferred was only ancillary to the transferor's business.

8

It is now clear that the Directive and TUPE are capable of applying not only to outsourcing exercises, but also to insourcing exercises and changes of service provider. An early UK case on service provision change was Dines and ors v (1) Initial Health Care Services Ltd (2) Pall Mall Services Group Ltd 1995 ICR 11, CA, in which the Court of Appeal considered whether TUPE applied where a health authority changed the contractor responsible for carrying out cleaning services. Referring to the ECJ case law discussed above, the Court decided that it was possible to conclude that there had been a 'relevant transfer' between the two contractors, which took place in two phases: (i) the handing back of the cleaning services by the first contractor to the health authority, and (ii) the handing over of the cleaning services by the authority to the second contractor.

Although it is clear that the Directive and Reg 3(1)(a) of the 2006 Regulations **1.18** *can* apply to service provision changes, the question of whether they actually *do* apply to a given set of facts has often proved difficult to answer. The problems that courts and tribunals have faced over the years in this regard are rehearsed at length in 'What is an "economic entity"?' and 'When does an economic entity retain its identity?' below. To remove the uncertainty, the Government introduced a new rule in the 2006 Regulations – Reg 3(1)(b) – to make it clear that the majority of service provision changes *are* now covered by TUPE. We discuss this rule – again, later in this chapter – in the section on 'Service provision changes'.

Reorganisation within a group of companies. In Allen and ors v Amalgamated **1.19** Construction Co Ltd 2000 ICR 436, ECJ, the European Court held that the Directive, and hence TUPE, can apply to a business transfer between two companies within a group. This is so even where the companies have the same ownership, management and premises, and are engaged in the same activity. Simply put, this is because there *is* a change of employer in such circumstances – the two group companies in the Allen case were distinct legal persons, each having specific relationships with their employees. It followed, held the ECJ, that the Directive would apply where a group company decided to subcontract to another company in the same group work and labour for driveage work in mines, provided that the transaction involved the transfer of an economic entity the identity of which was retained after the transfer.

Court orders. The transfer rules can apply where a court orders the transfer of **1.20** a business. In Berg and anor v Besselsen 1990 ICR 396, ECJ, the European Court held that there was a transfer of an undertaking to which the Directive applied when a lease/purchase agreement recognised under the law of the Netherlands was terminated by judicial decision. In that case, the business – a bar/discotheque – was owned and run by B, which transferred its operation, along with its employees, to S under a lease/purchase agreement. Under this type of agreement, the ownership of the business did not pass to S at this point. In time, the Dutch Court set aside the lease/purchase agreement before ownership had transferred, and ordered the business to be returned to B. The ECJ decided that there had been a transfer covered by the Directive when the business passed to S, and that there had also been a transfer covered by the Directive when the business returned by court order to B. Thus, B was responsible for all the arrears of pay due to employees for the period when S ran the business.

1.21 Regulatory interventions. A regulatory intervention may also lead to a TUPE transfer. In Rose v Dodd 2005 ICR 1776, CA, the Law Society, using its statutory powers under the Solicitors Act 1974, intervened in the practice of Reynolds and Dodd when the principal of the firm was suspected of dishonesty. The Law Society appointed as its agents another firm of solicitors to carry out the intervention and take full control of Reynolds and Dodd. A couple of months after the intervention, the firm's business was transferred, with court approval, to another firm of solicitors. The Court of Appeal held that employment of R, an employee of Reynolds and Dodd, had transferred under TUPE to the new firm.

1.22 Companies struck off the Register. In Charlton and anor v Charlton Thermosystems (Romsey) Ltd and anor 1995 IRLR 79, EAT, Mr and Mrs Charlton were the sole directors and shareholders of a heating company. The company was struck off the Register of Companies for failing to file annual accounts, and was dissolved. Thereafter, however, Mr and Mrs Charlton continued to run the business. The EAT upheld a tribunal's finding that a relevant transfer had occurred, stating: 'Although the company was dissolved on 30 October 1990, the business retained its identity in the hands of Mr and Mrs Charlton, formerly directors of the company, who continued the operation, using the same assets and employees as the company had.'

Similarly, in Karalia Ltd v Eracli EAT 453/97, the EAT held that a TUPE transfer had occurred where the transferor, E Ltd, had been struck off the Register, and its business had continued immediately in the hands of a newly created company, A Ltd.

1.23 Public and private sector. Regulation 3(4)(a) of the 2006 Regulations provides that 'these Regulations apply to public and private undertakings'. It is clear that transfers both to and from the public sector can be covered by the rules. See 'The public sector' below for further details.

1.24 Insolvency. If a business gets into extreme financial difficulties, an insolvency practitioner can be appointed either to keep the business running with a view to the sale of the whole or part of it as a going concern, or to wind it up and sell off its assets. Put extremely simply, the Directive and Reg 3(1)(a) of the 2006 Regulations will apply to a transfer instigated by an insolvency practitioner in the former set of circumstances, but not the latter. We discuss this issue more fully in 'Insolvency' below.

What is an 'economic entity'? 1.25

Under Reg 3(1)(a) there is a 'relevant transfer' of an undertaking or part of an undertaking only where 'there is the transfer of an *economic entity which retains its identity*' (our emphasis). The italicised wording, which mirrors that of Article 1.1(b) of the Directive, is derived from the ECJ's decision in Spijkers v Gebroeders Benedik Abattoir CV and anor 1986 2 CMLR 296, ECJ. In Jouini v Princess Personal Service GmbH 2007 IRLR 1005, ECJ, the European Court had to consider whether an economic entity had been transferred in circumstances where some of the administrative personnel and temporary employees of an employment business were employed by another temporary business. It held that Article 1(1)(b) of the Directive must be interpreted as applying to such a situation although it was for the national court to decide whether the grouping of staff in the particular instance amounted to an economic entity.

In Whitewater Leisure Management Ltd v Barnes and ors 2000 IRLR 456, EAT, the Appeal Tribunal advised that 'it will normally be best and clearest for an employment tribunal to deal first with the question of whether there was a relevant and sufficiently identifiable economic entity, and then proceed, whatever be the answer to that question, to ask and answer whether there was... a relevant transfer of any such entity'. The EAT in Cheesman and ors v R Brewer Contracts Ltd 2001 IRLR 144, EAT, agreed, adding that 'whilst we do not say that it is invariably an error of law not to raise those two questions as separate questions or to fail to deal with them in that order, a tribunal which so fails runs a real risk of error'. Thus, when distilling UK and ECJ case law into guidance as to what amounts to a relevant transfer (which we set out below), the EAT in Cheesman attempted 'to divide considerations between those going to whether there is an undertaking and those, if there is an undertaking, going to whether it has been transferred'. In this chapter, we adopt the EAT's approach, focusing in this section on what might constitute an economic entity, before turning to examine the circumstances in which such an entity can be said to have retained its identity.

'Economic entity' is defined by Reg 3(2) of the 2006 Regulations (and indeed 1.26 by Article 1.1(b) of the Directive) as 'an organised grouping of resources which has the objective of pursuing an economic activity, whether or not that activity is central or ancillary'. Without more, this rather abstract definition is not particularly helpful. Thankfully, however, its meaning can be teased out by examining the body of case law that gave rise to it.

Before we turn to examine Reg 3(2) in detail, it should first be noted that, in essence, the question of whether an economic entity exists is a *question of fact* for the employment tribunal to decide. Since appeals from a tribunal to the EAT lie only on questions of law, and not on questions of fact, decisions in this area are in theory difficult to challenge. Nevertheless, an error of law can arise

11

if a tribunal, carrying out its assessment of the facts, fails to take into account a relevant factor, takes into account an irrelevant factor, or reaches an unsustainable conclusion on the facts found. Given that the definition of 'economic entity' in Reg 3(2) of the 2006 Regulations and the case law giving rise to it is fairly complicated, arguments as to which factors are relevant and which are irrelevant have become commonplace.

1.27 **The Cheesman guidelines.** Having trawled through decisions of both the UK courts and the ECJ, the EAT in the Cheesman case (above) set out the following principles with regard to the question of whether there is an 'economic entity' in existence:

- there needs to be a stable economic entity, which is an organised grouping of persons and of assets enabling (or facilitating) the exercise of an economic activity that pursues a specific objective. There will not be such an entity if its activity is limited to performing one specific works contract. It has been held that the reference to 'one specific works contract' is to be restricted to a contract for building works

- in order to be such an undertaking it must be sufficiently structured and autonomous but will not necessarily have significant tangible or intangible assets

- in certain sectors such as cleaning and surveillance the assets are often reduced to their most basic and the activity is essentially based on manpower

- an organised grouping of wage-earners who are specifically and permanently assigned to a common task may, in the absence of other factors of production, amount to an economic entity

- an activity is not of itself an entity; the identity of an entity emerges from other factors, such as its workforce, management staff, the way in which its work is organised, its operating methods and, where appropriate, the operational resources available to it.

As with the Reg 3(2) definition of 'economic entity', which we set out above, the Cheesman guidance is unlikely to leave non-TUPE experts much the wiser unless it is unpicked. Below, we explain the key principles in more detail and examine the cases in which they were laid down.

1.28 **Organised grouping of resources.** The expression 'organised grouping of resources' found in Reg 3(2) derives from the case of Süzen v Zehnacker Gebäudereinigung GmbH Krankenhausservice 1997 ICR 662, ECJ, in which the ECJ ruled that the term 'economic entity' refers to 'an organised grouping of persons and assets facilitating the exercise of an economic activity which pursues a specific objective'. The ECJ also pronounced that an economic *activity*, in itself, is not sufficient to amount to an economic *entity*, stating that 'an entity cannot be reduced to the activity entrusted to it. Its identity also emerges from other factors, such as its workforce, its management staff, the way in which its work is organised, its operating methods or indeed, where appropriate, the operational resources available to it.'

In many 'standard transfer' situations it will be self-evident that there is an organised grouping of resources – comprising, for example, physical and intangible assets (the latter including goodwill and intellectual property rights), the workforce, premises, customers, operating systems, etc. However, where this is unclear – perhaps where there is a transfer of part of a business only, or a service provision change – the following principles should be applied.

Entity must be sufficiently structured and autonomous. In Francisco Hernández **1.29** Vidal SA v Gómez Pérez and ors 1999 IRLR 132, ECJ, and Sánchez Hidalgo and ors v Asociación de Servicios Aser and Sociedad Cooperativa Minerva and another case 1999 IRLR 136, ECJ, the ECJ explained that a group of resources pursuing an economic activity must be 'sufficiently structured and autonomous' in order to constitute an economic entity. In the following two cases the EAT suggested that, on the facts, no such structure and autonomy existed:

• **Wynnwith Engineering Co Ltd v Bennett and ors** 2002 IRLR 170, EAT: the claimants in this case took early retirement from British Aerospace, and were thereafter provided as agency workers to British Aerospace by W Ltd. When they were dismissed, they brought tribunal claims, in the course of which the question arose whether there had been a 'relevant transfer' from British Aerospace to W Ltd. A tribunal held that there had been such a transfer, but this decision was overturned by the EAT. The EAT noted that, in considering whether there had been an economic entity, the function of the employees had to be taken into account. In this case the employees carried out different functions across various parts of the employer's business. The fact that they shared the same employment status because they had taken early retirement and worked on short-term contracts was not sufficient to establish the existence of an economic entity that retained its identity after a transfer

• **Whitewater Leisure Management Ltd v Barnes and ors** (above): a leisure centre was managed by W Ltd under a management contract. W Ltd also managed other operations. Six employees of W Ltd's senior management team were involved with the centre, but the majority of their time was spent managing other aspects of W Ltd's business. A second group of W Ltd's employees at the centre – the core team – consisted of a manager, two assistant managers and 11 other full-time employees. A third group of employees included a general mix of part-time, casual and seasonal staff. W Ltd ran the Centre for six years, but then lost the contract to do so to the in-house team of the East Riding Yorkshire Council. None of the six senior managers moved to the Council, remaining employed by W Ltd. Of the 'core' team, seven of the 14 employees were taken on by the Council and seven stayed with W Ltd. The majority of the third group remained with W Ltd. The employees who *did* move across claimed that their continuity of employment had been preserved owing to the operation of TUPE. A tribunal disagreed, and the EAT upheld the tribunal's decision. In doing so, the EAT stated that, in this case, it was arguable that there had not been a stable and discrete entity, or a sufficiently structured and autonomous entity, because of the fact that the leisure centre was so intricately bound up with the rest of the outgoing contractor's operations. The senior management was plainly not discrete in so far as it spent the majority of its time working in other areas; and even if the management team was left out of account, it remained highly arguable that the entity in question was not autonomous.

1.30 ***Entity need not be 'separate' in the hands of the transferor.*** The above cases emphasised that, in order for a standard transfer to take place, a structured and autonomous economic entity must exist. In Fairhurst Ward Abbotts Ltd v Botes Building Ltd and ors 2004 ICR 919, CA, however, the Court of Appeal held that, where a transfer of a *part* of an undertaking takes place, the part in question need not *itself* exist as a discrete economic entity prior to its transfer.

The facts of the Fairhurst Ward case were as follows. In April 1996 the London Borough of Southwark awarded B Ltd a three-year contract for the maintenance and alteration of its void domestic dwellings (the 'Major Voids Contract'). A number of the Borough's employees, including the eight individuals involved in this case, transferred to B Ltd under TUPE. Towards the end of B Ltd's contract, the Borough decided to divide in two the geographical area covered by the original Major Voids Contract and invited separate tenders in respect of the two areas. FWA Ltd won the contract for Area 2. In B Ltd's opinion, TUPE applied to transfer the eight employees in question from it to FWA Ltd. FWA Ltd, however, refused to take the employees on. Consequently, from April 1999 the eight found themselves without an employer, and they launched proceedings in the employment tribunal claiming that they had been unfairly dismissed by either FWA Ltd or B Ltd. Naturally, the question arose whether a relevant transfer had occurred. When the case reached the Court of Appeal, FWA Ltd argued that the contract relating to Area 2 could not have transferred under TUPE because it had not existed as an identifiable economic entity before the alleged transfer took place.

1.31 The Court of Appeal accepted that, in order for TUPE to apply to a transfer, a stable, economic entity – being an organised grouping of persons and assets enabling or facilitating the exercise of an economic activity that pursues a specific objective – must be identifiable as existing, in the hands of the transferor, before the transfer takes place. However, neither legislation nor case law requires, in order for TUPE to apply to the transfer of *part* of an undertaking, that the part in question itself exists as an identifiable, stable, economic entity prior to its transfer. It is sufficient that part of an economic entity becomes identifiable as a separate economic entity on the occasion of the transfer separating the part from the whole. The Court noted that the aim of the Directive and of TUPE is to preserve the continuity of employment relationships within an undertaking. In its view, this aim does not require a distinction to be drawn between a case where the part of an undertaking transferred was identifiable as a discrete part before the transfer, and a case where the part transferred became identifiable as a separate entity only at the time of the transfer. In the circumstances, the Court upheld an employment tribunal's decision that TUPE applied in this case.

Significant assets not required. It is established that although an 'economic **1.32** entity' must be 'sufficiently structured and autonomous', it will not necessarily have significant tangible or intangible assets. As the ECJ noted in Francisco Hernández Vidal SA v Gómez Pérez and ors (above), in certain labour-intensive sectors of the economy, such as cleaning and surveillance, those elements are often minimal. With this in mind, the Court concluded that 'an organised grouping of wage earners who are specifically and permanently assigned to a common task may, in the absence of other factors of production, amount to an economic entity'.

An 'economic entity' may have only one employee. In Schmidt v Spar- und **1.33** Leihkasse der früheren Ämter Bordesholm, Kiel und Cronshagen 1995 ICR 237, ECJ, the ECJ held that the fact that an economic activity is performed by a single employee is not sufficient, in itself, to preclude the application of the Directive. The Court concluded that the Directive covers a situation 'in which an undertaking entrusts by contract to another undertaking the responsibility for carrying out cleaning operations which it previously performed itself, even though, prior to the transfer, such work was carried out by a single employee'. The Schmidt decision was expressly approved by the ECJ in Süzen v Zehnacker Gebäudereinigung GmbH Krankenhausservice (above). Yet, as we have seen, the ECJ in Süzen went on to define the term 'economic entity' as 'an organised grouping of *persons* and assets' (our emphasis). Does this suggest that more than one employee is actually required?

The EAT had the opportunity to ponder this matter in Dudley Bower Building Services Ltd v Lowe and ors EAT 856/01. It was called upon to consider an employer's appeal against a tribunal's finding that a set of maintenance duties performed essentially by a single employee had amounted to an economic entity capable of being transferred under TUPE. The employee in question was L, who was employed by WSA Ltd to perform 'response maintenance' of various pieces of electrical equipment at RAF Cosford. This work comprised 'package six' of WSA Ltd's building management duties at the site. In time, WSA Ltd lost its contract and the MoD accepted a tender from S Ltd. S Ltd then sub-contracted the 'package six' duties to WB, which did not take L on. L brought claims against WSA Ltd, S Ltd and WB, arguing that his employment had been

15

protected by TUPE. The tribunal upheld his claims, and DBBS Ltd, which in the meantime had acquired WB, appealed against the tribunal's decision. It argued that, in the light of the ECJ's comments in cases such as Süzen, the performance of contractual duties by a single employee was not, in itself, sufficient to amount to an economic entity. In this case, 'package six' had consisted of nothing more than the performance of a number of duties by L, in respect of which there had been no management role, and which could not be described as sufficiently structured or autonomous to attract the application of the transfer rules.

1.34 Like the tribunal before it, however, the EAT accepted that there is no reason in principle why work performed by a single person cannot amount to an economic entity. It noted that the Schmidt decision had not been overruled or disapproved and stated that, in its view, the words 'grouping of persons' contained in Süzen and other cases did not suggest that more than one employee is required for such an entity to exist. The EAT noted, however, that the ECJ in Schmidt did not decide that the performance of contractual duties by a single employee is *in itself* sufficient to indicate the existence of a stable economic entity. Whether an entity is sufficiently structured and autonomous for the Directive (and thus Reg 3(1)(a)) to apply to its transfer will depend on the facts of the case. The EAT pointed out that 'at one extreme, if the activity consists of no more than one cleaning lady and her mop, an economic entity may not exist, whereas if the task to be performed is complex and sophisticated and requires careful planning, specification and costings, it may be that an entity exists even though the work is performed by a single employee'.

Turning to the facts of the case in question, the EAT held that there had been material upon which the tribunal had been entitled to decide that a transferable economic entity had been in existence. Although the 'package six' duties had been performed essentially by one employee, the facts 'demonstrated a well established, sophisticated operation'. A complex pricing structure had been laid down; each task had needed to be authorised and prioritised; and the performance of the duties had taken place within a disciplined and technical framework. Accordingly, the EAT dismissed DBBS Ltd's appeal.

1.35 **Requirement of stability – single specific works contracts not covered.** In the aforementioned cases, reference to the term 'stable economic entity' was often made by the courts when describing that which is capable of being transferred under the Directive. Although the word 'stable' does not appear in the Directive's definition of an economic entity (and nor, for that matter, is it found in the 2006 Regulations), the ECJ, in Ledernes Hovedorganisation, acting for Rygaard v Dansk Arbejdsgiverforening, acting for Strø Mølle Akustik A/S 1996 IRLR 51, ECJ, emphasised that 'stability' of an entity is a prerequisite of the Directive's application. This is reflected in the Cheesman guidance, which we set out above.

In the Rygaard case, R was employed by a firm of carpenters, SP, which was contracted by SAS to build a canteen. SP told SAS that they wanted another company, SM, to complete the final stages of the work. SM subsequently entered into a contract with SAS, agreeing to do so. The question arose as to whether SP's employees who had been working on the building project were protected by the Directive, meaning that their employment transferred to SM. When this matter was referred to the ECJ, that court explained that a distinction must be drawn between the mere loss of a contract and the transfer of a stable entity. To be stable, the entity has to have an expectation of continuing or future work, with its activity not limited to the performance of one specific works contract. The ECJ went on to hold that the Directive did not apply where there was a transfer from one undertaking to another of building works with a view to the completion of those works in circumstances where the transferor merely made available to the new contractor certain workers and materials for carrying out the works in question. Such a transfer could come within the terms of the Directive only if it included the transfer of a body of assets enabling the activities or certain activities of the transferor undertaking to be carried on in a stable way.

The UK courts and tribunals have, in general, downplayed the significance of **1.36** the Rygaard case, deciding that it limits the Directive's application only in narrowly defined circumstances. Three case illustrations:

- **Balfour Beatty Power Networks Ltd and anor v Wilcox and ors** 2007 IRLR 63, CA: H plc provided street lighting services, under a number of different contracts, for WPB. In time, it lost two of these contracts – a jointing contract and an aerial supply contract – one of which was awarded to BB Ltd and the other to Interserve. The new contractors did not take on all the employees dedicated to the contracts in question, and some of the spurned employees brought tribunal claims, arguing that TUPE applied. An employment tribunal held, for various reasons, that no relevant transfer had occurred from H plc to BB Ltd, but that such a transfer had taken place from H plc to Interserve. Interserve appealed to the EAT and then to the Court of Appeal, which held that the tribunal had not erred in finding that the aerial supply contract had amounted to a stable economic entity capable of transferring under TUPE from H plc to Interserve, even though there was no guarantee that the contract would continue and where, in fact, the contract was lost shortly after the transfer. Lord Justice Buxton stated that 'an enterprise may be stable as a matter of practical and industrial reality, even though its long-term future is not secured'

- **Argyll Training Ltd v Sinclair and anor** 2000 IRLR 630, EAT: AIE was set up to provide training to enterprise companies in Scotland. It subcontracted the provision of training services in the Argyll area to another company, BEST, which was responsible for, among other things, the placement of trainees with employers. S was employed by BEST as a training adviser. Her work was directed exclusively to the contract with AIE and she had sole responsibility for organising placements in Argyll. In May 1998, having learned that it had lost its contract with AIE, BEST terminated all training placements and made S redundant. A few weeks later another contractor, ATL, took over the arrangements for the former BEST trainees with retrospective effect. Of the 42 trainees who had been on BEST's books, 21 transferred to ATL's. S succeeded with a tribunal claim that she had been dismissed in connection with a transfer of an undertaking from BEST to ATL, and ATL appealed to the EAT. It argued, with reference to the ECJ's decision in Rygaard, that TUPE had not applied in this case, as the activity in question had been limited to one specific contract. The EAT, however, was not persuaded by ATL's argument. Having examined the cases of Spijkers and Schmidt (above), both of which were referred to in the Rygaard decision, the EAT stated that there was no basis for automatically excluding all single-contract undertakings from the possibility of transferring under the Directive. The EAT felt supported in this regard by the Süzen case (above), in which a school's contracted-out cleaning services transferred from one contractor to another. If the relevant undertaking in Süzen was the cleaning of the particular school, that could be described as an activity limited to one specific contract. However, the ECJ in Süzen had clearly not regarded the entity as being insufficiently stable to attract the Directive's application. The EAT concluded that the proposition derived from Rygaard – that the Directive does not apply to an activity 'limited to performing one specific works contract' – must 'be taken to be restricted to single specific contracts for building works'. Thus restricted, the Rygaard principle could not assist ATL, whose appeal was dismissed

- **BSG Property Services v Tuck and ors** 1996 IRLR 134, EAT: T and 13 others were employed by Mid-Bedfordshire District Council in the Housing Maintenance Direct Services Organisation (DSO) to carry out maintenance on council houses. In 1992 the Council decided that the DSO could no longer carry out the maintenance services economically. It gave the DSO employees notice of dismissal, and signed a contract with BSG under which that organisation agreed to provide the services. BSG did not take on the DSO employees, instead using a pool of self-employed workers to carry out the work. The DSO employees brought tribunal claims arguing that TUPE had applied, meaning that they had been unfairly dismissed by BSG, the transferee employer. The tribunal upheld their claims and BSG appealed to the EAT. It argued that TUPE had not applied in this case as there had been no 'stable economic entity' as required by the ECJ's ruling in Rygaard. In its view, the 'entity' in question had 'lacked organisational stability'. At best, the 'activity' amounted to 'the opportunity to carry out response maintenance work essentially under a series of works contracts, as and when required'.

The EAT, however, dismissed BSG's appeal, stating that 'the requirement of "the stable economic entity" has to be read in the context of [the Rygaard] case and is apt to exclude activities under a short-term, one-off contract'. In the EAT's view, the 'continued and recurrent maintenance activities in this case' did not fall within this description, and were capable of transferring under the transfer rules.

The most restrictive approach seen in the above cases was that of the EAT in **1.37** Argyll, which decided that the 'Rygaard principle' – that the Directive does not apply to an activity 'limited to performing one specific works contract' – is relevant only to single, specific contracts for building works. The EAT's decision in Argyll was referred to specifically in the Cheesman guidelines (above) as to what amounts to an economic entity. It is worth bearing in mind, however, that the Cheesman guidelines appeared hot on the heels of the Argyll decision, meaning that Argyll was fresh in the EAT's mind at that time. In the years following the Cheesman guidelines, courts and tribunals have at times moved away from restricting Rygaard to the building arena.

In Mackie v Aberdeen City Council 2006 All ER 297, CA, for example, the Court of Session decided that Rygaard applied to prevent the application of TUPE, even though the 'entity' under scrutiny was not concerned with building works. In that case, M was employed by S Ltd, which agreed to provide to the Council an 'operational smart card system' to be used for the cash-free payment of meals by school children and as a bus pass for senior citizens. The contract was for a fixed price and for a fixed task. Towards the end of the contract, M was offered employment with the Council. Though her new post involved some tasks related to the card scheme, she was primarily involved in work which went beyond anything she had undertaken at S Ltd. In time, she brought a number of claims before an employment tribunal, and the issue arose as to whether her move from S Ltd to the Council had been covered by TUPE. The matter eventually came before the Court of Session (Inner House), which held that the tribunal had been correct to conclude that this case had involved the performance of a single contract of limited duration which, on the authority of Rygaard, could not amount to a stable economic entity capable of transferring under Reg 3(1)(a). It was clear that S Ltd had a contract to perform a particular and clearly defined task – the production of the smart card. The running of the smart-card system was always intended to be a matter for the Council. The Court stated: 'It is evident from the authorities that where the work in which the employee of the alleged transferor employer is involved is that of a single, one-off contract, there cannot be said to be an undertaking to which TUPE applies and it is in that context that the term "stable economic entity" is used.'

'Economic activity' does not require pursuit of profit. Prior to 1993, Reg **1.38** 2(1) of the 1981 Regulations provided that TUPE applied only to the transfer of a 'commercial venture'. The word 'commercial' is inextricably linked with the pursuit of profit and, accordingly, old Reg 2(1) cast considerable doubt on the possibility that TUPE could apply to non-profit oriented entities, such as charities and the public sector.

The 'commercial venture' requirement was removed, however, in the light of the ECJ's decision in Dr Sophie Redmond Stichting v Bartol and ors 1992 IRLR 366, ECJ, which we discussed in 'Transfer "to another person"' above. To recap, the Dr Sophie Redmond Foundation was funded by grants from the local authority to provide assistance to drug addicts in the Netherlands. In time, the local authority decided to terminate its subsidy to the Redmond Foundation and switch it to the Sigma Foundation, which did similar work. Considering whether the Directive could apply to transfer employees from Redmond to Sigma, the ECJ stated: 'In accordance with the approach of the Court to give a sufficiently broad interpretation to the concept of "legal transfer" in Article 1.1 of the [Directive] there is a legal transfer where a public body decides to terminate a subsidy paid to one legal person as a result of which the activities of that person are terminated and transferred to another legal person with similar aims.' The tenor of the ECJ's decision made it clear that the restriction of the application of TUPE to 'commercial ventures' was contrary to the Directive. Indeed, the ECJ expressly adopted the Commission's contention that the fact that the transaction in this case arose out of the grant of subsidies to foundations whose services were not remunerated did not prevent the transaction constituting a 'legal transfer' within the meaning of Article 1.1.

1.39 Now, Reg 3(4)(a) of the 2006 Regulations (and Article 1.1(c) of the Directive) codifies the principle laid down in the Dr Sophie Redmond case, providing that 'these Regulations apply to public and private undertakings engaged in economic activities *whether or not they are operating for gain*' (our emphasis).

1.40 **Activities may be 'central or ancillary'.** The last part of Reg 3(2) states that an economic activity can amount to an economic entity capable of transferring under the Regulations 'whether or not that activity is central or ancillary'. This wording makes the simple point – pertinent in particular to service provision changes – that the fact that a transferred activity is unconnected to the transferor's central activity does not exclude that operation from the scope of the Regulations.

The language of Reg 3(2) in this regard is taken from the ECJ's decision in Rask and anor v ISS Kantineservice A/S 1993 IRLR 133, ECJ. There, R was employed by Philips in a company canteen until 1 January 1989 when, following the contracting out of the canteen services, she was taken on by the contractor, ISS. ISS attempted to change some of R's terms and conditions, but R refused to accept the changes and, as a result, was dismissed. R sought compensation before the national court in Copenhagen, which referred questions to the ECJ as to whether the Directive had applied. The ECJ held that the situation where a company entrusts the responsibility for operating part of its business, such as a canteen, to another company, which thereby assumes responsibility as employer with regard to the employees working in that part, is capable of attracting the transfer rules. It went on to state: 'The fact that, in such a case, the activity transferred is only an ancillary activity of the transferor undertaking not necessarily related to its objects cannot have the effect of excluding that transaction from the scope of the Directive.'

A ship does not in itself amount to an economic entity. Article 1.3 of the **1.41** Directive states that 'this Directive shall not apply to seagoing vessels'. Endeavouring to reflect this, Reg 2(2) of the 1981 Regulations stated that 'references in these Regulations to the transfer of part of an undertaking are references to a transfer of a part which is being transferred as a business and, accordingly, do not include references to a transfer of a ship without more'.

In Castle View Services Ltd v Howes and ors 2000 SLT 696, Ct Sess (Inner House), the Court of Session decided that old Reg 2(2) did not automatically exclude all crew members of seagoing vessels from TUPE protection. The Court set out an example of a shipping company with two vessels. In the Court's view, if one of those vessels were to be sold to another company, TUPE would not apply: there will be a transfer of a ship, but nothing more. This, the Court pointed out, is consistent with the concept expressed in the Spijkers case (above) that the sale of an asset does not constitute the sale of part of a business. On the other hand, if the whole of the shipping company's business was sold – including both vessels – there would be a transfer of a business, which 'would constitute more than the mere transfer of the ship or ships'. In this scenario, stated that court, 'on a proper construction of Regulation 2(2) the crews of the vessels would not be excluded from the benefit of the Regulations'.

In the light of the Court's decision, the Government, in its consultation **1.42** document on the 2006 Regulations, expressed the view that old Reg 2(2) was 'declaratory only and adds nothing of substance to the effect of the Regulations, since the sale of a ship (with its crew) could not in itself constitute a relevant transfer in any event, unless it was sold as part of a business undertaking'. For this reason, the provision was not retained.

Public administration. Regulation 3(4)(a) of the 2006 Regulations states that **1.43** 'these Regulations apply to public and private undertakings engaged in economic activities'. However, Reg 3(5), reflecting ECJ case law, then provides that 'an administrative reorganisation of public administrative authorities or the transfer of administrative functions between public administrative authorities is not a relevant transfer'. We examine Reg 3(5), together with other matters to consider when a public sector employer is involved in a potential transfer situation, under 'The public sector' below.

21

1.44 When does an economic entity retain its identity?
It is one thing to identify an 'economic entity', but another thing altogether to conclude that such an entity 'retains its identity' following a transfer. Nevertheless, if the entity in question does *not* retain its identity, the transaction will fall outside both the Directive and Reg 3(1)(a) of the 2006 Regulations. The retention of identity issue has presented UK courts and tribunals with all manner of problems over the years, owing to the confusing messages from the European Court of Justice.

As with the question of whether an economic entity exists, the question of whether such an entity retains its identity is, at its heart, a *question of fact* for the employment tribunal. As we have noted, appeals from a tribunal to the EAT lie only on questions of law, and not on questions of fact. However, owing to the conflicting nature of the ECJ's decisions as to which factors should be taken into account in different sets of circumstances, it has regularly been possible for parties to appeal to the EAT, arguing that tribunals have failed to apply the law emanating from the European Court correctly.

1.45 Introduction – the Spijkers test. We start our examination of this somewhat tricky issue by focusing on the seminal case of Spijkers v Gebroeders Benedik Abattoir CV and anor 1986 2 CMLR 296, ECJ, from which the phrase 'retains its identity' is derived. In that case the ECJ stated: 'The decisive criterion for establishing the existence of a transfer within the meaning of the Directive is whether the entity in question retains its identity.' In its view, 'it is necessary to consider whether, having regard to all the facts characterising the transaction, the business was disposed of as a going concern'. This 'will be apparent from the fact that its operation is actually being continued or has been taken over by the new employer with the same economic or similar activity'. Furthermore, in order to decide whether such retention of identity has occurred, 'it is necessary to take account of all the factual circumstances of the transaction in question', including:

- the type of business or undertaking

- the transfer or otherwise of tangible assets such as buildings and stocks

- the value of intangible assets at the date of transfer

- whether the majority of the staff are taken over by the new employer

- the transfer or otherwise of customers

- the degree of similarity of activities before and after the transfer, and

- the duration of any interruption in these activities.

1.46 However, the ECJ continued, the above are merely factors in the overall assessment and 'cannot therefore be considered in isolation'. This suggests that no single factor is decisive, and that not all the 'criteria' need to be satisfied in order for the Directive – and thus Reg 3(1)(a) of the 2006 Regulations – to apply. This 'multifactoral' approach did not provide the formulaic certainty that the business community might have wished for.

Things became even more unclear in the mid-to-late 1990s, when the ECJ reached a series of arguably conflicting decisions as to when it could be said that an economic entity retains its identity following a service provision change (SPC). The uncertainty in this regard gave rise to a plethora of case law at both European and domestic level.

Below, we set out the main principles with regard to retention of identity as **1.47** established by the EAT in Cheesman and ors v R Brewer Contracts Ltd 2001 IRLR 144, EAT. We then go on to examine some of the aspects of the 'Spijkers test' in more detail, before turning to the problems that have arisen in the SPC arena.

The Cheesman guidelines. The EAT's main guidance on the 'retention of **1.48** identity' issue was laid down in 2000, in the case of Cheesman v R Brewer Contracts Ltd (above). This guidance simply summarises the extensive case law which we explore in more detail below, and does not provide a great deal of enlightenment in itself. Having said that, it highlights the pertinent issues and acts as a useful reference point. Moreover, the principles set out in Cheesman have held much sway in UK courts and tribunals in recent years. In Project 90 Ltd v Oswald and anor EAT 0388/05, for example, the EAT remitted a matter to that tribunal with an express direction to consider the Cheesman guidance while determining whether a relevant transfer under Reg 3(1)(a) had taken place.

In Cheesman, the EAT examined the convoluted ECJ case law before stating that the following principles apply:

- the decisive criterion for establishing the existence of a transfer is whether the entity in question retains its identity, as indicated, among other things, by the fact that its operation is actually continued or resumed

- in a labour-intensive sector it is to be recognised that an entity is capable of maintaining its identity after it has been transferred where the new employer does not merely pursue the activity in question but also takes over a major part, in terms of their numbers and skills, of the employees specially assigned by his predecessors to that task. That follows from the fact that in certain labour-intensive sectors a group of workers engaged in the joint activity on a permanent basis may constitute an economic entity

- in considering whether the conditions for existence of a transfer are met it is necessary to consider all the factors characterising the transaction in question, but each is a single factor and none is to be considered in isolation

- among the matters thus falling for consideration are the type of undertaking, whether or not its tangible assets are transferred, the value of its intangible assets at the time of transfer, whether or not the majority of its employees are taken over by the new company, whether or not its customers are transferred, the degree of similarity between the activities carried on before and after the transfer, and the period, if any, in which they were suspended

- in determining whether or not there has been a transfer, account has to be taken, among other things, of the type of undertaking or business in issue, and the degree of importance to be attached to the several criteria will necessarily vary according to the activity carried on

- where an economic entity is able to function without any significant tangible or intangible assets, the maintenance of its identity following the transaction being examined cannot logically depend on the transfer of such assets

- even where assets are owned and are required to run the undertaking the fact that they do not pass does not preclude a transfer

- where maintenance work is first carried out by a cleaning firm and then by the owner of the premises concerned, the mere fact does not justify the conclusion that there has been a transfer

- more broadly, the mere fact that the service provided by the old and new undertaking providing a contracted-out service or the old and new contract-holder are similar does not justify the conclusion that there has been a transfer of an economic entity between predecessor and successor

- the absence of any contractual link between transferor and transferee may be evidence that there has been no relevant transfer but is certainly not conclusive as there is no need for any such direct contractual relationship

- when no employees are transferred, the reasons why that is the case can be relevant as to whether or not there was a transfer

- the fact that the work is performed continuously with no interruption or change in the manner or performance is a normal feature of transfers of undertakings but there is no particular importance to be attached to a gap between the end of the work by one subcontractor and the start by the successor.

1.49 **Focus is on transferring entity's identity.** In applying the Spijkers test, courts and tribunals must focus on the identity of the entity transferred rather than on the nature of the transferor's and the transferee's businesses as a whole. The EAT made this point in Playle and ors v Churchill Insurance Group Ltd and ors EAT 570/98. There, C Ltd, an insurance company which marketed and sold its own policies, acquired the business of CGA Direct, which was not licensed to trade as an insurance firm in its own right, from CGA Group. A tribunal chairman, considering whether this transaction gave rise to a TUPE transfer, pointed out that the nature of the two businesses – CGA Group and C Ltd – was inherently different, and that what C Ltd had essentially been concerned with was the acquisition of CGA's customer lists. The chairman went on to find that TUPE had not applied in this case. The EAT, however, overturned the chairman's decision. The mere fact that the transferee's business was different in nature to the business which it had acquired was immaterial. By concentrating on the similarity (or lack of it) between the transferor and the transferee, the tribunal had missed the main issue, which was whether the transferring entity had retained its identity post-transfer.

Since the focus must be on the transferring entity's identity, the question of how that entity is defined is clearly an important one. In Camden Primary Care Trust and University College London v Skittrall and ors EAT 0078/05 and 0107/05 the EAT concluded that a tribunal had erred in defining an economic entity too narrowly, and consequently in finding that no TUPE transfer had taken place. In that case the degree-level education in podiatry offered by University College London (UCL) was taken over by the University of East London (UEL). The parties agreed that TUPE applied and all relevant staff were offered employment with UEL. Six staff objected to the transfer and an employment tribunal was asked to decide, by way of preliminary issue, whether there had been a relevant transfer. The tribunal found that no transfer had resulted, as the economic entity in question – 'the provision of a University of London BSc Honours degree in podiatry by UCL' – had not retained its identity after the changeover. The tribunal stated that the economic entity which came into being following the changeover – 'the provision of podiatric education in the form of a UEL BSc Honours degree in podiatry' – was a distinct undertaking. The EAT, however, overturned this decision. If the economic entity was the provision of a UCL degree in podiatry, its identity could not have been retained unless UCL had been successful on re-tender. In other words, the tribunal had defined the economic entity in such a way that no relevant transfer could occur. The EAT noted that a purposive approach to the application of TUPE is necessary in order that employees might be protected when a change of employer occurs, before concluding that the tribunal's decision could not stand.

Type of entity. One of the relevant factors identified by the ECJ in Spijkers was 'the type of business or undertaking'. As the ECJ pointed out in Süzen v Zehnacker Gebäudereinigung GmbH Krankenhausservice 1997 ICR 662, ECJ, 'it follows that the degree of importance to be attached to each criterion for determining whether or not there has been a transfer within the meaning of the Directive will necessarily vary according to the activity carried on'. **1.50**

Similarity of activities. In Spijkers, the ECJ stated that 'the degree of similarity of activities before and after the transfer' was a relevant factor going to the issue of whether an economic entity has retained its identity. **1.51**

Where the nature of a business changes significantly upon its acquisition – for example, where X buys a café and thereafter runs it as a jewellery shop – there is little difficulty in concluding that the economic entity has not retained its identity. Some cases, however, are not as clear-cut – an example being Mathieson and anor v United News Shops Ltd EAT 554/94. There, a hospital shop operating from a portacabin was redeveloped, and the hospital invited people to tender to run the new shop. The old shop had sold newspapers, magazines, confectionery and flowers. The new one sold the same goods, with the exception of flowers, as well as other items such as clothes, electrical equipment, cards and toys; opened for longer hours; and was run on a commercial basis. Applying Spijkers, a tribunal held that there had not been a relevant transfer as differences in stock, hours and commercial attitude meant that the new shop was a different business. This decision was upheld by the EAT.

1.52 On the other hand, minor changes in the way in which activities are carried out might not change the essential identity of the entity being transferred. This point is neatly illustrated by the case of Porter and anor v Queen's Medical Centre (Nottingham University Hospital) 1993 IRLR 486, QBD. There, the High Court held that a relevant transfer occurred where the supply of paediatric and neonatal services moved from two District Health Authorities to an NHS Trust. The Court said that the fact that the business was carried out in a different way following the transfer did not preclude the application of the 1981 Regulations. It went on to say that the provision of medical services is a type of undertaking in which it is particularly likely that different ways of carrying on the undertaking may be adopted without destroying its identity. The Court emphasised that while the methods of caring will be modified and improved as medical science advances, the object of the undertaking will not change.

Similarity of activities before and after the transfer is not necessarily the be all and end all. It is simply one element of the Spijkers test. As we highlighted in 'What is an "economic entity"?' above, the ECJ in Süzen v Zehnacker Gebäudereinigung GmbH Krankenhausservice stated that 'an entity cannot be reduced to the activity entrusted to it. Its identity also emerges from other factors, such as its workforce, its management staff, the way in which its work is organised, its operating methods or indeed, where appropriate, the operational resources available to it.' We discuss the Süzen case and the impact it had on service provision changes later in this section.

1.53 In Klarenberg v Ferrotron Technologies GmbH 2009 ICR 1263, ECJ, the claimant worked as the head of a unit in a company in Germany which developed and manufactured certain products for the steel industry. K sold the rights over a number of products that had been developed by the unit headed by the claimant, together with the production hardware and inventory of materials for the relevant products to FT GmbH. The products sold were incorporated into the range offered by FT GmbH and some employees who had worked in the relevant unit were engaged by FT GmbH and integrated into its organisational structure, carrying out work in relation not only to the products that had been sold but also to their own other products. The claimant sought a declaration that there was a relevant transfer of his employment to FT GmbH. On a reference by the national court, the ECJ ruled that when assessing if the economic entity had retained its identity after the transfer, this required the retention *not of* the specific organisation of the elements of production but of such a functional link of interdependence and complementarity between those elements as enabled the transferee to use them to pursue an identical or analogous economic activity, even if after the transfer they were integrated in a new and different organisational structure. The Court concluded that it was for the national court to ascertain, in the light of those considerations and making a global assessment of all the facts characterising the transaction, whether the identity of the economic entity transferred had been preserved.

Interruption of activities. Another relevant factor with regard to retention of **1.54** identity mentioned by the ECJ in Spijkers was 'the duration of any interruption in [the] activities'. In Landsorganisationen i Danmark v Ny Mølle Kro 1989 ICR 330, ECJ, the European Court considered whether a transfer of an undertaking under the Directive could have occurred where the 'change of employer' took place while the business in question was not functioning. In that case H, the owner of a tavern business, leased one of its taverns to L. However, in January 1981 H rescinded L's lease owing to L's breaching its terms. The tavern – which was operated on a regular basis only during the summer – was closed until March 1981, when H began to manage it herself. The national court referred a number of questions to the ECJ, which stated that 'the fact that the undertaking in question was temporarily closed at the time of the transfer... certainly constitutes one factor to be taken into account in determining whether a business was transferred as a going concern'. The Court continued, however, to state that such a closure does not in itself preclude the application of the Directive. That was true in particular 'in the case of a seasonal business, especially where, as in this case, the transfer takes place during the season when it is closed. As a general rule, such closure does not mean that the undertaking has ceased to be a going concern.'

The ECJ repeated much of this reasoning in the later case of P Bork International A/S (in liquidation) v Foreningen af Arbejdsledere i Danmark and ors 1989 IRLR 41, ECJ. There, Bork leased a beech wood veneer factory from OTF. The lease terminated on 22 December 1981, and during that month Bork dismissed all the factory's employees. On 31 December JI purchased the factory from OTF and brought it back into operation on 4 January 1982, taking on more than half of the staff previously employed by Bork. When some of the affected employees brought claims, the national court referred questions relating to the Directive's application to the ECJ. Referring to the Ny Mølle Kro case, the ECJ noted that a temporary closure was a relevant factor when considering whether a business was transferred as a going concern. It pointed out, however, that such a closure and the consequential absence of staff at the time of the transfer

27

were not in themselves sufficient to preclude the existence of a transfer of an undertaking within the meaning of the Directive. Furthermore, the Court stated: 'That is true, in particular, in circumstances such as those of this case, where the undertaking ceased to operate only for a short period which coincided, moreover, with the Christmas and New Year holidays.'

1.55 As the EAT pointed out in Gardner Merchant Ltd v Ryan and ors EAT 1337/95, however, if a transfer of an undertaking is to occur despite a temporary cessation of activity, it is paramount that the business carried on after such cessation is the same as that which was carried on before. In that case, GM Ltd had a contract to provide canteen and related services to COI. When the operation of the contract became unprofitable, GM Ltd gave notice to terminate the contract, which it was legally entitled to do. The response of COI was to shut the restaurant. GM Ltd, seeking to avoid making redundancy payments to the employees assigned to the contract, argued that there had been a relevant transfer of the canteen services back to COI. This argument was rejected by both the employment tribunal and the EAT. Here, there had not been a temporary cessation of the canteen services, only for those services to be resumed by COI at a later date. Rather, the undertaking had ceased to be when GM Ltd terminated its contract.

1.56 **Entity subsumed post-transfer.** In 'What is an "economic entity"?' above, we examined the case of Fairhurst Ward Abbotts Ltd v Botes Building Ltd and ors 2004 ICR 919, CA. There, the Court of Appeal emphasised that where there is a transfer of a part of a business, the part in question need not exist as an identifiable, stable, economic entity prior to its transfer in order for TUPE to apply. It is sufficient that part of such an entity becomes identifiable as a separate economic entity on the occasion of the transfer separating the part from the whole.

But what happens when an entity which *is* identifiable prior to a transfer becomes subsumed or fragmented in the transferee's business? In Farmer v Danzas (UK) Ltd EAT 858/93 F was employed by his own transport business, F Ltd. In essence, his business was to supply D Ltd with lorries and drivers so that D Ltd could provide a transport service called Eurapid to its customers. For this purpose, F leased and maintained the lorries and had accommodation in D Ltd's offices. In time, D Ltd decided to move the Eurapid service to its main site. It took the view that it needed to employ a manager to look after the Eurapid business and offered F the position on condition that F Ltd ceased trading. F accepted the post and started working for D Ltd on 1 October 1991. F Ltd's drivers were also taken on by D Ltd, and at first they continued to operate the Eurapid service as they had before – the only difference being that F Ltd's name had been taken off the lorries. By January of the following year, most of the drivers had been fully integrated into D Ltd's business. Thereafter, the leases on the lorries that had been taken out by F Ltd were allowed to lapse, and most of the vehicles were replaced by the end of 1992.

F was dismissed in early 2002 and brought a complaint of unfair dismissal. The **1.57** preliminary issue for the tribunal was whether F had the two years' continuous employment then required to bring such a claim. This depended on whether there had been a TUPE transfer of the business of F Ltd to D Ltd, preserving his continuity of service. The tribunal was satisfied that F Ltd had a business or an undertaking which was capable of being transferred and that D Ltd had acquired an identifiable part of that business. Moreover, D Ltd had been able to carry on substantially the same activities as F Ltd without interruption. The tribunal concluded, however, that because D Ltd had always intended to integrate F Ltd's business into its own, the business transferred had not retained its identity, meaning that no TUPE transfer had occurred. F appealed to the EAT, which overturned the tribunal's decision. The EAT held that there is no rule that an economic entity ceases to retain its identity merely because its economic activity is subsumed into the transferee's business. Such a rule would emasculate the working of the Directive and the Regulations, since all businesses are likely to want to integrate the activities of a newly acquired entity into their own. In order for TUPE to apply, it is sufficient that the transferred undertaking retains its identity *immediately* after the moment of transfer. In the instant case, F Ltd's drivers did exactly the same work immediately following the transfer as they had done before, using the same equipment and serving the same customers, and the transferee was able to carry on the activities of F Ltd without interruption. What happened subsequently was neither here nor there. F's appeal was therefore allowed.

Contrast the situation in the Farmer case with that in AEEU and ors v Lyndon Scaffolding plc EAT 1242/99. The claimants in that case were employed by L plc at Ferrybridge power station, in order to fulfil L plc's contract with Powergen to provide scaffolding services at the site. When L plc's contract came to an end, Powergen invited tenders not simply for the scaffolding work but for a combination of scaffolding, insulation and cleaning services. L plc – a specialist scaffolding firm – was not invited to tender. The contract was won by Cape, which did not accept that a relevant transfer from L plc had occurred with regard to the scaffolding work. The claimants lost their jobs and brought unfair dismissal claims before an employment tribunal. The tribunal decided, as a preliminary issue, that no transfer of an undertaking had occurred. One factor it took into account was that the nature of Cape's contract with Powergen was fundamentally different from that made earlier between L plc and Powergen. The L plc contract was for the supply of scaffolding services only. On the other hand, although the Cape contract included scaffolding services, it also covered cleaning and insulation services, with all three under one management. On appeal, the employees argued that the tribunal had erred in elevating this factor into one determinative of the transfer question. They relied

29

on the words of Morison J in the Farmer case (above) that there is nothing to suggest that an economic entity ceases to retain its identity merely because the economic activity is subsumed into the transferee's business. Moreover, they argued that the fact that the scaffolding service provided by L plc was subsumed into a wider contract entered into by Cape was actually irrelevant to the question of whether TUPE applied. The EAT, however, upheld the tribunal's decision. Unlike in the Farmer case, the tribunal here had not isolated one factor as being determinative of the transfer question, but had weighed up all the relevant factors. Furthermore, the EAT continued, if the nature of the service formerly provided differs materially from that provided by the incoming contractor, this is a factor which a tribunal is entitled to take into account in considering whether the former economic entity has retained its identity. Accordingly, the employees' appeal was dismissed.

1.58 Note that in the discussion on 'Service provision changes – retention of identity not required' below, we consider whether the AEEU case would have been decided differently under the new service provision change rules contained in Reg 3(1)(b) of the 2006 Regulations.

1.59 **Entity fragmented post-transfer.** An example of a case concerning fragmentation upon a transfer is Astle and ors v Cheshire County Council and anor 2005 IRLR 12, EAT. There, the Council outsourced certain architectural services to SGI, but thereafter became concerned about SGI's performance. The Council decided to terminate SGI's contract and to adopt what it referred to as a 'market economy' approach, under which a panel of consultants would be engaged to provide the services instead of a single contractor. Owing to this fragmentation upon the transfer, both an employment tribunal and the EAT concluded that the economic entity prior to the transfer had not retained its identity, meaning that TUPE did not apply.

1.60 **Transfer of assets.** It is well established that a transfer under the Directive and Reg 3(1)(a) of the 2006 Regulations can take place even though no assets transfer from the transferor to the transferee. The case of Merckx and anor v Ford Motors Co (Belgium) SA 1997 ICR 352 ECJ, involved Anfo Motors, a Ford dealer selling motor vehicles in several areas of Brussels. Ford decided to cease using Anfo, of which it was the majority shareholder, and instead began working with an independent dealer, Novarobel. The question arose whether a transfer of an undertaking had occurred between Anfo and Novarobel, and a number of issues were referred to the ECJ. That court concluded that the fact that neither tangible nor intangible assets were transferred from Anfo to Novarobel was not conclusive of the question as to whether an undertaking retained its economic identity. In fact, the ECJ continued, the purpose of an exclusive dealership for the sale of motor cars of a particular make in a particular sector remains the same even if it is carried on under a different name, from different premises with different facilities.

Shortly after the Merckx decision, the ECJ noted in Süzen v Zehnacker Gebäudereinigung GmbH Krankenhausservice (above) that the importance of asset transfer will fluctuate depending on the type of entity transferred. The Court stated that 'where in particular an economic entity is able, in certain sectors, to function without any significant tangible or intangible assets, the maintenance of its identity following the transaction affecting it cannot, logically, depend on the transfer of such assets'. However, similar logic suggested that the transfer of assets would be an extremely important factor in asset-reliant sectors – a point thereafter emphasised in Oy Liikenne Ab v Liskojärvi and anor 2001 IRLR 171, ECJ. We debate the issues arising from the Süzen and Oy Liikenne decisions, which were concerned with service provision changes, at length below.

Before moving on, it seems sensible to pose the question of what 'transfer of **1.61** assets' actually means. When will that particular box of the Spijkers test be ticked? The following two cases provide some useful insights in this regard, emphasising that a transfer of assets can occur whether or not the actual *ownership* of such assets changes hands:

* **Ablcr and ors v Sodexho MM Catering GmbH and anor** 2004 IRLR 168, ECJ: the management authority responsible for an Austrian orthopaedic hospital contracted out its catering services for patients and staff to Sanrest. Under the outsourcing agreement, Sanrest prepared meals on the hospital premises, using water, energy and all necessary small and large equipment provided by the hospital. Some years later, the management authority terminated its agreement with Sanrest and awarded the contract to Sodexho, which proceeded to perform the catering operation using the hospital's facilities. Sodexho denied Sanrest's contention that what had occurred amounted to a transfer of an undertaking under the Directive, and refused to take any of Sanrest's employees on. Sanrest dismissed the employees, who brought claims arguing that their employment had transferred to Sodexho. The Supreme Court of Austria referred the matter to the ECJ which, in ruling that there had been a transfer of an undertaking in the circumstances, confirmed that there had been a transfer of assets from Sanrest to Sodexho, despite the fact that the assets in question were owned by the hospital throughout. The ECJ stated: 'the tangible assets needed for the activity in question – namely, the premises, water and energy and small and large equipment, ([including] the appliances needed for preparing the meals and the dishwashers) – were taken over by [the new contractor]'

* **Güney-Görres and anor v Securicor Aviation and anor** 2006 IRLR 305, ECJ: SA employed 295 workers to carry out airport security under a contract it had with the German Government. In 2003 the Government terminated this contract and awarded it to KAV, which took on 167 of SA's employees and used the aviation security equipment owned by the Government. Some of

the employees who found themselves without work brought claims arguing that their employment had transferred from SA to KAV under the national transfer rules implementing the Directive. The German court hearing the claims noted that, under ECJ case law, an asset transfer is one of the criteria characterising a transfer of an undertaking. However, that court was unsure what the phrase 'asset transfer' actually meant. It decided to ask the ECJ whether, as German case law suggested, an asset transfer only takes place if the assets are used by the incoming contractor for its own purposes on an independent commercial basis. In this case, there was absolutely no scope for KAV to use the aviation security equipment – which was the property and the responsibility of the German State – for its own purposes. It could neither obtain any additional economic benefit from that equipment nor determine the manner or extent of its use. The ECJ held that 'the transfer of the assets for independent commercial use is not an essential criterion for a finding that there was a transfer of those assets from the original contractor to the new contractor'.

1.62 **Change of location.** In Merckx and anor v Ford Motors Co (Belgium) SA, which we discussed above, the ECJ confirmed that the fact that an economic entity, post-transfer, operates at a different location does not necessarily mean that its identity has not been retained. The Court stated: 'The purpose of an exclusive dealership for the sale of motor vehicles of a particular make in a certain sector remains the same even if it is carried on under a different name, from different premises and with different facilities. It is also irrelevant that the principal place of business is situated in a different area of the same conurbation, provided that the contract territory remains the same.'

Of course, when it comes to the contracting out of services, a change of location might well mean that there is no transfer of the assets required to carry out the activity from the outgoing contractor to the incoming contractor. The absence of such a transfer might go a long way towards a finding that no standard transfer under Reg 3(1)(a) has taken place, as we discuss below.

1.63 **Intention of the parties.** Generally, the Directive and the 2006 Regulations apply automatically if there is a relevant transfer, whether or not the parties want them to. However, the parties' views as to whether the Regulations apply *may* be taken into account by an employment tribunal in some circumstances.

In Lightways (Contractors) Ltd v Associated Holdings Ltd 2000 IRLR 247, Ct Sess (Inner House), L Ltd tendered for a contract to provide street lighting maintenance for Renfrewshire Council, bidding on the express basis that TUPE applied. L Ltd won the contract, but then proceeded on the basis that TUPE did not apply. Litigation ensued, and eventually the Court of Session held that an employment tribunal, in finding against L Ltd, had been entitled to take into account its expressed intention prior to the transfer. The Court said that it was legitimate, in determining whether or not a relevant transfer had taken place, to have regard not only to the events directly constituting the transaction, but also to the surrounding circumstances. Therefore, a serious statement prior to the transfer that TUPE applied could throw light on the true nature of the transaction.

Service provision changes. Earlier in this chapter we saw that cases such as **1.64** Rask and anor v ISS Kantineservice A/S 1993 IRLR 133, ECJ, demonstrated that the Directive, and hence Reg 3(1)(a) of the 2006 Regulations, can apply to service provision changes (SPCs) arising from outsourcing, insourcing or re-tendering exercises.

However, the question of when an entity can be said to have retained its identity following an SPC has caused much gnashing of teeth in UK courts and tribunals, which have struggled over the years to derive coherence from the ECJ case law on this point. Below, we analyse the main issues that have arisen, many of which can be traced back to the ECJ's decision in Süzen v Zehnacker Gebäudereinigung GmbH Krankenhausservice 1997 ICR 662, ECJ (above).

We reiterate that under the 2006 Regulations the vast majority of SPCs will fall **1.65** within the scope of TUPE in any event, owing to new Reg 3(1)(b), which we examine in the section on 'Service provision changes' below. It follows that the vexed issue of whether an economic entity has retained its identity following an SPC is no longer as central to the TUPE regime as it once was. Nevertheless, the case law in this regard is worthy of examination for two reasons: first, it enhances our understanding of the Reg 3(1)(a) test that is still conclusive to all transfers *other than* SPCs; and, secondly, owing to some of the exceptions to new Reg 3(1)(b), *some* SPCs will still have to satisfy the traditional Reg 3(1)(a) 'retention of identity' if they are to be covered by the 2006 Regulations.

The inclusive approach in Schmidt. The case of Schmidt v Spar- und Leihkasse **1.66** der früheren Ämter Bordesholm, Kiel und Cronshagen 1995 ICR 237, ECJ, concerned S, who had been employed by a bank to clean its branch office. In February 1992 the bank decided to outsource this cleaning work to Speigelblank, the firm already responsible for cleaning most of the bank's other premises. The bank dismissed S, who was offered re-engagement by Speigelblank on new terms, which she rejected. S brought a claim in respect of her dismissal to the German Labour Court, and the question arose whether the Directive had applied, meaning that S's employment had transferred to Speigelblank under the national transfer provisions. Unsure as to the answer to this question, the Court referred the matter to the ECJ.

The ECJ rejected the argument put forward by the German and UK governments that the Directive could not apply in a case such as this owing to the absence of a transfer of any tangible assets. Referring to the Spijkers case, the ECJ stated that 'the safeguarding of employees' rights, which constitutes the subject-matter of the Directive... cannot depend exclusively on consideration of a factor which

33

the Court has in any event already held not to be decisive on its own'. The ECJ went on to proffer the view that 'the similarity in the cleaning work performed before and after the transfer, which is reflected, moreover, in the offer to re-engage the employee in question, is typical of an operation which comes within the scope of the Directive and which gives the employee whose activity has been transferred the protection afforded to him by that Directive'.

1.67 The EAT, when interpreting the Schmidt decision in cases such as Isles of Scilly Council v Brintel Helicopters Ltd and ors 1995 IRLR 6, EAT, seemed to reduce the 'retention of identity' issue in the SPC arena to a single question: are the activities being carried out after the transfer broadly similar to those which were carried out before? If the answer to this question was yes, then TUPE applied. This was a simplistic approach, which involved the EAT's essentially ignoring a number of factors identified as relevant by the ECJ in Spijkers. Nevertheless, it brought with it the advantage of certainty, in that almost all SPCs would be covered by the Regulations. This certainty was dismantled, however, by the ECJ's decision in Süzen v Zehnacker Gebäudereinigung GmbH Krankenhausservice (above).

1.68 *Süzen – transfer of assets or employees required.* In the Süzen case S, a cleaner, worked for ZG, a company that had a contract to carry out cleaning in a school in Bonn-Bad-Godesberg, Germany. ZG's contract was terminated with effect from 30 June 1994 and S was dismissed along with seven of her colleagues. The school then entered into a cleaning contract with another company with effect from 1 August 1994. That company did not employ S, and S instituted proceedings before the German Labour Court. That court sought a preliminary ruling from the ECJ as to whether the Directive applied in these circumstances, meaning that S's employment had transferred to the new cleaning contractor.

The ECJ began by highlighting the established key criterion for determining whether there has been a transfer of an undertaking – namely, whether there is an identifiable economic entity that had retained its identity after the alleged transfer. Furthermore, the Court purported to affirm the list of relevant factors set out in the Spijkers case, stating that 'it is necessary to consider all the facts characterising the transaction in question, including in particular the type of undertaking or business; whether or not its tangible assets, such as buildings and moveable property, are transferred; the value of its intangible assets at the time of the transfer; whether or not the majority of its employees are taken over by the new employer; whether or not its customers are transferred; the degree of similarity between the activities carried on before and after the transfer, and the period, if any, for which those activities were suspended'.

1.69 Having set out this list of factors, the ECJ went on to resile from the Schmidt decision, which we set out above. The Court stated that it does not automatically follow that there is a transfer of an economic entity merely because the service provided by the old and the new contractors is similar, since an entity cannot be reduced to the activity entrusted to it. Rather, 'its identity also emerges from other factors, such as its workforce; its management staff; the way in which its work is organised; its operating methods, or indeed, where appropriate, the operational resources available to it'. Consequently, the ECJ continued, the mere loss of a service contract to a competitor cannot in itself indicate the existence of a transfer of an undertaking covered by the Directive.

The ECJ then pointed out that 'the degree of importance to be attached to each criterion for determining whether or not there has been a transfer within the meaning of the Directive will necessarily vary according to the activity carried on'. So while accepting that in labour-intensive sectors such as cleaning, an economic entity – amounting to a group of workers engaged in a joint activity on a permanent basis – is able to function without any significant tangible or intangible assets, the ECJ put the cat among the pigeons by suggesting that such an entity is only capable of retaining its identity following a transfer when the new contractor 'does not merely pursue the activity in question but also takes over a major part, in terms of their numbers and skills, of the employees specially assigned by his predecessor to that task'. It went on to conclude that 'the Directive does not apply to a situation in which a person who had entrusted the cleaning of his premises to a first undertaking terminates his contract with the latter and, for the performance of similar work, enters into a new contract with a second undertaking, if there is no concomitant transfer from one undertaking to the other of significant tangible or intangible assets or taking over by the new employer of a major part of the workforce, in terms of their numbers and skills, assigned by his predecessor to the performance of the contract'.

This was controversial. On the one hand, the ECJ seemed to affirm the **1.70** 'multifactoral' Spijkers test with regard to retention of identity. On the other hand, it stated that, in order for the Directive to apply to an SPC, a transfer of either assets or employees is essential. Furthermore, where the entity in question has no significant assets, the ECJ suggested that a single factor – the transfer or otherwise of the majority of the workforce in terms of numbers and skills – would be determinative of the retention of identity issue.

In the light of this, the Court of Appeal, in Betts and ors v (1) Brintel Helicopters Ltd (2) KLM ERA Helicopters (UK) Ltd 1997 ICR 792, CA, took the view that the Süzen case represented 'a shift in emphasis, or at least a clarification of the law, and that some of the reasoning of earlier decisions… may have to be reconsidered'. In Betts, the Court felt obliged by Süzen to reverse a High Court decision that a relevant transfer had taken place when Shell changed the supplier of its helicopter transport contract from Brintel to KLM. The Court of Appeal noted that the activity carried out before and after the change of contractor was very similar. Crucially, however, no staff or other significant assets were transferred. The incoming contractor had simply obtained a fresh

35

contract for supplying helicopter services to the oil rigs, which it carried out from a different land base using different helicopters and different crews. In those circumstances, no transfer of an undertaking had occurred.

1.71 *Labour-intensive entities – why was the workforce not taken on?* It was not long, however, before the UK courts and tribunals became aware of some of the difficulties of the Süzen ruling, particularly with regard to SPCs in labour-intensive sectors. The thrust of Süzen was that since the workers themselves comprise the principal assets of a labour-intensive undertaking, such as cleaning, the transfer of the 'major part of the workforce, in terms of their numbers and skills' is necessary in order for the undertaking to retain its identity and thus in order for the Directive to apply. Accordingly, a strict interpretation of Süzen suggested that a prospective transferee in a labour-intensive sector could avoid the operation of the Directive (and hence fall outside what is now Reg 3(1)(a) of the 2006 Regulations) by the simple expedient of not taking on a major part of the outgoing contractor's workforce.

To many, it seemed both bizarre and unsatisfactory that the operation of a measure specifically designed to protect employees from being dismissed in the context of a transfer would be made entirely dependent on whether the incoming contractor voluntarily takes on the employees who are affected. At the very least, the test appeared to be circular in its reasoning. In order to avoid this outcome, UK courts and tribunals strived to avoid interpreting Süzen strictly with regard to labour-intensive transfers. They did this in two ways. First, they emphasised that the ECJ in Süzen had affirmed the multifactoral test laid down in the Spijkers case, meaning that all relevant factors – and not just the transfer or otherwise of the employees – needed to be considered. Secondly, they suggested that one such relevant factor was a prospective transferee's *motive* for refusing to take the relevant employees on. If the motive was simply to avoid the application of TUPE, the case would be assessed as if the employees had, in fact, transferred.

1.72 Below, we set out three important cases in which this approach of the UK courts manifested itself:

- **ECM (Vehicle Delivery Service) Ltd v Cox and ors** 1999 ICR 1162, CA: A Ltd lost a contract with VAG to deliver cars from Grimsby to local car dealerships and delivery centres. The majority of A Ltd's work was thereafter performed by a different company, ECM Ltd. None of A Ltd's employees who had worked on the VAG contract were taken on by ECM Ltd and they claimed that they had been unfairly dismissed. An employment tribunal decided that there had been a relevant transfer from A Ltd to ECM Ltd, meaning that the employees had been protected by TUPE. When the case reached the Court of Appeal, ECM Ltd argued with reference to the Süzen case that, since it had not taken A Ltd's employees on, no relevant transfer could have occurred. The Court of Appeal rejected this argument. In Lord

Justice Mummery's view 'the importance of Süzen has... been overstated' and 'the ruling... should be seen in its proper context'. Because Süzen did not claim to mark a departure from previous case law, such as Spijkers, it remained the case that it is for the national court to assess all the facts characterising a transaction in order to determine whether a transfer of an undertaking had taken place. This is what the tribunal in this case had done. It had noted the differences in the way the new contractor carried out the contract – for example, unlike A Ltd, ECM Ltd had no administrative staff in Grimsby and did not deliver to local delivery centres – but had pointed out, on the other hand, that the customers and the work carried out remained essentially the same. Moreover, Mummery LJ continued, 'the tribunal was entitled to have regard, as a relevant circumstance, to the reason why those employees were not appointed by [ECM Ltd]. The Court of Justice has not decided in Süzen or in any other case that this is an irrelevant circumstance or that the failure of the transferee to appoint any of the former employees of the transferor points conclusively against a transfer'. Accordingly, the Court upheld the tribunal's decision, concluding that it had made no error of law

- **ADI (UK) Ltd v Willer and ors** 2001 IRLR 542, CA: ADI Ltd provided security services at a shopping centre. Its contract came to an end and the incoming contractor, FSG Ltd, refused to take on the nine security officers who had been performing the work. ADI Ltd dismissed the officers, some of whom brought unfair dismissal claims before an employment tribunal. Both the tribunal and the EAT concluded that no TUPE transfer had taken place, meaning that the employees had not transferred from ADI Ltd to FSG Ltd. ADI Ltd appealed against this decision to the Court of Appeal. Having noted that this case concerned a labour-intensive entity, and having considered the Süzen decision, the Court accepted that there would clearly have been a relevant transfer for the purposes of TUPE had FSG Ltd taken on the security officers who were dedicated to the relevant contract. But since FSG Ltd had not, in fact, taken the employees on, the Süzen case suggested that no relevant transfer had occurred. Despite this, however, the majority of the Court found a way of upholding ADI Ltd's appeal. Referring to the ECM case (above), the majority noted that it was necessary to have regard, as a relevant circumstance, to the reason why FSG Ltd did not employ the security officers in question. The majority then went one step further, holding that if the reason for FSG Ltd's declining to employ the officers was that it wished to avoid the operation of TUPE, the tribunal should have assessed the case as if the officers had, in fact, been taken on by that company. So, if the reason or principal reason for FSG Ltd's not taking on the employees was to avoid the application of TUPE, a relevant transfer had occurred in this case. Otherwise, there had been no such transfer. The Court remitted the case for the tribunal to consider FSG Ltd's motive for declining to take on ADI Ltd's security officers. Note, however, that Lord

37

Justice Simon Brown, in his minority judgment, was adamant that the ECJ jurisprudence did not support the approach taken by the majority. He concluded, interpreting Süzen strictly, that the decisive factor was that FSG Ltd had not taken on ADI Ltd's workforce. In his view, the reason for the incoming contractor's refusal to take the workforce on was 'immaterial'

- **RCO Support Services Ltd and anor v Unison and ors** 2002 ICR 751, CA: the Aintree Hospitals NHS Trust (the Trust) administered two hospitals in Liverpool – Walton Hospital and Fazakerley Hospital. Over a four-year period, the Trust phased out all its in-patient wards and operating theatres at Walton and reopened them at Fazakerley. The cleaning services at Walton, which had been contracted out to IHS Ltd, and the catering services at Walton, which had been provided by the Trust, 'transferred' to RCO Ltd, which ran both cleaning and catering at Fazakerley. RCO Ltd denied that TUPE applied. However, it was prepared to employ some of the relevant staff on its own terms and conditions. In the event, none of the cleaners or caterers applied to work for RCO Ltd, and some of them brought unfair dismissal claims before an employment tribunal. The tribunal decided that there had been relevant transfers from IHS Ltd to RCO Ltd in respect of the cleaning staff, and from the Trust to RCO Ltd in respect of the catering staff. When the case reached the Court of Appeal, the Court upheld the tribunal's decision. It did so notwithstanding that none of the relevant workforces had been taken on by RCO Ltd and that there had been no significant transfer of assets. In the Court's view, the limits set out in Süzen did not mean that the Directive can never apply in a contracting-out case if neither assets nor workforce are transferred. Furthermore, the Süzen decision should not be read as singling out, to the exclusion of all other circumstances, the particular circumstance of none of the workforce being taken on and treating that as determinative of the transfer issue in every labour-intensive case. Such an interpretation would run counter to the retention of identity test in the Spijkers decision, which warned against considering single factors in isolation. The tribunal in the instant case had correctly followed the Spijkers approach. Moreover, the tribunal had not erred in treating RCO Ltd's willingness to take on the existing staff as a factor supporting the retention of the identity of the cleaning and catering undertakings – the Süzen decision did not require the tribunal to exclude from its consideration of all the facts characterising the transaction the circumstances of the decision by the putative transferee not to take on the workforce.

1.73 More recently, the EAT examined a prospective transferee's motive for failing to take on an outgoing contractor's workforce in the case of Astle and ors v Cheshire County Council and anor 2005 IRLR 12, EAT. Cheshire County Council had for many years provided its own architectural services. In 1994 it contracted these services out to KD, and the relevant Council employees transferred under TUPE. In 1999 the Council awarded the contract to another contractor, SGI. Again TUPE applied, and the staff of KD, including 65 ex-Council employees, transferred to SGI. In time, the Council became concerned about SGI's performance, and felt that some of the staff who had originally been employed by the Council were part of the problem. The Council decided to terminate SGI's contract and to adopt what it referred to as a 'market economy' approach, under which a panel of consultants would be engaged to provide the services instead of a single contractor. The Council temporarily took over some of the responsibilities until the new arrangements were put in place. However, none of the relevant employees were taken on by the Council, and they brought tribunal claims arguing that they had transferred to the Council under TUPE.

The employment tribunal found that the Council did not want the SGI staff to continue to carry out the architectural services, and that 'the Council was therefore most concerned to avoid a TUPE transfer'. It also noted, however, that the Council had genuinely decided that the best way to deliver the services was by a panel of consultants rather than a workforce. The tribunal went on to conclude that the reason the Council did not accept the workforce back 'was not to defeat TUPE, but because it had given the responsibility of carrying out the provision of architectural services to a panel of consultants; thus the Council did not require a workforce to operate the business. In these circumstances the question of whether, had the workforce been transferred, [there would] have been a [TUPE] transfer, does not arise.' The fact was, the workforce did not transfer. Applying the multifactoral test in Spijkers, the tribunal concluded that no relevant transfer had taken place. On appeal, the EAT upheld the tribunal's decision. There were no grounds for overturning the conclusion that, although the Council had *wished* to avoid the consequences of TUPE, its reason for not taking on the contractor's workforce was not to thwart the operation of the Regulations as such, but to implement the new structure as the best method of delivering the services in question. Far from being a case in which the new scheme or structure that the employer had put in place was without commercial or economic justification, the Council's new way of operating was plainly sensible. While another tribunal might have reached a different conclusion on the facts, the tribunal in the instant case had heard all the evidence and had made no error of law.

Often a client decides to change the contractor performing a service owing to **1.74** concerns about the performance of the staff dedicated to the contract. In the following two cases clients did precisely this. Moreover, they instructed the incoming contractors not to take on the outgoing contractors' workforces. The new contractors obeyed these instructions and the employees concerned brought tribunal claims invoking TUPE. It fell to the EAT to grapple with the question of whether relevant transfers had occurred. In both cases, the EAT decided that the reason the employees were not taken on was the client's instruction, and *not* the transferee's wish to avoid TUPE. Accordingly, no relevant transfers had taken place:

- **Williams v Lockhart Security Services Ltd** EAT 1395/01: W worked as a security guard for L Ltd at the Darlington Retail Park (DRP). When L Ltd lost the guarding contract, DRP awarded a new contract to A Ltd. In doing so, it stipulated that it wanted none of the former L Ltd employees to continue working at its site. A Ltd thus declined to take W on, and he brought claims before an employment tribunal which gave rise to the question of whether a relevant transfer had occurred from L Ltd to A Ltd. The tribunal held that there had been such a transfer, but the EAT overturned its decision. The EAT concluded that where no physical assets or employees were transferred from L Ltd to A Ltd, and where the reason A Ltd had not taken on the employees dedicated to the contract was that they were prevented from doing so due to objection by the client, DRP, the economic entity had not retained its identity, meaning that no relevant transfer had occurred

- **Carlisle Facilities Group v Matrix Events and Security Services and ors** EAT 0380/04: CFG employed 32 security officers for Sea France on its cross-channel ferries. Sea France became dissatisfied by the general level of performance of the CFG staff, terminated the contract, and awarded it to MES, telling MES that it did not want any of CFG's staff to carry out the work. MES did not take the employees on, and some of them brought tribunal claims. The question arose as to whether there had been a relevant transfer from CFG to MES. An employment tribunal examined the reason why MES did not take the CFG security guards on, and decided that its decision not to do so could not be categorised as a ploy to avoid the Regulations. Rather, the reason why MES did not take the employees on was that Sea France had been dissatisfied with their performance. In so finding, the tribunal noted that it would have been easier for MES to have employed some of CFG's employees than to advertise for new labour. The tribunal went on to conclude that, since there were no relevant assets and none of the relevant employees had been taken on by MES, TUPE did not apply. On appeal, the EAT found no fault with the tribunal's decision.

1.75 The above two decisions are not without their difficulties. Essentially, they return us to the much criticized 'circular' situation discussed above – namely, that if the transferee, for whatever reason, chooses not to voluntarily take on the transferor's workforce, then a relevant transfer of a labour-intensive entity will not occur for the purposes of the Directive or Reg 3(1)(a) of TUPE. Moreover, the decisions chime with the radical approach recommended by the Advocate General in his Opinion in the Süzen case. He took the view that if the client does not want the incoming contractor to take on the relevant employees in an SPC situation, that should be sufficient to preclude the Directive from applying. This approach (which was not, in fact, adopted by the ECJ in its final decision in the Süzen case) does not sit easily with the principal purpose of the Directive, which is to protect employees' rights.

Having said all that, cases such as Williams and Carlisle Facilities Group would now almost certainly fall within the TUPE regime, owing to the new SPC rules contained in Reg 3(1)(b) of the 2006 Regulations – see 'Service provision changes – what difference will the new rules make?' below.

Oy Liikenne – Asset-reliant entities require asset transfer. We have seen how **1.76** the UK courts and tribunals attempted to downplay the importance of the Süzen decision, preferring to believe that it fitted harmoniously into the body of previous ECJ case law. However, a spanner was thrown into the works by the ECJ in Oy Liikenne Ab v Liskojärvi and anor 2001 IRLR 171. ECJ. Not content with upholding Süzen, the ECJ in Oy Liikenne went one stage further. It concluded that the absence of the transfer of a substantial body of *physical assets* in a case where the undertaking in question is heavily asset-dependent leads inexorably to the conclusion that the Directive does not apply.

The facts in Oy Liikenne were thus. Following a tender procedure, the Greater Helsinki Joint Board awarded the operation of a number of the city's bus routes to OL. The outgoing contractor, HL, dismissed the 45 drivers who had worked on the routes. 33 of the drivers (including L and J) applied to be taken on by OL. All were successful, but were engaged on less favourable conditions than those which they had enjoyed under HL. No vehicles or significant assets connected with the operation of the bus routes were transferred to OL from HL, although OL leased two buses from HL for a few months while waiting for the delivery of 22 new buses. L and J brought actions against OL claiming that, owing to the operation of the Directive, they were entitled to terms and conditions no less favourable than those that they had enjoyed prior to the transfer. A Finnish court referred the matter to the ECJ.

Referring to its previous decision in Süzen, the ECJ noted that a labour-intensive **1.77** entity, based essentially on manpower, is capable of maintaining its identity after a transfer where the new employer takes over a major part, in terms of their numbers and skills, of the employees employed by its predecessor. However, it continued, bus transport cannot be regarded as an activity based essentially on manpower. It requires substantial plant and equipment. The ECJ held that in a sector such as scheduled public transport by bus, where the tangible assets contribute significantly to the performance of the activity, the absence of a transfer to a significant extent from the old to the new contractor of such assets must lead to the conclusion that the entity does not retain its identity. In such circumstances, the Directive will not apply. So, on the facts of Oy Liikenne, in the context of a change in the contractor responsible for operating scheduled bus services, the absence of a transfer of the actual buses used by the previous operator meant that there could be no transfer to which the Directive applied.

41

This decision was surprising on several counts. First, many of the traditional 'Spijkers' factors pointing to a business transfer were present. For instance, there was a transfer of the customer base – albeit that the customer base in question took the form of bus passengers and therefore comprised a 'captive audience'. Secondly, a majority of the employees employed by the outgoing contractor to operate the bus routes were, in fact, taken on by the incoming contractor, without any break in their employment. Had this been a case of the transfer of a labour-intensive activity, the employees themselves would have been viewed as assets of the business, and as principal assets at that. And thirdly, one of the consistent propositions laid down by the ECJ in the pre-Süzen jurisprudence is that the transfer of physical assets is not a prerequisite for the transfer of an undertaking – see, for example, Merckx and anor v Ford Motors Co (Belgium) SA 1997 ICR 352, ECJ. In Oy Liikenne, however, far from downplaying the importance of physical assets, the ECJ conferred upon them such importance as to make them decisive of the question of whether or not the Directive applied – at least in a case of an asset-dependent undertaking such as municipal transport services.

1.78 The ECJ adopted a similar approach to the importance of asset transfer in Abler and ors v Sodexho MM Catering GmbH (above), but strangely enough reached the diametrically opposite outcome. The Abler case concerned a change of contractor responsible for providing catering services for an orthopaedic hospital in Austria. The old contractor, Sanrest, had prepared meals on the hospital premises, using water, energy and all necessary small and large equipment provided by the hospital. When management authority responsible for the hospital terminated its agreement with Sanrest, the new contractor, Sodexho, used the same equipment. However, it denied Sanrest's contention that what had occurred amounted to a transfer of an undertaking under the Directive, and refused to take any of Sanrest's employees on. Sanrest dismissed the employees, who brought claims arguing that their employment had transferred to Sodexho. When the Supreme Court of Austria referred the matter to the ECJ, the European Court stated that the catering activities in this case were based essentially on equipment – namely, the premises, water and energy and small and large equipment, including the appliances needed for preparing the meals and the dishwashers. This equipment was used both before and after the transfer – in fact, a defining feature of the situation was the express and fundamental obligation to prepare the meals in the hospital kitchen and thus to take over those tangible assets. The ECJ concluded: 'The transfer of the premises and the equipment provided by the hospital, which is indispensable for the preparation and distribution of meals to the hospital patients and staff is sufficient, in the circumstances, to make this a transfer of an economic entity.'

1.79 *UK courts downplay the importance of Oy Liikenne.* Despite the Oy Liikenne decision, the UK courts have stuck to their guns and continued to emphasise the multifactoral approach advocated in Spijkers. In downplaying the importance of Oy Liikenne, their message has been twofold. First, the ECJ did *not* mean to lay down a principle that an asset transfer must occur if an asset-reliant entity is to retain its identity following a transfer. Secondly, even if the ECJ *did* lay down such a principle, it will not necessarily affect a great number of cases. This is because tribunals are not obliged to decide that economic entities are *either* labour-intensive *or* asset-reliant. Many entities will fall somewhere in between these extremes. The following cases illustrate these points:

- **P&O Trans European Ltd v Initial Transport Services Ltd and ors** 2003 IRLR 128, EAT: Shell UK Ltd had a substantial fleet of in-house vehicles, used to transport the majority of its fuel products. Some of the transporting work, however, was carried out by contractors. Under an arrangement with Shell, both P&O and ITS provided backup petroleum delivery services. In late 1998 Shell decided to contract out the whole of its delivery function and P&O won the national contract as from 1 August 1999. As a result, Shell terminated its existing arrangement with ITS. P&O took on all of Shell's drivers and a large part of its fleet of vehicles. P&O also took on ITS's drivers, but none of its vehicles. The question arose whether a relevant transfer had occurred from ITS to P&O. A tribunal found that the business carried on by P&O was essentially the same as that carried on by ITS. However, no tangible assets had been transferred, in that P&O had not taken on any of ITS's vehicles. The tribunal considered this an important factor, as a delivery service was dependent upon the use of such vehicles. However, it also noted that all ITS's drivers had been transferred; Shell remained the customer; and there was no suspension of activity when P&O took on the contract. Having weighed up all these factors, the tribunal concluded that ITS's activity of providing a backup delivery service had retained its identity having been taken over by P&O, and that there had thus been a relevant transfer. P&O appealed to the EAT, relying on the ECJ's decision in Oy Liikenne to argue that, in an asset-intensive industry such as the delivery of petroleum products by tanker, the absence of a transfer of tangible assets or a significant part of them must lead to the conclusion that there is no relevant transfer. The EAT, however, upheld the tribunal's decision, stating that the Oy Liikenne case did not lay down a principle that in all cases of asset-intensive industries the absence, to a significant extent, of a transfer of such assets would always lead to the conclusion that no transfer had taken place. Rather, the ECJ had made it clear that the approach in deciding whether a transfer of undertaking has occurred remains multifactoral

- **Scottish Coal Co Ltd v McCormick and ors** 2005 All ER 104, Ct Sess (Inner House): from 1988 onwards C Ltd carried out mining activities at an opencast mining site in Ayrshire, pursuant to contracts with S Ltd. C Ltd possessed the necessary heavy excavating plant, dumper trucks and ancillary equipment to carry out these activities. It also erected workshops and office

43

buildings on site. In April 2001 S Ltd took over C Ltd's activities at the site. S Ltd did not acquire C Ltd's plant or equipment as part of this transaction, since C Ltd did not wish to sell it. The majority of C Ltd's former employees returned to the site to work for S Ltd, resuming the same mining activities they had performed prior to the transaction. Some of the workforce brought claims before an employment tribunal, contending that the transaction between the two companies had been a transfer of an undertaking for the purposes of TUPE. The employment tribunal, feeling that this was a complicated case in which no single factor proved decisive, eventually concluded that the economic entity in question retained its identity after the transfer, meaning that TUPE applied. When the EAT upheld the tribunal's decision, S Ltd appealed to the Court of Session, contending that both the tribunal and the EAT had failed to follow the guidance set down by the ECJ in Oy Liikenne. In S Ltd's view, that case illustrated that the primary step in determining whether there has been a transfer of an undertaking is to characterise the undertaking as either 'asset-reliant' or 'labour-intensive'. It stated that C Ltd's mining operation had clearly been an 'asset-reliant' undertaking, unable to operate without the use of its plant and equipment. Since no plant had been transferred, no relevant TUPE transfer could have taken place. The Court of Session rejected this argument. It did not read either Oy Liikenne or Abler as 'laying down an invariable requirement that, in the context of a claimed TUPE transfer, a given business must necessarily be characterised as either "asset-reliant" or "labour-intensive", as if those were mutually exclusive categories that defined exhaustively the range of possibilities that could arise'. Rather, there would appear to be an unlimited 'range of intermediate possibilities'. Oy Liikenne and Abler illustrated 'the position at one end of the spectrum when a transfer must include the production assets of the entity. In intermediate cases, it must always be an issue for the fact-finding tribunal whether, on an appreciation of all relevant facts and circumstances, the undertaking in question can be said to have been transferred for the purposes of the 1981 Regulations'

- **Balfour Beatty Power Networks Ltd and anor v Wilcox and ors** 2007 IRLR 63, CA: H plc provided street lighting services for WPD under a number of different contracts. One such contract related to the maintenance of overhead lines and the replacement of poles. H plc leased the vehicles and specialist equipment required to carry out these activities. When H plc lost this contract to Interserve, these leased items did not transfer and Interserve made alternative arrangements. However, the new contractor did take on the majority (although not all) of the dedicated workforce. The employees who were not taken on brought tribunal claims, and argued successfully that their employment had transferred to Interserve owing to the operation of TUPE. When the case reached the Court of Appeal, Interserve argued that, in the present case, assets such as vehicles and tools were important to the performance of the contract and that, in light of the Oy Liikenne decision, the fact that they had not been transferred prevented the Directive and hence Reg 3(1)(a) of TUPE from applying. The Court, however, upheld the tribunal's decision. Lord Justice Buxton approved the comments of the Court of Session in the Scottish Coal case above, expressing considerable doubts as to whether the ECJ had intended to lay down a rule as stark as that which Interserve suggested. In any event, he continued, this case presented an issue not yet addressed by the ECJ – namely, the relevance of the fact that the assets in question were leased by the transferor. He stated: 'They can... be better characterised as tools and equipment, rather than assets in the technical sense, and it is difficult to see them as an integral part of the former business... It is in this case difficult to see how exactly "transfer" of the leased assets would operate, or how the existence of those assets can override the general obligation to approach the case on a multifactoral basis.'

Conclusion. After a long period of uncertainty following the ECJ's decisions in **1.80** Süzen and Oy Liikenne, the approach of the UK Courts and tribunals has essentially come full circle. When answering the question of whether an economic entity has retained its identity following a service provision change, meaning that a relevant transfer has occurred under Reg 3(1)(a) of TUPE, a tribunal should take all the relevant factors into account. However, although this situation is clearer than it has been for many years, the multifactoral test still does not provide contractors with the certainty they would wish for. There will still be many sets of circumstances in which the retention of identity question will prove extremely difficult to answer.

Thankfully, most SPCs will in any event now be covered by the transfer rules owing to Reg 3(1)(b) of the 2006 Regulations, which, in order to put an end to the prevailing uncertainty and the inevitability of litigation that resulted, was specifically designed to ensure that such 'transfers' fall within TUPE's scope. We discuss new Reg 3(1)(b) in 'Service provision changes' below.

Entity situated In the United Kingdom immediately prior to transfer 1.81
Regulation 3(1)(a) of the 2006 Regulations states that a 'relevant transfer' under that provision only occurs where the transferring undertaking or business or part of undertaking or business is 'situated immediately before the transfer in the United Kingdom'.

Thus, on its face, Reg 3(1)(a) applies to standard transfers taking place within the United Kingdom, and to standard transfers from the United Kingdom outwards (presuming that the entity in question manages to retain its identity despite an arguably significant change of circumstances). It will *not* apply to transfers *into* the United Kingdom from elsewhere. However, if the transfer is from another country subject to the Directive, it would seem that some sort of transfer regime should take effect based on the national law equivalent to TUPE of the country concerned. We focus on issues surrounding transfers from the United Kingdom to elsewhere, and from elsewhere to the United Kingdom, in Chapter 9.

1.82 The Court of Appeal examined the meaning of 'the United Kingdom' for the purposes of Reg 3(1)(a) in Addison and ors v Denholm Ship Management (UK) Ltd and ors 1997 IRLR 389, CA. It decided that the territorial scope of the United Kingdom is confined to its land and territorial waters and does not extend to the UK sector of the Continental Shelf of the North Sea. It followed that the transfer of a contract for the supply of crew to a 'flotel' adjoining an oil installation in the UK sector of the Continental Shelf was not covered by TUPE.

Note that Reg 3(4)(b) clarifies that TUPE can apply to a business transfer notwithstanding that:

● the transfer is governed or affected by the law of another country, or

● the employment of the employees in the undertaking transferred is governed by the law of another country.

1.83 Furthermore, Reg 3(4)(c) provides that a relevant transfer can occur even where persons employed in the undertaking, business or part transferred ordinarily work outside the United Kingdom. The DTI Guide explains: 'For example, if there is a transfer of a UK exporting business, the fact that the sales force spends the majority of its working week outside the UK will not prevent the Regulations applying to the transfer, so long as the undertaking itself (comprising, among other things, premises, assets, fixtures and fittings, goodwill as well as employees) is situated in the UK.'

1.84 Service provision changes

In 'Standard transfers' above we saw that, in recent years, the circumstances in which the EU Acquired Rights Directive and TUPE will apply to service provision changes (SPCs) have proved difficult to pin down. The decisions of the ECJ have been inconsistent in this regard, giving rise to much litigation and commercial uncertainty.

In the 2005 Consultation Document the UK Government made clear its dissatisfaction with this state of affairs. It stated: 'Ideally, everyone should know where they stand... so that employers can plan effectively in a climate of fair competition and affected employees are protected as a matter of course.' It was with this ideal in mind that the Government drafted Reg 3(1)(b) of the 2006 Regulations. Introduced under a power contained in S.38 of the Employment Relations Act 1999, this goes beyond the Directive's requirements and brings the vast majority of SPCs within the TUPE fold. The Government expressed its hope that the new SPC rule will 'ensure a "level playing field" for contractors bidding for service contracts', and mean that businesses and employees 'will be (at least to some extent) "insulated" from the effects of any further developments in ECJ jurisprudence on the application of the Directive'.

The upshot is that there are now two different routes by which a 'relevant **1.85** transfer' can come about. The first is where the occasionally confusing Directive-driven definition – contained in Reg 3(1)(a) and discussed at length in 'Standard transfers' above – is satisfied. The second is where a 'service provision change' as defined by new Reg 3(1)(b) takes place. We should point out that Reg 3(1)(a) and Reg 3(1)(b) are not mutually exclusive, and that many SPCs will meet both sets of criteria. Nevertheless, a fair percentage of SPCs that are not covered by Reg 3(1)(a) will fall within Reg 3(1)(b).

Essentially, it makes no difference to the relevant employees whether it is Reg 3(1)(a), Reg 3(1)(b) or both that apply. The exception that proves this rule – Reg 21(5) – is a transitional provision, which is therefore of diminishing relevance. This provides that, in respect of SPCs taking place on or before 4 May 2006, and falling solely under Reg 3(1)(b), the information and consultation rules contained in Regs 11 and 12 (see Chapter 8) do not apply.

We now turn to examine the new, wide-ranging SPC provision that is Reg 3(1)(b), focusing in particular on the issues that, despite the Government's wish for commercial certainty, seem ripe for litigation.

The three types of SPC   1.86
Regulation 3(1)(b) states that the 2006 Regulations apply to 'a service provision change' where the conditions set out in Reg 3(3) are satisfied (see 'The Reg 3(3) conditions' below). Reg 3(1)(b) goes on to define three types of service provision change, as follows:

- where 'activities cease to be carried out by a person ("a client") on his own behalf and are carried out instead by another person on the client's behalf ("a contractor")' – Reg 3(1)(b)(i). This is the exercise commonly known as 'contracting out' or 'outsourcing'

- where 'activities cease to be carried out by a contractor on a client's behalf (whether or not those activities had previously been carried out by the client on his own behalf) and are carried out instead by another person ("a subsequent contractor") on the client's behalf' – Reg 3(1)(b)(ii). This concerns a change of contractor, usually following a re-tendering process, and is sometimes referred to as 'second generation contracting out'

- where 'activities cease to be carried out by a contractor or subsequent contractor on a client's behalf (whether or not those activities had previously been carried out by the client on his own behalf) and are carried out by the client on his own behalf' – Reg 3(1)(b)(iii). This is called 'contracting in' or 'insourcing'.

1.87 **What are 'activities'?** Each of the three SPC scenarios set out above involve 'activities' ceasing to be carried out by one person and subsequently being carried out by another. However, although the word 'activities' is clearly crucial to the workings of the new SPC regime, it is not defined in the 2006 Regulations.

In its response to consultation, published in February 2006, the Government made a number of points with regard to the term 'activities'. First, it surmised that 'in most cases, it should be clear what roles or functions comprise the activities in question and therefore which individuals will be transferred along with the service provision change'. By logical extension, however, that leaves some cases in which this issue will be far from clear, and where further guidance would be helpful. Unfortunately, the Government's next statement, that 'the term "activities" is more precise than some of the other alternatives suggested and is sufficiently broad to capture the nature of the service provision that the Government intends should be within this provision', did not exactly get to the nub of the issue. We explore some of the difficulties that this lack of clarity might pose in 'Retention of identity not required' below.

1.88 The Government went on to make reference to the case of Fairhurst Ward Abbotts Ltd v Botes Building Ltd and ors 2004 ICR 919, CA (for which, see 'Standard transfers – what is an "economic entity"?' above). The Fairhurst decision made it clear that a standard transfer can occur where what is transferred is not a separate economic entity in the hands of the transferor, as long as it becomes identifiable as such an entity on the occasion of the transfer. In the Government's view, 'this approach to what constitutes an economic entity applies equally to the construction of activities in the context of a service provision change'. Nevertheless, we suggest that the 'activities' must be identifiable as separate to some degree prior to the transfer, as Reg 3(1)(b) will not apply unless, under the transferor, there was 'an organised grouping of employees' which had 'as its principal purpose the carrying out of the activities concerned' – see 'The Reg 3(3) conditions' below.

The meaning of 'activities' has been considered by the EAT in a number of recent cases. These are discussed under 'Professional business services not excluded'.

1.89 **Definition of 'contractor'.** The term 'contractor', according to Reg 2(1), also includes sub-contractor. Accordingly, Reg 3(1)(b) can cover sub-contracting by a client's contractor and changes of sub-contractor.

1.90 **Definition of 'transferor' and 'transferee'.** One peculiarity of a TUPE transfer in a second-generation contracting-out scenario is that there is no direct relationship between the outgoing and incoming contractor. In effect, the contract is always transferred via the client for whom the service is being performed.

Regulation 2(1) states that 'in the case of a service provision change falling within regulation 3(1)(b), "the transferor" means the person who carried out the activities prior to the service provision change and "the transferee" means the person who carries out the activities as a result of the service provision change'. This clarifies that the client will effectively be left out of the equation in a second-generation case, and fits well with Reg 3(6)(a), which provides that a relevant transfer 'may be effected by a series of two or more transactions'.

The Reg 3(3) conditions   1.91
Each of the conditions set out in Reg 3(3) must be met if an SPC is to be covered by Reg 3(1)(b). These are as follows:

- 'immediately before the service provision change there is an organised grouping of employees situated in Great Britain which has as its principal purpose the carrying out of the activities concerned on behalf of the client' – Reg 3(3)(a)(i)

- 'immediately before the service provision change the client intends that the activities will, following the service provision change, be carried out by the transferee other than in connection with a single specific event or task of short-term duration' – Reg 3(3)(a)(ii), and

- 'the activities concerned do not consist wholly or mainly of the supply of goods for the client's use' – Reg 3(3)(b).

We now turn to examine these conditions in greater detail.

Organised grouping of employees carrying out the activities   1.92
The first of the conditions that must be satisfied in order for a 'service provision change' covered by Reg 3(1)(b) to occur is that 'immediately before the service provision change there is an organised grouping of employees situated in Great Britain which has as its principal purpose the carrying out of the activities concerned on behalf of a client' – Reg 3(3)(a)(i).

'Organised grouping of employees'. So, just as there will be no economic 1.93
entity capable of transferring under Reg 3(1)(a) where there is no organised grouping of *resources* (see 'Standard transfers' above), there will be no SPC under Reg 3(1)(b) where there is no organised grouping of *employees*.

The DTI Guide states that this requirement is intended 'to confine the Regulations' coverage to cases where the old service provider (i.e. the transferor) has in place a team of employees to carry out the service activities, and that team is essentially dedicated to carrying out the activities that are to transfer'. The Guide goes on to give an example where this requirement would not be met: 'if a contractor was engaged by a client to provide, say, a courier service, but the collections and deliveries were carried out each day by various different couriers on an ad hoc basis, rather than by an identifiable team of employees,

49

there would be no "service provision change" and the Regulations would not apply'.

1.94 Note that Reg 2(1) of the 2006 Regulations explains that 'references to "organised grouping of employees" shall include a single employee'. This linguistically awkward statement doffs its hat to the case of Schmidt v Spar- und Leihkasse der früheren Ämter Bordesholm, Kiel und Cronshagen 1995 ICR 237, ECJ (see 'Standard transfers – what is an "economic entity"?' above), in which the ECJ held that the fact that an economic activity is performed by a single employee is not in itself sufficient to preclude the application of the transfer rules.

The decisions in the following cases provide some useful insights into how employment tribunals will determine whether particular employees from part of an organised grouping of resources:

* **Hunt v Storm Communications Ltd and ors** ET Case No.2702546/06: H worked for Storm Communications Ltd ('Storm'), a PR agency, as an account manager. Her job description did not specify that she would work for any one client in particular but, in fact, she spent the majority of her time during the five year period of her employment working on the Brown Brothers Wines ("BBW") account. Two other individuals – a junior account executive, and a freelancer who had formerly been Storm's BBW account director – also worked on the account during this period, but to a much lesser degree. In June 2006, BBW informed Storm that it would be inviting tenders for its PR requirements. Storm pitched to retain the work, but was unsuccessful with its bid, and BBW awarded the new contract to Wild Card Public Relations Ltd ('WildCard'). Storm informed H that it believed that her employment would transfer to WildCard pursuant to TUPE. However, WildCard refused to accept that H was to transfer to it, arguing that since (a) H had no contractual obligation to carry out BBW work and (b) the records provided to it by Storm suggested that H only worked on the BBW account for 55 per cent of her time, H was not, therefore, 'essentially dedicated' to that account. H brought a number of claims against Storm and WildCard, including unfair dismissal based on the contention that TUPE 2006 had applied to transfer her employment to Wildcard. The employment tribunal held that this case concerned a change of contractor – from Storm to WildCard – rather than an 'insourcing' from Storm back to BBW, followed by a subsequent 'outsourcing' to WildCard. Although in the period between 28 July and 2 October, BBW had undertaken its own PR activities, this was only on a 'caretaker'" basis, and it did not truly take those activities back in-house. The tribunal also accepted H's evidence that the BBW account in fact provided some 70 per cent of her work and that, on that basis, H's 'principal purpose' was carrying out specialist PR services on behalf of BBW. Accordingly, H was held to be part of the 'organised grouping

of employees...which ha[d] as its principal purpose' the performance of PR activities for BBW. In contrast, the freelancer who had worked on that account was not employed by Storm, so she could not be part of a 'grouping of employees'. And although the junior account executive who worked on the BBW account was an employee, his contribution was deemed to be ad hoc, peripheral and not sufficiently specialist to be considered to be 'dedicated' to the BBW account

- **Williams v Executive Committee of the North Wales Society for the Blind** ET Case No.2902095/06: W was one of five rehabilitation officers employed by NWSB to make a rehabilitation team. W and an assistant were also supplied by NWSB to provide rehabilitation services to Conway County Borough Council. W spent 50 per cent of her time on duties related to the contract with the Council and the remainder on other activities within NWSB. When W was made redundant, she claimed that her employment had been transferred to the Council under TUPE by way of either a standard transfer or SPC. The tribunal held that W and her assistant did not, of themselves, comprise a stable economic entity, since they were not sufficiently structured or autonomous applying the test laid down in Cheesman and ors v R Brewer Contracts Ltd 2001 IRLR 144, EAT. For example, W had no line management over her assistant and their work was supervised by the Council's senior rehabilitation officer. Having found that there was no stable economic entity, the tribunal also found that there was no organised grouping of employees for the purposes of Reg 3(1).

In Royden v Barnetts Solicitors, ET Case No.2103451/07 the employment **1.95** tribunal held that two employees of a solicitors firm who spent the majority of their time on work referred to it by one institutional client were protected by Reg 3(1)(b)(ii) when the client decided to contract out the work to another law firm.

'Principal purpose'. In order for Reg 3(1)(b) to apply, the *principal purpose* of **1.96** the organised grouping of employees must be the carrying out of the activities on behalf of the client.

Single specific client. The 2005 Consultation Document stated that the **1.97** 'principal purpose' requirement will 'exclude from the extended coverage cases where there is an organised grouping of employees, but their principal purpose is to carry out service activities on behalf of clients in general, rather than a single specific client'. The Government provided the example of a travel agency, where the purpose of an established team of staff was to meet the travel booking needs of five different clients rather than of one client in particular. In the Government's view, 'if one of those five clients decides to switch to a different contractor for the supply of these services, there will be no transfer under [Reg 3(1)(b)]'.

51

Deciding whether this requirement is satisfied will not always be straightforward. Take, for example, a group of staff at Contractor Ltd, who devote Monday to Wednesday each week to providing a service to one client (A), and spend the rest of each week providing the same service to a number of other clients (B, C, D, E and F). What will be the position if client A decides to end its contract with Contractor Ltd, and engage a different company, Cheaper Ltd, to provide the service? Will there be an SPC within Reg 3(1)(b) from Contractor Ltd to Cheaper Ltd?

1.98 In one sense, the principal purpose of the relevant group of employees is to carry out the 'activities' on behalf of client A. That is what the employees spend the majority of their time doing, and, as the DTI Guide states, a team of employees does not need to work *exclusively* on the activities that are to transfer in order for Reg 3(1)(b) to apply. In another sense, however, the group's principal purpose is to carry out the activities in question for a number of different clients – a situation similar to that of the travel agency in the DTI's example, where Reg 3(1)(b) would *not* apply. This latter interpretation would almost certainly be preferable if, for instance, the employees were spending a lot of time working for client A simply because of a recent influx of work from that client, whereas the more normal pattern has been to carry out less work for client A and much more work, say, for clients B and C.

Scenarios such as this, which seem neither black nor white, will almost certainly lead to litigation. In this regard, it will be interesting to see the extent to which tribunals take into account the extensive case law concerning the question of whether individual employees are 'assigned' to the entity/grouping transferred – the test that is applied, where there *is* a relevant transfer, to determine *which* employees will move over to the transferee under Reg 4 (see Chapter 2 under '"Assigned" to undertaking transferred'). On their face, the group 'principal purpose' test of Reg 3(1)(b) and the individual 'assignment' test involve similar considerations. However, even if a tribunal were to see these tests as analogous, this would not bring it much closer to reaching a conclusion as to the principal purpose of the group of employees in our example. This is because the case law on the assignment issue is not exactly a beacon of clarity. In essence, it simply establishes that assignment is a matter for the tribunal to determine by weighing up all the facts of the case, meaning that no one factor – for example, the percentage of time an employee spends working in the transferring entity – is necessarily determinative.

1.99 **The problem of fragmentation.** Difficulties might also arise where a contract involving a number of different activities is repackaged and effectively transferred to two or more different employers. This issue was raised by the Employment Lawyers' Association, among others, during consultation on the 2006 Regulations, and the Government addressed it briefly in the DTI Guide. In its view, Reg 3(1)(b) will 'potentially cover situations where just some of those activities in the original service contract are re-tendered and awarded to a new contractor, or where the original service contract is split up into two or more components, each of which is assigned to a different contractor. In each of these cases, the key test is whether an organised grouping of employees has as its principal purpose the carrying out of the activities that are transferred.'

Let us consider another hypothetical example. A company, Odd-job Ltd, has a contract to carry out maintenance work (heating, lighting, etc), building work and landscape gardening for Client Ltd. Client Ltd decides to terminate this contract, and invites tenders for three different contracts – maintenance, building and landscape gardening. Three different companies – Maintenance Ltd, Building Ltd and Gardening Ltd – are successful. Given the 'organised grouping of employees' and 'principal purpose' tests contained in Reg 3(1)(a)(i), it seems that the application or otherwise of the new SPC rules to these changes would depend on how Odd-job Ltd's employees carried out the work prior to the 'transfers'. Two alternative scenarios:

- Odd-job Ltd employed nine employees to carry out the maintenance, building and gardening work for Client Ltd. These employees were jacks of all trades, each of whom spent an equal amount of time carrying out maintenance, building and gardening activities. Here, these nine employees comprised the only identifiable 'grouping', and the principal purpose of that grouping was carrying out *all* the activities comprising Odd-job Ltd's contract. In other words, there was no group of employees dedicated to any one of the maintenance activities, the building activities or the gardening activities. Thus, owing to Reg 3(3)(a)(i), there could be no SPC transfer from Odd-job Ltd to Maintenance Ltd, Building Ltd or Gardening Ltd

- Odd-job Ltd had in place three dedicated groups of staff performing the contract for Client Ltd – one each for maintenance, building and landscape gardening. Each group consisted of a manager and two team members. In these circumstances there was clearly, prior to the transfer, an organised grouping of three employees with the principal purpose of carrying out the maintenance activities on behalf of Client Ltd; another organised grouping of three with the principal purpose of carrying out the building activities; and a third organised grouping with the principal purpose of carrying out the landscape gardening activities. Reg 3(1)(b) would apply in these circumstances, transferring these dedicated groups to Maintenance Ltd, Building Ltd and Gardening Ltd respectively.

The above scenarios illustrate two extremes. In reality, things are unlikely to be **1.100** as straightforward as this, so let us try something a little more complicated. Again, nine Odd-job Ltd employees combined to carry out the maintenance, building and landscape gardening work for Client Ltd. One of those was a manager, responsible for overseeing the entire contract. Three of the remaining eight employees spent all their time carrying out the maintenance work. The other five employees divided the majority of their time equally between building and gardening, but helped out with the maintenance work when required. When Maintenance Ltd took over the maintenance activities, would there be a Reg 3(1)(b) SPC transfer from Odd-job Ltd to Maintenance Ltd? There are two alternative conclusions that might be drawn, as follows:

- prior to the transfer, there was no organised grouping of employees whose principal purpose was carrying out the maintenance activities in question. Thus, there could be no SPC transfer from Odd-job Ltd to Maintenance Ltd. The 'organised grouping of employees' test of Reg 3(3)(a)(i) is analogous to the 'organised grouping of resources' test used to identify an economic entity for the purposes of the standard transfer rules (see 'Standard transfers – what is an "economic entity"?' above). It follows that an 'organised grouping of employees' must be a structured and autonomous team, dedicated to carrying out the specific activities in question. In this case, no such team existed, as the maintenance work was intricately bound up with the rest of Odd-job Ltd's operations. Management time was divided across the maintenance, building and gardening activities. Furthermore, of the eight employees that performed the maintenance work, only three spent the majority of their time on it. The maintenance work was not the 'principal purpose' of the grouping of employees as a whole

- it could be said that, prior to the transfer, there was an organised grouping of employees whose principal purpose was carrying out the maintenance activities, meaning that there was an SPC transfer from Odd-job Ltd to Maintenance Ltd under Reg 3(1)(b). It would not accord with the purpose of Reg 3(1)(b) to deny TUPE protection to the three employees dedicated to the maintenance work simply because those activities formed part of a larger set of activities carried out by Odd-job Ltd. As the Government stated in its response to consultation on the 2006 Regulations – with reference to the case of Fairhurst Ward Abbotts Ltd v Botes Building Ltd (above) – the transferring 'activities' need not be identifiable as separate in the hands of the transferor prior to the transfer. Nor should TUPE protection be denied on the basis that a manager and other employees not dedicated to the maintenance work were involved in its performance.

1.101 In the absence of detailed guidance, both the above interpretations are possible. On a strict reading of the Regulations, the former is arguably preferable. However, this would create a loophole through which a number of service provision change scenarios could pass, and would not achieve the Government's stated aim of ensuring that 'affected employees are protected as a matter of course'.

Since the Regulations became law, there have been a number of EAT decisions dealing with the problem of fragmentation in the context of service provision changes. These cases involve transfers between a single transferor and two transferees and multiple transferors and transferees:

- **Kimberley Group Housing Ltd v Hambley** 2008 ICR 1030, EAT: L Ltd, contracted with the Home Office to provide accommodation and support services for the Teesside area from offices in Middlesbrough and Stockton. The Home Office then re-tendered the contract and ended up splitting the Teesside area between two new contractors, K Ltd and A Ltd. In Stockton, K Ltd won 97 per cent of the work. In Middlesbrough, K Ltd won 71 per cent of the work and A Ltd won 29 per cent. Three ex-employees of L Ltd based in Middlesbrough and another three from Stockton brought proceedings against both of the new contractors for redundancy payments and unfair dismissal. An employment tribunal decided, as a preliminary issue, that there had been a service provision change from Ltd to the two new contractors and that liability for the sums owed to the employees should be apportioned between those contractors. On appeal, the EAT was concerned with whether there had been a service provision change and, if so, the effect of this on the six employees who had brought claims. It agreed with the employment tribunal that there was a service provision change in relation to each of the new contractors. In reaching that conclusion, however, there had been no need for the tribunal to make a quantitative comparison of the proportional amount of activities carried on by the transferor before the transfer and after it by the putative transferee, though this may have been important in relation to identifying to whom employees transferred where there is more than one transferee. The EAT then turned to consider the consequences given that Reg 4 applied in respect of the six claimants. It rejected the possibility that there could be any splitting of liability as between transferees, whether this reflected the proportional split of work between the new contractors or otherwise. Contrary to the tribunal's approach, it was not permissible to divorce a contract from the rights and liabilities under it. Therefore, although the activities could be split between more than one transferee, the rights and liabilities in respect of each affected employee could only transfer to one of those transferees. In determining to whom the rights and liabilities transferred, the EAT held that the factors set out in Duncan Web Offset (Maidstone) Ltd v Cooper 1995 IRLR 633, EAT, should be followed. These included but were not limited to the amount of time spent and the amount of value given by the employee; the terms of the employment contracts showing what the employee could be required to do; and how the cost of employing the employee was apportioned. The EAT stated that the 'overall principle' is to focus upon 'the link between the employee and the work or activities which are performed'. On this basis, and with regard to the Stockton-based claimants (where K Ltd had won 97 per cent of the work), the EAT held that their employment had transferred to K Ltd. Regarding the Middlesbrough-based claimants (where the split was 71 per cent to K Ltd to 29 per cent to A Ltd), the EAT determined the case solely on the basis of the work split, and accordingly held that all rights, duties and liabilities under those employees' contracts should also pass to K Ltd

- **Thomas-James and ors v Cornwall County Council and ors** ET Case No.1701021/07: the claimants were employed by Cornwall County Council to provide free legal advice and assistance via the telephone and post to members of the public under a contract with the Legal Services Commission (LSC). Cornwall CC was one of 17 providers of this service. Following a re-tendering, LSC reduced the number of providers to nine. Cornwall CC was one of the outgoing providers, and its work was dispersed across the remaining nine service providers. The ET concluded that there needed to be an 'identifiable nexus' between the work that had been carried out by Cornwall CC and the work allocated under the new contract to the new contractors. While the activities in an SPC did not need to retain their identity, it still had to be possible to identify the activities in the hands of the outgoing contractor so as to see whether the same activities had been taken over under another contract. In the instant case, the incoming work was, both before and after re-tendering, allocated on a rotational basis as between the providers and it was not therefore possible to identify the activities previously carried out by Cornwall CC in the hands of any of the new nine providers. As such, there was no relevant transfer

- **Clearsprings Management Ltd v Ankers and ors** EAT 0054/08: C Ltd was one of four private contractors who were awarded one of the contracts to provide an accommodation and support service to asylum seekers in the North West. Those contracts came to an end in October 2005 and the various contractors (including C Ltd) each entered into a further short-term contract until 30 June 2006 so that the service continued to be provided during the process of contractual re-tender. Once this process was completed, new contracts were awarded to three of the existing contractors but C Ltd was unsuccessful. There was then a transition period from 20 March 2006 to 30 June 2006 when C Ltd and the new contractors continued each to provide the asylum service in the North West, and during that period responsibility for asylum seekers was gradually taken over solely by the new contractors. The EAT held that the employment tribunal had been entitled to find that the activity carried on by C Ltd was so fragmented following the transfer that no relevant transfer took place. None of the claimants (all former employees of C Ltd) were dedicated to a service transferred to any one of the new service providers and the allocation of responsibility for asylum seekers to individual claimants showed 'no discernible pattern'. The EAT contrasted the position in this case with that in Kimberley Group Housing Ltd v Hambley (above) where a much larger percentage of the activities was taken over by a single putative transferee in both of the geographical regions affected by the transfer.

Organised grouping must be 'situated in Great Britain'. In respect of service 1.102 provision changes, the Regulations only apply where there is an organised grouping of employees *situated in Great Britain* immediately before the service provision change. It follows that Reg 3(1)(b) only applies to SPCs within Great Britain or from Great Britain outwards – not to transfers into Great Britain from elsewhere.

For the purposes of Reg 3(1)(b) it is the 'organised grouping of employees' that must be within Great Britain. Nevertheless, Reg 3(4)(c) provides that a relevant transfer can occur even where some employees ordinarily work outside the United Kingdom. The DTI Guide gives an example to demonstrate how the Reg 3(4)(c) provision works in the context of the Reg 3(1)(b) SPC rules. That example is of a contract to provide website maintenance, which comes to an end and is taken over by another contractor. If, of the organised grouping of employees that has performed the contract, one of the IT technicians works from home outside 'the United Kingdom', that should not prevent the Regulations from applying. On the other hand, if the whole team of IT technicians worked from home outside 'the United Kingdom', then Reg 3(1)(b) would not apply, since there would be no 'organised grouping of employees' within that territory.

Northern Ireland. The reference to 'Great Britain' in Reg 3(1)(b) might at first 1.103 seem surprising. As we saw in 'Standard transfers' above, Reg 3(1)(a) covers the transfer of undertakings 'situated immediately before the transfer in the United Kingdom'. That is, Great Britain *and* Northern Ireland. The reason for the exclusion of Northern Ireland from the Reg 3(1)(b) SPC provision is that S.38 of the Employment Relations Act 1999, which contains the power of the Secretary of State to extend TUPE protection to 'circumstances in which there is no transfer, or no transfer to which the Community obligation applies', does not apply to that Province. However, protection equivalent to that afforded by Reg 3(1)(b) of the 2006 Regulations has been extended to Northern Ireland by the Service Provision Change (Protection of Employment) Regulations (Northern Ireland) 2006 SI 2006/177.

Cross-border transfers. With increasing globalisation and the expansion of 1.104 outsourcing across international borders, the issue of how and when the Regulations apply to cases with an international element is clearly of importance. Under Reg 3(1)(b), the main requirement is simply that of an organised grouping of employees situated in Great Britain immediately *before* the SPC. Thus, it seems at least arguable that an SPC involving, for example, a call centre that moves from the United Kingdom to India could be covered by the Regulations. This possibility was discussed by the EAT in Holis Metal Industries Ltd v GMB

57

and anor 2008 ICR 464, EAT. We explore this issue in Chapter 9, under 'Transfers from and to the United Kingdom'.

1.105 Not single specific events or tasks of short duration
The second of the three conditions required for a 'service provision change' covered by Reg 3(1)(b) to occur is that it must be shown that 'immediately before the service provision change the client intends that the activities will, following the service provision change, be carried out by the transferee other than in connection with a single specific event or task of short-term duration' – Reg 3(3)(a)(ii). This effectively inserts into the SPC test the principle established in Ledernes Hovedorganisation, acting for Rygaard v Dansk Arbejdsgiverforening, acting for Strø Mølle Akustik A/S 1996 IRLR 51, ECJ, that a transferring business must be stable and capable of continuation. We discuss the Rygaard case and its effect in 'Standard transfers – what is an "economic entity"?' above.

In the 2005 Consultation Document the Government explained that the aim of Reg 3(3)(a)(ii) 'is to ensure that the extension of scope does not catch those cases where a client buys in services from a contractor on a one-off basis, without intending to enter into an ongoing relationship with that contractor, and then subsequently buys in similar services from a different contractor'. It gave the example of a client engaging a contractor to organise a single conference on its behalf, stating that it would not be appropriate for the project team to transfer if the client subsequently engaged a different contractor to arrange another, similar conference.

1.106 The Reg 3(3)(a)(ii) wording is not without its difficulties. One possible interpretation is that the provision excludes from TUPE activities (i) all single specific events, and (ii) all tasks of short-term duration. This would suggest, for example, that the award of a contract relating to a single specific event would be excluded, no matter how long that event is intended to take. An alternative reading is that an event or task must be both 'single specific' and 'of short-term duration' if the Reg 3(3)(a)(ii) exclusion is to apply.

It is the latter meaning that the Government intended. The DTI Guide gives an example involving two different contracts for the provision of security to the Olympic Games. The first contract, providing security advice to the event organisers over a period of years up to 2012, would relate to a single specific event, but its longevity would mean that it would not be excluded by Reg 3(3)(a)(ii). The second contract, to protect the athletes' security during the Games itself, would be a single specific event that was of a sufficiently short duration to come within the exclusion and thus fall outside the new SPC rules.

1.107 Of course, even accepting that the Government's interpretation is correct, there is a huge difference between a contract covering a two-week period and another covering a five-year period. At what point between two weeks and five years an event or task ceases to be of short-term duration is, for now, anybody's guess.

In Williams and anor v Solo Services Group and anor ET Case No.1605833/09, the employment tribunal accepted the submission that cleaning activities undertaken by a contractor between 30 March to January 2010 were of a short-term duration and were connected with a single specific event, namely the closing down of the site. There was a clear intention to cease activities and close the entire factory. In those circumstances, there was no service provision change and therefore no relevant transfer.

'The client intends'. The Reg 3(3)(a)(ii) exclusion will only apply if, immediately **1.108** before the transfer, the client intends that the activities will be carried out by the transferee other than in connection with a single specific event or task of short-term duration.

In the 2005 Consultation Document the Government explained that Reg 3(3)(a)(ii) is 'designed to avoid creating a loophole that would enable the application of the extended provision [that is, Reg 3(1)(b)] to be avoided simply by the client and the contractor entering into a succession of short-term, one-off contracts (e.g. to take an extreme case, a succession of daily contracts for the cleaning of an office building) for what was in truth always intended to be an ongoing service provision arrangement. It is for this reason that the client's intention has been made part of the test.' Nevertheless, Reg 3(3)(a)(ii) *will* operate to exclude an SPC from TUPE 'even if the client happens to engage a particular contractor on a number of separate occasions to provide one-off services on its behalf... if this is simply coincidental or fortuitous and, on each occasion, the client has no intention that this arrangement should become an ongoing, "preferred supplier" one'.

The Government went on to explain that 'if a dispute arises over this issue, the **1.109** court or employment tribunal hearing the case will have to decide what the client's intention was based on the evidence before it'.

Not wholly or mainly for the supply of goods   1.110
The third condition that must be satisfied for a relevant SPC transfer to occur under Reg 3(1)(b) is set out in Reg 3(3)(b). This provides that the activities in question must 'not consist wholly or mainly of the supply of goods for the client's use'.

The DTI Guide set out the following example to explain the intended scope of this condition: 'The Regulations are not expected to apply where a client engages a contractor to supply, for example, sandwiches and drinks to its canteen every day, for the client to sell on to its own staff. If, on the other hand, the contract was for the contractor to run the client's staff canteen, then this exclusion would not come into play and the Regulations might therefore apply.'

59

In the 2005 Consultation Document, where the canteen example first appeared, the Government added: 'Even if the contractor, as part and parcel of the latter arrangement... supplies the food and drink to be served in the canteen, it is likely that this will be ancillary to those main activities; and the goods – the food and drink – will in any event be for direct sale to and consumption by the canteen's customers, not for the use of the client, so the circumstances will not fall within [Reg 3(3)(b)].'

1.111 As with many questions posed by TUPE, that of whether 'activities' consist wholly or mainly of the supply of goods might not always be easy to answer. Consider the following example. Supplier Ltd has a contract to supply specialist machinery to Big plc, its one major client. The contract also provides that Supplier Ltd will be responsible for servicing and repairing the machinery provided. If Big plc terminates this contract and enters into a similar contract with Goods Ltd, will the Reg 3(3)(b) exclusion take effect to prevent an SPC transfer from Supplier Ltd to Goods Ltd?

Here, it would seem that the main purpose of the *contract as a whole* is the supply of goods, with the service provision aspect – the service and repair of the machinery supplied – appearing to be merely ancillary to that purpose. So, at first glance, one might think that the transfer of the contract to Goods Ltd would fall within the Reg 3(3)(b) exclusion, and that no SPC transfer under Reg 3(1)(b) would occur. However, it is important to note that Reg 3(3)(b) does not talk about the contract consisting wholly or mainly of the supply of goods. Rather, it is the *activities concerned* that must consist wholly or mainly of the supply of goods if the exclusion is to apply. Arguably, there are two sets of 'activities' transferring from Supplier Ltd to Goods Ltd in our example: first, the activities concerning the supply of goods, to which the Reg 3(3)(b) exclusion would apply; and secondly, the service and repair activities, to which the exclusion would not apply. In other words, the goods activities might be severable from the service activities for the purposes of the new SPC transfer rules.

1.112 This hypothesis finds some support from the Government's response to consultation on the draft 2006 Regulations, in which it clarified, with reference to the case of Fairhurst Ward Abbotts Ltd v Botes Building Ltd and ors (above), that the transferring 'activities' need not be identifiable as separate in the hands of the transferor prior to the transfer. On this reading, presuming that Supplier Ltd had a dedicated team of staff whose principal purpose had been carrying out Big plc's ongoing service and repair needs, this team would be protected by Reg 3(1)(b) and would thus transfer to Goods Ltd.

If this were the case, what would become of Supplier Ltd's other team of staff, who were dedicated to making and supplying the machinery to Big plc? They would not transfer to Goods Ltd under the new SPC rules owing to the Reg 3(3)(b) supply of goods exclusion. However, they would still be protected by the 2006 Regulations, and hence transfer, if they could show that a relevant transfer under Reg 3(1)(a) occurred. As discussed in 'Standard transfers' above, there will be a relevant transfer under Reg 3(1)(a) where there is an economic entity that transfers and thereafter retains its identity. This test, it goes without saying, is extremely complicated. However, some relevant factors with regard to the question of 'retention of identity' might be whether any significant assets or employees pass from Supplier Ltd to Goods Ltd, and whether the activities were carried out in a similar way before and after the transfer.

Professional business services not excluded   1.113
In the 2005 Consultation Document, the Government sought views as to whether 'professional business services' should be excluded from Reg 3(1)(b). If they were not, the Government explained, 'a relevant transfer would occur under [Reg 3(1)(b)] in a case where, for instance, a client had engaged a firm of consultants to provide it with business advice on an ongoing basis, and subsequently decided to reassign that contract to a different firm of consultants – assuming that, prior to the reassignment, the first firm had set up an organised grouping of employees with the principal purpose of meeting that client's needs'. Two reasons suggested for introducing an exclusion were that 'service provision changes involving "white collar" services such as chartered accountancy, business consultancy, legal advice and computer software design rarely give rise to difficulties in practice' and 'the professionally qualified employees who are key to providing such services are – by virtue of having skills that are generally highly sought-after by employers – less in need of additional legal protection'.

In the event, however, the proposal that professional business services be excluded from Reg 3(1)(b) was dropped. The Government acknowledged that there were strong arguments against this exclusion, as set out in the consultation document. For example, it seemed only fair that white-collar workers would benefit from the same protection as their blue-collar counterparts, and it would have been 'conceptually and legally problematic to draw a clear distinction between professional business services and other types of services'.

So, there is no reason why an SPC transfer under Reg 3(1)(b) could not take 1.114 place where a large professional services company, such as a law firm, has a team dedicated to meeting the needs of one important client, and where that client decides to change its adviser. Of course, the transferor law firm might not wish to lose some or all of the lawyers that were dedicated to the contract in question, and some of those lawyers might not wish to transfer. We examine the transferor's and the employees' options in such a situation in Chapter 2 under 'Objecting to the transfer' and 'Employees retained by transferor'.

Recent examples of cases involving professional services include Hunt v Storm Communication ET Case No.270254/06 and Royden and ors v Hammonds

61

Direct and Barnetts Solicitors ET Case No.2103451/07 (both previously discussed under 'Organised grouping of employees carrying out the activities' above); and Ward Hadaway Solicitors v Love and ors EAT 0471/09 (discussed under 'Retention of identity not required' below).

1.115 **Retention of identity not required**
Unlike the test for standard transfers under Reg 3(1)(a) (see 'Standard transfers' above), there is no express requirement that, in order for Reg 3(1)(b) to apply to an SPC, the 'activities' in question 'retain their identity' after the transfer. The Reg 3(1)(b) SPC test is almost exclusively focused on the situation immediately *before* the transfer, and pays no heed, for example, to whether the transferee takes over the transferor's assets or employees. Furthermore, in its response to consultation on the 2006 Regulations, the Government stated that 'there is no implied requirement for [the] activities to be carried out by the transferee in an identical manner'.

1.116 **Innovative bids.** In a consultation document published in September 2001 the Government initially proposed that there would be an exclusion from the new SPC rules where an incoming contractor envisaged carrying out the activities in question in a new or 'innovative' manner. In other words, the transfer rules would not apply if the activities were carried out differently post-transfer. However, this proposal did not find its way into either the draft or the final Regulations.

In the 2005 Consultation Document the Government explained why the proposal was dropped: 'If the incoming contractor intends to carry out the service activities in a novel manner – for instance, using a computerised process in place of a previous manual one – it is likely that some of the employees who have been performing the activities for the old contractor (or, in the case of an initial contracting-out, the client) will lack the necessary skills and will have to be made redundant. There are, however, clear advantages in providing for the organised grouping of employees to transfer to the new contractor before any redundancies are made... If the employees remained with the old contractor, the likelihood is that they would all have to be made redundant... Some, however, may be able to retain their jobs with the new contractor, if they happen to have the skills necessary to adapt to the new working methods, or can be easily retrained, or can be reallocated to other parts of the new contractor's business. This would be in line with the employment protection aim of the Regulations, and would also be likely to assist the new contractor in reducing recruitment and training costs. Additionally, and importantly, treating all contractors – including those making "innovative bids" – on an equal footing will contribute towards the key policy objective of creating a "level playing field" in tendering exercises, and increased certainty and confidence for all concerned.'

Transferor and transferee must carry out the same activities. We have seen **1.117** that Reg 3(1)(b) has no express 'retention of identity' requirement, and that the transferor and the transferee need not carry out the 'activities' in the same way in order for an SPC transfer to occur. However, the three definitions of 'service provision change' in Reg 3(1)(b) (see 'The three types of SPC' above) share a requirement that the 'activities' are carried out before the transfer by one person, and after the transfer by another. It follows, then, that the 'activities' (as opposed to the manner in which they are carried out) must be identifiable as 'the same' pre- and post-transfer if an SPC transfer is to occur.

Whether 'activities' can be said to be the same pre- and post-transfer depends very much on how they are defined – and, as we saw in the discussion on 'The three types of SPC' above, neither the Regulations nor the DTI Guide are particularly helpful in this regard. However, there have been a number of recent decisions which are instructive:

- **Metropolitan Resources Ltd v Churchill Dulwich Ltd** 2009 IRLR 700, EAT: Migrant Helpline (MH), on behalf of the Home Office, had a contract with CD Ltd to provide accommodation to asylum seekers. The claimants were all employed by CD Ltd at Barry House in East Dulwich. In mid-September 2006, MR Ltd began to provide accommodation to MH on a short-term basis for asylum seekers at Coombe Farm in Croydon. This became the Home Office's preferred site. A contract was entered into between MH and MR Ltd with effect from 26 January 2007, following which all asylum seekers who would previously have been allocated to Barry House were instead allocated to Coombe Farm. The remaining 10–15 asylum seekers left at Barry House were dispersed over the next few weeks and were not replaced. The contract with CD Ltd expired at the end of March 2007 without being renewed. The employees claimed that their employment had transferred to MR Ltd. An employment tribunal held that 'activities' under Reg 3(1)(b)(ii) had to be defined relatively broadly and, in this case, they comprised the provision of good quality accommodation to asylum seekers and associated administration and reporting services on behalf of MH. The tribunal concluded that essentially the same activities were taken over by MRL, so that there was a service provision change. The EAT on appeal upheld these findings. It accepted the tribunal's view that the activities carried out by MR Ltd were not different merely because they were carried out from different premises. Those activities were essentially the same, notwithstanding that extra services were carried out by MR Ltd, that MR Ltd's operation began and continued without any of CD Ltd's employees, management or otherwise, and that there were differences in terms of security between Coombe Farm and Barry House. The EAT held that 'some additional duty or function is unlikely – unless the addition is of such substance that the activity then being carried on is no longer essentially the same as that carried on by the predecessor – to negate the existence of a transfer under Reg 3(1)(b)'

- **OCS Group v Jones and anor** EAT 38/09: OCS, a catering contractor, managed the catering operation at BMW's car plant at Cowley. Under the contract, OCS operated a centrally located restaurant serving cooked breakfast and hot and cold lunches and a bar facility supported by four satellite catering stations and a general shop. However, following the take over of the contract by MIS, the catering service was substantially reduced to the provision of five dry goods kiosks (offering sandwiches and salads). An employment tribunal concluded that there was no SPC. On appeal, OCS contended that the tribunal should have found that the general activity – the provision of food – was the same under both contracts. However, the EAT held that the activity carried out by MIS was substantially different to OCS in that prepared cooked food – whether hot or cold – was no longer required. The tribunal's decision that there was no SPC was accordingly upheld

- **Ward Hadaway Solicitors v Love and ors** EAT 0471/09: WH had been a member of a panel that provided legal services to the Nursing and Midwifery Council (NMC). The NMC decided to tender out its work to a single provider, Capsticks, with effect from the date of expiry of its contract with WH on 1 October 2007. However, all work in progress as at that date, which was expected to last for at least six months, remained with, and was completed by, WH. A question arose whether TUPE applied. The employment tribunal accepted that there was an organised grouping of employees whose principal purpose had been the carrying out of activities on behalf of the NMC. However, it concluded that the 'activities' in question comprised the work in progress that WH was dealing with as at 1 October 2007, all of which remained with WH itself. There was therefore no change in the identity of the firm carrying out those activities. The tribunal also concluded that the activities carried out by Capsticks were sufficiently different from those carried out by WH not to amount to the same activities. On appeal, the EAT held that the tribunal had been entitled to conclude that the relevant 'activities' were simply those composed of the work in progress and not the expectation of future work which was awarded to Capsticks.

- **Gumbley and ors v Excel Europe Ltd and anor** ET Case No.1306658: Land Rover (LR) had contracted with JC to manufacture and supply sequenced seats for its Range Rover 2006 model. JC in turn sub-contracted with EE Ltd to transport the seats to LR's premises in Solihull from JC's site in Redditch. LR decided to terminate its contract with JC and instead contract with a different company, LC, to manufacture and supply seats for its Range Rover 2007 model. LC then subcontracted with BL Ltd to transport the seats to Solihull from LC's site in Coventry. The question arose whether, following this change, the employees employed by EE Ltd were transferred under TUPE to BL Ltd. An employment tribunal held that there had been a relevant transfer by virtue of Reg 3(1)(b) since the activity of transporting seats to LR in accordance with LR's requirements remained broadly unchanged when carried out by BL Ltd as it had under EE Ltd. The seats were being delivered to LR using the same trailers and stillages (i.e. pallets) albeit that they were transported from a different address. Changes to the seats were merely cosmetic in nature and were made in the context of the fact that LR updated its models from time to time

- **TGWU and ors v Mitie Cleaning (North) Ltd** ET Case No.2405555/05: R1 employed 30 employees to provide cleaning services to R2. Owing to financial difficulties, R2 informed R1 that it intended to terminate the cleaning contract and to absorb the cleaning functions into the roles carried out by its existing employees. All of R2's employees were required to take responsibility for keeping their own immediate area clean, rotas were devised for communal areas and all employees were required to spend around two hours a week cleaning. An employment tribunal held that there was no SPC as the way in which the cleaning was to be carried out by R2's employees was different to how it was previously carried out by R1

- **Matthews v Secretary of State and ors** ET Case No.1100675/08: the claimants were employed by D&P Contracting (London) Ltd and were informed by two directors that the company was insolvent. The whole of the workforce were subsequently told to go and carry out refurbishment work for Viking Projects Contracting Company at the National Gallery and when that contract ended, they worked on a new contract at the science museum. The tribunal held that TUPE applied as the whole of the workforce was taken over and carried on working in a business activity that was broadly unchanged

- **Williams and anor v Solo Services Group and anor** ET Case No.1605833/09: RCS was contracted to carry out industrial and domestic cleaning at D Ltd's factory. In March 2007, RCS lost the contract to SSG, which continued to employ two of RCS's employees. Towards the end of 2008, D Ltd decided to close the factory and sold some of its machines along with the factory itself. However, it continued to be permitted to use the premises under a leaseback arrangement. In March 2009, D Ltd informed SSG that its own operatives would do any necessary cleaning when the contract with SSG came to an end. By that stage, production had almost ceased, machines were no longer cleaned and the only cleaning was to clear up any spillages. When the two employees issued claims for redundancy pay and breach of contract, SSG argued that D Ltd was liable to pay these as there had been an SPC when D Ltd took the cleaning services back in-house. The tribunal held that there was no relevant transfer under Reg 3(1(b)(iii) as the activities had changed

from around 70 per cent industrial cleaning to cleaning of spillages on an ad
hoc basis with no industrial element.

1.118 It is interesting to contrast the last-mentioned case above with Aziz and anor v
CPS Security Ltd and anor ET Case No 2301878/07. In that case an employment
tribunal held that there was a SPC when services provided by CPS Ltd
comprising 24 hours a day security, seven days a week was taken over by R2,
which then provided security services from Mondays to Fridays during day-
time only, six hours' security on Saturdays and a mobile patrol twice in the
evenings. The services were deemed to be essentially the same before and after
the service provision change.

1.119 Public and private sector

According to Reg 3(4)(a) the new SPC rules apply to public and private
undertakings engaged in economic activities, whether or not they are operating
for gain. So, for example, privatisations, and outsourcing by central or local
government of ancillary services to the private sector, can be covered. However,
as with standard transfers (above), there will be no relevant transfer under Reg
3(1)(b) where there is an administrative reorganisation of public administrative
authorities or a transfer of administrative functions between public
administrative authorities – Reg 3(5). We discuss what this means under 'The
public sector' below.

1.120 What difference will the new rules make?

The Final Regulatory Impact Assessment with regard to the 2006 Regulations
estimated that between 2,500 and 4,500 businesses, employing between 60,000
and 100,000 employees, are involved each year in a service provision change
not involving a public sector service. It assumed that, prior to the new rules
taking effect, 65 per cent of these SPCs were clearly 'standard transfers' under
the traditional Reg 3(1)(a) test and were recognised and treated as such; 10 per
cent were clearly not standard transfers; and the remaining 25 per cent were
legally uncertain. The Assessment went on to state its expectation that the new
Reg 3(1)(b) test will bring the majority of the uncertain SPC cases within the
TUPE fold; together with a proportion of the 10 per cent which currently
clearly lie outside TUPE. It concluded that, overall, 85–90 per cent of service
provision changes will be covered by the 2006 Regulations. Note that public
sector transfers were not included in these statistics since public sector employees
have, for some years, enjoyed 'TUPE-equivalent' protection upon a transfer
whether or not the Regulations technically apply – see 'The public sector' below.

To illustrate the impact of the new rules in a more practical way, we set out
three cases, decided before the 2006 Regulations took effect and discussed in
'Standard transfers' above, in which no relevant transfer under Reg 3(1)(a)
occurred. We consider whether these cases would have involved SPC transfers
under the new Reg 3(1)(b) regime:

- **Williams v Lockhart Security Services Ltd** EAT 1395/01: W was one of three employees working as security guards for L Ltd at the Darlington Retail Park (DRP). When L Ltd lost the guarding contract, DRP awarded a new contract to A Ltd. In doing so, it stipulated that it wanted none of the former L Ltd employees to continue working at its site. A Ltd thus declined to take W on, and he brought claims before an employment tribunal which gave rise to the question of whether a relevant transfer under Reg 3(1)(a) had occurred from L Ltd to A Ltd. The tribunal held that there had been such a transfer, but the EAT overturned its decision on the basis that, since neither L Ltd's assets nor its employees were taken on by A Ltd, the 'economic entity' in question had not retained its identity. If this case had been decided under the 2006 Regulations, there *would* have been an SPC transfer under new Reg 3(1)(b). The guarding activities were carried out before the transfer by L Ltd and after the transfer by A Ltd. Furthermore, each of the Reg 3(3) conditions (see 'The Reg 3(3) conditions' above) were met. Immediately before the service provision change, L Ltd had in place an organised grouping of employees which had as its principal purpose the carrying out of the guarding activities on behalf of DRP; DRP intended that those activities would be carried out by A Ltd after the service provision change on an ongoing basis; and the activities in question did not consist wholly or mainly of the supply of goods for DRP's use

- **AEEU and ors v Lyndon Scaffolding plc** EAT 1242/99: the claimants were employed by L plc at Ferrybridge power station, fulfilling L plc's contract with Powergen to provide scaffolding services at the site. With L plc's contract drawing to an end, Powergen invited tenders not only for the scaffolding work but for a combination of scaffolding, insulation and cleaning services. L plc – which was a specialist scaffolding firm – was not invited to tender. The new contract was won by Cape, which did not accept that a relevant transfer from L plc had taken place with regard to the scaffolding work. The claimants lost their jobs and brought unfair dismissal claims before an employment tribunal. The tribunal decided, as a preliminary issue, that no relevant transfer under Reg 3(1)(a) had occurred from L Ltd to Cape since the scaffolding 'economic entity' had not retained its identity. In this regard, the tribunal took into account that the nature of Cape's contract with Powergen was fundamentally different from that earlier made between L plc and Powergen. The L plc contract was for the supply of scaffolding services only. On the other hand, although the Cape contract included scaffolding services, it also covered cleaning and insulation services, with all three under one management. The EAT upheld the tribunal's decision. However, if this case had been decided under the 2006 Regulations, there *would* have been an SPC transfer from L plc to Cape under Reg 3(1)(b). The scaffolding activities were performed before the transfer by L plc, and after the transfer by Cape. The fact that Cape organised the scaffolding activities in a different manner, and that those activities formed only part of its contract with Powergen, would have been insufficient to take the case outside the new Reg 3(1)(b) SPC regime. Furthermore, each of the Reg 3(3) conditions were met. Immediately before the service provision change, L plc had in place an organised grouping of employees which had as its principal purpose the carrying out of the scaffolding activities on behalf of Powergen; Powergen intended that those activities would be carried out by Cape after the service provision change on an ongoing basis; and the activities in question did not consist wholly or mainly of the supply of goods for Powergen's use

- **Astle and ors v Cheshire County Council and anor** 2005 IRLR 12, EAT: the Council outsourced architectural services to SGI, but thereafter became concerned about SGI's performance. The Council decided to terminate SGI's contract and to adopt what it referred to as a 'market economy' approach, under which a panel of consultants would be engaged to provide the services instead of a single contractor. Owing to this fragmentation, both an employment tribunal and the EAT concluded that the 'economic entity' in question had not retained its identity after the transfer, meaning that there was no 'standard transfer' under Reg 3(1)(a). In our view, common sense suggests that this case would fall outside TUPE even now, regardless of the new Reg 3(1)(b) SPC rule. As we explained in 'The three types of SPC' above, the Regulations require the 'activities' to be carried out after the transfer either by the client itself or 'by another person'. Although this does not *necessarily* preclude a transfer of a single set of activities to more than one person, it does not seem to envisage a transfer to several consultants. A transfer of the employees concerned to one or all of the consultants would be completely unworkable.

1.121 ## Insolvency

If a business gets into extreme financial difficulties, an insolvency practitioner can be appointed either to wind up the business or to keep it running with a view to the sale of the whole or part of it as a going concern. In assessing whether the Directive, and hence Reg 3(1)(a) of TUPE, applies to a transfer in an insolvency context, it is crucial to have an understanding of the purpose of the insolvency proceedings in question. This has been made clear by the European Court of Justice in the following cases:

- **Abels v Administrative Board of the Bedrijfsvereniging voor de Metaalindustrie en de Electrotechnische Industrie** 1987 2 CMLR 406, ECJ: the Dutch company for which A worked experienced financial difficulties and was given judicial leave to suspend debt payments. Thereafter, the company was placed into liquidation, and the liquidator transferred its business to another company. A was taken on by the new company, but became embroiled in a salary dispute. When he brought a claim before the national court, the question arose as to whether the transfer of A's employment had been covered by the Directive. The national court referred this matter to the ECJ, which held that the Directive does not apply to a transfer where the 'transferor' has been declared insolvent with a view to the realisation and distribution of the undertaking's assets on behalf of its creditors. The ECJ stated, however, that the Directive could apply to a transfer from an insolvent company where the main aim of the insolvency procedure in place was to protect the assets of the business and to ensure that the business continued to trade by means of an agreement to suspend payment of the transferor's debts

- **D'Urso and ors v Ercole Marelli Elettromeccanica Generale SpA (in special administration) and ors** 1992 IRLR 136, ECJ: in 1981 the Italian Minister of Industry issued a decree commencing 'special administration proceedings for large undertakings in difficulties' in respect of EMG, the company for which the claimants worked. At the same time the organisation was authorised to continue trading under that procedure. In September 1985 the whole undertaking was transferred to another company called Nuova EMG, which had been specially formed for this purpose. Many employees were taken on by the new company, but the claimants were not. They sought a declaration that their contracts of employment had continued with Nuova EMG under the provisions of the Italian Civil Code, which implemented the Directive into Italian law. The national court referred the matter to the ECJ, which made the point that the application of the Directive in an insolvency context depends on the purpose of the particular insolvency procedure in question. As the Abels case made clear, the Directive applies to the transfer of an insolvent business where the purpose of the insolvency procedure is to enable the undertaking to continue trading, but does not apply in the context of compulsory liquidation proceedings designed to dispose of an insolvent company's assets

- **Jules Dethier Équipement SA v Dassy and anor** 1998 ICR 541, ECJ: on 15 May 1991 the Belgian Commercial Court in Huy made an order putting SPRL – which employed D – into liquidation. On 5 June 1991 the liquidator dismissed D, and on 27 June transferred SPRL's assets to JDE under an agreement approved by the Commercial Court. When D brought an action, the question arose of whether his employment had transferred from SPRL to JDE. The national court referred the question of whether the Directive applied in such circumstances to the ECJ. In the ECJ's view, it was clear from the previous case law of the European Court that the crucial question to be asked in determining whether the Directive applies to the transfer of an undertaking that is subject to an administrative or judicial procedure is: 'What is the purpose of the procedure in question?' If the answer is not immediately conclusive, then account should also be taken of the form of the procedure – in particular, whether the undertaking continues or ceases trading – and also of the Directive's objectives. The facts of the instant case disclosed that the undertaking continued to trade while it was being wound up by the court. In such circumstances, continuity of the business was assured when the undertaking was transferred. There was accordingly no justification for depriving the employees of the rights guaranteed under the Directive.

1.122 So, it appears that so long as an insolvency practitioner runs the business and retains its goodwill in order to make it viable for sale, the Directive, and hence the 2006 Regulations, will apply to any eventual transfer to an outside purchaser. On the other hand, where an insolvent business has been broken up and the assets sold off, it would appear that neither the Directive nor Reg 3(1)(a) of the 2006 Regulations takes effect.

The EAT had the opportunity to examine the above case law in Perth and Kinross Council v Donaldson and ors 2004 IRLR 121, EAT. There, Perth and Kinross Council contracted out its housing maintenance work to NCS Ltd. That company later ran into financial difficulties and a liquidator was appointed. On 16 January 2001 a court made an order for NCS Ltd to be wound up. The Council and NCS Ltd then entered into an informal arrangement, on terms accepted by the liquidator, whereby the company continued to carry out maintenance as and when required. The Council placed orders for work on a day-to-day basis on the understanding that the arrangement could be terminated at any time without notice. The Council became dissatisfied with the company's deteriorating performance, and terminated the arrangement with effect from 31 May 2001. As from that date the Council undertook the maintenance work itself. NCS Ltd ceased trading because the liquidator was unable to find any more work for it to carry out. A dispute arose as to whether there had been a transfer of an undertaking from NCS Ltd to the Council, within the meaning of TUPE, when the latter resumed the work in-house. An employment tribunal held that a transfer had taken place, and the Council appealed to the EAT.

1.123 Before the Appeal Tribunal, the Council relied on the ECJ's decision in the Abels case (above) to argue that no TUPE transfer had occurred. In Abels, the ECJ had held that the Directive does not apply to the transfer of an undertaking where the transferor has been declared insolvent and the purpose of the transfer is the realisation and distribution of the undertaking's assets on behalf of its creditors. The Council argued that it followed that complete insolvency, as in the instant case, excluded the application of TUPE. The EAT agreed with the Council's submissions. Since the ECJ had made it clear that the Directive did not apply in a case of irretrievable insolvency and cessation of business, it followed that the 1981 Regulations – which as secondary legislation made under the European Communities Act 1972 could not go beyond the scope of the protection provided by the Directive – did not apply in this case either.

Thus, there had been no relevant transfer when the Council took back work that it had contracted out to a company that had become insolvent and ceased to trade. In any event, the EAT continued, the ad hoc arrangements that had operated between the Council and NCS Ltd following the company's liquidation could not be regarded as establishing a stable economic entity (for which, see 'Standard transfers – what is an "economic entity"?' above). By the time of the cessation of business brought about by the Council's declining to offer any more work, there was simply nothing left to transfer. Nothing passed between the parties, therefore, and the liquidator had simply brought the business to an end because there was no more work for it to do.

Note that it is entirely possible that situations such as that in the Perth and **1.124** Kinross case would, if decided now, amount to an SPC transfer under new Reg 3(1)(b). As we discussed in 'Service provision changes' above, this provision offers TUPE protection over and above that required by the Directive in the SPC arena. Essentially, it would have been sufficient for the purposes of Reg 3(1)(b) if the maintenance activities in question were carried out by an organised grouping of NCS Ltd's employees prior to the transfer, and by the Council thereafter.

We discuss the issue of insolvency at length in Chapter 6. There, we focus in particular on the new provisions (Regs 8 and 9) that were introduced by the 2006 Regulations with a view to assisting the rescue of failing businesses. The main substantive differences that apply in the context concern the ability of the purchaser of an insolvent business to effect changes to employees' contractual terms and conditions and the degree to which the purchaser inherits the transferor's pre-transfer liabilities.

The public sector   **1.125**

Regulation 3(4)(a) provides that the 2006 Regulations apply to *public and private* undertakings engaged in economic activities whether or not they are operating for gain. This mirrors the wording of Article 1.1(c) of the Directive, which in turn reflects established case law. Thus, it is clear that transfers from public to private sector (and vice versa) can be covered by the Directive and hence the Regulations. Two brief examples:

- **Sánchez Hidalgo and ors v Asociación de Servicios Aser and Sociedad Cooperativa Minerva and another case** 1999 IRLR 136, ECJ: a Spanish municipality had entrusted the provision of its home-help services to an outside contractor. That contract came to an end and a new contract was awarded to a different undertaking. The ECJ held that the Directive could apply to the change of contractor – the fact that the service contract was awarded by a public body did not preclude the Directive's application

71

- **Mayeur v Association Promotion de l'Information Messine (APIM)** 2000 IRLR 783, ECJ: M was employed as a publicity manager by APIM, a private non-profit-making association which aimed to promote the French City of Metz. In time, APIM was dissolved and the municipality took over its activities. The ECJ held that the Directive applies where a municipality, a legal person governed by public law operating within the framework of specific rules of administrative law, takes over activities relating to publicity and information concerning the services which it offers to the public, where such activities were previously carried out, in the interests of that municipality, by a non-profit-making association which was a legal person governed by private law.

1.126 The question of whether the Directive and the Regulations apply to transfers *within* the public sector is more complicated. Nevertheless, as we shall see, the Cabinet Office's Statement of Practice *Staff Transfers in the Public Sector* (2000) aims to ensure that TUPE-style protection is afforded to employees in such circumstances.

1.127 **Transfer of public administrative functions**
While Reg 3(4)(a) provides that the 2006 Regulations apply to public and private undertakings, Reg 3(5), which also mirrors Article 1.1(c) of the Directive, states that 'an administrative reorganisation of public administrative authorities or the transfer of administrative functions between public administrative authorities is not a relevant transfer'.

The origin of the Reg 3(5) public administration exclusion is the ECJ's decision in Henke v Gemeinde Schierke and Verwaltungsgemeinschaft 'Brocken' 1996 IRLR 701, ECJ. That case involved H, who was employed as secretary to the Mayor of the municipality of Schierke, Germany. In July 1994 Schierke and other municipalities were reorganised, as permitted by the local government law for the Land of Saxony-Anhalt. As a result, all the tasks of the municipality of Schierke were transferred to a new local government body covering a number of municipalities, and the municipal administration of Schierke was dissolved. H lost her job and brought a claim that her contract of employment had been transferred to the new local government body. The ECJ held that there was no transfer of an undertaking in these circumstances. It stated that 'the concept of a "transfer of an undertaking, business or part of a business" does not apply to the transfer of administrative functions from a municipality to an administrative collectivity such as the one in question in the main proceedings'. It pointed out that the transfer 'related only to activities involving the exercise of public authority. Even if it is assumed that those activities had aspects of an economic nature, they could only be ancillary.'

1.128 The ECJ's emphasis in Henke on the importance of activities being of 'an economic nature' does not sit easily with its earlier comments in Dr Sophie

Redmond Stichting v Bartol and ors 1992 IRLR 366, ECJ (see 'Standard transfers – what is an "economic entity"?' above) that the application of the Directive is not restricted to 'commercial ventures'. Perhaps unsurprisingly, then, the Henke public administration exclusion has been interpreted narrowly. Two case examples:

- **Collino and anor v Telecom Italia SpA** 2002 ICR 38, ECJ: the Italian Minister for Posts and Telecommunications dissolved ASST, the state body responsible for operating certain public telecommunications services, and granted the exclusive concession in respect of those services to a state-owned company, Iritel. The question arose whether this could amount to a transfer of an undertaking within the meaning of the Directive. The ECJ held that the Directive applies where a public body transfers, by means of an administrative concession, the operation of a non-profit-making public telecommunications service to a state-owned company. It was settled case law that the Directive applies to all transfers of entities which are engaged in economic activities, whether or not they operate with a view to profit. Furthermore, the fact that the service transferred in the instant case was the subject of a concession by a public body did not exclude application of the Directive, since the activity in question was a business activity and not merely the exercise of public authority

- **Dundee City Council v Arshad** EAT 1204/98: a local government reorganisation took place in Scotland. As a result, a residential home 'transferred' from an abolished regional council to new unitary authorities. The EAT held that the 'Henke exclusion' did not take effect in these circumstances, and that the Directive and TUPE were capable of applying.

Nevertheless the DTI Guide states that the exclusion in Reg 3(5) means that 'most transfers within central or local Government are not covered by the Regulations'. Owing to this, the Government has taken steps outside those required by the Directive in order to ensure that employees 'transferring' within the public sector are afforded protection. We now consider what these steps have been. **1.129**

TUPE-equivalent protection **1.130**

As stated above, both the Directive and the 2006 Regulations provide that neither a reorganisation of a public administration nor the transfer of administrative functions between public administrations will amount to a 'relevant transfer'. As the DTI Guide notes, however, 'intra-governmental transfers are covered by the Cabinet Office's Statement of Practice "Staff Transfers in the Public Sector", which in effect guarantees TUPE-equivalent treatment for the employees so transferred'. In addition, the Statement of Practice and other Codes have an impact upon outsourcing *from* the public sector, affecting the employment conditions that the public sector, in its capacity

73

as a contracting party, will expect first and subsequent generation contractors to provide for employees. The relevant documents include:

- *Statement of Practice on Staff Transfers in the Public Sector (2000):* this applies directly to central government departments, the NHS, local government (where adopted by the relevant local authority) and public private partnerships. It provides that contracting-out exercises to the private sector and voluntary organisations (including second-generation contracting out), and transfers between different parts of the public sector, will be conducted on the basis that staff will transfer and the principles of TUPE should be followed, unless there are exceptional circumstances. Furthermore, there should be appropriate arrangements to protect the occupational pensions, redundancy and severance terms of staff in all these types of transfer. In this regard, appended to the Statement is guidance entitled *A Fair Deal for Staff Pensions*, under which incoming contractors are expected to provide transferring employees with pension rights broadly comparable to those which they enjoyed prior to the transfer

- *Code of Practice on Workforce Matters in Local Authority Service Contracts 2003*: this applies where a local authority or best value authority (such as a police or fire authority) transfers employees to a private or voluntary sector contractor under a contract to provide services. It will form part of the service specification and conditions for all such contracts, and makes it clear that local authorities will apply the principles set out in the Cabinet Office Statement of Practice on Staff Transfers in the Public Sector (above). The Code's primary focus, however, is on combating the problem of the so-called 'two-tier' workforce – and to that end is concerned with the terms and conditions of employees who join the contractor *after* the transfer takes place, traditionally on less favourable terms and conditions than their ex-public sector colleagues. The Code states, for example, that 'where the service provider recruits new staff to work on a local authority contract alongside staff transferred from the local authority, it will offer employment on fair and reasonable terms and conditions which are, overall, no less favourable than those of transferred employees'. The Code suggests that a company which fails to comply with its provisions might face difficulty in obtaining contracts, explaining that 'contractors who intend to cut costs by driving down the terms and conditions for staff, whether for transferees or for new joiners taken on to work beside them, will not provide best value and will not be selected to provide services for the council'.

1.131 Note that the *Code of Practice on Workforce Matters in Public Sector Service Contracts 2005* – which extended the reach of the local authority Code mentioned above to the wider public sector, including the Civil Service, the NHS and maintained schools (subject to some exceptions, such as where the Retention of Employment Model for NHS PFI contracts applies) – was withdrawn on 13 December 2010 and replaced by a set of voluntary, non-statutory *Principles of Good Employment Practice*. It is likely that the 2003 Code will also be withdrawn in due course.

The Statement and Code will continue to hold sway in public sector transfers regardless of the extended coverage of the 2006 Regulations with regard to service provision changes generally (see 'Service provision changes' above). This is because some of the protections they offer – in the context of pension provision in particular (often a highly valuable benefit in public sector contracts) – exceed those conferred by the 2006 Regulations and the Transfer of Employment (Pension Protection) Regulations 2005 SI 2005/649 (see Chapter 3 for further details).

In Law Society of England and Wales v Secretary of State for Justice and Office **1.132** for Legal Complaints 2010 EWHC 352, QBD, the High Court was asked by the Law Society to make declarations about the applicability of TUPE and the Cabinet Statement of Practice in the context of the imminent cessation of the Law Society's Legal Complaints Service (LCS) and its replacement with a new independent Office for Legal Complaints (OLC). In particular, the Law Society sought declarations on whether the cessation of the function of the LCS and the start of the function of the OLC: (i) will be a transfer of administrative functions between public administrative authorities within the meaning of Reg 3(5) of TUPE (see under 'Transfer of administrative functions' above); (ii) will be a transfer within the scope of the Statement of Practice; (iii) will amount to a relevant transfer under TUPE; or (iv) will fall within the scope of Reg 3(5) of TUPE, but will be outside the scope of the Statement of Practice.

Applying the 'multi-factorial' approach in Cheesman (see under 'Standard transfers – what is an "economic entity"?' above), the High Court concluded that the change from the LCS to the OLC will not comprise a relevant transfer. It found that:

- the LCS is an 'undertaking', as it has a relatively autonomous identity, separate from the Law Society

- it is also an 'economic entity', as it pursues an ancillary economic activity (providing redress or compensation for complainants)

- there would be no transfer of the LCS undertaking to the OLC – the simple fact that services provided by an old and a new undertaking are similar does not mean that there has been a TUPE transfer. A number of other factors (including, in particular, whether significant tangible or intangible assets or a major part of the workforce in terms of numbers and/or skills have transferred) must be considered (see Süzen v Zehnacker Gebäudereinigung GmbH Krankenhausservice 1997 IRLR 255, ECJ – discussed under 'Standard transfers – what is an "economic entity"?' above). In the instant case, although the activity that the OLC is due to carry out will be similar to that carried out by the LCS, none of the tangible or intangible assets of the LCS or its existing case load will be transferred to the OLC

- the LCS will not retain its identity within the OLC. The OLC's independence, wider range of powers and obligations mean that its culture and approach will be very different from that of the LCS.

1.133 Given the Court's ruling, it was not strictly necessary to consider if the proposed transfer would be a transfer of an administrative function within the meaning of Reg 3(5). However, the High Court judge did go on (obiter) to hold that it was. Equally, it was not necessary to consider if the Statement of Practice applied in the circumstances of the instant case as there was no relevant transfer.

1.134 When does the transfer occur?

Presuming that the TUPE Regulations do apply to a given set of circumstances, the next crucial question is *when* the relevant transfer takes place. As we discuss in Chapter 2, only those employees assigned to the transferring undertaking 'immediately before the transfer' will transfer automatically to the transferee under Reg 4.

In most cases, the question of when a transfer occurs will be extremely simple to answer. The EAT's decision in Wheeler v Patel and anor 1987 ICR 631, EAT, is authority for the proposition that, where a transfer is effected by a contractual agreement, the date of the transfer is that on which the relevant contract was completed. If a transfer is effected by a series of transactions, however, things become a little more complicated.

1.135 **Series of transactions.** Regulation 3(6) of the 2006 Regulations provides that 'a relevant transfer may be effected by a series of two or more transactions'. As we saw in 'Transfer "to another person"' above, this reflects a number of decisions of the ECJ, such as that in Foreningen af Arbejdsledere i Danmark v Daddy's Dance Hall A/S 1988 IRLR 315, ECJ. That case saw IC's lease of a restaurant/bar terminated by the landlord, PT, which thereafter concluded a new lease with DDH. The ECJ held that the fact that the transfer of the restaurant from IC to DDH took place in two phases – first from IC to PT, and then from PT to DDH – did not exclude the applicability of the Directive.

Often, where a transfer is effected by a series of two or more transactions, the transfer process happens over a period of time. In such circumstances, it might be difficult to identify a particular transfer date, and hence identify the group of employees assigned to the undertaking 'immediately before the transfer'. Recognising this, Reg 4(3) of the 2006 Regulations provides that where a transfer is effected by a series of transactions, an employee will transfer to the transferee if he or she was assigned to the transferring entity 'immediately before any of those transactions'. To an extent an anti-avoidance provision, it suggests that there need not always be one all-important cut-off point, but that there might be a series of dates immediately before which an employee can be employed in the undertaking if he or she is to be caught by the transfer rules.

The Directive, however, places a fairly large spanner in the works. Article 3.1, **1.136** which states that 'the transferor's rights and obligations arising from a contract of employment or from an employment relationship existing on *the date of a transfer*... shall... be transferred to the transferee' (our emphasis), suggests that a specific transfer date must be identified. Indeed, this is the conclusion that the ECJ arrived at in the case of Celtec Ltd v Astley and ors 2005 ICR 1409, ECJ.

The Celtec decision – 'the date of a transfer' must be identified. In the Celtec **1.137** case (above) the ECJ ruled that the 'date of a transfer' in Article 3.1 of the Directive is a particular point in time that cannot be postponed to another date at the will of the transferor or transferee. Both the choice of the word 'date' and the requirement for legal certainty indicated that the transferring must be identified at a particular point in the transfer process and not in relation to the length of time over which that process extends. The date in question, the Court continued, is that on which responsibility as employer for carrying on the business of the undertaking moves from the transferor to the transferee. With the ECJ having reached its decision, the case returned to the House of Lords. The task for their Lordships in Celtec Ltd v Astley and ors 2006 ICR 992, HL, was to examine the convoluted facts of the case in order to determine the 'date of the transfer'.

The facts of the Celtec case were as follows. In 1989 the Government decided to set up a number of Training and Enterprise Councils (TECs) in England and Wales to take over the training and enterprise responsibilities carried out by the Department of Employment (DoE). To assist with the transition, it was agreed that civil servants working in training and enterprise roles in the DoE's area offices would be invited to volunteer for three-year secondments to the newly created TECs. The first secondment began in 1990, with the last ending in 1996. The North East Wales TEC commenced business in 1990, and in September of that year A, H and O – three civil servants with responsibility for vocational training in North Wales – started three-year secondments there. In December 1991 the Secretary of State for Education and Employment, with the agreement of the TECs, announced that secondments would be phased out at the end of each of the TECs' fifth year of operation. As part of this move, seconded civil servants were free to choose whether to take up any offer of employment with the TECs or to return to the Civil Service after their secondments for redeployment. In 1993 H, O and A resigned from the Civil Service to take up employment with North East Wales TEC, which later became C Ltd. In 1998 C Ltd decided to effect redundancies, and, in the context of the calculation of redundancy payments, the question arose as to whether the claimants' continuous service with C Ltd should be aggregated with their service as civil servants with the DoE. They contended that it should, since their continuity had been protected by TUPE.

1.138 An employment tribunal found that there had been a transfer of an undertaking from the DoE to what became C Ltd. It noted, however, that in order for the claimants' continuity to be preserved by TUPE, they had to show that they had been employed by the DoE 'immediately before the transfer'. Thus, a preliminary issue arose as to when the undertaking in question transferred. Addressing this matter, the tribunal held that the transfer took place over several years – from the time the first secondment began in 1990 until the last one ended in 1996. It further held that each time a secondee became directly employed by C Ltd, this constituted one in a series of transactions by which the transfer was effected. As the secondees in question had been employed by the DoE immediately before the transaction that brought about their direct employment by the TEC, the tribunal held that the employees' continuous employment with the DoE had been preserved after the transfer. In time, this issue progressed to the House of Lords, which, as we saw above, learned from the ECJ that a specific date of transfer had to be identified. It followed that if the claimants had not been employed by the DoE immediately before that specific date, they had not, in fact, transferred under TUPE, and thus had lost their continuity of service when the identity of their employer changed.

The majority of the House of Lords (Lords Bingham, Hope and Carswell) held that, on these facts, the relevant transfer had occurred in September 1990, when the claimants were first seconded to the TEC, even though this was contrary to what all the parties understood to be the case at the time. In Lord Bingham's words: 'It is plain from the findings made below that Celtec set up in business in September 1990 and the employees seconded from the Department were the core of the business: without them there could have been no effective transfer. It is scarcely an exaggeration to say that they were the business.' Accordingly, their employment transferred from the DoE to the TEC/C Ltd under TUPE at that time – with their continuity preserved – notwithstanding that they had not resigned from the Civil Service in order to accept direct employment with the TEC until three years later.

1.139 **Difficulties arising from Celtec.** As Lord Mance pointed out in his dissenting judgment in the Celtec case, the decision of the majority is problematic in that it suggests that employees – whom the transfer rules are meant to protect – could find themselves employed by the transferee without even realising it and without their informed consent. This will be of particular concern to organisations such as the NHS, which frequently use 'partnership agreements' and other similar secondment arrangements when conducting outsourcing of services to the private sector. In Chapter 2, under 'Problems of secondment arrangements', we examine the impact of Celtec on such arrangements. Also in Chapter 2, under 'Employed "immediately before" transfer – transfers effected by series of transactions', we shall discuss what Celtec means for Reg 4(3) of TUPE. As set out above, this provides that where a transfer is effected by a series of transactions, an employee will transfer to the transferee if he or she was assigned to the transferring entity 'immediately before any of those transactions'. In other words, it suggests that a wider group of employees than that employed in the undertaking immediately before the 'date of the transfer' might receive TUPE protection. Frustratingly, neither the ECJ nor the House of Lords in Celtec turned their minds to Reg 4(3), despite its clear relevance to the issue at hand.

2 Who transfers?

General effect of transfer on employees

Who is an 'employee' for TUPE purposes?

Contracts 'otherwise terminated by' transfer

Employed 'immediately before' transfer

'Assigned' to undertaking transferred

Objecting to the transfer

Employees retained by transferor

Problems of secondment arrangements

Under UK common law, the relationship of an individual employee and his or her employer is governed primarily by the contract of employment between them. It is, in theory, an entirely *personal* relationship. Therefore, on general common law principles, that particular employee is taken to contract with that particular employer and neither party can arrange unilaterally for another party to fulfil his or her contractual obligations. But what is the effect of this rule when the employer wants to sell the business in which the employee works? At common law, the application of the rule meant that an employer could not, without the consent of the employee concerned, arrange for the purchaser of the business to take over the employee's employment contract – Nokes v Doncaster Amalgamated Collieries Ltd 1940 AC 1014, HL. The House of Lords in that case said that the freedom of an employee to choose the employer for whom he or she wanted to work constituted 'the main difference between a servant and a serf'. **2.1**

As a consequence of the common law position, the transfer of an undertaking constituted a repudiatory breach of an employment contract – i.e. a breach entitling the employee to treat the contract as terminated. This is because, while the employee was still ready and willing to perform his or her duties under the contract, the employer was no longer able to continue employing the employee in accordance with the terms of that contract. The virtue of the common law position was that employees were free to terminate their contracts with the transferor on the occurrence of such an event. The main disadvantage, however, was that any subsequent employment with the purchaser of the business (the transferee) involved a fresh contract, which might have been on less favourable terms. Another disadvantage was that the vendor of the business (the transferor) could take the opportunity of terminating some of his employees' contracts if that best suited his needs – where, for example, he wished to reduce his overheads to secure a better price for the business.

2.2 In 1977 the United Kingdom became subject to European obligations designed to protect employees involved in the transfer of an undertaking (see the Introduction to this Handbook). These obligations were set out in the EU Acquired Rights Directive, which, following subsequent amendments, was reissued in its entirety as Council Directive No.2001/23 of 12 March 2001 'on the approximation of the laws of the Member States relating to the safeguarding of employees' rights in the event of transfers of undertakings, businesses or parts of undertakings or businesses' ('the EU Acquired Rights Directive'). One of the aims of the Directive, in both its original and its amended form (the amendments essentially codifying interpretation by the European Court of Justice), is to ensure that employees of a transferred business should continue to be employed by its purchaser. To this end, Article 3.1 of the Directive states: '*The transferor's rights and obligations arising from a contract of employment or from an employment relationship existing on the date of a transfer shall, by reason of such transfer, be transferred to the transferee.*' This sets out the principle of automatic transfer of employment contracts. Thus, Article 3.1 of Directive 2001/23 involves what may be regarded as a radical departure from UK common law principles on contracts of employment. The effect required by this provision is now implemented in domestic law by Reg 4 of the Transfer of Undertakings (Protection of Employment) Regulations 2006 SI 2006/246 (TUPE), which replace the 1981 Regulations of the same title.

In this chapter we discuss the issue of how to identify which members of the transferor's workforce have their contracts (and thus employment) automatically transferred by virtue of Reg 4. In the next chapter, we address the related issue of which rights, powers, duties and liabilities transfer – along with the employment of transferred employees – to the transferee.

2.3 ## General effect of transfer on employees

Regulation 4(1) of TUPE states: 'Except where objection is made under paragraph (7), a relevant transfer shall not operate so as to terminate the contract of employment of any person employed by the transferor and assigned to the organised grouping of resources or employees that is subject to the relevant transfer, which would otherwise be terminated by the transfer, but any such contract shall have effect after the transfer as if originally made between the person so employed and the transferee.'

The wording of the provision differs only slightly from that used in the 1981 Regulations. Such changes as have been made are designed to incorporate well-established developments in case law and to reflect more closely what the Government considers to be the correct interpretation of the EU Acquired

Rights Directive. The reference to 'the organised grouping of resources or employees that is subject to a relevant transfer' is intended to encompass both types of relevant transfer provided for under the 2006 Regulations – i.e. a 'standard' transfer and a service provision change (see Chapter 1 for details). This concept derives from the ECJ's test of what amounts to an 'economic entity' capable of transferring under the Directive, and replaces the definition of 'undertaking' as used in the 1981 Regulations, although no change of substance has been effected by the different definition. Whenever references are made in this chapter to 'transfer of an undertaking', these should be taken as being shorthand for a transfer of the organised grouping of resources or employees comprising the economic entity in question.

The basic rule – 'novation' of the contract 2.4
Regulation 4(1) is central to the operation of the Regulations in that it establishes that the employment of employees who are subject to it transfers to the transferee. As Lord Justice Balcombe said in Secretary of State for Employment v Spence and ors 1986 ICR 651, CA: 'The paragraph has two effects: first, that a relevant transfer does not terminate a contract of employment; and the second effect, commencing with the word "but", is that there is a statutory novation of the contract.' The first effect is intended to override the common law contractual position (discussed above).

Statutory novation. The crucial part of Reg 4(1) so far as effecting the transfer 2.5 of employment is concerned is the final clause – 'but any such contract shall have effect after the transfer as if originally made between the person so employed and the transferee'. The stipulation that employment contracts shall have effect after the transfer as if originally made between the person so employed and the transferee is an example of a *statutory novation*. This is simply legal terminology for the substitution of a third party for one of the original parties to a contract. Under general contractual principles, any contract of whatever kind may be novated, but this normally happens by the consent of all the parties concerned and not by the intervention of statute. However, it should be noted that the effect of the particular novation or substitution provided for by Reg 4(1) is not to assign or transfer the contract but rather to extinguish the original contract and replace it by another. As a result, the transferee 'steps into the shoes' of the transferor and takes over all rights and obligations of the transferor under the contract as if the transferee had contracted with the employees concerned from the date on which they were originally employed by the transferor.

Effect of the novation. The fact that this consequence flows from the provision 2.6 of Reg 4(1) might, on the face of it, appear to make most of Reg 4(2)(a) – discussed in detail in Chapter 3, 'What transfers?' – otiose. That provision specifically stipulates that 'without prejudice to [Reg 4(1)]... all the transferor's rights, powers, duties and liabilities under or in connection with any [contract transferred by virtue of Reg 4(1)] shall be transferred by virtue of this regulation to the transferee'. Reg 4(2)(b) further provides that any act or omission done by the transferor prior to the transfer in respect of the contract transferred or a person assigned to the transferred undertaking is deemed to have been done by the transferee. The express provision for the 'transfer' of contractual rights and duties in Reg 4(2) is arguably unnecessary in view of the statutory novation effected by Reg 4(1). That said, Reg 4(2) serves to spell out in the plainest terms the full effect and logic of what follows once a contract is transferred to the transferee as a result of its novation.

The power of Reg 4(1), when it applies, is that it in effect reverses the position under UK common law as described at the start of this chapter. Rather than the transfer operating to bring about the termination of the contract (and with it the employment) of all employees employed by the transferor, the statutory provision operates to preserve the contract (and the employment under it) with the transferee as a successor to the original employer.

2.7 **Limitations on 'automatic transfer of employment' rule.** However, it is important to note that Reg 4(1) does not necessarily apply to every member of the transferor's workforce. Various limitations on the transfer of contracts are contained within the wording of Reg 4(1) itself, and for this reason the language of the regulation has to be carefully analysed. Were it not for these limitations, it would be possible to speak accurately of Reg 4 effecting the 'automatic' novation of contracts of employment and the employment regulated under such contracts. But the fact that there are limitations means that it is perhaps better to paraphrase Reg 4 as effecting the *quasi automatic transfer* of employment, especially since – as we shall see – employees are entitled to object to their employment transferring.

Scrutiny of Reg 4(1) shows that there are five limitations or 'caveats' to its operation. The first is gleaned from its opening words, which are '*Except where objection is made under paragraph (7)*'. This is a reference to the right of anyone whose employment would otherwise be transferred by virtue of Reg 4(1) to object to the transfer, with the consequence of preventing Reg 4(1) and (2) from operating to transfer either the contract of employment or the rights, powers, duties and liabilities thereunder to the transferee. If a valid objection is made, Reg 4(1) will not apply. This is a crucial protection of the rights of employees caught up in a transfer situation and it – along with the other caveats – is discussed in detail later below.

2.8 Secondly, Reg 4(1) speaks of the transfer not operating 'so as to terminate the *contract of employment* of any person *employed* by the transferor' (our emphasis). This shows that the statutory novation and the rights associated with it only apply to members of the transferor's workforce who are 'employees' employed under a 'contract of employment' as defined by the Regulations. As we shall see later in this chapter, the definition of 'employee' appears to go

84

somewhat wider than the equivalent definition for statutory rights purposes (including unfair dismissal) under the Employment Rights Act 1996 (ERA). But anyone who does not fall within this extended definition will not have their employment transferred by virtue of Reg 4 to the transferee.

Thirdly, and immediately following on from the wording discussed above, Reg 4(1) states that it is directed only to employees 'assigned to the organised grouping of resources or employees that is subject to the relevant transfer' (our emphasis). This means that any employee who is not actually 'assigned' to the undertaking being transferred will not be subject to the transfer of employment provisions of Reg 4. What is meant by 'assigned' is fully discussed below. It should be noted that this wording is new to the 2006 Regulations, but reflects the position that had already become established under the earlier TUPE Regulations as a result of decisions of the European Court of Justice determining to whom the principle of automatic transfer applies.

Fourthly, and straying for a moment outside the actual wording of Reg 4(1), **2.9** Reg 4(3) provides that the reference to 'a person employed by the transferor and assigned to the organised grouping of resources or employees' in Reg 4(1) is a reference 'to a person so *employed immediately before the transfer*, or would have been so employed if he had not been dismissed in the circumstances described in regulation 7(1)' (our emphasis). Thus, Reg 4 will not bite in respect of an employee who is not employed by the transferor and assigned to the transferred undertaking 'immediately before' its transfer to the transferee. As we shall see, the identification of precisely when the transfer takes place is therefore crucial. We shall also see that the reference in Reg 4(3) to Reg 7(1) essentially means that an employee will be 'deemed' to have been employed 'immediately before the transfer' if he or she has been unfairly dismissed prior to the transfer and the sole or principal reason for the dismissal is the transfer itself or a reason connected to the transfer that is not an 'economic, technical or organisational reason entailing a change in the workforce'.

Fifthly, Reg 4(1) contains one last potential limitation on the operation of the automatic transfer principle that it enshrines. This centres on the words '*which would otherwise be terminated by the transfer*'. Putting these words within the general context of the regulation, Reg 4(1) provides that 'a relevant transfer shall not operate so as to terminate the contract of employment of any person employed by the transferor... which would otherwise be terminated by the transfer'. Applying strict logic, we can deduce from this that only contracts of employment that would otherwise automatically terminate as a result of the transfer are caught by Reg 4(1). This demands the question: Which contracts are these? It is no use pretending that there is a simple or obvious answer to this. Indeed, it is true to say that the words 'which would otherwise be terminated by the transfer' – which also appeared in the antecedent provisions of Reg 5(1) of the 1981 Regulations – have given rise to a large amount of academic debate. Even though there has never been general agreement among TUPE experts as to whether, and to what extent, the words actually limit the application of the principle of automatic transfer, it is interesting that, despite this, the same wording has been retained in the 2006 Regulations without any attempt being made to illuminate its opaque meaning. As we shall see, the provision is unlikely to represent a major limitation on the operation of Reg 4, although it may have some bearing in a case where an employee agrees to be retained in the service of the transferor following a relevant transfer.

2.10 Summary of principle of novation

Summarising, then, the basic rule of novation enshrined in Reg 4 in the order in which each of the individual elements of the rule are discussed below: the contract of employment of anyone employed by the transferor will be automatically transferred to the transferee, as well as all rights, powers, duties and liabilities under it, *unless*:

- the person concerned is not an 'employee' as defined by the 2006 Regulations

- he or she is regarded as being employed on a contract that would not otherwise be terminated by the transfer

- he or she is not employed by the transferor 'immediately before' the transfer

- he or she is not 'assigned' to the undertaking being transferred, or

- he or she makes a valid objection to the transfer.

2.11 Each of these caveats or qualifications is considered separately below. However, it is worth pointing out that although these limitations are highly technical and the discussion around them involves complex legal analysis, the vast majority of transfers will be unaffected by them. In most cases, it will be self-evident which of the transferor's workers are 'employees' for the purposes of the Regulations and which of these are employed by the transferor immediately before the transfer. Similarly, it will be clear whether or not an employee is assigned to the relevant undertaking at the time of the transfer.

2.12 Who is an 'employee' for TUPE purposes?

Not every member of a transferor's workforce is necessarily covered by the protections accorded by the 2006 Regulations. In common with most of the statutory rights conferred by the ERA – including the right to claim unfair dismissal and entitlement to a statutory redundancy payment – the TUPE protections in respect of the transfer of contracts (Reg 4) and the specific protection against unfair dismissal (Reg 7) apply to 'employees' employed by the transferor under a contract of employment.

It would have been helpful when ascertaining exactly who is and who is not an 'employee' for this purpose if the definition of 'employee' under the Regulations were exactly the same as that for unfair dismissal and redundancy purposes under the ERA. Unfortunately, this is not the case. For reasons explained below, not only is the definition of 'employee' under the 2006 Regulations wider than under the ERA, but its unique formulation means that there is no exact equivalent in any other legislation. So while it is true that anyone who is an employee for the purposes of the ERA will fall within the TUPE definition of 'employee', it is also true that a further 'subset' of workers – to use a neutral term – may come within the protections of TUPE. The big problem lies in identifying this subset – a task made difficult by the lack of precision in the TUPE definition combined with the paucity of cases in which that definition has been scrutinised by the appellate courts.

Definition of 'employee' and 'contract of employment'　　2.13
'Employee' is defined for the purposes of the Regulations in Reg 2(1) as: 'any individual who works for another person whether under a contract of service or apprenticeship *or otherwise* but does not include anyone who provides services under a contract for services' (our emphasis).

'Contract of employment' is defined in Reg 2(1) as '*any agreement* between an employee and his employer *determining the terms and conditions of his employment*' (our emphasis). This definition is crucial because the entire thrust of Reg 4 is to effect the transfer of the contract of employment of any employee who is employed by the transferor and assigned to the undertaking being transferred immediately before the transfer. It will be immediately observed that the Regulations provide for a wide-reaching definition of 'contract of employment' in that the definition embraces any agreement devised in the context of an employment relationship that determines the terms and conditions applicable to that relationship.

Three certainties emerge from these definitions, namely that:　　2.14

• any person employed under a contract of service will be covered by TUPE

• any apprentice employed under a contract of apprenticeship will similarly be covered

• anyone who merely provides services under a contract for services (i.e. someone in business on their own account or an independent contractor) will not be covered.

Apart from the above, nothing else is spelt out about who does and who does not come within the definition of 'employee' for TUPE purposes, other than that the scope of the definitions embraces a wider group of persons than merely those employed under a contract of service. The uncertainty is almost entirely caused by the two words 'or otherwise' within the definition, since these raise

87

the crucial question: what is meant by a person who works for another under 'a contract of service... or otherwise'? Case law helps in establishing the parameters, but not a lot.

2.15 The insertion of the vague words 'or otherwise' into the Reg 2(1) definition of 'employee' and the broad scope given to the definition of 'contract of employment' are explicable in terms of the EU Acquired Rights Directive. Article 3.1 of the Directive provides that: 'The transferor's rights and obligations arising from a contract of employment *or from an employment relationship* existing on the date of a transfer shall, by reason of such transfer, be transferred to the transferee'. The substance of this provision is implemented into UK law by Reg 4 of the 2006 Regulations. In enacting the original version of TUPE, the then Conservative Government felt it had to give full cognisance to the words emphasised by italics above because those words clearly envisaged that rights arising not just from a contract of employment but from an employment relationship had to be transferred. Hence, the words 'or otherwise' were added into the definition of 'employee'. All of this was explained in the Court of Appeal's decision in Askew v Governing Body of Clifton Middle School and ors 2000 ICR 286, CA. In that case, Lord Justice Peter Gibson referred to the Parliamentary debates on the initial TUPE Regulations, where Lord Lyell, on behalf of the then Government, noted that '[the] wider definitions of "employee" and "contract of employment" are to embrace the wider concept of what appears in the Directive as "employment relationship"' (Hansard 10.12.81, HL Debates, col 1496).

The relationship between the definitions of 'employee' and 'contract of employment' was analysed by the Court of Appeal in the Askew case. It was pointed out that the TUPE definition of 'employee' includes but goes beyond how an employee is defined for the purposes of the ERA. The TUPE definition of 'contract of employment' is likewise given an extended meaning to include any agreement between an 'employee' (as defined by Reg 2(1)) and an employer determining the terms and conditions of the employee's employment. Hence, 'contract of employment' is defined in TUPE to include not only contracts of service and apprenticeship – i.e. to cover contracts that would be 'contracts of employment' as under the ERA – but also any other agreement that records or evidences 'an employment relationship' as required by the Directive. But, as Lord Justice Chadwick made clear, the relevant definitions are not framed to include an employment relationship in which there is no agreement whatsoever between the so-called employee and employer determining the terms and conditions of employment. Nor, as we shall see below, does the phrase 'contract of employment' extend to a non-contractual agreement. The reason for this is simple: the employment relationships to which the TUPE Regulations were intended to apply must be relationships that are capable of being protected by those Regulations. In particular, the relationships must be ones that provide some basis for the application of Regs 4(1) and 5(1) – the transfer of employment contracts and collective agreements to the transferee – or that give rise to rights capable of being protected under Part X of the ERA (unfair dismissal) and thus provide a foundation for the application of Reg 7(1), which protects against unfair dismissal by reason of the transfer.

Limits on scope of extended definitions   2.16
As explained above, the addition of the words 'or otherwise' to the definition of employee given in Reg 2(1) clearly contemplates an extension of the definition of employee beyond merely those employed under contracts of service or apprenticeship. But this extension has its limits. These are outlined below.

Requirement for contractual relations. TUPE protection can only extend to 2.17 individuals who work for another under some kind of contract. In other words, for Reg 4 to apply, there must be a contractual relationship between the individual and the transferor. This was made clear by Peter Gibson LJ in Askew (see above), when he stated: 'In my judgment, it is clear that TUPE proceeds on the basis that there must be a contract. One gets that from the application of the *euisdem generis* rule to "contract of service or apprenticeship or otherwise" in the definition of "employee", from the definition of "contract of employment" as meaning any agreement between an employee and his employer determining the terms and conditions of his employment, and from [what is now Reg 4(1) of the 2006 Regulations], which proceeds on the footing that there will be a contract of employment by the transferor in the undertaking or part transferred. TUPE also proceeds, consistently with the Directive, on the footing that the employee is employed by the transferor and will become the employee of the transferee.' Gibson LJ is basically relying on the rule of statutory interpretation that, where general words follow specific words, those general words are interpreted in the light of the specific words – for example, in the phrase 'cats, dogs and other animals', 'other animals' will be interpreted by the court as referring to domestic animals similar to cats and dogs.

Contract must be with the transferor. The second limitation to the expansive 2.18 definition of 'employee' in Reg 2(1) is related to the first limitation discussed above. Not only must the basis on which work undertaken by the individual on behalf of the other be underpinned by a contractual agreement, but that other has to be the actual or legal person who is the 'transferor' of the undertaking being transferred. This was again made clear by the Court of Appeal in Askew. There, a teacher was initially employed by the local education authority (LEA) to work at a particular school. Following a reorganisation, the school ceased to be run by the LEA and the responsibility for its operation was transferred to the school's governing body. Following the termination of his employment by the LEA, the claimant applied to the governors for re-employment but was unsuccessful. At first instance, an employment tribunal conclusively determined as a finding of fact that the school comprised the undertaking being transferred. On that basis, the Court of Appeal upheld the governors' argument that neither

89

TUPE nor the Acquired Rights Directive applied to transfer the claimant's employment from the LEA to the school's governing body. This was because the claimant's contract of employment – and, for that matter, employment relationship (using the extended language of the Directive) – was not with the transferor (the school) but with the LEA. As a result, the claimant was never employed by the transferor, with the result that what is now Reg 4 of the 2006 Regulations did not apply.

Lord Justice Ward explained his reasoning for reaching this conclusion in this way: '[The claimant] depends on the definition of employee in Reg 2(1). He submits that although his contract of service is with the LEA, he "otherwise" also "works for" the old governors in that, as he works at the school which they govern, he must to some extent work for them... [T]hat construction unnaturally strains the language. It forces the adverb "otherwise" to qualify the words "works for" rather than the word "contract". On his construction an employee means... an individual who works for a person under a contract of service or apprenticeship or (who works for a person in some other way). The more natural meaning is an individual who works for a person under a contract of employment or apprenticeship or (under some other contract). So I reject that argument.' Chadwick LJ, agreeing, concluded that: 'I am not persuaded that the provisions of the Acquired Rights Directive require – or enable – the court to give the words "or otherwise" in TUPE Reg 2(1) a meaning which extends the definition of "employee" to an individual (X) who works for another person (Y) under an arrangement which, as between X and Y, is non-contractual.'

2.19 **Contract must provide for personal service.** A further limiting factor is that the TUPE definition of 'employee' explicitly requires the employment relationship to be one whereby the individual *works for another person* under one of the relevant types of contract. Essentially, this boils down to the relationship needing to be one of employment rather than some other arrangement. This was made clear by the Court of Appeal in Cowell v (1) Quilter Goodson Co Ltd (2) QG Management Services Ltd 1989 IRLR 392, CA, where it was held that the TUPE Regulations did not apply to an equity partner of a firm that, following incorporation, was transferred as a limited company, which then employed the former partner under a contract of employment. In the judgment of Lord Donaldson MR (with whom the other members of the Court of Appeal agreed), an equity partner was someone who provides services under a contract for services and was not therefore an 'individual who works for another person whether under a contract of service or apprenticeship *or otherwise*' at the time of the transfer. Rather, the relationship, which was between the claimant partner and the other partners of the firm, was predicated on people carrying on business in common with a view to profit as governed by the Partnership Act 1890. That relationship was not one of employment; nor did the partnership agreement constitute a contract of employment or any kind of contract under which the individual worked for another person.

Exclusion of those engaged under contracts for services

2.20

The definition of employee in Reg 2(1) expressly excludes 'anyone who provides services under a contract for services'. This phrase is generally used to describe any contract under which services are provided that is not a contract of employment or apprenticeship. Occasionally, however, the phrase has a more specific and limited meaning, intended to be confined to contracts entered into by independent contractors. In that case, a contract with someone who is held not to be an employee, an apprentice or an independent contractor can properly be described as a 'contract sui generis' rather than a contract for services – see Construction Industry Training Board v Labour Force Ltd 1970 3 All ER 220, Div Ct, where the Divisional Court held that the contracts of workmen who were neither independent contractors nor engaged under a contract of service should be described as 'contracts sui generis' (i.e. of a unique kind). If this is applied to Reg 2(1), then an individual employed under a contract sui generis would presumably be an 'individual who works for another person whether under a contract of service or apprenticeship or otherwise' and thus fall within the definition of 'employee'.

There is a compelling reason why the phrase 'contract for services' as used in Reg 2(1) should bear its restrictive rather than its more general meaning. Were it simply to mean any contract that is not a contract of employment or apprenticeship, then it would be difficult to see how anyone who is potentially brought within the definition of 'employee' by the words 'or otherwise' would not be immediately excluded by the qualification 'does not include anyone who provides services under a contract for services'. A better reading of the phrase 'provides services under a contract for services' is that it effectively means 'provides services as an independent contractor under a contract for services'.

Workers

2.21

Having dissected the components of the definitions of 'employee' and 'contract of employment' in Reg 2(1), and the limitations that apply to the extended meaning of both terms, we now turn to examining particular types of individual or atypical worker. In each case the question is the same: Would the employment of such an individual by the transferor be subject to Reg 4, with the result that his or her 'contract of employment' is transferred to the transferee?

Certain statutory protection rights in the United Kingdom extend to individuals who do not technically work under a contract of service. This is sometimes signalled by use of the term 'worker' in place of the term 'employee' in the relevant legislation, in which case 'worker' is defined as one who either works under a contract of employment or works under 'any other contract, whether express or implied and (if it is express) whether oral or in writing, whereby the individual undertakes to do or perform personally any work or services for another party to the contract whose status is not by virtue of the contract that of a client or customer of any profession or business undertaking carried on by the individual'. This formula currently appears in the Working Time Regulations 1998 SI 1998/1833, the National Minimum Wage Act 1998, the Employment Relations Act 1999 in respect of the right to be accompanied at a grievance or disciplinary hearing, and the Part-time Workers (Prevention of Less Favourable Treatment) Regulations 2000 SI 2000/1551.

2.22 Distilling the definition into its constituent elements, the following are shown to be necessary for an individual to come within the definition of 'worker':

- there must be a contract, whether express or implied, and, if express, whether written or oral

- that contract must provide for the individual to carry out personal services; and

- those services must be for the benefit of another party to the contract who must not be a client or customer of the individual's profession or business undertaking.

In Byrne Brothers (Formwork) Ltd v Baird and ors 2002 ICR 667, EAT, the Appeal Tribunal laid down a helpful test to identify who comprises a 'worker' under the above definition. It held that the effect of the definition was to create an intermediate category of protected workers, who on the one hand are not employees but who on the other hand cannot be regarded as merely carrying on a business on their own account. The EAT said that to draw a distinction in a particular case would involve all or most of the same considerations that arise when deciding if somebody is an employee (e.g. degree of control, method of payment, provision of equipment, level of risk, etc). The effect of the definition of 'worker', however, is to lower the 'pass mark' so that persons who fail to reach the high mark necessary to qualify as employees may still qualify as workers. Adopting very similar reasoning, the EAT in JNJ Bricklaying Ltd v Stacey and ors EAT 0088/03 ruled that the relevant distinction is between workers whose degree of dependence is essentially the same as that of employees, and contractors who have more of an arm's-length and independent position and can therefore be regarded as being able to look after themselves.

2.23 In Bacica v Muir 2006 IRLR 35, EAT, the Appeal Tribunal cautioned that the mere rendering of a service personally is not sufficient to make a person a 'worker' under the statutory definition of worker in the employment protection provisions mentioned above. It is crucial not to ignore the last clause in the definition, which makes it clear that if a person renders services or performs work on the basis that the person to or for whom he or she does so is a customer of his or her business, he or she is not then to be regarded as a worker. Such work or service may well be rendered on a personal basis – for instance, it is well within the competence of many self-employed sole traders to do so and many secure business on the basis of selling their personal skills. In that case the EAT ruled that a claimant who carried out painting work for a company under the Construction Industry Scheme Regulations and whose accounts were submitted to the Inland Revenue on a self-employed basis was not a worker within the meaning of the Working Time Regulations 1998.

In the light of the above, the following are examples of those who have been held to be 'workers' engaged under a contract to provide personal service:

- a joiner working as a labour-only subcontractor. (Note that a contractual prohibition on substitution of the individual worker by another joiner without prior written consent was found not to prevent the contract being one to provide personal services) – Cavil v Barratt Homes Ltd EAT 0208/03

- a self-employed joiner who worked a 39-hour week exclusively for a firm of building contractors (notwithstanding that the worker completed his own tax return, paid his own tax and national insurance and provided his own hand tools) – Torith Ltd v Flynn EAT 0017/02

- bricklayers engaged under a building company's standard terms and conditions containing clauses that were inconsistent with a requirement to perform the work personally. (The Court of Appeal accepted that the factual background of the case, including the company's method of payment to each individual bricklayer, pointed strongly to the conclusion that, in reality, the contracts with individual workers required them to perform the work personally) – Redrow Homes (Yorkshire) Ltd v Wright and another case 2004 IRLR 720, CA.

Would workers of this kind come within the extended definition of 'employee' **2.24** in Reg 2(1) of the 2006 Regulations? Although there is no direct case authority on the point, it is highly arguable that they would. This is because such workers would appear, for the purposes of Reg 2(1), to be individuals who work for another person whether under a contract of service or otherwise. Provided that the requirement of personal service is met and that the putative worker is not exclusively providing his or her services as an independent contractor, then the only remaining requirement – as established by the Court of Appeal in the Askew case (see above under 'Limits on scope of extended definitions') – is that the employment relationship is regulated by a contract of some kind. In the absence of such a contract, the individual would not, in any event, be regarded as a worker for the purposes of the relevant employment legislation where that definition applies. So long as such a contract exists, then, in our view, the individual will be a worker for the purposes of the employment protection legislation and come within the extended definition of 'employee' under Reg 2(1).

Assuming that such workers would qualify for TUPE protection, a question as to the precise ambit of that protection might well arise. If such workers are not employees for the purposes of claiming, say, unfair dismissal, then they do not suddenly become entitled to such rights merely because their employment transfers following a transfer of an undertaking. Reg 7(6) in this regard expressly ensures that an individual who is otherwise excluded from claiming unfair dismissal cannot rely upon the provisions in the Regulations for deeming a dismissal by reason of the transfer to be unfair – see, further, Chapter 4 under 'The TUPE unfair dismissal regime – protected employees'.

More generally, it is well established that the objective of both the Acquired Rights Directive and TUPE is to preserve existing rights rather than augment or create new ones. This was made clear by the ECJ in Viggósdóttir v Íslandspóstur HF 2002 IRLR 425, ECJ, when it stated that 'the objective of the Directive… is not to improve the situation of an employee following a transfer, but merely to preserve his acquired rights'. Taking its cue from this, the EAT in Computershare Investor Services plc v Jackson EAT 0503/06 has stated: 'We accept that one cannot use TUPE to advance upon a position which was not there on the date of the transfer'. This means that if individuals who are not employees employed under a contract of service nonetheless fall within the extended definition of 'employee' for the purposes of Reg 2(1), then, following the transfer, they will be entitled to enforce the same – but only the same – statutory rights against the transferee as they had with the transferor.

2.25 Those in 'employment' for the purposes of discrimination law

The same reasoning can, subject to one further qualification, be applied in the case of those who come within the scope of UK anti-discrimination legislation. This, now codified in the Equality Act 2010 (EqA), uses neither the term 'worker' nor the term 'employee' to determine who is covered, but instead extends coverage to those in 'employment'. This is defined in S.83(2) EqA as 'employment under a contract of service or of apprenticeship or a contract personally to do any work or labour'. The definition is thus similar to, but wider than, that of 'worker' discussed above.

The protection against discrimination thus extends not only to those employed under contracts of employment or apprenticeship but also to those employed 'under a contract personally to do any work or labour'. Two elements are necessary to fall within this type of contract:

• a requirement for a contract to exist; and

• a requirement that such contract provides for the work or labour under it to be executed personally.

2.26 The first of these requirements is, as we have seen, common both to the definition of 'worker' in employment protection legislation where that concept is used and to 'employee' in Reg 2(1) of the 2006 Regulations. Without a contract of some kind – be it express or implied – neither of the relevant definitions will be satisfied.

The second requirement – that the contract, if not one of employment or apprenticeship, must nonetheless provide for personal execution of work or labour – has been interpreted to mean that it must have as its *dominant purpose* the execution of work or labour – Mirror Group Newspapers Ltd v Gunning 1986 ICR 145, CA. This means that the contracting party must perform the essential part of the work personally, although he or she is free to assign or delegate other aspects to another person without falling outside the definition of 'employment'.

With this in mind, would an individual employed on a contract personally to **2.27** perform work or labour as defined above come within the definition of 'employee' under Reg 2(1) of TUPE? Chadwick LJ in the Askew decision certainly seemed to think so when he observed: '"Employee" includes a person who is not employed under a contract of employment in the sense that that phrase is used in the [ERA]; the definition in Reg 2(1) is at least as wide as that adopted by the legislature for the purposes of the Sex Discrimination Act 1975.' Although his Lordship did not go on to amplify his reasoning in this regard, it seems fairly clear that an individual who has an agreement the dominant purpose of which is to provide for him or her to personally do work for another would be an 'employee' for the purposes of Reg 2(1), since he or she would be an 'individual who works for another person under a contract of service... *or otherwise*'. Furthermore, that contract would comprise a 'contract of employment' as defined in Reg 2(1) in that it is 'an agreement between an employee and his employer determining the terms and conditions of his employment'.

An important caveat applies here. This concerns the fact that, unlike the definition of 'worker' previously discussed, the definition of 'employment' in the anti-discrimination legislation does not contain an express exclusion for independent contractors. Such persons would include those who provide personal services for a client or customer in the course of practising a profession or running a business on their own account. For the most part, contractors of this kind receive protection from discrimination by virtue of specific provisions contained within the anti-discrimination legislation dealing with contract workers. However, in exceptional circumstances, such workers might also be able to bring themselves within the definition of 'employment' – see, for example, Kelly and Loughran v Northern Ireland Housing Executive 1998 ICR 828, HL, where the majority of the House of Lords held that a contract between a solicitor and a client for the retention of that solicitor's legal services could fall within the definition of 'employment' provided that the contract is one personally to execute work, one of the partners of the firm bringing the claim is a contracting party, and it is envisaged that that partner would be the individual who would have undertaken to provide the services personally. In any case where these conditions are met by a contractor, the individual concerned would be shut out of TUPE protection on account of the exclusion in the definition of 'employee' in Reg 2(1) of 'anyone who provides services under a contract for services'. As we have seen, however, there is a strong case for giving a restrictive meaning to the concept of 'contract for services' in this particular context – see under 'Exclusion of those engaged under contracts for services' above.

2.28 Agency workers

'Agency workers' are individuals engaged by an employment business who are assigned to work for clients of the business, usually under temporary worker agreements. The legal rights of such workers is an area fraught with difficulties since, even in the context of basic statutory rights such as unfair dismissal and redundancy entitlement, it is often unclear whether such workers are employees of the employment business, the client (i.e. end-user), or neither.

In the context of TUPE, the question often arises as to whether the employment of an agency worker assigned by an employment business to work for an end-user transfers following a transfer of the end-user's undertaking. In the absence of a direct contractual relationship between worker and end-user, recent case law suggests that the worker is highly likely to fall outside the relevant definition of 'employee' in Reg 2(1). This is because the only express agreement that he or she is likely to have is with the employment business. Rarely will there be any kind of written contractual agreement with the end-user. Thus, applying the Court of Appeal's decision in James v London Borough Council 2008 ICR 545, CA, the worker would not be an 'employee' employed under a 'contract of employment' with the transferor. And, in order for TUPE to apply, it is well established that the relevant contract has to be one to which the transferor is a party – see Clifton Middle School Governing Body v Askew 2000 ICR 286, CA. An agreement with a third party under which the individual is seconded or assigned to work for the transferor does not count – see 'Limitations on scope of extended definitions' above.

2.29 Non-employees who are 'protected' as employees

Although, as we have seen, the Acquired Rights Directive applies to transfer the rights of those employed under an 'employment relationship' as well as under a contract of employment, the scope of 'employment relationship' in this regard has been held to extend only to 'persons who, in one way or another, are protected as employees under the rules of law of the Member State concerned' – see Mikkelsen v Danmols Inventar A/S (in liquidation) 1986 1 CMLR 316, ECJ. On one interpretation of this, the ECJ is saying no more than that the Directive applies only to those who are defined as 'employees' under national law. In that case, the definition of 'employee' for TUPE purposes would begin and end with the definition given in Reg 2(1). However, on a broader interpretation of the ECJ's ruling, the Court might be taken to be saying that the Directive must be construed as extending not only to those who are employees but also to those who, under national legislation, are treated as employees for the purposes of employment protection rights. Potentially, this would mean that the definition of 'employee' in Reg 2(1) would need to be interpreted as embracing a small but significant group of individuals who, though they are technically not 'employees' who work under a contract of employment, nevertheless receive the same or similar protections against unfair dismissal and redundancy as if they were.

Apart from Mikkelsen, no other case appears to have tackled this issue, so **2.30** uncertainty remains. But were it the case that the Directive (and therefore TUPE) does extend to individuals who are treated as employees for employment protection purposes, then with specific regard to the United Kingdom the following groups of individuals are protected against unfair dismissal as 'honorary' employees:

- *Crown servants*: although such workers are said to be 'appointed' rather than 'employed', and their appointment is 'at will and terminable by the Crown without notice', they receive the same protection against unfair dismissal as do ordinary employees by virtue of S.191(1) ERA. The same applies in respect of most other statutory employment rights

- *House of Commons and House of Lords staff*: Ss.194 and 195 ERA provide that unfair dismissal rights apply to 'relevant members' of staff of the two Houses of Parliament

- *persons employed in the police service*: although generally excluded from unfair dismissal rights, some members of the police service – i.e. those who hold the office of constable or are appointed as police cadets – are entitled to bring unfair dismissal claims on limited grounds, namely health and safety and protected disclosure (i.e. whistleblowing) – Ss.43KA and 134A ERA

- *mariners*: those employed on a ship registered in Great Britain, who are ordinarily resident in Great Britain and who do not ordinarily work outside Great Britain are entitled to unfair dismissal protection – S.199 ERA.

Of course, in practice, most of the categories of individual mentioned above are **2.31** unlikely to be caught up in a transfer of an undertaking to which the 2006 Regulations apply. Of those that are listed, the most likely affected group are Crown servants, but it is improbable that the 'Mikkelsen question' will arise in respect of them since for many years it has been standard practice for TUPE to be faithfully applied to transfers (such as outsourcing) affecting the Civil Service and government departments.

2.32 Employees employed abroad

The 2006 Regulations apply to the transfer of an undertaking situated in the United Kingdom immediately before the transfer, and, in the case of a service provision change, where there is an organised grouping of employees situated in the United Kingdom immediately before the service provision change. However, neither Reg 4 nor any other provision deals specifically with the position of employees who, though employed in the undertaking (or part) transferred, ordinarily work abroad. The question arises whether the employment of such employees is transferred under Reg 4.

By virtue of Reg 3(4)(c), the Regulations expressly apply to a transfer of an undertaking, business or part of an undertaking or business situated in the United Kingdom, even where persons employed in the undertaking or part transferred ordinarily work outside the United Kingdom. It will be noted that this provision deals with the definition of a relevant transfer rather than the effect that such a relevant transfer has on employees employed in the undertaking who ordinarily work abroad. But the implication is – and there is nothing to contradict this – that such employees would be covered by Reg 4 provided they are actually 'assigned' to the undertaking (or part) being transferred at the time of the transfer. The issue of assignment is covered under '"Assigned" to undertaking transferred' below.

2.33 Contracts 'otherwise terminated by' transfer

Regulation 4(1) (set out at the beginning of this chapter) establishes the basic premise that a relevant transfer will not operate to terminate the 'the contract of employment of any person... *which would otherwise be terminated by the transfer*' (our emphasis). This implies that the 'automatic transfer of employment' rule applies to contracts of employment that would be terminated by the transfer and is inapplicable to those contracts of employment that would not be so terminated. However, this aspect of the wording of Reg 4(1) – which is identical in this regard to the previous wording in Reg 5(1) of the 1981 Regulations – has caused some difficulty because it is not at all clear which employment contracts would 'otherwise' be terminated by the transfer.

2.34 Are employment contracts 'otherwise' terminated by transfer?

The assumption that appears to underlie this provision is that, in the absence of the TUPE Regulations, transfers of an undertaking may, in and of themselves, cause the automatic termination of contracts of employment. In so implying, it is probable that the Parliamentary draftsman was seeking simply to reflect the common law position that the Regulations are intended to reverse. This, as we have seen in the introduction to this chapter, is based on two legal principles: (1) that employment contracts cannot be transferred unilaterally; and (2) that a transfer is likely to constitute a repudiatory breach of such contracts. However, for reasons explained below, the notion that such a repudiatory breach would according to the common law have the effect of automatically bringing about the termination of a contract of employment may well be technically erroneous. If that is the case, then the Regulations appear to have been based on a misapprehension as to the true common law effect of a transfer on contracts of employment.

Under general contract law, a breach by a party that goes to the root of a contract entitles the other party either to accept the repudiation (in which case the contract is terminated and the innocent party has the right to sue for damages), or to refuse to accept the repudiation (in which case the contract is not terminated and the innocent party may stand and sue for specific performance of the original contract). An unaccepted repudiation is 'a thing writ in water' – Howard v Pickford Tool Co Ltd 1951 1 KB 417, CA. In other words, a repudiatory breach in and of itself does not have the effect of automatically terminating the contract – the innocent party chooses whether or not to bring it to an end. This is known as the 'elective' theory of termination. So far as employment contracts are concerned, it has been a matter of some controversy whether the elective theory applies. On one view, it governs repudiatory breaches of contracts of employment just as much as any other kind of contract – see, for example, Gunton v Richmond-upon-Thames London Borough Council 1980 ICR 755, CA. On an alternative view, employment contracts are an exception to the general need for acceptance of the repudiatory breach, and hence such contracts terminate automatically by the unilateral actions of one party – see Stapp v Shaftesbury Society 1982 IRLR 326, CA. This is known as the 'automatic' theory of termination – i.e. the contract automatically terminates without the innocent party electing to accept the repudiation as ending the contract.

This difference of approach is of some significance when considering the meaning **2.35** of the phrase 'the contract of employment of any person employed by the transferor and assigned to the organised grouping of resources or employees that is subject to the relevant transfer, which would otherwise be terminated by the transfer' in Reg 4(1). If the elective theory applies, then Reg 4(1) proceeds on a misconception about the effect of a transfer on a contract of employment at common law because, on a strict interpretation, a transfer would not, in itself, terminate such a contract. Actual termination would only occur if the employee accepted the repudiatory breach brought about by the transfer as terminating the contract. Thus, if the 'elective' theory of repudiation is correct, it would follow that contracts of employment subsisting at the time of the transfer would not fall into the category of those which would 'otherwise be terminated by the transfer' for the purposes of Reg 4(1), and so would not be subject to the novation rule which that regulation goes on to provide. Clearly, such an interpretation would make the Regulations circular in operation, as no contract of employment would be novated under them on the occurrence of a transfer.

99

It seems certain, therefore, that in the specific context of TUPE, the phrase '[contract] which would otherwise be terminated by the transfer' in Reg 4(1) must be interpreted as resting on the assumption that the transfer itself automatically terminates employment contracts. That is the only way that the key provision of the Regulations – the automatic transfer of employment to the transferee – could be made to work. Authority for so construing Reg 4(1) can, to some extent, be gleaned from the decision of the House of Lords in Litster and ors v Forth Dry Dock and Engineering Co Ltd (in receivership) and anor 1989 ICR 341, HL. In that case Lord Oliver considered what was meant by the reference in what is now Reg 4(1) of the 2006 Regulations to a contract being terminated 'by' a transfer. His Lordship accepted that the phrase could embrace a number of different possibilities. He stated: 'If nothing at all occurs to disturb the relationship of master and servant apart from the simple unannounced fact of the transfer of business by the employer, it is the transfer itself which constitutes the repudiatory breach which, apart from Reg 4(1), "terminates" the contract. If, however, the employer, contemporaneously with the transfer, announces to his workforce that he is transferring the business and that they are therefore dismissed without notice, it is, strictly, the oral notification which terminates the contract; yet it could not, as a matter of common sense, be denied that the contract has been "terminated by the transfer" of the business... Similarly, if the employer, a week, or it may be a day, before the actual transfer, hands to each employee a letter announcing that he is proposing to transfer his undertaking at the close of business on the transfer date, at which time the employees are to consider themselves as forthwith dismissed, it could hardly be contended under the Regulations that their employment had not been terminated by the transfer, even though, at the date of the notice, the dismissal might be capable of taking effect independently, in the event, for instance, of the actual transfer of the business being postponed to a date or time later than the expiry of the notice. In each hypothetical case the employer's repudiation of the contract of service is differently communicated but its essential quality of a repudiation by the transfer of the undertaking remains the same and the contract can quite properly be described as having been terminated by the transfer.'

2.36 Clearly, Lord Oliver's construction of what is now Reg 4(1) means that, for the purposes of that regulation, contracts of employment subsisting at the time the transfer takes place will be automatically transferred on the basis that, apart from the Regulations, they would have been terminated 'by' the transfer. This approach is certainly in keeping with the obligations imposed upon Member States under the Acquired Rights Directive: Article 3.1 (which is set out at the beginning of this chapter) does not contain any wording equivalent to 'contracts which would otherwise be terminated by the transfer', and any detraction from the automatic transfer principle in Article 3.1 caused by a restrictive interpretation of these words in Reg 4(1) would clearly be in breach of the Directive.

It is interesting to note that in the original draft of the current Regulations published by the DTI in 2005, the reference to employment contracts that 'would otherwise have been terminated by the transfer' was omitted altogether. The explanation for this, according to the Public Consultation Document accompanying publication of the draft regulations, was that 'the Government considers these words add nothing of value to the meaning of the provision, and risk creating an unintended loophole in the Regulations' coverage – in that it has been argued by some commentators that they might have the effect of allowing the transferor to retain employees who would otherwise automatically transfer, on the basis that if they were to be retained, their employment would not be terminated by the transfer. This is contrary to the policy intention underlying the provision.' Why, then, was the previous wording reinstated in the final version of the new TUPE Regulations? The explanation – as given by the DTI in its published response to the public consultation in February 2006 – was that the Government was persuaded by some respondents to the consultation that the original wording offered valuable scope for transferors to retain the services of employees who would otherwise transfer. The precise reasoning for this view is not further explained. Presumably, however, it was thought that the contracts of employees who agree with the transferor to be retained or who are permanently reassigned to a different part of the transferor's business before the transfer would not be contracts that would 'otherwise be terminated by the transfer'. This possibility is further explored below.

Contracts to which Reg 4(1) might not apply   2.37
If, then, ordinary contracts of employment are to be interpreted as comprising contracts that would otherwise be terminated by the transfer, the question arises: Which (if any) contracts of employment would not so terminate, with the result that employment under them would not automatically transfer under Reg 4(1)?

There is little case authority to assist in answering this question. But it is submitted that not every case of a transfer will amount to a repudiatory breach, even assuming that in the ordinary case such a transfer does indeed bring about the automatic termination of employment contracts. The following are scenarios where an employee's contract with the transferor might, at common law, be regarded as surviving the transfer intact:

Contracts containing wide-ranging mobility/flexibility clauses. Where the 2.38
terms of an employee's contract of employment include a wide job description, the employee may be contractually required to work in any part of the employer's business to do work which corresponds to that description. If, then, part of the business in which the employee is currently employed is to be sold, the transferor may be in a position to employ the employee in another part of the business under the terms of the contract between them. In this situation the transfer would not constitute a repudiatory breach of contract and therefore

101

would not, apart from the Regulations, have resulted in the termination of the employment contract at common law. In consequence, Reg 4(1) would not operate to transfer that employee's contract to the transferee.

A similar outcome might result where an express flexibility contractual clause exists allowing the employer to require the employee to work in different parts of the business and/or at a different location and/or doing different types of work. If such a contractual term enables the transferor to ensure that the employee is, at the time of the transfer, employed in a part of the business that is not to be transferred, then once again Reg 4(1) will not operate to novate the employee's contract with the transferee. In this scenario, the question would also arise as to whether the employee is 'assigned to the organised grouping of resources or employees' (i.e. the undertaking) immediately before the transfer. The issue of 'assignment' is discussed in detail under '"Assigned" to undertaking transferred' below.

2.39 **Agreement that employee will be retained by transferor.** Sometimes, without making any formal objection to the transfer, the transferor and the employee enter into some kind of agreement whereby the former retains the services of the latter following the transfer. Such agreements may come about by the parties giving express consideration to the matter and reaching a position that reflects their mutual self-interest. However, they sometimes take a more passive form – whereby the parties simply carry on without reference to the transfer as if it has never happened.

Such retention of employees potentially causes considerable headaches from a legal point of view because, strictly speaking, the only way in which Reg 4(1) can be prevented from applying to an employee employed in the undertaking and assigned to it immediately before the transfer is for him or her to exercise the right to object conferred by Reg 4(7). This, as we shall see under 'Objecting to the transfer' below, entails the employee adopting a proactive rather than a passive approach to voicing his or her objection to the transfer, and any such objection brings with it a particular set of legal consequences.

2.40 One way of 'accommodating' retention of the employee by the transferor within the scheme of the Regulations would be to regard the contract of employment between employee and transferor as not otherwise terminating by reason of the transfer. Such a proposition was accepted by the EAT in Direct Radiators Ltd v Howse and anor EAT 130/86, although it is fair to say that in other cases – for example, Visionhire Consumer Electronics Ltd t/a Visionhire v Easton EAT 20/87 – the courts have expressed disquiet about this way of dealing with the situation, preferring to analyse the matter in terms of the employee entering into a new or at least varied contract with the transferor. In view of this difference of opinion, it is interesting to bear in mind the Government's view when enacting the 2006 Regulations. As we pointed out earlier, the original draft left out the phrase '[contract]... otherwise terminated by the transfer', but this was reinserted into the final version of Reg 4(1) on the grounds that it might be of practical advantage to transferors wishing to retain the services of employees who would otherwise transfer. The issue of the retention of employees following relevant transfers is discussed in more detail under 'Employees retained by the transferor' below.

Agreed contractual variations. In a case where the contract of employment **2.41** would otherwise be terminated by the transfer, it is possible that an employee might consent to vary his or her contract in time to avoid the application of the automatic transfer of employment rule in Reg 4(1). So, for example, if, just prior to the transfer occurring, the employee agreed to be reassigned to another part of the transferor's business and so ceased to be assigned to the undertaking being transferred, his or her contract of employment might remain unaffected by Reg 4(1) as it would not 'otherwise be terminated by the transfer'. In such a case, there is a further reason why Reg 4(1) would not apply: the employee would not have been 'assigned to the undertaking immediately before the transfer' as now required by the wording of Reg 4(1). Similar reasoning would apply if the consensual variation concerned the introduction into the contract of a wide-ranging mobility or flexibility clause, or to an arrangement whereby the employee agreed to be seconded outside the part of the business being transferred.

Employed 'immediately before' transfer   2.42

Once it has been established who, among the transferor's workforce, are 'employees' employed under 'contracts of employment' for the purposes of Reg 2(1), the next logical step in determining to whom the automatic transfer of employment rule in Reg 4(1) applies is to decide whether such employees are employed by the transferor and assigned to the transferred undertaking at the time of the transfer. Three separate issues may be relevant to this:

- when does the transfer take place?

- which of the transferor's employees are employed '*immediately* before the transfer'? (This is because Reg 4(1) only bites in respect of those employed by the transferor and who are, it would seem, also assigned to the transferred undertaking 'immediately before the transfer')

- in a case where the transfer is effected by two or more transactions, is the employee to be regarded as having been employed in the undertaking and assigned to it immediately before the first of those transactions? If so, then Reg 4(1) will apply to transfer his or her employment even if he or she has ceased to be employed/assigned by the end of the transfer process.

Although these issues are very much interrelated, we examine each of them in turn below.

2.43 When does the transfer occur?

Fixing the time of the relevant transfer is crucial because it is that point in time that is used to determine whether employees were in the employment of the transferor and assigned to the transferred undertaking for the purposes of the application of Reg 4. Only the contracts of employment of those employees (and not employees who are no longer employed as at the relevant date) automatically transfer to the transferee under Reg 4(1) – subject to the right of individual employees to object to the transfer. The time of the transfer also fixes the terms of the contracts of employment – i.e. the rights, powers, duties and liabilities – that are inherited by the transferee in accordance with Reg 4(2).

2.44 **The Celtec decision.** In view of these important consequences, the European Court of Justice and the UK courts have recently ruled that all relevant transfers must be regarded as taking place on a particular *date* rather than across a period of time. In Celtec Ltd v Astley and ors 2005 ICR 1409, ECJ, the European Court scrutinised the meaning of the words 'the date of a transfer' in the context of Article 3.1 of the old Acquired Rights Directive (No.77/187), which stipulated that 'the transferor's rights and obligations arising from a contract of employment or from an employment relationship *existing on the date of a transfer* within the meaning of Article 1.1 shall, by reason of such transfer, be transferred to the transferee' (our emphasis). This provision – which is now to be found in Article 3.1 of Directive 2001/23 – forms the foundation on which Reg 4(1) and (2) of TUPE 2006 is based. The ECJ ruled that the 'date of a transfer' is the date on which the responsibility as employer for carrying on the business of the undertaking moves from the transferor to the transferee. That date, the Court emphasised, is a particular point in time that cannot be postponed to another date at the will of the transferor or transferee. Thus, contracts of employment or employment relationships existing on the date of the transfer between the transferor and the workers assigned to the undertaking transferred are deemed to be handed over on that date to the transferee, regardless of any alternative date that might have been agreed between the parties.

In coming to this conclusion, the ECJ reasoned that the reference to the 'date of a transfer' in Article 3.1 is designed to identify the workers who may rely on the protection established by that provision. Both the choice of the word 'date' and the requirement for legal certainty indicated that the workers in question must be identified at a particular point in the transfer process and not in relation to the length of time over which that process extends.

2.45 The Celtec case had originally been referred to the ECJ by the House of Lords, and it was therefore returned to the Lords to enable the ECJ's ruling to be applied to its particular facts (see 2006 ICR 992). In the light of the ECJ's ruling, the crucial matter to be determined by their Lordships was the date of the transfer – i.e. the date on which responsibility as employer for carrying on

104

the business of the transferred unit moved from the transferor to the transferee. This proved to be no easy task, given the complex factual matrix involved.

The case arose in the context of the setting up of private company Training and Enterprise Councils (TECs) in the early 1990s. In September 1990 the claimants, who were civil servants employed by the Department of Employment, were seconded on a voluntary basis to the North-East Wales TEC (Newtec) – which later became C Ltd – for a three-year period, during which all parties assumed they remained employed by the DoE. In November 1991, just over a year after Newtec was set up, the Government announced that secondments to the TECs would be phased out at the end of the fifth year of each TEC's operations and that, as part of this process, the civil servants involved would be given the choice of returning to the Civil Service or taking up employment with C Ltd. At the end of their three-year period of secondment (i.e. in 1993), the claimants all chose the latter option. In 1998, C Ltd decided to effect redundancies and the question arose as to whether, in the claimants' case, their redundancy entitlements should be calculated on the basis that their continuous service with C Ltd should be aggregated with their service as civil servants with the DoE. They contended that it should, on the basis that the TUPE Regulations applied to transfer their employment to C Ltd. However, to make good that claim, they had to show that they continued to be employed by the transferor – the DoE – as at the 'date of the transfer'. If, at any time prior to that date, they had already become employed by C Ltd, they would be unable to rely on Article 3.1 of the Directive to transfer their accrued service because that provision only applies to contracts or employment relationships in existence as at the date of the transfer.

2.46 The majority of the House of Lords (Lords Bingham, Hope and Carswell) held that, on these facts, the transfer had occurred in September 1990 when the claimants were first seconded to the TEC, even though this was contrary to what all the parties understood to be the case at the time. It was even contrary to what the claimants themselves had contended at all points prior to the House of Lords hearing. In Lord Bingham's words: 'It is plain from the findings made below that Celtec set up in business in September 1990 and the employees seconded from the Department were the core of the business: without them there could have been no effective transfer. It is scarcely an exaggeration to say that they were the business.' Accordingly, their employment transferred from the DoE to the TEC/C Ltd at that time, notwithstanding that they did not resign from the Civil Service in order to accept direct employment with the TEC until three years later.

Lord Rodger, on the other hand, was concerned that this conclusion might have the effect of 'obliterating what had actually happened and of putting in its place an entirely fictitious version of events' whereby the claimants were in effect never seconded to the TEC. He therefore took the view that the date of the transfer did not coincide with the commencement of the employees' secondment from the Civil Service to the TEC in 1990 but occurred three years later when they resigned to take up direct employment with the TEC. In his judgment, that was the date on which the responsibility as employer for carrying on the business of the undertaking moved from the DoE to the TEC. On this basis, his Lordship agreed that the claimants remained in the employment of the DoE at the date of the transfer, with the consequence that their period of continuous employment as civil servants transferred at this point to C Ltd.

2.47 Lord Mance delivered a dissenting judgment. He highlighted the fact that the claimants had submitted at every stage of the case that they were seconded by the Department of Employment to TEC Ltd during the period of September 1990 to 1993. At no point had they claimed that the transfer took place in September 1990, with the result that their employment with the transferee had started on that date. His Lordship thought that the case ought to be remitted to the employment tribunal for it to consider the new point and to make necessary additional factual findings. In so concluding, he drew attention to some of the problems associated with the conclusion that the transfer had occurred in September 1990. In particular, he observed that if the claimants unwittingly became employees of C Ltd at that date, the larger number of DoE employees who thought they were choosing to remain civil servants and volunteering to be seconded to C Ltd or another TEC must, in law, have also ceased to be civil servants in 1990. This would mean that, when given the choice between employment in the civil service or employment with the TEC in 1993, those who had elected to 'revert' to the Civil Service at this point would sustain a break in their continuity of employment.

2.48 **Practical difficulties caused by Celtec.** In most cases, the date of the transfer will be self-evident. Where the transfer is effected by a contractual agreement, the EAT's decision in Wheeler v Patel and anor 1987 ICR 631, EAT, is authority for the proposition that, when deciding when a TUPE transfer took place, the relevant date is the date when the contract for the transfer was completed. However, the Celtec case illustrates the particular problems sometimes involved in identifying the precise date of the transfer in the context of complex transfers that take place in 'instalments'. This is often the case in outsourcing transactions or where a transfer occurs within a complex corporate structure in which employees are employed by a subsidiary to provide services to another subsidiary whose business is transferred.

Prior to Celtec, tribunals tended to get round these problems mainly by relying on provisions in the Regulations stipulating that a relevant transfer can be effected by a series of two or more transactions, and ensuring that employees will be regarded as having been employed immediately before the transfer so long as they are employed immediately before any of those transactions. It is a deeply frustrating aspect of Celtec that neither the ECJ nor the House of Lords dealt with these provisions and explained their impact on the requirement to pinpoint the actual date of the transfer. This is an issue to which we shall return in the discussion on 'Transfers effected by series of transactions' below.

The Celtec case also demonstrates that, in the absence of an explicit objection **2.49** by employees to the transfer of their employment, Reg 4 can sometimes operate to transfer employment even though the parties may be completely ignorant that this has happened. This particular problem is further considered under 'Objecting to the transfer' below.

On a related matter, there is finally the question of what impact the House of Lords' decision will have on secondment arrangements when these become embroiled in a TUPE transfer. This is of particular concern to organisations such as the NHS, which frequently use 'partnership agreements' and other similar secondment arrangements when outsourcing services to the private sector. We examine this issue in detail under 'Problems of secondment arrangements' at the end of this chapter.

Meaning of 'immediately before the transfer'   **2.50**

Returning to Reg 4(1), it will be recalled that this provides that the contract of employment of any employee 'employed by the transferor and assigned to the organised grouping of resources or employees that is subject to the relevant transfer' will, unless the employee formally objects, be transferred to the transferee. The first part of Reg 4(3) elucidates this. It says: 'Any reference in [Reg 4(1)] to a person employed by the transferor and assigned to the organised grouping of resources or employees that is subject to a relevant transfer, is a reference to a person *so employed immediately before the transfer*, or who would have been so employed if he had not been dismissed in the circumstances described in regulation 7(1)' (our emphasis). This wording differs somewhat from the equivalent provision in the 1981 Regulations – Reg 5(3) – in respect of the description of the transferred entity: in place of 'organised grouping of resources or employees' in Reg 4(3), old Reg 5(3) used the phrase 'undertaking or part of one'. However, for present purposes, what is material are the words 'employed immediately before the transfer', and these remain unchanged from the wording used in the original provision.

In practice, clarity as to the date of the transfer will suffice in most cases to determine whether an employee was employed by the transferor at the relevant time. Although, as we have seen above, it can sometimes be difficult to ascertain the precise date of the transfer, in the vast majority of cases this will not be so. Occasionally, however, the mere fact that an employee is employed in, and assigned to, the undertaking transferred on the date of transfer will not be enough. In such cases, the question of whether Reg 4(1) applies comes down to whether the employee was employed (or deemed to be so) at the precise moment of the transfer. This issue only arises where members of the transferor's

107

workforce have been dismissed prior to the transfer, leaving them vulnerable to the argument that, as they were not employed by the transferor and assigned to the undertaking 'immediately before the transfer', neither their employment nor any liability for their dismissal transfers to the transferee.

2.51 The term 'immediately before' has, as we shall see below, been strictly and literally interpreted by the courts, with the consequence that the protection of Reg 4(1) applies only to employees still employed by the transferor at the very moment of the transfer. On the other hand, the courts have also taken steps to ensure that this interpretation does not lead to the application of the 'automatic transfer of employment' principle being thwarted where the sole or principal reason for pre-transfer dismissals is the transfer itself.

2.52 **'Immediately before' means at moment of transfer.** Prior to the Court of Appeal's decision in Secretary of State for Employment v Spence and ors 1986 ICR 651, CA, it was widely thought that the phrase 'immediately before the transfer' could properly be construed as spanning a period of time. Thus a person dismissed on a Friday could nevertheless be regarded as employed immediately before a transfer even if this did not occur until the following Monday. This 'liberal interpretation' was sought to be justified by reference to the aims of the Acquired Rights Directive, which was to protect employees' rights. The concern was that if transferors could simply dismiss employees shortly before the transfer as a means of ensuring that they were not employed 'immediately before the transfer', the consequence would be that what is now Reg 4 would not apply to transfer their contracts of employment to the transferee.

However, in Spence the Court of Appeal unequivocally rejected this approach in favour of a strict and literal construction of what is now Reg 4(3). In that case, S and Sons went into receivership on 16 November 1983. Since there was no guarantee of a successful outcome to the receiver's negotiations for the sale of the business, the receiver decided to cease trading and dismiss all the employees. As a result the workforce was dismissed with immediate effect at 11 am on November 28. At 2 pm on the same day the agreement for the sale of the business was concluded. The workforce was re-employed by the new owners the following morning. S and 20 others applied for redundancy payments in respect of their dismissal by S and Sons. Both the tribunal and the EAT upheld their claims, and the Court of Appeal took the same view. It unanimously held that Reg 4(1) only applied to contracts subsisting at the very moment of transfer and that the words 'employed immediately before the transfer' in Reg 5(3) had to be interpreted in that sense. Since the new owners had not acquired the contracts of employment from the transferor, the employees were entitled to redundancy payments by the receiver of S and Sons.

2.53 The general effect of the Court of Appeal's decision was that an employee could be dismissed just a matter of hours or even minutes before the transfer and yet be left unprotected by Reg 4(1) and (2), with the consequence that any liability for the dismissal would not cross to the transferee. This left employees at the mercy of the transferor's solvency. If insolvent, an employee would have little hope of financial redress against his or her former employer.

Employees deemed to be employed 'immediately before' transfer. After the Spence decision, it became increasingly clear that the dismissal of employees before a transfer in order to avoid the TUPE Regulations was likely to be in breach of the Acquired Rights Directive. The European Court of Justice put the matter beyond doubt in P Bork International A/S (in liquidation) v Foreningen af Arbejdsledere i Danmark and ors 1989 IRLR 41, ECJ, when it held that the requirements of Article 4.1 of the Directive (which corresponds to the protection against unfair dismissal contained in what is now Reg 7 of the 2006 Regulations) were mandatory. That Article provides that the transfer of an undertaking 'shall not in itself constitute grounds for dismissal by the transferor or the transferee' (although dismissals for 'economic, technical or organisational reasons entailing changes in the workforce' [ETO dismissals] are permissible). The ECJ held that where an employee is dismissed in breach of Article 4.1 with effect from a date before the transfer, he or she must 'be considered as still employed by the undertaking on the date of the transfer'. Thus, the obligations of the employer towards the employee concerned would be fully transferred from the transferor to the transferee under Article 3.1 (which corresponds to Reg 4 of the 2006 Regulations). 2.54

Small wonder that, in the light of the Bork ruling, the Spence decision came under close scrutiny by the House of Lords as soon as it was given the opportunity to consider the matter. This came in the seminal case of Litster and ors v Forth Dry Dock and Engineering Co Ltd (in receivership) and anor 1989 ICR 341, HL. The facts were somewhat similar to those in Spence. FDD went into receivership in September 1983. Another company, FEE, was set up to acquire the business of FDD. All the employees of FDD were dismissed with immediate effect at 3.30 pm on 6 February 1984. The transfer of the business occurred at 4.30 pm. Only a few of the former employees of FDD were subsequently engaged by FEE, which ended up with a similar sized workforce to FDD, although it paid them lower wages than FDD had paid to its employees. The House of Lords held that it was necessary to give a purposive construction to what was then Reg 5(3) in order to give effect to the meaning of the Directive. What this actually involved was reading words into Reg 5(3) so that, after referring to a person employed immediately before a transfer, the provision read as if there were inserted '*or would have been so employed if he had not been unfairly dismissed in the circumstances described in Reg 8(1)*'. Their Lordships felt that the employees of FDD were unfairly dismissed under Reg 8(1) (now Reg 7(1)) for a reason solely connected to the transfer, and so must be deemed to have their contracts of employment 'statutorily continued' up to the point of transfer. In that way, the protection of Reg 5 would be triggered

109

and the transferee automatically then took over the employment contracts and liability arising from their termination.

2.55 Following Litster, and particularly in light of the House of Lords' addendum to the wording of Reg 5(3), the legal position can be summarised as follows. A dismissal that takes effect before a transfer for a reason connected with it is automatically unfair under what was then Reg 8(1) (now Reg 7(1)) and for the purposes of the operation of what was then Reg 5 (now Reg 4), the dismissed employees are therefore deemed to have been employed 'immediately before the transfer'. Liability for the dismissals will as a result be passed on to the transferee.

This position has now been consolidated into the express wording of Reg 4(3) through the addition of the words 'or would have been so employed if [the employee] had not been dismissed in the circumstances described in regulation 7(1)'. There is no doubt that this promotes the protection of employees' rights following transfer of the businesses in which they are employed and ensures that the Regulations are seen to be compliant with the requirements of the Directive as established by the ECJ in the Bork case.

2.56 It is important to note that none of this means that the interpretation given to the words 'employed immediately before the transfer' by the Court of Appeal in Spence is wrong. Indeed, the House of Lords in Litster did not overrule the Spence decision. And nor does anything in the 2006 Regulations require a less strict interpretation to be given to the notion of 'immediately before'. In Litster, their Lordships noted that, unlike the facts of the case before them, there had been no collusion in Spence between the transferor and transferee aimed at effecting pre-transfer dismissals as a means of evading the operation of the 'automatic transfer of employment' rule. The employees had been dismissed before an actual transfer deal had even been agreed at a time when the receiver was under pressure by the creditor bank to stop paying wages. In these circumstances, their dismissals were not rendered unfair by what is now Reg 7(1) since they were genuinely for an ETO reason. Given that the dismissals had taken place before the transfer – albeit only by a matter of hours – the upshot was that the employees were not employed (or deemed to be employed) 'immediately before' (i.e. at the moment of) the transfer, and the employment tribunal's decision that liability for their dismissals did not cross to the transferee was, therefore, correct on the facts.

In view of this, it is clear that Spence still applies for the purpose of interpreting the phrase 'immediately before the transfer'. The position is that, in order for Reg 4 to operate, the employee must in every case be employed at the moment of the transfer. But in view of the 'deeming' provision introduced by judicial interpretation in Litster and now codified in the wording of the 2006 Regulations themselves, most employees dismissed prior to a transfer will find themselves reaping the benefit of a fiction by which they are treated as having been employed at the moment of the transfer even though, in actual fact, they were not.

Outside of an insolvency context – for which specific provision is now made in the 2006 Regulations (see Chapter 6) – it will be rare that pre-transfer dismissals will not be rendered automatically unfair by Reg 7(1). Only dismissals entirely unconnected to the transfer (dismissals on grounds of capability or misconduct, for example), or transfer-connected dismissals that are nonetheless for genuine 'economic, technical or organisational reasons entailing a change in the workforce', fall outside Reg 7(1). Only in respect of these dismissals, therefore, will it be possible to say that an employee was not employed at the moment of the transfer or deemed to be so.

Whenever a genuine ETO reason for a pre-transfer dismissal is made out, or where the reason for dismissal is patently unconnected to the transfer, then – subject to two caveats mentioned below – the employee will be shut out of the protection of Reg 4(1). This is because, in the light of Spence, he or she will *not* actually have been employed 'immediately before the transfer' and cannot claim, within the terms of Reg 4(3), that he or she 'would have been so employed if he [or she] had not been dismissed in the circumstances described in regulation 7(1)'. **2.57**

The two caveats mentioned above are, first, that if an employee is on notice of dismissal and the notice does not expire until after the transfer has occurred, he or she will still be employed 'immediately before the transfer', so that his or her employment will transfer to the transferee and, along with it, any liability for the dismissal.

Secondly, in a case where an employee is dismissed prior to the transfer but pursues an internal appeal, if the appeal is successful the original dismissal effectively 'vanishes'. This means that the employee will be regarded as continuing to have been employed by the transferor 'immediately before the transfer'. The EAT confirmed that this is so in G4S Justice Services (UK) Ltd v Anstey and anor 2006 IRLR 588, EAT, when it held that the contracts of employment of employees who had been summarily dismissed by the transferor, but whose internal appeals against those dismissals were still pending at the date of the transfer, were transferred to the transferee under what is now Reg 4(1). Although the contractual obligation to hear and determine the appeals lay, notwithstanding the transfer, with the transferor, once those appeals had been determined in favour of reinstatement, the original dismissals were expunged and the claimants were to be treated as having been employed by the transferor up until the transfer date. **2.58**

Transfers effected by series of transactions
2.59
As we saw in Chapter 1, 'Identifying a "relevant transfer"', under 'Standard transfers', the definition of 'relevant transfer' includes a transfer that is 'effected by a series of two or more transactions' – Reg 3(6). The issue of what potentially comprises such 'transactions' was also explored in that chapter. The second

111

part of Reg 4(3) addresses the problem of identifying whether employees who were employed at some point during a transfer process that occurs in stages are to be regarded as being employed 'immediately before the transfer'. This, as we have seen, is crucial since only employees employed immediately before the transfer (or deemed to be so) are subject to the 'automatic transfer of employment' principle in Reg 4(1).

The wording of the second part of Reg 4(3) can only really be understood in the context of the entire regulation. This states that: 'Any reference in [Reg 4(1)] to a person employed by the transferor and assigned to the organised grouping of resources or employees that is subject to a relevant transfer, is a reference to a person so employed immediately before the transfer, or who would have been so employed if he had not been dismissed in the circumstances described in regulation 7(1), including, *where the transfer is effected by a series of two or more transactions, a person so employed and assigned or who would have been so employed and assigned immediately before any of those transactions*' (our emphasis).

2.60 An analysis of the italicised part of Reg 4(3) above shows that an employee will be regarded as being employed 'immediately before the transfer' in any case where the transfer has been effected by a series of transactions, provided that he or she either:

- was employed immediately before (i.e. at the moment of) any one of the transactions in question, or

- would have been so employed had he or she not been unfairly dismissed in the circumstances described in Reg 7(1) – i.e. dismissal by reason of the transfer itself or for a reason solely or principally connected to the transfer that was not an ETO reason.

The employee will be viewed in the former scenario as having actually been employed at the time of the transfer. In the latter scenario, he or she will be deemed to have been so employed.

2.61 It seems clear from this that Reg 4(3) effectively provides that an employee who has been dismissed for a reason entirely unrelated to the transfer (e.g. misconduct or incapability) will nonetheless be regarded as having been employed immediately before the transfer provided that he or she can show that he or she was actually employed immediately before 'any' of the transactions in the series. In such a case, Reg 4(1) and (2) will apply to transfer any liability for the dismissal to the transferee. Equally, if all that precludes the employee from being employed immediately before any one of the transactions is that he or she was unfairly dismissed by the transferor in the circumstances described in Reg 7(1), then he or she will be deemed to have been employed immediately before the transfer.

The rationale underpinning this appears to be that, once the transfer process has begun, employees should receive the full protection of Reg 4 and that it should be the transferee who becomes responsible on the completion of the transfer for any liabilities for dismissals made by the transferor during that process. Where the transfer process is straightforward – i.e. comprises a single transaction – then, as we have seen under 'Meaning of "immediately before the transfer"' above, protection will only be conferred if the employee is actually employed at the moment of the transfer or deemed to be so as a result of having been unfairly dismissed for a reason falling within Reg 7(1). Unlike the employee dismissed during an extended transfer process, an employee whose contract is terminated prior to a single transaction transfer for a reason entirely unrelated to the transfer will not benefit from Reg 4 because he or she will not actually have been employed at the moment of the transfer, and nor will he or she be deemed to be so.

Is the 'series of transactions' provision compatible with European law? Since **2.62** the EU Acquired Rights Directive contains no equivalent provision for dealing with transfers effected by two or more interrelated transactions, it is clear that Reg 4(3) extends by some margin the protection conferred on employees in this situation. In view of this, are the 2006 Regulations incompatible with the Directive? The mere fact that the Regulations enlarge on the protection guaranteed by the Directive does not mean that they are incompatible. S.38 of the Employment Relations Act 1999 confers powers on the Secretary of State to make provision for implementing any European obligation relating to the treatment of employees on the transfer of an undertaking. In particular, S.38(2) empowers the Secretary of State to 'make the same or similar provision in relation to the treatment of employees in circumstances other than those to which the Community obligation applies'. Therefore, provided that the national rule or law in question expands rather than diminishes the scope of protection accorded by the relevant EU Directive, it will not be ultra vires (i.e. beyond the legal scope of) the Directive.

A more thorny issue as to compatibility arises in relation to recent decisions of the ECJ and the House of Lords interpreting Article 3.1 of the Directive. These decisions – in Celtec Ltd v Astley and ors 2005 ICR 1409 (ECJ) and 2006 ICR 992 (HL) – have been discussed in detail under 'When does the transfer occur?' above. To recap, it was established by the ECJ that, for the purposes of determining which employees were subject to the 'automatic transfer of employment' rule in Article 3.1, it was necessary to identify the precise date of the transfer. Given that the Celtec case was a UK case brought under the 1981 TUPE Regulations, one might have thought that the 'series of transactions' provision in what was then Reg 5(3) would have received considerable attention, especially from the House of Lords. Unfortunately, and rather bizarrely, it did not.

113

2.63 It will be recalled that the facts of the case entailed a number of transactions by which the claimants were transferred from the Department of Employment to a private Training and Enterprise Council (TEC). Initially, the employees were seconded to the TEC but remained employed by the DoE. Three years later, they elected to become employed by the TEC; and three years after that, the DoE terminated all remaining secondment arrangements. An employment tribunal concluded that there had been a relevant transfer, which had commenced in September 1990 when the claimants were first seconded to the TEC and which was only completed in 1996 when the final secondments ended. Since the claimants had been employed immediately before the first of the transactions, this was sufficient in the tribunal's view to establish that TUPE applied to transfer the period of continuous employment built up with the transferor (the DoE) to the transferee (the TEC).

The tribunal's decision was appealed, and during all stages up to and including the Court of Appeal, the legal arguments centred on the tribunal's findings and conclusion that the employees were employed immediately before the transfer in accordance with Reg 5(3). However, when the matter reached the House of Lords, their Lordships decided that the case should be referred to the ECJ. At this stage, the focus shifted away from the wording of the TUPE Regulations and onto the Directive. The question became whether, for the purposes of the 'automatic transfer of employment' provision in Article 3.1 of the Directive, it was necessary to establish a single specific 'date' for the transfer. The ECJ ruled that it was. And from that point onwards, the 'series of transactions' provision in the TUPE Regulations was lost sight of. On the case being returned to the House of Lords, the sole question that their Lordships addressed was 'when was the date of the transfer for the purposes of Article 3.1?' A 3:2 majority concluded that the crucial date was the date the claimants had first been seconded to the TEC.

2.64 So where does this leave Reg 4(3)? As at the date of the publication of this Handbook, no other appellate decision has provided any elucidation on the matter. However, it is submitted that all that Celtec establishes is that it is necessary, in the context of a transfer effected by a number of separate transactions, to identify a specific date by which the transfer is regarded as finally having taken place. At that point, employees who are employed (or deemed to be so) in the transferor's undertaking are entitled to have their employment transferred to the transferee under Reg 4(1) (or its equivalent – Article 3.1). On this view, the fact that the UK Government has chosen to extend such protection to any employee employed immediately before at least one of the transactions does not pose a problem. The effect of Reg 4(3) is to regard such an employee as having been employed at the date of the transfer whatever date that occurs. This does not mean that it is not necessary – as the Celtec case requires – for the 'date' of the transfer to be identified. For one thing, it will be that date which determines the cut-off point for establishing according to national law which employees are actually employed by the transferor and assigned to the undertaking on the relevant date and which are not. And for another, it will be from that date that the transferee legally acquires the rights, powers, duties and liabilities in respect of any contracts of employment inherited from the transferor by virtue of Reg 4(2).

Arguably, in light of the above, the most useful lesson to be gleaned from the House of Lords' decision in Celtec is that the actual date of the transfer may come much earlier in the transfer process than the parties anticipated or understood to be the case. Certainly, it came as a surprise to many legal commentators that the House of Lords found that the date of the transfer was the earliest possible date that it could have occurred – i.e. the date when the claimants were first seconded to the transferee on a voluntary basis. It is difficult to avoid the impression that what lay behind their Lordships' conclusion was their determination to provide an equitable outcome for the employees in that particular case. In most instances when something takes place by stages, the outcome is not finalised until the last of those stages. Nothing in Celtec precludes the same common sense applying in the context of TUPE. So, for this reason, when faced with cases entailing a complicated transfer process, most tribunals are likely to conclude that the transfer has been effected by the last (or certainly one of the later) transactions in the series.

2.65 The virtue of Reg 4(3) is that it enables protection to be accorded to employees right from the start of the transfer process. As we have seen, this may include an employee who was employed immediately before one of the transactions in question but who was dismissed before the last of these for a reason entirely unrelated to the transfer. Although the Regulations do not spell out precisely what happens to the employee's employment between the date of dismissal and the date of the transfer, it would make sense for Reg 4(3) to be interpreted so that the employment is deemed to continue during the interim period. Then, as from the date of the transfer (probably at the end of the series of transactions), Reg 4(1) and (2) operates to transfer the employment (and any liability for the pre-transfer dismissal) to the transferee.

Must employee be assigned to undertaking 'immediately before' the transfer?

2.66

It is generally assumed from the wording of Reg 4(3) that, for the automatic transfer principle in Reg 4(1) to operate, an employee must show not only that he or she is employed by the transferor 'immediately before the transfer' but also that he or she is, at that time, assigned to the organised grouping of resources or employees that is the subject of the transfer. However, the actual wording of Reg 4(3) is ambiguous in this respect, since there is an argument that, given a strict and literal reading, the 'immediately before' condition applies only to the employment by the transferor and not to assignment to the organised grouping of resources. This argument is set out in detail under

115

'"Assigned" to undertaking transferred – assignment "immediately before" transfer' below. Suffice it to say here that it is unlikely that a literal reading accords with the Parliamentary intention behind Reg 4(3), and, except when discussing the particular issue of interpretation, the assumption made in this chapter is that an employee must be both in and assigned to the transferred undertaking or part at the moment of the transfer in order for Reg 4(1) to be triggered.

2.67 'Assigned' to undertaking transferred

Regulation 4(1) preserves the contract of any employee who, on the occurrence of a relevant transfer, is 'employed by the transferor *and assigned to the organised grouping of resources or employees* that is subject to the relevant transfer' (our emphasis). The italicised phrase expands on the equivalent provision in the predecessor Regulations, which simply used the words 'employed by the transferor in the undertaking or part transferred'. The change in wording reflects the substantial body of case law that had already evolved prior to enactment of the 2006 Regulations on the scope of the 'automatic transfer of employment' provisions in the Acquired Rights Directive and the 1981 TUPE Regulations. For this reason, although the UK cases referred to in this section were decided on the basis of the old wording, it is likely that they will continue to provide valid guidance for interpreting the current wording of Reg 4(1).

Except for the fact that Reg 2(1) stipulates that assigned means 'assigned other than on a temporary basis', the Regulations offer scant guidance as to when an employee will be regarded as being assigned to an undertaking or business (or part business) transferred. This is unfortunate, since the issue is sometimes surprisingly difficult to determine, especially where, for complex commercial reasons, a number of subsidiary companies are spun off by a parent company and employees end up being engaged by one subsidiary company to service the employment needs of other subsidiaries.

2.68 Usually, this difficulty presents itself within the context of intra-group transfers, but a similar problem can arise where the transfer is to an outside purchaser – particularly if only one part of the transferor's undertaking is sold off. In such a case, if the employee has performed many duties across different parts of the business as a whole, it can be hard to say whether he or she was employed in and assigned to the particular part transferred. Directors and group managers are classic examples of people who often have a global or group-wide remit. But any employee with wide-ranging responsibilities or a multi-faceted job description might also be caught up in this conundrum.

116

General test for determining 'assignment'   2.69

As already mentioned, the 2006 Regulations provide little help in ascertaining whether an employee is 'assigned' to the undertaking or part transferred. However, in Botzen and ors v Rotterdamsche Droogdok Maatschappij BV 1986 2 CMLR 50, ECJ, the European Court considered the matter within the context of the EU Acquired Rights Directive. Indeed, it was the ECJ's decision in that case which first established that the basic test for working out whether the 'automatic transfer of employment' rule applied should be whether an employee is assigned to the part of the undertaking transferred.

The ECJ's ruling in Botzen. The Botzen case involved a company that had got   2.70
into financial difficulties, as a result of which a new company was set up to acquire that company's activities. The old company's marine, general engineering, heavy machinery and turbine departments were all sold to the new company, but the general administrative, personnel, ship repair or offshore parts of its business were not. The question arose as to whether the claimants, who were mainly employed in the non-transferred parts of the transferor's business but who performed some duties for the transferred parts, were entitled to have their employment transferred to the new company in accordance with Article 3.1 of the Directive. The Dutch national court decided to refer the matter to the ECJ for a preliminary ruling.

To appreciate fully the ECJ's decision, it is useful first to consider how the Advocate General, Sir Gordon Slynn, proposed that the question should be answered. He observed: 'The only exception I would admit to the requirement that an employee must be "wholly" engaged in that part of the business [which transfers] would be where an employee was required to perform other duties to an extent which could fairly be described as de minimis [which means so minor or trivial as to be legally insignificant]. On the other hand, if a worker in fact is engaged in the activities of the whole business or in several parts then he cannot be regarded for the purposes of the Directive as an employee "of" the part of the business transferred.' Although the Advocate General's test was a strict one, it had the virtue of precision and certainty. According to his test, unless an employee was wholly employed in carrying out duties for and on behalf of the part of the undertaking transferred, then, subject to de minimis, the Directive would not apply to transfer his or her employment to the transferee.

However, the ECJ's judgment side-stepped the Advocate General's formulation   2.71
and offered something far less clear-cut. The Court ruled that: 'An employment relationship is essentially characterised by the link existing between the employee and the part of the undertaking or business to which he is assigned to carry out his duties. In order to decide whether the rights and obligations under an employment relationship are transferred under Directive 77/187 by reason of a transfer within the meaning of Article 1.1 thereof, it is therefore sufficient to establish to which part of the undertaking or business the employee was

----

117

assigned.' No further elucidation was given as to what the ECJ meant by 'assignment'. It simply left it to national courts to determine as a question of fact to which part of a business employees are assigned.

2.72 **UK case law interpreting Botzen.** It is therefore necessary to see how courts and tribunals in the United Kingdom have approached the matter in the light of the Botzen ruling. The first thing that is clear is that it will be an error of law for a tribunal to direct itself in accordance with the Advocate General's opinion in that case. In Kavanagh v Coral Racing Ltd and anor EAT 231/97 the EAT overturned a tribunal's decision that, on the basis of Sir Gordon Slynn's test, it was necessary for an employee to be wholly (or very substantially) engaged in the business or part of the business transferred. In that case, a tribunal had held that the claimant, who was a managerial supervisor, was not assigned to the undertaking transferred even though around 80 per cent of her time was spent doing tasks connected to the part of the undertaking that was transferred. Since she was also expected to perform other tasks and responsibilities that were not transferred and it was those responsibilities that justified the managerial role and commanded the commensurate salary, the tribunal concluded that she was not actually employed in the transferred undertaking. Allowing the employee's appeal, the EAT held that it was not necessary for an employee to be employed full time or substantially full time in the part transferred so long as he or she can properly be regarded as assigned to that part.

The same point concerning Botzen was made even more forcibly in OCO Mechanical Engineers Ltd v Bissett and ors EAT 06/98, where the EAT's then President Mr Justice Morison observed that: 'It is wrong for parties to cite the opinion of the Advocate General in Botzen without drawing attention to the fact, as it unquestionably is a fact, that the European Court of Justice itself did not accept the opinion as laying down the correct test to be applied... Accordingly, in future, we would not expect in the light of that decision, parties to rely on what was said by the Advocate General in that case, on this point.'

2.73 **A question of fact.** In the light of Botzen, and given that the concept of 'assignment to the undertaking or part transferred' has not been statutorily defined, the UK courts have sought in a number of cases to set out a general conceptual framework for dealing with the issue. The first point habitually stressed is that the issue of assignment is *a question of fact* to be determined by a tribunal considering *all the relevant circumstances* of the particular case – see Buchanan-Smith v Schleicher and Co International Ltd EAT 1105/94, as endorsed by the Court of Appeal in Jones and anor v Darlows Estate Agency 1998 EWCA Civ 1157.

2.74 **Time spent on duties for transferred undertaking.** A second point highlighted by Mr Justice Mummery in the Buchanan-Smith case was that an employee may be regarded as being assigned to the transferor's business or undertaking even if he or she spends time looking after other parts of the employer's business. In the case of an employer carrying on two undertakings, an employee *may* be assigned to one of those undertakings even though engaged in the activities of the other. This proposition flows directly from the ruling in Botzen to the effect that a person does not have to be engaged exclusively in the business or part transferred to be regarded as being 'assigned' to it. In this regard, Mummery J warned that the discharge by an employee of duties involving the use of assets or the discharge of beneficial administrative duties for the part transferred are insufficient to constitute 'assignment' to the undertaking.

The case law also demonstrates that the issue of assignment cannot necessarily be determined simply by establishing the relative percentages of time spent by the employee on activities associated with the part of the undertaking that is transferred compared with any part that is not. We shall examine the relevance of time spent in the part of the business transferred in more detail under 'Assignment to part of business only' below.

Typical scenarios where problems of assignment arise. The problem of **2.75** determining who is assigned to the undertaking being transferred tends to be particularly acute in the context of certain fairly common factual situations. Three such situations were identified by Mr Justice Morison in Duncan Web Offset (Maidstone) Ltd v Cooper and ors 1995 IRLR 633, EAT, as follows:

- X has a business in which he employs a number of persons. X transfers part of that business to Y

- a person is employed by X to work in Y's business and Y transfers that business to Z

- X, which is part of a group of companies, employs a number of people on X's sole business. The whole of X's undertaking is transferred by X to Y. Some of X's employees worked partly for X and partly for other parts of the group.

Helpfully, Morison J offered the following observations in respect of each of these scenarios.

Regarding the first (i.e. a 'part-only transfer'), in order to determine which **2.76** employees were employed in the part transferred it is necessary simply to ask which employees were assigned to the part transferred. Another way of putting the same question is to ask, as the Court of Appeal did in Gale v Northern General Hospital NHS Trust 1994 ICR 426, CA, whether a particular employee was 'part of the... human stock or resources' of the part transferred. Morison J in Duncan Web Offset acknowledged that difficult questions of fact often have to be determined by a tribunal to establish who was and was not 'assigned' to the part of the business that has been transferred; and, for this reason, it

119

declined to give general guidance on the matter. However, he accepted that some of the factors that *may* be relevant included:

- the amount of time spent on one part of the business or the other

- the amount of value given to each part by the employee

- the terms of the contract of employment showing what the employee could be required to do

- how the cost to the transferor of the employee's services was allocated between different parts of the business.

2.77 With regard to the second (i.e. 'the service company') scenario, the EAT observed that, on its face, TUPE would not apply so as to transfer the employment of the employee to the transferee, since the employee must actually be employed by the transferor in order for what is now Reg 4 to apply. However, Morison J emphasised that tribunals will be astute to ensure that the Regulations are not circumvented by the use of devices such as service companies, or by complicated group structures that conceal the true position. Thus, it might be possible to say that if the person always and exclusively worked on Y's business, then X was employing him on behalf of and as agent for Y. Alternatively, there may be circumstances in which X might be regarded as a party to the transfer, even if not expressly named in the contract of sale. Or it may be that the employee remained employed by X, who had other work for him or her to do. These would be matters for the tribunal to decide on the particular facts.

Finally, with regard to the third ('transfer of subsidiaries within a group') scenario, Morison J thought that in most cases where the transferor's entire business is sold to a purchaser, X's employees would be regarded as having been assigned to the undertaking transferred. However, in the case of a part-transfer only, he acknowledged there may be cases where it could be said that, despite being employed by X, some employees might in reality be assigned to the business of another part of the group that was not transferred. This recognises that the contract of employment test – i.e. what the employee is required to do according to his or her contract – is not the only matter for consideration, and that an employee might be employed by one company within the group but assigned to the business of another. The EAT again observed that it expected that tribunals would keep in mind the purposes of the Acquired Rights Directive and the need to avoid complicated corporate structures from getting in the way of a result that gives effect to that purpose.

2.78 Having set out the general guidance on 'assignment', it is useful to turn to the scenarios identified by the EAT in the Duncan Web Offset case to see how tribunals have resolved the question of assignment in practice.

Assignment to part of the business only

2.79

As was recognised by the first of the three factual situations outlined by Morison J in the Duncan Web Offset (Maidstone) Ltd v Cooper and ors 1995 IRLR 633, EAT (discussed under 'General test for determining "assignment"' above), one of the more common situations in which issues of assignment arise is where X transfers a part of his business or undertaking to Y. This may appear to be a simple scenario, but it masks the very difficult questions of fact that will often need to be determined before a tribunal is in a position to decide whether an employee was assigned to the particular part of the business/undertaking transferred. The cases below demonstrate this point well:

- **Buchanan-Smith v Schleicher and Co International Ltd** EAT 1105/94: B-S was one of only five employees of T Ltd, whose business was divided between the selling and the servicing of shredding machines. B-S dealt with the organisation and running of the service side, but was also involved in aspects of the sales side. Following financial difficulties the sales side was closed down and the service side transferred to S Ltd. On the question of whether B-S was assigned to the part of the business transferred (i.e. service of the shredding machines), an employment tribunal ruled that the fact that she had worked in both the sales and the service sides of the business meant that she was not 'assigned' to the service side. On appeal, the EAT held that the tribunal had adopted the wrong approach. It noted that the tribunal had itself found that it was B-S who ran and organised that part of the undertaking. It was also significant that the transfer of the sales side was accompanied by the closure of the rest of the company. There was therefore no longer any sales part to which B-S or any other employee of T Ltd could be regarded as assigned or allocated. The correct view was that B-S had been assigned to that part of T Ltd's business transferred to S Ltd

- **MRS Environmental Services Ltd v Dyke and anor** EAT 93/96: D worked for St Albans District Council on what was known as the Harpenden Town Council Work, looking after the village greens, the war memorial, the churchyard, the public hall and the council offices in that town. In 1994, the Council contracted out the Harpenden Town Council Work to MRS Ltd under a TUPE transfer. W duly became employed by MRS Ltd, carrying out the same duties, which took up 75 per cent of his time, and spending the remaining 25 per cent of his time working for the Council on services that remained their responsibility. When the Harpenden contract came up for renewal, MRS Ltd lost the contract to another bidder, M, who disputed that D was not assigned to the transferred part of the undertaking. An employment tribunal came to the conclusion that D 'worked for a significant amount of time in the part of the undertaking transferred and that he was therefore allocated to that part'. On appeal, the EAT found no error of law in the tribunal determining the question of assignment in this case solely by

121

reference to the amount of time D worked in the part transferred. The EAT noted that, in certain circumstances, the measure of time might be the only relevant factor and that, as M could not point to any other factor which the tribunal ought to have taken into account, the tribunal's findings of fact could not be disturbed

- **Moseley v Service Direct (UK) plc** EAT 0482/01; 1157/00: M was employed by ST Ltd as a telesales executive in the telesales department. His role entailed selling telecommunications equipment to, and furthering marketing projects with, dealers, as well as selling further products to existing customers who had service contracts, using the customer database operated by the service and maintenance department to do this. ST Ltd decided to sell off its service and maintenance department to SD plc. 50 or so employees went to work for that company but M was not one of them. Initially, he remained with ST Ltd, but, after being made redundant only two months later, he accepted new employment with SD plc as a telesales executive. However, a short while later, SD plc also decided to close its telemarketing department and M was made redundant once again. When M sought to claim for unfair dismissal, the tribunal had to decide, as a preliminary issue, whether M's employment had been transferred from ST Ltd to SD plc so as to give him sufficient continuity of employment to bring the claim. The tribunal found that M had not been subject to a relevant transfer as the telemarketing department in which he worked was not an 'integral part' of the service and maintenance operation that transferred; only those employees who were 'wholly and exclusively' concerned with the service and maintenance operation transferred to SD plc. The EAT dismissed M's appeal, rejecting his argument that the tribunal had not approached the matter of assignment correctly in that it had not referred to the term 'assignment' but instead focused on whether M was 'integral' to the part transferred. The EAT also declined to attach any significance to the fact that ST Ltd's telemarketing department closed soon after the transfer, which M argued implied that the department had 'little life left' without the service and maintenance department

- **Birmingham City Council v Gaston and ors** EAT 0508/03: between 1975 and 1979, G worked as a plumber in the Council's Housing Department, during which time he was allocated to Contract B, one of four housing repair contracts, each of which related to a different geographical zone within the Council's remit. In 1979, G was elected Chief Federation Steward for the recognised trade union, a position he held up until the relevant transfer in 2001. During this time, he was a full-time shop steward and did no work as a plumber, except for his participation on an out-of-hours rota covering all four zones. In April 2001, Contracts A and B were transferred to the second respondent, and Contracts C and D to a different transferee. For the purpose of G's unfair dismissal claim, an employment tribunal was asked to address the question of whether G was assigned, at the time of the transfer, to the part of the undertaking transferred to the second respondent. The tribunal found that he was not. For the last 20 years, plumbing had formed no part of G's day-to-day activities; instead, he had undertaken duties as a shop steward in relation to employees assigned to all four contracts, as well as employees who remained with the Council after the transfer. The Council appealed to the EAT, contending that the tribunal had failed to attach weight to G's contractual position and had failed to make sufficient findings of fact. The EAT rejected these arguments, and also rejected the contention that G's position was analogous to that of a seconded employee. While a seconded employee might remain assigned to the particular part of the undertaking in which he or she normally worked, in the same way as might someone on extended sick leave or a sabbatical, it was highly improbable that this was so in the case of an employee absent for 22 years, particularly one who had in that time performed work extraneously to the part of the undertaking to which he had originally been assigned

- **CPL Distribution Ltd v Todd** 2003 IRLR 28, CA: T was employed by CPL as personal assistant to B, who was the manager of the company's concessionary coal business and later took on the additional role of CPL's business acquisitions manager. CPL subsequently sold the concessionary coal business to GF and a question arose as to whether T was employed in that particular part of CPL's business. She had kept a log of the correspondence she had dealt with which showed that most of her work related to the concessionary coal business. After the sale of the contract for that business, B continued to be employed by CPL solely in respect of the acquisitions management part of its business. An employment tribunal held that, on these facts, T was 'effectively assigned' to B, but not to the concessionary coal business that had been transferred. In the tribunal's view, the correct analysis was that T's post as personal assistant to B was potentially redundant after the transfer and that the employer should have dealt with the situation as a redundancy rather than treat T as being assigned to the contract that had transferred. CPL's appeals to the EAT and subsequently to the Court of Appeal were dismissed. In the Court of Appeal's view, the tribunal had been entitled on the facts to find that, since the concessionary coal business was but one area of B's responsibility and that a substantial part of his time was taken up with carrying out other duties for CPL, he could not be said to have been assigned to the transferred part of the business. Equally, as B's personal assistant, T was also involved in those other duties and was likewise not assigned to the concessionary coal business at the time that it transferred. The fact that the majority of the typing carried out by T was in relation to the concessionary coal business was not of itself conclusive evidence of assignment since a personal assistant's duties would normally be broader than just typing

123

- **Williams v Advance Cleaning Services Ltd and anor** EAT 0838/04: W was employed as a project leader within the Train Care Division of ERS Ltd, which held three contracts for cleaning services on trains operating out of London train stations and at the stations themselves. W had extensive experience in project and personnel management, and it was for that reason that he was appointed to the Train Care Division in the first place, in the hope that he could improve performance on one of the three contracts – the 'London terminals contract' – which was proving particularly difficult to administer. In August 2003, ERS Ltd lost the London terminals contract to the respondent, ACS Ltd, and soon after went into liquidation. W brought a claim for unfair dismissal against both ERS Ltd and ACS Ltd, and it fell to be decided as a preliminary issue whether his employment had been transferred from the former to the latter. It was common ground that the change of contractor involved a transfer of a part of ERS Ltd's undertaking. It was also accepted that W spent most of his time on the London terminals contract (i.e. more than 50 per cent of his time and possibly as high as 70 per cent). The tribunal found that W was at all times a project manager in the employ of ERS Ltd. Historically, he had moved from one project to another and, had work been available, he would have moved on to the next project after the London terminals contract had been lost. He never became an integral part of the London terminals contract, and so was not assigned at the time of the transfer in the part of the undertaking transferred. On appeal, the EAT reminded itself that the question of assignment is one of fact and accordingly refused to interfere with the tribunal's conclusion

- **Mowlem Technical Services (Scotland) Ltd v King and anor** 2005 CSIH 46 Ct Sess (Inner House): K was a branch manager for a private company in charge of running a council's housing maintenance contract. He was responsible for all of the contracts run by the company (including those with bodies other than the council) but the council contract represented 80 per cent of the company's work. In 2001 the council decided to terminate the housing maintenance contract and to bring the work back in-house but K was not on the list of employees to be transferred back to the council. On his claim for unfair dismissal by reason of a relevant transfer, an employment tribunal found that, although the contract was an 'undertaking' and it had been transferred, K was not wholly or predominantly assigned to that undertaking. He had had periodic meetings with the council, but the contract was managed on a day-to-day basis by an assistant, G. Two other employees who were found to have transferred spent around 80 per cent of their time actually working on the contract. The EAT dismissed K's appeal, as did the Court of Session (Inner House) on further appeal. The Court held, applying the test in Duncan Web (cited above), that time spent working on a particular project was only one factor to consider in determining whether an employee was assigned to that project when it transferred under TUPE.

124

On this basis, it accepted that the employment tribunal had come to a perfectly proper conclusion on the evidence – particularly in relation to the differences between the jobs done by K and G. Whereas G's duties were intimately related to the performance of the contract in question, K's were of a much more general nature relating to the conduct, supervision and financial arrangements of the branch as a whole.

Perhaps the most significant and generally applicable point to emerge from these cases is that the problem of ascertaining assignment will rarely be simply a matter of making a mathematical calculation as to the proportionate amounts of time an employee spends working for different parts of a business. Only in one of the above cases – MRS Environmental Services Ltd v Dyke – was this approach found to be appropriate, and it may be no coincidence that the employee in that case was a manual worker rather than a manager or executive. The amount of time actually spent working for a particular part of a business is arguably a more reliable guide to the issue of assignment in the case of manual work than it is in the case of so-called 'white collar' work. **2.80**

Employees engaged by service/holding companies **2.81**
Morison J in Duncan Web Offset (Maidstone) Ltd v Cooper and ors 1995 IRLR 633, EAT (discussed under 'General test for determining "assignment"' above) thought that, on its face, the 'automatic transfer of employment' rule in what is now Reg 4 would not apply in the case of an employee employed by X to work in Y's business where Y transfers that business to Z. Typically, 'X' in this scenario comprises a service (or labour-supply) company or a holding company operating within a corporate group, and Y is either the parent or a trading subsidiary within that group. The reason why, conceptually speaking, Reg 4 does not apply is that the employee is not actually employed by the transferor (Y) at all. It will be remembered that for the 'automatic transfer of employment' rule to operate, a contract of employment has to exist between the transferor and the employee concerned – see Askew v Governing Body of Clifton Middle School and ors 2000 ICR 286, CA, and the discussion on 'Definition of "employee" and "contract of employment"' in the section on 'Who is an "employee" for TUPE purposes?' above.

However, Morison J also commented that courts and tribunals will be astute to ensure that employers do not use devices such as service or holding companies, or, for that matter, complex corporate structures, as a means of deliberately avoiding the protection which the TUPE Regulations are intended to provide. His Lordship hinted that where there is a legitimate suspicion that such devices are being used for this purpose, tribunals will lift the corporate veil or else use the law of agency to establish that the employee was effectively assigned to the organised grouping of resources/employees being transferred.

2.82 It should be noted that the facts of Duncan Web Offset were not such as to cause the EAT to give detailed consideration to lifting the corporate veil in that case: the Appeal Tribunal was able simply to uphold the tribunal's conclusion that the claimants had been assigned to a subsidiary company which was sold by receivers notwithstanding that they carried out responsibilities for other subsidiaries that were not sold. The tribunal had reached this conclusion on the basis of a straightforward assessment of what duties the claimants carried out in practice.

2.83 **Piercing the 'corporate veil'.** In practice, there is little evidence that tribunals are as willing as Morison J thought they would be to lift the corporate veil to determine the reality of the relationship between subsidiaries within a complex corporate structure. This is primarily because fundamental principles of company law are at stake. Each company within a group of companies is regarded as a separate legal entity possessed of separate legal rights and liabilities – see Solomon v A Solomon and Co Ltd 1897 AC 22, HL. Any liabilities that one of the subsidiaries incurs will rarely be passed on to the parent or other subsidiary companies within the group or on to associated companies over whom the parent has control, even if these remain solvent while the liable subsidiary does not. A 'corporate veil' effectively shields one company from the liabilities of another, and the courts are reluctant to pierce the veil except where it is being relied on as a device or façade to conceal impropriety or the true facts of the situation – see Ord and anor v Belhaven Pubs Ltd 1998 BCC 607, CA, and, specifically in relation to a TUPE transfer case, Print Factory (London) 1991 Ltd v Millam 2007 ICR 1331, CA.

There have been few cases decided within the context of TUPE where employees are (or have become) employed by a service company supplying the labour needs of a transferred subsidiary. In Brookes and ors v Borough Care Services Ltd and anor 1998 ICR 1198, EAT, the Appeal Tribunal rejected the argument that the TUPE Regulations or the Acquired Rights Directive required, as a matter of 'purposive interpretation', the corporate veil to be pierced to enable two separate companies to be treated as a single entity. In that case BCS, a company limited by guarantee, ran a number of care homes. In 1995 it decided to transfer the care homes to the voluntary sector. CLS, an industrial and provident society, made a successful bid for the homes and set up a company to which the homes would be transferred. Originally CLS's intention was to acquire BSC's business in the form of a TUPE transfer, but it changed track after becoming concerned that it might not lawfully be able to alter the acquired employees' terms and conditions after the transfer. So instead, CLS acquired the homes by taking control of BCS: it became the sole member of BCS and CLS's members became the directors of BCS. Even though it was conceded that this method of acquisition was specifically intended to avoid the TUPE Regulations coming into play, the EAT rejected all the bases upon which the employees contended that a relevant transfer had nevertheless occurred. It affirmed that there can be no relevant transfer for the purposes of TUPE where a limited liability company is acquired via a change in the identity of the company's members or shareholding as there is no change in the legal personality of the company concerned and therefore no transfer from one legal person to another – see Chapter 1 under 'Standard transfers – transfer "to another person"'.

In another case – Banking Insurance and Finance Union v Barclays Bank plc **2.84** and ors 1987 ICR 495, EAT ('the BIFU case') – the EAT showed itself to be equally reluctant, in the absence of suspected impropriety, to look behind such an arrangement to conclude that employees had, de facto, been employed by the transferred company. In the BIFU case, Barclays Bank plc decided to set up a new investment bank, Barclays de Zoete Wedd Ltd (BZW), to be formed by a merger between Barclays Merchant Bank subsidiary (BMB) and associated firms of stockbrokers and jobbers in which Barclays had a controlling interest. The staff who worked for BMB were seconded from and employed by Barclays itself. However, instead of transferring them along with BMB's enterprise directly to BZW, Barclays set up a further subsidiary, Barclays de Zoete Wedd Services Ltd (BZW/S), to which the employment of those members of staff was transferred. Barclays then planned to transfer BMB's business, unencumbered by the staff, direct to BZW and 'transfer' the staff from BZW/S to BZW under a labour supply agreement. The employees' trade union, BIFU, complained to a tribunal that Barclays was in breach of its duty under the 1981 Regulations to inform and consult the union about the transfers. Barclays contended that there had been no relevant transfer, denying that the transfers between Barclays, BMB, BZW and BZW/S constituted a series of transactions forming a single transfer.

Although the employment tribunal expressed unease about the position, accepting that 'unscrupulous employers can adopt these sort of procedures to evade their responsibilities under the Regulations', it found that no such ulterior motive lay behind the corporate manoeuvres in this case. The tribunal concluded that, as no good will or assets had been transferred, there had been no relevant transfer. In upholding that conclusion, the EAT rejected the claimants' argument that assets had been transferred in the sense of a pool of available employees, and that good will had likewise been transferred in the form of the customer lists acquired by BZW from Barclays. Finally, the EAT rejected the argument that the decision as to whether there had been a transfer was affected by the fact that the tribunal had found that 'moral pressure' had been asserted on the employees to force them to agree to becoming employed by the newly created service subsidiary, BMZ/S. About this, the EAT simply observed: 'There may well be cases where something more than moral pressure is exercised where a tribunal would be entitled to say that that constituted a transfer. In the present case the effect of the moral pressure in our judgment is of no legal consequence.

127

As was pointed out in argument, if no staff had elected to transfer there could have been no transfer.'

2.85 Although the BIFU case was decided comparatively early on in the history of TUPE and was concerned with whether there had been a relevant transfer rather than whether the claimants were assigned to the undertaking transferred, the facts and decision of the case demonstrate how difficult it is for employees employed by service companies to show that they have been assigned to a trading subsidiary that is sold off. It must be borne in mind that, for Reg 4(1) to apply, an employee has to be '*employed by the transferor* and assigned to the organised grouping of resources or employees immediately before the transfer'. Mere assignment is not sufficient. Were it to be so, it would be a lot easier for employees to argue that the corporate veil should be lifted so as to focus on the realities of the situation regarding to whom the employees were assigned to work as opposed to by whom they were legally employed.

Two of the decisions discussed below, under 'Employees with global or group-wide responsibilities', provide further instances of where, in the context of TUPE, the question of piercing the corporate veil arose. In Michael Peters Ltd v (1) Farnfield (2) Michael Peters Group plc 1995 IRLR 190, EAT, the Appeal Tribunal declined to lift the veil so as to conclude that a director with global responsibilities across a large corporate group was, de facto, employed in and assigned to the particular subsidiaries transferred for TUPE purposes. However, by way of contrast, in Sunley Turriff Holdings Ltd v Thomson and ors 1995 IRLR 184, EAT, the Appeal Tribunal in Scotland upheld a tribunal's decision to lift the veil in circumstances where the employee was employed by one subsidiary but the transferee had acquired a different subsidiary – comprising a shell company without employees or physical assets – for whom the employee worked prior to the transfer. By choosing to lift the corporate veil, the tribunal was able to establish to its satisfaction that, in reality, the transferred undertaking had acquired a large part of the business of the subsidiary by whom the employee was legally employed, and that he had therefore been assigned to the part of the undertaking transferred.

2.86 The Sunley Turriff case perhaps provides a faint ray of hope to employees employed by service companies who seek to convince a tribunal to lift the corporate veil as a means of enabling them to satisfy the 'employment' and 'assignment' conditions of Reg 4. But, for the reasons outlined above, the instances of where this course of action is adopted will be rare.

2.87 **One company acting as agent for the other.** A different possibility contemplated by the EAT in the Duncan Web Offset case is that, in an appropriate case, employees employed by a service or holding company might be regarded as being employed and assigned to a sister company through the process of agency. Take, for example, the situation where employees are employed by company X, which supplies its services to another subsidiary company, Y, and it is Y that is bought by an outside purchaser. Is it possible to argue that in employing the employees X was acting as agent for Y, with the result that the employees' employment transfers to the new owner of Y?

This argument was unsuccessfully advanced in Brookes and ors v Borough Care Services Ltd and anor 1998 ICR 1198, EAT, as a basis for contending that two separate companies, BSC and CSL, should be treated as a single entity in circumstances where CSL obtained the control of BSC by effectively acquiring BSC's shares and members with the intention of circumventing the application of TUPE. The facts of the case have already been discussed above. Suffice it to say here that the EAT rejected the argument that BSC should be treated as acting as agent for CLS and as employing the employees as agents of CLS rather than on its own behalf. That argument was doomed to failure because, as a mere share acquisition, no change occurred in the legal personality of the acquired company, BSC. The Brookes decision is not therefore a very reliable guide as to the prospect of the agency argument succeeding in a different situation where a trading subsidiary is sold off to an outside purchaser but the subsidiary employing the staff who carry out the work on behalf of the trading subsidiary is not sold.

Perhaps more telling is Zabaxe Ltd v Nicklin and ors EAT 123/89, in which a **2.88** relationship of agency was found to have arisen in a TUPE context between two subsidiary companies. In that case, one of the subsidiaries employed employees and the other was responsible for paying them. The EAT characterised the latter as an 'invoicing company' acting as an agent for the former. Admittedly, this was largely on the basis of concessions made by the principal company during the tribunal hearing and, unfortunately, the EAT was not called upon to analyse the matter further because the TUPE issues were overtaken by a procedural matter concerning adjournment of the proceedings. Even so, the Zabaxe case lends some support to the notion of agency operating within a service company set-up.

Implied contract of employment in tripartite relationship. The other **2.89** possibility is that a contract of employment might be 'implied' between the employee and the company in receipt of his or her services. This is analogous to the tripartite relationship between (i) an agency worker, (ii) the agency supplying his or her services, and (iii) the end-user of those services. We have already seen in the discussion on whether agency workers are 'employees' for TUPE purposes that the law on the status of such workers is in a state of flux – see 'Who is an "employee" for TUPE purposes? – agency workers' above. However, as things stand at the present time, there does appear to be the possibility that a contract of employment can, in some circumstances, come into being between an agency worker and an end-user if there is a long-term relationship between them. Were similar reasoning to be applied to the relationship between an employee, service company and its trading subsidiary,

129

then Reg 4(1) might well operate to transfer the implied contract of employment between the employee and the trading subsidiary to any purchaser of that subsidiary. However, this is likely to remain a long-shot argument while doubts continue to be expressed in the agency worker case law about the ability of the courts to imply contracts other than on the ground of necessity.

2.90 ## Employees with global or group-wide responsibilities

As previously pointed out, a TUPE transfer involving associated companies within the same corporate group can often give rise to the problem of identifying to which of the subsidiaries an employee is assigned. This is particularly so where the employee has overarching or 'group-wide' responsibilities. This comes within the third scenario canvassed by the EAT in Duncan Web Offset (Maidstone) Ltd v Cooper and ors 1995 IRLR 633, EAT (outlined under 'General test for determining "assignment"' above). The following are examples of this:

- **Michael Peters Ltd v (1) Farnfield (2) Michael Peters Group plc** 1995 IRLR 190, EAT: MPG plc ('the Group') was the holding company for 25 subsidiary companies in the United Kingdom and abroad. The Group and four of the subsidiaries were based at the same premises in London and between them carried on the business of design consultancy. F was employed by the Group as Chief Executive and was responsible for overseeing the financial management and running of all the subsidiary companies. In August 1990, following the appointment of receivers, the business of four of the subsidiary companies was sold to an outside purchaser, CLK. One of the subsidiaries was MP Ltd (the transferee), which continued to trade under the same name after the transfer. F, who had been made redundant before the sale, complained that he had been unfairly dismissed for a reason connected with the transfer. Although an employment tribunal upheld his claim, the question of whether he had been employed in and assigned to the undertaking transferred only emerged as a result of the transferee's appeal to the EAT. In allowing the appeal, the EAT noted that the tribunal had made the crucial finding of fact that F was responsible for the running of the Group as a whole and was therefore to be taken to be assigned to the Group and not to any of the individual subsidiaries. In the EAT's view, this was not a case where it was appropriate to 'pierce the corporate veil' and to say that the business of the four companies was, in reality, the business of the Group. This was so notwithstanding that it was a Group company that owned the good will of the business, that only it was empowered to recover debts, and that it was that company which owned and transferred certain assets, including the premises, to CLK

- **Sunley Turriff Holdings Ltd v Thomson and ors** 1995 IRLR 184, EAT: T was employed as company secretary and chief accountant of both LC and LC(S), two subsidiaries of the L Group, although his contract of employment was with LC. In January 1993 receivers were appointed to the group. They sold the business of LC(S) to STH, but T was told that he was not one of the employees who were to be transferred to STH. He remained working for the receivers until they made him redundant a couple of months later. T brought unfair dismissal proceedings against STH, claiming that he was employed in the part of the undertaking that had been transferred and that his contract of employment had therefore passed to the transferee. In deciding this issue, the employment tribunal took the unusual step of lifting the 'corporate veil' in order to see precisely what had been transferred. It found that LC(S) was a shell company with no employees, no separate accounting records and no proper bank account. What STH had really purchased was all contracts in the name of LC and LC(S), together with employees engaged in that part of the business transferred. On the evidence, the tribunal held that T was one of these employees. On appeal, the EAT upheld the tribunal's finding, stating that it was entitled to find as it did in the light of the Botzen case on the basis that T had been 'assigned' to the part transferred

- **Jones and anor v Darlows Estate Agency** 1998 EWCA Civ 1157, CA: J, a Regional Operations Director for a chain of estate agents based in Cardiff, had responsibility for a regional office comprising 20 branches in Wales and 11 branches in Devon. X – J's secretary and PA – carried out administrative and clerical functions associated with J's work. Following a TUPE transfer, the Welsh branches were sold to a new owner, but J and X were not taken on. An employment tribunal found that neither had been assigned to the undertaking transferred. The matter went to the Court of Appeal, which agreed with the tribunal that J's managerial and administrative responsibilities covered the business of the Wales and West of England region as a whole without assignment to one part of that business as opposed to the other. The fact that a greater proportion of both J's and X's recent time was spent on dealing with the branches in Wales did not alter this conclusion

- **Prosperis Ltd and anor v Spencer and anor** EAT 0988/03: S was engaged in July 2000 as an Executive Consultant by WEFS Ltd under an employment contract. This stated that he may at any time be 'transferred to work for another company within the same Group of companies as the employer, whether on a temporary or permanent basis'. The Group was a non-trading holding company with three subsidiaries: WEFS Ltd, Ward Evans Corporate ('Corporate') and One Direct Solutions Ltd ('One Direct'). There was also an independent costs centre, One Life, which was a trading name for WEFS Ltd's mortgage business and was part of its corporate structure. Throughout his time with WEFS Ltd, S was effectively the 'right-hand man' to D, who at all material times was a director of WEFS Ltd, and was also at various times Managing Director of WEFS Ltd, One Life and One Direct. For about the first 18 months of his employment, S worked on WEFS Ltd business; in early 2002 he was asked to focus his attentions on the mortgage business

131

of One Life; in July 2002 he took on the role of Management Training Coordinator for the whole Group; and in September 2002 he began dealing with training issues in the customer service department of One Direct. When the companies went into administration in December 2002, the business and assets of WEFS Ltd were sold by receivers to HLW, which denied liability for S's employment, claiming that he was not assigned to WEFS Ltd at the time of the relevant transfer. An employment tribunal found that he was so assigned, and HLW appealed. The EAT dismissed the appeal. The tribunal had correctly characterised the situation as belonging to the third category identified by the EAT in Duncan Web Offset – S was one of WEFS Ltd's employees who worked partly for WEFS Ltd and partly for other parts of the Group. The tribunal had found, in essence, that S was employed by WEFS Ltd as a trouble-shooter to be moved from job to job as required. He was not assigned to any other part of the Group because none of the tasks he undertook were intended to lead to a permanent transfer away from WEFS Ltd

- **(1) Tibbitt v Wagon plc and ors; (2) McNabb v Wagon plc and ors** EAT 0121–2/02: both claimants were employed in senior positions within the group of companies comprising HW Holdings Ltd ('Holdings'), HW Engineering Ltd ('Engineering') and HW Environmental Ltd ('Environmental'). Environmental had been created specifically to develop a particular product, the Environmental Vehicle Emission Control ('EVEC'), whose inventor took a 40 per cent holding in the company. Environmental had no employees, although it did have expenses by way of salaries and travel which were met by Engineering. At the relevant time, T was Managing Director of Environmental and M was Manager of Business Development and Marketing in Holdings, with responsibility for Environmental. Both concentrated their efforts on the EVEC project. In October 2000, Holdings and Engineering went into receivership, and W plc bought Engineering and certain assets belonging to Holdings. It was accepted that the purchase engaged TUPE, and most of the employees employed by Engineering went over. The claimants, however, did not, although four other employees who spent substantial amounts of their time on EVEC did. W plc asserted that the claimants were not assigned to the part of the undertaking that transferred. Deciding the issue of assignment, an employment tribunal weighed, on the one hand, the facts that T had been employed on paper by Engineering throughout; that the whole of that business transferred; and that all three companies were closely connected. Furthermore, T still spent a considerable amount of time on duties relating to Engineering, and both claimants used Engineering's assets in the performance of their duties. On the other hand, Environmental had been deliberately set up as a separate company and T was its Managing Director; the claimants were expected to spend a majority of their time on the EVEC project, which was the preserve of Environmental;

and Environmental was not a wholly-owned subsidiary. On balance, the tribunal concluded that as there was no transfer of Environmental, nor was there a transfer of the claimants' contracts of employment. The EAT dismissed their appeal. There was ample evidence on which the tribunal could conclude that Environmental had sufficient organisational structure to meet the criteria of the third category identified by the EAT in Duncan Web Offset, which structure included the claimants. The tribunal had therefore been entitled to find that the claimants were assigned to the work of Environmental, which did not transfer, rather than to Engineering or to the part of Holdings that did.

Some might feel that it is hardly in keeping with the purpose of the 2006 **2.91** Regulations or the Acquired Rights Directive that an employee can be dismissed on account of the transfer of the major and most viable part of a business – as occurred in the Michael Peters case (above) – and yet be denied the protection of the Regulations because he or she is held not to have been assigned to work in the particular parts of the undertaking transferred. Indeed, it was probably considerations of this kind that prompted the tribunal and the EAT in the Sunley Turriff case to pierce the corporate veil in order to reach the conclusion that the employee was assigned to the particular associated company comprising the transferred undertaking in that case. But, as has already been made clear under 'Employees engaged by service/holding companies' above, the courts have repeatedly stressed that only in very limited circumstances is it appropriate to adopt this device for achieving 'justice' in a particular case.

Assignment 'immediately before the transfer'   2.92
In this chapter we have seen that if an employee is to transfer from transferor to transferee under Reg 4 of the 2006 Regulations, he or she must be employed by the transferor 'immediately before the transfer' within the meaning of Reg 4(3). Furthermore, the employee must be 'assigned to the organised grouping of resources or employees' transferred, within the meaning of Reg 4(1). But must the employee be *assigned to the organised grouping of resources or employees immediately before the transfer*?

Legal commentary on the 2006 Regulations has generally assumed so. But a closer analysis of the actual wording of Reg 4(3) suggests the position may be more complex.

The problem can best be identified by dissecting the elements of Reg 4(3) into **2.93** three parts, and italicising the words of significance for these purposes:

* part 1:   'Any reference in [Reg 4(1)] to a person *employed* by the transferor and *assigned* to the organised grouping of resources or employees that is subject to a relevant transfer,

133

- part 2: is a reference to a person *so employed* immediately before the transfer, or who would have been *so employed* if he had not been dismissed in the circumstances described in regulation 7(1),

- part 3: including, where the transfer is effected by a series of two or more transactions, a person *so employed and assigned* or who would have been *so employed and assigned* immediately before any of those transactions.'

2.94 The first thing to note is that the words 'and assigned' do not appear anywhere in the second part of Reg 4(3), in marked contrast to the third part dealing with transfers effected by a series of transactions. The regulation thus does *not* include the following words depicted by square brackets: 'Any reference in [Reg 4(1)] to a person employed by the transferor and assigned to the organised grouping of resources... is a reference to a person so employed [and assigned] immediately before the transfer'. Nor does it go on to say 'or who would have been so employed [and assigned]'. Therefore, a literal reading of the actual wording of the second part of Reg 4(3) would more naturally lead to the conclusion that the requirement to be employed 'immediately before the transfer' relates only to being employed by the transferor and not to being assigned to the organised grouping of resources.

On its face, this is surprising, since nowhere in the DTI's Response to the Public Consultation on the initial draft of the 2006 Regulations published in February 2006 was any suggestion made by the Government that it intended such a result. In view of this, it is tempting to look past the drafting peculiarities of Reg 4(3) to construe it as requiring that, for Reg 4(1) to operate, the employee must be employed in and assigned to the undertaking immediately before the transfer. That outcome could be achieved by construing the first mention of the phrase '*so employed*' in the second part of Reg 4(3) as being short-hand for the reference to 'a person *employed by the transferor and assigned to the organised grouping of resources or employees*' in part one. But what is odd is that the Parliamentary draftsman appeared to make a deliberate decision to add the words 'and assigned' twice in the third part of Reg 4(3). This makes it absolutely expressly clear, in the context of a relevant transfer that is effected by a series of transactions, that the employee will be deemed to have been employed 'immediately before the transfer' provided that he or she is employed by the transferor *and* assigned to the undertaking immediately before any of the relevant transactions.

2.95 Applying normal rules of statutory interpretation, the draftsman is usually assumed to have chosen his or her words deliberately. In which case, why did he or she choose to use the phrase 'so employed and assigned' twice in the third part and not at all in the second part of Reg 4(3), where the phrase is limited to the words 'so employed'? If it was thought that the words 'and assigned' were useful for the sake of clarity in part 3, why were they thought unnecessary in part 2?

134

The lack of any case law focusing on this issue means that any explanation is necessarily speculative. One possibility is that the particular wording of Reg 4(3), if given a strict and literal reading, helps guard against the transferor being able to 'cherry-pick' which employees go across to the transferee by preventing the issue of assignment being entirely dependent on whoever happens to be assigned to the transferred undertaking at the time of the transfer. Certainly, as the Response to the public consultation on the draft regulations made clear, this was a matter of concern for the Government. But if that is the mischief to which the drafting of Reg 4(3) was addressed, a different problem emerges: if the employee only has to be employed by the transferor, and not necessarily assigned to the undertaking, immediately before the transfer, what would stop him claiming the protection of Reg 4(1) if he or she had ceased to be assigned to the undertaking weeks, months or even years before the transfer?

The practical difficulties that result from a literal reading of Reg 4(3) drive one **2.96** to conclude that, despite the drafting uncertainties, a straightforward reading of the first and second parts of that regulation produces a more sensible outcome. This view can to some extent be supported by the stipulation in Reg 2(1) that '"assigned" means other than on a temporary basis'. Arguably, the determination of whether the employee's assignment to the transferred undertaking was permanent or temporary requires (or at least implies) that a specific date and time is identified by which to make that assessment. How else would it be possible to say whether a change in the pattern of an employee's assignment sometime before the transfer was permanent or merely temporary?

The remainder of this section therefore proceeds on the assumption that Reg 4(3) provides that the automatic transfer of employment rule in Reg 4(1) bites only if the employee is employed by the transferor *and* assigned to the organised grouping of resources or employees *'immediately before the transfer'*.

How Reg 4(3) applies. The precise meaning of the phrase 'immediately before **2.97** the transfer' has been examined under 'Employed "immediately before" transfer' above. Essentially, the phrase has been interpreted to mean that an employee must be actually be employed and assigned *at the moment of the transfer* or be *deemed* to be so. The deeming provision comes into play if, prior to when the transfer occurs, an employee is unfairly dismissed in the circumstances described in Reg 7(1) – that is to say, dismissed by reason of the transfer or for a reason related to it that is not an 'economic, technical or organisational reason entailing changes in the workforce'. In the event of such an unfair dismissal, the employee will be 'deemed' to have been employed at the moment of the transfer. And provided that the employee can also show at the time of dismissal that he or she was assigned to the undertaking, business or part transferred in accordance with the test for assignment as discussed in this section, Reg 4(1) will operate to transfer his or her employment to the transferee.

135

Regulation 4(3) also deals with the situation where a transfer is effected by a series of two or more transactions. Again, this has been discussed under 'Employed "immediately before" transfer' above. Essentially, if the employee can show that he or she is both employed by the transferor and assigned to the undertaking transferred immediately before any of the transactions in the series, then he or she is regarded as having been so employed and assigned 'immediately before' the transfer. Furthermore, the employee will be deemed to have been employed immediately before a relevant transaction if he or she would have been so assigned had he or she not been unfairly dismissed for the purposes of Reg 7(1).

2.98 **Relevant case law.** There is not much case law that considers the issue of the 'immediately before' stipulation in Reg 4(3) specifically in the context of assignment. The point is, however, taken up in the two cases outlined below:

- **J Murphy and Sons Ltd v Fox and anor** EAT 1222/96: F had been employed since 1986 by JM Ltd as a general operative. Although his work had taken him to various parts of the country, prior to October 1995 he had never worked at JM Ltd's main depot, from which a major maintenance contract with British Gas was serviced. However, from that date F was allocated work at the depot and carried out general duties in relation to the British Gas contract until mid-December 1995, when he was informed that JM Ltd had lost the contract to another company, N Ltd. F was told that, as from 8 January 1996, his employment would automatically be transferred to N Ltd under TUPE. He brought a claim of unfair dismissal against M Ltd, relying on the contention that, as he had never been assigned to the relevant undertaking (the British Gas contract), his employment had not transferred. An employment tribunal agreed. It asked itself the question: To which part of M Ltd's undertaking was F assigned at the date of the transfer? The tribunal answered this by looking at the 'reasonable expectations of the parties' as at October 1995 when F was first assigned to work at the main depot, and concluded, in the light of his previous employment history, that the expectation was that his assignment there was not permanent. M Ltd appealed, contending that the approach adopted by the tribunal had been erroneous. The EAT agreed. It held that, in determining the question of assignment, the tribunal had wrongly considered F's employment history and whether the British Gas work was temporary or permanent. The EAT observed: '[What is now Reg 4] provides that the employee need only be employed immediately before [the] transfer. There is no requirement for a long-term view of the previous employment.' Since he was assigned to the transferred work at the relevant time, F's employment was automatically transferred to H Ltd, and accordingly M Ltd was not liable to him for unfair dismissal

- **United Guarding Services Ltd v St James Security Group Ltd and anor** EAT 0770/03: H was employed by S Ltd as a security officer. Clause 4 of her contract provided that she would normally be based at 50 Broadway, Westminster, where S Ltd had a commercial contract to supply security services – although she could also be required to work at different sites within reasonable travelling distance if given a written direction to that effect. In practice, she exclusively worked at 50 Broadway until September 2002. At that point, a dispute arose between H and her manager, P, after which she worked at other sites for S Ltd over a three-week period. She then commenced employment tribunal proceedings alleging, among other things, that she had been unfairly dismissed and requesting that she be reinstated to her 'permanent' site from which she claimed to have been unfairly removed as a result of P's harassment and bullying. S Ltd's ET3 asserted that H had not actually been dismissed, and that, following an investigation into her allegations against P, it had found the allegations to be unfounded. As a result, it was prepared to continue employing her at a different site to avoid her coming into contact with P. Prior to the tribunal hearing, S Ltd lost the service contract in respect of 50 Broadway, and its operation was taken over by a different company, U Ltd, from 29 April 2003. In view of this, H amended her ET1 to claim that the change of contractor comprised a TUPE transfer and that, as she was assigned to the security undertaking at 50 Broadway, her employment had transferred to U Ltd. The tribunal found that H's position was 'analogous to "suspension" or something of that kind', in that, pending the resolution of her claims, her employment was continuing even though she was not actively working for the employer. The tribunal further held that she had been assigned to 50 Broadway at the time of the transfer and that her employment had accordingly transferred to U Ltd. On U Ltd's appeal, the EAT ruled that the tribunal had asked itself the right question – whether H was 'assigned' to 50 Broadway 'immediately before the transfer' – but had erred in concluding on the facts that she was so assigned. The proper approach was to apply a two-stage test by asking: (a) what was the employee's contractual place of work? and (b) would she have been required to work there immediately before the transfer? If that test had been applied, there could only have been one answer: that H's contractual place of work, in the absence of a direction under clause 4 of her contract, was 50 Broadway, but that she would not have been required to work there immediately before the transfer on 29 April 2003. Since she was not allowed to work at those premises 'at all', she could not be said to be assigned to the contract to supply security services at the relevant time.

In both these cases, the EAT effectively decided that taking a 'snapshot' of the position at the date of the transfer determined whether the employees concerned were to be regarded as 'assigned' to the business or part transferred. Some may feel that the recent history of the respective employees' employment was **2.99**

137

somewhat underplayed in favour of looking at the precise position as it existed at the time of the transfer. But the requirement to be assigned 'immediately before the transfer' encourages tribunals to adopt a snapshot approach. This has led to qualms being expressed that the position can be artificially engineered by the use of temporary assignments to shift employees in and out of certain parts of an undertaking in order to allow the transferor to retain those employees who are highly valued or 'dump' onto the incoming employer those who are regarded as a problem.

It is likely, however, that this concern about cherry-picking is dealt with to some degree by the stipulation in Reg 2(1) of the 2006 Regulations that the word 'assigned' means 'assigned other than on a temporary basis'. This is considered in more detail below. It suffices to say here that, had a similar provision been contained in the 1981 Regulations, the cases above might have been decided differently on their facts – especially J Murphy and Sons Ltd v Fox. There, the EAT rejected the view that, even if F's assignment to work on the British Gas contract was temporary, this could not affect the conclusion that he was assigned to the contract at the point when responsibility for operating it transferred. In view of Reg 2(1), such a view could no longer be sustained. Admittedly, in that case, the employee was contending that his employment had not been automatically transferred because he had not been assigned to the relevant undertaking at the time of its transfer, whereas in more typical TUPE cases employees argue the exact opposite. But this does not alter the fact that any employee who would now wish to challenge the pattern of assignment that just happened to exist at the time of the transfer will find Reg 2(1) a useful tool in his or her armoury.

2.100 **Temporary assignment**

As mentioned above, Reg 2(1) defines 'assigned' as meaning 'assigned other than on a temporary basis'. The DTI's 'Employment rights on the transfer of an undertaking: a guide to the 2006 TUPE Regulations for employees, employers and representatives' (the DTI Guide) explains that this means that 'the new employer does not take over the contracts of any employees who are only temporarily assigned to the "organised grouping". Whether an assignment is "temporary" will depend on a number of factors, such as the length of time the employee has been there and whether a date has been set by the transferor for his return or re-assignment to another part of the business or undertaking.'

Although there was no equivalent to Reg 2(1) in the 1981 Regulations, case law had already established that an employee who was only temporarily assigned to the undertaking being transferred at the time of the transfer would not have his or her employment automatically transferred to the transferee – see Securiplan v Bademosi EAT 1128/02. In that case the claimant had worked for 21 years as a security officer at a Cable and Wireless (C&W) site for which his employer, S, provided security services. The claimant sustained an accident at work in July 2000 and when he was fit enough to return to duties there was no longer a vacancy for him at the C&W site. So, in January 2001, S placed the claimant at Marylebone magistrates' court, where he continued to work all year. S knew that the claimant was unhappy at the new site, and on 3 December 2001 told him that he could return to work at the C&W site in January 2002. However, on 6 December, S's contract to provide security at the court was abruptly terminated and the contract awarded to C Ltd. S declined to continue employing the claimant, as a result of which the claimant brought a number of tribunal claims against the company. Upholding these, an employment tribunal rejected S's argument that the claimant was assigned to the magistrates' court contract on the date when S lost that contract, and that his employment had therefore automatically transferred to C Ltd.

On appeal, the EAT upheld the tribunal's decision. His Honour Judge McMullen **2.101** QC, giving the EAT's judgment, observed that: 'We are not able to interfere with the express finding, that upon his return from industrial injury the vacancy at Cable and Wireless no longer existed, but the [claimant] was *assigned on a temporary basis* elsewhere. The judgment as to what is temporary and what is permanent is a matter for the employment tribunal.' Accordingly, the claimant's employment had not transferred. Instead, he was to be taken to have reverted to his duties either at the C&W site straightaway or to other temporary assignments pending his return to that site at the beginning of January 2002.

Secondment. It is submitted that a similar approach should be taken in most **2.102** cases where, at the time of the transfer, an employee is seconded from outside into the transferred undertaking, or vice versa. However, it is true that particular difficulties concerning the application of TUPE can arise if the secondment arrangement is a transaction in a series of transactions leading to the transfer, as was the case in Celtec Ltd v Astley and ors 2006 ICR 992, HL. As a result of the House of Lords' decision in that case, employees may find themselves regarded as having been 'assigned' to the undertaking to which they are seconded and thus transferred automatically to the transferee. This is a problem that may especially affect the public sector, where secondment arrangements (such as those that underpin the NHS Retention of Employment Model) are fairly commonplace. The issues that may arise are discussed in detail under 'Problems of secondment arrangements' at the end of this chapter.

Employees subject to mobility or flexibility clauses **2.103**

Can an employee be said to be 'assigned' to a particular part of the business transferred if, under his or her contract of employment, he or she can be assigned to another part of the business under a mobility or flexibility clause? The answer is 'Yes' if, at the time of the transfer, the transferor has not sought to exercise the right to reassign under the contractual clause in question; and 'No' if the employee has genuinely been reassigned under the clause at some point before

139

the transfer or, in the case of an employee who was absent at that time, would have been reassigned had he or she returned to work before the transfer.

In Securicor Guarding Ltd v Fraser Security Services Ltd and ors EAT 350/95 S Ltd had a contract to supply security services to D Ltd at its site in Caerphilly. Two of S Ltd's employees were employed on a permanent basis as security guards at that site, although one of them did overtime work at other sites. However, a term of their contracts headed 'Mobility of employment' stipulated that, 'should the interests of the company demand it, you may be required to serve at [S Ltd's] head office in London or at one of the company's branches'. Following a competitive tendering exercise, D Ltd decided to terminate S Ltd's contract and award it to another company, FS Ltd, who then declined to take on the two employees. S Ltd had no other work available at any of its other sites, so the employees were dismissed. They claimed unfair dismissal against both S Ltd and FS Ltd. On the preliminary question of whether TUPE applied to transfer their employment to FS Ltd, a tribunal ruled, among other things, that the employees had not been 'assigned' to the activities carried on at the Caerphilly site because under the mobility clause they could be required by S Ltd to work elsewhere.

2.104   The EAT allowed S Ltd's appeal, giving short shrift to the tribunal's reasoning. The employees had been the permanent staff assigned solely to D Ltd's Caerphilly site unless and until transferred to another site. The fact that one of them performed additional overtime duties elsewhere was immaterial. In the words of His Honour Judge Peter Clark: 'It would be standing TUPE on its head to hold that because the transferee will not honour a relevant employee's existing terms and conditions of employment, and because the contract between the employee and the transferor contains a mobility clause, that has the effect of compelling the *transferor* to retain the employee on his existing terms.'

In a case where the evidence is that a mobility clause option has been validly exercised by the transferor so as to assign an employee to a part of its undertaking that is not the subject of the relevant transfer, then the employee will not be regarded as being 'assigned' to the undertaking transferred. This, in effect, is what happened in United Guarding Services Ltd v St James Security Group Ltd and anor EAT 0770/03 – discussed in detail under 'Assignment "immediately before the transfer"' above.

2.105 **Employees absent at the time of the transfer**
Where the employee was absent before the transfer, whether by reason of long-term sickness, maternity or paternity leave, suspension, strike action, lay-off, sabbatical leave or any other legitimate absence from the workplace, the question is always whether, upon returning to work, he or she would have been assigned to the undertaking or part transferred. That question should be answered by looking at the position as it obtained immediately before the transfer.

140

In Fairhurst Ward Abbotts Ltd v Botes Building Ltd and ors 2004 ICR 919, CA, the Court of Appeal confirmed that the issue of whether an employee on sick leave at the time of a transfer is employed in the undertaking or part of an undertaking transferred is a factual matter, which will be determined by reference to where he or she would be required to work if fit to do so. On this basis, an employment tribunal had erred in holding that the claimant, owing to his sickness absence from the part of the undertaking to which TUPE applied, had not been transferred. Although the Court, by a majority, ordered that the case be remitted to the tribunal for determination of where the employee would have been required to work had he not been on sick leave, Lord Justice May dissented on the basis that there was no need for the matter to be remitted as the tribunal had already found that the claimant had, some months before the transfer, been 'assigned' by the outgoing contractor to the part transferred. Therefore, in reality, he was in the same position as six other employees whom the tribunal had found had transferred under TUPE.

An employment tribunal made a similar finding in Nethercoat v Firm Security Group Ltd ET Case No.33642/95. That case involved N, who worked at Sheerness for a security firm. In November he was sent on an assignment to another location, and a month later had an accident causing him to be absent until the end of March. In the meantime, his firm's contract with the Sheerness operation was transferred to another company. When N returned to work at Sheerness, the new contractor disputed that his contract had been transferred to it, but an employment tribunal found that he had been employed in and assigned to the undertaking immediately before the transfer.

Employees subject to pending disciplinary processes

2.106

Are employees subject to pending disciplinary processes and appeal hearings deemed to be employed immediately before the transfer within the meaning of Reg 4(3)? This issue was considered by the EAT in G4S Justice Services (UK) Ltd v Anstey and anor 2006 IRLR 588, EAT. At the date of the transfer of the business, two employees were awaiting the outcome of internal appeals against their dismissals for gross misconduct. However, the transferee refused to reinstate them as they were not regarded as having been employed by the transferor immediately before the transfer. The EAT held that the successful appeal hearing had the effect of expunging the original dismissals and so the employees should be treated as having been employed by the transferor up to the date of the transfer.

In Russell v First Security Guards ET Case No.2700189/09 the employee was employed as a team manager supervising a team of security personnel at Credit Suisse premises. He was suspended pending investigations into allegations of misconduct on 22 August 2008. During the period of suspension, his employer proposed to transfer the security contract on which he worked to the transferee. The employee was excluded from the list of transferring employees and he only

141

became aware of this on the day of the transfer. The transferee refused to employ the employee as the transferor had previously excluded him as a transferring employee. An employment tribunal held that the employee was assigned to the contract that was transferred to the transferee and his dismissal on the date of the transfer by the transferee was automatically unfair.

2.107 ## Bogus or 'fraudulent' assignments

In Carisway Cleaning Consultants Ltd v Richards and anor EAT 629/97 the transferor's ruse to dump an unwanted employee into the part of the undertaking to be transferred was characterised by the EAT as 'fraudulent'. The claimant in that case, R, had worked for 19 years for C Ltd, a cleaning company with contracts to clean several of Sainsbury's stores. In October 1995, while based at the Ladbroke Grove store, the claimant was suspended pending an investigation into poor performance and alleged falsification of clock cards. The following day C Ltd offered him the choice of working at the store in Chesham, which he accepted and for which he received a significant pay increase. But unbeknown to him, C Ltd already knew that it had lost the contract to supply cleaning services at that store, and only two days after the claimant starting work at Chesham, it wrote to inform him that his employment was to be transferred to the new contractor, CCS. The claimant's name had not been included on any list of employees supplied by C Ltd to CCS. Following the transfer, R worked for a few weeks for CCS, but it did not work out and his employment was terminated.

The claimant brought tribunal proceedings against both C Ltd and CCS for unfair dismissal. An employment tribunal upheld the claim against C Ltd on the basis that the claimant had never been assigned to the part of C Ltd's undertaking that had transferred to CCS. It found that C Ltd had been attempting, by sleight of hand, to use the TUPE Regulations to offload a long-serving employee against whom there had been complaints and who enjoyed the employment protection rights that went with a lengthy period of continuous employment. In its view, the claimant could not be considered as part of the undertaking that was transferred, since he had been gulled into working for that undertaking.

2.108 The EAT's judgment rejecting C Ltd's appeal is notable not so much for the fact that it upheld the employment tribunal's decision but for the trenchant words it used to describe the employer's actions in this case. His Honour Judge Hull QC, who gave the EAT's judgment, observed that in the wholly exceptional circumstances of the instant case, the employee had been 'defrauded' into moving to the undertaking that was about to be transferred. The transferor's action might well have been a fraud not only against the employee but also against the transferee, especially since the transferor had increased the employee's salary to such a degree that the cleaning contract that the transferee was to take over would have been totally profitless. The tribunal had correctly

142

concluded that the transferor had acted fraudulently, and, as HHJ Hull found, what is fraudulent is void. Accordingly, the claimant was not employed in the part of the undertaking that was transferred, with the result that what is now Reg 4 did not apply to cause his contract to be transferred automatically to the transferee.

The EAT also dealt with the transferor's argument that the tribunal should have gone on to consider whether the claimant, having continued to work at the Chesham store once he knew that a transfer was imminent, had thereby waived the fraud. In its view this contention was unsound as there was nothing in the evidence to suggest that the claimant had decided to take that course and, in any event, the full extent of the transferor's fraud upon him did not come to light until the tribunal hearing.

The Carisway decision is intriguing given that the employee in question was **2.109** indisputably working in the relevant part of the undertaking both immediately before and after it was transferred, and, on their face, there was nothing in the Regulations to prevent the transfer of his employment to the transferee. It may be that the stipulation that 'assigned' in the context of the 2006 Regulations means 'assigned other than a temporary transfer' would be a matter that would be considered by a tribunal were similar facts to arise in a future case. Ostensibly, however, the claimant in Carisway had been permanently reassigned to the undertaking at the time of its transfer in the sense that his removal to the Chesham store was not intended to be merely a temporary arrangement. It would seem that the EAT's reasoning, without expressly saying so, was really based on considerations of public policy. Given its comment that the fraud arguably operated against the transferee as well as the employee, it is interesting to consider whether, in a case where a fraudulently assigned employee nonetheless wishes to become employed by the transferee, the latter could argue that he was not bound to take on the employee in the light of the transferor's conduct. Applying the assertion that what is a fraud is void, the transferee might well succeed in avoiding the application of Reg 4(1).

Difficult issues arising from assignment to part of business   2.110
When only a part of a business is transferred, and employees are judged to be assigned to the part transferred, logistical and practical problems can arise in respect of the employee's job under the transferee. Two such problems are discussed below.

Position where employee's post-transfer role is reduced. It is clear from the **2.111** discussion above of the requirement to be assigned to the undertaking that the most common scenario in which difficult questions arise is where the employee concerned works some of the time for one part of the transferor's business and the remainder of his or her time for another part of the business. Assuming that the employee is found to have been assigned to the transferred part and is taken

143

on by the transferee, what happens if he or she is left without a full-time job? Assume, for example, that prior to the transfer Y worked full time for Z Ltd, but that 70 per cent of his time was spent working in part A of the transferor's business, and 30 per cent in part B. If only part A is subject to a TUPE transfer, that would mean that, under the transferee, Y may lose 30 per cent of his role. What are the legal consequences of this?

Obviously, if the transferee is in a position to offer sufficient work of the kind that Y was doing for the majority of his time so that the 30 per cent difference can be made up, there should be no difficulty. Alternatively, it might be that some new aspect could be added to Y's transferred role to enable him to continue working full time. Or he might simply accept employment on a part-time basis. However, if none of these options are viable, the transferee might well have to consider making Y redundant. Technically, the situation would appear to meet the statutory definition of redundancy in S.139(1)(b) ERA – i.e. that there has been a diminishment in the requirement for employees to carry out work of a particular kind. The definition of redundancy is discussed in IDS Employment Law Handbook, 'Redundancy' (August 2008), Chapter 2. It is worth pointing out that although the dismissal in this context would almost certainly be transfer-connected, it would likely be for an 'economic, technical or organisational reason entailing a change in the workforce' and so would be potentially fair – see Chapter 4 for details.

2.112 **Different parts of business subject to different transfers.** One scenario that, though far from common, may throw up even more difficult issues so far as TUPE is concerned would be if separate purchasers bought different parts of a transferor's business in circumstances where, prior to the transfer, the employee worked in both parts. Assuming the separate sales each constituted a relevant transfer, the question would arise of whether it is possible for an employee to be 'assigned' to two or more parts of the transferor's business at the same time. If so, would this mean that following the transfer of the separate parts, the employee becomes employed by the two different transferees?

The scenario outlined above occurred in Hassard v McGrath and ors 1996 NILR 586, NICA. The facts of that case were somewhat involved but centred upon the decision of the Northern Ireland Housing Executive to outsource its business of maintaining and repairing its housing stock, which was being administered through the direct labour organisation (DLO) which the Executive had previously set up. The claimant worked as a joiner in the Fermanagh district of the DLO's operation, and that district was divided into four modules, 010, 020, 030 and 040. Each module comprised a particular housing estate or set of estates. The claimant's recent pattern of working showed that he worked in varying amounts for all four modules. One of the bidding contractors, D, was appointed by the Executive to service the maintenance work of modules 010 and 030 (for which, when amalgamated, the claimant had spent 25 per cent of his time working). A separate bidder, M, was appointed to deal with modules 020 and 040 (for which the claimant worked 73.39 per cent of his time). The issue arose as to whether the change of contractors comprised separate relevant transfers and whether the claimant had been assigned, at the time of the transfers, to one or both or neither of the transferred parts of the DLO's undertaking.

An industrial tribunal in Northern Ireland held that the appointments of the **2.113** bidders amounted to separate relevant transfers; that the claimant was assigned equally to the two parts of the undertaking that were the subject of those transfers; and that he thereupon became employed by two different employers, D and M. On appeal, the Northern Ireland Court of Appeal overturned that decision. It pointed out that if the tribunal's conclusion was correct, the claimant's contract of employment with the Executive became two contracts of employment and that, following the transfer, he became employed by the two contractors in differing proportions. The Court thought that was not a palatable conclusion. In its view, 'an employee is only protected by the [Acquired Rights] Directive or the TUPE Regulations if before the transfer he was assigned solely to one part of the undertaking transferred to a transferee'.

Although decisions of the Northern Ireland Court of Appeal are not, strictly speaking, binding on tribunals or the EAT in Great Britain, its decisions are of highly persuasive value, particularly in a context like TUPE where the relevant legislation does not materially differ. In any case, the NICA's decision is, it is submitted, a sensible one.

Objecting to the transfer
2.114

As discussed at the start of this chapter, the TUPE Regulations oust the common law rule that an employer may not transfer a contract of employment to a third party without the express consent of the employee. By virtue of Reg 4(1), an employee who is employed, or is deemed to be employed, in the organised grouping of resources or employees being transferred at the time of the transfer has his or her contract automatically transferred to the transferee. This reflects the position – as it has been found to be by the European Court of Justice – under the EU Acquired Rights Directive. In Rotsart de Hertaing v J Benoidt SA (in liquidation) and anor 1997 IRLR 127, ECJ, the European Court ruled that the contracts of employment and employment relationships existing on the date of the transfer between the transferor and the workers employed in the undertaking automatically pass to the transferee by the mere fact of the transfer. Moreover, by reason of the mandatory nature of the Directive, and in order not to deprive workers of the protection afforded by the Directive, the transfer of employment contracts automatically takes place regardless of the intentions of the transferor or the transferee and cannot be obstructed by the transferee's refusal to fulfil his obligations towards the transferred employees.

145

2.115 **Position under the Acquired Rights Directive**
Apart from causing the employee's contract to be transferred to the transferee, the 2006 Regulations also ensure that all the transferor's rights, powers, duties and liabilities under that contract pass to the transferee – Reg 4(2). The priority attached to the automatic transfer of the transferor's rights and duties over any objections that the employees concerned may have about it was confirmed by the ECJ in the Dutch case of Berg and anor v Besselsen 1990 ICR 396, ECJ. There, the question put to the European Court was whether the employment obligations of a transferor are transferred automatically to the transferee on the transfer of an undertaking. If so, did it then follow that an employee's consent to such a discharge of the transferor's obligations was unnecessary and that any objections by him or her could not prevent it? The claimant argued that his consent was required. The ECJ decided that Article 3.1 of what is now Directive No.2001/23 – upon which Reg 4(1) is based – must be interpreted as meaning that the transferor is discharged from all contractual employment obligations owed to transferred employees following a relevant transfer, and that this legal consequence was neither conditional on the consent of the employees concerned nor affected by any objections they might have.

The judgment in the Berg case was thought to be clear authority for the principle that the automatic transfer of employment contracts was a legal consequence of a relevant transfer, which was unaffected by any objections employees might have. However, the relevance of an employee's objections to the automatic transfer of his or her employment contract came under the ECJ's scrutiny in Katsikas v Konstantinidis 1993 IRLR 179, ECJ, a case concerning the rights of an employee who had been dismissed because of his objection to working for the transferee to whom his employer's business was transferred. The ECJ considered the principle established in the Berg case but decided that it had no bearing on the issue in the case before it. Berg concerned an employee's objection to the transfer of his employer's obligations entered into prior to the transfer, not to the transfer of his own contract of employment. The Court pointed out that, if the Directive were to be interpreted as obliging employees to work for the transferee rather than simply permitting them to do so on the terms and conditions agreed with the transferor, this would call into question the fundamental right of employees to select their employer. The ECJ concluded, therefore, that Article 3.1 did not prevent employees from opposing the automatic transfer of their contract of employment. On the other hand, neither did Article 3.1 oblige Member States to provide for the continuance of the contract with the transferor. The fate of the employment contract was left to the discretion of individual Member States.

2.116 In Merckx and anor v Ford Motors Co (Belgium) SA 1997 ICR 352, ECJ, the European Court advanced the case law on objection to the transfer even further. What was of interest in the Merckx case was whether, in circumstances where the reason for the employee's objection to the transfer is that he or she will

146

incur a substantial and detrimental change to his or her terms and conditions, the employee is to be regarded as having been dismissed and so entitled to recover any redundancy payment or compensation due. The Court ruled that where the contract of employment or employment relationship is terminated because the transfer involves a substantial change in working conditions to the detriment of the employee, the employer is to be regarded, by virtue of Article 4.2 of the Directive, as responsible for the termination. A change in the level of remuneration awarded to the employee constitutes a substantial change in working conditions, so that where the contract or employment relationship is terminated by the employee because the transfer involves such a change, the employer will be liable to pay compensation on the ground that he has dismissed the employee.

Position under TUPE Regulations   2.117

In so far as the Katsikas case left it to Member States to determine the effect on an employee's existing contract where he or she objects to the transfer, the UK Government addressed the position by implementing specific amendments to Reg 5 of the 1981 Regulations. These provided that, in the event of an objection being voiced to the transferor or transferee, the Regulations would not operate to transfer the employee's contract (or any rights, duties or liabilities in respect of it) to the transferee – old Reg 5(4A). However, in that situation, the employee's contract of employment would be terminated on the date of the transfer, but he or she would not be treated as having been dismissed for any purpose – old Reg 5(4B).

Following these changes, there was some confusion as to the interplay between these new provisions and the pre-existing right of an employee, by virtue of old Reg 5(5), to terminate his or her contract of employment without notice if a substantial change is made in his working conditions to his detriment. The question was whether such a right was compatible with, and survived, the new stipulation in old Reg 5(4B) that where the employee exerts his or her right to object to the transfer, that causes the termination of his or her employment with the transferor but the termination will not be treated as a dismissal for any purpose. How, then, could the employee bring any claim (such as unfair constructive dismissal) based on the termination?

The Humphreys decision. The position was rapidly made clear by the Court   2.118
of Appeal in Humphreys v University of Oxford and anor 2000 ICR 405, CA. In that case the Court ruled that where an employee, prior to a proposed transfer, objected to the transfer under old Reg 5(4A) and the objection was based on an anticipated detrimental change in his or her working conditions, the contract with the transferor terminated as soon as the transfer took place. And despite the stipulation in old Reg 5(4B) that termination in these circumstances does not constitute a dismissal for any purpose, the employee retained the right to sue the transferor for constructive dismissal under Reg

147

5(5). That is because old Reg 5(4B) had to be read, in order to give effect to the purpose of the Acquired Rights Directive, as being subject to Reg 5(5), which preserves the employee's right to claim that he has been constructively dismissed in a case where the employee anticipates that the transfer will lead to a substantial and detrimental change in his working conditions.

The facts of the Humphreys case concerned an employee who worked for the University setting and marking GCSE and A-level exam papers. Under his existing terms, he had life tenure up to the age of 67. On being informed that his post was to be transferred to a separate examining body, he objected in writing, stating his reason to be that the transfer involved a significant change in his working conditions that was to his detriment. His concern was that the transferee would only be in a position to guarantee three years of employment up to the age of 65. Following his objection, he brought a claim against Oxford University in the High Court for damages for wrongful dismissal covering the unexpired period of his tenure. The University applied to have the employee's action struck out on the ground that it was misconceived. The High Court judge rejected that application and, on appeal by the University, the Court of Appeal ruled that he had been right to do so. The judge had properly interpreted the provisions of Reg 5 of the 1981 Regulations as entitling the employee to argue that, having objected to becoming employed by the transferee and thereby bringing his employment with the transferor to an end as soon as the transfer occurred, he could nevertheless claim that he had been constructively dismissed by the transferor on the ground that any transfer of his employment to the transferee would have caused a substantial change in his working conditions to his detriment.

2.119 Prior to the Humphreys case, the EAT in Sita (GB) Ltd v Burton and ors 1998 ICR 17, EAT, expressed the opinion that any anticipation by employees that the transferee will fail to meet his obligations cannot found a claim of unfair constructive dismissal against the transferor because what is at risk is the preservation after the transfer of the employee's current terms in his contract with the transferor. The EAT's reasoning was that the TUPE Regulations provide an absolute answer by way of remedy to any attempt by the transferee to alter those terms unlawfully after the transfer. The EAT did not consider that the conduct of an employer could be regarded as sufficiently drastic with regard to the obligation of mutual trust and goodwill if it did nothing to alter the remedies available to the employee upon transfer. However, the Court of Appeal in the Humphreys case decided that the employee's right to claim constructive dismissal under what was then Reg 5(5) survived his objection to the proposed transfer and that the transferor was the appropriate defendant.

2.120 **Outline of 'objection' provisions under TUPE 2006**. The provisions dealing with the right of objection and its effect on the employee's contract of employment are now to be found in Reg 4(7)–(11) of TUPE 2006. These largely mirror the right of objection that was contained in the old Regulations as amended, but with some important changes of wording discussed under 'Objection on basis of "Substantial changes to working conditions"' below. The Regulations provide as follows:

- Reg 4(7) states that the rules in Reg 4(1) and (2) providing for the automatic transfer of employment and of contractual rights and liabilities, etc 'shall not operate to transfer the contract of employment and the rights, powers, duties and liabilities under or in connection with it of an employee who informs the transferor or the transferee that he objects to becoming employed by the transferee'

- Reg 4(8) states 'subject to paragraphs (9) and (11), where an employee so objects, the relevant transfer shall operate so as to terminate his contract of employment with the transferor but he shall not be treated, for any purpose, as having been dismissed by the transferor'

- Reg 4(9) states that 'where a relevant transfer involves or would involve a substantial change in working conditions to the material detriment of a person whose contract of employment is or would be transferred under [Reg 4(1)]', then, except in the specific context of insolvency, 'such an employee may treat the contract of employment as having been terminated, and the employee shall be treated for any purpose as having been dismissed by the employer'

- Reg 4(11) states that all the above provisions as well as the automatic transfer of employment rule in Reg 4(1) 'are without prejudice to any right of an employee arising apart from these Regulations to terminate his contract of employment without notice in acceptance of a repudiatory breach of contract by his employer'.

Putting all of these provisions together, the position is that, where an employee **2.121** objects to the transfer, (a) the automatic transfer of employment rule will not operate, but (b) the transfer will have the effect of terminating the employee's contract with the transferor, and (c) he or she will not, for any purpose, be considered to have been dismissed by the transferor, *except* (d) where the transfer involves or would involve a substantial change in the employee's working conditions to his or her material detriment. In that case the employee is entitled to treat the contract as having been terminated and that termination will constitute a dismissal for any purpose. Finally, (e) none of the above affects the employee's general legal right to resign without notice in response to a repudiatory breach of contract by the employer – whether the employee is employed by the transferor at the time of resignation or has become employed by the transferee after a relevant transfer.

It will be seen that Reg 4(7)–(11) codifies and makes explicit the position under the previous Regulations as interpreted by the Court of Appeal in the Humphreys case (see above). In particular, Reg 4(9) spells out that where the employee's objection to the transfer results in him or her resigning because the transfer involves (or is anticipated to involve) a substantial change to his or her working conditions, then this is an exception to the rule that such objection will not be regarded as a dismissal for any purpose. And Reg 4(11) contains a separate provision that now makes it explicit that the specific provisions under TUPE are without prejudice to the employee's right 'apart from these Regulations' to resign in the face of a repudiatory breach of contract by the employer. Again, this codifies the position as decided by the Court of Appeal in Humphreys, when it rejected the view taken by the EAT in Sita (GB) Ltd v Burton and ors that any anticipation by an employee that the transferee will fail to meet his obligations under TUPE cannot found a claim of unfair constructive dismissal against the transferor (see above).

2.122 Timing of the objection

On the face of it, the wording of Reg 4(7) implies that any objection to a transfer has to be made by the employee before (or at the latest, at the time of) the relevant transfer. That is because the provision stipulates that the rules providing for the automatic transfer of the contract of employment and the rights, duties and liabilities under the contract do not apply to an employee 'who informs the transferor or the transferee that he objects to becoming employed by the transferor'. If, therefore, the employee remains silent, and simply goes across to the transferee without demur, it is difficult to see how he or she can later claim to have objected to becoming employed by the transferee within the terms of Reg 4(7). However, does this literal interpretation have to give way in circumstances where the employee did not know about the imminent change of employer?

This was the question that faced the High Court in New ISG Ltd v Vernon 2008 ICR 319, ChD. There, the employee was kept in the dark about the identity of his new employer following the sale of the transferor's business by joint administrators. When, two days after the transfer, he learned of the identity of the transferee, he resigned and subsequently went to work for a competitor. The new transferee immediately sought to enforce restrictive covenants in the employee's contract, contending that this had been transferred automatically in accordance with Reg 4 of TUPE. Initially, the transferee was successful in obtaining a temporary injunction restraining the employee from working for the competitor. However, on review, a High Court judge lifted this on the basis that the employee, by resigning as soon as he found out about the transfer, had in effect objected to the transfer within the meaning of Reg 4(7). This had the consequence that his contract of employment had not transferred, so the transferee was not in a position to enforce the restrictive covenants contained within it. The judge rejected the transferee's argument that the employee's objection was ineffective because it was made after the transfer had occurred.

The employee had not known of the identity of the transferee before the date of the transfer and had submitted a letter of resignation within two working days of the transfer. In those circumstances, while the wording of Reg 4(7) envisaged that an employee must object before or at the time of the transfer of the undertaking for the objection to be valid, the judge reasoned that a purposive approach was necessary to give force to the principle behind the right to object.

There are limits, however, to the extent to which the courts will allow an **2.123** employee to object after a transfer has occurred. In Capita Health Solutions Ltd v McLean and anor 2008 IRLR 595, EAT, an employee employed by the BBC had deep reservations about the imminent transfer of her employment as an occupational nurse to CHS Ltd, which was due to take over the entirety of the BBC's HR department, including its occupational health service. These reservations were expressed by way of a grievance alleging that the change of employer entailed a significant change to the employee's role and pension benefits. However, in subsequent dealings, the employee and the BBC agreed that she would go to work for CHS Ltd for the six-week period during which she was working out her notice of resignation, and that she would continue to be paid by the BBC during this period. At the end of the six weeks, the employee duly resigned and claimed unfair dismissal against both CHS Ltd and the BBC and the issue arose as to whether the transferor – i.e. the BBC – should be regarded as a proper respondent to the proceedings. This depended on whether the employee had validly objected to the transfer: if not, her employment would have transferred to CHS Ltd, making it the sole respondent potentially liable for the unfair dismissal.

The EAT ruled that the act of going to work for the transferee under a temporary secondment arrangement in circumstances where the employee was fully aware of the change in the identity of the employer was wholly inconsistent with having evinced an objection to the transfer. What, in fact, the employee's approach showed was that she was agreeable to working for CHS Ltd, albeit for only six weeks: this was wholly inconsistent with her claim that she had objected to the transfer. In the EAT's view, the intention of the parties, while a relevant consideration, was not determinative of the question of whether an objection within the meaning of Reg 4(7) had been made. This was wholly an objective matter to be decided by the facts and circumstances of the case at issue. Furthermore, the fact that the BBC had continued to pay the employee during the secondment period was irrelevant, as was the fact that the employee was working out notice given prior to the transfer. In Lady Smith's judgment, 'if... it had been intended that objecting employees be required or able to work out notice periods that ran on after the date of the transfer, it is more than reasonable to have expected that to be provided for in the Regulations... That is not to say that an objecting employee cannot be employed by the transferor employer after the transfer date, but the transferor is not obliged to retain such an employee in his employment. Any such employment would be under a new contract.'

2.124 Potentially draconian consequences of objecting

It will be seen from the above that, if the exceptions contained in Reg 4(9) and (11) do not apply, the effect of an employee objecting to the transfer is draconian. Although the employee's employment with the transferor is not transferred to the transferee according to his or her wishes, the employment automatically comes to an end at the point where the relevant transfer occurs, but that termination is not regarded as a 'dismissal' for any purpose whatsoever. This means that any remedy that the employee might ordinarily have sought as a result of being dismissed is unavailable. Furthermore, the normal protections in respect of contractual rights that the employee would have when his or her employment transfers under Reg 4(1) and (2) do not apply. Therefore, should the employee enter into a new contract after the transfer with the transferor (or, for that matter, the transferee), the employer can potentially insist on new and less favourable terms and conditions of employment without risking a finding that those terms have been varied by reason of the transfer and are accordingly void. However, in Capita Health Solutions v McClean and anor 2008 IRLR 595, EAT, the Appeal Tribunal held that an employee who had objected to her employment transferring to an outsourcing company, but who had subsequently agreed to work on a six-week secondment with the transferee, had not validly objected to the transfer. In the EAT's view, her acceptance of the secondment indicated that she was prepared to – and in fact did – work for the transferee and that this was inconsistent with a valid objection. As a result, the automatic transfer principle applied to transfer her employment to the transferee.

It might have been thought that in view of the legal consequences that flow from an objection to the transfer, the transferor would be under some obligation to explain the situation to the employee. But, as we see below, there is no such obligation. This means that the 'substantial change to working conditions' exception in Reg 4(9), which basically requires the employee to have good cause for objecting to the transfer, is of major importance in determining the employee's legal position if he or she chooses not to transfer to the transferee. The scope of this exception is discussed below.

2.125 Objection on basis of 'substantial change to working conditions'

As we have seen in the discussion on 'Position under the Acquired Rights Directive' above, the ECJ in Merckx and anor v Ford Motors Co (Belgium) SA 1997 ICR 352, ECJ, required Article 3.1 of the Directive to be read as making the transferor responsible for termination of an employee's contract of employment if the latter has objected to the transfer by reason of the fact that it would entail a substantial and detrimental change being made to his or her working conditions. In Europièces SA v Sanders 2001 1 CMLR 25, ECJ, the European Court subsequently made it clear that it was for the national courts to decide whether the working conditions proposed by the transferee involved or would involve a substantial change for this purpose.

152

The Merckx ruling is transposed into UK national law by what is now Reg 4(9) and (11) of the 2006 Regulations. As explained above, these provide that where the relevant transfer involves or would involve a substantial change in working conditions to the material detriment of an employee employed by the transferor, the employee may treat the contract of employment as having been terminated, and the employee shall be treated for any purpose as having been dismissed by the transferor – Reg 4(9). This right is without prejudice to any right of an employee arising apart from the Regulations to terminate his contract of employment without notice in acceptance of a repudiatory breach of contract by his employer – 4(11).

Although the parameters of what is meant by 'substantial change to working **2.126** conditions' in this context are not certain, what is nonetheless clear is that the phrase potentially extends to changes to non-contractual terms and conditions and may even cover the environmental or moral concerns of the employee. Certainly, in enacting the new Regulations, the Government took the view that the recasting of these provisions had made it clearer than under the previous Regulations that the substantial change to working conditions to the employee's material detriment does not necessarily have to be so serious as to amount to a repudiatory breach of contract such as to found a classic case of constructive dismissal. This point is discussed in greater detail in Chapter 4.

It is important to observe that Reg 4(9) includes the rider that a substantial change to working conditions must be to the employee's 'material' detriment. Although the employee may object to the transfer for any reason he or she wishes, he or she will only be entitled to rely on the freestanding right to terminate the contract of employment by reason of a substantial change to working conditions falling short of a repudiatory breach if it is shown not just that such a change has been or will be made but also that it is to the employee's material detriment. The equivalent provision under the 1981 Regulations merely spoke of 'where a substantial change is made in [the employee's] working conditions to his detriment'. The addition of the word 'material' was presumably intended to import an element of objectivity into the question of whether a substantial change has been made to the employee's working conditions. Although the word 'substantial' already serves to rule out merely minor or trivial changes, the fact that proven substantial changes have also to be shown to be to the employee's material detriment suggests that the bar has been raised somewhat by the 2006 Regulations. Apart from that, the issue of whether the employee has suffered a material detriment will no doubt be a question of fact for the tribunal to decide having regard to the relevant circumstances of the case.

Is change of employer's identity a 'substantive change'? Another alteration **2.127** made to the 'objection' provisions by the TUPE Regulations 2006 (compared to the position under the predecessor Regulations) concerns the provision

153

dealing with a substantive change made to working conditions. The 1981 Regulations contained a stipulation at Reg 5(5) that a mere change in the identity of the employer could not constitute a substantial change in working conditions to the employee's detriment, unless the employee could show that it was a significant change and was to his detriment. This stipulation does not find its way into the 2006 Regulations. One view might be that the role of the words 'significant change' in Reg 5(5) of the 1981 Regulations is now taken up by the requirement for there to be a 'material' detriment in Reg 4(9) of the 2006 Regulations.

It may be the case, therefore, that a simple change in the identity of the employer will continue to give employees the right to refuse to transfer and bring a claim in the same circumstances, albeit via differently drafted provisions. This prospect may be of particular significance, for example, in situations where a function of a large internationally recognised company is contracted out to a small unknown contractor: on the one hand, it might well be argued that an employee transferring in such circumstances would suffer a loss in status that could prejudice him or her in the job market in the future, and that this would constitute a substantial change in working conditions that is materially detrimental. On the other hand, it could be contended that a mere perception of a loss in status is not a 'material' detriment. The courts' view as to which approach is correct could have a significant impact on the ability of large companies to contract out in this manner, especially where labour-intensive functions are concerned: if all the employees concerned are able to object to the transfer and seek compensation, the transfer will not be able to go ahead because there will be no organised grouping of employees to transfer.

2.128 Care must be taken in situations where the transfer involves a change in location and this is said to be the substantial and materially detrimental change: if the employee has a mobility clause in his or her contract requiring him or her to work at various locations, a substantial detrimental change may not exist, and any resignation will be without compensation. The DTI Guide simply says that what might constitute a substantial change in working conditions 'will be a matter for the courts and the tribunals to determine in the light of the circumstances of each case. What might be a trivial change in one setting might constitute a substantial change in another. However, a major relocation of the workplace which makes it difficult or much more expensive for an employee to transfer, or the withdrawal of a right to a tenured post, is likely to fall within this definition.'

2.129 **Dismissal by 'employer'.** Regulation 4(9) states that where there is a substantial change in working conditions to the material detriment of the employee, 'such an employee may treat the contract of employment as having been terminated by the employer'. Similarly, the constructive dismissal provision of Reg 4(11) refers to a repudiatory breach of contract 'by the employer'. It is significant that neither regulation specifies whether the employer in question is the transferor or the transferee. This appears to be deliberate: it allows for the fact that the employee's decision to terminate the contract in either situation might occur before the transfer or after it. In other words, an employee can resign and claim that he or she has suffered a materially detrimental change to working conditions while still employed by the transferor or after the transfer has occurred when, technically, the employee has become employed by the transferee.

The same is true in the case of a resignation precipitated by a repudiatory breach of contract. If the breach and resignation occur before the transfer, then the relevant employer against whom the employee would bring a claim of constructive dismissal is the transferor. In some circumstances, however, liability for unfair dismissal will pass to the transferee even though the constructive dismissal was an act done by the transferor. If the reason for the constructive dismissal is transfer-connected but not for an ETO reason within the meaning of Reg 7(1), then the employee will be deemed to have been employed immediately before the transfer, and liability for his or her unfair dismissal will pass to the transferee by virtue of Reg 4(2) – see 'Employed "immediately before" transfer' above. If the transfer is not transfer-connected, or is for an ETO reason, then, provided the contract is terminated by the employee resigning prior to the transfer, liability will remain with the transferor. Where the repudiatory breach and resignation in response to it occurs after the transfer, then the 'employer' in question for the purposes of Reg 4(11) would be the transferee.

Meaning of 'objection'   2.130
Unfortunately there is no definition in the 2006 Regulations to clarify precisely what conduct will qualify as raising an objection. Reg 4(7) simply states that there will be no transfer of an employee's contract where that employee informs the transferor or the transferee that he objects to the transfer. Cases decided under the 1981 Regulations will continue to be applicable, however, and it has been held that there is a valid objection to the transfer where there is a refusal to give consent, and that refusal is communicated to either the transferor or the transferee in advance of the transfer – Hay v George Hanson (Building Contractors) Ltd 1996 IRLR 427, EAT.

In the Hay case the employee argued that he had not objected to the transfer, and that his employment had therefore automatically transferred to the transferee. An employment tribunal held otherwise. It found that the employee had taken all possible steps within his capacity to resist the transfer. For example, he had sought alternative employment with the transferor, without success, and after the transfer had continued to seek through his union a redundancy package from the transferor. At one stage the transferee had written to the employee informing him that in its opinion his behaviour meant that he was objecting to the transfer, but received no reply from either him or his union.

155

On appeal, the EAT upheld the tribunal's decision. It stated that the word 'object' in the context of what was then Reg 5(4A) of the 1981 Regulations means a refusal to consent to the transfer, and that such a state of mind does not amount to an effective objection unless and until it is conveyed to the transferor or the transferee. That said, objection could be imparted by either word or deed, or by both. In each case, it would be a question of fact whether the employee's state of mind amounted to a refusal to consent to the transfer and whether that state of mind was in fact brought to the attention of the transferor or transferee prior to the transfer.

2.131 The wording of old Reg 5(4A) (which remains unchanged in new Reg 4(7)) was criticised by the EAT in Hay. It pointed out that, taken in its general context, the word 'object' could reflect a state of mind short of refusal, and that it was obvious that all manner of means might be used whereby information might be conveyed to the intended recipient. Furthermore, the regulation was silent as to the timing of the objection, and nor was there a requirement that any employee objecting to the transfer should be informed of the consequences of his objection by the transferor. Nevertheless, the EAT felt able to construe Reg 5(4A) in accordance with what it perceived to be the general scheme of the relevant provisions as a whole, which was to protect the right of an employee not to be transferred to another employer against his or her will. Thus, it concluded that the word 'object' effectively means a 'refusal to accept' the transfer, and that it is necessary for that refusal to be conveyed to the transferor or the transferee by either word or deed.

Where an objection is clearly to the disadvantage of the employee – as it was in the Hay case – it might have been thought that it would take unequivocal evidence to persuade a tribunal that the employee had objected to being transferred. It cannot have been the aim of the ECJ in the Katsikas ruling to provide employers with a means of evading the purpose of the Directive. Even without the assistance of a purposive interpretation, however, the EAT's approach is arguably open to question. Its method of ascertaining whether an employee has objected seems to be a matter of finding out whether the employee's words or deeds revealed a withholding of consent, and then to determine whether or not that state of mind was in some way or other transmitted to either of the relevant parties. But what Reg 4(7) actually provides for is that the employee's contract will not transfer if the employee 'informs the transferor or the transferee that he objects'. It might be contended that those words, on their plain and ordinary meaning, require some kind of formal and unambiguous notification to the existing employer or the transferee: they do not appear to leave room for an objection to be inferred solely from an employee's actions, which may be a reflection of genuine misgivings about a pending transfer – a state of affairs that arguably existed in the Hay case – even if those misgivings are communicated to the relevant parties.

A more generous approach, so far as employees' rights are concerned, was **2.132** taken in Euro-Die (UK) Ltd v Skidmore and anor EAT 1158/98. In that case, the employee was anxious about his employment protection rights in the event that his employment was terminated by the transferee, and therefore refused to work for the new employer without first receiving assurances from the transferor that his continuity of employment would be protected. When these were not forthcoming, he decided not to present himself for work after the transfer and claimed unfair constructive dismissal, against both the transferor and the transferee. An employment tribunal found that the employee had been constructively dismissed by the transferor and that the transfer was the principal reason for his dismissal. The dismissal was therefore automatically unfair under what is now Reg 7(1) of TUPE 2006. Liability for the dismissal, however, passed to the transferee by virtue of what is now Reg 4(1). On the transferee's appeal, the EAT ruled that the transferor's failure to give an assurance in respect of a matter as crucial as the protection of the employee's continuity of employment amounted to a fundamental breach of the implied term of trust and confidence and agreed with the tribunal that the resulting constructive dismissal was automatically unfair. Most interestingly, for present purposes, the EAT rejected the transferee's contention that, by raising his concerns about the preservation of his continuity of employment, the employee had objected to becoming employed by the transferee for the purposes of Reg 5(4A) (now Reg 4(7)) so as to prevent the automatic transfer of his contract. Since it was clear that the employee had no absolute objection to working for the new employer but had simply declined to do so unless he was given an assurance about his continuity, Reg 5(4A) did not apply to prevent the automatic transfer of his contract or to prevent the transferee being liable for the constructive dismissal of the employee under Reg 5(2) (now Reg 4(2)).

What is clear is that there is no requirement that an employee's refusal to consent to the transfer be informed: the only requirement is that the refusal be clearly communicated. In Ladies' Health and Fitness Club Ltd v Eastmond and ors EAT 0094/03 an employment tribunal had found that the employees' objection to the transfer had not been properly informed, and could not therefore amount to an effective objection for the purposes of the Regulations. The EAT disagreed. After considering a petition signed by the employees that had not been shown to the tribunal, it remitted the question of whether or not there had been an objection to the tribunal for reconsideration, saying: 'It appears to us clear that if there is an objection within the Regulation, the fact that it may be high-handed, ignorant, over-reactive or simply misconceived would not affect the position, although... it might be that on analysis what occurred did not amount to an objection if someone in fact does not know what they are doing.' This latter qualification may be crucial where an employee does not understand the effect of a formal objection in circumstances where the transfer does not involve any significant change in working conditions that is

157

materially to his or her detriment. An employee may wish to voice opposition to a transfer while ultimately feeling powerless to resist it, and may make empty threats without realising that they may technically be resigning. Eastmond suggests that such employees may still transfer.

2.133 In Senior Heat Treatment Ltd v Bell and ors 1997 IRLR 614, EAT, employees were held not to have objected to becoming employed by the transferee in circumstances where they accepted the transferor's option of 'opting out' of the transfer of the business in return for receiving severance packages. Since the employees had, before the date of the transfer, entered into contracts of employment with the transferee to take effect immediately after the transfer, the EAT held that it had been open to the employment tribunal to find that, notwithstanding their agreement to 'opt out' of the transfer, they had not objected to it. In consequence, their contracts of employment were automatically transferred to the transferee and their continuity of employment remained unbroken for the purposes of claiming redundancy payments and compensation for unfair dismissal against the transferee. This case demonstrates that the operation of Reg 4(1) of the TUPE Regulations cannot be avoided by persuading an employee to opt out of the Regulations, unless the decision to opt out constitutes a genuine objection to the transfer within the meaning of Reg 4(7). In this regard, care will have to be taken when drafting compromise agreements – discussed in Chapter 10, 'Practical aspects of transfers', under 'Avoidance of TUPE provisions – waiver of rights'. The EAT sensibly pointed out that in the Senior Heat case the employees clearly had no objection to the transfer since they had in fact agreed to go and work for the transferee.

A similar conclusion was reached by the EAT in Capita Health Solutions Ltd v McLean and anor 2008 IRLR 595, EAT (discussed in detail under 'Timing of the objection' above). Indeed, in that case, it was clear that the employee did have marked objections going to the change in the identity of the employer and voiced these by raising grievance and giving notice of resignation. However, what scuppered her case that she had 'objected' to the transfer within the strict terms of Reg 4(7), was – according to the EAT – that she agreed to go to work for the transferee under a 'secondment' arrangement during the six weeks she was working out her notice.

2.134 **Remedies available to an objecting employee**
The options available to an employee who does not wish to transfer to the transferee on a relevant transfer are essentially these:

• to terminate the contract with notice on the ground that a substantial change has been (or will be) made to working conditions to his or her material detriment

158

- to resign (with or without notice) on the ground that the employer has repudiated the contract in circumstances entitling the employee to terminate the contract without notice by reason of the employer's conduct

- to otherwise object to the transfer.

Under the first option, the employee will be regarded as having been dismissed by the transferor – Reg 4(9). Under the second option, the employee – assuming a repudiatory breach has occurred – will be regarded as having been constructively dismissed – Reg 4(11). In both these cases, subject to what is said below, the employee will be entitled to claim unfair dismissal provided he or she has sufficient qualifying service to do so. Under the third option, although the Regulations provide that the contract will thus be terminated, the employee will not be treated as having been dismissed by the transferor for any purpose (including claiming unfair dismissal) – Reg 4(7) and (8).

While the provisions of Reg 4(7)–(9) and (11) clearly allow an employee to **2.135** elect to resign rather than transfer to the transferee, such a decision may prove to be a high-risk strategy. Unless the employee can be confident either that the transfer will involve a substantial change in working conditions that is materially to his or her detriment, or else that he or she has grounds for claiming constructive dismissal, then the termination of his or her contract will not be treated 'for any purpose' as a dismissal by the transferor. Thus, any claim for unfair dismissal, constructive dismissal or a contractual or statutory redundancy payment will be ruled out.

Where the transfer will only involve a change in identity of the employer, this change in itself will have to amount to a substantial change in working conditions that is materially detrimental (see above) before any claim will be possible. In most cases, it seems, the choice will be to either work for the transferee or to resign and leave empty-handed.

Unfair dismissal. Assuming that the employee is able to show that the transfer **2.136** involves (or will involve) a substantial change in working conditions to his or her material detriment, then he or she may terminate the contract. In that case, as made clear by Reg 4(9), the termination will be deemed to be a dismissal by the transferor. But what kind of 'dismissal' is it? In Humphreys v University of Oxford and anor 2000 ICR 405, CA (see under 'Position under TUPE Regulations' above), the Court of Appeal assumed that it would be a constructive dismissal, thus conferring upon the employee the right to claim unfair dismissal against the transferor on that basis. However, this case was decided when the relevant provision as contained in the 1981 Regulations referred to 'the right of an employee arising apart from these Regulations to terminate his contract of employment without notice if a substantial change is made in his working conditions to his detriment'. It was therefore apparent that only changes amounting to a repudiatory breach of contract entitling the employee to resign

159

without notice could comprise a 'substantial change to working conditions'. As we have seen, however, the Regulations have been reformulated to allow employees to terminate their contracts as a result of a change of this kind even if the change is not so fundamental as to amount to a repudiatory breach of contract.

The problem is that, in order to claim unfair dismissal, the employee has to show that he or she has been 'dismissed' within the meaning of S.95(1) ERA. The general assumption has been that a dismissal for the purposes of Reg 4(9) equates to a constructive dismissal under S.95(1)(c) ERA, which is defined as occurring where 'the employee terminates the contract under which he is employed… in circumstances in which he is entitled to terminate it without notice by reason of the employer's conduct'. The difficulty here is that the deemed dismissal of an employee who terminates the contract because the employer has substantially changed his or her working conditions within the meaning of Reg 4(9) will not fall within the S.95(1)(c) category of dismissal if the change in question falls short of being a repudiatory breach of contract. That is because anything less than a repudiatory breach will not comprise a circumstance in which the employee 'is entitled to terminate [the contract] without notice'. For rather complex reasons – fully set out in Chapter 4 under 'Material detriment dismissals' – we submit that the better view is that dismissal in the circumstances described in Reg 4(9) should be regarded as an express dismissal by the employer as defined by S.95(1)(a) ERA. If correct, this at least establishes a cogent basis for a 'dismissal' upon which a claim of unfair dismissal can be founded.

2.137 Another reason why it is important to establish the precise nature of a Reg 4(9) dismissal is that different statutory dispute resolution procedures may apply depending on whether the dismissal is constructive or express. Again, this matter is discussed in Chapter 4.

Whether the dismissal is express or constructive, it is of course insufficient simply to establish that there is a dismissal to succeed in a claim of unfair dismissal: the dismissal in question must also be shown to have been unfair. It may be that a Reg 4(9) dismissal is potentially fair as being for an 'economic, technical or organisational reason entailing a change in the workforce' (ETO) within the meaning of Reg 7(2), though there are dangers here if the transferor seeks to rely on or anticipate a potential ETO reason that the transferee might have for dismissal once the transfer has occurred – see Chapter 4. In any event, the employee would still need to show that dismissal was not reasonable in all the circumstances for the purposes of S.98(4) ERA. Relevant factors in that determination would include, for example, an absence of proper consultation, or a failure to offer the employee suitable alternative employment that is available.

2.138 **Constructive dismissal on other grounds.** Regulation 4(11) states that nothing in Reg 4(1), (7), (8) and (9) prejudices the employee's right, arising apart from the Regulations, simply to resign in response to his employer's repudiatory breach. This, as has previously been mentioned, preserves a right to claim constructive dismissal, and indicates that the grounds for constructive dismissal claims may be based on something other than where a substantial change in working conditions is made to the employee's material detriment. The test of constructive dismissal is well established. The focus is on the employer's conduct that has provoked the employee to resign, which must be shown either to constitute a significant breach going to the root of the contract or exhibit an intention no longer to be bound by an essential term of the contract, and in either case must be serious enough to entitle the employee to resign without notice – Western Excavating (ECC) Ltd v Sharp 1978 ICR 221, CA. Any employee who resigns by reason of such conduct will be regarded as having been dismissed within the meaning of S.95(1)(c) ERA – see above. This will lay the foundation for a claim of unfair dismissal or, for that matter, breach of contract. In the case of an unfair dismissal claim, the dismissal will have to be shown to have been unfair for liability to arise.

Anticipatory breach of contract by transferee. An interesting question arises **2.139** whether an employee can rely on Reg 4(9) or Reg 4(11) to resign prior to the transfer in anticipation of a detrimental change being made to his or her working conditions or a repudiatory breach of contract by the transferee. If so, then it would appear from the Court of Appeal's decision in Humphreys v University of Oxford and anor 2000 ICR 405, CA, that the transferor will be left with residual liability for the dismissal regardless of whether the effective date of termination occurs before or after the transfer. In that case the Court accepted that, although the language of what was then Reg 5(5) was more appropriate to a case where an employee treats him or herself as dismissed after a transfer once a threatened change has become reality, Reg 5(5) had to be interpreted to apply also where the employee objects because a proposed transfer would result in such a change. The Court also ruled that an employee's objection to the transfer of his or her employment to the transferee had the effect of preventing his or her contract of employment from automatically passing to the transferee under what is now Reg 4(1). Instead, the employee's contract with the transferor terminated immediately upon the transfer. And since, in those circumstances, the transferee never becomes his or her employer, the employee had no right to claim against the transferee in respect of the termination. Rather, it is the transferor who is left with residual liability for any unfair dismissal.

There is no reason to suppose that the Court of Appeal's reasoning with regard to the employee's ability to terminate the contract by reason of an anticipatory change to working conditions or a repudiatory breach by the employer would not continue to apply now that the two elements of Reg 5(5) have been separated into two different provisions (i.e. Reg 4(7) and (11)). However, there is greater ground for caution regarding the Court's position on whether it is the

161

transferor or the transferee who is liable for any resulting unfair dismissal. These matters are considered in further detail in Chapter 4 under 'Constructive dismissals'.

2.140 **Redundancy payment.** If an employee's objection and subsequent resignation on account of a substantive change being made to his or her contract constitutes an ETO reason that satisfies the statutory definition of 'redundancy', then provided that no suitable alternative employment is available with the transferor, the employee will be redundant and ought to be able to claim a statutory redundancy payment. This position was confirmed by the EAT in Gorictree Ltd v Jenkinson 1985 ICR 51, EAT. In this regard, Reg 7(3)(b) stipulates that where an ETO reason for dismissal is made out, the dismissal will be regarded as having been by reason of redundancy if the statutory test for redundancy as set out in S.98(2)(c) ERA applies, or otherwise for a 'substantial reason of a kind such as to justify the dismissal of an employee holding the position which that employee held' within the meaning of S.98(1)(b) ERA.

2.141 **Limitation on claiming notice pay.** Regulation 4(10) adds a new provision not present in the 1981 Regulations. This specifies that 'no damages shall be payable by an employer as a result of a dismissal falling within paragraph (9) in respect of any failure by the employer to pay wages to an employee in respect of a notice period which the employee has failed to work'. This makes it clear that even where an employee objects to the transfer because it will involve a significant change in working conditions that is materially detrimental (thereby in most cases representing an anticipatory repudiatory breach of contract), no notice pay claim will be possible: the employee is required to work out his or her notice period even though under normal circumstances he or she would be entitled to resign immediately and obtain notice pay as part of any claim. However, since working for the transferor will have to cease on the date of the transfer, a question mark is raised over whether the transferor will be obliged to continue paying the employee for any period of notice that cannot actually be worked owing to the fact that the contract is terminated by the transfer before the notice period expires. What happens if the transferor stops paying the employee? For the same reason, it is also possible that notice pay will be available when a transferor dispenses with the employee's services immediately upon an objection being made, since the employee will again be unable to work out his or her notice period through no fault of his or her own.

2.142 **Injunctions.** The general rule on injunctions is that a court will not force the parties to a contract of employment to work together once it has been breached. This is known as the rule against 'specific performance'. However, before the right to object to the automatic transfer of an employee's contract was accepted, the TUPE Regulations had precisely the same effect as an order for specific performance in that they compelled the employees concerned to work for a particular transferee. This naturally raised the question of whether employees could obtain an injunction to prevent the transfer from taking place and thus putting them in that position. In Newns v British Airways plc 1992 IRLR 575, CA, this issue was considered by the Court of Appeal. The Court began by noting that what is now Reg 4 changed the common law position whereby an employer could not transfer an employee to another employer without the employee's consent and instead provided for a statutory novation of the employee's contract. Thus, the effect of Reg 5 was that the transfer of an undertaking no longer constituted a repudiatory breach of contract. As there was no breach, the Court concluded that an employee was not entitled to an injunction to restrain the transfer. It should be noted that this position is subject to the qualification that where the transfer involves a significant change in the employee's working arrangements which is to his detriment – such as a change in location where there is no clause in the contract requiring mobility – the transfer will constitute a repudiatory breach enabling the employee to resign and claim constructive dismissal. Whether an injunction to restrain a transfer is available in such circumstances is not clear.

The Court did, however, leave open the possibility that an injunction might be granted where it was demonstrated that the employer had acted – or would act – in breach of the general duty of good faith in transferring the employee. As there are no authorities on the point, it remains to be seen what would constitute a breach of good faith in this context.

Is employee's knowledge of transfer necessary?   2.143

Regulation 4(1) makes no reference to an employee's knowledge (or otherwise) of a transfer and contains no requirement that notice of the transfer be given to employees. In view of this, there remains some uncertainty as to the interesting question of whether an employee's contract of employment may be transferred along with his or her employer's business without his or her knowledge. Does a lack of knowledge fatally undermine the employee's right to be able to object to the transfer?

This question was first raised in Photostatic Copiers (Southern) Ltd v Okuda and Japan Office Equipment Ltd (in liquidation) 1995 IRLR 11, EAT. In that case the employee claimed not to have received a memorandum from his employer, the transferor, to the effect that a TUPE transfer was about to occur and his employment would henceforth be transferred to the transferee. The EAT upheld an employment tribunal's decision that the automatic transfer of a contract of employment under what is now Reg 4(1) of TUPE 2006 does not take effect unless the employee is given notice of the transfer and of the identity of the transferee. As a result, the employee remained employed by the transferor until he was dismissed by it after the transfer had occurred.

Two later decisions of the EAT took the opposite view and, in so doing, **2.144** expressly declined to follow the Photostatic Copiers decision. In Secretary of

163

State for Trade and Industry v Cook and ors 1997 ICR 288, EAT, the Appeal Tribunal held that the decision in Photostatic Copiers was inconsistent with the purpose of the EU Acquired Rights Directive and should not be followed in future by tribunals. There was no precondition that a TUPE transfer could only be effective if the employee knew of the transfer and the identity of the transferee. If there were such a requirement, unscrupulous employers would simply refuse to disclose what was happening, the EAT said. Therefore, if it were good law that the Regulations could only have effect if employees have the requisite knowledge, the very protection that the Directive and Regulations are designed to provide would be significantly undermined.

The EAT further took the view that there is no need to import such a precondition into the Regulations. An employee who is misled will not suffer any disadvantage, the EAT said. In relation to an employee dismissed immediately before the transfer, liabilities pass, as a matter of law, to the transferee. In relation to an employee who would have objected to being transferred had he known what was happening, he has lost nothing of value.

2.145 The accuracy of this latter proposition must be doubted. It is not necessarily true that an employee who is transferred without his knowledge, and who would have objected had he or she been aware of the transfer, has lost nothing of value. In many cases there will be a right to object to the transfer and claim compensation. Nonetheless, a differently constituted EAT took the same view in MRS Environmental Services Ltd v Dyke and anor EAT 93/96. In that case a local authority employed a groundsman whose work was contracted out to a private company. That company later lost the contract, and told the groundsman that his employment would transfer to the new contractor, whose identity it did not know. The contractor, however, did not contact the groundsman, who claimed that he had been unfairly dismissed. The EAT held that, under the 1981 Regulations, statutory novation took effect regardless of whether the parties had consented or knew each other's identities. The earlier decision in Photostatic Copiers could not be followed. The groundsman's contract of employment was therefore deemed by what is now Reg 4(1) to have transferred automatically to the new contractor, and he was, under what is now Reg 7(1), to be treated as having been unfairly dismissed. All obligations which the company had owed to him came to an end when the transfer was deemed to have taken place, and the transferor was not therefore liable, liability having passed to the transferee.

The question of the extent to which an employee has to be made aware of a transfer in order to be in a position to object to it arose for consideration in the House of Lords' decision in Celtec Ltd v Astley and ors 2006 ICR 992, HL. Other aspects of this case, including its particular facts, have been extensively discussed earlier in this chapter in the section on 'Requirement to be employed "immediately before" transfer'. In addressing the issue of knowledge of the transfer, their Lordships began by pointing out that the basic proposition that the right to automatic transfer of employment under Article 3.1 of the Directive may not be made subject to the consent of either the transferor or transferee nor of the employees themselves is subject to a single exception. This is that it is open to an employee, whose contract of employment would otherwise be transferred automatically on the date of the transfer, to withdraw from this arrangement by declining to enter the employment of the transferee. Application of that exception depends, first, on the employee being in a position to choose whether or not to enter the employment of the transferee after the date of the transfer and, secondly, on the employee in fact exercising that choice by deciding of his or her own free will not to do so.

The House of Lords proceeded to hold that the exception did not apply in the **2.146** instant case because, although the employees were in a position on or after the date of the transfer to choose of their own free will not to work for the transferee, they did not do so. In 1990, the employees had agreed to be seconded from their positions as civil servants with the Department of Education to a newly created Training and Enterprise Council (TEC). In 1993, when given the choice, the particular claimants elected to become employed by the TEC rather than return to work for the DoE. A transfer was found to have occurred back in 1990 when the secondment arrangement was first put in place. On this basis, their Lordships concluded that the claimants' employment had transferred to the TEC at that time because they continued to do the same jobs after the transfer of the undertaking to the TEC, albeit in the belief that they remained in the employment of the Civil Service. In their Lordships' view, the exception to the automatic transfer rule did not work the other way round, so as to give effect to an employee's wish to remain in the employment of the transferor while continuing to be employed in the unit to which he has been assigned after its transfer to the transferee. The inevitable conclusion in the particular case, therefore, was that the claimants' contracts of employment had been transferred automatically to the transferee, with continuity of employment, on the date of the transfer.

There is no doubt that the House of Lords' decision is problematic in some ways, in that it suggests that employees, whom the transfer rules are meant to protect, could find themselves employed by the transferee without even realising it and possibly without their informed consent. In the Celtec case, it was very much in the employees' interests for the House of Lords to hold that they had in fact been transferred, as otherwise they would have lost their accrued employment rights with the transferor. But there could be cases in the future where the application of the principle set out by the House of Lords could work against an employee who in effect finds him or herself working for a new employer without realising that this is the case. It remains to be seen what, if anything, could be done to ameliorate the position of employees in this situation.

— **165**

2.147 It should be remembered that the 2006 Regulations impose separate obligations to inform and consult about any proposed transfer. Reg 13(2) imposes an obligation to inform and consult representatives of any affected employees about any proposed transfer. Reg 13(10) and (11) provide that where there are no employee representatives to consult, there is a duty to invite elections, and where no such invitation is taken up within a reasonable time, the duty is to provide the relevant information to the affected employees individually. Failure to comply with consultation requirements will result in liability to pay compensation of up to 13 weeks' pay to each employee under Reg 15, and, by virtue of Reg 15(9), transferee and transferor will be jointly and severally liable for the payment of any such compensation (although the transferee may have a remedy against the transferor in respect of any failure to provide adequate 'employee liability information' in advance of the transfer). These provisions are discussed in detail in Chapter 8.

As a result of these duties, in most cases employees will be aware of an impending transfer, and the problem of some employees potentially losing their right to object will not therefore arise. It might be argued that a complete failure to inform and consult by the transferor amounts to a breach of mutual trust and confidence, which would entitle the employee who would otherwise have objected to resign and claim constructive dismissal against the transferee (the liability arguably created by the transferor's breach having been transferred by operation of Reg 4(2)). This situation would press transferees to require indemnities against any such liability, which in turn would effectively pass liability back to the transferor for its failure.

2.148 Employees retained by transferor

Subject to the right to object to the transfer (see above), the contract of any person employed in and assigned to the undertaking at the moment of its transfer automatically passes over to the transferee under Reg 4(1). However, where the transferor and the transferee agree that certain staff employed in the undertaking to be transferred are to remain in the employment of the transferor, the question arises as to whether Reg 4(1) still applies to transfer the contracts of those employees. The general view that has emerged from the cases (although they are not consistent) is that the application of Reg 4(1) can only be avoided where there is also a contractual arrangement to that effect between the transferor and the employees concerned before the transfer takes place.

The cases below (all of which were decided under the 1981 Regulations) illustrate the different ways in which the courts have tackled the issue of whether the employment of an employee retained by the transferor after a relevant transfer is automatically transferred to the transferee:

- **Direct Radiators Ltd v Howse and anor** EAT 130/86: H was employed by S as a bookkeeper in S's business. That business was sold to D Ltd on 28 February 1985. Before the transfer, D Ltd had made it clear that it did not require H's services. S retained H from 28 February to 5 April 1985 to help with clerical and bookkeeping work relevant to the collection of outstanding business debts owed to him. She was then dismissed and claimed a redundancy payment from D Ltd. A tribunal upheld her claim, finding that the transferee, D Ltd, had become H's contractual employer liable in respect of her contract by virtue of Reg 5(1) of TUPE 1981. As a result, it was liable to pay H a redundancy payment. On appeal to the EAT, D Ltd argued that Reg 5 could not apply because H had been retained after the transfer under a contract of employment with S and, therefore, she was not at the time of the transfer working under a contract that 'would otherwise have been terminated' by reason of the transfer for the purposes of Reg 5(1). The EAT accepted that if the relationship between S and H after February 28 was a contractual one, then D Ltd's argument was well founded. However, the tribunal had failed to make a clear finding as to whether H was still working for S under an employment contract after the transfer and so remitted the case for determination on that point

- **Visionhire Consumer Electronics Ltd t/a Visionhire v Easton** EAT 20/87: an employee was offered a new contract with the transferee which was to take effect a week after the transfer. In the meantime, the employee continued working for the transferor. The EAT rejected the transferee's argument that, because the employee had been retained by the transferor, Reg 5 did not effect the automatic transfer of his employment contract since it was not one which would 'otherwise have been terminated by the transfer'. Mr Justice Popplewell commented that: 'Apart from the fact that [the transferee's argument] would, in the view of the industrial members, cause immense difficulty as a matter of practice in industry and lead to grave disadvantages for the workforce, it does not in our view accord with what Reg 5 says... If it is intended to retain part of the staff after a transfer then that would have to be done by a novation of contract between the transferor and the employee before the transfer'

- **A and G Tuck Ltd v Bartlett and A and G Tuck (Slough) Ltd** 1994 IRLR 162, EAT: B had worked as a production manager for S since 1966. In 1983 S took over another company, H. From 1989 onwards, B worked for both companies but remained an employee of S throughout. On 10 August 1992, B discovered that S had been sold to C while he was on holiday. B's name was not on the list of employees who were transferred to C, but his employer asked him to assist C in the running of S for two weeks, which he did. On 12 August C invited B to work for him; an arrangement that S supported. C subsequently dismissed B and he complained that his dismissal was unfair. The EAT rejected the argument that Reg 5(1) applied to transfer

167

B's contract to the transferee on the basis that, because B was kept on by the transferor, he was not in the position where his contract 'would otherwise have been terminated by the transfer'.

2.149 In reality, the claimant in the last-mentioned case did transfer to the transferee, even though he was not recognised as being formally employed by it until two weeks after the transfer. The ruling that the automatic transfer of employment rule did not apply in his case in fact made little difference given that his dismissal occurred within a sufficiently short period of the transfer date such that his continuity of employment remained intact. However, given that there was no express novation of the employee's contract with the transferor, that he did go to work for the transferee, and that the relevant transfer happened without his knowledge, one wonders whether the same conclusion that the employee's employment did not automatically transfer to the transferee would be reached were a case on similar facts to arise now. It could be argued that this is precisely the kind of situation in which the TUPE Regulations were intended to intervene and transfer the contract of employment automatically. In finding otherwise, the EAT's judgment would appear to be inconsistent with the House of Lords' decision in Celtec (discussed above) – and particularly the view expressed in that case that it is not open to an employee to go to work for the transferee and yet argue that he or she remains employed by the transferor once the transfer takes place.

2.150 It is submitted that, in general, the analysis of the EAT in the case below is the best way of approaching the operation of Reg 4(1) in a case where an employee is retained by the transferor after the transfer. The Appeal Tribunal concluded that the operation of the 'automatic transfer of employment' rule could only be avoided in such a situation by an express agreement with the employees concerned:

- **Sunley Turriff Holdings Ltd v Thomson and ors** 1995 IRLR 184, EAT: T was employed by LC to work as company secretary and chief accountant of LC and LC(S), two subsidiaries of a group. Receivers were appointed to the group, who sold LC(S) to STH. T was not included in the list of employees to be transferred to STH; he was told that he was to remain employed by LC. T continued to work for the receivers until they made him redundant shortly after the transfer. T claimed a redundancy payment from STH, the transferee, on the basis that he was employed in the undertaking which had been transferred to it. The tribunal found that there had been a transfer to which the Regulations applied and that T was employed in the part transferred, but STH appealed to the EAT against that finding. STH argued that T's employment had not automatically transferred to it because his employment with LC had continued after the date of the transfer. The EAT decided that if an employee continues to work for a transferor after a transfer which, under the Regulations, legally has the effect of transferring his or her employment to the transferee, then that continued employment must be as a result of a new agreement, or a variation of the previous agreement, between the transferor and the employee. While there was a great deal of uncertainty about T's position, Reg 5, in the EAT's view, was imperative in its terms and must apply whatever misunderstandings there may have been. The EAT considered that it would be contrary to the objectives of the Regulations to allow uncertainty to prejudice the position of employees to whom they applied. The receivers had been mistaken in their view that T's contract continued with LC and the EAT upheld the tribunal's finding that T had done nothing which might suggest that he had agreed to continue in the employment of LC. T, therefore, succeeded in his claim against STH.

In reaching its conclusion, the EAT considered the Direct Radiators decision **2.151** (above) and commented that that case must have been decided on the assumption that something had occurred following the transfer to terminate the employment with the transferee brought about by the Regulations and to bring into existence the new employment with the transferor. On this basis, the EAT reasoned that its decision in the instant case was not inconsistent with the decision in Direct Radiators.

The Sunley Turriff case makes it clear that a mistaken belief that the Regulations do not apply to a particular employee cannot defeat the principle of the automatic transfer of contracts of employment under the Regulations. The EAT also stated that there may be circumstances in which it would be possible to infer that an employee who continues in the transferor's employment may be taken to have agreed to do so. However, it seems that when there is confusion or misunderstanding, the employee who continues to work for the transferor is unlikely to jeopardise his or her position in relation to the application of the Regulations.

Problems of secondment arrangements   2.152

The decision of the House of Lords in Celtec Ltd v Astley and ors 2006 ICR 992, HL, has been extensively discussed elsewhere in this chapter. However, its implications for the continued use of secondment arrangements have yet to be analysed in any depth. Such arrangements are especially widely used by public sector employers as part of the Public Finance Initiative (PFI) under which public services are outsourced to private sector contractors. So, for example, under the 'Retention of Employment model' (REM) deployed across the National Health Service following any outsourcing of cleaning, catering, laundry, portering and security services, NHS employees are seconded to incoming private contractor firms. This is to ensure that they retain their favourable terms, including membership of the NHS Pension Scheme and access to NHS pay scales. Indeed, it is the retention of public sector pay and pension rights that is usually the main driver behind such arrangements.

169

Although the application of the REM in theory only applies to the NHS, similar arrangements have been applied elsewhere in the public sector where PFI is used to effect the contracting out of public services. Although secondment is not as prevalent in the private sector, it is sometimes used – particularly with regard to professional and managerial staff.

The Celtec case concerned employees employed by the Civil Service who were seconded in September 1990 to work for a new enterprise council, which later became Celtec Ltd (C Ltd), in order to provide vocational training on behalf of the Department of Education. In July 1993, the claimants were given the choice between continuing to work for the DoE or becoming employed by C Ltd. They chose the latter option, although many of their colleagues chose the former. It was later accepted that a relevant transfer of the DoE's training service to C Ltd had occurred at some point but it was not clear precisely when. A majority of the House of Lords ruled that the relevant date was September 1990 when the claimants had first been seconded, and not, as the parties had assumed, 1 July 1993 when the claimants had elected to enter the employ of C Ltd. This meant that the employment of employees (including the claimant) had been transferred automatically to C Ltd back in September 1990 even though they, the DoE and C Ltd were all oblivious of this at the time.

2.153 The House of Lords' ruling creates considerable difficulties for all those who utilise secondment arrangements of the kind described above. This is because the entire strategy underpinning these arrangements is to prevent what is now Reg 4 from applying to transfer the contracts of employees to the recipient of the employees' services following the outsourcing of the service in question. As we have seen in Chapter 1, the 2006 Regulations introduced a new definition of 'relevant transfer' that makes it far more likely that a change of service provider will constitute a transfer to which the Regulations apply. And as the Celtec case makes clear, the 'automatic transfer of employment' is likely to apply to all employees who happen to be assigned to the 'organised grouping of employees' supplying the service on the date when the change of service provider occurs regardless of their expectations or wishes in the matter. This means that their employment with the transferor will cease and they will become employed by the transferee. If that happens in a secondment context, the seconded employees will no longer be eligible for membership of their former employer's pension scheme.

2.154 The objection route

The question arises whether it will be possible for arrangements such as the NHS REM to survive the Celtec decision. It might be thought that the most obvious way around the problem is that, just prior to a change of service provider, employees formally object to the transfer to ensure that Reg 4(1) does not operate to transfer their employment to the incoming contractor. Indeed, that is the tactic currently deployed by the REM. The difficulty, however, is that the act of actually going to work for the transferee is, according to Lord Hope (one of the Lords who made up the majority decision in Celtec), completely incompatible with the suggestion that the employee has objected to the transfer. His Lordship emphasised that the sole reservation to the operation of the automatic transfer of employment rule is where the employee objects to the transfer. In this regard, 'it is a fundamental right of the employee to be free to choose his employer. So he cannot be obliged to work for an employer whom he has not freely chosen: Katsikas v Konstantinidis 1993 IRLR 179, ECJ, para 32. From this it follows that it is open to an employee whose contract of employment would otherwise be transferred automatically from the transferor to the transferee on the date of the transfer of his own free will to withdraw from this arrangement by declining to enter the employment of the transferee... That, then, is the extent of the sole reservation... It does not... work the other way round. It does not enable effect to be given to an employee's wish to continue to be employed by the transferor while continuing to be employed in the unit to which he has been assigned after its transfer to the transferee. But the application of the rule that he can withdraw from the arrangement depends on two things: first, that the employee is in a position to choose whether or not to enter the employment of the transferee after the date of the transfer; and second, that he in fact exercises that choice by deciding of his own free will *not* to do so.'

Assuming Lord Hope's analysis to be correct, it will be seen that the 'objection route' cannot therefore be relied upon in a secondment situation even if, unlike the claimants in the Celtec case, all the parties were fully cognisant of the fact of the transfer and of the date it occurred. Effective objection to the transfer simply cannot go hand in hand with the subsequent act of working for the transferee (see also the recent case of Capita Health Solutions Ltd v McLean and anor 2008 IRLR 595, EAT – discussed under 'Objecting to the transfer – timing of the objection' above – which supports Lord Hope's view).

2.155 One of the major implications of this is that the seconded employee will risk incurring a break in his or her continuity of employment once the secondment arrangement is concluded and he or she returns to working for the transferor. This can be seen from the particular facts of the Celtec case. As it turned out, the majority's decision worked out well for the particular claimants in that case: they had argued that they had continuous employment with C Ltd dating back to at least 1993. In the event, they were handed a windfall when the House of Lords ruled that their continuity stretched as far back as September 1990 when the relevant transfer was found to have occurred on the basis that that was when the secondment agreement was first put in place. The problem, however, is that what was true of the claimants must, in all logic, have been equally true of the large number of employees who elected in July 1993 *not* to become employees of C Ltd and instead to return to work for the DoE. Since the transfer of their employment would presumably have likewise occurred in

September 1990, they, like the claimants, would have ceased to be employed by the DoE from that date and instead have become employed by C Ltd. This meant that the legal effect of their election in July 1993 was not so much that they *continued working* for the DoE as that they *entered into new employment* with it three years after they had ceased to be employed as civil servants and had become employed by C Ltd. Since no relevant transfer was found to have occurred in July 1993 to transfer C Ltd's undertaking back to the DoE, the employees' continuity of employment with C Ltd must be judged to have broken and begun afresh with the DoE. This is so even though the employees in question were under the impression that they had remained employed by the DoE all along.

Perhaps the solution lies along the lines of the decision in New ISG Ltd v Vernon 2008 ICR 319, ChD, where the High Court adopted a pragmatic approach towards whether an employee had objected to the transfer within the terms of Reg 4(7). The Vernon case has been discussed in detail under 'Objecting to the transfer – timing of the objection' above. In that case the High Court held that an employee who had not been informed of the change in the identity of his employer had not been accorded a valid opportunity to object to the transfer. Accordingly, his action in working for the transferee for a couple of days until he was actually informed of the transfer did not preclude him making an objection at that point. While it is true that this scenario is very different from that in Celtec, it may well be that tribunals will be keen to adopt a similarly pragmatic approach to any case where an employee, through no fault of his or her own, would otherwise be denied the freedom of choice implicit in the 'objection provision' of Reg 4(7).

2.156 The Reg 4(1) route

Such are the practical and legal difficulties that the Celtec decision may cause when secondment arrangements are caught up in a TUPE transfer. Is there anything that can help the parties to such arrangements to ensure that seconded employees remain employed by the transferor? A possible solution would be for the parties to rely heavily on the words 'which would not otherwise have been terminated by the transfer' in Reg 4(1). We have seen in the section on 'Contracts "otherwise terminated by" transfer' above that this wording appears to preclude the application of the automatic transfer of employment rule to any contract of employment that would not, at common law, have been terminated automatically by reason of the transfer. Although the precise scope of this qualification is not clear, it might be that it would be found to extend to secondment arrangements based on the rationale explained in the examples given below:

- Example 1: if the secondment is time-limited to achieve a particular objective, it may be argued that such arrangements are not TUPE transfers within the meaning of Reg 3(1) but are new and specific contractual arrangements that lie outside the contract of employment. Since the intention of the parties entering into such arrangements is for the employee to return to the seconder in due course, it might be argued that that the resulting contractual relations are not caught by the automatic transfer of contracts of employees employed immediately before the transfer under Reg 4(1)

- Example 2: If the parties to a relevant transfer have agreed in advance that employees will continue to be employed by the transferor but will be seconded to work for the transferee, then so long as the employees in question enter into such an arrangement of their own free will, they might arguably be taken to be employed on contracts that would not otherwise terminate as a result of the transfer. So if, by way of example, employees of a local authority are seconded to an NHS body, the local authority would have to retain responsibility for all the services to which the employees are assigned. If the authority retains overall managerial control and ensures that the employees owe their duties to the seconder, rather than to the host directly, the secondment is likely to be held to be genuine.

It is true – as we have seen in the discussion on 'Employees retained by **2.157** transferor' above – that this analysis has not tended to find much favour in the few appellate cases where the words 'would not otherwise have terminated' have come under scrutiny. But none of those have dealt with the situation where there is a formal secondment agreement of the kind used in the public sector. It may well have been considerations of this kind that induced the Government to retain the wording in the new version of TUPE, having originally disclosed its intention to remove it.

3 What transfers?

Overview

Rights and liabilities relating to the individual

Collective rights and liabilities

Rights and liabilities that do not transfer

Continuing liability of the transferor?

The primary value of any business often lies not in its tangible assets but in its **3.1** goodwill, intellectual property and contracts with clients or customers. Most transfers of undertakings will entail the transfer of these intangible assets. But any purchase of an economic entity will also involve the acquisition by the transferee of 'hidden' rights and liabilities, particularly given that, by virtue of Reg 4 of the Transfer of Undertakings (Protection of Employment) Regulations 2006 SI 2006/246 (TUPE), the transferee will acquire not only the staff assigned to the entity transferred – as we discussed in Chapter 2 – but various rights, powers, duties and liabilities that go with those employees and their contracts of employment.

Overview   3.2

Regulation 4(2) states that on the completion of a relevant transfer:

- all the transferor's rights, powers, duties and liabilities under or in connection with any such contract shall be transferred to the transferee – Reg 4(2)(a) and

- any act or omission before the transfer is completed, of or in relation to the transferor in respect of that contract or a person assigned to that organised grouping of resources or employees, shall be deemed to have been an act or omission of or in relation to the transferee – Reg 4(2)(b).

These provisions are subject to a number of other regulations which qualify their impact – see below under 'Rights and liabilities that do not transfer'.

It is important to note that the two limbs of Reg 4 are distinct. This was stressed by the EAT in Perry's Motor Sales Ltd and anor v Lindley EAT 0616/07 (discussed in detail under 'Rights and liabilities relating to the individual – statutory rights' below). In that case, the EAT held that liability for a dismissal rendered unfair by virtue of S.104 of the Employment Rights Act 1996 (enforcement of a statutory right) could crystallise on the transfer and become a liability transferred to the transferee by virtue of Reg 4(2)(b) even though it was not a liability that transferred under Reg 4(1)(a).

175

3.3 Ignorance of the duties or liabilities that attach to a contract, or of any relevant acts or omissions of the transferor, will not prevent Reg 4(2) applying. Article 3.2 of the EU Acquired Rights Directive (No.2001/23) makes this clear: 'A failure by the transferor to notify the transferee of any such right or obligation shall not affect the transfer of that right or obligation and the rights of any employees against the transferee and/or transferor in respect of that right or obligation.' Indeed, employment rights and obligations transfer irrespective of the wishes of the parties – Rotsart de Hertaing v J Benoidt SA (in liquidation) and anor 1997 IRLR 127, ECJ, and Celtec Ltd v Astley and ors 2005 ICR 1409, ECJ (and even if the employees themselves are unaware of the fact of the transfer or of the identity of the transferee – Secretary of State for Trade and Industry v Cook and ors 1997 ICR 288, EAT). It is therefore vital for transferees to carry out careful and comprehensive due diligence when acquiring an undertaking. Copies of contracts of employment do not, as we shall see, contain a comprehensive list of the various employee-related duties and liabilities with which the transferee is likely to be encumbered.

It was in order to help address this issue that the Government included, in the 2006 Regulations, a new obligation on the transferor to notify the transferee of certain 'employee liability information' – Reg 11. This limited statutory list includes basic information about the employees; the information contained in their particulars of employment; information about relevant collective agreements; and information about disciplinary action, grievances or legal action from the last two years before the date of the transfer. We discuss the new obligations in detail in Chapter 8, under 'Employee liability information'. What is important to note here is that the statutory obligations provide the transferee with basic protection only. Employees are likely to benefit from more extensive contractual benefits than would be contained in their statutory particulars of employment, and the fact that a right of action arose more than two years ago does not necessarily mean that it will not be actionable now. Therefore, irrespective of the new statutory protections, transferees should, as before, conduct full due diligence and require relevant warranties and indemnities to be included in the acquisition documentation – see Chapter 10 for practical advice in this regard.

3.4 Note that Reg 4(2)(a) refers to the rights, powers, duties and liabilities *of the transferor* under the employment contract. In discussing the implications of employment contracts transferring to the transferee, it is common to think more in terms of the rights of *employees* under the contract, particularly given that the aim of the Regulations is to preserve employees' rights. The point is, to a degree, academic, as an employee's right is the counterpart to an employer's liability. But it is important, for the purposes of understanding how Reg 4(2)(a) applies, to realise what it says.

The effect of Reg 4(2) is to protect the rights of employees *as they exist at the time of the transfer*. (For discussion as to when a transfer is likely to be regarded as having taken place, see Chapter 1, under 'When does the transfer occur?') It does not create or increase rights. Two cases demonstrating this:

- **Computershare Investor Services plc v Jackson** 2008 ICR 341, CA: J started work with a bank in 1999 which did not have a severance pay scheme. She transferred to CIS plc in 2004. CIS plc had a severance pay scheme, the terms of which differed depending on whether the employee 'joined' before or after 2002. When J was made redundant in 2005 she was treated as having length of service extending back to 1999, but it was the terms of the post-2002 joiner scheme which were applied to her. An employment tribunal found that she should have been entitled to benefit from the pre-2002 joiner scheme. That decision was overturned by the EAT and, on further appeal, the Court of Appeal held that the EAT's decision was correct. Lord Justice Mummery noted that the object of the relevant Directive was to ensure that employees' rights are safeguarded in the event of a transfer rather than to improve on existing rights – Viggósdóttir v Íslandspóstur HF 2002 IRLR 425, ECJ. On this basis, the effect of what is now Reg 4(1) is not to give a transferred employee access to employment benefits other than those to which the employee was entitled before the transfer of the undertaking. In the instant case, the fact that the claimant's employer calculated her severance pay on the basis of her deemed continuity of service from 1999 was irrelevant to the question of whether she was a post-2002 entrant within the meaning of the employer's enhanced severance terms. That question was determined by the date when, as a fact, she joined the employer's employment. It was not possible to make artificial use of the TUPE Regulations for the purpose of interpreting the employer's contract for enhanced severance pay in a way which displaced the correct finding of fact that J began work for the transferee in 2004 or which miraculously transformed her from being a post-2002 new entrant into a pre-2002 entrant

- **Werhof v Freeway Traffic Systems GmbH and Co KG** 2006 IRLR 400, ECJ: W was employed by Siemens in Germany under a contract of employment which was governed by a collective agreement and wage agreement negotiated between the trade union for the industry and the employers' association of which Siemens was a member. On 1 October 1999 Siemens transferred the part of its business in which W worked to FTS. FTS was not a member of any employers' association that concluded collective agreements. In May 2003 the trade union and the employers' association concluded a new collective agreement which provided for an increase in the wage rate and an additional payment. W commenced proceedings against FTS claiming the difference between his basic salary and the sum provided for in the new collective agreement, plus the additional payment. The German court asked the ECJ whether a transferee who inherits a collective agreement but was not an original party to it is bound by collective agreements subsequent to the one in force at the time of the transfer. The ECJ noted that under the Directive the rights and obligations arising from the collective agreement were automatically transferred to the new employer even though the latter was not a party to it. However, the ECJ stated, the Directive's objective is merely to safeguard rights and obligations in force on the day of the transfer. Article 3.3 makes it clear that the terms and conditions of the collective agreement in force at the time of transfer are to continue to be observed only until the date of its termination or expiry, or the entry into force or application of another collective agreement. This wording does not indicate that the Community legislature intended the transferee to be bound by collective agreements other than the one in force at the time of the transfer. FTS was, therefore, not liable for the additional payments.

3.5 The Regulations cannot be used to improve upon existing rights; but neither may such rights be diluted as a consequence of a relevant transfer. It is ironic that, as a result of the 'non-dilution' principle, transferring employees seem to acquire an extra degree of protection – a quasi-statutory assurance that their contracts cannot be varied – which they would not have had in the absence of the transfer, or had the transfer fallen outside TUPE's protection: see Chapter 5, 'Changing terms and conditions', under 'Varying terms in a TUPE context', for further discussion.

As the cases above demonstrate, the rights and obligations that are capable of being transferred upon a relevant transfer encompass a wide range – including both those that attach to the individual employee and those that are collectively negotiated (although there is inevitably some crossover between the two). Using these two broad categories, we now consider the particular rights, powers, duties, liabilities, acts and omissions that transfer under TUPE, before turning to the significantly more limited list of rights, powers, duties, liabilities, acts and omissions that do not transfer.

3.6 Rights and liabilities relating to the individual

The most obvious sets of rights and liabilities that transfer on the completion of the relevant transfer are those appertaining to the transferred employee's contract of employment. Indeed, express reference is made to the contract of employment in Reg 4(2), which speaks of 'all the transferor's rights, powers, duties and liabilities under or in connection with any *such contract*' (our emphasis). 'Such contract' is a reference back to Reg 4(1), which stipulates that 'a relevant transfer shall not operate so as to terminate the contract of employment of any person employed by the transferor and assigned to the organised grouping of resources or employees that is subject to the... transfer'.

As we shall see, however, Reg 4(2) is apt to transfer even non-contractual rights and benefits as well as those that have contractual status.

Contractual and discretionary rights and benefits 3.7

The more obvious rights and liabilities which transfer are those contained by way *of express terms* in an employee's contract of employment. These may include, for example, job title and function; place of work; hours of work; salary; holiday entitlement; enhanced contractual sick leave and pay; enhanced contractual maternity leave and pay; length of contract where it is fixed term; notice provisions; and so on. In the absence of contractual documentation, note that express terms may have been agreed orally between the parties, although to some extent these should be recorded in the employee's statutory statement of particulars of employment. Orally agreed terms are no less valid and are capable of transfer. But even the most obvious contractual terms may have hidden implications for the recipient transferee. Take the following examples:

- *job title or description* – these may not always be contractual but are likely to be so, especially where an employee is relatively senior. Where an undertaking's day-to-day activities are little affected by the transfer and an employee is of lower-than-managerial status, there should be no difficulty in his or her retaining a pre-transfer title or description. However, employees of executive or managerial level may be required to slot into a new management structure upon transfer and thereby sacrifice their pre-transfer designation or function. This is permissible by virtue of Reg 4(5) if it is for an economic, technical or organisational reason entailing changes in the workforce, but not otherwise – see Chapter 5

- *length of notice period* – it has been known for executives to seek to protect their position by insisting upon a substantial notice period. Where such rights have been renegotiated with the transfer in mind, they are likely to be void under Reg 4(4). This provides that any purported variation of a contract of employment that is to be transferred is void if the sole or principal reason for the variation is the relevant transfer or a reason connected with the transfer that is not an economic, technical or organisational reason entailing changes in the workforce. However, where this is not the case the notice period, however long, will continue to apply after the transfer. Transferees should therefore look out for onerous notice rights in the course of their pre-transfer due diligence.

Of course, a contract is not limited to its express terms. Other types of 3.8 contractual term include:

- *implied terms* – terms that are not spelt out in so many words but which parties are taken to have agreed either because they are too obvious to need recording, or because they are part of the custom and practice of the business or industry, or because they can be logically deduced from the conduct of

179

the parties. Terms may also be implied if they are necessary to give 'business efficacy' to the agreement as a whole

- *incorporated terms* – terms that are incorporated into individual contracts from other sources such as collective agreements or works rules

- *statutory terms* – terms that are derived from provisions contained in statutes affecting the employment relationship, such as the insertion by the Equal Pay Act 1970 of an 'equality clause' into every individual contract of employment.

Terms falling within any of the above categories are, with certain caveats, capable of transferring to the transferee under Reg 4(2).

3.9 Normal contractual principles apply to determine the precise nature of what transfers. For example:

- **Learning and Skills Council v Barfoot and ors** EAT 0621/03: the London East Technical and Enterprise Council (LETEC) established a contractual bonus scheme for some of its employees in September 1998. LETEC sent letters to the employees setting out the terms of the new scheme and stating that the 'bonus structure' would cease at the end of 2000. In June 2000, a further letter was sent indicating the level of bonuses for the period 1 April 2000 to 31 March 2001. On 26 March 2001, the Learning and Skills Council (LSC) acquired the employees upon a TUPE transfer. It decided not to reintroduce a contractual bonus scheme, and paid bonuses to the employees on a discretionary basis. The employees brought a tribunal claim in respect of an unauthorised deduction of wages, alleging that they had not been paid the bonuses to which they were contractually entitled. On the evidence, the tribunal found that although the contractual bonus scheme ceased at the end of 2000, a contractual obligation to pay a bonus after that remained. The EAT, however, allowed LSC's appeal. It held that contractual documents had to be given the meaning which the documents would convey to a reasonable observer having all the background knowledge which would reasonably have been available to the parties in the situation in which they were at the time of the contract. No such reasonable observer, having given the letter mature thought and having all the background knowledge available to the parties at the time, would have thought that it meant that, although the terms of the bonus scheme which was then being established would cease at the end of 2000, the employees' entitlement to a contractual bonus under some other bonus structure would continue indefinitely. The EAT remitted the claim to a fresh tribunal for reconsideration.

We consider rights and liabilities arising from all four main types of contractual term at various points below. But what is the situation regarding non-contractual working arrangements and expectations, and discretionary rights and benefits?

180

Non-contractual working arrangements. Some commentators and tribunals 3.10
have implied or assumed that if there is no contractual basis to a particular
term, then it will not transfer – unless it can be argued that a refusal to provide
it constitutes a breach of an implied contractual term, such as the duty to
maintain the employee's trust and confidence. For example, in London Borough
of Newham v Smith and anor EAT 1345/00 the EAT had to consider whether
working arrangements that the transferring employees had had with the
London Borough of Waltham Forest passed to the London Borough of Newham
upon a relevant transfer. The EAT said this: 'The tribunal firstly and primarily
had to decide... whether the working arrangements operated by Waltham
Forest which we have described were embodied into the contracts of employment
of the employees at the time of the transfer. If they were, the effect of Reg 5
[now Reg 4] would have been to transfer the contractual obligations of the
transferor, Waltham Forest, in respect of those arrangements to the transferee,
Newham. If they were not, then no obligations in respect of those arrangements
existed and there was nothing in respect of those arrangements which could be
transferred by way of contractual obligation to Newham.' On the facts of the
case, a system under which employees could be called out for emergency work
outside normal working hours was found to be non-contractual, and therefore
'in respect of those arrangements, no obligations passed to Newham', but a
system whereby employees were allowed free use of the employer's vans for
travelling to and from work was a contractual arrangement, which Newham
was, therefore, obliged to uphold. Note, too, the decision of the EAT in Jefferies
v Powerhouse Retail Ltd EAT 1328/95, upholding a tribunal's conclusion that,
since certain enhanced redundancy terms were not incorporated into the
claimant's contract, 'those terms cannot have transferred under [the 1981
Regulations] when the transfer took place'.

However, there are problems with this approach. The wording of Reg 4(2) is
not limited to matters arising from the contract of employment. Regulation
4(2)(a) provides for the transfer of rights, powers, duties and liabilities not only
'under' the contract but also 'in connection with' the contract – it is hard to see
why this phrase should be added if it was not to extend the rights, powers,
duties and liabilities that are capable of transfer to those which are not
themselves part of the contract but somehow assist in its performance.
Furthermore, Reg 4(2)(b) attributes to the transferee any act or omission by the
transferor, not only in respect of a novated contract, but also in respect of a
person assigned to the relevant undertaking. This wording – not limited to
those matters which can be described as rights, powers, duties or liabilities – is,
arguably, capable of covering the transferor's actions in maintaining for his
employees a non-contractual emergency cover system, such as that examined in
London Borough of Newham, for example. In Secretary of State for Employment
v Spence and ors 1986 ICR 651, CA, the Court of Appeal concluded that the
wording of Reg 5(2)(b) (now replaced by Reg 4(2)(b) but with slightly different

181

wording), 'clearly can have the effect of transferring obligations other than contractual obligations'. And as Peter Gibson LJ put it in the combined appeal of (1) Martin v Lancashire County Council (2) Bernadone v Pall Mall Services Group Ltd and ors 2001 ICR 197, CA (in relation to the question of whether or not tortious liability transferred – see under 'Tortious and other civil liabilities' below): under sub-paragraph (a) 'rights etc are not limited to those under the contract but include those "in connection with" the contract. That prepositional phrase is far wider and it does not suggest that the rights etc need be contractual. That is supported by sub-paragraph (b) of Reg 5(2) [now Reg 4(2)(b)]. It is not just what is done by the transferor in respect of the contract that is deemed to have been done by the transferee but also anything done by the transferor in respect of the employee. That does not suggest that it is limited to what will result in contractual rights and liabilities.'

3.11 Although the cases mentioned above all concerned the 1981 Regulations, the position is the same under the 2006 Regulations. Reg 5(2)(b) of TUPE 1981 referred to 'anything done... in respect of... a person employed in that undertaking', and Reg 4(2)(b) of TUPE 2006 refers to 'any act or omission... in respect of... a person assigned'. Indeed, if anything, the inclusion of the new concept of omissions in Reg 4(2)(b) makes the scope of the 2006 Regulations wider than that of its predecessor in this respect. Finally, note also that the existence of Reg 4(6), which excludes liability for criminal offences from the operation of Reg 4(2), suggests that Parliament felt that Reg 4(2) was potentially capable of transferring liabilities of a patently non-contractual nature.

In addition to the reasoning above in respect of the specific wording of the TUPE Regulations, the language of the Acquired Rights Directive also envisages that non-contractual rights and obligations should transfer. Article 3.1 expressly applies to rights and obligations of the transferor arising from an '*employment relationship*' and not just from an employment contract. In the Martin case (above) Peter Gibson LJ observed: 'It would seem to me to be surprising if the rights and obligations were to be limited to contractual claims and to exclude claims in tort. Why should there be such a dividing line (in accordance with the distinction in English law between tort and contract) in a [European] Directive? It is the more surprising when the language used in the Directive is broad ("arising from") and when it is not only a contract of employment but also an employment relationship (which is plainly something different) from which the rights and obligations must arise.' 'Employment relationship' is not a defined term but it seems doubtful whether the wording adopted by the United Kingdom – 'in connection with' the employment contract – adequately implements the Directive in this regard – although Reg 4(2)(b), as we have discussed, has a potentially broader extent, covering as it does acts and omissions in relation to the *person assigned* to the transferred entity. In any event, however, if Reg 4, when taken as a whole and construed literally, does not effect the transfer of all rights and obligations envisaged by the Directive, then following the ruling of

Lord Templeman in Litster and ors v Forth Dry Dock and Engineering Co Ltd (in receivership) and anor 1989 ICR 341, HL, the courts must give it a purposive construction to ensure that it effects the transfer of all rights and obligations envisaged by the Directive. Lord Oliver envisaged that such a construction would be applied even though it may involve some departure from the 'strict and literal application of the words which the legislature has elected to use.'

It is clear, then, that statutory and civil rights and duties transfer in addition to **3.12** contractual matters, and for the purpose of determining what transfers it should therefore be unnecessary (as Peter Gibson LJ implied in Martin) to impose a strict delineation as to what is or is not contractual. But what happens to non-contractual working practices of the kind with which the EAT in both the London Borough of Newham and Jefferies cases (above) were concerned? One can understand a reluctance to hold that non-contractual working conditions are capable of transfer, because of the vast impracticalities of replicating the precise working environment of an organised grouping in the hands of the transferee. But it is, we submit, the entirely logical continuation of the above analysis. The better view, surely, is that non-contractual working arrangements and benefits *do* pass to the transferee, but that the same principles affect their application and enforcement in the transferee's hands as they did before the transfer. In other words, non-contractual working practices under the transferor remain non-contractual working practices under the transferee – and the transferee is at as much liberty to resile from them as the transferor would have been. (This is subject to any implied contractual obligation to exercise discretions in a non-capricious way, and to the right of the employee to be treated as having been dismissed if he or she resigns on the ground that a substantial change has been made to working conditions that is to the employee's material detriment. This latter right – conferred by Reg 4(9) – is not dependent on the change amounting to a breach of contract – see Chapter 4, under 'Material detriment dismissals', for full details.)

At this stage of the analysis, therefore, it is highly pertinent to determine whether or not a particular practice or procedure is contractual. Usual principles will apply to determine whether or not a procedure or policy has been incorporated into the contract. Take the following examples, all of which relate to the incorporation or otherwise of enhanced redundancy terms:

- **Quinn and ors v Calder Industrial Materials Ltd** 1996 IRLR 126, EAT: Q and others were dismissed for redundancy by CIM Ltd, a company forming part of a group. The employees complained to an industrial tribunal that the employer was in breach of contract in that it had not paid enhanced redundancy compensation under the terms of a policy issued throughout the group containing guidelines on the payment of additional sums in the event of redundancy. Although there was no written term entitling the employees to such compensation, they claimed that a term was implied

183

into their contracts on the ground of the employer's established custom and practice. The employment tribunal decided, however, that the employer had not breached the claimants' contracts and, on appeal, the EAT held that the tribunal had not erred. This was so notwithstanding that enhanced payments had been made on each occasion that redundancies had occurred after the date when the policy was formulated. The issue was what terms the parties had agreed. The relevant question was whether, taking account of all the circumstances – which included (but was not limited to) whether the policy had been drawn to the attention of the employees or followed without exception for a substantial period – the inference could be drawn that the employer intended to become contractually bound by the term. Applying this approach, it was clear that the redundancy payments policy in question had not been incorporated into any agreement and had not been communicated to the employees. That was a significant factor because a positive act of communicating terms to employees might well give rise to an inference that the employer intends to be bound by them. On the other hand, that inference cannot be drawn merely because terms are repeatedly applied. The fact that it was clear, at least from the employer's point of view, that payment was not automatic but required a decision on each occasion also went against an inference that the employer intended to be bound by the enhanced redundancy terms. Although the employees may reasonably have expected the policy to apply to them, it was not possible to infer that the right to enhanced redundancy payments had been incorporated into their contracts of employment

- **Alexander and ors v Standard Telephones and Cables Ltd (No.2)** 1991 IRLR 286, QBD: as a result of technological change STC Ltd considered making redundancies. It took into account the following selection criteria: length of service, skill, aptitude, performance, attendance record and work-approach. The employees disputed that they had been lawfully dismissed for redundancy, contending that it was a requirement of the collective agreements that selection for redundancy should be carried out on the basis of length of service alone. They claimed that the terms of the relevant collective agreement were expressly incorporated into their individual contracts of employment – or impliedly incorporated as a matter of contractual intent – and that in failing to adhere to the selection procedure in the collective agreement, STC Ltd was in breach of contract. The employees' statutory written statements of particulars included a provision that 'the basic terms and conditions of your employment by this company are in accordance with and subject to the provisions of [listed] relevant agreements', although the statements made no mention of redundancy terms. The High Court summarised the principles to be applied in determining whether a part of a collective agreement is incorporated into individual contracts of employment as follows: it is the contractual intention of the parties to the agreement – the employee and the employer – which must be ascertained. In so far as that intention is to be found in a written document, that document must be construed on ordinary contractual principles but, where there is no document or where the document is incomplete or inconclusive, the parties' contractual intention has to be ascertained by inference from the other available material, including collective agreements. Where a document is expressly incorporated by general words it is still necessary to consider whether any particular part of that document is apt to be a term of the contract; if it is inapt, the correct construction of the contract may be that it is not a term of the contract. Where it is not a case of express incorporation, but a matter of inferring contractual intent, the character of the document and the relevant part of it and whether it is apt to form part of the individual contract are central to the decision as to whether or not the inference should be drawn. The wording of the statements of written particulars was not sufficient to show an express incorporation of the redundancy procedure agreements, particularly as the written statements did not specifically deal with redundancy matters, implying that these were not a 'basic' term or condition to which the statement referred. Nor was it possible to infer, as a matter of contractual intent, that the selection procedure contained in the collective agreements had been incorporated into the individual contracts of employment. Where none of the other clauses of the collective agreement were apt to be incorporated, it would require a cogent indication that the clause setting out the basis for redundancy selection was to have a different character and was to be incorporated for it to have that effect. In the present case, the wording of the relevant clause was too weak to support an inference of incorporation when considered in context. It followed that the selection of the employees for redundancy was not in breach of any term of their contracts of employment and their claim would therefore be dismissed

- **Anderson v Pringle of Scotland Ltd** 1998 IRLR 64, Ct Sess (Outer House): A had been an employee of PS Ltd for many years. A collective agreement between the employers and A's union, the GMB, included a redundancy procedure that provided for selection on the basis of 'last in, first out' (LIFO). In 1997 the employer proposed to make some 290 employees redundant on the basis of a selective scheme to which neither A nor the union had agreed. A would have been made redundant under the proposed selection criteria, whereas if the LIFO scheme had been adhered to he would have been retained. A claimed that the LIFO method of selection formed a term of his employment contract. He sought an interim interdict (the Scottish term for an interlocutory injunction) preventing his employer from implementing its proposed system of selection or any selection criteria other than LIFO pending the full trial of the issue. The first question before the Court of Session was whether A had shown an arguable case that the LIFO procedure was incorporated into his contract of employment. On this matter the Court was satisfied that he had established a prima facie case that the whole of the collective agreement was incorporated into his contract. Accordingly, it was arguable that he was contractually entitled to require the employer to operate the LIFO method of selection. The Court of Session granted an interim interdict in favour of the employee, prohibiting his employer from making selections for redundancy on any basis other than LIFO.

3.13 If a disciplinary or redundancy procedure is of a contractual nature, and a transferred employee is dismissed by the transferee in breach of it following the transfer, he or she is likely to have a claim for wrongful dismissal against the transferee. If the transferor is responsible for the breach, the transferee will acquire liability for it if the employee would otherwise have transferred – see also under 'Unfair and wrongful dismissal' below. However, it is important to note that even if such arrangements are of a non-contractual nature, allowing the transferee to end or replace them as he wishes, an affected employee may yet have a claim. Normally, an employee may only claim constructive dismissal in response to a repudiatory breach of contract. However, a serious breach of a particular policy may amount to a breach of the implied term of trust and confidence, even if the policy itself is non-contractual (for example, imposing unreasonable disciplinary sanctions (short of dismissal) that are outside the range of sanctions provided by the relevant disciplinary procedure – Abbey National plc v Holmes EAT 406/91). Further, Reg 4(9) provides that if a relevant transfer involves or would involve a substantial change *in working conditions* to the material detriment of the transferring employee, then he or she can treat the contract as terminated and will be treated as having been dismissed by the employer. He or she may then be able to claim unfair dismissal, without the need to demonstrate a breach of contract – see Chapter 4, under 'Material detriment dismissals' for further details.

3.14 **Discretionary rights and benefits**. A discretionary right or benefit involves an element of uncertainty in that its application or value is unascertainable until the relevant discretion is exercised. We take the view that regardless of this element of uncertainty, discretionary rights and benefits pass to the transferee under Reg 4(2)(a), as liabilities and powers under or in connection with the employment contract. What the transferee can then do is entirely dependent upon the terms of the relevant right or benefit, and the extent to which the discretion has already been exercised. The usual rules relating to the exercise of discretionary powers in employment contracts will apply – see the discussion of Martin and ors v South Bank University 2004 ICR 1234, ECJ, under 'Contingent rights' below.

In Moir v First Security ET Case No.2204146/09 M's contract provided that company sick pay would be paid at her employer's discretion subject to the provision of a medical certificate and that payment would not be made if employees unreasonably refuse to undergo a medical examination or refuse to

186

allow the employer to request a medical report from their GP. M was taken ill and was on sick leave for three months during which he was only paid statutory sick pay. When his employment transferred under TUPE, the transferee refused to award him contractual sick pay since its own employees were only entitled to SSP. An employment tribunal held that while the contract clearly provided a discretion, it was equally clear from the wording that company sick pay would be paid provided there was no reason to believe that employees were abusing the system or being uncooperative. M's claim for company sick pay was upheld as the transferee had only exercised its discretion by giving consideration to its own circumstances rather than those that it acquired following the transfer.

Wherever a benefit scheme itself is discretionary (i.e. not contractual in nature), **3.15** it will not transfer under TUPE. So, for example, in Davies v Crown Records Management Ltd ET Case No.3302274/08 an employment tribunal held that a discretionary bonus scheme operated by the transferor entitling the employee to a bonus of 40 per cent of basic salary (reduced to 5 per cent after the transfer) did not transfer to the new employer under Reg 4. The operation of the scheme was entirely at the discretion of management as to whether it operated at all and upon what terms. Contrast this decision with Bousted v Reliance Security Services Ltd ET Case No.1701352/07 (see under 'Enhanced redundancy schemes' below), a case involving the operation of an enhanced redundancy compensation scheme that was held to have been transferred following a transfer even though the benefits payable under it were referred to as 'ex gratia' payments and the terms of the scheme were not expressly incorporated into the employee's contract or staff handbook.

Liability for past breaches of contract. The transferee inherits liability under **3.16** Reg 4(2)(b) for the transferor's past breaches of contract – such as arrears of wages – in addition to the responsibility to maintain ongoing rights and benefits. This liability for past breaches is not limited to obligations arising out of the contract existing on the date of the transfer, but also those arising from previous contracts with the transferor – DJM International Ltd v Nicholas 1996 ICR 214, EAT (which considered inherited liability for a discrimination claim – see 'Statutory rights' below) – although claims will be subject to length of service limitations.

Continuity of employment   3.17
Continuity of employment is preserved in the event of a relevant transfer, although it is not entirely clear whether the TUPE Regulations themselves have the effect of preserving continuity or whether this is governed by the Employment Rights Act 1996 (ERA). S.218 ERA specifically preserves continuity of employment following a change of employer in relation to the transfer of a business or undertaking and in relation to a change in the partners of a firm (provided, of course, that the employee remains in employment) – see Chapter 7 for more detail. It is clear, certainly, from the underlying policy and objectives

187

of the Directive, and from relevant case law, that continuity must be preserved whenever the Directive (and the national law that implements it) applies. For instance, in Collino and anor v Telecom Italia SpA 2002 ICR 38, ECJ, the European Court stated that in calculating the rights of a financial nature attached to employees' length of service, such as a termination payment or salary increases, the transferee 'must take into account the entire length of service of the employees transferred, both in his employment and that of the transferor'.

As Collino demonstrates, the fact that a relevant transfer does not break continuity of employment for transferring employees may significantly affect the nature of the liabilities towards those employees that are preserved in the context of a relevant transfer. First, length of service may affect whether a particular employee is *entitled* to certain statutory rights. Secondly, length of service may have an impact upon the *calculation* of certain statutory or contractual benefits. We now examine these possibilities in turn.

3.18 **Entitlement to statutory rights.** In usual cases, an employee is required to have one year's service to claim unfair dismissal – S.108(1) ERA. Put simply, a transferee who acquires an employee who was employed by the transferor for the previous nine months will become liable to that employee for unfair dismissal after only a further three months following the relevant transfer, and not one year as would be the case if it had taken on a new employee in a context that was not transfer-related. The length of service provisions are disapplied in most 'automatic unfair dismissal' cases. For our purposes, the most significant of these is a claim of unfair dismissal for asserting TUPE rights under S.104(4)(e) ERA. In such cases, continuity of employment ceases to be relevant. However, note that one year's qualifying service *is*, unusually, required for claims that a dismissal is 'automatically unfair' under Reg 7(1) of the Regulations (because the reason for it is either the relevant transfer or a reason connected with the transfer that is not an 'ETO reason') – see MRS Environmental Services Ltd v Marsh and anor 1997 ICR 995, EAT, and the section on the TUPE unfair dismissal regime in Chapter 4.

Another statutory right which may be affected by the transferred employee's continuity of employment is the right to claim statutory redundancy pay. Two years' service is required – S.155 ERA. An employee with 18 months' service at the point of transfer will not need to start counting again before he or she becomes entitled to claim statutory redundancy pay.

3.19 **Calculating benefits.** It is common for employers to seek to encourage loyalty or motivation, or reward the experience, of their workers by incorporating a service-related element into the calculation of contractual benefits. (This is permitted, within certain parameters, by Reg 32 of the Employment Equality (Age) Regulations 2006 SI 2006/1031.) Clearly, the fact that continuity is preserved on a transfer can greatly enhance the value of such benefits, and service-related statutory benefits, to the employee – to the transferee's corresponding detriment. Note that, in Computershare Investor Services plc v Jackson 2008 ICR 341, CA (discussed under 'Overview' above), in spite of the dispute over when the claimant *joined* the severance pay scheme, her employer never failed to take into account her pre-transfer employment for the purpose of calculating *length of service* under the scheme – to the employee's considerable financial advantage.

Calculating the period of continuous employment. It is likely that the **3.20** employee's continuity has to be calculated in accordance with the detailed rules contained in Ss.210–219 ERA. The date on which the period of continuous employment started is usually the date on which the employee started work with the transferor. However, note that if the employee was subject to a previous TUPE transfer, the start date will be earlier.

Continuity of employment will have other, practical implications for the transferee that should not be overlooked. For example, employees who are transferred while absent on sick leave or maternity leave will not restart their leave at the point of transfer: the transferee will be credited with the length of leave such employees have taken and whatever pay they have received for the purposes of applying the relevant absence and pay policies. And, in another example, the reference period for assessing employees' average weekly working hours under the Working Time Regulations 1998 SI 1998/1833 will 'roll over' the transfer date, so the transferee will need to take account of hours worked by employees in the weeks leading up to the transfer in assessing whether they are averaging under the statutory limits.

Note that even if the acquired employees have no rights under TUPE – because, **3.21** for example, the acquisition does not constitute a relevant transfer – their employment may nevertheless be deemed to be continuous under S.218 ERA – see Chapter 7 for fuller details.

Unfair and wrongful dismissal   **3.22**
In Chapter 4, 'Unfair dismissal', we discuss at length the extent to which employers, whether transferors or transferees, can effect dismissals fairly in a transfer situation – and in what circumstances an employee's own decision to leave his or her employment can amount to a dismissal, giving rise to a potential unfair dismissal claim. Here, we consider who – transferor or transferee – shoulders the liability for unfair and wrongful dismissals that are carried out around the time of – or otherwise in connection with – a relevant transfer.

TUPE-related dismissals. Regulation 7(1) of the 2006 Regulations, which **3.23** implements Article 4.1 of the Acquired Rights Directive, provides that certain TUPE-related dismissals will be automatically unfair. It provides that where, either before or after a relevant transfer, any employee of the transferor or

189

transferee is dismissed, the employee shall be treated for ERA purposes as unfairly dismissed if the sole or principal reason for dismissal is:

- the transfer itself, or

- a reason connected with the transfer that is not an economic, technical or organisational reason entailing changes in the workforce (an 'ETO reason' – for the meaning of which, see Chapter 4, under 'Dismissals potentially fair for an "ETO reason"'.

As discussed in Chapter 2, an employment contract and the liabilities in respect of it will only transfer if the employee in question is employed by the transferor and assigned to the transferring entity immediately before the transfer, *or would have been so employed if he had not been dismissed in the circumstances described in Reg 7(1)* – Reg 4(3). In other words, the transferee will (almost) always be liable for dismissals that are automatically unfair under Reg 7(1). If the reason for the dismissal is the relevant transfer itself, then the dismissal will be automatically unfair under Reg 7(1) and, owing to Reg 4(3), liability for the dismissal will pass to the transferee. If the reason for the dismissal is connected with the transfer, and is not an ETO reason, the dismissal will be automatically unfair under Reg 7(1), and, again, liability will pass to the transferee – see Litster and ors v Forth Dry Dock and Engineering Co Ltd (in receivership) and anor 1989 ICR 341, HL. (Note that there is no obligation upon the transferee to re-employ employees who were unfairly dismissed by the transferor in such circumstances, although the transferee is responsible for all liabilities relating to those employees. However, as the DTI's guidance 'Employment rights on the transfer of an undertaking – a guide to the 2006 TUPE Regulations for employees, employers and representatives' (the DTI Guide) – points out, an obligation to re-employ could, theoretically, arise were a tribunal to uphold a claim of unfair dismissal and order reinstatement or re-engagement.)

3.24 However, there are two exceptions to the principle that liability for such unfair dismissals transfers. First, Reg 7(1) protects '*any* employee of the transferor or transferee' (our emphasis) – not just those who have been assigned to the organised grouping to be transferred. This means that a transferor will retain liability in respect of employees who are not assigned to the undertaking – and therefore are unaffected by Reg 4(1) and (2) – even if they have been unfairly dismissed under Reg 7(1) for a non-ETO reason connected with the relevant transfer. For the second, more limited, exception, see the discussion on anticipatory breach of contract under 'Constructive dismissal' below.

3.25 **Wrongful dismissal.** In addition, the effect of Reg 4(2) is that the transferee will inherit liability for any pre-transfer breach of employment contract by the transferor or for that matter any other act or omission in respect of relevant employees. For example, if the unfairly dismissed employee was given insufficient notice, or dismissed in breach of a contractual disciplinary or redundancy procedure, his or her claim of wrongful dismissal will also lie at the door of the transferee, who may thus be liable for damages for pay in lieu of notice. Note that this is not the case in respect of an employee who relies on Reg 4(9) (see 'Material detriment dismissals' below), because Reg 4(10) provides that 'no damages shall be payable by an employer as a result of a dismissal falling within paragraph (9) in respect of any failure by the employer to pay wages to an employee in respect of a notice period which the employee has failed to work'. There is no such restriction where an employee claims unfair constructive dismissal under normal principles.

Dismissals unconnected with a relevant transfer. Where an employee is **3.26** dismissed by the transferor, before the transfer, in circumstances that are entirely unconnected with the transfer – for example, for misconduct – Reg 7(1) will not apply to make the dismissal automatically unfair. For this reason, the dismissed employee will not be 'employed by the transferor' immediately before the transfer within the meaning of Reg 4(1) and (3). Therefore, his or her contract of employment and associated rights, powers, duties and liabilities will not transfer to the transferee under Reg 4(2)(b) unless he or she was dismissed on notice and that notice expired only after the date on which the transfer occurred. Clearly, if the dismissal is effected by the transferee after the transfer, the transferee will bear liability for it, even if the misconduct occurred before the transfer. The fairness or otherwise of the decision to dismiss will be assessed by applying the normal reasonableness test set out in S.98(4) ERA. It is possible that in such circumstances the dismissed employee's claim of unfair dismissal may relate to the way in which the disciplinary process that commenced before the transfer was conducted by the transferor. If that is the case, and assuming that the employee was assigned to the transferred undertaking, Reg 4(2)(b) ensures that whatever the fault of the transferor in relation to the initial conduct of the disciplinary procedure, this will be attributed to the transferee upon the relevant transfer, as an 'act or omission' in respect of the employee. This will be the case even if the subsequent dismissal itself bears no relation to the transfer. Transferees should be careful in such circumstances to 'remedy' the pre-transfer failings of the disciplinary procedure by ensuring that any appeal conducted after the transfer amounts, in effect, to a rehearing – and, of course, by insisting upon appropriate warranties and indemnities against the transferor in respect of such risks – see Chapter 10 for practical advice in this regard.

Transfer-connected dismissals for an ETO reason. If the transfer-connected **3.27** reason for a pre-transfer dismissal, express or constructive, is an 'ETO reason', then it will not be automatically unfair under Reg 7(1). In these circumstances, liability for the dismissal (which might yet be unfair under the reasonableness test set out in S.98(4) ERA) will not pass to the transferee, regardless of the fact that the dismissal was transfer-connected – see, for example, Thompson v SCS Consulting Ltd and ors EAT 0034/00. Transferees will, however, bear liability for ETO dismissals they carry out themselves, whether before the transfer in

191

relation to their existing workforce, or after the transfer in respect of transferred employees.

3.28 **Constructive dismissals.** A 'constructive dismissal' occurs where an employee resigns, with or without notice, in response to a repudiatory breach of contract on the part of his or her employer. In such circumstances the employee will be treated as having been 'dismissed' within the meaning of S.95(1)(c) ERA, and thus (provided he or she has the requisite qualifying service) will be able to bring an unfair dismissal claim under that Act. So, employers who unilaterally seek to make changes to the employment relationship or its terms and conditions, prompted by the transfer or a reason connected with it, risk provoking employees to resign and claim unfair constructive dismissal. Reg 4(11) specifically provides that other provisions in Reg 4 are 'without prejudice to any right of an employee arising apart from these Regulations to terminate his contract of employment without notice in acceptance of a repudiatory breach of contract by his employer'.

As a general rule, Reg 7(1) and (2) apply whether dismissals are express or constructive. So, with regard to a constructive dismissal that is shown to be by reason of a relevant transfer, or for a reason connected with the transfer that is not for an 'ETO reason', the dismissal will be automatically unfair under Reg 7(1). Liability will (usually) pass to the transferee if the constructive dismissal occurs while the employee is employed by the transferor before the transfer, and will rest with the transferee if the dismissal occurs after the transfer.

3.29 Generally, where an employee does nothing in response to an employer's repudiatory breach of contract, he or she is likely to be regarded as having sanctioned it, thereby affirming the contract, and will lose the right to resign and claim that he or she has been constructively dismissed. Note however that where a detrimental change to terms and conditions occurs in connection with a relevant transfer under TUPE, case law suggests that such a change will be void, even where the employee in question purports to agree to it. Logically, therefore, an employee will be able to claim constructive dismissal years after the initial breach, notwithstanding his or her inaction at the time – despite the principle that the objective of the Directive is not to improve on employees' existing rights. Transferees need to be aware of their extended potential liability in this regard.

3.30 *Anticipatory breach of contract.* Where an employer manifests a clear intention to commit a breach of contract at some date in the future, an employee can resign and claim constructive dismissal in anticipation of the breach of contract. Clearly, where a transferring employee resigns after the transfer, in anticipation of a breach of contract by his or her new employer, the transferee will be liable if the constructive dismissal is found to be unfair. But who will be liable if an employee, while still employed by the transferor, anticipates a change being made to his or her fundamental terms and conditions by the transferee and, in view of this, resigns and claims unfair constructive dismissal before the transfer?

It seems that the answer to this will depend on whether the employee is taken to have formally objected to the transfer. The rationale upon which this proposition is based is complex, and is explained in detail in Chapter 4, under 'Constructive dismissals – resignation in anticipation of a breach by the transferee'. Suffice to say here that in Humphreys v University of Oxford and anor 2000 ICR 405, CA, the Court of Appeal considered the interrelationship between the right to object to the transfer under what is now Reg 4(8) and the right to claim constructive dismissal by reason of an anticipated repudiation by the transferee under what is now Reg 4(11). The Court ruled that, notwithstanding that Reg 5(4B) stipulated that, where an employee objects, the relevant transfer will operate to terminate his or her employment with the transferor and that termination shall not be regarded as constituting a dismissal for *any* purpose, the employee's right to claim unfair constructive dismissal against the transferor was nonetheless preserved. This was because what is now Reg 4(7) is, by virtue of Reg 4(11), subject to 'any right... arising apart from these Regulations' to claim constructive dismissal.

However, the Court made it clear that, in order for the transferor to be regarded **3.31** as having constructively dismissed the employee by reason of the transferee's anticipated repudiatory breach, the employee's objection to the transfer would have to be one of substance (i.e. a fundamental change in working conditions). If, on the other hand, the employee's objection was merely based on the fact that the identity of his employer was about to change as a result of the imminent transfer, that would not be a repudiatory breach of contract. In these latter circumstances, the employee would simply be left with the legal consequences specified by Reg 4(8) when an objection to the transfer is made – i.e. the relevant transfer would serve automatically to terminate the employee's contract, but he or she would be unable to claim to have been 'dismissed' for any purpose whatsoever.

Although, in a case where the employee has both objected to the transfer and resigned on the basis of constructive dismissal, the Court of Appeal in Humphreys makes it clear that liability for the dismissal will remain with the transferor, it would appear that the position is different where the employee resigns in the face of a fundamental breach of contract by the transferor but does not formally object to the transfer. In Euro-Die (UK) Ltd v Skidmore and anor EAT 1158/98 the EAT ruled that any liability for constructive dismissal in these circumstances will pass to the transferee if the dismissal was automatically unfair as a result of what is now Reg 7(1) – i.e. if the dismissal is by reason of the transfer or for a reason connected to it that is not an ETO reason. If, however, there is an ETO reason for the constructive dismissal within the meaning of Reg 7(2), the liability for it would not transfer but would instead

193

remain with the transferor. A full explanation of the rationale upon which the EAT reached this conclusion is given in Chapter 4 under 'Constructive dismissals – resignation in anticipation of a breach by the transferee'.

3.32 There is no doubt that the rules regarding which employer – transferor or transferee – is liable with regard to a pre-transfer constructive dismissal can yield quirky results. On the one hand, where an employee, owing to his or her anticipating a repudiatory breach by the transferee, both objects to a relevant transfer and successfully claims constructive dismissal, the transferor will be liable for that dismissal through little or no fault of his own (see the Humphreys case). On the other hand, where an employee does not formally object to the transfer but successfully claims unfair constructive dismissal on the back of a failure on the part of the transferor, where such failure is connected with the relevant transfer, liability is likely to pass to the transferee under TUPE, through little or no fault of the transferee's (see the Euro-Die case). This analysis illustrates why it is extremely important that both transferor and transferee consider carefully the nature of the warranties and indemnities that are to be contained in the transfer agreement, under which the parties can essentially decide between themselves who is to bear the liabilities for transfer-connected dismissals – see Chapter 10 for the practicalities.

3.33 **Material detriment dismissals.** Where an action by the transferee, actual or anticipatory, is not sufficient to amount to a repudiatory breach of contract for the purposes of a constructive dismissal claim, the employee might nevertheless be entitled to 'resign' and treat him or herself as dismissed under Reg 4(9). This provides that, if a relevant transfer involves or would involve 'a substantial change in working conditions to the material detriment of a person' whose contract of employment is transferring, 'such an employee may treat the contract of employment as having been terminated, and the employee shall be treated for any purpose as having been dismissed by the employer'. This form of dismissal – new to the 2006 Regulations – is discussed in detail in Chapter 4 under 'Material detriment dismissals'.

It is important to note that the substantial change to working conditions that forms the basis of a Reg 4(9) dismissal need not amount to a repudiatory breach of contract, or even to a breach of contract at all, following the wording of Reg 4(9) (which statutorily reverses the Court of Appeal's decision in Rossiter v Pendragon plc and Crosby-Clarke v Air Foyle Ltd 2002 ICR 1063, CA). The circumstances in which Reg 4(9) can operate are therefore potentially much wider than the normal concept of constructive dismissal. There is nothing, however, to prevent an employee claiming unfair dismissal on the basis both of material detriment dismissal under Reg 4(9) and constructive dismissal under Reg 4(11).

3.34 Regulation 4(9) states that where a relevant transfer involves or would involve substantial changes to the employee's material detriment, the employee may treat the contract as having been terminated and the employee will be treated as having been dismissed 'by the employer'. The employer in question will, we suggest, be the transferor where the effective date of termination occurs before the transfer takes place, and the transferee if the relevant date falls after the transfer. Subject to what is said below, however, it is submitted that liability for a pre-transfer dismissal would pass to the transferee in any event under Reg 4(2) and (3) if, as is often likely to be the case, the dismissal is shown to be by reason of the transfer or for a transfer-related reason that is not an 'ETO reason' under Reg 7(1).

This is subject to the caveat we discussed under 'Anticipatory constructive dismissal' immediately above. If an employee formally objects to the transfer, then Reg 4(7) precludes the contract of employment and the rights, powers, duties and liabilities under or in connection with it from transferring to the transferee. Thus, where an employee objects to the transfer within the meaning of Reg 4(7) and successfully claims material detriment dismissal under Reg 4(9), liability in these circumstances would not be transferred, but would remain with the transferor.

Statutory rights 3.35

Many rights of employees as against their employers are derived not from the terms of their employment contracts but from statute. Some, such as the right to equal pay for men and women, are inserted into the contract expressly by legislation, while others, such as rights under health and safety legislation, are not referable to the contract (with the proviso that breaches of such rights may also constitute breaches of implied contractual terms such as the obligation on the employer to provide a safe system of work and a safe workplace). Clearly, all employees benefit from such rights to the extent that they are covered by the relevant legislation, so the transferee will bear such responsibilities towards its 'new' employees simply by virtue of being their current employer. But to what extent is the transferee liable for the transferor's breaches, committed before the transfer, of the transferred employees' statutory rights?

The brief answer is that the transferee does inherit liability for the statutory rights of transferred employees, with the exception of liability under a continuation order – see 'Continuation orders' below – and the partial exception of the duty to inform and consult in relation to a relevant transfer – see under 'Collective rights and liabilities – duty to inform and consult' below. If a statutory right or liability of an employer can be said to have arisen under or in connection with an employment contract, then it will be transferred by Reg 4(2)(a).

Take the following example, which related to the equality clause which is 3.36 deemed to be included in every contract under which a person is employed at an establishment in Great Britain – S.1(1) Equal Pay Act 1970. The term 'equality clause' is defined in S.1(2), but in brief is intended to ensure parity of terms and conditions between men and women engaged on like work, work rated as equivalent, or work of equivalent value, and to prevent less favourable treatment of a woman compared with a man, or vice versa:

- **Armstrong and ors v Newcastle upon Tyne NHS Hospital Trust** EAT 0158–59/04 (the case subsequently came before the Court of Appeal on other points): the Newcastle Health Authority made bonus payments, before 1985, both to its domestic ancillary workers, most of whom were female, and to its porters, most of whom were male. In that year, the domestic work was put out to tender, and an in-house tender was accepted. As a result, the domestic staff lost the right to bonuses, whereas bonus payments to porters continued. In 1991 responsibility for the Authority's four hospitals was divided between two new hospital trusts, the Royal Victoria Infirmary and Freeman. In 1998, RVI and Freeman merged, becoming the Newcastle upon Tyne NHS Hospital Trust (the NHT). In 2001 a group of female domestic workers brought equal pay claims against the NHT. They argued that their work was of equal value to that of male porters working at RVI, who continued to receive the bonus payments to which the domestic workers were no longer entitled. One of the issues before the EAT was: What were the effects on the equality clause of the two TUPE transfers, in 1991 and again in 1998? The EAT observed that the effect on the employees' contracts was that they were deemed always to have been with the respondent Trust. From any date when a claimant's contract commenced, the equality clause operated to vary her contract of employment and that contract, as varied, remained in force.

3.37 As compensation in equal pay claims may extend back over six years, the transferee's liability in such cases is, potentially, very great. However, the Armstrong case should be contrasted with cases where an equal pay claim relates to an employee's pension rights. The pension rights, as modified by the equality clause, are incapable of transferring under TUPE following Reg 10 – see under 'Pensions' below.

3.38 **Statutory rights associated with employment relationship.** Even if an employee's statutory right does not clearly arise from association with the employment contract, it is likely that the transferee will nevertheless pick up responsibility for it. The Acquired Rights Directive clearly intends liability for employees' statutory rights to be transferred. As we discussed under 'Contractual and discretionary rights and benefits' above, Article 3.1 expressly applies to all rights and obligations of the transferor arising from an *employment relationship* and not just in respect of an employment contract. In Martin and ors v South Bank University 2004 ICR 1234, ECJ, the European Court considered that it was clear from Article 3 that – except where provided by Article 3.4 – all the transferor's rights and obligations arising from the contract of employment or employment relationship were transferred to the transferee, regardless of whether the rights and obligations in question derived from statutory provisions or were implemented by such provisions.

The EAT's decision in Alamo Group (Europe) Ltd v Tucker and anor 2003 ICR 829, EAT, concerned whether a transferee inherited the transferor's liability to pay employees compensation for his failure to consult with employee representatives regarding a proposed transfer under what is now Reg 13 of the 2006 Regulations (for which, see under 'Collective tights and liabilities – duty to inform and consult' below). The EAT took the view that as the employment relationship includes not only contractual rights but also rights and liabilities from statute and regulations that neither party can exclude, it would make no sense for the legislature to intend to exclude statutory or regulatory rights that it had introduced for the very purpose of protecting employees. Reg 4 therefore applied, the EAT said, to rights and obligations derived from statute and regulations, even if not expressly or impliedly incorporated in the contract of employment, provided these exist 'in connection with' the contract of employment or (following the wording in the Directive) 'the employment relationship'. After all, in the seminal cases of Litster and ors v Forth Dry Dock and Engineering Co Ltd (in receivership) and anor 1989 ICR 341, HL, and (1) British Fuels Ltd v Baxendale and anor (2) Wilson and ors v St Helens Borough Council 1998 ICR 1141, HL, it was established that liability for unfair dismissal under Reg 7 is transferred in accordance with Reg 4, notwithstanding that protection against unfair dismissal is a statutory and not a contractual right.

Failure to fulfil statutory obligations. Regulation 4(2)(b) of TUPE 2006 is **3.39** capable in itself of effecting the transfer of statutory rights such as those mentioned above, as it attributes to the transferee *any act or omission* of or in relation to the transferor in respect of the transferred employment contract or *in respect of the employee* assigned to the transferred undertaking. This includes an employer's omission to fulfil his statutory responsibilities towards his employees that are independent of the employment contract, as well as those that are implied or incorporated into the contract. An example:

- **DJM International Ltd v Nicholas** 1996 ICR 214, EAT: N transferred under TUPE to DJM. She had previously been employed full time but had been forced by her previous employer to retire at 60 and re-employed by it on a part-time basis. When DJM later made her redundant, she brought several claims against it, including sex discrimination relating to her forced retirement. The EAT held that the issue was not whether the alleged act of sex discrimination was in respect of a particular contract, but whether it was in respect of a person employed in the undertaking transferred. Under Reg 5(2) of the 1981 Regulations (which Reg 4(2) of TUPE 2006 has since replaced), any 'things done' by a transferor were deemed to have been done by the transferee, so DJM was potentially liable for the alleged discrimination.

197

3.40 The position was confirmed in Taylor v Serviceteam Ltd and London Borough of Waltham Forest, Romford County Court, 24.10.97 Case No.RM602374 – see under 'Tortious and other civil liabilities' below – in which the court held that liability for failure to operate a safe system of work and for breach of an employer's statutory duty was a liability arising 'in connection with' an employment contract under what is now Reg 4(2)(a). A breach of statutory duty also amounted to an act 'done… in respect of' an employee within the meaning of Reg 4(2)(b). On the facts of the case, the transferor's potential liability for breach of statutory duty (and in tort) in respect of an employee's personal injury passed to the transferee by virtue of Reg 4(2).

In Perry's Motor Sales Ltd and anor v Lindley EAT 0616/07 the EAT held that liabilities that 'crystallise' on the transfer are capable of transferring to the transferee. In this case, L was dismissed by the transferor prior to the transfer on the instruction of the transferee. The unusual facts were that L had previously worked for the transferee and had brought claims against it. After the transfer, she brought tribunal proceedings against the transferee arguing that, although she had been employed for less than one year, her dismissal had been automatically unfair under S.104 ERA on the ground that she had been dismissed for seeking to enforce a statutory right (i.e. the right to claim unfair dismissal when previously employed by the transferee). Both the employment tribunal and the EAT agreed that L's dismissal by the transferor should be treated as an act of the transferee by virtue of Reg 4(2)(b). The EAT specifically rejected the contention that, because the claimant was never in the position to bring S.104 dismissal proceedings against the transferor on the basis of a previous claim since she had never actually brought such a previous claim, then no such liability could pass to the transferee under Reg 4. Mr Justice Wilkie, giving the judgment of the Appeal Tribunal, stated: 'The transferor, by its actions prior to the transfer, can, by Reg 4(2)(b), cause to crystallise, on the transfer, a liability in the transferee, whose actions they are deemed to be, which was not a liability of the transferor prior to the transfer, which does not transfer under Reg 4(2)(a), but which, nonetheless, is a liability of the transferee as the employer of the claimant.'

3.41 However, in Coutinho v Vision Information Services (UK) Ltd and anor EAT 0469/07, the EAT held that liability for an act of victimisation committed by a transferor after a relevant transfer in relation to a former employee whose contract terminated prior to that transfer, was not an existing liability of the transferor at the date of the transfer and thus could not pass to the transferee. The act did not fall within Reg 4(2)(a) or Reg 4(2)(b) as it took place *after* the transfer. The claimant's claim for victimisation against the transferee was therefore struck out by the tribunal.

3.42 **TUPE does not augment statutory rights.** Just as the application of TUPE protection cannot create or increase contractual or collectively agreed rights upon relevant transfer (as we saw from the decision in the Computershare and Werhof cases discussed under 'Overview' at the beginning of this chapter), so neither can it artificially augment an employee's statutory rights. In Cross and anor v British Airways plc 2006 ICR 1239, CA, C and G worked for British Caledonian Airways Ltd (BCA) until 1988, when the company merged with British Airways plc (BA). Under their terms and conditions with BCA, C and G had a contractual retiring age (CRA) of 60. Following the merger, they became employed on BA's terms and conditions, which included an earlier CRA of 55 for all flight crew. When BA terminated their employment upon their reaching 55, C and G brought tribunal claims arguing that they had been unfairly dismissed. BA argued that the tribunal had no jurisdiction to hear the unfair dismissal claims because C and G had reached the normal retiring age (NRA) for the job they were doing – 55 – and were therefore excluded, under S.109 ERA, from the right not to be unfairly dismissed. The main issue for determination was whether C and G's statutory NRA of 60 had transferred with them by operation of TUPE. The matter reached the Court of Appeal, which noted that, while there is a presumption that an employee's NRA is the same as his or her CRA, an NRA must in fact be determined by reference to the facts at the time of dismissal and not at the time the contract was entered into or at the time of the transfer. Furthermore, determining an NRA is an objective test – one concerned with how the facts affect all employees in the employee's position, and not merely the individual employee in question. The essential issue, as summarised by Lord Justice Peter Gibson in Barclays Bank plc v O'Brien and ors 1994 ICR 865, CA, is 'what, at the effective date of termination of the applicant's employment and on the basis of facts then known, was the age which employees of all ages in the group could reasonably regard as their NRA?'

Having made the above observations, the Court of Appeal agreed with BA that an NRA is subject to change, both pre- and post-transfer, depending on the facts at the time of dismissal. 'It is not something that is capable... of being frozen in perpetuity as at the moment of transfer.' This is because statute requires that it be determined according to the NRA of employees in the same position at the time of dismissal. Put another way, the Court of Appeal accepted that if an employee's NRA may vary, then 'there is nothing there to transfer or to preserve as at the time of transfer'. All that is transferred is a right not to be unfairly dismissed before reaching the NRA, whatever that may be at the time of dismissal. The Court of Appeal therefore dismissed the appeal and upheld the EAT's decision that C and G had an NRA of 55 (and were thus excluded from the right not to be unfairly dismissed).

That the TUPE Regulations can be relied upon to confer statutory entitlements **3.43** that did not exist at the time of the transfer is also demonstrated by Secretary of State for Employment v Anchor Hotel (Kippford) Ltd 1985 IRLR 452, EAT – a case that arose in the context of an employer's claim to a statutory redundancy payment rebate. The question arose as to whether the transferor, who had given employees notice to terminate their employment which expired on the same date as that on which the transfer of the business took effect and who had made redundancy payments to them following the transfer, was entitled to claim a rebate from the National Insurance Fund. The EAT accepted the Secretary of State's contention that no rebate was due in as much as the transferor was never liable to make the redundancy payments because that liability had been transferred to the transferee of the business pursuant to what is now Reg 4 of the 2006 Regulations. In particular, since the employees were employed 'immediately before' the transfer, their contracts and all liabilities under or in connection with their contracts transferred to the transferee, and it was therefore the transferee rather than the transferor who was legally required to make any redundancy payments.

3.44 **Other statutory rights**. In addition to discrimination, unfair dismissal and redundancy claims and equal pay rights, statutory rights or liabilities which will pass to the transferee include those relating to the minimum wage; minimum notice period; annual leave and other working time rights (for example, any opt-out entered into by the employee may continue to apply); protection with regard to trade union membership; rights for part-time or fixed-term workers; the right to return from maternity leave, and other family-related rights. See below for a discussion as to protective awards.

3.45 **Tortious and other civil liabilities**
We saw under 'Contractual and discretionary rights and benefits' above that the Court of Appeal in Secretary of State for Employment v Spence and ors 1986 ICR 651, CA, ventured to suggest that the wording of old Reg 5(2)(b) (which is now replaced in amended form by Reg 4(2)(b)) appeared to have 'the effect of transferring obligations other than contractual obligations: for example... they may well embrace obligations arising in tort'. This hesitancy now seems odd, as it has become well established that the transferee inherits liability in respect of the tortious acts of the transferor in so far as such acts are committed against a person employed in the transferred undertaking. Such liability is acquired not just under the 'acts and omissions' provision of Reg 4(2)(b) but also under the basic provision transferring all the transferor's rights, powers, duties and liabilities under or in connection with the employee's contract of employment in Reg 4(2)(a). The point was tested in the following case:

• **Taylor v Serviceteam Ltd and London Borough of Waltham Forest**, Romford County Court, 24.10.97 Case No.RM602374: T was employed by the London Borough of Waltham Forest ('the Borough') as a refuse collector. In May 1994 he sustained an injury to his wrist while retrieving a bin that had slipped into a dustcart because it was the wrong size for the loading mechanism. T alleged that his employer was negligent and had breached the Manual Handling Operations Regulations 1992 SI 1992/2793, which obliged employers, so far as reasonably practicable, to avoid the need for employees to undertake manual handling operations that involved a risk of injury. In August 1994 the Borough's refuse collection service was contracted out, under TUPE, to S Ltd, who became T's new employer. T sought to recover compensation for his injury from S Ltd, and the Romford County Court had to decide, as a preliminary issue, whether the Borough's potential liability for negligence or breach of statutory duty had passed to the transferee by virtue of Reg 4(2)(a). The Court considered that although liability for negligence or for breach of statutory duty was not a liability under an employment contract within the meaning of Reg 4(2)(a), an employer's duty to operate a safe system of work arose by virtue of the existence of a contract of employment. Accordingly, liability for failure to operate a safe system of work and for breach of an employer's statutory duty was a liability arising 'in connection with' an employment contract under Reg 4(2)(a). A tortious act or breach of statutory duty also amounted to an act 'done... in respect of' an employee within the meaning of old Reg 5(2)(b) (now Reg 4(2)(B) but with slightly different wording). It followed that the transferor's potential liability in tort and for breach of statutory duty in respect of the personal injury sustained by the employee passed to the transferee of the undertaking by virtue of Reg 4(2).

Tortious liability for personal injury/negligence. Tortious acts, in the **3.46** employment context, can often be categorised in a number of different ways, as the above case demonstrates. The common law tort of negligence may also interface with a breach of the implied contractual term to provide a safe system of work, or breaches of statutory duties contained in health and safety legislation. However, given that the question as to whether a liability passes is referable to the 'employment relationship' – according to the Directive – it does not normally matter in which way a claim is framed (other than the fact that the duty to mitigate loss applies to damages claims for breach of contract in the way that does not apply to claims in tort). In the combined cases of (1) Martin v Lancashire County Council (2) Bernadone v Pall Mall Services Group Ltd and ors 2001 ICR 197, CA, the Court of Appeal held that an employee's personal injury claim was capable of transfer whether the claim was pleaded in negligence, contract or breach of statutory duty. Indeed, the fact that the employees in those cases, who chose to sue in negligence, could alternatively have sued in contract for breach of an implied term to provide a safe system or place of work, substantiated the point that the employer's liability for negligent breach of his duty of care could be said to be 'in connection with' the contract of employment within the meaning of Reg 4(2)(a).

The cases discussed above dealt with circumstances in which an employee sustained an injury before the transfer, and the issue was whether liability for that injury transferred to the transferee. What is the situation where a *risk* of injury is evident before the transfer, but the injury itself is not sustained until after the transfer? The result is likely to depend upon the extent to which the employer should have been aware of the risk to the employee – in other words, if the employee brought the issue to his attention or if the risk was objectively obvious. In a transfer situation, if the transferor was or should have been aware of the risk, but did nothing about it, this omission will be imputed to the transferee under Reg 4(2)(b), so that when and if the injury is sustained the transferee will not be able to hide behind the transfer to avoid liability. This drives home the need for the transferee to undertake probing due diligence – and to obtain appropriate indemnities and warranties in respect of information provided to him by the transferor – see Chapter 10 for advice on these matters.

3.47 **Transfer of transferor's personal injury insurance cover.** The decision in Martin v Lancashire County Council (above) was also significant in that it addressed the problem of personal injury insurance. Before the Court of Appeal's decision, where an employee was injured before the transfer, and liability for that injury passed to the transferee upon transfer, the transferee would not be able to take advantage of the transferor's insurance under the Employers' Liability (Compulsory Insurance) Act 1969. This was because the transferor's insurer would only incur liability where the *transferor* was liable (the principle of secondary liability). Such liability would not, however, arise where the transferor offloaded its liability to the employee onto the transferee at the moment of transfer as a result of Reg 4(2). The problem was exacerbated by the fact that the transferee could not claim under its own employer's compulsory liability insurance policy, as this would not cover injuries to an employee that occurred before the employee entered the transferee's employment.

In the Taylor case (see above) the county court registered its concern that 'although the [Acquired Rights] Directive is intended to safeguard employees' rights, one of the curious consequences of such transfer of such rights to the transferee is that whereas an employee would be certain to recover (all other things being equal) damages from the transferor or its insurance company because of compulsory employer's liability insurance, the transferee would probably not have such cover for an event occurring before the undertaking was transferred to it. The transferee might well not be able to meet the cost of a liability about which it knew nothing and for which it would not otherwise have been responsible. In that event the employee's rights would not have been safeguarded.' Given that the limitation period for commencing personal injury proceedings is three years, transferees prior to the decision in Martin could be faced with potentially substantial claims arising from acts that occurred some time before the transfer. Were such a transferee in financial difficulty and unable to meet such claims, the injured transferring employee would be severely prejudiced. The only solution was for the transferee to ensure that the transferor gave appropriate and comprehensive warranties and indemnities.

Fortunately, the issue of whether a transferor's right to an indemnity under an **3.48** employer's liability insurance policy could be a transferable right within the meaning of Reg 4(2)(a) came directly before the Court of Appeal in Martin. The employees in the joined appeals were a refuse collector and a catering assistant respectively, who had each been injured at work before their employments were transferred under TUPE, and sought damages from their new employers. Having found that tortious liabilities were capable of transfer under Reg 4(2) (see above), the Court went on to consider whether a transferor's right to be indemnified in respect of tortious liabilities under his employer's liability insurance passes to the transferee under Reg 4(2). S.1(1) of the Employers' Liability (Compulsory Insurance) Act 1969 obliges all employers who are not exempted to insure against liability in respect of personal injuries sustained by employees arising out of and in the course of their employment. The Court noted that although employees do not have a right of action under that Act, it was enacted for their benefit, ensuring that employers were able to meet any personal injury liability arising. Given the Court's decision that the transferor's liability to an employee in tort was a liability 'in connection with' the contract of employment within the meaning of Reg 4(2)(a), the transferor's vested or contingent right to recover from its insurers in respect of the tortious liability therefore also amounted to a vested or contingent right in respect of a liability 'in connection with' the contract. Although the right to recover an indemnity was a right under the contract of insurance – and not 'under' the contract of employment within the wording of Reg 4(2)(a) – that right was nonetheless 'in connection with' and 'arising from' the contract of employment because the liability being insured was a liability for bodily injury or disease sustained by the employees arising in the course of their employment. Accordingly, the Court concluded that Reg 4(2)(a) was not limited to the transfer of rights and liabilities only as between the employee and the transferor.

The main problem, even after the decision in Martin, was that not every employer is obliged to take out insurance covering possible personal injury claims by his employees. Public sector companies, for example, are exempted from the requirement to take out personal injury insurance by S.3 of the Employers' Liability (Compulsory Insurance) Act 1969. So a transferee buying from a public sector company could inherit an uninsured claim that it might be unable to meet. The TUPE Regulations 2006 specifically addresses this point in Reg 17 by imposing on the transferor and transferee joint and several liability in respect of being liable for personal injury sustained by employees – see under 'Continuing liability of the transferor' below. But Martin will still be relevant in cases regarding insurance that is affected by the Employers' Liability (Compulsory Insurance) Act 1969. It should be carefully noted in this regard that the principle established by that case, while welcome, does not leave either transferees or transferred employees entirely protected. Where, for example, the transferor has failed in some respect to comply with the insurance policy –

203

perhaps by not notifying the insurer of relevant information – the insurer may refuse to pay out, or the transferee may find that there is an excess to pay. The lesson to be drawn from this is that warranties and indemnities can never be dispensed with.

3.49 **Transfer of other tortious liabilities.** Most cases in relation to the transfer of tortious liability relate to personal injury claims, but other tortious claims (such as those based on misrepresentation or negligent misstatement) are also capable of transfer. One example:

- **Hagen and ors v ICI Chemicals and Polymers Ltd and ors** 2002 IRLR 31, QBD: the claimants comprised some 439 employees who were originally employed in the Central Engineering Resource section of ICI Chemicals and Polymers Ltd until August 1994, when ICI divested that part of its business to Redpath Engineering Services (RES). It was common ground that TUPE applied and all of the employees' contracts of employment transferred to RES. The employees were considerably reluctant to transfer out of ICI because of, among other things, ICI's culture of job security and its favourable pension scheme. The case was unusual in that the managements of both ICI and RES accepted that the deal would not go ahead without the support of the workforce as a whole. Although the employees eventually agreed to the transfer, they later claimed that they had been persuaded to do so because of certain promises given and representations made to them by ICI (the transferor) and RES (the transferee). The employees claimed that these representations were in fact false and as a consequence they had been misled and had suffered loss. They brought actions in the High Court seeking damages on the basis of, inter alia, negligent misrepresentation. The High Court found that ICI was in breach of an implied term in the employees' contracts of employment and an equivalent duty in tort to take reasonable care over the accuracy of the representations made to the employees. ICI had negligently misrepresented to the employees the extent to which the pensions on offer from RES were 'broadly comparable' to the pensions provided by the ICI scheme. The Court found that the employees had relied on the representations to their detriment in agreeing to the transfer going ahead, and that had the employees known the true position under the RES pension scheme they would, on the balance of probabilities, have successfully renegotiated so that no one was more than 2 per cent worse off. The question then arose as to whether Reg 4 operated so as to pass ICI's liability for negligent misrepresentation to RES. The High Court held that following the Court of Appeal's decision in Martin v Lancashire County Council (see above), a transferor's liability to his employees in tort is, in principle, capable of passing to a transferee, particularly where it mirrors a contractual liability. It is a liability that arises 'in connection with' a contract of employment within the meaning of Reg 4(2)(a)). However,

Reg 10 provides that Reg 4 does not apply to liabilities arising under or in connection with so much of the contract as relates to an occupational pension scheme. Where, as on the facts in this case, the transferors had negligently misrepresented the benefits to be conferred under an occupational pension scheme, their liability was 'in connection with' that part of the contract relating to the scheme. Accordingly, the transferor's liability was caught by Reg 7 and did not pass to the transferee – see under 'Rights and liabilities that do not transfer – terms relating to pensions' below.

Vicarious liability. Employers are also *vicariously* liable for the torts of their 3.50 employees committed in the course of employment. So, where one employee commits a tortious act against another, it seems likely that the injured employee could claim against a transferee who had inherited the transferor's vicarious liability for the unlawful act. However, this may not extend to a transferor's vicarious liability to a third party for an employee's tort. Although there is no case law on the matter, it is probable that Reg 4(2) is best interpreted as transferring only liabilities of the transferor vis-à-vis his employees (as opposed to liabilities owed by him to third parties as a result of his own employees' tortious acts, which surely was not within the protectionist aim of the Acquired Rights Directive). Whatever the doubt, however, it would surely be the case that occupier's liability to a third party visiting the premises would not be transferred, since it would arise wholly independently of employment contracts or an employment relationship, and thus not fall within the ambit of Reg 4(2).

Illegal workers of the transferor. Prior to the Immigration, Asylum and 3.51 Nationality Act 2006 (IANA), the transferee could rely on the transferor's immigration status checks carried out before the transfer. It was therefore unnecessary for the transferee to carry out its own checks on the immigration status of the transferred employees. However, on and after 29 February 2008, a transferee that acquires employees as a result of TUPE must carry out its own checks to avoid a civil penalty – currently a fine of up to £10,000 in respect of each individual. Guidance issued by the UK Border Agency (UKBA), entitled 'The Prevention of illegal working: Comprehensive Guidance for Employers on preventing illegal working', states that: 'Employers who acquire staff as a result of a Transfer of Undertakings (Protection of Employment) Regulations transfer are provided with a grace period of 28 days in which to undertake the appropriate document checks and establish an excuse, following the date of transfer.' If the transferee fails to carry out the checks on any transferring employee within 28 days it will not be able to avoid civil liability in relation to that employee.

As a result of the UKBA guidance, the transferee cannot argue that it does not need to carry out checks as those carried out by the transferor are deemed, by virtue of Reg 4(2)(b), to have been carried out by the transferee. The statutory

205

defence in S.15(3) IANA to the civil penalty does not transfer from the transferor to the transferee.

3.52 The UKBA Sponsorship and Employers' Helpline has confirmed that the 28-day limit applies even if a transferee has a high number of transferred employees. The UKBA Helpline recommends that if an employer wishes to establish a statutory excuse it should prioritise completing the checks within the 28-day grace period. If an employer cannot complete the checks in time, and suspects that an employee is working illegally, it should contact the helpline and ask for a reference number. This can then be quoted to apply for a penalty reduction should the transferee be found to be employing illegal workers.

While the UKBA guidance is silent on the matter, liability in respect of the transferor failing to carry out immigration status checks is likely to transfer to the transferee under Reg 4(2) since it is highly arguable that the liability is 'in connection with' a transferred contract of employment. Therefore, the transferee would be wise to obtain indemnities and warranties in respect of the transferor's failure to have carried out such checks and its consequential liability for a civil penalty.

3.53 *Transferred employee on limited leave to remain.* If a transferred employee has limited leave to remain in the United Kingdom, and no statutory excuse has previously been established, a check will need to be completed within the 28-day grace period. The transferee would not need to do a document check until the next annual check required for those on limited leave if:

* a statutory excuse had already been established by the transferor, and

* the anniversary for the annual check for those on limited leave was more than 28 days away.

3.54 *Transferred employees who commenced work for transferor before February 2008.* The UKBA Sponsorship and Employers' Helpline has also confirmed that if the transferred employee commenced work for the transferor prior to February 2008, the transferee will have a statutory defence if:

* checks based on the April 2004 guidelines had been carried out at the time of employment

* the transfer was in accordance with TUPE; and

* there was true continuity in the employee's terms and conditions.

If the transferor carried out no checks on an employee who commenced work prior to February 2008, provided the transfer was in accordance with TUPE, and there was true continuity in the employee's terms and conditions, the UKBA Helpline has stated that there would be no legal requirement to establish a statutory excuse. However, whether or not checks were carried out at the

206

time of employment by the transferor, the transferee is advised to carry out the necessary checks within 28 days in order to establish a statutory excuse.

Transfer of transferor's status as a 'sponsor'. Under the United Kingdom's 3.55 points-based immigration system, employers who wish to employ migrants from outside the European Economic Area need to be registered as a 'sponsor' with the UKBA. This registration does not pass to the transferee on a TUPE transfer. Where a transferee acquires 'sponsored' employees as a result of a transfer it must apply for a sponsor licence, if it does not already have one, within 28 days of the transfer. If its application is unsuccessful, all migrants who were due to transfer will have their permission to stay and work in the United Kingdom curtailed. The transferor must provide the UKBA, within 28 days of the change, with the details of any migrants who will transfer to the transferee by emailing SCOC@ukba.gsi.gov.uk.

Further details on action the transferor and transferee should take in relation to sponsored employees can be found on www.ukba.homeoffice.gov.uk.

Mobility clauses   3.56

Where transferred employees have mobility clauses in their contracts, the question may well arise after the transfer whether the transferee will be entitled to enforce an equivalent mobility clause appropriate to its own place of business. This issue has been considered by the EAT in Tapere v South London and Maudsley NHS Trust 2009 IRLR 972, EAT. In that case, T's employment was transferred in April 2007 from Lewisham Primary Care Trust (LPCT) to South London and Maudsley NHS Trust (SLMT) following a TUPE transfer. After the transfer, SLMT attempted to relocate T to another hospital site in reliance upon the mobility clause in her contract with LPCT, which permitted relocation 'to similar locations *within the Trust*'. However, T did not wish to be relocated and brought a claim against SLMT under Reg 4(9) on the ground that she had been subjected to a substantial change to working conditions to her material detriment in respect of which she was entitled to claim unfair dismissal. An employment tribunal rejected that claim, ruling that the mobility clause was not in this case restricted, post-transfer, to the transferor's (LPCT's) geographical location, but that the benefit of it transferred, entitling SLMT to transfer T to any of the locations at which it operated. In so holding, the tribunal concluded that the words 'within the Trust' in the mobility clause did not add anything: an employer with a mobility clause would only transfer an employee to other locations which that employer itself owned or operated.

On appeal, the EAT was adamant that the phrasing of a contractual mobility clause fell to be construed in view of the facts and circumstances at the time the contract containing the clause was entered into. Where, in a TUPE context, there are practical impediments to permitting the clause to be implemented by the transferee with precisely the same benefits and obligations, then the

207

equivalent of these can be substituted provided that neither benefit nor burden is increased or enlarged (the concept of 'substantial equivalence'). It was not necessary to consider substantial equivalence if the relevant contractual term can be continued, post-transfer, without practical difficulty. In the instant case, the words 'within the Trust' could not be regarded as surplus or meaningless. They were plainly words of definition, which restricted the intended geographical area to which the mobility clause applied. The interpretation adopted by the employment tribunal had increased the scope of the geographical area in which the employee could be required to relocate. This resulted in the terms of her contract being altered to her disadvantage and in her employment being less protected after the transfer than it was before. The tribunal had erred in finding that there had been no dismissal within the terms of Reg 4(9).

The EAT's approach to the mobility clause in the Tapere case (above) underlines the fact that the practical difficulties experienced by a transferee cannot be invoked to override or modify an employee's contractual rights.

3.57 Restrictive covenants

Restrictive covenants and clauses preventing the disclosure of confidential information are often set out in the employment contract, or at least in an agreement that is collateral to the employment contract, and therefore, from a straightforward reading of Reg 4(2)(a), the benefit of these should pass to the transferee upon a relevant transfer. However, as the courts have identified, problems arise from attempting to transfer such employer-specific rights and obligations.

First, there is a question of enforceability. Restrictive covenants are strictly speaking contrary to public policy, so will be enforced by the courts only where the restraint can be shown to be no wider than is reasonably necessary to protect the legitimate business interests of the employer. For this reason, covenants are usually 'tailor-made' to suit the needs of that particular employer in relation to his products, customers and catchment area. Were it to be applied, literally, to a different employer, with possibly different products, customers and catchment area, a covenant may cease, as drafted, to be reasonable, and thus be unenforceable.

3.58 Related to this, the question arises as to whether Reg 4(2) can possibly have the effect of transferring the benefit of a restrictive covenant to a purchaser whose specific needs may be very different. The Court of Session in McCall v Initial Supplies Ltd, unreported 2.5.90, Ct Sess, doubted that it could. To hold otherwise, the Court reasoned, would mean that in certain situations the substitution of the transferee could radically alter the rights and duties of the parties to the contract of employment. To take an example, a restrictive covenant which prohibits the poaching of an employer's customers may be reasonable in the context of a small company. However, if that company is transferred to a large multinational, the group of customers to whom the restriction purportedly applies may increase substantially, both in numerical and geographical terms. Another argument could be that the whole purpose of the Directive (and therefore the purpose of the national law that implements it) is to protect employees who are subjected to a transfer. As restrictive covenants are in the interests of the employer, surely TUPE has no place in seeking to preserve them.

In Morris Angel and Son Ltd v Hollande and anor 1993 ICR 71, CA, however, the Court of Appeal confirmed that restrictive covenants *do* transfer under TUPE. The question is rather how the transferred covenant should be interpreted. The covenant in question, which was contained in H's service agreement, restrained him from dealing after his dismissal with persons who had done business with the employer or its subsidiaries in the previous year. H was dismissed at the time that the company for which he worked was transferred to MA Ltd under TUPE. The Court found that what is now 4(1) gave the purchasing employer standing to enforce the covenant to restrain the employee from dealing with former clients of the transferred undertaking. However, the covenant could not be read in a way that restricted H from dealing with those who had been customers of the transferee in the year leading up to the transfer, since that would be to radically alter the nature of the agreement (and H had not been seeking to deal with those customers in any event). As Dillon LJ put it: 'Such an obligation was not remotely in contemplation when the service agreement was entered into and I can see no reason why [Reg 4] should have sought to change the burden on the employee.' However, the Court went on to hold that Reg 4(1) required the covenant to be read, purposively and retrospectively, as though it had been agreed between H and the transferee as *owner of the undertaking*. This gave the transferee standing to enforce the covenant in respect of persons who had been clients of the transferred undertaking in the year prior to dismissal. This solution also deals with the problem of enforceability, discussed above, as the reinterpreted covenant was no wider than it was before. The Court also dealt with the issue of the protective purpose of TUPE: 'There is no doubt that the protection of employees' rights was the primary objective but any contract of employment is a complex of rights and obligations on each side, and in Litster v Forth Dry Dock and Engineering Co Ltd, Lord Templeman summed up the effect of the EEC Directive as being that upon the transfer of a business from one employer to another the benefit and burden of a contract of employment between the transferor and a worker in the business should devolve on the transferee.'

The distinguishing factor between the McCall and Morris Angel decisions is **3.59** probably that in Morris Angel the employee was dismissed immediately after the transfer and so the transferred undertaking and its clients could still be seen as a separate entity from the rest of the transferee's business. Thus, it remains to be seen whether Morris Angel establishes a general rule or whether it turns

209

to a large extent on its own facts. In particular, the Court did not have to consider what meaning the covenant might have had if the employee had been dismissed six or 12 months after the transfer. If Morris Angel does establish a general rule, its effect will be to freeze the scope of, for example, a non-dealing covenant as at the date of the transfer, and any dealings that the employee has after his dismissal with persons who became customers of the transferee after the transfer will not be caught by it. Even with the benefit of the Court of Appeal's approach in Morris Angel, the restrictive covenant may cease to provide suitable protection for the new owner. If covenants are to receive a limited interpretation following transfer, it would be advisable for transferees to renegotiate more appropriate ones once the transfer has taken place so as to make them more relevant to the transferee's business, and thus more likely to be enforced by the courts. But considerable care ought to be taken in this regard. Any such renegotiated covenants could be set aside under Reg 4(4) on the basis that the reason for the variation is 'connected with the transfer' and 'not an economic, technical or organisational reason entailing changes in the workforce' – see Credit Suisse First Boston (Europe) Ltd v Lister 1999 ICR 794, CA, and the discussion in Chapter 5, under 'Varying terms in a TUPE context'.

The problem, however, does not end there. What are the consequences for the transferor? If it transfers only part of its business, at the point of transfer the transferor loses the benefit of the restrictive covenant for the retained part of its business. This issue may be best addressed by warranties or indemnities between the transferor and the transferee. The transferor will also lose the benefit of provisions as to confidential information, whether express or implied. Remember, too, the principle that an employer may not enforce the benefit of a contract where he has committed a repudiatory breach of it. As the transferee inherits any breaches of contract from the transferor, his ability to enforce restrictive covenants may be jeopardised.

3.60 In New ISG Ltd v Vernon 2008 ICR 319, ChD, the identity of the transferee was withheld by the transferor. Upon learning of the identity of their new employer, a number of employees objected to the TUPE transfer. The transferee sought interim injunctions to enforce restrictive covenant clauses in the employees' contracts of employment. The transferee argued that the right to object to the TUPE transfer must be exercised before the transfer and, as the employees did not do so, they could not prevent Reg 4 from operating to transfer the benefit of the restrictive covenants to it. The High Court held that, in the circumstances, the employees' objection could be treated as if it had occurred before the transfer, since no valid opportunity had been accorded to the employees to object to the change of employer before then. The objection had retrospective effect and prevented the operation of TUPE from automatically transferring the employees' contracts of employment containing the restraint of trade clause to the transferee. Therefore, the transferee employer's application for injunctive relief was refused.

Share option schemes 3.61

Share options commonly form part of an employee's overall remuneration. If they are expressed as a contractual entitlement, it would seem that they should be transferred by Reg 4(2) – and even if a share option scheme has non-contractual status, it may well have a 'connection' with the contract within the meaning of Reg 4(2)(a). Liabilities under it would accordingly be transferred to the transferee. The same would appear to be the case with an employee's right to participate in a profit-sharing scheme (see below). But a conclusion that liability to continue a share option scheme passes to the transferee upon a relevant transfer is likely to cause considerable practical difficulties. Where, for example, the business of a company is sold to a trading partnership it will be impossible for the partnership to provide the employees with the same rights to buy shares in the new, unincorporated, business. There may therefore be convincing commercial grounds for stopping employees from participating in share option schemes upon the occasion of a relevant transfer. However, the transferee in such situations could be in breach of contract and have to face claims for damages, which could be substantial, or even claims of constructive dismissal. Executive employees in particular may lose out on the chance to obtain future share options, as well as the opportunity to exercise existing rights.

However, the case law demonstrates that it is by no means a given that rights under share option schemes may be enforced against the transferee following a relevant transfer. The precise terms of a scheme are likely to be decisive in determining whether it is capable of surviving the transfer of a business, as the case below illustrates:

- **Chapman and anor v CPS Computer Group plc** 1987 IRLR 462, CA: C and E were employed by a subsidiary of CPS and were entitled to participate in CPS's share option scheme. They could not exercise their rights in the scheme until a specific period of time had passed unless, at any time before the end of that period, one of a number of events intervened – for example, if they were dismissed for redundancy. CPS sold the subsidiary and C and E sought to exercise their options, claiming that they had become redundant because CPS had ceased to carry on the business in which they were employed, despite the fact that what is now Reg 4 applied to transfer their contracts to the purchaser. In the course of its decision, the Court of Appeal held that although Reg 4 transferred the claimants' employment, it did not affect their rights to exercise their options under the share option contract, which was a separate and discrete contract and so was not transferred by Reg 4(2). On the facts of the case, therefore, the sale of the business triggered the claimants' rights to exercise their options.

211

3.62 We take the view that it is likely that this point would be decided differently today. Given the Court of Appeal's decision in (1) Martin v Lancashire County Council (2) Bernadone v Pall Mall Services Group and ors 2001 ICR 197, CA (see under 'Tortious and other civil liabilities' above) – that 4(2)(a) could extend even to a transferor's right against a third party insurer – so long as the right related to a liability 'under' or 'in connection with' the employment contract – it seems unlikely that a contract that contained benefits connected with the employment contract (or at the very least with the employment relationship), would not be covered by Reg 4(2)(a), even if that contract was 'separate and discrete'. However, there is at least one scenario in which share option rights might not be capable of transfer. Reg 4(2)(a), as we have seen, operates to transfer the 'rights, powers, duties and liabilities' *of the transferor* under or in connection with the employment contract. Where an employee owns options over stock in a group company *that is not the transferor*, it is arguable that those options are incapable of transfer under Reg 4(2)(a). The same could apply to a profit-sharing scheme where an employee of a subsidiary receives benefits from another group company calculated on the basis of the profits of the group of companies as a whole.

Even if Chapman was wrongly decided and share options contained in collateral contracts are capable of transfer under Reg 4(2)(a), it may well be the case that TUPE preserves rights in any share option scheme after the transfer only to the extent that the rules of the scheme allow. The employment contract itself may permit an employee to be a member of such a scheme, but the rules may provide employers with a unilateral right of termination and exclusion of liability. Whether rules of this nature were enforceable was at issue in the cases of Micklefield v SAC Technology Ltd 1990 IRLR 218, ChD, and Levett v Biotrace International plc 1999 IRLR 375, CA. In Micklefield, a clause in a share option agreement stating that the option holder had to continue to be employed in order to exercise the option granted, and would be deemed to have waived his right to damages for loss of his option rights as part of any claim for compensation for loss of office, was held to exempt the employer from liability to pay compensation for loss of rights under the option scheme. In the circumstances, the plaintiff was not entitled to recover damages for loss of his option rights even if he could show that he had been wrongfully dismissed just before the date when the option became exercisable. In Levett, however, the Court of Appeal took a different line, holding that an employee who was summarily dismissed by a company in breach of his contract of employment was entitled to exercise an option to purchase shares that the company had previously granted him. Although the rules of the share option scheme provided that the option would lapse in the event of the employee being dismissed following disciplinary action, the unlawfulness of the dismissal prevented the employer from relying upon it to deprive the employee of his rights under the scheme. That was because the general rule of construction – that a party to a contract cannot take advantage of his or her own wrongdoing – applied in the absence of any clear wording to the contrary within the scheme's rules. So it seems that, while share option schemes are capable of transfer, the extent to which a transferee is bound by them will depend upon the rules of the scheme (including any condition excluding the employer's liability for damages for the cessation of share option rights) and the circumstances which apply.

However, if a transferee inherits liability under a share option scheme, it will **3.63** still find itself faced with the difficulties outlined above of applying that scheme in practice. In such circumstances, it is likely that the obligation on the transferee is to provide a 'substantially equivalent' scheme – see Mitie Managed Services Ltd v French and ors 2002 IRLR 512, EAT (discussed in the section immediately below).

Profit-sharing schemes, profit-related pay and performance- **3.64** related pay

Profit-related or performance-related schemes usually provide for a payment to be made to an employee in respect of past performance, whether related to the business or of the individual, calculated over a reference period. Problems may occur, therefore, where a profit-sharing scheme is based on the overall performance of a company that is selling only part of its business – in order to continue such a scheme, the purchaser of that part would have to have inside access to details of the transferor's overall performance. Or, where the payment date for a profit-related or performance-related scheme falls after the date of a relevant TUPE transfer, the transferee will (assuming it inherits the transferor's liabilities under such a scheme) have to calculate payments due by reference to work done during a qualifying period with the transferor. However, such potential logistical difficulties have not prevented the courts holding that liabilities under such schemes transfer under Reg 4(2):

- **Unicorn Consultancy Services Ltd v Westbrook and ors** 2000 IRLR 80, EAT: W and others were employed by WSA Ltd, a company forming part of the Atkins Group. The employees belonged to a profit-related pay scheme and had all worked for the full profit year for the scheme, from 1 April 1996 to 31 March 1997. On 31 March 1997 the contract on which the employees were engaged came to an end and a new contract was awarded to UCS Ltd. The transfer – a 'relevant transfer' for the purposes of TUPE – took place on April 1. The employees brought employment tribunal proceedings against UCS Ltd on the ground that the new employer had a continuing duty to pay them profit-related pay. The EAT held that under Reg 4(2)(a) the transferor's liability to pay profit-related pay to its employees transferred to the transferee upon a relevant transfer. In addition, Reg 4(1) and (2)(b) meant that the rules of the scheme had to be interpreted on the basis that the employees' contracts were to have effect after the transfer as if they had been made between the employees and the transferee. So where the

213

rules provided that 'only those employed' in a company in the Atkins Group at a particular date would receive payment, this was to be construed as merely requiring employment in the undertaking transferred, not as requiring continued employment by a company within the Atkins Group. The employees therefore qualified for payment of profit-related pay.

3.65 The Unicorn case makes it clear that if the performance period has expired, the transferee is obliged to make payment. Where the reference period for calculating the payment spans the transfer, however, more difficult problems potentially arise. Following the transfer, how can profits continue to be calculated by reference to the profits of the transferor – with whom the relevant employees no longer have any connection, and who no longer has any control over the performance of the entity transferred? Or, where the name of the transferee is simply substituted for that of the transferor – to quote Lord Coulsfield's obiter observation in McCall v Initial Supplies Ltd, unreported 2.5.90, Ct Sess – 'an employee whose remuneration included an annual bonus related to his employer's profits for the year would... be entitled to claim a bonus related to the acquirer of the undertaking, if the acquisition had taken place during the year'. This would have the effect of radically altering the rights and obligations of the parties, if the new owner was considerably more (or less) profitable than the old. In Unicorn, Mr Justice Charles acknowledged these difficulties when he expressed his obiter opinion that where a TUPE transfer takes place during the profit period, a transferee might be under an obligation to provide a replacement scheme, or make payments equivalent to those earned under the transferor's scheme – and that this would accord with the underlying purpose of TUPE. The EAT has since had the opportunity to address this issue directly in Mitie Managed Services Ltd v French and ors 2002 IRLR 512, EAT.

F was employed by a company which was part of the Sainsbury's group, and was entitled under her contract to the benefits of an Inland Revenue-approved profit-sharing scheme ('the Sainsbury's Scheme'). Under the Sainsbury's Scheme, eligible employees received either cash payments or awards of shares in the parent company. The size of such payments or awards related to the annual consolidated profits of the group. On 17 May 1999 the part of the undertaking in which F was employed transferred to PBMS Ltd under TUPE. Following the transfer, F and six colleagues brought an application in an employment tribunal under S.11 ERA seeking a declaration as to their particulars of employment with PBMS Ltd. The employees argued that, by virtue of what is now Reg 4, they were entitled to continue to receive payments and awards of shares under the Sainsbury's Scheme, for which their new employer, PBMS Ltd, would be liable. The tribunal considered that all existing contractual terms had transferred under Reg 4 and had to be honoured or lawfully varied, however inconvenient that might be. It held, therefore, that the employees' contracts continued to contain a clause entitling them to payments and awards under the Sainsbury's Scheme. PBMS Ltd appealed to the EAT.

214

Before the appeal hearing, a further transfer of the undertaking took place, this **3.66** time to MMS Ltd, which was substituted for PBMS Ltd as the appellant. MMS Ltd argued that it would be impossible for it to carry out obligations that the employment tribunal said had transferred, since it had no way of accessing the confidential information required to operate the Sainsbury's Scheme and no ability to issue shares in Sainsbury's. Further, MMS Ltd argued that it would be odd if the employees' pay were to be determined by reference to the profits of a company for which they no longer worked. MMS Ltd stated that these problems could be avoided if the EAT were to take a broad approach to Reg 4 and argued, by reference to the Unicorn case, that the employees' rights could be safeguarded if they were entitled to participate in a different profit-sharing scheme, operated by reference to the performance of the employing entity. The employees argued for a strict interpretation of Reg 4 as set out by the tribunal – if the legislature had intended to create a special rule in respect of profit-sharing schemes then it would have been done so expressly, in the same way that it created an express rule to exclude pension schemes. They cited in support the decision of the ECJ in Abels v Administrative Board of the Bedrijfsvereniging voor de Metaalindustrie en de Electrotechnische Industrie 1987 2 CMLR 406, ECJ, in which the Court held that the existence of a specific exclusion for pension schemes led to the conclusion that all other rights of employees must transfer.

The EAT held that the employment tribunal had erred in finding that, following a transfer of an undertaking, contractual terms relating to profit-related pay had been preserved word-for-word under the transferring employees' contracts, thereby entitling the employees to continue to participate, at the transferee's expense, in a profit-sharing scheme operated by the transferor. Any interpretation of Reg 4(2) should avoid giving rise to absurdities or injustices. In this case, the transferee was unable to issue shares in the transferor company and was not entitled to confidential information belonging to the transferor. The entitlement found by the employment tribunal would be impossible for the transferee to perform and, accordingly, the tribunal's construction of Reg 4(2) produced a result that was absurd and unjust. In the light of the decision of the ECJ in Abels, it would be difficult if not impossible to argue that a profit-related pay entitlement could not be the subject of a transfer, but that case is not conclusive as to precisely what transfers by way of contractual entitlement in relation to a particular scheme. The EAT concluded that, in a case such as this, the transferred employees were entitled to participate in *a scheme of substantial equivalence* but one that was free from unjust, absurd or impossible features. Such an approach was consistent with the purpose of the Regulations and of the Directive to protect workers and, more particularly, to safeguard their rights upon a change of employer. The EAT therefore allowed the transferee's appeal and remitted the case to the employment tribunal to determine appropriate particulars substantially equivalent to the transferor's profit-sharing scheme.

215

3.67 This is not the first time that the courts have had to take a broad view of Reg 4 in order to produce a workable result: see for example Morris Angel and Son Ltd v Hollande and anor 1993 ICR 71, CA (discussed under 'Restrictive covenants' above), in which the Court of Appeal had to consider the effect of Reg 4 on a restrictive covenant restraining the employee from dealing with the transferor's clients following termination of employment. In Mitie, the EAT anticipated that in most cases a transferee company would be able to negotiate an equivalent scheme with the employees or their unions, failing which an application could be made to an employment tribunal for a determination of the relevant particulars of employment, under S.11 ERA. It is possible that the validity of a 'substantially equivalent' scheme might be open to challenge by a disgruntled employee in the light of the House of Lords' decision in (1) British Fuels Ltd v Baxendale and anor (2) Wilson and ors v St Helens Borough Council 1998 ICR 1141, HL, on the basis that an agreement to vary the terms of employment had been reached by reason of the transfer of the undertaking. However, Mr Justice Maurice Kay in his judgment in Mitie considered that the issue was not consensual variation of the profit-related pay entitlement, but 'what has been transferred in the absence of such consensual variation'. In any event, employees have the right, under Reg 4(9), to treat their employment as having been terminated, if a relevant transfer involves a 'substantial change' in their working conditions to their material detriment – see Chapter 4 under 'Material detriment dismissals'.

More recently, the issue was revisited by an employment tribunal in Tomlin v EDS Ltd ET Case No.2702211/07. T began working for Vodafone Ltd in October 1999 and his employment was transferred to EDS Ltd in January 2007. He claimed that EDS Ltd had breached his contract in that he had lost the opportunity to participate in a share save and incentive scheme operated by his previous employer. The tribunal dismissed his claim as the share scheme T had referred to was, in fact, provided by Vodafone Group plc, which was not the transferor. Further, in order for the transferee to create a tax free scheme similar to that operated by Vodafone, it would have been necessary for the EDS Group to create a scheme that was open to all of its employees, including those employed by EDS Ltd. However, EDS Group was not the transferee either. The tribunal held that the scheme fell outside the scope of TUPE as it would not be appropriate to expect third parties who have nothing to do with the TUPE transfer to create schemes of this nature.

3.68 **Contingent rights**
As we discussed at the beginning of this chapter, TUPE protects only those employment rights that exist at the time of the transfer, not those which arise subsequently. It might be argued, therefore, that contingent rights – those which have not fully matured at the time of the transfer, but are expressed to crystallise upon, for example, the employee's dismissal – are also excluded from the scope

of the Regulations. However, this is not the case, as the European Court ruled in Martin and ors v South Bank University 2004 ICR 1234, ECJ.

In that case, M, D and W were lecturers at an NHS nursing college, employed under the General Whitley Council (GWC) conditions of service. Included in these conditions were the terms of the Collective Agreement on Premature Payment of Superannuation and Compensation Benefits. For employees aged between 50 and retirement age, who had at least five years' service within the NHS Superannuation Scheme, this provided for early retirement with immediate payment of a retirement pension and compensation in three circumstances: dismissal for redundancy; voluntary early retirement on organisational change; and early retirement in the interests of the efficiency of the service. In November 1994 the nursing college became part of SBU, and the claimants' employment transferred under TUPE. The claimants chose to remain on their existing terms of employment but joined the Teachers' Superannuation Scheme, as they were unable to continue their membership of the NHS retirement scheme following the transfer. In January 1997 SBU wrote to all staff aged over 50 offering them early retirement in the interests of the efficiency of the service. M and D accepted. The terms offered for early retirement in the higher education sector differed from those provided to NHS employees by the GWC conditions of service. Under the applicable regulations, a teacher aged 50 or over who took early retirement because of redundancy or in the interests of the service was entitled to an early retirement pension based on actual years of pensionable service, and a lump sum. However, whereas NHS employers were obliged to pay an additional compensatory annual allowance and lump sum when an employee took early retirement, employers in the higher education sector had a discretion whether or not to pay such additional benefits. Furthermore, NHS employers were obliged to credit the employee with a prescribed number of additional years' service when calculating the compensatory benefits, but employers in the higher education sector had a discretion to determine how many years' service with which to credit the employee.

3.69 The claimants contended that they were entitled to the more favourable NHS terms of early retirement instead of SBU's terms. The employment tribunal referred a number of questions to the ECJ for a preliminary ruling, including whether rights that are contingent upon dismissal or early retirement by agreement with the employer are subject to Article 3.1 of the Directive, and therefore transfer with the transfer of an undertaking, or whether they fall within the exclusion in Article 3.4 relating to pension schemes (for which, see under 'Rights and liabilities that do not transfer – terms relating to pensions' below). The ECJ considered that it was clear from Article 3 that – except where provided by Article 3.4 – all the transferor's rights and obligations arising from the contract of employment or employment relationship are transferred to the transferee, even if their implementation is contingent on a particular event, the occurrence of which may depend on the will of the employer.

This case indicates that if, following the transfer, the transferee exercises its power to grant early retirement, it becomes bound by the rights and obligations of early retirement established by the employee's contract of employment or employment relationship with the transferor. But the principle is applicable to liabilities of the transferor under other contingent rights of the employee too: see, for example, under 'Golden parachutes' below.

3.70 Golden parachutes

So-called 'golden parachute' clauses may be included in the contracts of senior executives. These trigger the payment of a liquidated sum upon the occurrence of a specified event – typically dismissal, but also sometimes where the business is subject to a takeover. In principle, there is nothing to prevent liability under a golden parachute passing to the transferee under Reg 4(2)(a), as a liability of the transferor under the employment contract of an employee assigned to the relevant transfer. Where the golden parachute is triggered to 'open' on the occasion of a relevant transfer, the transferee will therefore become immediately liable to the employee for payment. Even where the clause does not crystallise upon transfer, the latent liability will pass to the transferee – see 'Contingent rights' below. The liability may be substantial, as such payments – being structured as a debt as opposed to compensatory – are not subject to mitigation by the executive and must be paid in full.

A transferee may possibly succeed in having a golden parachute clause set aside if it can argue that the clause was negotiated by the executive with the prospective transfer in mind. However, as a general rule, Reg 4(4) provides that any purported variation of a contract of employment that is to be transferred is void if the sole or principal reason for the variation is the relevant transfer or a reason connected with the transfer that is not an economic, technical or organisational reason entailing changes in the workforce – see further Chapter 5.

3.71 Compromise agreements

It is common for employers to use compromise agreements to seek to protect themselves against potential claims from employees whom they have made redundant (or whose employment has otherwise been terminated) – all the more so where an employee is dismissed in the context of a TUPE transfer, as the parties are likely to feel even more uncertain as to their position in law. We discuss the extent to which compromise agreements are effective to compromise an employee's rights under TUPE – and whether it is effective to use compromise agreements to manage the dismissal of employees for the purpose of re-engaging them post-transfer, on different terms and conditions – in Chapter 5 under 'Alternative strategies for effecting changes'; and Chapter 10 under 'Avoidance of TUPE provisions'. Here, we consider the extent to which the transferee can benefit from a compromise agreement that was made between the transferor and an employee who was (or would have been had he or she not been dismissed) assigned to the transferring entity.

There is little case law on the subject. But if a compromise agreement can be argued to contain benefits for the transferor 'in connection with' the employment contract, within the meaning of Reg 4(2)(a), then those benefits will pass to the transferee. It might be argued that while a compromise agreement may indeed seek to compromise an employee's contractual claims, it is likely to relate also to the settlement of statutory employment claims (given that employment-related statutory claims cannot, as a rule, be settled except through the means of a formal compromise agreement or Acas-conciliated settlement). However, this would be an unduly restrictive objection. Following the ruling of Lord Templeman in Litster and ors v Forth Dry Dock and Engineering Co Ltd (in receivership) and anor 1989 ICR 341, HL, the courts must give the TUPE Regulations a purposive construction to ensure that they affect the transfer of all rights and obligations envisaged by the Acquired Rights Directive. And Article 3.1 of the Directive states that the transferor's rights and obligations transfer to the transferee upon a relevant transfer, where they arise from an employment contract 'or from an *employment relationship*'. It seems likely that a compromise agreement effected between the transferor and an employee will contain rights arising from their employment relationship.

Another objection might be that if the point of the Directive is to protect **3.72** employees' rights upon a relevant transfer, why should it seek to impute to the transferee rights to enforce a compromise agreement as against the employee? A compromise agreement, though perhaps in the employee's financial interest, hardly protects his or her employment rights. However, the wording of Article 3.1 of the Directive is clear – the rights of the transferor, as well as his obligations, pass to the transferee. And, following Litster, 'upon the transfer of a business from one employer to another the benefit and burden of a contract of employment between the transferor and a worker in the business should devolve on the transferee'.

Sometimes the parties to a transfer will adopt a belt and braces approach and seek to enter into tripartite agreements – between the transferor, transferee and employee – compromising the employee's rights. Such an agreement, if entered into before the transfer, would have to be very clearly worded to enable the transferee to enforce it, as the employee would be compromising his or her rights against the transferee in respect of claims that do not yet exist – see Royal National Orthopaedic Hospital Trust v Howard 2002 IRLR 849, EAT, and University of East London v Hinton 2005 ICR 1260, CA. However, if for any reason settlement agreements are not concluded before the date of the transfer, the transferee must ensure that he is a party to them in order to benefit from their terms. In Thompson and ors v Walon Car Delivery and anor 1997 IRLR 343, EAT, BRS Automotive Ltd lost a contract for car distribution with Saab to

WCD. WCD did not want to take on the relevant BRS employees, so BRS began to negotiate settlement terms with those employees. In the event, while settlement terms were reached in draft form by the date of the transfer, these were not formalised, through Acas conciliation, until a few days after the transfer. The EAT held that liability for the employees' unfair dismissals passed to the transferee at the moment of transfer, and the transferee could not rely on a compromise agreement entered into between the transferor and the employee *after* the date of the transfer, to avoid such liability. (Note that the situation might have been different had the employees attempted to make claims for breach of contract against the transferee instead of unfair dismissal, given the tribunal's finding that the terms of the compromise agreement, which included settlement of contractual claims, were 'in place' by the date of the transfer. In so far as a settlement fulfils the common law requirements for a binding legal contract, it will be effective to compromise contractual claims.)

3.73 If the benefit of a compromise agreement, entered into between the transferor and the employee before the transfer, passes to the transferee, the transferee will be protected against any claim made against him by the employee according to its terms, to the extent that the agreement is valid. This will, however, leave the *transferor* without the benefit of the compromise agreement (see under 'Continuing liability of the transferor?' below). The transferor should therefore seek to address this issue in negotiating indemnities against the transferee – see Chapter 10 for practical advice in this respect. (Where the circumstances are right, however, a transferor may be able to benefit from a sum paid to an employee under a compromise agreement with the *transferee*, after dismissal on the date of the transfer. The EAT held in Steele v Boston Borough Council EAT 1083/01 that an employee who was *not* assigned to the entity transferred had not made a valid compromise agreement with the transferee because he was not its employee. But the sum paid to him by the transferee as purported consideration for that agreement could be taken into account when calculating compensation under his subsequent claim for unfair dismissal against the *transferor*.)

3.74 Pensions

We consider in some detail, under 'Rights and liabilities that do not transfer' below, the situation regarding terms relating to pensions. Occupational pension schemes are expressly excluded, by Reg 10, from the operation of Regs 4 and 5, and therefore liabilities of the transferor relating to employees' rights and benefits under occupational pension schemes do not, as a rule, transfer to the transferee.

However, the transferee must not assume that he will thereby escape any responsibility relating to pensions. Note the following:

- Reg 10 applies only to occupational pension schemes (as defined by S.1 of the Pensions Schemes Act 1993). Therefore Reg 4 will apply to transfer in full any rights, powers, duties and liabilities that relate to non-occupational pension schemes such as a personal pension scheme. And under Reg 5, the transferee will inherit the terms of any collective agreement relating to a personal pension scheme – see under 'Collective rights and liabilities – collective agreements' below

- Reg 10(2) provides that any provisions of an occupational pension scheme which do not relate to benefits for old age, invalidity or survivors shall not, for these purposes, be treated as being part of the scheme. In other words, Regs 4 and 5 *will* apply to transfer liability relating to rights and benefits under any part of an occupational pension scheme that does *not* relate to benefits for old age, invalidity or survivors: see discussion of Beckmann v Dynamco Whicheloe Macfarlane Ltd 2003 ICR 50, ECJ and Martin and ors v South Bank University 2004 ICR 1234, ECJ under 'Rights and liabilities that do not transfer – terms relating to pensions' below

- although terms relating to occupational pension schemes do not pass (subject to the exclusion in Reg 10(2) discussed above), UK law provides that the transferee must make available for eligible transferring employees, after the transfer, a minimum level of future pension benefits. The relevant provisions are set out not in TUPE but in the Pensions Act 2004 and the Transfer of Employment (Pension Protection) Regulations 2005 SI 2005/649. Again, for more detail see under 'Rights and liabilities that do not transfer – terms relating to pensions' below

- Reg 10(1) excludes the operation of Regs 4 and 5 only. In other words, the transferee will continue to bear responsibilities under other provisions in the TUPE Regulations relating to occupational pension schemes. For example, it will be obliged to include as a matter for information and consultation under Reg 13 any measure that it proposes to take in relation to affected employees' pension rights and benefits.

In Whitney v Monster Worldwide Ltd 2010 EWCA Civ 1312, CA, the Court **3.75** of Appeal upheld a High Court decision that assurances given to an employee that he would be no worse off if he transferred to a new money purchase scheme following the closure of his employer's final salary scheme in 1989 amounted to a binding guarantee. It did not matter that the assurances were not recorded in a single document, as there was a 'unanimity of view that there was a contract'. The guarantee therefore transferred to the transferee by novation alongside a TUPE transfer.

In an analogous case, the High Court in Hagen and ors v ICI Chemicals and Polymers Ltd and anor 2002 IRLR 31, QBD, held that liability for a negligent misstatement made by the transferor about pension rights and benefits was transferred to the transferee. The Court ruled that a transferor employer owed a duty both in contract and in tort to take reasonable care to ensure the accuracy

221

of statements made to employees regarding a proposed transfer of the undertaking in which they were employed. Where, therefore, a false impression was created in the minds of employees by representations made about the value of pension benefits under a scheme operated by the transferee, the transferor was liable for breaching an implied term to take reasonable care in making statements and for making a negligent misrepresentation. However, the transferor was not similarly liable for expressing his own view that the transfer would be in the best interests of the employees even though his opinion proved to be erroneous, since the transferor had no special knowledge or skill which would make it reasonable for the employees to rely on that opinion rather than their own.

3.76 Changes to contractual retirement ages

In Power v Regent Security Services Ltd 2008 ICR 442, CA, a case decided under the 1981 Regulations, P's employment was transferred to RSS Ltd in July 2005. Shortly before the transfer the new employer sent P a letter, the effect of which was to increase his contractual retirement age from 60 to 65. However, in September 2005 RSS Ltd informed P that he would be retired on his 60th birthday, which was in November of that year. P brought a claim of unfair dismissal. RSS Ltd contended that P had reached his normal retirement age and was therefore barred from claiming unfair dismissal by S.109 of the Employment Rights Act 1996. An employment tribunal found that P's normal retirement age for the purposes of the ERA was the same as his contractual retirement age. However, it went on to hold that the contractual variation of P's retirement age to 65 had been made in connection with the transfer of P's employment and was therefore void under Reg 12 of the 1981 Regulations (now Reg 18 of the 2006 Regulations) and he was not, therefore, entitled to rely upon the variation even though it was to his advantage. Accordingly, P's retirement age was 60, as it had been prior to the transfer, and S.109 ERA applied to exclude the tribunal's jurisdiction.

On appeal, both the EAT and the Court of Appeal held that the tribunal had erred. The aim of the Acquired Rights Directive (No.77/187) (since replaced by Directive No.2001/23) and of the implementing TUPE Regulations is to safeguard the acquired rights of employees on the transfer of an undertaking. Safeguarding the acquired rights of employers was not the aim. Allowing a transferee employer to rely on TUPE in order to prevent a transferred employee from taking the benefit of a varied term agreed by the employer by reason of the transfer is not required either by the aim of, or by the provisions of, the Directive and TUPE. The Court of Appeal expressly approved the EAT's reasoning that it would be inconsistent with the aim of protecting the workforce to refuse them benefits contractually conferred by the transferee. An employee's rights on a transfer are not being safeguarded if he or she is prevented from taking the benefit of a term that was agreed with the transferee on or after the transfer. The safeguarding of an employee's acquired rights on the transfer of an undertaking means that a transferred employee who wishes to take the benefit of the original retiring age of 60 agreed with the transferor is entitled to do so as against the transferee. If the retiring age is then varied by agreement with the transferee, the employee must be treated as obtaining an additional right, not as waiving an acquired right. Neither the public policy reflected in the Directive and TUPE nor the reasoning in the previously decided cases prevents an employee from reaching an agreement with the transferee employer under which he or she obtains an additional right by reason of the transfer. The transferred employee can then choose between enforcing the transferred acquired right or the newly obtained right.

The narrow point of interest in the Regent Security services case is that an **3.77** employee who, following a relevant transfer, is subject to a change in his or her contractual retirement age is entitled to rely both on his or her original term or the varied term, whichever is to his or her advantage. This indicates that a post-transfer variation of a term relating to retirement will be regarded by the courts as being subject to the specific rules relating to variation of contract in TUPE – discussed in detail in Chapter 5. Any such variation that the employee regards as detrimental is likely to be void. The wider point of interest in the case is that the Court of Appeal has interpreted the restrictions on transfer-related changes as applying only to changes that are detrimental to the employee. This has led to accusations that the court has sanctioned a 'pick 'n' mix' approach, whereby an employee who has entered into a new or varied contract with the transferee is entitled to choose whichever pre- and post-transfer terms he or she prefers. Despite these complaints, the Regent Security Services decision remains the leading authority on the matter and is binding unless or until overruled by the Supreme Court.

Enhanced redundancy schemes   3.78
There have been a number of decisions in relation to whether enhanced redundancy schemes transfer under TUPE. Examples of these are discussed below.

An enhanced redundancy compensation scheme was held to transfer to the transferee in Bousted v Reliance Security Services Ltd ET Case No.1701352/07. In this case, B worked for a series of companies as a security and fire safety officer from 1983 and his employment was transferred under TUPE on a number of occasions. His previous employers had made several redundancies in the past and on each occasion the same enhanced redundancy payments were automatically made. The terms of these were published on company notice boards even though they were referred to as 'ex-gratia' payments in severance documents. However, in B's case, the transferee refused to honour the terms of the enhanced redundancy scheme that had been operated by his previous employer. An employment tribunal held that B was entitled to the

223

enhanced terms of severance although they had not been expressly incorporated into his contract of employment or referred to in the staff handbook. The tribunal took account of the fact that the ex-gratia payments had been published by the transferor and had, without exception, been automatically paid to clerical staff made redundant in the past.

3.79 Sometimes the focus in a TUPE context will not be on whether the scheme as a whole transfers, but whether the specific rules under such schemes that govern whether particular employees qualify for enhanced benefits apply to employees transferred under TUPE. This was the case in Jackson v Computershare Investor Services plc 2008 ICR 341, CA. There, the claimant had worked for the transferor since 1999 under a contract of employment that contained no provision for enhanced redundancy pay. In June 2004 her employment transferred under TUPE to CIS plc, which operated a dual system of redundancy terms that offered more generous benefits to those who had joined it before 1 March 2002. When the claimant was made redundant in 2005 she argued that since the operation of TUPE meant that she was to be treated as having continuity of employment with CIS plc dating back to 1999, she should be afforded the benefit of the pre-March 2002 redundancy terms. CIS plc disagreed, and the claimant brought claims of unfair dismissal and breach of contract for non-payment of enhanced contractual severance pay. The employment tribunal found as a matter of fact that J had joined CIS plc at the point of transfer in 2004. However, it held that since what is now Reg 4(1) required that a transferred employee's contract of employment shall be deemed to have originally been made with the transferee, it was appropriate to treat J as having joined CIS plc before 2002. As a result, she was entitled to the enhanced redundancy payment. CIS plc successfully appealed to the EAT and the claimant further appealed to the Court of Appeal.

The Court of Appeal, agreeing with the EAT, held that it is not the purpose of the TUPE Regulations to place transferred employees in a better position than they were in prior to the transfer. Thus, the claimant, whose employment transferred under the Regulations in 2004, had no right to be treated as a pre-2002 entrant for the purposes of the transferee employer's enhanced redundancy scheme, notwithstanding that she was deemed to be continuously employed by the transferee from the date on which she started employment with the transferor. So far as the employer's redundancy scheme was concerned, the date of the employee's joining the company was an objective fact that was unaffected by the deeming provisions of TUPE.

3.80 It will be interesting to see whether the same approach is taken where an employer's redundancy provisions are based on length of service, rather than a specific joining date. If, for example, the employer's terms stated that anyone with more than five years' service with the company was entitled to an enhanced redundancy package, then on one view it might be argued that the employee's pre-transfer service, which is deemed by virtue of Reg 4(1) and (2) to be with the transferee, should be included in the calculation of whether she had the requisite five years' service. But the employer might be able to argue, on the basis of the Court of Appeal's decision in the instant case, that it was only years of actual (as opposed to deemed) continuous employment with his company that counted for the purposes of his or her redundancy scheme.

Another issue that might arise is what happens if the transferee is forced to amend the transferor's enhanced redundancy scheme because it is not legally compliant? This happened in Corrie v Excel Europe ET Case No. 202589/07 where the transferor's scheme provided that employees with at least ten years' service would receive redundancy compensation based solely on their age – 26 weeks' pay for those under 31, rising to 104 weeks for those aged 50 and then reducing by five weeks each year up to the age of 62. The transferee sought to amend these provisions to ensure compliance with age discrimination legislation and to harmonise all terms across its group of companies. The claimant's union protested against this purported variation, arguing that the scheme was protected by TUPE and could not be amended to the detriment of transferred employees. An employment tribunal held that the scheme was non-contractual but that, even if it had been, its original terms were unlawfully discriminatory. Accordingly, the employee's claim for enhanced redundancy compensation was dismissed.

Collective rights and liabilities 3.81

The capacity of the TUPE Regulations 2006 to automatically transfer collective rights, duties and liabilities is considerable. This is partly because many such rights and liabilities, etc, though contained within collective agreements made between employers and recognised trade unions, are often incorporated into employees' individual contracts of employment, and so transfer by virtue of Reg 4(2) as explained above. But it is also because separate provisions in TUPE – namely, Regs 5 and 6 – provide respectively for collective agreements and trade union recognition agreements to be transferred to the transferee on the completion of a relevant transfer. It is these latter provisions that this section focuses upon.

Collective agreements and pay bargaining arrangements 3.82

Collective agreements, though negotiated with the employer or employers' association by a trade union, seek to regulate the employment relationship and, as such, may be expressly incorporated, in whole or in part, into individual contracts of employment. However, whether or not their terms have contractual effect in this way, the TUPE Regulations 2006 provide that collective agreements

225

continue to apply as soon as the transferee acquires the undertaking following a relevant transfer. Reg 5(a) stipulates that:

- any collective agreement made by or on behalf of the transferor with a trade union recognised by him in respect of any transferring employees, that is in force immediately before the transfer, shall have effect after the transfer in so far as it applies to any relevant employees, just as if it had been made by or on behalf of the transferee with the union

- anything done under or in connection with the collective agreement (as it applies to the employee), by or in relation to the transferor before the transfer, shall, after the transfer, be deemed to have been done by or in relation to the transferee.

3.83 'Collective agreement' has the meaning given to it by S.178(1) of the Trade Union and Labour Relations (Consolidation) Act 1992 (TULR(C)A), which is 'any agreement or arrangement made by or on behalf of one or more trade unions and one or more employers or employers' associations and relating to one or more of the matters specified [in S.178(2)]'. Those matters are: terms and conditions of employment or physical working conditions; engagement, non-engagement, dismissal or suspension of workers; allocation of work; matters of discipline; union membership or non-membership; facilities for trade union officials; machinery and procedures for negotiation and consultation on any of the above matters and on trade union recognition. The definition in S.178 applies not only to formal written agreements but also to 'arrangements' – so any unwritten arrangements between the transferor and a union are nevertheless capable of transfer. However, a collective agreement that covers only matters outside the scope of S.178(2) – perhaps concerning the development of business strategy – will not be subject to Reg 5 and so will not continue to have post-transfer effect. If a collective agreement contains matters within the list in S.178(2) as well as matters outside it, it will nevertheless constitute a 'collective agreement' within the meaning of S.178(1) and thus be transferred under Reg 5. Arguably, in such a case the non-S.178(2) matters covered by the agreement will have effect after the transfer, along with the rest of the agreement, to the extent that they apply to 'any relevant employees', according to the wording of Reg 5.

Regulation 5(a) also states that anything done by the transferor in respect of a collective agreement is treated as having been done by the transferee. Presumably matters such as commitments made by the transferor during pay negotiations would be covered by this phrase.

3.84 It has been argued that if a transferee is bound by the terms of an incorporated collective agreement because of the effect of Reg 4(2) – as opposed to Reg 5(a) – then this renders Reg 5(a) otiose. However, the significance of Reg 5 lies primarily in ensuring the continuity of a collective agreement unless and until

226

it terminates or is replaced. Such continuity is particularly important, from a legal point of view, where legislation imposes a duty – say, on tribunals – to take account of the contents of collective agreements. For example, agreed procedures in collective agreements concerning time off for union matters for union officials and members will be significant when tribunals are deciding in accordance with the Acas Code of Practice on Time Off for Trade Union Duties and Activities (2003) whether an employer has unreasonably refused time off – see Ss.168–170 TULR(C)A. Additionally, a collective agreement covering redundancy procedure and selection criteria might be relevant to any claim by an employee covered by the collective agreement that his or her redundancy dismissal was procedurally unfair.

It should be emphasised that Reg 5 transfers the effect of collective agreements only in respect of employees whose contracts of employment are transferred under the Regulations. So an employee engaged *after the transfer* by the transferee will not be covered automatically by a transferred collective agreement. This is illustrated, in relation to the EU Acquired Rights Directive (No.2001/23), by the decision of the European Court of Justice in Landsorganisationen i Danmark v Ny Molle Kro 1989 IRLR 37, ECJ. In that case, H owned a tavern, which she let to L. A few months later L concluded an agreement with the relevant employees' association, under which she agreed to comply with a prior collective agreement that had been negotiated with the employers' association in so far as it applied to employees who were members of the association. At the beginning of 1981 L breached the lease, and H took over operation of the tavern. In May 1983 H engaged a waitress to work over the summer. Subsequently, the Danish Trades Union Congress brought an action against H on the ground that the wage she paid to the waitress was not the same as that due under the collective agreement, which was binding on H due to the effect of the Danish equivalent of the TUPE Regulations. The Danish court referred several questions to the ECJ. In the course of its answer, the ECJ held that the obligation on the transferee to observe the terms and conditions of a collective agreement applied only in respect of employees employed at the time of the transfer, and not in respect of those engaged after the transfer.

3.85 Regulation 5(b) provides that as well as taking over a collective agreement, the transferee takes over 'any order made in respect of that agreement' in so far as it applies to the relevant employees. It is unclear what this is intended to cover. Perhaps Parliament envisages that the Central Arbitration Committee's remit will one day extend to making orders about the scope or application of specific collective agreements, which, currently, is a matter for negotiation between the parties (subject to the definition of 'collective agreement' in S.178(1) TULR(C)A, above, and matters for collective bargaining that may be imposed by the compulsory recognition procedure – see under 'Trade union recognition' below).

227

Note that Reg 10 expressly excludes any terms relating to occupational pension schemes from the operation of Reg 5 (just as it excludes any such terms in individual contracts from the operation of Reg 4 – see under 'Rights and liabilities that do not transfer – terms relating to pensions' below). Terms in collective agreements relating to other sorts of pension schemes, or relating to terms within occupational pension schemes that do not relate to benefits for old age, invalidity or survivors, will transfer.

3.86 **Harmonisation of different collective terms.** A transferor is likely to experience problems where existing employees are covered by a collective agreement that is incompatible with any other agreement covering transferred employees. However, unlike the harmonisation of contractual terms – as to which see Chapter 5 under 'Harmonising terms and conditions' – the harmonisation of collective agreements that are not legally binding will not be hindered by provisions of the Regulations. This, of course, is subject to the point made above that a transferee may be legally bound by the terms of a collective agreement to the extent that such terms are incorporated into the individual contracts of employment of the employees transferred. In that case, such rights will be automatically transferred by virtue of Reg 4(2), and any variation of those terms in order to harmonise them with the terms applicable to the transferee's existing workforce is likely to be rendered void by Reg 4(4) – see Chapter 5 under 'Varying terms in a TUPE context'.

3.87 **Presumption that collective agreements legally unenforceable.** Although Reg 5 is clear that collective agreements transfer to the transferee on a relevant transfer, there are significant questions as to the effect this will have upon the transferee in practice. The main reason for this is the presumption in UK law that collective agreements are not legally enforceable. Initially, this presumption arose out of the common law – see, for example, Ford Motor Co Ltd v Amalgamated Union of Engineering and Foundry Workers and ors 1969 2 QB 303, QBD – but it is now codified on a statutory basis in S.179 TULR(C)A. (The presumption does not apply in respect of collective agreements made between 1971 and 1974. However, in practice, many such agreements, if still applicable today, expressly state that they are not intended to be legally enforceable.) The presumption as to non-enforceability is rebutted by virtue of S.179(2) where the parties have expressly agreed in writing that the contrary intention applies – which they very rarely do. Thus, if a collective agreement was only binding 'in honour' on the transferor of an undertaking before the transfer, it will likewise only be binding in honour on the transferee following the transfer.

This position may not have been anticipated by the European legislators. The wording of Article 3.3 of the Directive seems to indicate an assumption that collective agreements will be enforceable as against the transferee, since it states that: 'Following the transfer, the transferee shall continue to observe the terms and conditions agreed in any collective agreement on the same terms applicable to the transferor under that agreement, until the date of termination or expiry of the collective agreement or the entry into force or application of another collective agreement.' However, the position in UK law has not yet been challenged and it would be anomalous if collective agreements acquired enforceability in the United Kingdom only by virtue of a TUPE transfer.

Effect of incorporated terms. The legal unenforceability of collective **3.88** agreements does not mean, however, that they can necessarily be ignored by the transferee after a transfer takes place. As we noted above, the terms of a collective agreement can be *incorporated* into individual contracts of employment. The EAT considered whether terms had been so incorporated in the following case:

- **Glendale Grounds Management v Bradley** EAT 484/97: B, a maintenance worker, originally employed by Nottinghamshire County Council, found himself with a new employer, GGM, after his work was contracted out. The TUPE Regulations 1981 applied to the transfer. A clause in B's contract provided that his terms and conditions of employment were subject to collective agreements negotiated nationally by the National Joint Council (NJC). They were incorporated into his contract of employment 'after approval by the County Council'. B claimed that he was entitled to a pay increase in accordance with the NJC agreement – a claim that the employment tribunal upheld. On appeal, the EAT ruled that the tribunal had erred and that B's contract did not incorporate the NJC agreement. This was because it was plain as a matter of construction of the employee's contract as a whole that the expression 'County Council' in the clause referring to incorporating collective agreements approved by the Council was a reference to the employee's employer, which originally was Nottinghamshire County Council and, following the transfer, became GGM. Since, however, GGM had not approved the NJC agreement that contained the pay increase which B sought, the increase was not incorporated into B's contract of employment.

See also Alexander and ors v Standard Telephones and Cables Ltd (No.2) 1991 **3.89** IRLR 286, QBD (discussed under 'Rights and liabilities relating to the individual – contractual and discretionary rights and benefits' above) – and IDS Employment Law Handbook, 'Contracts of Employment' (2009), Chapter 2, for further discussion of incorporation of contractual terms from collective agreements.

In Werhof v Freeway Traffic Systems GmbH and Co KG 2006 IRLR 400, ECJ, the European Court held that where a transferred employee's contract contains a clause referring to a collective agreement that binds the transferor, a transferee who is not a party to that agreement is nonetheless obliged to observe its terms and conditions since they are preserved by the Directive. However, as we shall see in the more detailed discussion of this case below, the ECJ made it clear that

229

this does not extend to new collective agreements entered into by the transferor after the date of the transfer. In a UK transfer context, this principle has been confirmed by the Court of Appeal in Alemo-Herron v Parkwood Leisure Ltd 2010 ICR 793, CA, where the Court held that transferee employers were not bound by negotiations that are collectively agreed by third parties after a relevant transfer had taken place notwithstanding a clause in transferred employees' contracts of employment linking their pay rises to the outcome of such negotiations. Consistent with the decision in Werhof, a transferee was only committed to the terms of any collective agreement until such agreement terminated, expired or was replaced.

3.90 The conclusion reached by the Court of Appeal in the Alemo-Herron case (above) was, however, 'finessed' by the EAT in Worrall v Wilmott Dixon Partnerships Ltd EAT 0521/09. In that case the Appeal Tribunal upheld a tribunal's conclusion that a collectively agreed term that allowed a local authority to award extra pay to those employees seeking voluntary redundancy was not incorporated into the claimant's contract of employment. But even if the term had been so incorporated, it would not have bound a subsequent employer who inherited the contract by way of a TUPE transfer, since statutory regulations had removed the transferee's ability to make the award. The EAT asserted that the principle in Alemo-Herron that the rights of parties under a collective agreement must be assessed at the time of the transfer did not mean that subsequent legislative changes could be ignored. Although, as the Court of Appeal had made clear, incoming employers will not be bound by subsequent changes to the collective agreement itself, they will be bound by legislative changes that have an effect on the terms of such collective agreements.

When terms of an unenforceable collective agreement have been incorporated, they take legal effect as contractual terms that are directly enforceable between individual employees and the employer – Marley v Forward Trust Group Ltd 1986 IRLR 369, CA, and Robertson and anor v British Gas Corporation 1983 IRLR 302, CA. After a transfer, incorporated collective terms (which, as seen for example in the Alemo-Herron case above, may deal with crucial matters such as pay) will be directly enforceable against the transferee as part of an individual employee's contract of employment – but this will be because of the operation of Reg 4 and not because of Reg 5. Thus any incorporated terms will be unaffected by any unilateral withdrawal by the transferee from the collective agreement from which those terms derive.

3.91 It should be noted, however, that in Ralton and ors v Havering College of Further and Higher Education 2001 IRLR 738, EAT, the Appeal Tribunal ruled that, in the context of fixed-term contracts, an employment tribunal had correctly concluded that a transferee was not bound by the Acquired Rights Directive to continue to employ the claimants on the terms contained in a collective agreement after the termination of their existing fixed-term contracts that incorporated those terms and their re-employment under new contracts that did not incorporate those terms. In that case the claimants were employed by the local education authority on contracts that expressly incorporated the terms of the 'Silver Book' collective agreement. In 1993 their employment was transferred, under TUPE, to Havering College. When their fixed term contracts expired, they were re-employed on contracts for an indefinite term which did not incorporate the Silver Book terms. The EAT's reasoning for concluding that there had been no breach of the Directive (and therefore of TUPE) was that it was clear as a matter of UK law that, prior to the transfer, the transferor would have been at liberty to enter into new terms that did not incorporate the collective terms on the expiry of the fixed-term contracts. The claimants did not acquire a right to continued enjoyment of the incorporated terms merely because there had been a transfer to which the Directive applied. The purpose and effect of the Directive was not to alter the rights and obligations between employer and employee after a transfer but to safeguard and continue the existing rights and obligations for the protection of employees.

Are new collective agreements binding on the transferee? Even if collectively **3.92** agreed terms are found to be incorporated into the contracts of transferring employees, their precise wording, and the way in which they are construed, will have a significant impact upon the transferee following the transfer. Particular problems emerge where there is a change of service provider arising from the contracting out to an independent private contractor of a service previously operated in-house by a public authority. In this scenario, the case law shows that the difficulty lies in determining to what extent the transferee continues to be bound by negotiating mechanisms referred to in collective agreements even though, as a private employer, it is not represented in those mechanisms and cannot influence the negotiations. This happens where the collective agreements refer, for example, to a national JNC or other body such as the Whitley Council for the purposes of setting terms and conditions. One of two distinct issues can arise in this situation:

- where a transferred employee's contract incorporates the terms of a particular collective agreement, is the transferee bound, after the transfer, by *new* collective agreements that are negotiated by way of replacement by the same parties to that incorporated agreement?

- where a transferred employee's contract incorporates the terms of a particular collective agreement, is the transferee bound, after the transfer, by further negotiations between the parties under the terms of that agreement, such as pay bargaining?

We examine both of these issues in turn.

Although the TUPE Regulations are silent on this issue, the Directive is clear **3.93** that the obligation on the transferee to observe the terms of the transferor's

231

collective agreement lasts only 'until the date of termination or expiry of the collective agreement or the entry into force or application of another collective agreement' – Article 3.3. (Indeed, EU Member States are permitted by Article 3.3 to limit the period for observing the terms of a collective agreement – although the United Kingdom has not implemented such a limit.) Article 3.3 was examined by the ECJ in the following case:

- **Werhof v Freeway Traffic Systems GmbH and Co KG** 2006 IRLR 400, ECJ: W was employed by Siemens in Germany under a contract of employment governed by the framework collective agreement and the wage agreement in force for the North Rhine-Westphalia iron and steel, metal and electrical industry. The collective agreement had been negotiated between the trade union for the metal industry and the Metal and Electrical Industry Federation (the Federation), of which Siemens was a member. On 1 October 1999 Siemens transferred the part of its business in which W worked to FTS. FTS was not a member of any employers' association that concluded collective agreements. In May 2003 the Federation and the trade union concluded a new collective agreement, with effect from 1 June 2003, which provided for an increase in the wage rate and an additional payment. W commenced proceedings against FTS claiming, from 1 June 2003, the difference between his basic salary and the sum provided for in the new collective agreement and the additional payment. The German court asked the ECJ whether a transferee who inherits a collective agreement but was not an original party to it is bound by collective agreements subsequent to the one in force at the time of the transfer. The ECJ noted that the rights and obligations arising from the collective agreement were automatically transferred to the new employer even though the latter was not a party to it. However, the ECJ stated, the Directive's objective is merely to safeguard the rights and obligations of employees in force on the day of the transfer. Article 3.3 makes it clear that the terms and conditions of the collective agreement in force at the time of transfer are to continue to be observed only until the date of its termination or expiry, or the entry into force or application of another collective agreement. It further adds that Member States may limit the period for observing terms and conditions of a collective agreement provided that that period is not less than one year. The ECJ therefore concluded that the wording of the Directive does not indicate that the Community legislature intended the transferee to be bound by collective agreements other than the ones in force at the time of the transfer. Moreover, if future collective agreements were binding on a transferee who was not a party to the collective agreement, this would infringe its fundamental right not to join an association under Article 11 of the European Convention on Human Rights.

3.94 A year and a half before the ECJ's decision in Werhof, the EAT had similarly ruled in Ackinclose and ors v Gateshead Metropolitan Borough Council 2005

IRLR 79, EAT, that employees could not benefit from terms negotiated under a new collective agreement for local authority workers which, two years after the transfer, had replaced the agreement incorporated in the transferred employees' contracts.

Pay bargaining under the incorporated collective agreement. The specific 3.95 question as to whether transferred employees are able to benefit from pay increases negotiated following their transfer, under collectively agreed terms that are incorporated into their transferred contracts, has generated a considerable body of case law. Until recently, a number of these cases had concluded that transferees were bound by subsequent decisions under pay bargaining arrangements in which they had no active role. Such cases included BET Catering Services Ltd v Ball and ors EAT 637/96 and Whent and ors v T Cartledge Ltd 1997 IRLR 153, EAT. The latter entailed claimants who originally worked for the London Borough of Brent's street lighting department under contracts of employment providing that their pay and conditions would be set in accordance with the local authority's National Joint Council (NJC) collective agreement 'as amended from time to time'. The street lighting work was subsequently contracted out to an independent contractor, Cartledge, which then derecognised the trade union recognised by Brent and which was represented on the NJC. Cartledge wrote to the employees to inform them that the collective agreement would no longer have effect and that in future their pay would be determined on an individual basis. An employment tribunal dismissed the employees' claims that the failure to pay them the NJC-agreed rates constituted an unlawful deduction from wages contrary to Part 1 of the Employment Rights Act 1996. The EAT overturned that decision on appeal, holding that the transferee was bound by the NJC agreement, as it remained incorporated into individual contracts of employment even though the transferee had sought to terminate it. Therefore the employees retained the right to have the benefit of the terms negotiated by the NJC until the individual contracts of employment had been effectively varied by agreement or the employee had been dismissed and re-engaged on terms that did not include the NJC agreements.

The decision of the Court of Appeal in Glendale Managed Services v Graham and ors 2003 IRLR 465, CA, though dealing with a slightly different issue, appeared to lend support to the approach taken by the EAT in Whent. That case did not specifically concern the incorporation of a collective agreement as such. However, the written statements of particulars of the claimants stipulated that their rate of pay would 'normally be in accordance with the NJC' and further stated that 'any changes that subsequently may be made in your terms and conditions of employment will be separately notified to you or otherwise incorporated in the documents to which you have access'. At issue in the case was not whether a transferee could depart from the agreed NJC rate but rather in what circumstances it could do so. The employer had reserved an express

233

right to deviate from the nationally agreed pay structure, but where the contract provided that NJC rates would normally be paid – and in fact the employer regularly applied NJC pay increases without making a formal decision to do so – the Court of Appeal found an implied term that the employer would, at the very least, inform the employee if and when there was to be a departure from that norm. The transferee's decision to depart from the long-standing practice of honouring NJC pay rates without first notifying its employees meant that it was unable to rely on that contractual right – and there had therefore been an unlawful deduction from wages.

3.96 This line of cases, however, no longer commands the approval of the courts in the light of the ECJ's ruling in Werhof and the Court of Appeal's decision in Alemo-Herron (see above). In the latter, the Court of Appeal held that an employment tribunal had not erred in finding that a transferee was no longer bound to pay transferred employees in accordance with a collective bargaining agreement which was incorporated into the employees' contracts of employment. In so holding, the Court cited the Werhof ruling as authority for the proposition that Article 3 of the Acquired Rights Directive required a static interpretation of the burden upon transferees of employment contracts incorporating terms fixed from time to time by collective agreement. The ECJ in that case inferred from Article 3(2) that the Directive did not intend a transferee to be bound by any collective agreement other than the one in force at the time of the transfer. This conclusion was consistent with the objective of the Directive, which is to safeguard the rights and obligations of employees in force on the day of the transfer and is not intended to protect mere expectations to rights and hypothetical advantages flowing from future changes to collective agreements. Since Article 3(1) must always have borne the meaning set out in Werhof, even though it was not until 2006 that it came to be explained, it followed, according to the Court of Appeal, that the United Kingdom had no obligation when enacting TUPE to do more than incorporate a burden upon transferees that was co-extensive with that meaning. While the United Kingdom could have chosen to implement the Directive so as to give employees wider rights than those required by the Directive, and so imposed greater burdens on transferees, there was nothing in the language of Reg 5 to suggest that it had done so. The duty of the domestic courts is to interpret the Regulations consistently with Article 3(1), the meaning of which is to be found in Werhof.

3.97 Trade union recognition

Regulation 6 of the TUPE Regulations 2006 provides that where an independent trade union is recognised to any extent by the transferor in respect of employees of any description who become employees of the transferee after a relevant transfer, then the union is deemed to be recognised by the transferee to the same extent in respect of employees of that description. However, this transfer of recognition applies only where the transferred organised grouping of resources or employees 'maintains an identity distinct from the remainder of the transferee's undertaking' – Reg 6(1). Therefore, if the transferred workforce becomes integrated into the new employer's workforce following the transfer, union recognition will not be deemed to have been transferred. There is no equivalent restriction, however, on the application of Reg 5 concerning the effect of collective agreements after the transfer (as to which see above). Therefore, even if the transferred workforce fails to maintain a distinct identity following the transfer and a particular union loses recognition as a result, any collective agreement made by it may still continue to have effect.

Meaning of 'maintains an identity distinct'. Questions will inevitably arise **3.98** as to what constitutes maintaining a 'distinct' identity. If the organised grouping of resources or employees fails to maintain a distinct identity, it is in theory arguable that there has not been 'a transfer of an economic entity which retains its identity' within the meaning of Reg 3(1)(a) for the purpose of determining whether there has been a relevant transfer at all (in cases not involving a service provision change). We assume that Reg 6 is intended to apply in Reg 3(1)(a) types of transfer, and not just to service provision changes (which are covered by Reg 3(1)(b)). If so, the two phrases 'retains its identity' (Reg 3(1)(a)) and 'maintains an identity distinct' (Reg 6(1)) cannot have exactly the same meaning, because Reg 6(1) is predicated on the fact that there has been a relevant transfer to start with. In other words, the internal logic of the Regulations must allow for the possibility that an economic entity can retain its identity and yet fail to 'maintain an identity' distinct from the remainder of the transferee's undertaking. So, in order for Reg 6 to apply, the economic entity must retain its identity *a little bit more closely* than it had to in order to give rise to a relevant transfer in the first place. The rather tortuous nature of this reasoning perhaps indicates that the legislators did not anticipate such a disjunction.

However, there are ways round this difficulty. First, the wording of Article 6 of the Acquired Rights Directive may be helpful. This provides that employee representation shall be preserved following the transfer so long as the relevant undertaking *'preserves its autonomy'*. If Reg 6 is read in this light, it is easier to see that an economic entity may retain its identity following a transfer in terms of, for example, the activities it undertakes, and yet sacrifice to a new parent company its ability to make strategic decisions in respect of the administration and running of its business, in a way which would cause it to fall outside the scope of Reg 6 while still qualifying as a relevant transfer. Note, too, the EAT's decision in Farmer v Danzas (UK) Ltd EAT 858/93 that there is no rule that an economic entity ceases to retain its identity, for the purpose of identifying whether there has been a relevant transfer, merely because its economic activity is subsumed into the transferee's business, since all businesses are likely to want to integrate the activities of a newly acquired entity into their own. The EAT held that in order for the TUPE Regulations to apply, it is sufficient that the

235

transferred undertaking retain its identity *immediately after* the moment of transfer. On this basis, we would suggest that the proper interpretation of Reg 6(1) is that it requires that the transferred entity maintains its identity distinct from the remainder of the transferee's undertaking on a slightly more permanent basis than is required by Reg 3(1)(a).

3.99 **Independent union.** Unlike Reg 5 – which provides for the continuation of a collective agreement regardless of the status of the trade union with which it is made, so long as it is 'recognised' – only applies to an *independent union*. It seems likely that the independence of trade unions for the purposes of Reg 6 will be determined according to the definition of 'independent trade union' provided in S.5 TULR(C)A. This provides that an independent trade union is one that is not under the domination or control of an employer or group of employers or of one or more employers' associations, and is not liable to interference by an employer or group or association tending towards such control. In addition, S.8 TULR(C)A provides that if the Certification Officer has issued a certificate of independence to a trade union and the certificate is in force, then this is 'conclusive evidence for all purposes that a trade union is independent'. All of the main trade unions in the United Kingdom are listed with the Certification Officer with certificates of independence.

3.100 **Extent of recognition.** Regulation 6(2) provides for an independent trade union, which is recognised 'to any extent' by the transferor in respect of the transferred employees, to be recognised 'to the same extent' by the transferee after the transfer. This means that in each case the detail of the recognition arrangements needs to be examined in order to determine what precisely is transferred to the new employer. In practice, the bargaining issues in respect of which a union may be recognised can vary substantially. For example, under the statutory procedure for trade union recognition, the issues for collective bargaining are restricted to pay, hours and holidays, unless the parties have agreed to cover other matters – paras 3(3) and 54(3) of Schedule A1 TULR(C)A. In cases of voluntary recognition, the union may be recognised for only limited purposes, such as for representing union members who have individual grievance and disciplinary issues. It is possible that in this type of case, the union may not be recognised for the purposes of 'collective bargaining' as defined in the TUPE Regulations and so members will not be entitled to the statutory rights flowing from recognition discussed below.

It should be noted that Reg 10 – which excludes the application of Regs 4 and 5 from contracts of employment or collective agreements to the extent that they relate to an occupational pension scheme – does not affect the operation of Reg 6. Therefore if a union is recognised for bargaining in respect of pensions, it will continue to be recognised in this respect after the transfer.

3.101 What constitutes recognition is a mixed question of fact and law. Voluntary recognition is often established by a written collective agreement between the employer and trade union that sets out the details of the recognition that is being conferred, the procedures to be followed and what facilities will be provided to union representatives in respect of carrying out their duties. However, voluntary recognition can arise, without any express agreement, based on a clear and unequivocal course of dealings – see National Union of Gold, Silver and Allied Trades v Albury Brothers Ltd 1979 ICR 84, CA. Recognition can also arise from use of the statutory procedure for trade union recognition under which an employer may be compelled to recognise a union for collective bargaining purposes in certain circumstances. The provisions for statutory recognition claims are set out in Schedule A1 to the TULR(C)A. Where trade union recognition for collective bargaining purposes is granted after an application to the Central Arbitration Committee (CAC), then there can only be effective derecognition by agreement, or following the employer's use of the statutory derecognition procedure.

Voluntary and statutory recognition. Having made the distinction between **3.102** statutory and voluntary recognition, it is worth pausing to note that the DTI Guide takes Reg 6 to apply to cases of *voluntary recognition* only. It observes that 'where at the time of the transfer a union is recognised by the transferor employer via the statutory recognition procedure, then different arrangements apply... Regulations are to be made, in due course, under paragraph 169B of Schedule A1 [TULR(C)A] to ensure that declarations made by the CAC, and applications made to the CAC, are appropriately preserved in the event of a change in the identity of the employer.' At the time of publication of this Handbook, no such regulations have been issued, even in draft form.

The meaning of 'union recognition' for the purposes of Reg 6 is defined in Reg 2(1) as being the same as that in S.178(3) TULR(C)A, which defines this in terms of 'the recognition of the union by an employer, or two or more associated employers, to any extent, for the purpose of collective bargaining'. Reg 2(1) likewise refers to S.178(1) TULR(C)A for the meaning of 'Collective bargaining', which is there defined as negotiations relating to or connected with one or more of the matters set out in S.178(2). Those matters were listed in the discussion on 'Collective agreements' above.

No distinction between statutory and voluntary recognition is actually made in **3.103** Reg 6 itself. It is true that the statutory recognition procedure disapplies the meaning of collective bargaining given by S.178(1) (which is precisely the definition adopted by Reg 2(1) of TUPE) – paras 3(2) and 54(2) of Schedule A1 to the TULR(C)A. However, Reg 6 itself simply provides that where before the transfer an independent union is 'recognised' in respect of transferred employees, it shall be deemed to have been so 'recognised' by the transferee. Even if the statutory procedure does not use the definition of collective bargaining from S.178(1), it does not disapply the meaning of the term 'recognised' – from S.178(3) – which applies throughout the TULR(C)A. In practice a statutorily

237

recognised trade union is likely to conduct negotiations relating to or connected with precisely those matters contained within S.178(1), even if the definition is not expressly used. For completeness we assume in our discussion here that Reg 6 is apt to apply also to statutory recognition, while noting the indications given in the DTI Guide that the application of TUPE to declarations and applications under the statutory recognition procedure may, in time, be covered separately within the TULR(C)A itself.

3.104 **Effect of Reg 6.** The CAC's decision in National Union of Rail, Maritime and Transport Workers v Chubb Security Personnel Ltd (TUR1/412/2004, 29.4.05), CAC, illustrates the way in which the Regulations affect how the statutory procedure operates. There was an ongoing dispute between the union and S Ltd, the employer, as to trade union recognition. By virtue of para 22 of Schedule A1 to the TULR(C)A, when a majority of the bargaining unit are members of the union seeking recognition, the CAC will usually be obliged to make a declaration of recognition. Having established that union membership within the bargaining unit was over 50 per cent, the CAC was considering awarding recognition without a ballot. Meanwhile, the contract on which the relevant employees were engaged was taken over, pursuant to a TUPE transfer, by C Ltd. C Ltd wrote to the CAC arguing that no recognition declaration should be made and there should be a ballot, as it had not been provided with details of the situation. However, the CAC held that the fact that C Ltd might have been unaware of the details flowing from the transfer did not constitute a persuasive reason for holding a ballot in the interest of good industrial relations. The CAC decided to award recognition without a ballot even though there was a 'new employer' and so gave recognition to the union to conduct collective bargaining with C Ltd for the employees in the defined bargaining unit.

While a trade union may be recognised to a greater or lesser extent for the purposes of collective bargaining, the fact that it is recognised at all has significant legal consequences, whether the recognition is voluntary or under the statutory procedure. The statutory legal consequences for the union include:

- the right for its representatives to be informed and consulted about a relevant transfer under Reg 13

- the right for its representatives to be informed and consulted about collective redundancies under S.188(1) TULR(C)A

- the right to information for the purposes of collective bargaining under S.181 TULR(C)A

- the right of the union's representatives and trade union learning representatives to time off under Ss.168 and 168A TULR(C)A.

These consequences will have effect after the transfer to the extent that Reg 6 applies.

Is recognition legally binding? Regulation 6(2)(b) provides that where a **3.105** transferor before the transfer recognised an independent trade union in respect of transferring employees, then after the transfer 'any agreement for recognition may be varied or rescinded *accordingly*'. This implies that the same process for variation or rescission would apply after the transfer as it would have before – and therefore perhaps states the obvious. In most cases, trade union recognition by an employer is voluntary. Voluntary recognition is not legally binding, and so the employer may at any time, subject to the terms of the recognition agreement, derecognise the trade union. In other words, where a transferee is deemed by Reg 6 to have recognised a union in respect of transferred employees, the transferee could following the transfer proceed to derecognise the union. Unless the recognition agreement is stated to be legally binding, which is highly unlikely in practice, the union and union members will have no legal remedy (see (1) Associated Newspapers Ltd v Wilson (2) Associated British Ports v Palmer 1995 ICR 406, HL). However, derecognition may cause unrest among the affected employees, and possibly provoke a statutory trade union recognition claim. Were such a claim to succeed and the CAC to grant statutory recognition, then it would be far harder for the employer to derecognise the union and remedies would become available for any failure by the employer to comply with the statutory recognition procedure. If the parties were unable to reach agreement between themselves within the required time frame, the CAC would be obliged to specify the method of collective bargaining, and this would then become legally enforceable between the parties unless they then agreed that the specified method is not to be legally binding – see paras 31(3)–(5) of Schedule A1 to the TULR(C)A.

Does Reg 6 add anything to Reg 5? As discussed above, Reg 5(a) provides **3.106** that collective agreements have effect after a relevant transfer as if made by or on behalf of the transferee. The meaning of a 'collective agreement' covers a broad range of agreements or arrangements relating to any matter or matters that are suitable for collective bargaining – including recognition procedures. A collective agreement is capable of transfer even if it is not made by the transferor itself, so long as it is made on its behalf – so could potentially cover 'arrangements' imposed under the compulsory recognition procedure contained in Schedule A1 to the TULR(C)A. Given all this, it is arguable that Reg 6 adds nothing, in terms of substantive legal effect, to Reg 5.

Special rights for public sector transfers
3.107

Great care must be taken where a transfer involves the transfer of an economic entity from, to or within the public sector. This is because there are extensive protections, over and above those provided by the TUPE Regulations 2006, for the benefit of employees transferring within and out of the public sector. This is so whether or not the transfer in question is legally capable of protection under TUPE and European law.

239

3.108 **Rights under TUPE.** First, a reminder of the extent to which public sector transfers are protected by TUPE itself. Reg 3(4)(a) provides that the Regulations apply to 'public and private undertakings engaged in economic activities whether or not they are operating for gain'. This confirms that TUPE applies, for example, to the outsourcing of ancillary services from central or local government and government agencies to the private sector; privatisations; and transfers and service provision changes by charitable or 'not for profit' organisations – see further Chapter 1 under 'Standard transfers – what is an "economic entity"?'

However, there will be no relevant transfer in the case of 'an administrative reorganisation of public administrative authorities or the transfer of administrative functions between public administrative authorities' – Reg 3(5) – following the decision of the ECJ in Henke v Gemeinde Schierke and Verwaltungsgemeinschaft 'Brocken' 1996 IRLR 701, ECJ (again, see Chapter 1). The DTI Guide states that the exclusion in Reg 3(5) means that 'most transfers within central or local Government are not covered by the Regulations'. Nevertheless, such transfers will be accorded TUPE-equivalent treatment under the extra-TUPE provisions to which we now turn.

3.109 **TUPE-equivalent protection.** Special protections derived from a series of Statements, Guidance, legislative provisions and Codes of Practice have accorded, save in exceptional circumstances, TUPE-style protections to employees transferring in and out of the public sector. The relevant provisions make the observance of these protections mandatory. There are four of these so-called 'TUPE plus' arrangements.

3.110 *Cabinet Office Statement of Practice on Staff Transfers in the Public Sector 2000.* This is probably the most important of the practice documents for public sector transfers. It provides that where a transfer, such as a transfer under central government control, is excluded from TUPE because of Reg 3(5) (see above), it should nevertheless be treated as if TUPE applies to it – and that certain public sector bodies, such as the NHS, should treat TUPE as being applicable to almost all transfers in the public sector, whether or not it applies in fact. Accordingly, the Statement applies to transfers involving any of the following:

- central government departments and agencies
- local government (where adopted by the relevant local authority)
- the NHS
- public private partnerships (including contracting out and Public Finance Initiative (PFI) projects)
- internal transfers among public sector bodies generally
- second-generation and subsequent-generation outsourcing.

240

Although the Statement of Practice is not legally enforceable, it is generally followed in practice by private sector service providers, and compliance with it is usually stipulated in the outsourcing contract.

Section 38 of the Employment Relations Act 1999. Section 38 of the **3.111** Employment Relations Act 1999 gives the Secretary of State a power to make statutory instruments providing TUPE-equivalent protections to cases or classes of cases falling outside the scope of the Directive. This has so far been exercised in situations relating to rent officers (see the Transfer of Undertakings (Protection of Employment) (Rent Officer Service) Regulations 1999/2511, and OFCOM (see the Transfer of Undertakings (Protection of Employment) (Transfer to OFCOM) Regulations SI 2003/2715).

Staff Transfers from Central Government: A Fair Deal for Staff Pensions June **3.112** *1999.* This Guidance, first published in June 1999, was also appended to the Cabinet Office Statement of Practice (discussed above) when it was published in January 2000. It should be noted, however, that its application is only mandatory where a transfer involves staff being transferred out of the public sector into the private sector – i.e. in the context of public private partnerships (PPPs) – irrespective of whether these amount to transfers protected under TUPE. It does not therefore apply to transfers between public bodies. The Guidance provides that the following pension protections should apply in such transactions:

- *future pension benefits* – the private sector employer must offer a 'broadly comparable' scheme to the public sector pension scheme which the employees are leaving as a result of the transfer. This involves rigorous scrutiny of the alternative pension arrangements by an appropriately qualified actuary to ensure that there is no material detriment overall in terms of future accrual of pension rights for the individuals affected

- *accrued pension benefits* – more significantly, the Pensions Guidance (as updated by supplementary guidance, 'Fair Deal for Staff Pensions: Procurement of Bulk Transfer Agreements and Related Issues' issued in June 2004) provides that there must be a 'bulk transfer agreement' in place where staff become early leavers of the public sector pension scheme of which they were members prior to the transfer. Such an agreement effectively shields early leavers from suffering the normal disadvantages that apply when transferring out of a final salary (otherwise known as a defined benefit) pension scheme by attributing a higher transfer value for accrued benefits than would normally be the case. This can be a highly valuable benefit for affected staff and can increase the cost of bids by hundreds of millions of pounds in large-scale PPP transfers.

Code of Practice on Workforce Matters in Local Authority Service Contracts **3.113** *2003.* A problem with the Cabinet Office Statement of Practice (see above)

241

was that it did not protect non-public sector employees recruited to the private sector following the transfer, and therefore could not prevent the rise of the 'two-tier workforce'. This phrase refers to the difference between the terms and conditions that apply, following a transfer, to the transferee's existing workforce on the one hand and the employees whom it acquired as a result of the transfer on the other. In order to deal with this issue, the Best Value Code of Practice – also known as the 'Two Tier Workforce Code' – was introduced in 2003. This Code, which is enforceable by contract, ensures that the terms and conditions applicable to employees within local authorities are protected when they are transferred to independent contractors. Importantly, this also extends to the right to continuing access to the Local Government Pension Scheme (LGPS) or an alternative scheme of good quality (again, subject to actuarial analysis). This puts the onus on local authorities to choose contractors on the basis of their ability to deliver good services, by means other than cutting staff terms and conditions. Although the Code does not require that new (as opposed to transferring) employees be given terms and conditions identical to those of transferred staff, their terms and conditions must be fair and reasonable and in overall terms no less favourable. As part of the drive to end two-tier workforces, the Code also provides that new joiners will be offered reasonable pension provision. This may be membership of the LGPS, of a good quality employer pension scheme or of a stakeholder pension scheme with an employer contribution.

All of these instruments will continue to hold sway in public sector transfers irrespective of the tightening of TUPE protection resulting from the extended definition of transfers applicable to service provision changes (SPCs) generally. It is important to note that their practical significance in such transfers is undiminished, as some of the protections offered – in the context of pension provision in particular (often a highly valuable benefit in public sector contracts) – exceed those conferred by the TUPE Regulations 2006 and by Ss.257 and 258 of the Pensions Act 2004 and the Transfer of Employment (Pension Protection) Regulations 2005 SI 2005/649. The latter only impose a minimum level of future pension obligation on transferees – see under 'Rights and liabilities that do not transfer – terms relating to pensions' below. This statutory minimum provision does not compare with the strength of pension protection conferred by the Statements and Code of Practice mentioned above, and in particular the bulk transfer agreement protection of accrued benefits available to employees transferring from the public to the private sector under the 'Fair Deal on Staff Pensions' outlined above.

3.114 Note that the *Code of Practice on Workforce Matters in Public Sector Service Contracts 2005* – which extended the reach of the local authority Code mentioned above to the wider public sector, including the Civil Service, the NHS and maintained schools (subject to some exceptions, such as where the Retention of Employment Model for NHS PFI contracts applies) – was withdrawn on 13 December 2010 and replaced by the voluntary, non-statutory *Principles of Good Employment Practice*. It is likely that the 2003 Code will also be withdrawn in due course.

Retention of Employment Model (REM). The operation of the TUPE 3.115 Regulations can have particular disadvantages in the context of Private Finance Initiative (PFI) projects. From the employees' point of view, transfer from a public to a private employer can be perceived as giving rise to a gradual erosion of rights and benefits – especially with regard to pension rights. As for the PFI company and any sub-contractors, they will have to meet the higher cost of employing ex-public sector employees on transferred levels of pay and other benefits.

However, it was in the NHS that the application of TUPE to PFI projects, and particularly the outsourcing of 'soft' service jobs, provoked most industrial unrest. The NHS, stretched at the best of times, lost employees, and there was concern about the two-tier workforce that was developing whereby public sector employees were working side-by-side with private sector employees who were on less favourable terms and conditions. But most significantly, employees would lose the benefit of the NHS Superannuation Scheme. As far as this applies to non-clinical staff, it is structured in such a way that other employers cannot obtain admitted body status to the scheme, and therefore Codes on Best Value (see above) cannot be complied with.

It was in this context that in 2001 the Government announced its intention to 3.116 pilot a 'new model for ancillary staff in PFI hospitals' – now known as the Retention of Employment Model. The basic principle behind REM is that instead of TUPE applying to transfer the employment of front-line employees, they remain employed by the NHS and are seconded to and managed by the private sector partner on a long-term basis. As such, they remain on their existing terms and conditions and subject to existing NHS policies and procedures. The private sector partner, however, retains responsibility for providing the outsourced services, and management-level and supervisory staff transfer to it under TUPE as normal.

In order to ensure that such an arrangement does not fall foul of the TUPE Regulations by amounting to an agreement to contract out of it contrary to Reg 18 – see Chapter 10 under 'Avoidance of TUPE provisions' – the employees exercise their formal right to object to the transfer under Reg 4(7). They will then be treated as having resigned and can be re-employed by the NHS Trust on the same terms and conditions as before, but under long-term secondment to the private sector partner. Obviously, an employee does not have to exercise his or her right to object if he or she does not want to, but in that case he or she would stand to lose the special entitlements conferred by the REM agreement.

243

3.117 Duty to inform and consult

One issue that has vexed the courts has been whether or not liability in respect of the duty under Reg 13 to inform and consult representatives of affected employees – to the extent that it applies to the transferor – passes to the transferee upon a relevant transfer. (For full details of this duty, see Chapter 8.) The answer, since the coming into force of TUPE 2006, is yes, but not exclusively. Reg 15(9) provides that the transferee is *jointly and severally liable* with the transferor in respect of compensation payable to an employee for the transferor's failure to carry out any of various aspects of the Reg 13 duty.

3.118 Liability for failure to inform and consult. Regulation 15(9) was introduced in response to conflicting case law on this issue under the 1981 Regulations. In the following two cases, the EAT reached different conclusions:

- **Transport and General Workers' Union v James McKinnon, JR (Haulage) Ltd and ors** 2001 ICR 1281, EAT: the EAT held that the transferor's liability to pay compensation for its failure to inform and consult representatives prior to a relevant transfer did not pass to the transferee under what is now Reg 4(2) of the 2006 Regulations. TUPE would be construed in a way that ensures that a transferor has an incentive to comply with the information and consultation obligations imposed upon it during the transfer process. This required the conclusion that the transferor would retain the liability to pay compensation for its own failure to consult

- **Alamo Group (Europe) Ltd v Tucker and anor** 2003 ICR 829, EAT: the EAT reasoned that rights and obligations were subject to what is now Reg 4(2) of the 2006 Regulations if they arise under or in connection with the contract of employment or – in line with Article 3 of the Acquired Rights Directive – the employment relationship. Reg 4(2) applies to rights and obligations derived from statutory provisions, even if not expressly or impliedly incorporated in the contract of employment, provided the necessary 'connection' is made. The EAT thought that no distinction should be drawn between statutory liability to inform and consult under TUPE itself, and general liability arising out of the contract of employment on the other. The modern employment relationship includes both contractual rights and rights and liabilities derived from statute and regulations that neither party can exclude and which give added protection to employees. Had the legislature intended to exclude from the scope of Reg 4 statutory or regulatory rights introduced for the very purpose of protecting employees – such as those contained in what is now Reg 13 – it would have expressly done so.

3.119 The legislature clearly took note. The Government's chosen solution, found in Reg 15(9) of TUPE 2006, was to make the transferor and transferee *jointly and severally liable* – that is, both collectively and individually liable – where a *transferor* has failed to inform or consult in respect of affected employees. In deciding upon this course of action, the Government, in the 2005 consultation document on the draft new Regulations, reiterated the EAT's concern in the TGWU case that if liability were to pass wholly to the transferee, there would be little or no statutory incentive for the transferor to comply with the information and consultation requirements.

The DTI Guide explains how the system of joint and several liability works. It notes that it will be for the appropriate representatives or individual employees seeking redress to choose whether to take action against the transferor, the transferee or both. Furthermore, a party who is a sole respondent in such an action will have the possibility of joining others who are jointly liable in respect of the same liability. When this occurs, it will be for the employment tribunal to apportion the compensation between the two respondents fairly. Alternatively, the Guide continues, if judgment is given against a sole respondent, that respondent might be able to recover a contribution from others who are jointly liable in respect of the same liability by suing them in the civil courts. In such a case, liability would then be apportioned fairly, in line with the provisions of the Civil Liability (Contribution) Act 1978.

Where a court or tribunal is obliged to consider how liability should be **3.120** apportioned, it will focus on the extent of each respondent's responsibility for the damage in question. Since joint and several liability only arises in respect of the transferor's failure to inform and consult, and not the transferee's, one would imagine that the transferor will usually be required to pay most if not all of the compensation awarded.

Note that, however liability is to be apportioned by the tribunal, the transferor and transferee might have agreed between themselves, by way of indemnities, who will actually bear the cost for any failure on the part of the transferor to inform or consult – see Chapter 10 for details.

Liability in respect of unassigned employees. The duty that arises in respect of **3.121** Reg 13 is a duty to inform and consult representatives of 'affected employees'. These are defined as 'any employees of the transferor or the transferee *(whether or not assigned to the organised grouping of resources or employees that is the subject of a relevant transfer)* who may be affected by the transfer or may be affected by measures taken in connection with it' (our emphasis) – Reg 13(1). Any affected employee may bring a claim that an employer has failed to comply with a requirement of Reg 13 (or of Reg 14, which relates to requirements governing the election of employee representatives). So transferees should be aware that they may inherit liability (albeit on a joint and several basis) in respect of employees who are not assigned to the transferred undertaking and who are thereby not covered by the provisions in Reg 4(1) and (2). It seems unlikely that this can have been the Government's intention, given that the transferee will never have an employment relationship with such employees.

245

For further discussion of this apparent quirk, see Chapter 8 under 'Informing and consulting representatives – claims for failure to inform or consult'.

3.122 *Transferee's failure to provide information.* There is one situation in which the transferee will be solely liable for the transferor's failure to inform transferring employees. Reg 15(8)(b) states that where the transferor (after giving notice to the transferee in accordance with Reg 15(5)) shows that its failure to inform was due to the transferee's own prior failure to provide it with the information specified in Reg 13(4), the tribunal may order the transferee to pay appropriate compensation to such descriptions of affected employees as may be specified in the award.

3.123 **Failure to comply with a compensation order.** Thus far we have discussed the already rather complex issue of which of the commercial parties bears liability for a failure to inform and consult. The position is complicated yet further when one considers who bears liability for a failure to comply with a compensation order made by a tribunal in respect of an employer's failure to inform and consult.

If a tribunal makes an award of compensation under Reg 15 for failure to comply with a requirement of Regs 13 or 14 (concerning the duty to inform and consult and to make provision for the election of employee representatives), and the employer in question fails to pay it wholly or in part, the affected employee may complain to a tribunal – Reg 15(10). If the tribunal upholds such a complaint, it shall order the transferor or transferee as applicable to pay the complainant the amount owed – Reg 15(11). As we discussed above, Reg 15(9) provides that the transferee and transferor are jointly and severally liable in respect of an order for compensation made against the transferor. However, Reg 15(9) also provides that the parties are jointly and severally liable in respect of compensation payable under Reg 15(11). In other words, the transferee is jointly and severally liable with the transferor for a claim that either one of them has failed to comply with a compensation order.

3.124 This leads to an incongruous result. We saw above that where the transferor (after giving notice to the transferee in accordance with Reg 15(5)) shows that its failure to inform was due to the *transferee's* failure to provide him with the information specified in Reg 13(4), then the transferee is *solely liable* to pay compensation for the transferor's consequent failure to inform – Reg 15(8)(b). However, if the transferee then fails to pay up, and a tribunal upholds an employee's complaint about this, then, under Reg 15(11), the *transferor* will bear joint and several liability with the transferee for the transferee's failure. (Under Reg 15(11) the transferor will also be jointly and severally liable with the transferee for the transferee's failure to comply with a compensation order made under Reg 15(7) in respect of the transferee's failure to comply with its obligations under Regs 13 or 14.) Clearly this spreading of liability is in the best interests of the affected employees, but seems rather tough on the transferor, who was not liable for the original failure that led to the relevant compensation order. All of these potential outcomes need to be addressed carefully in the warranties and indemnities covering the transfer – in respect of which practical advice is given in Chapter 10.

Protective awards
3.125

The statutory duty on employers to inform and consult workplace representatives about large-scale redundancies is contained in S.188 TULR(C)A. This states that 'where an employer is proposing to dismiss as redundant 20 or more employees at one establishment within a period of 90 days or less, the employer shall consult about the dismissals all the persons who are appropriate representatives of any of the employees who may be affected by the proposed dismissals or may be affected by measures taken in connection with those dismissals'. Consultation must begin 'in good time' and must in any event begin:

* where 100 or more redundancies are proposed at one establishment within a 90-day period, at least 90 days before the first of the dismissals takes effect

* otherwise at least 30 days before the first dismissal takes effect – S.188(1A).

If a tribunal finds that an employer has acted in breach of S.188, the tribunal 3.126 must make a declaration to that effect and may make a 'protective award' – S.189 TULR(C)A. This is an award of pay up to a maximum 13 weeks (90 days) based on the statutory definition of a 'week's pay' but with no financial cap or ceiling being applied in respect of each week's pay. Protective awards are payable to those employees who have been dismissed as redundant, or whom it is proposed to dismiss as redundant, and in respect of whom the employer has failed to comply with the requirements of S.188 – S.189(3).

The duty to collectively consult commonly arises in the context of a relevant transfer as redundancies are often a by-product of a change in ownership. As with the duty to inform and consult under Reg 13 of TUPE 2006 (see above), there has been conflicting case law as to whether a transferor's duty to collectively consult and liability to pay a protective award in respect of his failure to comply with the collective consultation requirements in TULR(C)A passes to the transferee by virtue of Reg 4(2).

In Angus Jowett and Co Ltd v National Union of Tailors and Garment Workers 3.127 1985 ICR 646, EAT, the Appeal Tribunal held that an employer's duty to consult recognised unions over impending redundancies under S.188 TULR(C)A and liability for a protective award under that Act for failure to consult were not automatically transferred under what is now Reg 4(2). This was on the basis that such duties and liabilities were not 'under or in connection with any such contract' within the meaning of Reg 4(2)(a). In the words of Beldam J: 'It is true that the words "in connection with" are extremely wide; but it seems to us that the [transferor's] duties or liabilities which lead to the making of a declaration

247

and protective award... arise in connection not with any contract with an individual employee but by reason of a failure to consult recognised unions'.

The issue was revisited by the EAT 15 years later in Kerry Foods Ltd v Creber and ors 2000 ICR 556, EAT. WHL Ltd, which operated a sausage-making business near Plymouth, was in financial difficulties and on 24 January 1997 receivers were appointed. The receivers dismissed some of the employees on January 27 and a further ten employees were dismissed on January 31, the day that production ceased. Soon afterwards the business was sold to KF Ltd as a going concern. It refused to take on any of WHL Ltd's staff and the remaining employees were dismissed on the day the business was sold. No trade union was recognised by WHL Ltd and none of the staff were consulted regarding the redundancies or the transfer of the business. The employees complained to an employment tribunal that they had been unfairly dismissed and that they had not been consulted about the redundancies or the transfer. The tribunal found that there had been a relevant transfer and that responsibility for the employees' contracts passed to KF Ltd. In the course of its decision, the tribunal held that the employees were entitled to a protective award of four weeks' pay as there had been no collective consultation with them about the impending redundancies or transfer. KF Ltd was ordered to pay compensation and it appealed. The EAT held that the duty to consult employee representatives, whether or not there is a recognised union, is a right 'in connection with' an individual's contract of employment and therefore falls within the meaning of liabilities 'under or in connection with any... contract' for the purposes of what is now Reg 4(2)(a) of the 2006 Regulations. What is now Reg 4(2)(b), which attributes to the transferee any act or omission of or in relation to the transferor in respect of the transferred employment contract or in respect of the assigned employee) was also held to be wide enough to cover the failure to consult.

3.128 The EAT in the Kerry Foods case felt able to distinguish the earlier decision of Angus Jowett and Co Ltd v National Union of Tailors and Garment Workers 1985 ICR 646, EAT, as this was reached at a time when the Employment Protection Act 1975 and the TUPE Regulations 1981 only required consultation with recognised trade unions. The European Court of Justice had since made it clear that the EU Collective Redundancies Directive (No.75/129) was intended to protect the rights of employees as individuals. The TULR(C)A (and TUPE) now require consultation with 'appropriate representatives', who may be either trade union representatives or elected representatives of the employees affected by the transfer. In the light of this, the EAT felt that no valid distinction could any longer be drawn between liabilities arising in connection with individual contracts of employment on the one hand and liabilities arising in connection with a failure to consult on a collective basis on the other. The EAT therefore held that the transferor's liability for the failure by the receivers to consult passed to the transferee upon the completion of the transfer. It is highly likely that it would have reached the same conclusion had the issue been whether the transferor's liability to pay a protective award made against it passed to the transferee upon transfer.

It is therefore the case that an employer's liability for a failure to consult his employees or their representatives *will* pass to a transferee following a transfer of the undertaking. Note that the provisions in Reg 15(9) providing for joint and several liability (examined under 'Duty to inform and consult' above) apply only to the various obligations to inform and consult under the Regulations, and not to the collective consultation requirements in the TULR(C)A. However, the cases on that area – TGWU and Alamo – are likely to be relevant, by analogy, in any discussion as to the transfer or otherwise of liability for failure to collectively consult and liability for protective awards in respect of such failure.

Rights and liabilities that do not transfer   3.129

Certain rights and liabilities are expressly excluded from the principle of automatic transfer in the Regulations, mainly for public policy reasons. We examine these below.

Criminal liabilities   3.130

Regulation 4(6) of the TUPE Regulations 2006 states: 'Paragraph (2) shall not transfer or otherwise affect the liability of any person to be prosecuted for, convicted of and sentenced for any offence.' Accordingly, liability for a criminal offence committed by a transferor will not be transferred with the business to the transferee.

Some legislative breaches give rise to both criminal and civil liabilities. In the employment context, where an employer commits particular breaches of health and safety legislation, or of the Protection from Harassment Act 1997, for example, he may in appropriate circumstances be prosecuted for a criminal offence and be liable to be sued separately in a civil court. In such a case, following Reg 4(6), the transferee would not incur any criminal liability of the transferor. But would it become responsible for paying civil damages in respect of the original breach – for example, for failing to provide a safe system of work? As we have seen above, a transferor's tortious and civil liabilities are certainly capable of transferring to the transferee under Reg 4(2). Therefore, where a transferor has committed a tortious act before the transfer, and been prosecuted and sued for the relevant breach, it is likely that civil liability for it would pass to the transferee. However, what is the case where the transferor has committed an act before the transfer that *might* give rise to criminal and civil liability, but which has not yet prompted a prosecution or civil claim? Reg 4(6) makes it clear that Reg 4(2), in its entirety, is not to be read as either transferring criminal liability *or otherwise affecting* the criminal liability of a person. In other words, Reg 4(2)(b) – which provides that any act or omission

249

of the transferor before the transfer shall be deemed to have been an act or omission of the transferee following the transfer – cannot have the effect of attributing to the transferee potentially criminal acts or omissions of the transferor as this would *affect the liability* of the transferee to be prosecuted for a criminal offence. Arguably, this is the case even if that act or omission may also give rise to civil liability.

3.131 If this interpretation is correct, it has potentially nonsensical consequences. An affected employee, following the transfer, could not sue the transferee, because the transferee would not have been deemed to have committed the breach – but neither could he or she sue the transferor, because under Reg 4(2)(a), to the extent that the breach gave rise to civil liability, this would have 'transferred' to the transferee.

Note that an employer who fails to notify the Secretary of State about collective redundancies under S.193 TULR(C)A commits a criminal offence – S.194. Where a transferor proposes to dismiss as redundant 20 or more employees within a 90-day period, in the course of a TUPE transfer, it should note that it will not escape liability for failing to inform the Secretary of State in advance of the redundancies.

3.132 Terms relating to pensions
Occupational pension schemes are expressly excluded from the operation of Regs 4 and 5 of the 2006 Regulations. In this regard, Reg 10(1) provides that Regs 4 and 5 shall not apply:

- to so much of a contract of employment or collective agreement as relates to an occupational pension scheme – Reg 10(1)(a) or

- to any rights, powers, duties or liabilities under or in connection with any such agreement or otherwise arising in connection with that person's employment and relating to such a scheme – Reg 10(1)(b).

The exclusion of occupational pension schemes has the important consequence that employees' rights under such schemes do not automatically transfer to their employment with the transferee, even though their contracts are otherwise preserved by virtue of Reg 4(1). The Directive allows Member States to exclude pension schemes from transfer in their implementing legislation, so the Regulations are not in breach of the Acquired Rights Directive in this respect. Article 3.4(a) states that, unless Member States provide otherwise, the automatic transfer provisions do not cover 'employees' rights to old-age, invalidity or survivors' benefits under supplementary company or inter-company pension schemes outside the statutory social security schemes in Member States'.

3.133 Definition of occupational pension scheme. An 'occupational pension scheme' for these purposes is as defined by S.1 of the Pension Schemes Act 1993. Broadly, such a scheme aims to provide benefits to, or in respect of, people in a particular employment or employments, and is established by (or by persons who include) the employer, or a relevant employee, or an interested body. The administration of the scheme must either fall within the United Kingdom or within another country outside the EU. Where a pension scheme fails to meet this description – as will be the case in respect of a personal pension scheme, and, probably, a group personal pension scheme – the scheme will not fall within the exclusion in Reg 10 and will therefore pass to the transferee under Reg 4(2). Transferees would be well advised, therefore, when examining pension terms prior to acquisition, to ensure that purportedly occupational pension schemes meet the statutory definition.

Benefits for old age, invalidity or survivors. Regulation 10(2) of the 2006 **3.134** Regulations provides that any provisions of an occupational pension scheme that do not relate to benefits for old age, invalidity or survivors shall not, for the purposes of Reg 10, be treated as being part of the scheme. In other words, Reg 4 and the collective agreement provisions of Reg 5 *will* apply to transfer rights under any part of an occupational pension scheme that does *not* relate to benefits for old age, invalidity or survivors. Predictably, this provision – or at least Article 3.4 of the Directive from which it derives – has spawned a number of cases questioning what it means by old age, invalidity or survivors' benefits. In each of the following cases, the claimants were employed on the former General Whitley Council (GWC) conditions of service (now substituted by equivalent arrangements under the NHS 'Agenda for Change' initiative). The GWC was a system of establishing employment conditions in the public sector through joint negotiations between employers and employees. Section 45 of the GWC conditions of service provided for lump sum redundancy payments to be made to employees of various NHS bodies on dismissal by reason of redundancy, with such payments to be paid by the employer. Section 46 set out the terms of the Collective Agreement on Premature Payment of Superannuation and Compensation Benefits. For employees aged between 50 and normal retirement age who had at least five years' service within the NHS Superannuation Scheme, Section 46 provided for early retirement with immediate payment of a retirement pension and compensation in three circumstances: dismissal for redundancy; retirement in the interests of the efficiency of the service; or premature retirement following organisational change.

In Frankling and ors v BPS Public Sector Ltd 1999 ICR 347, EAT, the claimants were originally employed by the Eastbourne Hospitals NHS Trust. In September 1996 the Trust contracted out the claimants' department to BPS, and their contracts of employment were transferred under TUPE. In 1997 BPS made the claimants redundant. Although it paid them redundancy payments in accordance with Section 45 of the GWC conditions, it did not make any payments under Section 46. The claimants brought tribunal claims to enforce what they claimed to be their entitlements under Section 46. The tribunal held that the accelerated and enhanced early retirement benefits in Section 46 fell within the exclusion in

251

TUPE relating to occupational pension schemes, so the transferee was not obliged to provide these. In the course of rejecting the claimants' appeal, the EAT found that Section 46 'relates to an occupational pension scheme' within the meaning of what is now Reg 10(1) of the 2006 Regulations. The benefits guaranteed by Section 46 would accordingly be excluded from the operation of the automatic transfer of contract provisions in what is now Reg 4 unless it could be said that they 'do not relate to benefits for old age, invalidity or survivors' within the meaning of Reg 10(2). As to this, although the early retirement provisions of Section 46 were triggered by the fact that the claimants had been dismissed for redundancy, the provisions of a pension scheme did not cease to relate to benefits for old age merely because the employees had not taken retirement at the normal retirement age. 'Benefits for old age' are retirement benefits or benefits which come from retirement, whether compulsory or voluntary, and whether paid at normal retirement age or earlier. A benefit does not change its character or identity merely because it is enhanced or accelerated. The claimants' benefits were calculated by reference to age and years of service and were transmissible to survivors on death. It followed that the benefits falling due to redundant employees under Section 46 were 'old age' and 'survivors' benefits' within the meaning of Reg 10(2) and, as such, were excluded from the operation of TUPE by Reg 10(1). The transferee was therefore under no contractual obligation to provide the benefits under Section 46.

3.135 The correctness of the decision in Frankling was put in doubt, however, by two ECJ cases that followed it: Beckmann v Dynamco Whicheloe Macfarlane Ltd 2003 ICR 50, ECJ, and Martin and ors v South Bank University 2004 ICR 1234, ECJ.

In Beckmann, B worked within the NHS for the North West Regional Health Authority (NWRHA). On 1 June 1995 the body for which she worked was TUPE-transferred to DWM. B worked for DWM until her dismissal for redundancy on 6 May 1997. These benefits were administered pursuant to the NHS Superannuation Scheme Regulations 1995 and the NHS (Compensation for Premature Retirement) Regulations 1981, which provide, inter alia, that the benefits will be paid by the Secretary of State, who is then reimbursed by the NHS. On B's dismissal for redundancy, DWM paid her lump sum redundancy payments in accordance with Section 45 of the GWC conditions of service. However, although B met the conditions for receipt of benefits under Section 46, DWM did not provide her with any benefits under that section. B brought legal proceedings seeking a declaration that she was entitled to the Section 46 early retirement benefits and an order that DWM pay them.

3.136 The High Court referred to the ECJ the question of whether B's entitlement to the early payment of a pension and a retirement lump sum constituted a right to an old-age, invalidity or survivor's benefit within the meaning of Article 3.4 of the Acquired Rights Directive. On that point, the Court held that early retirement benefits paid in the event of dismissal for redundancy to employees who have reached a certain age are not old-age, invalidity or survivors' benefits within the meaning of Article 3.4, even if calculated by reference to the rules for calculating normal pension benefits. The exclusion of such benefits in Article 3.4 applied only to benefits paid from the time an employee reaches the end of his or her normal working life, as laid down by the pension scheme in question. Since the general objective of the Directive is to safeguard the rights of employees in the event of transfers of undertakings, the exceptions specified in Article 3.4 to the rule that the transferor's rights and obligations arising from contracts of employment, employment relationships and collective agreements transfer to the transferee have to be interpreted strictly. Accordingly, the exceptions could only apply to benefits listed exhaustively in Article 3.4 – i.e. old-age, invalidity or survivors' benefits – and the excepted benefits had to be construed in a narrow sense. In the ECJ's view, benefits can be classified as 'old-age benefits' within the meaning of Article 3.4 only when they are benefits paid from the time when an employee reaches the end of his or her normal working life as laid down by the general structure of the pension scheme in question. In the instant case, the particular payments made on dismissal for redundancy under Section 46 of the General Whitley Council (GWC) conditions of service could not be classified as old-age benefits because they were not to be paid out when an employee reached the end of her working life. This was so even though the benefits were determined by reference to the rules for calculating normal pension benefits. The respondent's argument that the early payment of benefits that are, by definition, old-age benefits does not alter their nature could not be accepted.

Similar logic was applied by the ECJ in Martin and ors v South Bank University 2004 ICR 1234, ECJ. In that case, M, D and W were lecturers at an NHS nursing college. In November 1994 the nursing college became part of SBU, and the claimants' employment transferred under TUPE. The claimants chose to remain on their existing terms of employment but joined the Teachers' Superannuation Scheme, as they were unable to continue their membership of the NHS retirement scheme following the transfer. In January 1997 SBU wrote to all staff aged over 50 offering them early retirement in the interests of the efficiency of the service. M and D accepted. The terms offered for early retirement in the higher education sector differed from those provided to NHS employees by the GWC conditions of service. Under the applicable regulations, a teacher aged 50 or over who took early retirement because of redundancy or in the interests of the service was entitled to an early retirement pension based on actual years of pensionable service, and a lump sum. However, whereas NHS employers were obliged to pay an additional compensatory annual allowance and lump sum when an employee took early retirement, employers in the higher education sector had a discretion whether or not to pay such additional benefits. Furthermore, NHS employers were obliged to credit the

253

employee with a prescribed number of additional years' service when calculating the compensatory benefits, but employers in the higher education sector had a discretion to determine how many years' service with which to credit the employee. The claimants argued that they were entitled to the more favourable NHS terms of early retirement instead of SBU's terms. An employment tribunal referred a number of questions to the ECJ for a preliminary ruling, including whether rights that are contingent upon dismissal or early retirement by agreement with the employer are subject to Article 3.1 of the Directive, and therefore transfer with the transfer of an undertaking, or whether they fall within the exclusion in Article 3.4 relating to pension schemes. The ECJ considered that it was clear from Article 3 that – except where provided by Article 3.4 – all the transferor's rights and obligations arising from the contract of employment or employment relationship are transferred to the transferee.

3.137 **Effect of Reg 10 exclusion.** Assuming, therefore, that a pension amounts to an occupational pension scheme as defined – and to the extent that it relates to benefits for old age, invalidity or survivors within the meaning of Reg 10(2) – what is the effect of the exclusion in Reg 10(1), from the transferee's perspective? The employee's right to be a member of the transferor's scheme, and his or her entitlement to benefits under it, do not pass to the transferee. This means that the transferee is not obliged to continue the transferor's scheme, and nor – as the High Court confirmed in Adams and ors v Lancashire County Council and anor 1996 ICR 935, ChD – is the transferee obliged (by TUPE or the Directive at least) to provide a replacement. In the Adams case, Lancashire County Council operated its own school catering service until 1993. It employed over 3,000 people, most of whom were part-time workers employed at a low hourly rate. All workers, however, were entitled to join the Local Government Pension Scheme. In 1993, the Council put its school catering service out to tender and the bid put in by BET Ltd, a private catering company, was successful. While it was accepted by the parties that BET's acquisition of the contract was covered by the TUPE Regulations, BET made it clear that it would not be offering access to a pension scheme to any employee who earned less than £15,000 a year. In response, 11 employees who earned less than that sum commenced High Court proceedings against both BET and the Council, claiming that they were entitled to equivalent pension rights in their employment with BET. The employees argued that the purpose of the Directive was to protect the pay and conditions of workers when their employment was transferred to a new employer following the transfer of an undertaking. Since Community law recognised pensions as a form of deferred pay, the transferee's refusal to offer pensions rights at least equivalent to those that the employees had enjoyed with the transferor meant that the employees were worse off in terms of pay than they had been before the transfer. In the employees' view, such unfairness was contrary to the general purpose of the Directive, which was to protect the terms and conditions of employment following a transfer.

The High Court held that occupational pension schemes were excluded from the scope of TUPE by virtue of Reg 10, and this was clearly compatible with the wording of Article 3 of the Directive. Accordingly, under the TUPE Regulations, the transferee was not required, following a relevant transfer, to give the transferred employees rights to an occupational pension scheme that were comparable to those that they had enjoyed with the transferor prior to the transfer.

Note that there are obligations *outside* TUPE for ongoing pension benefits to **3.138** be provided in appropriate circumstances (see below). Note too that in practice, at least in public sector transfers, it is often a condition of acquisition that pension protection be given to the acquired employees, particularly in contracting out or second generation outsourcing situations.

Neither the Regulations nor the Directive exclude pension rights from transferring in the sense that they *require* an existing arrangement to come to an end. There is nothing, bar logistical difficulties, to stop a transferee continuing arrangements voluntarily, and this may be desirable (if permitted by the rules of the scheme and by the Inland Revenue) if there is a prospect of the employees in a labour-intensive undertaking otherwise objecting to the transfer *en masse*, thereby preventing its execution. The transferor must carefully consider any promises it makes to the workforce in respect of post-transfer pension provision, however, as any misleading statements may give rise to liability for negligent misrepresentation (which, as we have discussed, will *not* pass to the transferee upon the transfer to the extent that it relates to an occupational pension scheme within the meaning of Reg 10(1) – see Hagen v ICI Chemicals and Polymers Ltd and ors 2002 IRLR 31, QBD, under 'Rights and liabilities relating to the individual – tortious and other civil liabilities' above).

Regulation 10(3) provides that any 'employee whose contract of employment **3.139** is transferred in the circumstances described in Reg 4(1) shall not be entitled to bring a claim against the transferor for (a) breach of contract or (b) constructive unfair dismissal under S.95(1)(c) [ERA]'. Thus, an employee is precluded from claiming unfair constructive dismissal on the ordinary basis in respect of loss or reduction in his or her rights under an occupational pension scheme in consequence of a relevant transfer. (Note, this does not apply to alleged breaches or dismissals that occurred before 6 April 2006 when the 2006 Regulations came into force.) The principle behind the introduction of this part of Reg 10 was that, given that rights to occupational pension schemes do not pass to the transferee upon a relevant transfer, an employee who loses such rights on account of the transfer might, theoretically, be entitled to sue the transferor for breach of contract or for constructive unfair dismissal based upon the loss sustained. Whether this was actually the case prior to the coming into force of Reg 10(3), or whether such rights simply dissipated upon transfer, was never tested directly in the courts – but the expression of Lord Justice Pill in

255

Powerhouse Retail Ltd and ors v Burroughs and ors 2004 IRLR 979, CA, that 'the pension terms *fall out* of the contract of employment with the transferee *and no further pension rights can be accrued* against the transferor' suggests that the latter was the likely position. The Powerhouse case was further appealed to the House of Lords, where it became known as Preston v Wolverhampton Healthcare NHS Trust (No.3) 2006 ICR 606, HL. In upholding the Court of Appeal's decision, nothing in Lord Hope of Craighead's speech (with which the other Law Lords agreed) suggests a view differing from that taken by Pill LJ.

The prohibition in Reg 10(3) in respect of claiming unfair constructive dismissal applies only in respect of S.95(1)(c) ERA. Does this mean that an employee *may* make a claim for constructive unfair dismissal against the transferor under Reg 4(9), on the basis that the loss (or prospective loss) upon the transfer of his or her occupational pension rights involves a substantial change in working conditions to his or her material detriment? Given that Reg 10(1)(b) excludes Reg 4 from applying to any rights, powers, duties and liabilities arising in connection with a person's employment which relate to an occupational pension scheme, this seems unlikely but not impossible.

3.140 **Obligation on Member States to protect immediate and prospective rights.** Although, as we discussed above, TUPE does not oblige a transferee to continue or replace a transferor's scheme, Article 3.4(b) of the Directive provides that Member States shall 'adopt the measures necessary to protect the interests of employees and of persons no longer employed in the transferor's business at the time of the transfer in respect of rights conferring on them immediate or prospective entitlement to old age benefits, including survivors' benefits'. In Walden Engineering Co Ltd v Warrener 1993 IRLR 420, EAT, the Appeal Tribunal concluded that Article 3.3 (the precursor to Article 3.4(b)) was clearly addressed to Member States and did *not* create any liability on a transferor or transferee in the private sector to protect interests under company pension schemes.

The interests that Article 3.4 requires Member States to protect are dual. First, they are required to protect rights conferring *immediate* entitlement to old age benefits. These are the rights which crystallise at the time of the transfer vis-à-vis the transferor's scheme – i.e. accrued pension rights. UK law seems fully to satisfy the requirement under Article 3.4, since under Ss.69–82 of the Pension Schemes Act 1993 occupational pension schemes must provide employees who have been in the scheme for two years with the right to a preserved pension upon leaving the scheme, whether or not a transfer has taken place.

3.141 Secondly, Member States are required to protect rights conferring *prospective* entitlement to old-age benefits. Although there is nothing in the TUPE Regulations that requires transferees to provide ongoing pension benefits to incoming staff, there are such requirements in legislation outside the scope of the Regulations. For some time, employees involved in transfers within or out of the public sector have benefited from special pension protections conferred by the 'Fair Deal for Staff Pensions' and related practice – discussed under 'Collective rights and liabilities – special rights for public sector transfers' above. However, now the Pensions Act 2004 (and in particular Ss.257 and 258 of that Act) along with the Transfer of Employment (Pension Protection) Regulations 2005 SI 2005/649 (both of which came into force on 6 April 2005) impose basic requirements on transferees in both public and private sector acquisitions to provide ongoing pension protection. These provisions require examination in some detail.

Future pension protections. First, which of the transferring employees are **3.142** covered by the protections? The initial requirement is that, immediately prior to the transfer, an occupational scheme is in force 'in relation to which the transferor is the employer' – S.257(1)(c)(i) Pensions Act 2004. Most occupational pension schemes will obviously satisfy this requirement. However, it should be noted that the definition of an occupational pension scheme in S.1 of the Pension Schemes Act 1993 also covers schemes that are established by persons other than the employer, such as interested bodies or indeed an employee in the relevant employment. This suggests that the members of such schemes could be left without any protection at all following a transfer. While their schemes will be excluded from transfer by virtue of Reg 10, since they fall within the definition of 'occupational pension schemes' in S.1, they would not qualify for the basic protections guaranteed under the Pension Act 2004 as their schemes would not satisfy the S.257(1)(c)(i) requirement.

Assuming that the transferor does have an occupational pension scheme immediately prior to the transfer, the minimal pension protections guaranteed under the 2004 Act and 2005 Regulations apply where the employee:

- is an active member of the scheme – S.257(2) or
- is not an active member but is eligible to be one – S.257(3) or
- is not and is not eligible to be an active member, but would have become eligible if his employment had not been curtailed – S.257(4).

The existing scheme may be a defined benefit scheme or money purchase **3.143** scheme. If any of the benefits that may be provided by the scheme are money purchase benefits, then for the pension protections to apply the transferor must be required to, or actually have made, contributions to the scheme in respect of the employee (or would have been required do so if the employee had been an active member). So if the scheme includes money purchase benefits but the employer has not and is not or would not be required to make contributions to it, the transferee will fall under no obligations to make any substitute pension provision for the employee who loses his or her rights under Regs 4 and 10.

257

Assuming the pension protections apply, S.258 of the Pensions Act 2004 puts the transferee under an obligation to provide a replacement scheme for his incoming employees. However, the transferee has a free choice as to what kind of pension scheme to implement. It may be:

- a defined benefit scheme in relation to which the level of benefits meets a statutory minimum standard or

- a stakeholder or money purchase occupational pension scheme to which the employer contributes at a specific rate.

3.144 Where the transferee adopts a *money purchase* (i.e. defined contribution) scheme, the transferee must secure that the employee is or is eligible to be an active member of either an occupational money purchase scheme or a stakeholder scheme into which the transferee makes 'relevant contributions'. These must amount to contributions that match those of the employee, up to 6 per cent of the employee's gross basic salary (not including fluctuating emoluments) – see S.258(2)(b) and Reg 3 of the Transfer of Employment (Pension Protection) Regulations 2005 SI 2005/649.

Where the transferee adopts a scheme that is *not a money purchase scheme*, the transferee must secure that the employee is or is eligible to be an active member of an occupational pension scheme which either:

- satisfies the statutory reference scheme test defined in S.12A of the Pensions Schemes Act 1993 (the minimum benefit standard required for defined benefit schemes to be contracted out of the State pension) or

- entitles the member to benefits of a value equal to at least 6 per cent of pensionable pay (as defined under the rules of the scheme) for each year of employment together with the total amount of contributions made by the member (contributions which, if required by the scheme, must not exceed a rate of 6 per cent of the member's pensionable pay) or

- provides for the transferee to make 'relevant contributions'. As above, these must amount to contributions that match those of the employee, of up to 6 per cent of the employee's gross basic salary (not including fluctuating emoluments) – see S.258(2)(c) and Reg 2 of the 2005 Regulations.

3.145 Note that there is no requirement that the transferee mirror any death or ill-health benefits that may have been included in the transferor's pension before the transfer.

By virtue of S.258(6) of the Pensions Act 2004, the employee can agree to contract out of these provisions.

Insolvency

The TUPE Regulations 2006 introduced new provisions not contained in the precursor Regulations aimed at promoting the 'rescue culture' in respect of businesses that are insolvent. It has always been the case that TUPE will apply where a business, or the underlying profitable part of it, is continued during the course of the insolvency proceedings and subsequently sold as a going concern by the insolvency practitioner. What is new is that the normal TUPE rules regarding the transfer or rights, duties and liabilities are modified to a greater or lesser extent depending on the nature of the insolvency proceedings in question. The aim of this is to encourage transferees to acquire businesses that have got themselves into financial or other trading difficulties by limiting the employment liabilities they take on.

The key changes introduced by Regs 8 and 9 of the 2006 Regulations are that:

* where the transferor is subject to bankruptcy or analogous insolvency proceedings instituted with a view to liquidating the transferor's assets under the supervision of an insolvency practitioner, both Regs 4 and 7 are disapplied in their entirety – Reg 8(7). This means that the transferee will not have to take on any of the employees assigned to the undertaking that is the subject of any relevant transfer. It also means that if such employees are voluntarily re-engaged by the transferee, none of the rights, duties, powers and liabilities under or in connection with their contracts of employment are automatically transferred; nor are the employees protected in the usual way against detrimental variation of their contractual terms or unfair dismissal by reason of the transfer

* where the transferor is the subject of 'relevant insolvency proceedings', Reg 4 will continue to apply except that certain core debts (such as statutory redundancy payments, payments in lieu of notice and unpaid holiday pay of up to six weeks) will not transfer but will instead remain with the transferor – Reg 8(5). These will become payable by the Secretary of State for Trade and Industry out of the National Insurance Fund. 'Relevant insolvency proceedings' for these purposes are defined in Reg 8(6) as 'proceedings which have been opened in relation to the transferor not with a view to the liquidation of the assets of the transferor and which are under the supervision of an insolvency practitioner'. In practice, this will cover administrative receiverships and administrations.

The provisions of Reg 8 and 9 are examined in detail in Chapter 6.

Continuation orders

We discussed above the extent to which statutory rights are transferred on a relevant transfer. One such right that has been found not to transfer is the benefit of an interim relief order for continuation of employment on the ground

259

of trade union-related discrimination, under S.164 TULR(C)A – an admittedly limited but interesting exception.

In Dowling v ME Ilic Haulage and anor EAT 0836/03 D was employed by a haulage company, IH, as a driver's mate. He was dismissed for gross misconduct on 15 December 2002 and brought a claim under S.152 TULR(C)A, alleging that the real reason for the dismissal was his participation in trade union activities as a shop steward. He also applied for interim relief. That application was heard on 3 February 2003 and a continuation order was granted. The hearing of D's unfair dismissal claim was listed to take place on 22 April 2003. Meanwhile, on 14 April, part of IH's business was acquired by another company, BL Ltd. The parties accepted that TUPE applied and BL Ltd was joined as a second respondent to the unfair dismissal claim. However, a tribunal chairman subsequently dismissed BL Ltd from the proceedings. Her reasoning was that, at the date of the transfer, D was not employed under a contract of employment for the purposes of Reg 4(1), and accordingly IH's obligations under the continuation order did not pass to BL Ltd by virtue of Reg 4(2)(a). D appealed to the EAT.

3.149 The appeal was heard by the then President of the EAT, Mr Justice Burton. He agreed with the tribunal chairman that the relationship that is effected by a continuation order is not a 'contract of employment' for the purposes of TUPE because it is purely statutory and unilateral, in that the employee receives pay but has no corresponding obligation to provide services. He rejected the argument that D's position was similar to that of an employee absent on maternity leave or long-term sick leave. In his view, an individual who is the subject of a continuation order is an ex-employee and there is no subsisting employment contract upon which Reg 4(1) can bite. D referred to the case of Litster and ors v Forth Dry Dock and Engineering Co Ltd (in receivership) and anor 1989 ICR 341, HL, in which the House of Lords held that Reg 4(1) must be construed purposively so that an employee dismissed before a transfer for a reason connected with it is deemed to have been employed in the undertaking immediately before the transfer. He argued that a similar analysis applied in the context of continuation orders. Burton J did not accept this analogy. In his view, it was much more difficult to construe Reg 4(1) as effecting a statutory continuation of the employment contract in the present context than it was in Litster, where the aim was to prevent the parties from evading the application of TUPE.

In any event, it was plain from the narrow wording of S.164 TULR(C)A that a continuation order was not intended to have this effect. S.164(1) prescribes two exclusive and limited purposes for which the contract of employment continues in force – pay and benefits, and calculation of the employee's period of continuous employment. Burton J made the additional point that, for the duration of a continuation order, an employer can do nothing to terminate its obligations under S.164, short of applying to the tribunal for variation or revocation of the order under S.165. Even if a continuation order were capable of effecting a statutory continuation of the employment contract, the contract created or continued by the order would not – indeed, could not – be terminated in the event of a transfer of the business. Thus, it was not a 'contract which would otherwise [have been] terminated by the transfer' within the meaning of Reg 4(1). Burton J concluded that a continuation order does no more than create, on the part of the former employer, a financial liability which does not pass to a transferee of the undertaking. Accordingly, he dismissed D's appeal.

This situation is exceptional and should be contrasted with that in which **3.150** employment is deemed to have continued following a successful appeal from a summary dismissal. In G4S Justice Services (UK) Ltd v Anstey and ors 2006 IRLR 588, EAT, A and S were summarily dismissed on 13 April 2005 for gross misconduct and lodged internal appeals against their dismissals. Their disciplinary procedure provided that, in the event of a successful appeal against dismissal, continuity of employment would be classed as unbroken service with full restitution of lost earnings. Before the employees' appeals were heard, however, their employer lost the contract on which they worked to another contractor, G4S, which took over on 1 May. Following the transfer G4S declined to hear the employees' appeals, claiming that it had never been their employer. As a result their appeals were heard by GSL, which allowed both and directed that they be reinstated. G4S refused to reinstate them on the basis that they had not been employed by GSL 'immediately before' the transfer within the meaning of Reg 4(3), with the result that their employment had not transferred to G4S under Reg 4(1) and (2). A and S subsequently brought claims of unfair dismissal against both GSL and G4S. The EAT upheld an employment tribunal's finding that the claimants' contracts of employment had transferred to the transferee under TUPE. Although the claimants had been summarily dismissed by the transferor, they had lodged appeals against those dismissals that were still pending at the time of the transfer. The EAT found that the contractual obligation to hear and determine the claimants' appeals against dismissal lay, notwithstanding the transfer, with the transferor. The transferor's subsequent decision to uphold those appeals and reinstate the claimants with full continuity of service had the retrospective effect that the dismissals were expunged and the claimants were employed 'immediately before the transfer'. Therefore, the obligation on the transferor to reinstate the claimants transferred to the transferee under the TUPE Regulations.

Continuing liability of the transferor?   3.151

Once Reg 4(2) of the 2006 Regulations has operated to transfer rights and duties to a transferee, it is not possible for a transferring employee to bring a claim against the transferor in respect of them. Equally, however, a *transferor* will no longer be able to assert any right transferred to the transferee against the transferred employees – which may be of particular consequence in relation to, for example, the loss of the right to enforce restraint of trade clauses and clauses relating to confidential information, or compromise agreements – see the sections on 'Restrictive covenants and confidential information' and 'Compromise agreements' under 'Rights and liabilities relating to the individual' above.

The ECJ ruled that this was the position in relation to the Acquired Rights Directive (No.2001/23) in Berg and anor v Besselsen 1990 ICR 396, ECJ. Its analysis of Article 3.1 showed that a relevant transfer entails the automatic transfer from the transferor to the transferee of the employer's obligations arising from a contract of employment or an employment relationship – subject, however, to the right of EU Member States to provide for joint liability of the transferor and transferee following the transfer. (Since Berg, the Directive has been amended to allow Member States to provide for *joint and several* liability – see below.) Therefore, the ECJ held, unless the Member States provide otherwise, the transferor is released from its obligations as an employer solely by reason of the transfer. This legal consequence is not conditional on the consent of the employees concerned, and cannot be prevented by their objection to the transfer.

3.152 In Stirling District Council v Allan and ors 1995 IRLR 301, Ct Sess (Inner House), the Court of Session confirmed that this is also the position under UK law in its implementation of the mandatory provisions of the Directive. In that case Stirling District Council conducted a competitive tendering exercise under which the contract on which the claimants worked was awarded to B Ltd. A and seven of his colleagues, who were dismissed for redundancy, initiated tribunal proceedings against the Council. The tribunal held that their dismissals were automatically unfair under what is now Reg 7(1) of the 2006 Regulations. However, it refused to uphold the claims against the Council on the basis that the employees had initiated proceedings against the wrong party, given that under Reg 4(2) rights and liabilities under contracts of employment are automatically assigned to the transferee where the employees were deemed to be employed immediately before the relevant transfer. The EAT allowed the employees' appeal. It took the view that it would be contrary to the Regulations' main purpose of protecting employees' rights if Reg 4(2) were to be regarded as transferring to the transferee exclusive responsibility for a dismissal carried out entirely by the *transferor* and taking effect before, or simultaneously with, the transfer. The Council appealed.

The Court of Session held that the tribunal had correctly held that liability to compensate the employees for the dismissals fell exclusively on the transferee. In concluding that the transferor was accordingly not liable for the unfair dismissals, the Court cited the following reasons:

- there was no ambiguity in Reg 4(2)(b)'s provision that, on completion of a relevant transfer, all the transferor's contractual liabilities towards his employees were transferred to the transferee. The word 'transferred' necessarily denotes that the transferor's liabilities, whether accrued or continuing, pass to the transferee and that the transferor is no longer subject to any such liabilities. Therefore, while it is true that the responsibility of an employer for the dismissal of an employee should not be excluded in the absence of express provision or necessary implication, Reg 4(2)(a) unambiguously and clearly provided such express provision

- it was a natural consequence of the subsequent provision in Reg 4(2)(b) – which states that anything done before the completion of the transfer by the transferor in relation to a contract of employment was deemed to have been done by the transferee – that the liability of the transferor for the act of unfair dismissal should be discharged. Again, this expressly and unambiguously excluded the transferor's responsibility for an employee's dismissal

- the employees' contention that the transferor remained liable was inconsistent with the terms of the Directive. The fact that Article 3 gave Member States the *option* of providing for the continued liability of the transferor, in addition to the transferee, clearly confirmed that the transferor did *not* remain liable unless provision to that effect had been made.

Although a decision of the Court of Session does not strictly bind the lower **3.153** courts in England and Wales, the decision in Allan was followed by the EAT in Secretary of State for Employment v Mapstone and ors EAT 1060/94, which noted that the Court of Session's decision was 'manifestly right' and 'whether or not that is binding upon us we should not dream of departing from such authority unless we were satisfied that it is wrong'. Indeed, the Court of Session in Allan took into account the obiter dictum of the EAT in Ibex Trading Co Ltd (in administration) v Walton and ors 1994 ICR 907, EAT, that 'use of the word "transfer" in its natural and ordinary meaning suggests a taking away from one and a handing over to another' – in holding that, in fact, 'the word cannot bear any other meaning in any circumstances'.

Joint and several liability **3.154**
As the Court of Session in Allan (above) noted, Article 3.1 of the Directive contains an option for Member States to provide for joint and several liability of transferor and transferee after the transfer, in respect of obligations which otherwise would fall exclusively on the transferee. The United Kingdom has opted to impose joint and several liability under TUPE in the following two areas only:

- liability to pay compensation for the transferor's failures to comply with its information and consultation requirements under Regs 13 or 14, and liability for either party's failure to pay compensation awarded to an employee in respect of such failures under Reg 15(7) or (8) – Reg 15(9); and

- liability for personal injury claims (so far as this relates to the employee's period of employment with the transferor) in situations where the transferor is not required to take out personal injury insurance under S.3(1)(a)–(c) of the Employers' Liability (Compulsory Insurance) Act 1969 – Reg 17(2).

3.155 The effect of joint and several liability is that an employee may sue either the transferor or the transferee or both for compensation. In that case, as the DTI Guide points out (in relation to cases under Reg 15(9)), 'where either the transferor or the new employer is the sole defendant, he may seek to join the other employer to the case' – or, where judgment is given against a sole defendant, he may be able to recover a contribution from the other potential defendant by suing him under S.1(1) of the Civil Liability (Contribution) Act 1978. Note that where a transfer occurs in a context in which the transferor is insolvent, the transferee may in effect end up bearing full liability itself, despite the provisions for joint and several liability in Regs 15(9) and 17(2).

3.156 **Joint and several liability in respect of failure to inform and consult.** We discussed fully the effect of the provisions as to joint and several liability in respect of failure to inform and consult under 'Collective rights and liabilities – duty to inform and consult', above. The provisions seek to address the problem raised by Alamo Group (Europe) Ltd v Tucker and anor 2003 ICR 829, EAT. In that case the EAT held that liability for a failure to inform and consult passed like any other liability to the transferee upon transfer – with the unjust effect that transferors could with impunity conduct perfunctory consultation exercises upon transfer.

3.157 **Joint and several liability for personal injury.** We discussed above the effect of the Court of Appeal's decision in (1) Martin v Lancashire County Council (2) Bernadone v Pall Mall Services Group Ltd and ors 2001 ICR 197, CA, under 'Rights and liabilities relating to the individual – tortious and other civil liabilities'. The Court there held that a transferor's right to be indemnified in respect of tortious liability under compulsory employers' liability insurance passes to the transferee under Reg 4(2). This is because the liability against which employers are obliged, by the Employers' Liability (Compulsory Insurance) Act 1969, to insure is liability for bodily injury or disease sustained by their employees arising out of and in the course of their employment – and, therefore, any right to be indemnified in respect of that liability is a right in respect of liability 'in connection with' and 'arising from' the contract within the meaning of Reg 4(2).

However, the Court's conclusion in Bernadone was not relevant where a transferor was not obliged to take out insurance covering possible personal injury claims by his employees. S.3(1)(a)–(c) of the Employers' Liability (Compulsory Insurance) Act 1969 provides that the following authorities and bodies are not required to effect insurance under the Act:

• health service bodies; National Health Service Trusts; NHS Foundation Trusts; Primary Care Trusts

- the Common Council of the City of London; London Borough Councils; councils of a county or county borough in Wales; councils constituted under S.2 of the Local Government etc (Scotland) Act 1994 in England and Wales or joint committees in Scotland which are so constituted as to include among their members representatives of any such council; joint authorities established by Part IV of the Local Government Act 1985

- the Broads Authority; the Strathclyde Passenger Transport Authority

- police authorities; the London Fire and Emergency Planning Authority

- the Commission for Equality and Human Rights

- employers that are exempted by regulations (as listed in Schedule 2 to the Employers' Liability (Compulsory Insurance) Regulations 1998 SI 1998/2573).

So a transferee acquiring a business from an NHS Trust, for example, could **3.158** inherit an uninsured claim that it might be unable to meet. It was to address this loophole that the TUPE Regulations 2006 introduced the provision in Reg 17(2) according to the transferor and transferee joint and several liability in respect of claims for personal injury arising out of an employee's employment with a potentially uninsured transferor. This, however, has served to give rise to a disparity between cases in which a transferor is from the private sector and those in which the transferor falls within the list of exempted bodies above. In the former, following the Martin decision, the transferee will inherit full liability for personal injury claims; in the latter, the transferee is jointly and severally liable with the transferor.

Possibility of dual employment   3.159
There remains one further hypothetical situation where the transferor may continue to bear liability in respect of individual transferred employees. The possibility was discussed in Chapter 2 that, in the context of a relevant transfer arising out of a service provision change, the identifiable group of employees assigned to the transferring activity worked on that activity for part only of their weekly working time. Could it be the case that if, say, those employees work from Monday to Wednesday on the activity to be transferred, that that part of their employment will transfer to the transferee but for the remaining two days the employees will continue to work for the transferor? If this were the case, the relevant employees would have dual employment following the transfer and the transferor would thus retain liability in respect of their employment to the extent that it was not transferred. It is probable, though, that whole-time dedication may be required on the part of employees to give rise to a relevant transfer – for a fuller discussion see Chapter 2, under '"Assigned" to undertaking transferred – difficult issues arising from assignment to part of business'.

265

4 Unfair dismissal

The Transfer of Undertakings (Protection of Employment) Regulations 2006 SI **4.1** 2006/246 (TUPE) severely restrict the circumstances in which employers – transferors or transferees – can effect dismissals fairly in a transfer situation. Reg 7, which implements Article 4 of the EU Acquired Rights Directive (No.2001/23), provides that a dismissal will be automatically unfair if the sole or principal reason for it is (i) a relevant transfer, or (ii) a reason connected with a relevant transfer that is not 'an economic, technical or organisational reason entailing changes in the workforce of either the transferor or the transferee'. This regime is, in essence, the same as that previously found in Reg 8 of the 1981 Regulations, albeit expressed in a clearer manner.

Regulation 7 augments, and hence cannot be divorced from, the general unfair dismissal law contained in the Employment Rights Act 1996 (ERA). Accordingly, we begin this chapter by giving a brief overview of the relevant ERA provisions. We then explain how the Reg 7 TUPE unfair dismissal rules fit together, before turning to examine in depth the two questions central to the Reg 7 regime: first, when will a dismissal be automatically unfair?; and secondly, what will amount to 'an economic, technical or organisational reason entailing changes in the workforce' (an ETO reason)?

Also in this chapter, we discuss at length the two routes by which an employee's **4.2** decision to leave his or her employment, taken in response to the actions of a transferor or transferee, can amount to a 'dismissal' giving rise to a potential unfair dismissal claim. First, as Reg 4(11) acknowledges, a constructive dismissal might occur where an employee resigns in response to a repudiatory breach of contract by his or her employer. Secondly, Reg 4(9) states that 'where a relevant transfer involves or would involve a substantial change in working conditions to the material detriment of a person whose contract of employment is or would be transferred... such an employee may treat the contract of employment as having been terminated, and the employee shall be treated for

---

267

any purpose as having been dismissed by the employer'. Having examined these provisions, we bring the chapter to a close by considering which employer – transferor or transferee – will be liable for unfair dismissals carried out around the time of a relevant transfer.

Note that we presume, for the purposes of this discussion, that a relevant transfer within the meaning of Reg 3 of the 2006 Regulations has taken (or is about to take) place. For an examination of what amounts to a relevant transfer, see Chapter 1.

4.3 Overview

This Handbook does not cover general unfair dismissal law in detail. In this section, however, we outline the main features of the unfair dismissal regime contained in the Employment Rights Act 1996 that can impact upon TUPE-connected dismissals. For a more detailed analysis of this area, see IDS Employment Law Handbooks, 'Unfair Dismissal' (2010) and 'Redundancy' (2008).

4.4 Who is eligible to claim unfair dismissal?

An individual must meet certain eligibility criteria in order to bring an unfair dismissal claim, whether or not such a claim is TUPE-connected. In summary:

- only 'employees' can claim – S.94(1) ERA. An employee is defined as 'an individual who has entered into or works under a contract of employment' – S.230(1). A 'contract of employment' is defined as 'a contract of service, whether express or implied and (if it is express) whether oral or in writing' – S.230(2)

- an employee must have been continuously employed by the employer for at least one year in order to claim – S.108(1) ERA

- only claims relating to 'employment in Great Britain' can be brought. However, expatriate employees working wholly outside Great Britain will be entitled to bring unfair dismissal claims in certain unusual circumstances – see Lawson v Serco Ltd and other cases 2006 ICR 250, HL.

4.5 Meaning of 'dismissal'

In order to succeed with an unfair dismissal claim, whether in relation to TUPE or otherwise, an employee has to show that he or she has been 'dismissed' within the meaning of S.95(1) ERA. This provides that a dismissal occurs in each of the following three circumstances:

- the employer terminates the employee's contract with or without notice – S.95(1)(a)

268

- the employee is employed under a fixed-term contract which terminates upon its expiry without being renewed on the same terms – S.95(1)(b)

- the employee terminates the employment contract, with or without notice, in circumstances where he or she is entitled to do so without notice owing to the employer's conduct (known as a constructive dismissal) – S.95(1)(c).

Reason for dismissal   4.6

Once an employee has established that a dismissal has occurred, the onus is on the employer to show that the reason or principal reason for dismissal is one of the potentially fair reasons set out in S.98(1) and (2) ERA: the employee's capability or qualification, conduct, redundancy (see 'Redundancy' below), inability to work owing to a statutory requirement, retirement, or dismissal 'for some other substantial reason of a kind such as to justify the dismissal of an employee holding the position which the employee held'.

Certain reasons for dismissal are *automatically* unfair – for example, dismissals by reason of trade union membership; pregnancy; and, as this chapter explains, the transfer of an undertaking where there is no 'economic, technical or organisational reason entailing changes in the workforce'.

Reasonableness   4.7

In addition to showing a fair reason for dismissal, in order to escape unfair dismissal liability the employer must also have acted reasonably in all the circumstances, having regard to equity and the substantial merits of the case – S.98(4) ERA. In other words, the employer must have acted reasonably in treating the reason as a sufficient reason for dismissal and have acted fairly and in accordance with relevant procedures.

With regard to reasonableness, the tribunal should not simply consider whether it would have dismissed in the circumstances and substitute its view for that of the employer – Iceland Frozen Foods Ltd v Jones 1983 ICR 17, EAT. Rather, the test to be applied is whether the employer's decision to dismiss fell within the range of reasonable responses available to it – see (1) Post Office v Foley (2) HSBC Bank plc v Madden 2000 ICR 1283, CA.

Procedural requirements   4.8

The fairness of a dismissal also depends on the employer's compliance with any contractual and statutory procedural requirements – for example, proper redundancy consultation and selection procedures. In dismissing, employers have to be sure that they comply with the revised Acas Code of Practice on Disciplinary and Grievance Procedures issued under S.199 of the Trade Union and Labour Relations (Consolidation) Act 1992. Arguably, the Code does not sit easily with non-fault dismissals such as those usually associated with relevant transfers, and there is an express exclusion in the case of redundancy dismissals.

269

However, as there is no such exclusion in the case of TUPE-related dismissals, it may be sensible for employers to err on the side of caution and familiarise themselves with the provisions of the Code, many of which are based on generally accepted standards of fairness and reasonableness. For a detailed discussion of the issue of ensuring fairness in the context of internal dismissal procedures, see IDS Employment Law Handbook, 'Unfair Dismissal' (2010), Chapter 3, under 'Fairness of internal procedure'.

4.9 Time limit

An unfair dismissal claim must be brought in an employment tribunal within three months of the effective date of termination or, if that is not reasonably practicable, within such further period as the tribunal considers reasonable – S.111(2) ERA.

4.10 Remedies

The remedies available to an unfairly dismissed employee are:

- reinstatement, i.e. an order that the employee be reinstated in his or her old job with no financial loss – S.114 ERA

- re-engagement, i.e. an order that the employee be re-engaged in a job comparable to that from which he or she was dismissed, or in other suitable employment – S.115, or

- compensation – Ss.118–124A ERA, which is the usual remedy. This is divided into a basic award calculated according to a set formula (subject to a current maximum (as at January 2011) of £11,400) and a compensatory award of such amount as the tribunal considers just and equitable in all the circumstances, having regard to the loss sustained by the employee as a consequence of the dismissal (subject to a current maximum (as at January 2011) of £65,300).

4.11 Redundancy

Dismissals effected by a transferor or transferee will often be by reason of redundancy. As we saw above, redundancy is one of the potentially fair reasons for dismissal set out in S.98(2) ERA.

4.12 Definition of redundancy. In order for this reason to be demonstrated, the definition of redundancy contained in S.139 ERA must be satisfied. Under that provision, an employee is dismissed by reason of redundancy where the dismissal is wholly or mainly attributable to the fact that:

- the employer has ceased or intends to cease to carry on the business either for the purposes of which or in the place where the employee was employed, or

- the requirements of the business for employees to carry out work of a particular kind or to carry out work in the place where the employee was employed have ceased or diminished or are expected to cease or diminish.

Even if there is a genuine redundancy situation, however, a redundancy dismissal will still be unfair under the ERA if the employer has not acted reasonably in all the circumstances – S.98(4) (see 'Reasonableness' above).

Pool for selection. The first thing that an employer must do in order to carry **4.13** out a fair redundancy dismissal is to identify the group of employees from whom those who are to be made redundant will be drawn. This group is known as the 'pool for selection'.

A employer generally has a good deal of flexibility in defining the pool – he need only show that he has applied his mind to the issue and acted rationally, from genuine motives. However, the following should be borne in mind:

- an employer will need to have justifiable reasons for excluding a particular group of employees from the selection pool where the excluded category do the same or similar work to those who are up for selection. In the context of redundancies made following a TUPE transfer, the selection pool should generally be from all employees of the transferee doing similar work, not just transferred staff

- a fair pool for selection is not necessarily limited to those employees doing the same or similar work. Employers might be expected to include in the pool those employees whose work is interchangeable.

Selection criteria. The next step is to apply reasonable selection criteria to **4.14** the pool of employees up for selection. There are no legal requirements as to the precise criteria that should be used, but they should not depend solely upon subjective opinion, so some criteria at least should be capable of objective assessment.

Note that some reasons for redundancy selection will render a dismissal automatically unfair – for example, maternity, race, disability, trade union membership or the assertion of a statutory right.

Consultation. After warning of the potential for redundancy, the employer is **4.15** obliged to consult individually with all employees provisionally selected for redundancy before any final decision to dismiss is taken. What constitutes a fair and proper consultation is a question of fact for the tribunal to determine, but clearly the consultation must be genuine. The employee should be provided with information regarding the reasons for the redundancy and for the employee's provisional selection for redundancy and, if applicable, his or her individual scores against the selection criteria. While the individual scores of other employees should not be disclosed, employees should be given an idea of how they scored comparatively. Discussions should also take place on the steps that have been or will be taken to avoid making the employee redundant, and in particular on the search for suitable alternative employment (see below). Notice of termination should not be served until consultation has concluded.

4.16 **Suitable alternative employment**. A dismissal may be considered unfair if no consideration is given to finding the employee another suitable job within the organisation or group. Since the fairness of a dismissal for redundancy is judged not simply at the date on which notice is given but also with regard to events up to the date on which it takes effect, a suitable vacancy arising during the notice period should be offered to the otherwise redundant employee.

4.17 **Redundancy payment.** Employees with at least two years' continuous employment will be eligible for a statutory redundancy payment, which is calculated according to a set formula in the same way as the basic award for unfair dismissal. However, an employee who refuses an offer of suitable alternative employment loses this right.

4.18 The TUPE unfair dismissal regime

Regulation 7(1) of the 2006 Regulations, which implements Article 4.1 of the EU Acquired Rights Directive, provides that certain TUPE-related dismissals will be automatically unfair. It states: 'Where either before or after a relevant transfer, any employee of the transferor or transferee is dismissed, that employee shall be treated for the purposes of Part X of the 1996 Act (unfair dismissal) as unfairly dismissed if the sole or principal reason for his dismissal is (a) the transfer itself; or (b) a reason connected with the transfer that is not an economic, technical or organisational reason entailing changes in the workforce.'

Regulation 7(2) and (3) then provide that Reg 7(1) shall not apply to render a TUPE-connected dismissal automatically unfair where there is an 'economic, technical or organisational reason entailing changes in the workforce' (an ETO reason) for it; and Reg 7(3) clarifies that, for the purposes of the general unfair dismissal provisions of S.98 ERA (see 'Overview' above), a dismissal for an ETO reason will be potentially (not automatically) fair either by reason of redundancy or for 'some other substantial reason'. The fairness or otherwise of such an ETO dismissal will be determined in the normal way, with reference to the S.98(4) reasonableness test.

4.19 In this section we explain how the structure of Reg 7 brings a clarity that was lacking under the previous TUPE unfair dismissal rules, which were contained in Reg 8 of the 1981 Regulations. We then consider which categories of 'employees' will be eligible to rely on the Reg 7 TUPE unfair dismissal regime. Later in this chapter we focus in more detail on the important questions of when a dismissal will be automatically unfair owing to Reg 7(1), and when a dismissal will be potentially fair owing to the employer's demonstrating an ETO reason.

272

Clarity brought by new Reg 7   4.20

Under the 1981 Regulations, the rules providing unfair dismissal protection upon a TUPE transfer – contained in Reg 8 – were the subject of much wrangling in the courts. Before explaining why, it is sensible to set out the relevant provisions.

Regulation 8(1) of the 1981 Regulations stated: 'Where either before or after a relevant transfer, any employee of the transferor or the transferee is dismissed, that employee shall be treated... as unfairly dismissed if the transfer or a reason connected with it is the reason or principal reason for his dismissal.' Reg 8(2) then provided: 'Where an economic, technical or organisational reason entailing changes in the workforce of either the transferor or the transferee before or after a relevant transfer is the reason or principal reason for dismissing an employee paragraph (1) shall not apply to his dismissal.'

ETO reason can be transfer-connected. The main uncertainty caused by the   4.21
structure of old Reg 8 was summarised by the Government in its 2001 consultation document on TUPE reform, as follows: 'A number of... cases have focused on the relationship between Regulation 8(1) and Regulation 8(2). A particular issue has arisen as to whether dismissals for a reason connected with the transfer – Regulation 8(1) – and dismissals for an ETO reason – Regulation 8(2) – are two mutually exclusive categories or whether the latter are a sub-set of the former.' To make more sense of what this debate was all about, and its importance, we set out a case in which it arose:

• **Warner v Adnet Ltd** 1998 ICR 1056, CA: W was made redundant around the time of the transfer of the business for which he worked, and claimed automatically unfair dismissal with reference to Reg 8 of the 1981 Regulations. An employment tribunal decided that W's dismissal was for a reason connected with a relevant transfer, which, in its view, meant that the dismissal was automatically unfair – by virtue of Reg 8(1) – unless there was an ETO reason for it – within the meaning of Reg 8(2). The majority of the tribunal then decided that there was indeed an ETO reason for the dismissal, as redundancies of non-essential staff had been necessary. The tribunal went on to conclude that W's dismissal had been reasonable in all the circumstances, and thus fair under the provisions of the ERA. W appealed to the EAT, and thereafter to the Court of Appeal. He argued that the provisions of Reg 8(1) and (2) of the 1981 Regulations were mutually exclusive. Thus, in his view, the tribunal's task had been to determine whether the reason for his dismissal fell within Reg 8(1) *or* Reg 8(2); was it a reason connected with a relevant transfer *or* an ETO reason? If there was a Reg 8(1) reason for his dismissal, W continued, then that was the end of the matter and the dismissal was automatically unfair. The Court of Appeal rejected W's argument and upheld the tribunal's decision. In its view, the tribunal had been correct to determine, first, whether the transfer (or a

━━━━━━━━━━━━━━━━━━━━━━━━━━━━━ **273**

reason connected with it) was the principal reason for the dismissal; and, as the answer to this question was 'yes', to go on to decide whether the reason for dismissal was also an ETO reason within the meaning of Reg 8(2). Since there had been an ETO reason, it followed that Reg 8(1) did not apply to render W's dismissal automatically unfair.

4.22 In the 2001 consultation document, the Government, largely agreeing with the Court's decision in the Warner case, stated: 'The Government considers that ETO reasons should properly be seen as a sub-set of reasons connected with the transfer. If this were not the case, the ETO exception in the Directive would be essentially superfluous, as it would be clear in any event that the Directive could have no impact on changes completely unconnected with the transfer.'

This approach is reflected in the drafting of new Reg 7(1), which, as stated above, provides: 'Where either before or after a relevant transfer, any employee of the transferor or transferee is dismissed, that employee shall be treated for the purposes of Part X of the 1996 Act (unfair dismissal) as unfairly dismissed if the sole or principal reason for his dismissal is (a) the transfer itself; or (b) a reason connected with the transfer that is not an economic, technical or organisational reason entailing changes in the workforce.' This wording makes it clear that employers can point to an 'ETO defence' in respect of dismissals carried out for *a reason connected with the transfer*. Note, however, that no such defence is available under Reg 7(1) where a dismissal is carried out *by reason of the transfer itself*. We discuss the difference between dismissals carried out by reason of the transfer itself and dismissals carried out for a transfer-connected reason in 'Automatically unfair dismissals' below.

4.23 **'Sole or principal reason'.** As stated above, Reg 8(1) of the 1981 Regulations provided that an employee would be unfairly dismissed if the transfer or a reason connected with it is 'the reason or principal reason' for the dismissal. The corresponding part of new Reg 7(1), however, requires the transfer or a reason connected with it to be 'the *sole* or principal reason' (our emphasis) for dismissal if the rule is to take effect.

In Kerry Foods Ltd v Creber and ors 2000 ICR 556, EAT, Mr Justice Morrison stated that, given its natural meaning, old Reg 8(1) seemed to render a dismissal automatically unfair 'where the transfer is the principal or *a* reason for the dismissal. In other words, on their face, the Regulations contemplate that a transfer may be the sole or *an* effective cause of the dismissal.' This reasoning suggested that even if a relevant transfer or a reason connected with it was only a *minor* reason for dismissal, with the principal reason being unconnected with the transfer, the dismissal could be automatically unfair under old Reg 8(1). The introduction of the word 'sole' into new Reg 7(1) clarifies that this is not, in fact, the case.

The three categories of dismissal

4.24

So, as the Government pointed out in the 2005 consultation document, new Reg 7 now makes it clear that dismissals carried out by a transferor or a transferee will fall into one of three categories, as follows:

- dismissals for which the sole or principal reason is either the transfer itself or a reason connected with the transfer that is not an ETO reason. These will be automatically unfair under Reg 7(1)

- dismissals for which the sole or principal reason is connected with the transfer but also an ETO reason. Owing to Reg 7(2) and (3), these will be potentially fair by reason of redundancy or some other substantial reason. Thus, they will be actually fair if the reasonableness test of S.98(4) ERA is satisfied (see 'Overview' above)

- dismissals for which the sole or principal reason is unconnected with the transfer – for example, where an employee is dismissed for gross misconduct or poor performance. The fact that such dismissals take place around the time of a relevant transfer is merely a coincidence and the 2006 Regulations will have no effect. The rules of the ERA will determine the fairness or otherwise of the dismissals in the normal way.

We discuss the first two of these categories – those with regard to which the 2006 Regulations have an impact – in 'Automatically unfair dismissals' and 'Dismissals potentially fair for an "ETO reason"' a little later in this chapter.

Which employees are protected?

4.25

We now consider who might benefit from the unfair dismissal protection afforded by Reg 7 of the 2006 Regulations. In this regard, we make two essential points:

- only those employees who are entitled to claim unfair dismissal under the ERA – for instance, those with a minimum of one year's qualifying service – will be entitled to claim automatically unfair dismissal under Reg 7

- Reg 7 protects not only those employees who are to move from the transferor to the transferee as a result of TUPE, but all employees of the transferor or the transferee eligible to claim unfair dismissal who are dismissed by reason of the transfer or for a transfer-connected reason.

Employees must be eligible to claim under the ERA. As stated in the introduction to this chapter, Reg 7 of the 2006 Regulations implements Article 4 of the EU Acquired Rights Directive. The first part of Article 4.1 makes it clear that 'the transfer of the undertaking, business or part of the undertaking shall not in itself constitute grounds for dismissal by the transferor or the transferee', and that 'this provision shall not stand in the way of dismissals that may take place for economic, technical or organisational reasons entailing changes in the

4.26

275

workforce' – principles that, as we have seen, are reflected in Reg 7(1). However, the second subparagraph of Article 4.1 states that 'Member States may provide that the first subparagraph shall not apply to certain specific categories of employees who are not covered by the laws or practice of the Member States in respect of protection against dismissal'.

So, as the High Court put it in R v Secretary of State for Trade and Industry ex parte Unison 1996 ICR 1003, QBD, the second subparagraph of Article 4.1 'permits or envisages derogation by Member States' from the principle that transfer-connected dismissals are not allowed. This fits in with the objective of the Directive, which, as the ECJ explained in Viggósdóttir v Íslandspóstur HF 2002 IRLR 425, ECJ, is 'not to improve the situation of an employee following a transfer, but merely to preserve his acquired rights'. In other words, if an individual has not already acquired the right to claim unfair dismissal, the Directive is not designed to step in to provide him or her with that right simply because he or she is dismissed in relation to a transfer.

4.27 Regulation 7(6) of the 2006 Regulations grasps the opportunity for derogation provided by Article 4.1. It clarifies that Reg 7(1) – which, as we have seen, renders certain transfer-related dismissals automatically unfair – will *not* protect an employee who is excluded from the right to claim unfair dismissal under the ERA. For example, then, Reg 7 will not protect:

• anyone who is not an 'employee' as narrowly defined by S.230 ERA (see 'Overview – who is eligible to claim unfair dismissal?' above)

• anyone who does not have the continuous service required by S.108(1) ERA in order to claim unfair dismissal (currently one year) – see MRS Environmental Services Ltd v Marsh and anor 1997 ICR 995, EAT.

4.28 Note that the definition of 'employee' contained in Reg 2 of the 2006 Regulations is considerably wider than that contained in S.230 ERA – see Chapter 2 under 'Who is an "employee" for TUPE purposes?' for details. The upshot of this is that there will be certain groups of individuals who are protected by TUPE generally, but will gain no benefit from the Reg 7 unfair dismissal provisions.

Employees need not be members of the transferring workforce. It is important to note that it is not just potentially transferring employees who are protected by Reg 7. The TUPE unfair dismissal rules cover 'any' employee of the transferor or the transferee – Reg 7(1). Reg 7(4) clarifies that 'the provisions of this regulation apply irrespective of whether the employee in question is assigned to the organised grouping of resources or employees that is, or will be, transferred'. The practical effect of this is that the following employees may be eligible to claim automatically unfair dismissal via Reg 7 (assuming they meet the other qualifying requirements – see 'Overview' above):

- those dismissed by the transferor prior to the transfer, whether or not they are employed in the undertaking or part of the undertaking to be transferred

- those retained by the transferor after the transfer but dismissed subsequently

- those who transfer under TUPE from the transferor to the transferee and are thereafter dismissed by the transferee

- those in the transferee's existing workforce who are dismissed before or after the transfer – for example, as a result of redundancy or a reorganisation exercise triggered by the influx of transferring employees.

Automatically unfair dismissals   4.29

As we saw in 'The TUPE unfair dismissal regime' above, Reg 7(1) of the 2006 Regulations provides that where, either before or after a relevant transfer, any employee of the transferor or transferee is dismissed, that employee shall be treated for ERA purposes as unfairly dismissed if the sole or principal reason for dismissal is:

- the transfer itself, or

- a reason connected with the transfer that is not an economic, technical or organisational reason entailing changes in the workforce.

So, if the sole or principal reason for the dismissal of an employee eligible to   4.30 claim unfair dismissal is the transfer itself, that is the end of the matter: the dismissal will be automatically unfair under Reg 7(1). On the other hand, if the sole or principal reason for the dismissal is a reason 'connected with' the transfer, that dismissal will only be automatically unfair under Reg 7(1) if the reason for dismissal was not also an 'ETO reason'.

We consider what might amount to an ETO reason in 'Dismissals potentially fair for an "ETO reason"' below. In this section, we focus on the circumstances in which it might be said that a dismissal is *by reason of the relevant transfer itself* or for *a reason connected with the relevant transfer*, within the meaning of Reg 7(1). This, it should be noted, is a question of fact to be determined by the employment tribunal in the circumstances of the case.

Dismissals by reason of the transfer itself   4.31
To reiterate, if the sole or principal reason for a dismissal is *the relevant transfer itself* – as opposed to a *reason connected with the transfer* – there is no 'ETO defence' available to the employer, and the dismissal is automatically unfair under Reg 7(1). So, when will the sole or principal reason for a dismissal be the transfer itself?

Arguably, the logical answer to this question is 'never'. After all, as we saw in Chapter 2, Reg 4(1) provides that 'a relevant transfer shall not operate so as to

277

terminate the contract of employment of any person employed by the transferor and assigned to the organised grouping of resources or employees that is subject to the relevant transfer'. In other words, the whole point of TUPE is that the transfer itself cannot *cause* a dismissal. Thus, it would seem, there must always be a reason other than the transfer itself if a dismissal is to take effect – even if that reason is as basic as the parties' ignorance of TUPE's requirements or the transferee's wish not to take on the employee in question.

4.32 Clearly, however, this interpretation is not that envisaged by Reg 7(1), and is not that favoured by the Government. In the 'Employment rights on the transfer of an undertaking: a guide to the 2006 TUPE Regulations for employees, employers and representatives' (the DTI Guide), when discussing the new rules with regard to changing terms and conditions in Reg 4(5), which use similar terminology to that of Reg 7, the Government stated: 'Where an employer changes terms and conditions simply because of the transfer and there are no extenuating circumstances linked to the reason for that decision, then such a change is prompted by reason of the transfer itself. However, where the reason for the change is prompted by a knock-on effect of the transfer – say, the need to re-qualify staff to use the different machinery used by the transferee – then the reason is "connected to the transfer".'

So, in the Government's view, where a dismissal is carried out because of the transfer and there are no 'extenuating circumstances' – that is, to take the Oxford English Dictionary definition, there are no circumstances making the dismissal 'seem less serious or more forgivable' – the dismissal will be by reason of the transfer itself rather than for a transfer-connected reason. Unfortunately, though, the Government's comments do not leave things particularly clear with regard to where the line should be drawn. What will amount to 'extenuating circumstances' and what will not?

4.33 This debate could fill many pages, but we suggest that it need not trouble tribunals unduly. That is because, as long as the sole or principal reason for a dismissal is not completely *unconnected* with a relevant transfer, the following reasoning would seem to apply:

- where the employer cannot point to an ETO reason for dismissal within the meaning of Reg 7(2), it will make no difference to the question of unfair dismissal liability whether the dismissal is categorised as being by reason of 'the transfer itself' or for a reason 'connected with the transfer'. In either case, the dismissal will be automatically unfair owing to Reg 7(1)

- where, on the other hand, an employer can establish an ETO reason for dismissal, it seems evident that the dismissal should be categorised as being for a reason 'connected with the transfer' rather than by reason of 'the transfer itself'. That is because the existence of an ETO reason suggests that, to adopt the Government's terminology, there were 'extenuating circumstances' surrounding the dismissal. It follows – where the dismissal is transfer-connected but for an ETO reason – that the Reg 7(2) exception to the Reg 7(1) automatically unfair dismissal rule will apply, rendering the dismissal potentially fair by reason of either redundancy or some other substantial reason (see 'Dismissals potentially fair for an "ETO reason"') below.

So, in our view, tribunals could adopt the following practical approach: **4.34**

- first, consider whether the sole or principal reason for dismissal is *either* the transfer itself *or* transfer-connected within the meaning of Reg 7(1) (without troubling unduly to determine which), as opposed to being unconnected with the transfer

- if the sole or principal reason for dismissal is unconnected with the transfer, determine the fairness of the dismissal in the normal way, with reference to S.98 ERA

- if the sole or principal reason for dismissal is either the transfer itself or transfer-connected, go on to consider whether the reason for dismissal is an ETO reason within the meaning of Reg 7(2)

- if the sole or principal reason for dismissal is either the transfer itself or transfer-connected, and the employer cannot establish an ETO reason for dismissal, conclude that the dismissal is automatically unfair under Reg 7(1)

- if the sole or principal reason for dismissal is either the transfer itself or transfer-connected, and the employer can establish an ETO reason for dismissal, conclude that the dismissal is to be categorised as being for a reason 'connected with the transfer' rather than by reason of 'the transfer itself', and that, owing to Reg 7(2) and (3) the dismissal is potentially fair by reason of either redundancy or for some other substantial reason. Go on to determine the fairness or otherwise of the dismissal with reference to the 'reasonableness test' contained in S.98(4) ERA.

A number of recent employment tribunal cases help to illustrate the interaction **4.35** between Reg 7(1) and 7(2). Two examples:

- **Voice v Eastgate Optometry Ltd** ET Case No.1400130/08: V was employed by Boots the Chemist to work 35 hours a week. He worked Mondays to Fridays and one Sunday in every four. His employment was transferred to EO Ltd under TUPE. EO wanted to maximise its profits by doing more work on Saturdays and so insisted that V worked on Saturdays, which he refused to do. When his grievance was dismissed, the employee resigned and claimed that he had been unfairly dismissed for a reason connected with the transfer under Reg 7(1). An employment tribunal held that it was the transfer that led to the decision to change the way the business was operated and, in turn, to the employee's dismissal. The principal reason for

279

the employee's dismissal was thus the transfer itself or a reason connected with the transfer. The tribunal went to hold that although there was a technical or organisational reason for the change, EO Ltd was unable to show that it 'entailed changes in the workforce', with the consequence that an ETO reason within the meaning of Reg 7(2) had not been made out. V was therefore automatically unfairly dismissed by virtue of Reg 7(1)

- **Gowers and anor v Brambleton Ltd** ET Case No.2403058/08: Following a TUPE transfer in November 2007, the claimants became employees of B Ltd. On 4 January 2008 they were called to a meeting and told they were at risk of redundancy. Further consultation meetings were held that month, following which the claimants were put on paid leave. By the end of January, they were informed that they were to be made redundant with effect from 1 February. B Ltd argued that there had been a reduction in their funding from the local authority as a result of a change in government funding, and that it was this that had necessitated the dismissals. On their claims that they had actually been dismissed by reason of the transfer or a reason connected with it, an employment tribunal held that the claimants' dismissals were automatically unfair under Reg 7(1). It took account of the employees' long service, the proximity of the dismissals to the transfer, and that there was no apparent ETO reason for the dismissals at the time they took place. Although the tribunal accepted that there was a change in government funding, B Ltd had not produced evidence to show when this had occurred or how it had affected its business.

4.36 In CAB Automotive Ltd v Blake and ors EAT 0298/07 the EAT scrutinised the wording of what is now Reg 7(1) in the context of dismissals effected by an administrator with one eye on slimming down an insolvent business to make it more attractive for eventual sale. On 4 May 2005, following the insolvency of a major client, I Ltd (a car interior design business) was put into administration. An administrator, M, was appointed to 'tidy up the business to sell to somebody else'. On 6 May, M told senior managers that the business needed to be 'cut back to the bone' and that all employees, except those involved in the operational needs of the sustainable business, were to be dismissed on the ground of redundancy. 72 employees were dismissed on that ground later that day. Around the same time, A Ltd, another company designing car interiors, also went into administration. A Ltd had a contract with Jaguar/Land Rover for the design of the interior of the new Land Rover Defender. Some of I Ltd's directors – who were not involved in the administration process – planned to take over that contract. On 12 May a new company, CAB Ltd, was formed from I Ltd and A Ltd, to service the Jaguar/Land Rover contract, and a day later CAB Ltd agreed with M that it would acquire I Ltd's assets and residual workforce. In August 2005 the dismissed employees presented claims of unfair dismissal against I Ltd and, in the alternative, CAB Ltd, on the basis that they had been unfairly dismissed for a reason connected with the transfer of I Ltd's business

280

to CAB Ltd. They contended that M's intention to slim down the business and find a buyer meant that the dismissals were 'connected with the transfer' within the meaning of what is now Reg 7(1) even though the identity of the eventual transferee was not at that time apparent.

An employment tribunal accepted this argument and held that the employees' dismissals were unfair. On appeal, the EAT held that the tribunal had failed to consider properly the central question under Reg 7(1): whether the transfer, or a reason connected with it, was *the* reason or principal reason for the claimants' dismissals. Instead, the tribunal – having incorrectly stated that Reg 7(1) applies where the transfer, or a reason connected with it, was *a* reason for the dismissals – had simply found that the dismissals were 'connected with the transfer'. That was not the same as finding that the transfer, or a reason connected with it, was *the* reason for the dismissals. In other words, a conclusion of automatic unfair dismissal would have required in the instant case an explicit finding to the effect that M had felt that transfer was a realistic possibility and that he had made the dismissals to encourage transfer. The EAT remitted the case to the tribunal to determine whether this was so. It also held that the tribunal had appeared to have incorrectly treated the ETO defence in what is now Reg 7(2) as being capable of applying only if Reg 7(1) did not – in other words, that Reg 7(1) and 7(2) were mutually exclusive. That was not the case.

4.37 The necessity to scrutinise the motives of the person who takes the decision to dismiss in order to determine whether the reason for dismissal was solely or principally the transfer itself was emphasised by the Court of Appeal in another insolvency case, Dynamex Friction Ltd and anor v Amicus and ors 2009 ICR 511, CA. In that case, the Court held (by a majority) that an employment tribunal had not erred in finding that the employees of an insolvent company had been dismissed by the administrator for the economic reason that he had no money to pay them, rather than for a reason connected with the transfer of the undertaking within the meaning of what is now Reg 7(1), notwithstanding the employees' allegations that the director of the insolvent company had stage-managed matters so that he might continue the business under a new name and free of its liabilities to the employees. The tribunal was wholly justified in taking the view that those matters could not have any relevance because they did not impinge upon the decision-making by the administrator.

In deciding whether a dismissal was for a reason connected with the transfer within the meaning of Reg 7(1), Lord Justice Ward (with whose judgment Lord Justice Rimer agreed) stressed that it is the person who took the decision to dismiss whose thought processes must be the subject of analysis. Once it was established in the instant case that it was the administrator's decision to dismiss the employees, then nothing done by the director of the company before that decision was taken or after it could have any bearing on the reasons why the administrator acted as he did. Although it was clear that the company director cynically manipulated the insolvency of the company and placed the company in administration with every expectation that it would soon fall into his hands unburdened by any liabilities to his former employees, it was the administrator who dismissed the employees and his actions were unsullied by the company director's scheming.

4.38 It is interesting to note the reasoning of Lord Justice Lawrence Collins in his dissenting judgment. He suggested that case law of the European Court of Justice supported a more liberal interpretation of the TUPE Regulations, under which it would be a relevant consideration that the director of the insolvent company 'stage-managed the administration and used the administrator as his unwitting tool to regain the business' without any liability to his former employees. In the view of Lawrence Collins LJ, the ECJ cases 'do not shut out the argument which the respondents make in this case, namely that the national court should not look solely at the motives of the legal entity which in law effects the dismissal. I do not say that they are bound to win if they can show stage-management by [the director of the insolvent company]. What I do say is that this is not a proper case for their claim to be, in effect, struck out on a point which has not been raised below and which has not been the subject of adequate findings of fact. It is a point which is of sufficient general importance to justify the further findings of fact which the EAT thought necessary, perhaps followed, at the appropriate stage, by a reference to the European Court.'

We now turn to the crucial question of when the sole or principal reason for a dismissal might, at the very least, be said to be 'connected with the transfer'.

4.39 Dismissals for a reason 'connected with' the transfer

As we have seen, where the reason for a dismissal is 'connected with' a relevant transfer, the dismissal will be automatically unfair under Reg 7(1) if the employer fails to mount a successful 'ETO defence'. Here, we examine when a dismissal will be 'connected with' a relevant transfer, as opposed to unconnected with it.

In P Bork International A/S (in liquidation) v Foreningen af Arbejdsledere i Danmark and ors 1989 IRLR 41, ECJ, the European Court held that it was for national courts to determine whether a dismissal was 'by reason of' a relevant transfer, by considering the objective circumstances in which the dismissal occurred. The ECJ stated that a court should take particular note of whether the dismissal in question took place at a time close to that of a relevant transfer, and whether the employee was subsequently re-engaged by the transferee.

So, in general, the closer in time a dismissal is to a relevant transfer, the more likely a tribunal will be to find that it is transfer-connected. In fact, where a dismissal takes place around the time of the transfer, there will be a strong presumption that it is so connected. However, as the case law we set out below demonstrates, timing is not everything. If an employer can show that the reason for a dismissal is genuinely conduct, capability, statutory bar or retirement, the dismissal will most likely not be transfer-connected, regardless of its timing. Furthermore, even where a dismissal occurs owing to an employer's need to reduce the workforce, the fact that it takes place around the time of a relevant transfer may be merely coincidental – that is, it might well have occurred regardless of the transfer process.

We now turn to consider some of the domestic case law – first, relating to pre-transfer dismissals, and then relating to post-transfer dismissals – in which courts and tribunals have considered whether the reason for dismissal was either by reason of a relevant transfer or transfer-connected.

Pre-transfer dismissals. An early, high-profile case in which pre-transfer **4.40** dismissals were held to be connected with a relevant transfer was that of Litster and ors v Forth Dry Dock and Engineering Co Ltd (in receivership) and anor 1989 ICR 341, HL. There, Forth Dry Dock and Engineering Co Ltd went into receivership in September 1983. In November of that year a new company, Forth Estuary Engineering Ltd, was incorporated with the objective of taking over the business of Forth Dry Dock, and the actual transfer was executed at 4.30 pm on 6 February 1984. At around 3.30 pm on the same day the entire workforce of Forth Dry Dock – about 25 employees – were handed letters dismissing them with immediate effect. The letters stated that no further funds were available for paying wages, accrued holiday pay or statutory notice pay and that any claims would have to be made against the Department of Employment. Within 48 hours of the dismissals the ex-employees of Forth Dry Dock learned that Forth Estuary was recruiting labour. A group of them filled in application forms for employment, but none were successful, and only three ex-employees of Forth Dry Dock were ever taken on by Forth Estuary. Forth Estuary, however, very soon had a workforce of similar size to Forth Dry Dock, having recruited from a pool of similar unemployed tradesmen who were willing to accept lower rates of pay. L and 11 other ex-employees of Forth Dry Dock presented unfair dismissal complaints with reference to TUPE. A tribunal upheld their claims – a decision that was eventually upheld by the House of Lords. Their Lordships recognised that it was clear on the facts that the dismissal of the existing workforce had been engineered by the receivers and the purchaser specifically with a view to preventing liabilities transferring under TUPE. In the circumstances, the dismissals were by reason of the transfer and automatically unfair owing to what was then Reg 8(1), and what is now Reg 7(1), of TUPE.

It is clear, however, that dismissals can be carried out just before a relevant **4.41** transfer without being connected with it. For instance, a struggling business might need to dismiss employees owing to financial constraints, regardless of the impending transfer. Below we set out three case examples in which pre-

283

transfer dismissals were held to be unconnected with the transfer, meaning that the TUPE unfair dismissal regime did not assist the employees concerned:

- **Secretary of State for Employment v Spence and ors** 1986 ICR 651, CA: S and Sons went into receivership on 16 November 1983. On Friday 25 November the receivers entered into negotiations with a company for the sale of the business. There was no guarantee of a successful outcome, and, when the deadline for the sale stipulated by S and Sons' principal customer passed, the receivers decided to cease trading and to dismiss all the employees. As a result, the assembled workforce was dismissed with immediate effect at 11 am on Monday 28 November. At 2 pm on the same day, the agreement for the sale of the business was concluded. The members of the workforce were told by the purchaser to report for work the following morning, at which point they were re-employed. S and 20 others applied for redundancy payments in respect of their dismissals by S and Sons. Before an employment tribunal their claims were resisted by the Secretary of State for Employment (on whom liability would have fallen because of S and Sons' insolvency) on the ground that the employees had not been redundant, but had transferred to a new employer under TUPE. The tribunal held, however, that the employees were entitled to redundancy payments, and the tribunal's decision was upheld by both the EAT and the Court of Appeal. On the facts, the dismissals were not transfer-connected within the meaning of what is now Reg 7(1). Rather, the receivers dismissed the workforce because, at the time of the dismissals, there was no prospect of work for the business

- **Longden and anor v Ferrari Ltd and anor** 1994 ICR 443, EAT: on 14 March 1991 K Ltd contacted the receivers of F Ltd with a view to a possible purchase of some or all of F Ltd's undertaking. K Ltd made what it termed a 'budgetary offer' for a division of F Ltd, but did not have sufficient information about the business to enter into a binding agreement. When K Ltd refused to sign the relevant documentation, F Ltd's receivers, who were under pressure from the company's bank, decided to 'pull the plug' – that is, to close down the undertaking, auction off its assets and dismiss its staff. K Ltd, however, thought it crucial that F Ltd should continue to operate while negotiations were ongoing, and on 27 March agreed to pay the receivers £4,000 to enable the company to keep 'ticking over' for another week. Also on 27 March, K Ltd supplied the receivers with the names of the F Ltd employees whom it believed it was essential to retain. The next day, the receivers gave the non-essential staff – including L – notice of dismissal. In the event, a sale took place from the receivers to K Ltd on 10 April. A tribunal dismissed L's complaint of unfair dismissal against K Ltd since, in its view, L had not been dismissed for a transfer-connected reason. He had been dismissed by F Ltd's receivers because of financial constraints, and because of pressure from the bank which had appointed them, and not because of an instruction from K Ltd. In its view, K Ltd's identification of the employees whom it was essential to retain did not carry with it a request that the other employees be dismissed. On appeal, the EAT upheld the tribunal's finding. There had been evidence on which the tribunal could reasonably have concluded that financial constraints and pressure from the bank were the reasons for the dismissal of employees on 28 March, and that neither the transfer on 10 April nor a reason connected with it was the reason or principal reason for those dismissals

- **Honeycombe 78 Ltd v (1) Cummins and ors (2) Secretary of State for Trade and Industry** EAT 100/99: In January 1998 HW Ltd ran into financial difficulties. On 15 January H – an insolvency practitioner – reported to Mr and Mrs G – the directors and shareholders of the company – that the sale of the business should be pursued, but that the only likely purchaser was a vehicle set up by Mr and Mrs G themselves. On 26 January an administration order was made and H was appointed administrator. On 27 January he dismissed all of HW Ltd's employees, and on 30 January concluded an agreement between HW Ltd and a new 'shelf' company to be purchased by Mr and Mrs G for the sale to the new company of HW Ltd's assets. That agreement was conditional on the obtaining of a court order, which was forthcoming on 6 February. On 11 February Mr and Mrs G purchased a shelf company called H Ltd and the parties concluded the agreement on that date. H Ltd took on all but four of HW Ltd's former employees. These four lodged tribunal claims, arguing that they had been dismissed for a transfer-connected reason contrary to TUPE. The tribunal found that it had been evident all along that any sale effected by H would be in favour of some legal body set up by Mr and Mrs G, and noted that the time span from H's appointment on 27 January to the conclusion of the agreement on 11 February was a period of 15 days. In these circumstances, the tribunal concluded that the claimants had been dismissed by reason of the transfer; that their dismissals were automatically unfair; and that liability for the dismissals passed to the transferee, H Ltd, under TUPE. H Ltd appealed to the EAT, pointing in particular to the tribunal's finding of fact that H had 'made it clear immediately on his appointment that he would not allow [HW Ltd] to trade and would dismiss the staff because there were no assets to pay them at that stage and that is what he did on 27 January'. H Ltd argued that, in the light of this, it was clear that the principal reason for dismissal was economic, and not connected to the transfer. H did not make the decision to dismiss in order to trim down the business for a sale. In fact, H reached his decision despite the outline proposal by Mr and Mrs G to purchase the business and keep on the staff. As at 27 January there was no certainty that a sale would be effected, and the economic reason for dismissal was paramount. The EAT accepted H Ltd's argument, concluding that the tribunal's decision had been plainly and unarguably wrong

285

- **Farmer v Victim Support** ET Case No.1400595/08: F was employed by Victim Support Gloucestershire as area manager. In 2006 the Government decided to increase funding for Victim Support, but required it to become a national organisation, and so local organisations were required to agree to merge into one. There were changes to the staffing structure in each of the local offices, and F's post became Enhanced Service Manager. He was required to apply for that post, but refused as he felt that the position should be given to him. As F did not apply for the new job, he was given formal notice of redundancy and his employment was terminated on 18 December 2007. Victim Support Gloucestershire subsequently transferred to Victim Support on 1 March 2008. An employment tribunal held that F had been unfairly dismissed for a reason connected with the transfer. Victim Support was anxious that the new system be in place before the transfer and it was the implementation of that system that led to F's dismissal. The tribunal noted that the Enhanced Service Manager role post-transfer was essentially the same as F's pre-transfer job. As there was no genuine redundancy situation, F was therefore unfairly dismissed for a reason connected with the transfer contrary to Reg 7(1).

4.42 *Need the transferee be identified?* Where a company is insolvent the receivers, administrators or liquidators will often feel the need to terminate the employment of some employees to increase the chance of a successful sale of the company's business. They may carry out these dismissals whether or not they have a purchaser lined up. This raises the question of whether, if at the time of dismissal there is no specific purchaser with whom negotiations are ongoing, the dismissals can nevertheless be 'connected with' a subsequent transfer of the business. In the two cases set out below the EAT reached conflicting conclusions in this regard:

- **Harrison Bowden Ltd v Bowden** 1994 ICR 186, EAT: NGS got into grave financial difficulties and in January 1991 went into receivership. The company was run on a day-to-day basis on behalf of the receivers by G. On 29 January 1991 G placed an advertisement in the *Financial Times* for the sale of the business as a going concern. The following day HB Ltd responded to the advert, showing interest in the business, but nothing more. On 31 January the majority of NGS's staff, including B, were dismissed by G, purportedly by reason of redundancy. A sale of the business to HB Ltd was completed on 8 February. When B claimed unfair dismissal, an employment tribunal decided that the 31 January dismissals were transfer-connected, as their object was to facilitate a proposed or possible transfer. HB Ltd appealed to the EAT, arguing that what is now Reg 7 only has effect where there is an actual, or at least a prospective, transferee at the moment of dismissal – which there was not in the present case as it had done no more than make enquiries about the sale of the business. HB Ltd pointed to the fact that Reg 7 speaks of dismissals being connected with 'the' transfer –

that is, the transfer to the specific transferee – as opposed to 'a' transfer that might occur sometime in the future. The EAT, however, held that the tribunal had not erred in holding that the dismissals by the receiver were for a reason connected with 'the' transfer (and indeed automatically unfair) even though no actual or prospective transferee had been identified when the dismissals were carried out, and even though the dismissals did not occur owing to collusion between the receivers and the eventual purchaser. The reason for the dismissals was to facilitate a transfer and, in that sense, the dismissals were connected with the transfer that took place at a later date

• **Ibex Trading Co Ltd (in administration) v Walton and ors** 1994 ICR 907, EAT: W was employed by ITC Ltd when, in August 1991, administrators were appointed to preside over the company's affairs. The administrators decided to free the company of its debts and then sell it. To this end they sought to reduce the size of the workforce and lower the wages of those who remained. On 16 October 40 of the 94 employees were given notice of dismissal for redundancy, and the dismissals took effect on 4 November. On 11 November the administrators received an offer for the business, and the sale – which amounted to a relevant transfer – was completed in the following February. W and some of his ex-colleagues brought unfair dismissal claims against both the transferor and the transferee. A tribunal rejected the notion that the complainants had been dismissed in connection with the transfer, and the EAT upheld this decision. Accepting the linguistic argument that had been rejected in Harrison Bowden (above), the EAT ruled that, while it could be said that the employees were dismissed for a reason connected with 'a' possible transfer, they had not been dismissed for a reason connected with 'the' transfer. At the time the employees were dismissed, no offer had been made for the business and any transfer was 'a mere twinkle in the eye and might well never have occurred'.

4.43 Faced with these inconsistent decisions, in Morris v John Grose Group Ltd 1998 IRLR 499, EAT, the Appeal Tribunal again turned its mind to this issue. There, it preferred the Harrison Bowden approach, rejecting that adopted in the Ibex case. The facts of the Morris case were as follows. M was a service manager for a Ford motor dealership, MMC Ltd, in respect of which receivers were called in on 27 September 1996. Almost immediately, the receivers decided that the workforce had to be slimmed down, in order that the business might keep trading with a view to its being sold as a going concern. At a staff meeting early on 30 September, M learned that he was one of those who were to be dismissed. Later that morning, the receivers held initial discussions with representatives of JGG Ltd, a potential purchaser, at a meeting arranged by Ford. The parties started formal negotiations in October and a deal was eventually struck on 5 November. M brought a tribunal claim, arguing that his dismissal had been automatically unfair under what is now Reg 7(1) of TUPE. The tribunal, following the approach of the EAT in the Ibex case, decided that

287

'the' transfer could not have been the reason for M's dismissal, because on 30 September 'the' transfer did not exist: the eventual transferee, JGG Ltd, had not even gone so far as to make an offer for the dealership. The most that could be said was that M had been dismissed by reason of 'a' transfer – an event that the receivers may have hoped for or expected, but which at the time of the dismissal was not near to happening.

On appeal, however, the EAT overturned the tribunal's decision. In its view, the words 'the transfer' appearing in Reg 7(1) do not necessarily have to refer to the particular transfer that has actually occurred. If the rule were interpreted otherwise, this would lead to unfair anomalies. For example, employees dismissed by reason of a particular anticipated transfer that did not, in the event, go through, but which was promptly replaced by another comparable transfer in circumstances where a transfer to someone was inevitable, would not have the benefit of Reg 7, even though they would have had such protection had the original transfer of an undertaking materialised. Accordingly, the EAT's statement in the Harrison Bowden case that no special significance should be attached to the use of the definite article 'the' in Reg 7 would be preferred to the alternative approach taken by the EAT in the Ibex case. In the light of this, the tribunal in the instant case should not have asked whether 'the' transfer to JGG Ltd, or a reason connected with 'the' transfer to JGG Ltd, was the reason for M's dismissal. Rather, it should have asked whether 'a' transfer to *any* transferee who might appear, or a reason connected with such a transfer, was the reason, or principal reason, for his dismissal.

4.44 In CAB Automotive Ltd v Blake and ors EAT 0298/07 the EAT ringingly endorsed the Morris case, suggesting that what is now Reg 7(1) can apply, for example, where a number of potential transferees are interested but, at the time of the dismissal, matters were at a very early stage. On balance, then, we suggest that if the reason for a dismissal is simply to help make a business a more attractive proposition to potential purchasers, that dismissal will, more than likely, be 'connected with' any transfer that does eventually take place, and hence, in the absence of an 'ETO reason', automatically unfair under Reg 7(1). However, it is the motives of the person who carries out the dismissal or, in the case of an insolvency administrator, requires dismissals to be effected, that have to be scrutinised. In the case of dismissals that occur in the context of administration, any ulterior motives of third parties are apparently irrelevant – see Dynamex Friction Ltd and anor v Amicus and ors 2009 ICR 511, CA (discussed under 'Dismissals by reason of the transfer itself' above).

4.45 **Post-transfer dismissals.** As stated above, timing is not everything. Nevertheless, it is fair to say that the further away the date of dismissal is from the date of the relevant transfer, the more sympathetic a tribunal is likely to be towards the employer's argument that the sole or principal reason for the dismissal was not transfer-connected. Take, for example, the following case in which dismissals took place more than two years after an outsourcing exercise to which TUPE applied:

- **Norris and ors v Brown and Root Ealing Technical Services Ltd** EAT 386/00: in 1994 the London Borough of Ealing contracted out its Technical Support Group (TSG) to B Ltd. On 1 April of that year B Ltd inherited the TSG workforce by operation of TUPE. B Ltd achieved the efficiency savings stipulated by its contract with the Borough for the first two years, but in 1996 started to experience problems owing to underfunding. Because of this, in October 1996 B Ltd offered the TSG employees cash sums payable upon their accepting new, less-favourable, terms and conditions. In December 1996 B Ltd gave notice of termination to the employees who had not agreed to revised terms and conditions and, upon the expiry of that notice in February 1997, dismissed those employees and re-engaged them on the new terms. A number of those employees applied to an employment tribunal claiming that their dismissals had been automatically unfair, in that the dismissals had been carried out for a reason connected with the TUPE transfer. The employment tribunal, however, accepted that B Ltd had carried out the dismissals since it was experiencing serious cash-flow difficulties, and that those difficulties had been caused by the underfunding of the contract between the company and the Borough, arising from an error in the original pricing schedule. The tribunal went on to note that B Ltd's decision to dismiss the employees had not been made until August 1996, which was two years and four months into its five-year contract, and that there had been significant intervening events between the relevant transfer and the dismissals. The tribunal concluded that the dismissals had not been connected with the relevant transfer and had not, therefore, been automatically unfair under Reg 7(1). It went on to hold, with regard to the provisions of S.98 ERA, that the dismissals, which had been carried out for 'some other substantial reason', had been fair. The EAT upheld the tribunal's decision.

4.46 However, there is no specific point in time after which a transferee has carte blanche to dismiss transferred employees. Each case will be decided on its own facts. As the following case demonstrates, a dismissal taking place a significant amount of time after a transfer might, once the surrounding circumstances are taken into account, be held to contravene Reg 7(1):

- **Taylor v Connex South Eastern Ltd** EAT 1243/99: T refused to accept changes to his terms and conditions (in particular, to his redundancy terms), which were introduced, for harmonisation purposes, around two years after his employment transferred under TUPE from British Rail to CSE. Owing to his refusal, T was dismissed, and he brought an unfair dismissal claim, arguing that he had been dismissed for a reason connected with a relevant transfer, contrary to TUPE. The employment tribunal hearing T's claim

289

accepted that there is no particular time limit after which dismissals will not be transfer-connected. However, it was in no doubt that the chain of causation weakens with the passage of time, and that two years appeared to be a long time to maintain a connection. The tribunal went on to conclude that, at the time of T's dismissal, there had long ceased to be any possibility of his being dismissed for a transfer-connected reason. On appeal, however, the EAT overturned the tribunal's decision. In doing so, it noted that the reason why the chain of causation tends to weaken over time is that time provides greater opportunity for intervening events to break it. But, if no such intervening events occur, the passage of time in itself will not weaken or break the chain. Turning to the facts of the case, the EAT found it 'abundantly clear' that it was one of the important terms transferred under TUPE that was the subject of CSE's attempt to change T's contract. In the circumstances, the EAT felt able to conclude that T's dismissal by reason of his refusing to accept the change was carried out for a reason connected with the transfer within Reg 7(1).

4.47 A similar conclusion was reached more recently in London Metropolitan University v Sackur and ors EAT 0286/06, in which the EAT upheld an employment tribunal's ruling that employees dismissed two years after a transfer, in order to effect harmonisation changes, had been dismissed for a reason connected with the original transfer.

In Vallance v Maes Corporation Ltd ET Case No.1101491/09 an employee who was employed as a chambermaid at a hotel was held to have been automatically and unfairly dismissed when she was dismissed by the transferee after it was awarded a contract to provide cleaning services to the hotel. The transferee had not checked the employee's previous employment history (including her length of service); nor was it aware of the latitude she had been given by the hotel regarding how she was permitted to carry out her duties. She was dismissed when she and a colleague left work without completing their allocation of rooms. On her claim of unfair dismissal, an employment tribunal held that the dismissal was substantively and procedurally unfair as well as being automatically unfair under Reg 7(1) in view of the fact that the transferee had failed to appreciate the employee's employment rights and the effect of the TUPE Regulations.

4.48 By way of contrast, however, in the case below the chain of causation between a relevant transfer and a dismissal *was* broken, even though the dismissal took place much closer to the time of transfer than in the Taylor and Sackur cases:

- **Rickards v Shipperley** EAT 0019/93: S and his wife were joint shareholders of Y Ltd. He was managing director and she was company secretary. As an employee of the company, S was remunerated by way of salary. In time, Y Ltd ran into financial difficulties, and on 30 June 1992 its stock and assets were sold to R. There was an understanding that R, who intended to carry on the business, would retain the existing employees and premises, and would continue to deal with the same suppliers and the same customers. However, it became almost immediately apparent that the suppliers would not maintain a relationship with the business if S remained involved in it. Owing to this, R gave S a note on 3 July which stated: 'Following my takeover of [Y Ltd's] business your services are no longer required. Your employment is terminated forthwith.' S brought a tribunal claim that he had been unfairly dismissed for a transfer-connected reason, contrary to Reg 7. The tribunal upheld his claim, but R appealed successfully to the EAT. The EAT bore in mind that there was a short period of time between the relevant transfer and the dismissal, and noted the unfortunate wording of the dismissal letter. Nevertheless, it felt unable to conclude that S's dismissal was for a transfer-connected reason. It stated: 'the transfer did not cause or contribute to the dismissal – what caused the dismissal was the attitude shown by the suppliers... The transfer may have *resulted* in the dismissal, in the sense that it highlighted and brought into focus one of the trading problems which faced this company, but it was not the *reason* for the dismissal... The reason for the dismissal was the continued participation in the business of a man with whom the suppliers of the business felt unable to deal.'

Validity of transfer-connected dismissals   4.49

Article 3 of the EU Acquired Rights Directive provides that the rights and obligations of the transferor with regard to the transferring employees will transfer to the transferee (see Chapter 3), and Article 4 provides that the transfer shall not in itself constitute grounds for dismissal unless there is an ETO reason entailing changes in the workforce (see above).

These provisions led to considerable debate as to whether transfer-connected dismissals should actually be *invalid*. This matter was central to the case of (1) British Fuels Ltd v Baxendale and anor; (2) Wilson and ors v St Helens Borough Council 1998 ICR 1141, HL. That case involved appeals from the Court of Appeal, which decided that, where an employee is dismissed by the transferor for a reason connected with the transfer that is not an ETO reason, and is thereafter taken on by the transferee on different terms and conditions, the dismissal is ineffective and the employee is employed by the transferee on the terms of the original pre-transfer contract. The House of Lords, however, disagreed with the Court of Appeal's decision, and confirmed that transfer-related dismissals *are* effective. It followed that employees who were dismissed prior to a transfer and then re-employed on new terms and conditions by the transferee could not argue that their dismissals were null and void. Rather than the original contracts themselves, all that passed to the transferee was the potential liability to compensate the employees for their dismissals.

291

4.50 In reaching this decision, their Lordships noted that there is no right under English law for a dismissed employee to insist that the employer continue to employ him or her. The nearest to such 'specific performance' countenanced by UK employment law is the ability of tribunals to order reinstatement under S.114 ERA. Note that ultimately, however, a transferee can refuse to comply with a reinstatement order, at the cost of an additional award of compensation as a penalty.

4.51 ## Dismissals potentially fair for an 'ETO reason'

We saw in 'The TUPE unfair dismissal regime' and 'Automatically unfair dismissals' above that a dismissal carried out *by reason of the relevant transfer itself* will, without doubt, be rendered automatically unfair by Reg 7(1) of the 2006 Regulations. However, Reg 7(2) and (3) provide that a dismissal carried out for a reason *connected with* such a transfer will not be automatically unfair 'where the sole or principal reason for the dismissal... is an economic, technical or organisational reason entailing changes in the workforce of either the transferor or the transferee before or after a relevant transfer'.

So, where an employer successfully demonstrates an 'ETO reason' for a transfer-connected dismissal – and, as the DTI Guide states, the onus is on the employer to do so – the dismissal will not be *automatically* unfair under Reg 7(1). However, it might nevertheless be unfair under the general unfair dismissal provisions of the ERA – see McGrath v Rank Leisure Ltd 1985 ICR 527, EAT. In other words, an 'ETO dismissal' is only *potentially* fair. Where such a dismissal occurs, the tribunal must determine the issue of fairness by applying the 'reasonableness test' contained in S.98(4) ERA, examining matters such as consultation, selection and dismissal procedures (see 'Overview' above).

4.52 In this section we focus on the meaning of the phrase 'economic, technical or organisational reason entailing changes in the workforce' contained in Reg 7(2), in order to ascertain the types of situation in which an employer might establish an ETO defence. Unfortunately, this key phrase is defined neither by Article 4 of the Directive, from which it was lifted, nor by the 2006 Regulations themselves. As a result, the task of determining the scope of the Reg 7(2) exception to the Reg 7(1) automatic unfairness rule has been left to the courts and tribunals.

Note that there are, essentially, two limbs to the employer's Reg 7(2) 'ETO defence'. First, there must be an 'economic, technical or organisational reason for dismissal', and secondly, that reason must 'entail changes in the workforce'. We consider case law concerning both of these limbs below.

292

Economic, technical or organisational reason 4.53

The first thing that an employer must do in order to rely on the Reg 7(2) 'ETO defence', and hence to avoid a finding that a transfer-connected dismissal is automatically unfair under Reg 7(1), is demonstrate that the sole or principal reason for the dismissal was an 'economic, technical or organisational' one.

At first glance, one might consider that most TUPE-connected dismissals will be carried out for an 'economic, technical or organisational' reason of some sort. However, as we shall see, the courts have been keen to interpret the words 'economic', 'technical' and 'organisational' narrowly in a TUPE context.

Economic reason. A case in which the EAT construed the word 'economic' 4.54 narrowly for the purposes of the Reg 7(2) ETO defence is Wheeler v Patel and anor 1987 ICR 631, EAT. That concerned the transfer of a shop from G to P. By a letter dated 12 December 1985 G told all the employees (including W) about the proposed sale, and said that the completion date would be 20 January 1986. The letter terminated their employment as from 17 January 1986. After completion, P engaged some of the dismissed employees, but he did not take on W. W claimed unfair dismissal, but a tribunal rejected her complaint. On appeal, the EAT established from the tribunal's findings that G's reason for dismissing W was either his concern to comply with the purchaser's wishes or his desire to make the sale proceed more easily. Either way, it was clear that the transfer of the business from G to P was the reason, or was connected with the reason for the dismissal. Therefore, the dismissal would be declared unfair under Reg 7(1), unless G could mount a successful ETO defence. Attempting to do so, he argued that his reason for dismissing W was 'economic' within the meaning of Reg 7(2). The EAT, however, rejected G's argument and upheld W's appeal. It held that an 'economic' reason for dismissal must relate to the *conduct of the business concerned*. Broader economic reasons were not relevant. It followed that G's desire to obtain an enhanced price for the business, or to achieve a sale by capitulating to demands by the purchaser to dismiss the workforce, did not constitute an 'economic' reason for dismissal. Accordingly, G's dismissal of W had been automatically unfair.

The approach adopted in the Wheeler case was affirmed by the EAT in Gateway Hotels Ltd v Stewart and ors 1988 IRLR 287, EAT. There, it was held that there was no 'economic' reason for dismissal for TUPE purposes where hotel employees were dismissed prior to a transfer in order to enhance the sale price of the business concerned.

It follows from these cases that if employees of a failing business are dismissed 4.55 solely in order to make the business a more attractive proposition for sale (especially if there is evidence of collusion between transferor and transferee), this is unlikely to be viewed as an ETO reason, meaning that such dismissals will almost certainly be automatically unfair under Reg 7(1).

293

However, as the following case demonstrates, the need to reduce a workforce in order to make a failing business viable as a going concern – an aim that might sometimes appear only subtly different to that of making a business more attractive for sale – is capable of amounting to an 'economic' reason for dismissal within the meaning of Reg 7(2):

- **Thompson v SCS Consulting Ltd and ors** EAT 0034/00: T was employed as a sales executive in the UK by SCS Ltd and subsequently by LS Ltd, both of which were wholly-owned subsidiaries of a Canadian company, LS Inc. In late 1998 the two subsidiary companies were in financial difficulty, and receivers were appointed. It was agreed that another company, OTUK Ltd, would acquire the assets of SCS Ltd and LS Ltd. On 23 December 1998 the receivers met with a representative of OTUK Ltd and informed him that, because of the lack of funds and the unsuccessful nature of the businesses to be sold, they proposed to dismiss the entire workforce immediately. However, OTUK Ltd wished some of the staff to remain. It was eventually agreed that those employees whom OTUK Ltd did not wish to retain would be dismissed prior to the transfer 'on the grounds that they are not required for the operation of the business and that it would not be economically viable for the business to continue if the dismissed employees remained in the employ of the vendors'. Some 25 employees, including T, were dismissed by the receivers on 29 December with immediate effect. The transfer to OTUK Ltd took place 11 hours later. T complained to an employment tribunal that he had been automatically unfairly dismissed for a reason connected with a relevant transfer. The tribunal found, however, that the businesses of SCS Ltd and LS Ltd had been overstaffed, inefficient and insolvent, and could only have been made viable as going concerns by reducing the workforce. It went on to hold that, in the circumstances, there had been an 'economic, technical or organisational reason' for the dismissals falling within Reg 7(2) and that, accordingly, T's dismissal was not automatically unfair under the Regulations. On appeal, the EAT upheld the tribunal's decision. Where, in order to make the businesses viable as going concerns, it was necessary for their workforces to be reduced, and where, left to their own devices, the receivers would have dismissed all of the employees, it had been open to an employment tribunal to find that there had been an 'economic' reason for dismissal, notwithstanding the fact that the subsequent transferee of the businesses had dictated which employees should be dismissed and which should be retained.

4.56 It is not just in insolvency situations that employees are dismissed for 'economic' reasons. Often, transferees will decide that redundancies are necessary for such reasons post-transfer. In fact, the example of an economic reason contained in the DTI Guide is one relating to 'the profitability or market performance of the transferee's business'. Below, we set out two cases in which a transferee

294 ———————————————————

employer was able to rely on an economic reason for dismissal within the meaning of Reg 7(2):

- **Whitehouse v Chas A Blatchford and Sons Ltd** 1999 IRLR 492, CA: W was employed by JS Ltd as one of 13 technicians working on the company's contract to supply prosthetic appliances to Sheffield's Northern General Hospital. In 1996 JS Ltd lost that contract to CAB Ltd. Owing to a reduction in annual funding from the health authority, the hospital required CAB Ltd to reduce the number of technicians from 13 to 12. On 1 April 1997 CAB Ltd began work on the contract, and took on all the relevant JS Ltd employees. After unsuccessfully seeking a volunteer for redundancy, CAB Ltd selected W as the employee to be dismissed. W claimed that he had been dismissed for a reason connected with the transfer contrary to what is now Reg 7(1) and that his dismissal was therefore automatically unfair. The employer resisted the claim on the ground that there was an ETO reason for dismissal. An employment tribunal noted that it was a condition of the contract with the hospital that the new contractor should reduce the contract price by reducing the number of technicians. In those circumstances, said the tribunal, a redundancy was inevitable. The tribunal concluded that W's dismissal was for an economic or organisational reason which entailed a change in the workforce, and that CAB Ltd had therefore established an ETO defence. The tribunal further held that the employer had acted reasonably in treating the ETO reason as a sufficient reason for dismissal, and thus rejected W's claim. This decision was upheld by the EAT and the Court of Appeal. After the transferee was awarded the contract, noted the Court, there was a demand for the services of 12 rather than 13 technicians. That would have been the case even if the transferor had retained the contract. In those circumstances, the transfer of the undertaking was the occasion for the reduction in the hospital requirements from 13 to 12 technicians, but it was not the cause of or the reason for that reduction. The circumstances in this case were in no way analogous to the position of the vendor of a business who, for the sole purpose of achieving the best price for the business, dismisses employees. In the instant case, the reduction in employees was directly connected with the provision of services under the contract

- **Meikle v McPhail (Charleston Arms)** 1983 IRLR 351, EAT: M was employed as a barmaid at a public house in Paisley. On 24 June 1982 McP took over the pub. One of the terms of his deal with the transferor was that he would take over most of the existing staff, including two full-time barmaids, one part-time barmaid and a cleaner. After consultations with his accountant McP realised that he had over-committed himself and that substantial salary savings would have to be made. On 28 June he dismissed all the staff, including M, except one full-time barmaid. M brought an unfair

295

dismissal claim before an employment tribunal. The tribunal held that M's dismissal had been connected with a relevant transfer, but accepted McP's argument that there had been an economic reason for the dismissal within the meaning of Reg 7(2). The tribunal went on to conclude that McP had made out an ETO defence and that, accordingly, M's dismissal had not been automatically unfair. Furthermore, McP had acted reasonably in carrying out the dismissal, meaning that it was fair for the purposes of the ERA. On appeal, the EAT upheld the tribunal's decision.

4.57 **Technical reason.** Assessing the scope of the phrase 'technical reason' is less problematic. The DTI Guide states that this includes 'a reason relating to the nature of the equipment or production processes which the [transferee] operates'. So, for example, where a transferee introduces new machinery that an employee does not have the necessary skills to operate, there might be a technical reason within the meaning of Reg 7(2) for the employee's dismissal.

Of course, in order to succeed with the ETO defence the employer would have to show that the technical reason 'entailed changes in the workforce' (see below). Furthermore, in order for the employer to avoid unfair dismissal liability under the ordinary provisions of the ERA, the dismissal must have been within the 'range of reasonable responses' available to it (see 'Overview' above). In some cases – perhaps where the employer has considerable resources and/or the skills in question are not particularly difficult to attain – it would be unreasonable for the employer to dismiss rather than to provide the employee with the training that would enable him or her to continue in employment.

4.58 **Organisational reason.** The DTI Guide states that the phrase 'organisational reason' includes 'a reason relating to the management or organisational structure of the [transferee's] business'. Two situations immediately spring to mind in which a transferee might be able to rely upon an organisational reason for dismissal. First, where the transferee simply does not require every member of the transferring workforce, as well as every member of his existing workforce, to carry out his needs. Secondly, where the transferee decides to reorganise job functions in order to carry on the transferring business, or provide the transferring service, in a different way. Three case examples:

- **Burstal v Compass Cleaning Ltd** ET Case No.1402457/02: a company lost the contract comprising 98 per cent of its work to R, and it was accepted that the company's employees transferred to R by the operation of TUPE. However, B, the assistant to the transferor company's managing director, was dismissed by R upon the transfer, and claimed unfair dismissal. In rejecting her claim, an employment tribunal noted that since the contract in question had been subsumed into R's operation, neither a managing director nor a managing director's assistant was required in respect of that contract. It followed that B's dismissal was for an ETO reason entailing changes in the workforce and hence was not automatically unfair

- **Porter and anor v Queen's Medical Centre (Nottingham University Hospital)** 1993 IRLR 486, QBD: a relevant transfer occurred where the supply of paediatric and neonatal services moved from two District Health Authorities to an NHS Trust. Following the transfer, the Trust decided to reorganise the way that the services would be performed, with a focus on the importance of highly developed specialisms. It did not re-engage P or N, two consultant paediatricians who had been dedicated to the services in question prior to the transfer, and instead carried out a recruitment process focusing on the desired specialisms – which included neonatology, neurology and community health care. P and N brought a legal action in the High Court, but the Court accepted that, owing to the reorganisation of the way in which the service was to be performed, the Trust had dismissed the claimants for an ETO reason

- **Radford v McKesson Information Solutions UK Ltd** ET Case No.2405482/09: R's employment was transferred from Capita to MIS Ltd when it won the contract for the provision of payroll services to various NHS Trusts. R's role prior to the transfer was to manage teams in Blackburn and Cambridge, and she was based in Darwen. MIS Ltd made it clear prior to the TUPE consultation that the only vacancies it had were based in Bangor and that employees who did not wish to relocate there would be at risk of redundancy. R wrote to MIS Ltd asserting her right to transfer under TUPE, stating that she therefore expected the transferee to provide details of suitable roles for her. She was told that as she did not wish to move to Bangor and had not expressed an interest in any other post, redundancy consultation would begin. Her employment was subsequently terminated on the ground of redundancy. In respect of her claim that she had been automatically unfairly dismissed within the terms of Reg 7(1), MIS Ltd maintained that the activities for which she was employed ceased to continue at the location at which she was employed, and that this comprised an ETO reason for dismissal. An employment tribunal, however, held that R was unfairly dismissed following a TUPE transfer and that there was no ETO reason. The work to be carried out in Bangor was the same as that which had been carried out in Darwen; looked at as a whole, the workforce remained substantially unchanged, so there was no organisational reason for the dismissal.

Although it will usually be the transferee who is likely to rely on an organisational **4.59** reason for carrying out transfer-connected dismissals, there are circumstances in which the transferor will be able to do so. For example, if a transferor employer loses a major contract, he might need to reorganise the workforce that he retains – i.e. those employees who were not dedicated to the contract in question – and, as a result, might feel the need to carry out redundancy dismissals. In such circumstances, these dismissals could well be for an organisational (or indeed an economic) reason within the meaning of Reg 7(2).

297

Most, if not all, of the above examples have concerned genuine redundancy situations. But what else might amount to an organisational reason for dismissal? It seems that dismissals, express or constructive, as a result of a transferee's wish to fundamentally alter hours of work, or to harmonise terms and conditions, would qualify. However, the major stumbling block for the employer in such circumstances will be establishing that such a reason 'entailed changes in the workforce' – the second limb of the Reg 7(2) test, to which we now turn our attention.

4.60 Entailing changes in the workforce

In order to avail himself of the Reg 7(2) ETO defence, an employer is not only required to point to an 'economic, technical or organisational reason' for dismissal, but is also obliged to demonstrate that such a reason 'entails changes in the workforce'. Below, we consider what both 'entailing' and 'changes in the workforce' mean in this context.

4.61 Meaning of 'entailing'. In the leading case of Berriman v Delabole Slate Ltd 1985 ICR 546, CA, Lord Justice Browne-Wilkinson said that, owing to the word 'entailing' in what is now Reg 7(2), 'the phrase "economic, technical or organisational reason entailing changes in the workforce"... requires that the change in the workforce is part of the economic, technical or organisational reason. The employers' plan must be to achieve changes in the workforce. It must be an objective of the plan, not just a possible consequence of it.'

This means that where an employer has an economic, technical or organisational reason for doing *something*, but that something does not *necessarily* entail 'changes in the workforce', any dismissals that happen to arise as a result of that reason will not fall within the Reg 7(2) 'ETO' exception. Put another way, 'changes in the workforce' must flow inexorably from, rather than be a possible end-result of, the employer's ETO reason.

4.62 The necessary link between an ETO reason and a 'change in the workforce' was lacking in the Berriman case. That involved B, a quarryman, who was paid £100 per week prior to transferring to DS Ltd under TUPE. Following the transfer, DS Ltd informed B that it intended to harmonise the terms and conditions of the transferring employees with those of its existing employees. Since this process was to involve a significant reduction in his pay, B resigned and claimed that he had been unfairly constructively dismissed for a reason connected with a relevant transfer, contrary to Reg 7(1). An employment tribunal rejected his claim on the basis that DS Ltd had established an ETO reason for dismissal under Reg 7(2). On appeal, however, the EAT and thereafter the Court of Appeal disagreed with the tribunal's decision. The Court of Appeal held that DS Ltd's 'organisational reason' for B's dismissal – the plan to harmonise terms and conditions – had not 'entailed' changes in the workforce (such changes being, as we shall see below, changes in either workforce numbers or workforce functions). The harmonisation process was not one that *necessarily* led to changes in the workforce. The most that could be said was that it might (not must) lead to the dismissal of any employees who did not fall into line.

Meaning of 'changes in the workforce'. The position under the case law as it **4.63** currently stands is that an employer must show one of two things in order to establish that an economic, technical or organisational reason for dismissal entailed (i.e. necessitated) 'changes in the workforce': either that the ETO reason entailed a change in the numbers of the workforce overall, or that it entailed a change in the functions of members of the workforce.

This position, like the meaning of the word 'entailing', discussed above, was established by the Court of Appeal in the leading case of Berriman v Delabole Slate Ltd. To recap, that case concerned an attempt by a transferee employer, DS Ltd, to harmonise the terms and conditions of its inherited workforce with those of its pre-existing workforce. B, an employee who transferred to DS Ltd under TUPE, resigned and claimed that he had been unfairly constructively dismissed for a reason connected with a TUPE transfer. His claim was eventually upheld by the Court of Appeal, which rejected the employer's argument that the dismissal had occurred for an ETO reason 'entailing changes in the workforce'. In this case, DS Ltd's 'organisational reason' for acting – namely, its wish to produce standardisation of pay terms – had led to B's dismissal, but B's position had thereafter been filled by a new employee who was prepared to accept DS Ltd's conditions of service. Such a scenario did not, in the Court's view, involve 'changes in the workforce' as required by Reg 7(2). In this regard, Lord Justice Browne-Wilkinson stated: 'To our minds, the word "workforce" connotes the whole body of employees as an entity: it corresponds to the "strength" or the "establishment". Changes in the identity of the individuals who make up the workforce do not constitute changes in the workforce itself so long as the overall numbers and functions of the employees looked at as a whole remain unchanged.'

The Berriman decision was clarified by EAT in Crawford v Swinton Insurance **4.64** Brokers Ltd 1990 ICR 85, EAT. There, an employee argued that, in the absence of a reduction in workforce numbers, a change in the identity of at least one of the employees must occur if there are to be 'changes in the workforce'. The EAT rejected this submission. In determining whether changes in the workforce have occurred, it reiterated that it is the workforce as an entity, rather than the identity of the individuals who make it up, that must be examined. With this in mind, the EAT was satisfied that there could be 'changes in a workforce' for the purposes of the ETO defence 'if the same people are kept on but they are given entirely different jobs to do'.

In the following cases, employers attempted to argue that, although there was no reduction in overall workforce numbers, transfer-connected dismissals were

299

carried out owing to changes to job functions, and hence owing to 'changes in the workforce' for the purposes of the Reg 7(2) ETO defence:

- **Lane v Dyno-Rod plc** ET Case No.17833/85: L was employed by R Ltd, which ran a drain cleaning business, as 'area manager'. When the business transferred to D-R plc, L's terms and conditions were substantially altered. His title became 'senior engineer', and his status and duties changed. Although his remuneration was initially substantially the same, L felt that his changed circumstances would reduce his earning capacity, so he resigned and claimed constructive dismissal. A tribunal held that D-R plc had constructively dismissed L in connection with a relevant transfer, but had made out an ETO reason for doing so which had entailed changes in its workforce. The fact that the company did not need an area manager – the reason which resulted in L's becoming employed as a senior engineer – showed that there had been a restructuring of the business, and that this had necessarily involved changes to the duties of at least one member of the workforce

- **Bullard and anor v Marchant and anor** 1986 ICR 389, EAT: B was employed as a part-time assistant in a newsagents. He was dismissed by the owner, M, just prior to the sale of the business – a relevant transfer – to P. P then offered B employment on the same number of working hours, but at different times of the day. B accepted the offer, but soon afterwards resigned and brought a tribunal claim with regard to his dismissal. A tribunal declined to find B's dismissal unfair, and B appealed to the EAT. The EAT held that B's dismissal had been automatically unfair owing to TUPE. With regard to the employer's ETO defence, there had been no 'changes in the workforce' within the meaning of Reg 7(2), but only changes in terms and conditions of employment falling outside the meaning of those words

- **Crawford v Swinton Insurance Brokers Ltd** 1990 ICR 85, EAT: following a relevant transfer to S Ltd, C had to change from typing and clerical work to selling insurance; had to work different, less-flexible hours; and lost the use of her company car. She resigned and brought an unfair constructive dismissal claim, contending that the reason for dismissal was transfer-related and was automatically unfair under Reg 7(1). An employment tribunal rejected her claim, holding that the principal reason for dismissal was an 'organisational reason entailing changes in the workforce' within the meaning of Reg 7(2), and so was not automatically unfair. Unlike the Berriman case (above), where the employer had sought simply to harmonise contractual terms, S Ltd's objective in this case had been to change the content of C's job. On appeal, the EAT noted that where the same employees are kept on after a relevant transfer, but are engaged in a different occupation, there is a change in the workforce for the purposes of the ETO defence. However, the EAT was not satisfied that the tribunal in this case had ascertained whether bringing

300

about a change in job functions was the *principal* reason motivating S Ltd in its decision to impose the contractual changes on C. The EAT thought that there were several potential reasons for the employer's plan, and that rationalisation of its organisation did not *necessarily* involve taking away C's car and taking away her right to flexible working hours. As a result, the case was remitted to the same tribunal for consideration of what was the principal reason for C's dismissal

- **Crown Leisure Ltd v Waldron** EAT 307/91: W was employed by the transferor as one of four service engineers who worked on fruit machines in clubs. Following a TUPE transfer, the new employer, CL Ltd, sought to impose detrimental changes to his hours, holiday and sick pay entitlement. W resigned and claimed constructive dismissal, arguing that his dismissal was automatically unfair under TUPE. An employment tribunal upheld his claim, and CL Ltd appealed to the EAT. It contended that W's dismissal was for an 'organisational reason entailing changes in the workforce', in that, instead of continuing to be general engineers who turned their hands to workshop repair, on-site servicing and installation, the claimant and his colleagues were required, after the transfer, to form part of a specialised corps separately comprising service engineers, installation engineers and workshop repair engineers. The EAT, however, upheld the tribunal's conclusion. In its view, there was no suggestion from the evidence that W was being asked to accept any significant change to his job description. The document containing the new terms and conditions was headed 'service engineers' – the exact same job title that had applied to W under the transferor. The EAT observed that 'the employers were... engaged in a perfectly understandable operation of trying to harmonise the terms and conditions of employment of the whole of their workforce... That may be perfectly understandable for commercial reasons, may be perfectly defensible in many ways, but it simply is not what Reg 8(2) [of the TUPE Regulations 1981] is talking about, because although the requirement that there shall be organisational reasons... may well be satisfied, there is no relevant change in the workforce entailed by those reasons'

- **Gibson v Ciro Cittero (Menswear) plc** EAT 1276/97: G was employed as a sales assistant at the Romford branch of a clothes store. In June 1996 the business was acquired by CCM plc, which already had more than 200 stores country-wide. Prior to the transfer, G had been a key holder for the branch and was paid an extra £20 a week (8 per cent of her total weekly earnings) for bearing that responsibility. Following the transfer, however, CCM plc decided that her key-holder duties should be transferred to a more senior manager, consistent with its general policy in other stores. G ended up resigning and claiming unfair constructive dismissal owing to the loss of her additional allowance. An employment tribunal found that, although she had been constructively dismissed, her dismissal was not unfair on account

301

of the fact that the reason for dismissal comprised an ETO reason entailing changes in the workforce. In particular, the tribunal ruled that there had been a change in G's job function, as she no longer had the role of key holder, and that this change was far from being a mere 'standardisation' in pay. Rather, it constituted an organisational reason entailing a change in the functions of a member of CCM Ltd's workforce. On appeal, the EAT accepted the tribunal's reasoning with regard to the question of whether CCM plc had an ETO reason for G's dismissal. However, it held that the tribunal had failed to consider whether the dismissal was nonetheless unfair under S.98(4) ERA as being unreasonable in all the circumstances, and remitted the case to a different tribunal for determination of that matter

- **Green v Elan Care Ltd** EAT 18/01: G was employed as the care manager at a residential home. The residential home business fell into financial difficulties and, in April 2001, was acquired by E Ltd. The acquisition amounted to a TUPE transfer. The principal shareholder of E Ltd – who had previously been employed in the care home as its financial manager – decided to implement a reorganisation of management, combining the functions previously performed by G and the care home's proprietor with his own functions. Thus, the jobs of three managers were to be merged into one. G was offered alternative employment as senior carer, but this meant that she would no longer be a manager and her annual salary would be reduced from £19,000 to £10,000. She declined the offer and was subsequently dismissed. G claimed that her dismissal was automatically unfair under Reg 7(1). In her view, her dismissal had been connected with the transfer, and had not been for an ETO reason entailing changes in the workforce within the meaning of Reg 7(2) since E Ltd had simply sought to change her terms and conditions. An employment tribunal rejected G's claim. It held that the proposal of alternative employment entailed a fundamental change to G's job functions, and hence that the reason for dismissal had been an ETO reason entailing changes in the workforce. On appeal, the EAT upheld the tribunal's conclusion. The EAT acknowledged that, under the proposed changes, the number of employees in the workforce was to remain the same. However, case law demonstrated that this did not prevent the tribunal from concluding that E Ltd's reason for dismissal fell within Reg 7(2). Furthermore, while a minor change in the functions of one employee or a small number of employees in a large workforce might not be sufficient for the purposes of that provision, where the steps taken by the employer involve a real change in functions in a substantial or key area of the workforce, it is open to a tribunal to find that changes in the workforce are entailed. In this case, had G accepted the proposal, she would have been retained in a wholly different and non-managerial position. The changes accordingly involved a wholesale reorganisation in the management structure and a reduction in the number of managers by at least one. In view of this, it was open to the tribunal to find that E Ltd's organisational reason for G's dismissal entailed changes in the workforce

* **London Metropolitan University v Sackur and ors** EAT 0286/06: In August 2002 the University of North London (UNL) and the London Guildhall University (LGU) merged to form London Metropolitan University (LMU). The merger was effected by a transfer of UNL to LGU, which, immediately upon that transfer, changed its name to LMU. The parties accepted that TUPE applied. Staff originally employed by LGU enjoyed slightly better terms and conditions than those who had been employed by UNL. LMU took the decision that the UNL terms and conditions were to be the standard form of contract for all new and existing staff, and in September 2004 it imposed the new terms on staff originally employed by LGU, dismissing and offering to re-engage those who refused to accept. A group of former LGU employees brought claims based on Reg 7(1) of TUPE, which were upheld by an employment tribunal. In its view, the dismissals were effected in order to harmonise terms and conditions, which, according to settled case law, was a transfer-connected reason. Furthermore, LMU had failed to establish an ETO reason entailing changes in the workforce. The Court of Appeal's decision in Berriman (see above) had established that 'changes in the workforce' means changes in the numbers or job functions of employees, neither of which was present here, as it was LMU's intention to retain all transferred staff in their existing roles. LMU appealed to the EAT, but the EAT upheld the tribunal's decision. In its view, Berriman remained good law, and was correctly applied by the tribunal.

Two conclusions can be drawn, with some certainty, from the above body of **4.65** case law. First, as the Berriman, Bullard and Sackur cases illustrate, in order to amount to a 'change in the workforce' within the meaning of Reg 7(2), a change in 'job function' must involve, to some extent at least, a change to the actual *tasks* that employees are required to perform. So, neither a simple harmonisation of terms and conditions (for more on which, see Chapter 5) nor a simple change in working hours will, in themselves, suffice. Transfer-connected dismissals arising from such changes are almost certain to be automatically unfair under Reg 7(1).

Secondly, as the EAT expressly decided in Crawford, where workforce numbers are not reduced but employees are given *entirely different jobs* to do, this will be sufficient to amount to 'changes in the workforce' for the purposes of the Reg 7(2) ETO defence. This analysis concurs with the DTI Guide, which states that 'a functional change could involve a new requirement on an employee who held a managerial position to enter into a non-managerial role, or to move from a secretarial to a sales position'. The cases of Lane and Green provide good examples of 'changes in the workforce' taking place post-transfer owing to employees' being required to perform different roles.

303

4.66 But these two scenarios – first, a simple harmonisation process which does not alter an employee's job function at all and, secondly, a reorganisation leading to an employee doing a completely different job – represent two extremes. What about a situation where, for an organisational reason, an employee's duties do change, but only in a fairly minor way? Will this amount to a 'change in the workforce' enabling the employer to rely on the Reg 7(2) ETO defence? On the one hand, the message from the Crown case seems to be that where an employee's duties remain *essentially* the same after the transfer as before it, the transferee might find it difficult to convince a tribunal that any change to terms and conditions was prompted by an ETO reason entailing a change of job 'functions'. On the other hand, in the Gibson case the EAT did not disturb a tribunal's finding that there had been a 'change in the workforce' where an employee lost a key-holding responsibility at a clothes store, even though she otherwise continued in the same role. This suggests that the wholesale changes to an employee's role envisaged by the Crawford case and the DTI Guide are not necessarily required for the employer's ETO defence to be invoked.

The meaning of 'entailing changes in the workforce' was clarified by the EAT in Nationwide Building Society v Benn and ors 2010 IRLR 922, EAT. In this case, B and 17 other employees were employed by the Portman Building Society (PBS) until their employment was transferred to the Nationwide Building Society (NBS) in August 2007 under TUPE. The employees argued that;

- NBS had altered their terms and conditions of employment to their detriment after the transfer in that their job roles and responsibilities were downgraded when they were assimilated into NBS roles; and

- there was a significant difference between the pre- and post-transfer roles and the assimilation process transferring them was itself a breach of mutual trust and confidence; and

- the NBS bonus scheme was less generous than the previous PBS scheme.

4.67 They resigned and brought claims of unfair constructive dismissal at the employment tribunal. An employment tribunal handled two of the claimants' cases as a test case. It held that that, while the claimants had been constructively dismissed, their dismissals were not automatically unfair as there was an ETO reason for them. The new roles the employees were required to perform post-transfer represented a diminution in skills and responsibilities. Following the transfer, the claimants were unable to continue selling products for which they were licensed and were losing their qualifications in that respect. However, the principal reason for the change in the claimants' roles and thus their dismissal was that NBS did not have in place the range of products or funds which would have enabled the claimants to continue to function at their previous level. The tribunal concluded that this amounted to an 'organisational' reason within the meaning of Reg 7(2). As to whether this was a reason 'entailing changes in the

304

workforce', the tribunal concluded that the lack of an equivalent product range to that which the employees had been able to offer customers pre-transfer entailed a change to the claimants' job functions which satisfied the requirements of Reg 7(2). Similarly, the change to the bonus scheme under the transferee had been connected with the claimants' job functions and was also made for an ETO reason.

In upholding the tribunal's decision on appeal, the EAT found no grounds for interfering with the finding that there was an ETO reason for the dismissals. The EAT rejected the employees' argument that NBS's harmonisation of roles, functions and remuneration could not constitute an organisational reason 'entailing changes in the workforce' because those changes affected only PBS employees rather than the transferee's workforce as a whole. Pointing out that TUPE applies not only to a transfer of an undertaking but also to a transfer of part of an undertaking, the EAT noted that it was the unchallenged conclusion of the tribunal that there was an organisational change of the group of employees which transferred from PBS to NBS. Reg 7(2) does not state that the ETO reason must entail changes in the entirety of the workforce. In the instant case, the organisational change affected a body of transferring employees, and the tribunal did not err in concluding that the claimants' dismissals were for an ETO reason.

The decision in the Nationwide Building Society case (above) demonstrates **4.68** that there does not have to be a radical change in employee function for Reg 7(2) to apply. More controversial is the conclusion that there can be an ETO reason which affects only the transferred employees. As applied to the facts of this case – and particularly in regard to the finding that the reduction in bonus was for an ETO reason – it might be argued that this comes close to permitting the kind of post-transfer harmonisation of terms and conditions which the Berriman case appeared specifically to exclude from the scope of the ETO defence.

Transferor cannot dismiss for transferee's ETO reason **4.69**
We saw above that, in order to amount to an ETO reason under Reg 7(2), the reason for a transfer-connected dismissal must relate to the conduct of the business concerned. We also saw that the Reg 7(2) 'ETO defence' can be relied upon in respect of dismissals carried out by either the transferor or the transferee.

That noted, we now turn to the interesting question of whether a *transferor* can establish an ETO reason for dismissal for Reg 7(2) purposes where he dismisses employees, prior to a transfer, for a reason relating to the *transferee's* future conduct of the business in question. Put another way, can a transferor 'borrow' the transferee's ETO reason, and carry out dismissals prior to the transfer that the transferee would be entitled to carry out after the transfer? Following a

305

number of years of conjecture, the Court of Session, in the recent case of Hynd v Armstrong and ors 2007 SLT 299, Ct Sess, answered this question firmly in the negative.

4.70 The Hynd case involved Morison Bishop, a law firm with offices in Edinburgh and Glasgow, which employed H, a corporate lawyer, in its Glasgow office. The partners in the firm decided to dissolve the partnership with effect from 31 July 2002, with the intention of forming two new firms: an Edinburgh-based firm called Morisons and a Glasgow-based firm called Bishops. Since Bishops was to concentrate on property law and litigation, the Glasgow partners of Morison Bishop anticipated a reduced requirement for corporate lawyers. Acting with the authority of the other partners in the firm, they made H redundant on 31 July 2002 – the date on which the partnership dissolved. On 1 August 2002 Morisons and Bishops each commenced practice. Following his dismissal, H initiated proceedings in an employment tribunal against the former partners of Morison Bishop and the partners of the new entity, Bishops, complaining that his dismissal was by reason of or connected with a relevant transfer, and was automatically unfair what is now Reg 7(1) of TUPE. The tribunal rejected H's claim. It observed that he had been dismissed by the partners of Morison Bishop (the transferor) in anticipation of the transfer of part of their undertaking to Bishops (the transferee) because the prospective partners in Bishops had decided, for economic and organisational reasons, that H would not be required for the future conduct of the business following the transfer. On that basis, the tribunal concluded that the dismissing employer had established an ETO reason for dismissal, which entailed changes in the workforce, under what is now Reg 7(2). H's appeal to the EAT was refused and he appealed once more, this time to the Court of Session. Before that Court, he argued that since he was dismissed by the transferor prior to the transfer, the 'ETO defence' would only apply if the ETO reason for his dismissal related to the transferor's own future conduct of the business. In other words, the transferor should not be entitled to rely on an ETO reason based on the anticipated future conduct of the business by the transferee.

The Court of Session (Inner House) turned first to the EU Acquired Rights Directive, holding that it was 'reasonably clear' that Article 4.1 did not permit dismissals by transferors in circumstances such as those in the instant case. With regard to dismissals by a transferor, Article 4.1 was naturally construed as limiting the ETO defence to dismissals for reasons which entailed changes in the transferor's own workforce. This conclusion was supported by two further considerations. First, if Article 4.1 were interpreted so as to permit a transferor to dismiss employees prior to the transfer because they were surplus to the transferee's requirements, there would be every incentive, where the transferor was insolvent, for redundancies to be effected by the transferor in advance of the transfer so that liabilities with regard to the redundant employees did not pass to the transferee and could, in practice, be avoided. That result would be inconsistent with the Directive's objective of protecting employees. Secondly, in a situation where the combined workforces of the transferor and transferee were greater than the transferee would require after the transfer, and where redundancies would therefore be necessary, such an interpretation of Art 4.1 would enable the selection of employees for redundancy to be made solely from the transferor's workforce, and would thus relieve the transferee of the need, which would otherwise arise, to consider all the employees of the combined workforces on an equal footing.

Next, the Court considered whether Reg 7(2) – which referred to an ETO **4.71** reason entailing changes in the workforce 'of either the transferor or the transferee before or after a relevant transfer' – could be construed in line with its preferred interpretation of the Directive. In order to do so, the Court reviewed the relevant authorities. In Wheeler v Patel (above) the EAT had held that a dismissal by the transferor in order to comply with a requirement of the intended transferee could not be an ETO reason for dismissal within the meaning of Reg 7(2). Such a reason did not relate to the conduct of the business; it related simply to the transferor's desire to achieve a sale. This reasoning was later affirmed by the Court of Appeal in Whitehouse v Chas A Blatchford and Sons Ltd (above), where that Court emphasised that, for an ETO reason to arise where an employee is dismissed by a transferor, the transferor's reason for dismissal must relate to its own future conduct of the business; a condition which could not be met where the transferor had no intention of continuing the business.

Taking these cases on board, the Court of Session concluded that Reg 8(2) of TUPE could be interpreted in line with Art 4.1 of the Directive. Thus, the right of an employer to dismiss for an ETO reason entailing changes in the workforce arose only where the employer dismissed an employee for a reason of its *own*, relating to its *own* future conduct of the business, and entailing a change in its *own* workforce. Accordingly, the Court held that the tribunal's conclusion that H's dismissal was for an ETO reason was based on a mistaken interpretation of the Regulations. On a correct interpretation, the only conclusion open to the tribunal was that the employer's ETO defence failed in this case, meaning that H's dismissal was automatically unfair.

In reaching its decision in the Hynd case, the Court acknowledged that, had H **4.72** not been dismissed by Morison Bishop prior to the transfer, he could have been fairly dismissed for an ETO reason by Bishops after the transfer. The message from the case to a transferee, then, is a simple one: in the absence of watertight warranties and indemnities from the transferor (for which, see Chapter 10), where a transferee believes that he has an ETO reason for carrying out dismissals, he should carry out those dismissals once the relevant transfer has occurred, rather than put pressure on the transferor to dismiss members of the workforce prior to the transfer. Any such dismissals carried out by the transferor are likely to be automatically unfair under Reg 7(1) and, as we shall see in 'Which employer will be liable?' below, liability for such dismissals will pass under TUPE to the transferee in any event.

4.73 ETO dismissals will be redundancy or SOSR

Under Reg 7(3)(b), where a transfer-connected dismissal is not rendered automatically unfair by Reg 7(1) – i.e. where the employer is successful with his 'ETO defence' – the reason for dismissal for the purpose of S.98 ERA will be either 'some other substantial reason' of a kind such as to justify the dismissal of an employee holding the position which that employee held, or, where the reason for dismissal fulfils the definition of redundancy in S.139 ERA, then the dismissal will be treated as a redundancy dismissal, and the employee's normal rights on redundancy – such as a redundancy payment and the right to claim that he had been chosen under an unfair redundancy selection – will apply. Reg 7(3)(b) addresses an anomaly under the 1981 Regulations, which provided that dismissal for an ETO reason connected to the transfer was always to be treated as being for some other substantial reason, meaning that no redundancy payment was technically required.

Most cases discussed above in which an ETO defence has been available to an employer have involved either the reduction in workforce numbers or dismissals owing to significant changes to job functions. Many of these are likely to meet the statutory definition of redundancy contained in S.139 ERA, in that the requirements of the business for employees to carry out work of a particular kind will have ceased or diminished.

4.74 Employers wishing to carry out ETO dismissals in connection with a relevant transfer should attempt to ascertain whether such dismissals will by reason of redundancy and, if they are, ensure that they jump through the necessary hoops with regard to selection, consultation and dismissal procedures. If they do not, the dismissals are likely to be rendered unfair by S.98 ERA. For discussion about the definition of redundancy, redundancy selection and consultation, see IDS Employment Law Handbook, 'Redundancy' (2008).

4.75 Constructive dismissals

To this point, this chapter has largely been concerned with the question of when a dismissal will be rendered automatically unfair by Reg 7 of the 2006 Regulations – in other words, when a dismissal will be by reason of a relevant transfer, or for a reason 'connected with' a relevant transfer that is not 'an economic, technical or organisational reason entailing changes in the workforce'.

We now cast our net wider and turn to the two routes (envisaged by Reg 4) by which an employee's decision to leave his or her employment, taken in response to the actions of a transferor or transferee, can amount to a 'dismissal' potentially giving rise to a unfair dismissal claim. In this section we focus on the traditional concept of 'constructive dismissal', which Reg 4(11) acknowledges can arise in a TUPE context, and in the next we discuss the new concept of 'material detriment' dismissal, which is specific to the TUPE regime.

A 'constructive dismissal', then, occurs where an employee resigns, with or **4.76** without notice, in response to a 'repudiatory breach' of contract on the part of his or her employer – that is, a breach going to the heart of the contract. In such circumstances, even where no express dismissal has occurred, the employee will be treated as having been 'dismissed' within the meaning of S.95(1)(c) ERA, and thus (providing that he or she has the requisite qualifying service) will be able to bring an unfair dismissal claim under that Act – see 'Overview' above.

Many of the cases discussed in the chapter thus far have concerned constructive rather than express dismissals, with such dismissals often arising owing to a transferee employer's wish to change transferring employees' contractual terms – see, for example, the leading case of Berriman v Delabole Slate Ltd 1985 ICR 546, CA, discussed at length under 'Dismissals potentially fair for an "ETO reason"' above. For more on changing terms and conditions for a reason connected with a relevant transfer, see Chapter 5.

Below, we start by explaining the concept of 'constructive dismissal' in more detail, before turning to consider how such a dismissal is treated by the 2006 Regulations. In particular, we examine what might ensue where an employee resigns, prior to a relevant transfer, owing to concerns about changes the transferee might make to his or her contractual terms.

What is a constructive dismissal? **4.77**

The basic elements of a constructive dismissal are reflected in one of the operative definitions of 'dismissal' found in the ERA. By virtue of Ss.95(1)(c) and 136(1)(c), an employer will be regarded as having dismissed an employee if the latter terminates his or her employment contract, with or without notice, in circumstances in which he or she is entitled to terminate it without notice by reason of the employer's conduct.

In Western Excavating (ECC) Ltd v Sharp 1978 ICR 221, CA, the Court of Appeal ruled that the employer's conduct giving rise to a constructive dismissal must involve a *repudiatory breach of contract*. In other words, it is only in response to a breach serious enough to constitute a repudiation of the contract that an employee is relieved of the obligation to give notice before resigning. As Lord Denning MR put it: 'If the employer is guilty of conduct which is a significant breach going to the root of the contract of employment, or which shows that the employer no longer intends to be bound by one or more of the essential terms of the contract, then the employee is entitled to treat himself as discharged from any further performance. If he does so, then he terminates the contract by reason of the employer's conduct. He is constructively dismissed.'

309

4.78 What might amount to such a repudiatory breach of contract? Although we do not intend to dwell on this question here – a full discussion of the issues is contained in IDS Employment Law Handbook, 'Contracts of Employment' (2009) – the following brief points should be noted:

- the obligation on an employer to pay employees their salary is so fundamental that a breach of this duty, such as a wage cut (see, for example, RF Hill Ltd v Mooney 1981 IRLR 258, EAT), is likely to be treated as repudiatory

- fringe benefits are commonly regarded as part of employees' remuneration, so a breach of a term relating to such benefits may well be repudiatory (see, for example, Triton Oliver (Special Products) Ltd v Bromage EAT 709/91, where the withdrawal of an employee's right to a company car founded a successful constructive dismissal claim)

- unilateral changes to an employee's job content (outside of those envisaged by the employment contract) and/or to an employee's status are likely to be repudiatory. See, for example, Marconi Radar Systems Ltd v Bennett EAT 793/82, in which B, a quality manager who returned from holiday to find that certain design work had been transferred from himself to his former deputy, was found to have been constructively dismissed

- an increase in or alteration of an employee's hours of work can amount to a repudiatory breach of contract – see, for example, Tawiah v Southern Derbyshire Mental Health Trust ET Case No.11547/94, in which such a breach occurred where the employer insisted that a nurse change from night shifts to day shifts

- whether or not an employee can claim constructive dismissal when the location of his or her workplace is changed depends largely upon how much mobility is built into the contract. If there is no express or implied mobility clause, the employer may be at risk of a constructive dismissal claim if he tries to relocate the employee. For example, in Strachan St George v Williams EAT 969/94 an employer's moving an audiotypist to an office that was a further hour away from where she lived was held to be a repudiatory breach of contract

- the common law implies a term into all contracts of employment that employers will not, without reasonable or proper cause, conduct themselves in a manner calculated or likely to destroy or seriously damage the relationship of trust and confidence between the parties – Courtaulds Northern Textiles Ltd v Andrew 1979 IRLR 84, EAT. A breach of this implied term, which can cover a very wide range of behaviour, will amount to a repudiatory breach of contract. It is this term that is most often cited in constructive dismissal claims.

4.79 It is important to note that, whether or not a repudiatory breach of contract has occurred, there will be no constructive dismissal unless the employee

310 ————————————————————————————————

'accepts' that breach by resigning, and thus bringing the contract to an end. The decision whether to accept the breach belongs exclusively to the employee, and often other less drastic options are available. One is that the employee may choose to 'stand and sue' on the contract – meaning that, rather than resign, he or she will take legal action for breach of contract, in which case the contract remains alive as between the contracting parties.

Alternatively, the employee might simply choose to look past the breach – i.e. effectively ignore it. If the employee fails to register any obvious protest about the breach, then at some point he or she is likely to be regarded as having sanctioned it, thereby affirming the contract. In such a case, the employer will no longer be in breach of contract and the employee will thus lose the right to resign and claim that he or she has been constructively dismissed. (That said, the TUPE regime complicates this analysis somewhat, since case law suggests that contractual changes to an employee's detriment are void if made by reason of a relevant transfer, even where the employee in question agrees to those changes – see below under 'Employee cannot affirm TUPE-connected contractual change' and, in more detail, in Chapter 5 under 'Varying terms in a TUPE context'.)

In summary, in order to show that he or he has been constructively dismissed, **4.80** an employee must establish the following:

- that there was a repudiatory breach of contract on the part of the employer

- that it was the employer's breach that actually caused the employee to resign. If there is a different reason for the employee's resignation, such that he or she would have left irrespective of the employer's conduct, then there has not been a constructive dismissal, and

- that the employee did not delay too long before resigning, thus affirming the contract and losing the right to claim constructive dismissal.

Preservation of constructive dismissal rights under TUPE – Reg 4(11) **4.81**
The 2006 Regulations expressly provide for the employee's normal constructive dismissal right to be preserved. In this regard, Reg 4(11) stipulates that 'paragraphs (1), (7), (8) and (9) [of Reg 4] are without prejudice to any right of an employee arising apart from these Regulations to terminate his contract of employment without notice in acceptance of a repudiatory breach of contract by his employer'.

In other words, none of the following in any way displace or limit the employee's right to claim constructive dismissal as a result of a repudiatory breach of contract by the employer:

- Reg 4(1), which provides for the automatic transfer of an employee's employment from the transferor to the transferee (see Chapter 2)

311

- Reg 4(7) and (8), which concern the employee's right to object to the automatic transfer of his or her employment (also discussed in Chapter 2)

- Reg 4(9), which provides an employee with an additional right to treat his or her contract as having been terminated where the relevant transfer involves or would involve a substantial change to working conditions to his or her material detriment (see 'Material detriment dismissals' below).

4.82 So, where there is a relevant transfer to which the 2006 Regulations apply, employers who unilaterally seek to make changes to terms and conditions or otherwise to the employer/employee relationship, prompted by the transfer or a reason connected with it, risk provoking employees to resign and claim unfair constructive dismissal. This is the case whether the changes are made prior to the transfer (by the transferor) or after the transfer (by the transferee).

As touched on in 'What is a constructive dismissal?' above, the kinds of change (or threatened change) that typically lead to employees resigning and claiming constructive dismissal are those that are made to remunerative benefits including pay and other remuneration, holiday, hours of work (including overtime and shift patterns), bonus and commission schemes, profit share, sickness benefit entitlement, pensions, and other fringe benefits such as car provision. Sometimes, however, the changes relate to the work the employees do or the place at which they are employed to do it. Such changes typically affect job descriptions, job functions and/or job status. Unless the scale of the change is minor, then in most cases a unilateral change to any of the above will be regarded as a repudiatory breach of contract entitling the employee to resign with or without giving notice. In addition, if the employer's conduct is such as to destroy or seriously damage the employment relationship, this will amount to a breach of the fundamental implied term of trust and confidence, such as to entitle the employee to resign and claim constructive dismissal.

4.83 Remember that even if a change is not of such a scale as to amount to a repudiatory breach, Reg 4(9) now confers a freestanding right for the employee to resign on the ground that the relevant transfer involves or would involve a change in working conditions to his or her material detriment. This new right is explored in detail under 'Material detriment dismissals' below.

4.84 **Employee cannot affirm TUPE-connected contractual change**
In 'What is a constructive dismissal?' above, we made the point that, generally, where an employee does nothing in response to an employer's repudiatory breach of contract, he or she is likely to be regarded as having sanctioned it, thereby affirming the contract, and will lose the right to resign and claim that he or she has been constructively dismissed.

However, owing to case law interpreting the EU Acquired Rights Directive and the TUPE regime, this analysis does not apply where a change to terms and conditions occurs in connection with a relevant transfer under TUPE. That is because, as we explain in Chapter 5 under 'Varying terms in a TUPE context', that case law suggests that contractual changes to an employee's detriment are void if made in connection with a relevant transfer, even where the employee in question purports to agree to them. Logically, then, where a transferee employer reduces a transferring employee's wages, or otherwise alters his or her terms and conditions to his or her detriment 'in connection with the transfer', the employee will be able, a number of years later, to claim constructive dismissal with regard to the ongoing breach, notwithstanding his or her inaction at the time.

Fairness/unfairness of constructive dismissals in a TUPE context   4.85
All that a constructive dismissal accords the employee is the right to regard him or herself as having been dismissed. It does not necessarily follow that the employee in question has been *unfairly* dismissed.

Assuming that a constructive dismissal has occurred, then, outside a TUPE context, the following must happen in order for the dismissal to be fair. First, the employer must show that there was a potentially valid reason for dismissal within the terms of S.98(1) and (2) ERA; and, secondly, provided that such a reason is shown, the tribunal must conclude that, in all the circumstances of the case, the employer had acted reasonably, within the meaning of S.98(4), to dismiss the employee for that reason within the ERA – see 'Overview' above.

What about a constructive dismissal occurring in connection with a TUPE   4.86
transfer? As a general rule, Reg 7(1) and (2) – the provisions dealing with dismissals carried out in a TUPE context, which were discussed at length above – apply whether or not dismissals are express or constructive. So, with regard to a constructive dismissal that is shown to be by reason of a relevant transfer, or for a reason connected with the transfer that is not an 'ETO reason' (i.e. an economic, technical or organisational reason entailing changes in the workforce), the dismissal will be automatically unfair under Reg 7(1) and, assuming that the employee has the necessary continuous service, he or she will be entitled to the usual remedies for unfair dismissal. But if the transfer-connected reason for the constructive dismissal is an 'ETO reason', then, in accordance with Reg 7(2), that reason will be regarded as being either for 'redundancy' or 'some other substantial reason of a kind such as to justify the dismissal of an employee holding the position which the employee held' for the purposes of Ss.98(1) and 135 ERA. In that case, the fairness or otherwise of the decision to dismiss will be assessed by applying the normal reasonableness test set out in S.98(4) ERA.

The above applies whether a constructive dismissal occurs while the employee is employed by the transferor prior to the transfer, or by the transferee after the transfer. Note that, in practice, any constructive dismissal that is shown to be

313

for a reason connected with a relevant transfer is likely to be automatically unfair under Reg 7(1), because the 'ETO' exception to the automatic unfairness rule has a fairly narrow compass. As discussed in 'Dismissals potentially fair for an "ETO reason"' above, the Court of Appeal in Berriman v Delabole Slate Ltd 1985 ICR 546, CA, concluded that the ETO exception will not apply unless there have been changes in the numbers of the workforce as a whole or in the job functions of members of the workforce. By and large, non-consensual changes to the fundamental terms and conditions of employment are not normally made with a view to changing numbers or functions. And the same is true of most other forms of repudiatory conduct on the employer's part, prompted by the transfer, that might provide the basis for a constructive dismissal claim.

4.87 However, difficulties are introduced into the otherwise straightforward picture described above where an employee resigns prior to a relevant transfer owing to concerns about what the transferee employer might do after the transfer. As we shall see below, a combination of various TUPE provisions and the case law interpreting those provisions conspire to make the legal position in this regard rather complex.

4.88 Resignation in anticipation of a breach by the transferee
The normal rule is that, where an employer manifests a clear intention to commit a breach of contract at some date in the future, an employee can resign and claim constructive dismissal in anticipation of the breach of contract. The question is how this plays out in a TUPE context.

There is no confusion where a transferring employee resigns *after the transfer*, in anticipation of a breach of contract by his or her new employer. Here, the normal rule as set out above will apply.

But can an employee, while still employed by the *transferor,* anticipate a change being made to his or her fundamental terms and conditions by the *transferee* and, in view of this, resign and bring a claim of unfair constructive dismissal *prior to the transfer*? And if so, will it be the transferor or the transferee who is liable? It is to these two tricky questions that we now turn.

4.89 Resignation prior to the transfer. The first appellate case to concern the question of an employee's resignation, prior to the transfer, owing to concerns about what the transferee might do after the transfer, was that of Sita (GB) Ltd v Burton and ors 1998 ICR 17, EAT. This case involved the transfer of services from a local authority to S Ltd. In the weeks leading up to the transfer B and P, who were members of the workforce that was to be transferred, became increasingly concerned about the behaviour of S Ltd, which they believed had no intention of respecting their terms and conditions of employment after the transfer. A few weeks before the transfer, B and P handed in their resignations and brought unfair constructive dismissal claims against both the authority and

S Ltd. An employment tribunal found that the behaviour of S Ltd, as the prospective transferee, in the weeks leading up to the transfer, was such as to lead a reasonable employee to suspect that his or her terms and conditions might change substantially after the transfer. This, in the tribunal's view, amounted to a breach of the implied contractual term of mutual trust and confidence, which entitled the employees to resign and claim constructive dismissal. The tribunal went on to hold that, since the sole cause of the employees' resignations was the transfer, their dismissals were in connection with the transfer and were therefore automatically unfair under what is now Reg 7(1). Furthermore, the liability for the dismissals passed to the transferee under what is now Reg 4(1).

S Ltd, however, was successful with its appeal. The EAT held that the tribunal had misdirected itself in law in so far as it held that the employees had been constructively dismissed by the prospective transferee. Since the employees were never employed by the transferee, there never existed any contract of employment which the transferee could have breached. In any event, the tribunal was also in error if its decision, properly understood, was that the transferor had constructively dismissed the employees by proceeding with the transfer in spite of the employees' reservations about the intentions of the transferee. It is only in the rarest of circumstances, the EAT said, that the duty of trust and confidence owed by an employer to an employee can be breached by reason of the actions of third parties. In the context of TUPE transfers, it may be possible that the consequences of the proposed transfer for the employees are so dire, whether in health and safety terms or otherwise, that the transferor's behaviour in going ahead with the transfer could destroy the relationship of trust and confidence with its employees. But it is not possible, as a matter of principle, for such a breach to occur where an employee's concerns relate solely to his terms and conditions following the transfer. The EAT reasoned that, since the 1981 Regulations required the transferee to honour existing terms, they provided a remedy to any attempt by the transferee to alter those terms unlawfully after the transfer. In the light of this protection enjoyed by employees involved in a transfer, the consequences of the transferor's proceeding with the transfer could not be drastic enough to give rise to a breach of the fundamental term of trust and confidence so as to entitle the employee to claim constructive dismissal against the transferor. Accordingly, the EAT overturned the tribunal's decision and rejected the employee's constructive dismissal claims.

The upshot of Sita seemed to be that an employee could not claim constructive **4.90** dismissal prior to a relevant transfer (whether against the transferor or the transferee), in anticipation of the transferee's failure to honour the transferring contractual or other legal obligations. However, the following two cases demonstrate that the position is not, in reality, that simplistic. In fact, the Humphreys case – a Court of Appeal decision which takes precedence over the

EAT's decision in Sita – suggests that an employee *can* claim constructive dismissal against the transferor on the back of an anticipatory breach of contract by the transferee, as long as the anticipated breach is one of substance:

- **Humphreys v University of Oxford and anor** 2000 ICR 405, CA: the employment of H, an academic with security of tenure, was due to transfer to a new employer under TUPE. H anticipated that, following the transfer, there would be several variations to his terms and conditions, including a fundamental change resulting in a shorter tenure than he had envisaged. Owing to this, he exercised his right under what is now Reg 4(7) to object to the transfer of his employment to the transferee. He combined his objection with a claim for damages for wrongful dismissal, in respect of the unexpired period of his tenure, on the basis that he had been constructively dismissed by the transferor. The transferor – for reasons discussed at length below – denied that H was entitled to claim constructive dismissal against it, and applied for an order that his claim be struck out. This application was rejected by a High Court judge and, on appeal, by the Court of Appeal. However, in allowing the claim to proceed, the Court of Appeal made it clear that, in order for a transferor to be regarded as having constructively dismissed an employee by reason of the transferee's anticipated repudiatory breach, the anticipated breach would have to be one of substance (i.e. a fundamental change in working conditions)

- **Euro-Die (UK) Ltd v Skidmore and anor** EAT 1158/98: S, whose employment was to transfer to a new employer under TUPE, was anxious not to lose his employment protection rights. He refused to work for the new employer in the absence of an assurance from the transferor that his continuity would be protected. When this was not forthcoming, he claimed unfair constructive dismissal against both the transferor and transferee. A tribunal, and thereafter the EAT, upheld his claim, holding that the transferor's failure to reassure the employee as to his continuity of employment was a fundamental breach of the implied term of trust and confidence, entitling him to treat himself as having been constructively dismissed. For reasons expanded upon below, the transferee was held liable for the dismissal, which was by reason of the transfer and thus automatically unfair under Reg 7(1). Note that the EAT (presided over by its then President, Mr Justice Lindsay) acknowledged that the outcome as to the unfairness of the dismissal in the case would have been different had the transferor told S that it was unsure about his rights and would seek advice. In those circumstances, the transferor would not have repudiated the contract by damaging the relationship of trust and confidence, and the employee would not have been found to be constructively dismissed.

4.91 **Which employer will be liable?** We saw above that the Humphreys and Euro-Die cases suggest that employees can resign and claim unfair constructive dismissal, prior to the transfer, owing to concerns they might have as to what the consequences of the transfer might be. The question arises, then, as to which employer – transferor or transferee – will be liable if such a claim is successful.

It seems that the conclusion in this regard will depend on whether the employee is taken to have formally objected to the transfer. The reasons for this require an analysis of the interplay between the employee's right to object to the transfer under Reg 4(7) and (8) of the 2006 Regulations (formerly Reg 5(4A) and (4B) of the 1981 Regulations) on the one hand, and the preservation of the right arising, apart from the Regulations, to claim constructive dismissal found in Reg 4(11) (formerly Reg 5(5)) on the other. Given the importance of the right to object in this context, it will be useful to provide a brief reminder of what this right comprises and its effect on the contract of employment before examining the Humphreys and Euro-Die decisions in more detail.

Background – the right to object. The employee's right to object to a relevant **4.92** transfer was considered in detail in Chapter 2 under 'Objecting to the transfer'. This right arises out of the general principles that employees cannot be compelled to enter into a contract of employment and an employer may not transfer a contract of employment to a third party without the employee's consent. In Katsikas v Konstantinidis 1993 IRLR 179, ECJ, the European Court held that the EU Acquired Rights Directive could not be interpreted so as to prevent employees from opposing the automatic transfer of their contracts of employment. The basis of this decision was that, if the Directive were interpreted as obliging employees to work for the transferee rather than simply permitting them to do so on the terms and conditions agreed with the transferor, this would call into question the fundamental right of employees to select their employer.

The UK Government responded to Katsikas by inserting two new provisions into the 1981 Regulations. Reg 5(4A) provided that an employee's contract of employment would not be transferred automatically on a relevant transfer if the employee informed the transferor or the transferee that he or she objected to becoming the employee of the transferee. And Reg 5(4B) stipulated that, where an employee so objected, the transfer had the effect of terminating the employee's contract of employment with the transferor, but that the employee was not to be treated for any purpose as having been dismissed. Consequently, it seemed, the employee would lose all rights to claim unfair dismissal, wrongful dismissal, redundancy or any other remedy based on his or her having been dismissed by the transferor. However, Reg 5(5) stated that the right to object was 'without prejudice to any right of an employee arising apart from these Regulations to terminate his contract of employment without notice if a substantial change is made to his working conditions to his detriment', while noting that 'no such right shall arise by reason only that... the identity of the employer changes unless the employee shows that, in all the circumstances, the change is a significant change and is to his detriment'.

4.93 Although the wording of these provisions has been somewhat altered by the 2006 Regulations, the substance of the specific provisions dealing with the right to object remains essentially the same. Old Reg 5(4A) now corresponds to Reg 4(7) of the 2006 Regulations and old Reg 5(4B) corresponds to Reg 4(8). Only in relation to old Reg 5(5) have the changes effected by the new Regulations led to a significant alteration, in that new Reg 4(9) and (11) separate the preserved right in relation to claiming constructive dismissal from the now apparently different right of the employee to treat the contract as having been terminated if a substantial change has been made to working conditions. Previously, Reg 5(5) had bundled these together, which meant that they were seen not as separate rights, but as a single provision aimed simply at preserving the employee's entitlement to claim constructive dismissal if a substantial change was made to his or her employment to his or her detriment as the result of a transfer.

4.94 *Position where an employee resigns and objects to the transfer.* It was in the Humphreys case (above) that the interrelationship between the right to object and the right to claim constructive dismissal by reason of an anticipated repudiation by the transferee was first considered. In essence, the Court of Appeal ruled that the right to claim constructive dismissal based on Reg 5(5) (now Reg 4(11)) survived any objection to the proposed transfer, but that it was the transferor who retained liability in respect of the dismissal. The process of reasoning by which the Court reached this conclusion is fairly complex.

Recall that the employee in that case, H, was an academic with security of tenure. He anticipated that after a relevant transfer there would be several variations to his terms and conditions, including a fundamental change resulting in a shorter tenure. In these circumstances, he objected to the transfer of his employment to the transferee, but also brought a constructive dismissal claim against the transferor. In defending the claim, the transferor conceded that H had formally objected to the transfer and agreed that, in view of Reg 5(4A) (now Reg 4(7)), his employment with it had terminated automatically upon the transfer. However, it denied that H was entitled to claim any damages in respect of the termination, and applied for an order that his claim should be struck out. The transferor's contention centred on the terms of Reg 5(4B) (now Reg 4(8)): it argued that the clear effect of this was to prevent the employee claiming that he had been dismissed 'for any purpose' once he had objected to the transfer of his contract. In other words, an employee who went down the 'objection route' lost the right to claim that the ensuing termination of his employment at the moment of the transfer could be treated for any purpose as a dismissal by the transferor.

A High Court judge rejected the employer's application to strike out and, on **4.95** appeal, the Court of Appeal confirmed that he had been right to do so. In its view, H's objection to the transfer had the effect of preventing his contract of employment from automatically passing to the transferee under TUPE. Instead, his contract with the transferor terminated immediately upon the transfer. Since, in those circumstances, the transferee never became his employer, the transferee could not have constructively dismissed him. However, in the Court's view, old Reg 5(5) meant that H's right to claim constructive dismissal against the transferor was preserved. This was because, owing to Reg 5(5), the provision in Reg 5(4B) (now Reg 4(8)) that an employee whose contract terminates following an objection under Reg 5(4A) (now Reg 4(7)) was not to be treated for any purpose as having been dismissed by the transferor, was subject to the right arising 'apart from [the] Regulations' to claim constructive dismissal.

As touched on above, however, the Court made it clear that, in order for the transferor to be regarded as having constructively dismissed the employee by reason of the transferee's anticipated repudiatory breach, the employee's objection to the transfer would have to be one of substance (i.e. a fundamental change in working conditions). If, on the other hand, the employee's objection was merely based on the fact that the identity of his employer was about to change as a result of the imminent transfer, that would not be a repudiatory breach of contract. In these latter circumstances, the employee would simply be left with the legal consequences specified by what is now Reg 4(8) when an objection to the transfer is made – i.e. the relevant transfer would serve automatically to terminate the employee's contract, but he or she would be unable to claim to have been 'dismissed' for any purpose whatsoever.

In respect of who would be potentially liable for H's constructive dismissal, **4.96** were his claim to succeed, the Court of Appeal accepted that, before Reg 5(4A) and (4B) were introduced by way of an amendment to the 1981 Regulations, a transferor's liability for a constructive dismissal carried out in connection with the relevant transfer would have passed to the transferee by virtue of Reg 5(2) (now Reg 4(2) of the 2006 Regulations – see Chapter 3). The Court ruled, however, that the effect of Reg 5(4A) and (4B) (now Reg 4(7) and (8)), when read with Reg 5(5) (now Reg 4(11)), was to ensure that, where the employee had objected to the transfer, any liability for the constructive dismissal of that employee would remain with the transferor. In particular, the Court pointed out that where an employee objects to the transfer, what is now Reg 4(7) expressly excludes the comprehensive transfer of rights, obligations and liabilities with regard to the transferring employee's contract, which would otherwise occur under what is now Reg 4(2). It followed that if H had been constructively dismissed by the transferor, any liability would remain with the transferor and not pass across to the transferee.

It is submitted that, on the authority of the decision in Humphreys, the analysis above continues to govern the position under the 2006 Regulations. If, for sound reasons, the employee anticipates that the transferee is likely to engage in conduct (such as imposing substantial contractual changes) which would repudiate the contract, and at the same time voices his or her objection to the transfer itself, Reg 4(7) will apply to ensure that the employee's employment is not transferred. Instead, as Reg 4(8) stipulates, the relevant transfer will operate to terminate the contract of employment. And although this same provision makes it clear that such termination will not be regarded as a dismissal for any purpose, the Humphreys ruling drives home the fact that this is 'without prejudice' to the right of the employee enshrined in what is now Reg 4(11) to terminate the contract by reason of a repudiatory breach by the transferor. The Court of Appeal's reasoning as to why the transferor retains liability for the constructive dismissal in these circumstances equally continues to be valid.

4.97 *Position where no objection to transfer accompanies resignation.* The outcome may well be different from that described above if an employee claims constructive dismissal prior to a relevant transfer, out of concern about the possible consequences of the transfer, but does not object to the transfer itself within the meaning of Reg 4(7) of the 2006 Regulations.

As discussed above, in Euro-Die (UK) Ltd v Skidmore and anor an employee, S, who had been anxious not to lose his employment protection rights in the event that his employment was terminated by the transferee, refused to work for the new employer in the absence of an assurance from the transferor that his continuity would be protected. The transferor did not provide this assurance, and S resigned and claimed unfair constructive dismissal against both the transferor and the transferee. A tribunal found that the employee had been constructively dismissed by the transferor and that the transfer was the reason for his dismissal. It held that the dismissal was therefore automatically unfair under Reg 7(1) (discussed at length in 'Automatically unfair dismissals' above) and that liability for the dismissal passed to the transferee by virtue of Reg 4(2) – see Chapter 3 for details.

4.98 The transferee appealed to the EAT. The reasoning of the Appeal Tribunal in dismissing the transferee's appeal contained three crucial planks, as follows:

- the transferor's failure to reassure the employee as to his continuity of employment was a fundamental breach of the implied term of trust and confidence entitling him to treat himself as having been constructively dismissed

- the simple fact that he had raised concerns about his continuity of employment did not mean that the employee was to be taken as having objected to becoming employed by the transferee for the purposes of what is now Reg 4(7) such as to prevent the automatic transfer of his contract to the transferee. It was clear that he had no absolute objection to working for the new employer, but had simply declined to do so unless he was given an assurance about the position as to his continuity

- the employment tribunal had correctly held that, since the employee's constructive dismissal occurred for a reason connected with the transfer that was not an 'ETO reason', it was automatically unfair under what is now Reg 7(1). Accordingly, liability for unfair constructive dismissal perpetrated by the transferor was transferred to the transferee under what is now Reg 4(2).

As to whether the transferor or the transferee was liable for the constructive **4.99** dismissal, the EAT was influenced by the fact the transferor's breach consisted not in threatening to change his conditions of employment, or in going ahead with a transfer when the transferee threatened to make such a change, but in failing to reassure the employee that his terms and conditions would be protected by the Regulations following the transfer. Lindsay J observed that if the employee's expression of concern in this case had amounted to an absolute objection to the transfer under what is now Reg 4(7), his contract would not have passed to the transferee by virtue of what is now Reg 4(2) and any liability for his constructive dismissal would have remained with the transferor in accordance with the Court of Appeal's ruling in Humphreys.

Conclusions and additional points. Drawing on the above, the following **4.100** points can be made with regard to an employee's claiming constructive dismissal in anticipation of a repudiatory breach on the part of the transferee employer:

- the Humphreys case, together with Reg 4(11), establishes that an employee who formally objects to a relevant transfer under Reg 4(7) is not precluded from resigning and claiming constructive dismissal. Where a resignation is made in conjunction with an objection to the fact of the transfer itself, however, any constructive dismissal claim will always be against the transferor, even though it may be based on an anticipated breach of contract by the transferee. Furthermore, if such a claim is made out, the transferor will be liable for any damages/compensation arising from it, as the employee's formal objection will prevent any such liability transferring to the transferee under Reg 4(2). So, if, for example, the transferor employer is insolvent, an employee should avoid formally objecting to the transfer for the purposes of Reg 4(7) if he or she has any designs upon receiving significant compensation for unfair constructive dismissal. In such circumstances, if the employee does not formally object; his or her claim for constructive dismissal is successful; and the dismissal is held to be in connection with the transfer but not for an ETO reason, the dismissal will be automatically unfair under Reg 7(1), meaning that liability for it will transfer to the transferee under Reg 4(2)

- the rules with regard to which employer – transferor or transferee – will be liable for a pre-transfer constructive dismissal can, at times, yield quirky

321

results. On the one hand, where an employee, owing to his or her anticipating a repudiatory breach by the transferee, both objects to a relevant transfer and successfully claims constructive dismissal, the transferor will be liable for that dismissal through little or no fault of his own (see the Humphreys case). On the other hand, where an employee does not formally object to the transfer but successfully claims unfair constructive dismissal on the back of a failure on the part of the transferor, where such failure is connected with the relevant transfer, liability is likely to pass to the transferee under TUPE, through little or no fault of *his* own (see the Euro-Die case). This illustrates why it is extremely important that both transferor and transferee consider carefully the nature of the warranties and indemnities that are to be contained in the transfer agreement, under which the parties can essentially decide between themselves who is to bear the liabilities for transfer-connected dismissals. We discuss warranties and indemnities, together with other issues surrounding the transfer agreement, in Chapter 10

- finally, note that where the anticipated action by the transferee is not sufficient to amount to a repudiatory breach of contract for the purposes of a constructive dismissal claim, the employee might nevertheless be entitled to 'resign' and treat him or herself as dismissed. This is because of the additional protection afforded by Reg 4(9), which takes effect where a relevant transfer involves or would involve a substantial change to a transferring employee's working conditions to his or her material detriment. We turn our attention to 'material detriment' dismissals immediately below.

4.101 Material detriment dismissals

Regulation 4(9) of the 2006 Regulations provides that, if a relevant transfer involves or would involve 'a substantial change in working conditions to the material detriment of a person' whose contract of employment is to transfer, 'such an employee may treat the contract of employment as having been terminated, and the employee shall be treated for any purpose as having been dismissed by the employer'.

In this section we explain the background to, and scope and detail of, Reg 4(9), before considering its relationship with the employee's rights to object to a relevant transfer under Reg 4(7), to claim constructive dismissal with reference to Reg 4(11), and to claim unfair dismissal under Reg 7 and the ERA.

4.102 Background to the introduction of Reg 4(9)
The first matter that requires consideration is the thinking that lies behind Reg 4(9), since it is substantially different from its predecessor contained in Reg 5(5) of the 1981 Regulations. The old regulation in effect integrated the right to claim constructive dismissal (now separately contained in Reg 4(11) – see 'Constructive dismissals' above) with the right of the employee to terminate

his or her contract of employment 'without notice if a substantial change is made in his working conditions to his detriment'.

Position under the 1981 Regulations. The origin of what is now Reg 4(9) lies   **4.103** in the EU Acquired Rights Directive, which, in its most up-to-date guise, stipulates in Article 4.2: 'If the contract of employment or the employment relationship is terminated because the transfer involves a substantial change in working conditions to the detriment of the employee, the employer shall be regarded as having been responsible for termination of the contract of employment or of the employment relationship.' Reg 5(5) of TUPE 1981 was drafted in very similar terms, providing that rules under the Regulations with regard to the automatic transfer of an employee's employment from the transferor to the transferee, and the employee's right to object to the transfer (in respect of both of which, see Chapter 2), operated 'without prejudice to any right of an employee arising apart from the Regulations to terminate his contract of employment without notice if a substantial change was made in his working conditions to his detriment'. That provision went on to stipulate that 'no such right shall arise by reason only that... the identity of his employer changes unless the employee shows that, in all the circumstances, the change is a significant change and is to his detriment'.

The scope of old Reg 5(5) and the extent to which it gave birth to a new right separate from the right to claim constructive dismissal became the subject of much judicial debate, both domestically and at European level. The main issue was whether the test to be used for interpreting that provision was the same as that used for constructive dismissal, so that there had to be a 'repudiatory breach' by the employer; or whether the provision was to be interpreted less restrictively in that the employee was only required to show a 'substantial change' in his or her working conditions to his or her detriment, so effectively creating another and less stringent test for the purposes of changes implemented to working conditions in a TUPE context.

In Merckx and anor v Ford Motors Co (Belgium) SA 1997 ICR 352, ECJ, the   **4.104** European Court stated that Article 4.2 of the Directive requires that if the contract of employment is terminated because the transfer involves a substantial change in working conditions to the detriment of the employee (for example, a change in remuneration levels), the employer must be regarded as having been responsible for the termination. This was so even though in that case the employee's pay depended on profit and turnover so that the previous level of income under his employment with the transferor could not be guaranteed – in other words, to use domestic terminology, even though there was not necessarily a repudiatory breach of contract. It seemed for a while that, in the light of Merckx, the courts in the United Kingdom had come down in favour of the view that Reg 5(5) provided for something more than merely a consolidation of the right to claim constructive dismissal where either the transferor or the

323

transferee repudiates the contract of employment by changing working conditions to the employee's detriment. In Rossiter v Pendragon plc 2001 IRLR 256, EAT, the Appeal Tribunal concluded that Reg 5(5) had to be interpreted as meaning that, where an employee suffered a substantial change in working conditions to his or her detriment, he or she had the right to claim constructive dismissal even if the employer's actions did not constitute a breach of contract, repudiatory or otherwise. The EAT asserted that such a purposive construction was necessary to give effect to Article 4.2, and was implicit in the ECJ's ruling in Merckx. The EAT also pointed to previous EAT decisions which suggested – albeit tentatively – that a different and less stringent test applied where changes to working conditions were prompted by the transfer of an undertaking compared to the position outside a TUPE situation.

This analysis did not survive, however, when the Rossiter case went to Court of Appeal, where it was joined with another case, Air Foyle Ltd v Crosby-Clarke. In allowing both appeals – reported at 2002 ICR 1063, CA – the Court of Appeal was adamant that Reg 5(5) did no more than reiterate the right to claim constructive dismissal on the usual basis. It held that the well-established test for constructive dismissal confirmed in Western Excavating (ECC) Ltd v Sharp 1978 ICR 221, CA (see 'Constructive dismissals' above) applied as much to a case that involves the transfer of an undertaking as it does to a case which does not. In support of that conclusion, Lord Justice Peter Gibson (with whom Jonathan Parker LJ and Sir Christopher Slade agreed) pointed to the particular wording of the regulation in question. Reg 5(5) expressly preserved rights that arose '*apart from these Regulations*'. The only right to claim constructive dismissal that arose apart from the 1981 Regulations was the right to terminate the contract 'without notice' in response to an employer's repudiatory breach. If there were to be a right to claim constructive dismissal by reason only of a substantial change in working conditions to the employer's detriment, without there being a breach of contract, that would be a new right arising, not apart from the TUPE Regulations, but by reason of those Regulations. It followed that only conduct by the transferor or transferee amounting to a repudiation of the contract would entitle the employee to terminate the contract and claim constructive dismissal.

4.105 In summary, the 1981 Regulations allowed employees to resign and claim constructive dismissal if their working conditions were varied to their detriment and that variation amounted to a repudiatory breach. In other words, Reg 5(5) did no more than preserve the common law right to constructive dismissal. A resignation in response to a change which was not so serious as to be repudiatory would not be treated as a constructive dismissal and employees would therefore not have any remedy based on dismissal. That is how the position lay until the enactment of the 2006 Regulations.

Position under the 2006 Regulations. As already noted, however, Reg 4(9) of **4.106** the 2006 Regulations now provides that 'where a relevant transfer involves or would involve a substantial change in working conditions to the material detriment of a person whose contract of employment is or would be transferred under [Reg 4(1)]', then 'such an employee may treat the contract of employment as having been terminated, and the employee shall be treated for any purpose as having been dismissed by the employer'. And Reg 4(11) separately provides that the right to object to the transfer (contained in Reg 4(7) and (8)), and the 'automatic transfer of employment' rule in Reg 4(1), 'are without prejudice to any right of an employee arising apart from these Regulations to terminate his contract of employment without notice in acceptance of a repudiatory breach of contract by his employer'. It is immediately apparent that, in contrast to the position under the 1981 Regulations, the 2006 Regulations have separated the provision dealing with substantial changes to working conditions from the employee's right 'arising apart from the Regulations' to resign and claim constructive dismissal.

The practical importance of this is that the 2006 Regulations – in line with the Directive and the Merckx decision – now confer an independent freestanding right on the employee to resign in the face of a substantial change to working conditions, whether or not this change amounts to a repudiatory breach of contract, and for such resignation to be treated as a dismissal by the employer for all purposes.

Scope of right under Reg 4(9)

4.107

The fact that the Reg 4(9) right now stands apart from the right of the employee to treat him or herself as constructively dismissed indicates that this freestanding right does not require the substantial change to working conditions to amount to a repudiatory breach of contract, or even to a breach of contract at all. All that needs to be shown is that a substantial change has been made to the employee's working conditions causing him or her material detriment.

The clear effect of Reg 4(9), then, is to reverse the Court of Appeal's decision in Rossiter (see 'Background to the introduction of Reg 4(9)' above) and to reinstate the position upheld by the EAT in that case – namely, that an employee is entitled to resign and be deemed to have been dismissed where his or her working conditions are substantially changed to his or her detriment irrespective of whether such a change comprises a breach of contract by the employer, repudiatory or otherwise. It is generally accepted that this serves to bring the TUPE Regulations back into line with the Acquired Rights Directive, and, in particular, with what Article 4.2 requires. That this was the legislative intention behind Reg 4(9) was expressly acknowledged by the Government in its Public Consultation Document on the draft regulations issued in March 2005.

325

4.108 The upshot is that the circumstances in which Reg 4(9) can operate are potentially far wider than the normal concept of constructive dismissal. Reg 4(11) continues to give the employee the right to terminate his or her employment without notice in acceptance of the employer's repudiatory breach of contract, but it might prove easier for employees to use the material detriment dismissal provisions, since they entail a less onerous test. However, it will be important to take on board the points made below when considering whether the conditions for claiming a material detriment dismissal under Reg 4(9) have been satisfied.

'Substantial change to working conditions' has to cause 'material detriment'. Although the phrase 'working conditions' is not defined for the purposes of Reg 4(9), and has not yet been clarified by case law, its scope is potentially wide. It may well cover a range of employee concerns regarding, for example, diminished promotion opportunities, pensions and benefits, trade union rights, health and safety, environmental or ethical issues, and lower commissions or shares in profits (even if purely a result of the different turnover or profitability levels of the transferee – see the Merckx case above). Depending on just how broad the concept of working conditions is held to be, it may even cover, in certain circumstances, something as simple as the transferee's identity.

4.109 The DTI Guide asks 'what might constitute a substantial change in working conditions?' and answers that question thus: 'This will be a matter for the courts and the tribunals to determine in the light of the circumstances of each case. What might be a trivial change in one setting might constitute a substantial change in another. However, a major relocation of the workplace which makes it difficult or much more expensive for an employee to transfer, or the withdrawal of a right to a tenured post, is likely to fall within this definition.'

However broad the concept of working conditions may or may not be, it is important to note that Reg 4(9) requires the substantial change to those conditions to be to the employee's *material detriment*. It is likely that detriment for this purpose will be construed widely in the way it has been in other contexts, most notably in discrimination law. In Shamoon v Chief Constable of the Royal Ulster Constabulary 2003 ICR 337, HL (a race discrimination case) the House of Lords specifically held that it was unnecessary for a complainant to demonstrate that he or she has suffered some physical or economic consequence in order to prove detriment for the purposes of a race discrimination claim, although an unjustified sense of grievance could not, in their Lordships' view, amount to a 'detriment'.

4.110 Regulation 5(5) of the 1981 Regulations merely required a substantial change to be to the employee's 'detriment'. The importation of the adjective 'material' into Reg 4(9) was made by the Government at a late drafting stage, presumably to import an element of objectivity into the question of whether a substantial change has been made to the employee's working conditions. Although the

326

word 'substantial' – which did already exist in the predecessor provisions and which reflects the language of Article 4.2 of the Directive – already serves to rule out merely minor or trivial changes, the fact that proven substantial changes have now to be shown to be to the employee's material detriment suggest that the bar has been raised somewhat higher by the 2006 Regulations. It should, however, be noted that the word 'material' does not appear in Article 4.2 of the Directive. This raises the question of whether, if tribunals were to allow its presence in TUPE to limit the circumstances in which employees are entitled to treat the contract as having been terminated, the Regulations would be compatible with the Directive, as they are obliged to be.

Aside from this, the issue of whether an employee has suffered a material detriment is pre-eminently a question of fact for the employment tribunal to decide having regard to the relevant circumstances of the case. This was confirmed in Europièces SA v Sanders 2001 1 CMLR 25, ECJ, where the European Court stated that it was for the national courts to decide whether the working conditions proposed by the transferee involved or would involve a substantial change to the detriment of the employee.

Many of the points made above are apparent from the EAT's decision in Tapere **4.111** v South London and Maudsley NHS Trust 2009 IRLR 972, EAT – the first major appellate case to consider Reg 4(9). In that case the Appeal Tribunal ruled that an employment tribunal erred in holding that a transferred employee who had been required to move to the transferee's workplace under the terms of a mobility clause was not entitled to treat herself as dismissed on the ground that the change of workplace constituted 'a substantial change in working conditions' that was to her 'material detriment', within the meaning of Reg 4(9). Whether or not there is a change in working conditions is a simple question of fact. Whether it is a change of substance will also be a question of fact, and the focus in determining that issue must be on the nature of the change. In the sense that the employee will not be the arbiter of whether the change is substantial, it might be said that the approach is objective, but the focus in determining whether the change is substantial must be on the nature of the change in question.

And as for the question of whether the change was to the material detriment of the employee, the correct approach to be adopted was analogous to the issue of whether a claimant has suffered a detriment in a discrimination claim. In that context, the House of Lords had made clear in Shamoon v Chief Constable of the Royal Ulster Constabulary 2003 ICR 337, HL, that detriment had to be judged from the employee's point of view. In the instant case, the change of location meant potential disruption to childcare arrangements and a longer journey or altered journey which the appellant did not find attractive. The questions that ought to have been asked were whether the employee regarded those factors as detrimental and, if so, whether that was a reasonable position

327

for the employee to adopt. The tribunal, in determining the matter by weighing the employee's position against that of the employer and deciding that the employer's position was reasonable, had looked at the matter from the wrong standpoint and thus misdirected itself as to the correct approach to Reg 4(9).

4.112 By holding that 'material detriment' should be interpreted subjectively and in line with Shamoon, the EAT has made it relatively easy for an employee to establish a Reg 4(9) dismissal. The focus in such cases is therefore likely to be on the reason for, and fairness of, the dismissal. It is important to remember that, if the principal reason for such a dismissal is the transfer or a reason connected with the transfer (other than an ETO reason entailing changes in the workforce), the dismissal will be automatically unfair under Reg 7(1) – see under 'Automatically unfair dismissals' above.

The following employment tribunal decisions also serve to illustrate what amounts to a 'material detriment':

- **Royden and ors v Barnetts Solicitors** ET Case No.2103451/07: the six claimants were employed by LLW, a law firm based in Liverpool. In 2007 they were among 23 staff affected when Barnetts Solicitors (BS) won a £1m contract to provide legal services to the Britannia Building Society, previously held by LLW. The employees worked at LLW's Birkenhead office but, following the transfer, they would have been required to work at BS's Southport office or at the Bradford or Manchester offices of Hammonds, a legal firm that collaborated with Barnetts in fulfilling Brittania work. Southport was the only location to which the claimants would consider relocating but they were reluctant to work there and resigned on 4 June 2007 on the ground that the transfer constituted a substantial change to their working conditions which was to their material detriment. An employment tribunal upheld their claim, concluding that by insisting the employees relocate to its own offices, BS had imposed a substantial and detrimental change to working conditions within the meaning of Reg 4(9) and that the resulting dismissals were unfair

- **Collyer v Boots Opticians Ltd** ET Case No.2602275/08: C's contract of employment with BO Ltd provided that she was entitled to 39 weeks' sick pay, although it also made clear that the sick pay scheme was discretionary and could be withdrawn at any time. Furthermore, BO Ltd was contractually entitled to withhold sick pay if it thought there were reasons for so doing. In 2008, BO Ltd announced a proposal to transfer the part of its business in which C worked to a new franchise business. When C heard of the proposal she tried to transfer out of the optical side back into the main Boots organisation, where her employment had begun in 1992. Her manager told her that he did not think that she would be allowed to do this as an information pack stated that only those staff for whom a transfer had already been agreed would be allowed to transfer out once a franchise proposal had been announced. The new franchisee proposed that the sick pay scheme be amended to provide for just two weeks' sick pay. When C became aware of this, she lodged a grievance. This was rejected on the day before the transfer and she resigned immediately upon being informed of the outcome of the grievance and claimed unfair dismissal on the basis of Reg 4(9). An employment tribunal held that the change in C's terms of employment was 'substantial' and to her detriment in that, had it not been for the proposed change to the sick pay scheme, she would not have resigned and would instead have transferred to the new organisation. The resulting dismissal was unfair because BO Ltd had failed to show that there was a substantial reason for making the change to the scheme.

Change in employer's identity – a substantial change? Another difference in **4.113** the wording of Reg 4(9) compared to the antecedent provision is that the reference to the identity of the employer has been omitted. Old Reg 5(5) provided that the 'automatic transfer of employment rule', as well as the right to object to the transfer, was without prejudice to the employee's right to terminate the contract without notice if a substantial change was made to his working conditions, but that 'no such right shall arise by reason only that... the identity of his employer changes unless the employee shows that, in all the circumstances, the change is a significant change and is to his detriment'. Although there was a good deal of academic speculation as to the circumstances in which a concern over the changing identity of the employer in a transfer situation might form the basis for an employee claiming a significant change in working conditions to his or her detriment, this does not appear to have been raised in any decided case. Notwithstanding that the identity of the employer is no longer specifically referred to in Reg 4(9), it is arguable that, if the change in the identity of the employer is materially detrimental to the employee – perhaps where the transferee has a bad reputation in the industry in question – he or she can resign and claim to have been dismissed under Reg 4(9) by reason of a substantial change having been made to his or working conditions.

Before or after the transfer. Regulation 4(9) can apply where the transfer **4.114** *'involves or would involve* a substantial change in working conditions' (our emphasis). This suggests that the employee may rely on Reg 4(9) whether he or she leaves employment before or after the transfer. Any employee who so resigns is deemed to have been dismissed by the employer (i.e., we presume, by the transferor or the transferee, depending on whether the effective date of termination is before or after the transfer).

Requirement to give notice? We observed in 'Constructive dismissals' above **4.115** that constructive dismissal is defined, in S.95(1)(c) ERA, in terms of the employee's right to terminate the contract *without notice* by reason of the employer's repudiatory conduct. This is the corollary of the employer's right to

329

terminate the contract without notice if the employee repudiates the contract by committing an act of gross misconduct. Just as an act of less serious misconduct does not relieve the employer from the obligation to give full contractual notice before terminating the employee's employment, an employee is not relieved of giving the normal contractual notice before resigning on account of a less serious breach of contract by the employer.

With regard to material detriment dismissals, as opposed to constructive dismissals, Reg 4(9) is silent on the matter of whether the employee should give proper notice before resigning on the basis that the transfer involves or would involve a substantial change to working conditions to his or her detriment. Given that the deemed dismissal is only triggered by the employee's resignation, it is difficult to fathom whether the party who should be giving notice is the employee or the employer. On the one hand, if the employee's resignation is by reason of a substantial change to working conditions that does not amount to a repudiatory breach, the logical position would be that the employee remains obliged to give notice before resigning. On the other hand, this sits uncomfortably with the fact that the resignation is deemed to be a dismissal for all purposes by the employer. Where an employer does the dismissing, it is he (not the employee) who is usually obliged to give notice. Probably the safest view is to assume that an employee is in a position to choose whether to give notice or not before resigning. If, however, he or she gives only partial notice or no notice at all, a specific provision of the 2006 Regulations – Reg 4(10) – applies to relieve the employer of the obligation to pay wages to the employee in respect of the period of notice not worked. This point is discussed immediately below.

4.116 **No right to claim damages for lost wages**
Regulation 4(10) of the 2006 Regulations stipulates that 'no damages shall be payable by an employer as a result of a dismissal falling within [Reg 4(9)] in respect of any failure by the employer to pay wages to an employee in respect of a notice period which the employee has failed to work'.

The effect of this is understandable only in terms of the fact that, where an employee resigns on the ground that a relevant transfer involves or would involve a substantial change in working conditions, such a resignation is deemed to be a dismissal by the employer. Recognising that, normally, an employer would be obliged to give notice before dismissing, Reg 4(10) disentitles the employee from claiming damages for wrongful dismissal in respect of wages not paid during the period of notice in circumstances where the employee chooses not to work out that notice in full or in part. This provision was added only at a late stage in the drafting of the new Regulations, when the Government was persuaded during the public consultation process that it was not right for the employer to be penalised for failing to give notice of termination in a situation where the employee resigned but was treated as having been dismissed by the employer.

It should be noted that Reg 4(10) speaks of 'any failure by the employer to pay 4.117
wages'. In the absence of a definition of 'wages', it is arguable that damages for
loss of other remunerative benefits (including pension loss, bonuses, profit-
related pay and fringe benefits) during the period of notice would be recoverable.

It is not clear, however, whether Reg 4(10) affects compensation for unfair
dismissal. In practice, employees who trigger dismissal by resigning within the
terms of Reg 4(9) will generally seek to claim unfair dismissal rather than
wrongful dismissal. It may be significant that Reg 4(10) states that 'no *damages*
shall be payable', since this could be seen as suggesting that the provision is
directed solely at wrongful dismissal claims given that the word 'damages' is
usually reserved for the awards payable in respect of claims at common law.
However, if 'damages' were to be interpreted more widely to cover any form of
monetary compensation, then it is arguable that employment tribunals would
have to exclude any unpaid wages for any period of unworked notice from its
assessment of the compensatory award for unfair dismissal.

Advantages of Reg 4(9) claim over constructive dismissal claim 4.118
As already mentioned, it is apparent that claims based on a Reg 4(9) dismissal
can be brought in response to changes to working conditions that fall short of
a repudiatory breach of contract. For example, there would be no repudiatory
breach of contract (and therefore no basis for a constructive dismissal claim) if
an employer changed the place of work in circumstances where the contract
contains a mobility clause. But the absence of a repudiatory breach would
prove to be no barrier to a Reg 4(9) claim. Employees often regard the
circumstances of a transfer as being detrimental, even where the transferor and
transferee have fully complied with their legal obligations.

In determining the relative merits and demerits of a constructive dismissal claim
and Reg 4(9) material detriment dismissal claim, it is instructive to consider the
alleged breaches of contract at issue in the Rossiter/Air Foyle conjoined cases
(discussed under 'Background to introduction of new right' above). These
involved changes to the operation of a commission scheme and changes to a
shift pattern and, in regard to both, the Court of Appeal found no repudiatory
breach of contract. Although that was fatal to the claimants' respective cases of
constructive dismissal, it is highly arguable that if these cases were to arise now
they would be decided differently in view of the new freestanding right to
complain of dismissal where the transfer involves a substantial change to
working conditions.

There is also a good case for arguing that a reduction in occupational pension 4.119
benefits following a relevant transfer could be grounds for a Reg 4(9) claim. It
is well known that an employee's rights under an occupational pension scheme
do not transfer under Reg 4(2) of the 2006 Regulations, save for the limited
extent provided for by the Transfer of Employment (Pension Protection)

331

Regulations 2005 SI 2005/649. Furthermore, Reg 10(3) of the 2006 Regulations precludes employees from bringing breach of contract or constructive dismissal claims arising out of a loss or reduction in rights under an occupational pension scheme in consequence of a relevant transfer. This exclusion, however, would not appear to apply to claims brought under Reg 4(9), as such claims are not concerned with a breach of contract. Given the minimal obligations imposed by the Pension Protection Regulations on transferee employers to provide a replacement pension scheme, there appears to be scope for transferred employees to bring Reg 4(9) claims. That said, it has to be remembered that just because the employee is treated as having been dismissed after resigning because of a substantial change being made to working conditions does not mean that the dismissal is necessarily unfair. The framework for judging the fairness of Reg 4(9) dismissals is considered under 'Enforcing the right to claim unfair dismissal' below.

On the other hand, there are two positive reasons why an employee might wish to claim constructive dismissal in addition to making a claim under Reg 4(9). If a repudiatory breach of contract is made out:

- the employee would be entitled to recover payment of wages in lieu of the unworked notice period. This is not the case in a claim based on Reg 4(9) – see 'No right to claim damages for lost wages' above

- the employer might find himself unable to enforce post-termination restrictive covenants. The basic rule is that a repudiatory breach of contract by the employer prevents him from enforcing express clauses in his favour designed to restrict the employee in his or her activities once the contract has ended – see General Billposting v Atkinson 1909 AC 118, HL.

4.120 Interrelationship with the right to object

We saw in 'Constructive dismissals – resignation in anticipation of a breach by the transferee' above that an employee who objects to a relevant transfer under Reg 4(7) is, in the normal course of events, left high and dry as far as remedies are concerned, because the termination of employment triggered by the objection is not regarded as a dismissal for any purpose – Reg 4(8).

However, Reg 4(8) is expressly made subject to Reg 4(9). This suggests that when Reg 4(9) applies, it overrides Reg 4(8) – meaning that an employee who formally objects to the transfer under Reg 4(7) *will* be considered dismissed if he or she can show that the transfer would have involved a substantial change in working conditions to his or her detriment. Nevertheless, it would seem (applying the logic of the Court of Appeal in Humphreys v University of Oxford and anor 2000 ICR 405, CA – again, see 'Constructive dismissals – resignation in anticipation of a breach by the transferee' above) that the employee's Reg 4(7) objection to the transfer has to be respected. The remaining effect of the objection in such circumstances would be to disapply Reg 4(2) – that is, the provision providing for the automatic transfer of the employee's contract and the rights and liabilities arising from it to the transferee. Thus, liability for the dismissal under Reg 4(9) could not transfer under Reg 4(2), meaning that it would be the transferor who retains any liability for it.

Enforcing the right to claim unfair dismissal 4.121

Regulation 4(9) states that employees who treat the contract as having been terminated in the circumstances covered by that regulation will be treated as if they have been dismissed by the employer even though, technically, they have not. This raises a number of practical and legal uncertainties:

- is the deemed dismissal an 'express' dismissal, a 'constructive' dismissal, or neither?

- do the provisions of Reg 7(1) and (2) dealing with automatically unfair dismissal and ETO reasons for dismissal, discussed at length in this chapter, apply?

Each of these issues will now be discussed in turn.

Express or constructive dismissal? With regard to the type of dismissal that 4.122 occurs when an employee treats his or her contract as having been terminated by the employer under Reg 4(9), the DTI Guide comments: 'The Regulations merely classify such resignations as "dismissals". This can assist the employee if he subsequently complains [of] unfair dismissal because he does not need to prove he was "dismissed".'

The difficulty left unaddressed by this is that, in order to claim unfair dismissal, the employee has to show that he or she has been 'dismissed' within the terms of the ERA. S.95(1)(a)–(c) of that Act defines three types of dismissal, only the following two of which have any potential relevance for present purposes:

- where 'the contract under which [the employee] is employed is terminated by the employer (whether with or without notice)' – S.95(1)(a) (an express dismissal), and

- where 'the employee terminates the contract... (with or without notice) in circumstances in which he is entitled to terminate it without notice by reason of the employer's conduct' – S.95(1)(c) (a constructive dismissal).

It is by no means clear which of these two types of dismissal applies where an 4.123 employee resigns by reason of a substantial change being made to his or her terms and conditions within the meaning of Reg 4(9).

Given that the resulting dismissal is triggered by the employee's choosing to treat the contract as terminated, it could be argued that the dismissal 'reads' more naturally as a constructive dismissal within S.95(1)(c) rather than an express dismissal under S.95(1)(a). But S.95(1)(c) dismissals are traditionally

333

predicated on the employee's resigning in view of an employer's repudiatory conduct. This can be contrasted with the position under Reg 4(9), where the substantial change to working conditions need not entail a repudiatory breach or even a breach of contract at all. Furthermore, S.95(1)(c) speaks of the *employee* terminating the contract. This is not on all fours with Reg 4(9), which provides that the 'employee may treat the contract of employment as *having been terminated*, and the employee shall be treated for any purpose as *having been dismissed by the employer*' (our emphasis).

4.124 Given the difficulties with regarding a Reg 4(9) 'material detriment' dismissal as a constructive dismissal falling within S.95(1)(c) ERA, is it possible to construe such a dismissal as an express dismissal by the employer within S.95(1)(a)? Well, it may be possible, but this would not sit particularly easily with the practical reality of the situation. A decision by an employee to treat his or her contract as having been terminated, for all that it may be *deemed* to be a dismissal by the employer, is not self-evidently an express dismissal by the employer. Rather, the dismissal is a legal construct over which the employer can hardly be said to have much effective control. Furthermore, a major drawback of concluding that a Reg 4(9) dismissal is an express dismissal by the employer within the meaning of S.95(1)(a) is the potential onerous and unintended consequences so far as the application of the statutory dispute resolution procedures is concerned. This issue is addressed below.

Having said that, a slight alteration to Reg 4(9) would, it seems, be enough to bring such a dismissal within S.95(1)(a). Reg 4(9) states that 'where a relevant transfer involves or would involve a substantial change in working conditions [the employee] may treat the contract of employment as having been terminated, and the employee shall be treated for any purpose as having been dismissed by the employer'. If this were to be read as though an additional comma were inserted after the word 'dismissed – so that it read 'as having been terminated, and the employee shall be treated for any purpose as having been dismissed, by the employer' – it would become clear that the employee could treat the contract as having *been terminated by the employer*. This is exactly the phrase used in the definition of express dismissal in S.95(1)(a).

4.125 A third option would be that, given the 'hybrid' characteristics of a Reg 4(9) dismissal, it may be that that tribunals will come to regard this as a new form of statutory dismissal rather than a constructive or express dismissal in the traditional sense. But this would be problematic to employees seeking to bring claims of unfair dismissal under Part X of the ERA, since such claims can only be brought if the employee has been dismissed on one of the bases set out in S.95(1)(a)–(c). It would be expected that tribunals would want to avoid such an outcome since it would clearly be contrary to the legislative intention behind Reg 4(9).

334

On balance, the stance generally adopted by most legal commentators is that the deemed dismissal provided for by Reg 4(9) is a 'quasi-constructive' dismissal, falling within S.95(1)(c) ERA. This may well be right, but, as we have explained, the language of S.95(1)(c) would need to be stretched somewhat to permit the employee to claim unfair dismissal on that basis.

Assessing fairness or unfairness of a Reg 4(9) dismissal. The DTI Guide poses the questions (i) whether it is unlawful for the employer to make substantial changes in working conditions, and (ii) whether it is automatically unfair when an employee resigns because such a change has taken place. In answering 'no' to both these questions, the Guide states that 'to determine whether the dismissal was unfair, the tribunal will still need to satisfy itself that the employer had acted unreasonably, and there is no presumption that it is unreasonable for the employer to make changes'. **4.126**

However, the problem for employers is that in many such cases the sole or principal reason for a Reg 4(9) dismissal will be the transfer itself or a reason connected with the transfer that is not an economic, technical or organisational reason entailing changes in the workforce ('ETO reason'). There is nothing in the Regulations to suggest that the rules in Reg 7(1) and (2) dealing specifically with the unfairness of TUPE-connected dismissals, discussed at length in this chapter, do not apply to a Reg 4(9) 'material detriment' dismissal just as much as they apply to other express and constructive dismissals. So, unless the reason for the Reg 4(9) dismissal is found to be entirely unconnected to the transfer or, if transfer-connected, for an ETO reason, the dismissal will be automatically unfair in any event.

Which employer will be liable? It is important to consider whether it would be the transferor or transferee who incurs liability if the employee resigns on the basis of changes in working conditions within the meaning of Reg 4(9). **4.127**

Regulation 4(9) states that where a relevant transfer involves or would involve substantial changes to the employee's material detriment, the employee may treat the contract as having been terminated and the employee will be treated as having been dismissed 'by the employer'. The employer in question will, we suggest, be the transferor where the effective date of termination occurs before the transfer takes place, and the transferee where the relevant date falls after the transfer. Subject to what is said below, it is submitted that liability for a pre-transfer dismissal would pass to the transferee in any event under Reg 4(2) and (3) (for details, see Chapter 3) if, as is often likely to be the case, the dismissal is shown to be by reason of the transfer or for a transfer-related reason that is not an ETO reason under Reg 7(1) – see 'Automatically unfair dismissals' above.

This is subject to a single but important caveat. If an employee formally objects to the transfer, then, as we have seen above, Reg 4(7) precludes the contract of employment and the rights, powers, duties and liabilities under or in connection **4.128** with it from transferring to the transferee. Thus, where an employee objects formally to the transfer under Reg 4(7) as well as successfully claiming material detriment dismissal under Reg 4(9), liability in these circumstances would not be transferred, but would remain with the transferor.

4.129 Which employer will be liable?

We finish this chapter by taking a brief look at which employer – transferor or transferee – will be liable for various types of dismissal taking place around the time of, or in connection with, a relevant transfer.

In the normal course of events, it is the employer who actually dismisses the employee who will be liable if a dismissal is found to be unfair. However, the provisions of TUPE complicate this somewhat where a dismissal is found to be carried out by reason of a relevant transfer, or for a reason connected with a relevant transfer. In such circumstances, where a dismissal is carried out by the transferor prior to the transfer, liability for that dismissal might end up with the transferee. This is due to the following:

- as discussed in Chapter 2, Reg 4(1) provides that the contract of any person employed by the transferor and assigned to the organised grouping of resources or employees that is subject to the relevant transfer shall have effect after the transfer as if originally made between the person so employed and the transferee. That is, except where the employee in question objects to the transfer in accordance with Reg 4(7)

- as discussed in Chapter 3, all the transferor's rights, powers, duties and liabilities in connection with a transferring contract – including, that is, unfair dismissal liability – will transfer to the transferee

- however, as discussed in Chapter 2, a contract, and liabilities in respect of it, will only transfer under the above rules if the employee in question is employed by the transferor and assigned to the transferring organised grouping *immediately before the transfer*, or would have been so employed *if he had not been dismissed in the circumstances described in Reg 7(1)* – Reg 4(3)

- where an employee is dismissed by the transferor prior to a relevant transfer, he or she will clearly not be employed by the transfer *immediately before the transfer*. However, the above shows that Reg 4(1)-(3) will nevertheless apply to transfer liability for the dismissal to the transferee if the dismissal was carried out *in the circumstances described in Reg 7(1)*. That is, as we have seen in this chapter, where the dismissal is automatically unfair owing to its being carried out by reason of the relevant transfer itself, or for a reason connected with the relevant transfer that was not an economic, technical or organisational reason entailing changes in the workforce.

336

Put another way, the transferee will (almost) always be liable for automatically **4.130** unfair dismissals under Reg 7(1). The only occasion when it will not be so liable is where:

- the automatically unfair 'dismissal' occurs owing to the *employee's* decision to leave employment in the circumstances envisaged by Reg 4(9) (see Material detriment dismissals' above) or Reg 4(11) (see 'Constructive dismissals' above), and

- the employee raises an objection to the relevant transfer under Reg 4(7).

In such circumstances, the effect of the employee's objection is to disapply the rules in Reg 4 with regard to the transfer of liability to the transferee. Thus, in these narrow circumstances, liability for the Reg 7(1) automatically unfair dismissal will remain with the transferor – see Humphreys v University of Oxford and anor 2000 ICR 405, CA.

The following general propositions can be made with regard to pre- **4.131** transfer dismissals:

- if the reason for the dismissal is the relevant transfer itself, then the dismissal will be automatically unfair under Reg 7(1) (see 'Automatically unfair dismissals' above) and, owing to Reg 4(1)–(3), liability for the dismissal will pass to the transferee. That is, unless the dismissal was a Reg 4(9) material detriment dismissal or a Reg 4(11) constructive dismissal AND the employee objected to the transfer within the meaning of Reg 4(7)

- if the reason for the dismissal is connected with the transfer, and is not an economic, technical or organisational reason entailing changes in the workforce within the meaning of Reg 7(2) (see 'Dismissals potentially fair for an "ETO reason"' above), the dismissal will be automatically unfair under Reg 7(1), meaning that, once more, liability will pass to the transferee owing to Reg 4(1)–(3). Again, that is, unless the dismissal was a Reg 4(9) material detriment dismissal or a Reg 4(11) constructive dismissal AND the employee objected to the transfer within the meaning of Reg 4(7)

- if the reason for the dismissal is connected with the transfer, but is an ETO reason entailing changes in the workforce, the dismissal will not be automatically unfair under Reg 7(1). In these circumstances, liability for the dismissal (which might be unfair under the reasonableness test set out in S.98(4) ERA) will not pass to the transferee, regardless of the fact that the dismissal was transfer-connected – see, for example, Thompson v SCS Consulting Ltd and ors EAT 0034/00

- if the dismissal is unconnected with a relevant transfer – for example, a gross misconduct dismissal which would have occurred whether or not a transfer was on the horizon – the 2006 Regulations will have no impact, and liability for the dismissal will remain with the transferor.

337

4.132 What happens if an employee claims that he was assigned to the undertaking that was sold and should therefore have transferred to the transferee but he was retained by the transferor and was made redundant a few months after the transfer? Who is liable in such a scenario and when does the limitation period start to run?

We would suggest that the answer to this tricky scenario lies in who has dismissed (or is deemed to have dismissed) the employee. If the employee claims that he should have transferred to the transferee on or after the date of the transfer and the transferee refuses to accept the novation of the employee's contract, then there would be an automatic unfair dismissal claim under Reg 7(1) against the transferee – in which case the claim would have to be brought against the transferee within three months of the date of the transfer. If, however, the employee remains employed by the transferor and is made redundant several months after the transfer, he could still potentially make a Reg 7(1) claim against the transferor – such a claim would have to be brought against the transferor within three months of the dismissal (not the date of the transfer). If the unfair dismissal claim against the transferor is successful, it is possible that liability would pass to the transferee under Reg 4(2)(a).

4.133 Given these complexities, the transferor and the transferee should always be fully aware of any potential liabilities regarding redundancy and unfair dismissal, and consider carefully what warranties and indemnities – which essentially allow the parties to decide who is to bear the costs of liabilities for dismissals connected with the transfer – should be included in the transfer agreement. The practical issues that the parties involved in a TUPE transfer need to bear in mind are discussed at some length in Chapter 10.

5 Changing terms and conditions

<table>
<tr><td>

Overview

Varying terms outside a TUPE context

Varying terms in a TUPE context

Types of variation permitted by TUPE

Harmonising terms and conditions

Alternative strategies for effecting changes

Effecting variations – practical considerations

</td></tr>
</table>

It is a basic principle of employment law that an employer can only change a **5.1** contract of employment with the agreement of the employee. Any attempt by an employer to impose a unilateral variation of a fundamental term of a contract would constitute a repudiatory breach entitling the employee to resign and claim constructive dismissal. Even outside the context of a relevant transfer, it is therefore often difficult to change terms and conditions. Given that the purpose of the Transfer of Undertakings (Protection of Employment) Regulations 2006 SI 2006/246 (TUPE) is to protect the rights of employees on a relevant transfer, it is not surprising that transferors and transferees face even greater legal and practical difficulties when seeking to make changes to contracts of employment.

As we have seen in Chapters 2 and 3, employees are protected on a transfer mainly by Reg 4(1) and (2) under which the new employer takes over the employment contracts of all those employed or deemed to be employed immediately before the transfer. The transferee assumes all the rights, powers, duties and liabilities which the transferor had under those contracts and is bound by their terms and conditions as if he were the original employer. This raises the question of whether a transferee can seek to vary the terms and conditions of transferred employees. Although the EU Acquired Rights Directive (No.2001/23) does not contain any express provisions relating to changing terms and conditions, it is now well established through case law at both European and domestic level that changes made by reason of the transfer are, for the most part, invalid. New provisions have been introduced under the TUPE Regulations 2006 that are intended to give greater certainty as to when and to what extent changes can be made, and to codify the existing case law.

In this chapter we discuss the basic employment law principles relevant to changing terms and conditions; the types of change to terms and conditions that are permitted under TUPE; and the practical considerations that surround this issue.

339

5.2 Overview

The provisions discussed in detail in this chapter, which set out the permitted and prohibited changes to terms and conditions, must be considered in conjunction with the provisions in the 2006 Regulations governing unfair dismissal (see Chapter 4, 'Unfair dismissal') as well as the general common law applicable to the variation of contractual terms. Given the complexity of this area, we summarise below the main relevant provisions of TUPE in this regard:

- changes in contracts of employment are permitted if the sole or principal reason for the variation is either: (a) a reason connected with the transfer that is an economic, technical or organisational reason entailing changes in the workforce ('ETO reason'), or (b) a reason entirely unconnected with the transfer (Reg 4(5))

- any variation of a transferred contract of employment will be void if the sole or principal reason for that variation is either (a) the transfer itself, or (b) a reason connected with the transfer that is not an ETO reason (Reg 4(4))

- if a relevant transfer involves or would involve a substantial change in working conditions to an employee's material detriment, he or she is entitled to resign on notice and claim breach of contract or, if he or she has sufficient continuous service, unfair dismissal (Reg 4(9)). However, the employer does not have to pay the employee his or her wages for any period of notice in respect of which the employee fails to work (Reg 4(10))

- nothing in the Regulations affects the employee's general right to resign without notice in response to a repudiatory breach of contract by the employer (i.e. constructive dismissal) (Reg 4(11))

- a constructive dismissal or a material detriment dismissal will be automatically unfair if it is found to be by reason of the transfer or a reason connected with the transfer that is not an ETO reason (Reg 7).

The remedies alluded to above in relation to constructive dismissal and material detriment dismissal claims are discussed only in outline in this chapter. Full details are given in Chapter 4.

5.3 Varying terms outside a TUPE context

A contract of employment consists of all the terms and conditions under which the employee works, whether written, oral or implied. Occasionally, a power may be expressed in the contract itself for the employer unilaterally to make (usually minor) changes in terms and conditions (i.e. without the need for the employee's consent). But in order for such a term to be effective, it must be clear, unequivocally incorporated into the contract and correctly exercised.

This usually means that the employer will be expected to follow a reasonable and fair procedure when making any changes, including undertaking a proper consultation and information process (with union representatives if appropriate), giving reasonable notice of the change and obtaining the written agreement of each employee.

Options where employees refuse to consent to contractual changes 5.4
If the desired contractual change cannot be agreed, the employer has three main options:

- to continue seeking the employee's agreement to the change (possibly in return for a financial or other incentive). If the employee continues to work under the new terms and conditions without protest he or she may be deemed to have accepted the change

- to unilaterally impose the required variation and run the risk of breach of contract and/or constructive unfair dismissal claims (see below); or

- to terminate existing contracts by giving contractual notice and combine this with an offer of re-engagement on the revised terms and conditions to come into effect on the day after the old contract expires. In these circumstances, there will be no breach of contract as proper notice has been given. However, the termination of the existing contract may be an unfair dismissal unless the employer can show that the principal reason for dismissal was the potentially fair reason of 'some other substantial reason of a kind such as to justify the dismissal of an employee holding the position which the employee held'. For example, there may be a pressing commercial reason for the changes. In order to be 'fair', the employer would also have had to follow a proper procedure at the very least, and will also have to show that the decision to require changes to the employee's terms was a reasonable one in all the circumstances of the particular case.

The unilateral imposition of a substantial detrimental change to terms and conditions and/or the failure to follow a proper procedure when seeking to reach agreement on new terms may amount to a repudiatory breach of contract entitling the employee to resign and sue in a civil action for wrongful dismissal. Alternatively, so long as the sum claimed for breach of contract does not exceed £25,000 and arises from, or is outstanding on, the termination of employment, the employee is entitled to bring such a claim in the employment tribunal. Damages for wrongful dismissal would usually be limited to the salary and value of remunerative benefits that the employee would have received had he or she been given proper contractual notice. In addition, if the employee has the necessary qualifying service, he or she might choose to bring a complaint of unfair constructive dismissal in the employment tribunal. If such a claim succeeds, the remedy of reinstatement is potentially available, although in practice this is rarely ordered by the tribunal. Any compensation would consist

341

of a basic award calculated according to a set formula equivalent to a statutory redundancy payment and a compensatory award of up to (currently, as at January 2011) £65,300 based on the employee's proven financial losses.

5.5 Constructive dismissal and breach of contract

A constructive dismissal situation can arise if an employer engages in conduct that is a fundamental (or 'repudiatory') breach of the contract of employment, or which indicates that he no longer intends to be bound by one or more of the contract's essential terms – see Western Excavating (ECC) Ltd v Sharp 1978 ICR 221, CA. Whether the breach of contract by the employer is so significant that it is capable of amounting to a repudiation will depend on the precise facts. Common examples include unilaterally reducing pay or status, changing job function or duties, or withdrawing a significant contractual benefit. In the face of such conduct, the employee is entitled to accept the fundamental breach by resigning from his or her employment with or without notice. In these circumstances he or she is treated as having been constructively dismissed for both common law and statutory purposes, and can therefore claim against his or her employer for breach of contract and, provided there is sufficiently continuous service, unfair dismissal.

The employee does not necessarily have to resign his or her employment to take legal action in respect of a repudiatory breach. One option is to remain in employment and sue in the civil courts for breach of contract or, in a case where the breach in question relates to pay, to bring an employment tribunal claim for unlawful deduction from wages under Part 1 of the Employment Rights Act 1996 (ERA). The availability of this option was confirmed by the House of Lords in Rigby v Ferodo Ltd 1988 ICR 29, HL. If, however, the employee remains in employment after the repudiatory conduct, there is an ever-present risk that he or she will be found to have affirmed the contractual change, with the consequence that the right to bring legal proceedings for constructive dismissal or breach of contract may be lost. For this reason, such an employee is always best advised to signal in the clearest possible terms his or her continuing protest against the breach and to bring legal action at the earliest opportunity.

Note that a more detailed discussion of changing terms and conditions and constructive dismissal can be found in IDS Employment Law Handbook, 'Contracts of Employment' (2009), Chapters 6 and 7.

5.6 Varying terms in a TUPE context

When variations to an employee's contract of employment are effected by reason of a relevant transfer or for a reason connected to the transfer, the law governing the ability of the employer to enforce such variations is fundamentally affected. Precisely how is discussed below.

342

Case law background 5.7

Prior to TUPE 2006 the principles governing changes to terms and conditions on a transfer were derived entirely from case law. The leading authority was Foreningen Af Arbejdsledere i Danmark v Daddy's Dance Hall A/S 1988 IRLR 315, ECJ, in which the European Court held that the provisions of the EU Acquired Rights Directive protecting workers' terms and conditions of employment could not be waived by the workers whom they are intended to benefit. This was so even if the disadvantages resulting from the waiver were offset by benefits which, taken together, meant that the worker was not worse off overall. The Court, however, stressed that the objective of the Directive was to achieve only partial harmonisation across EU Member States in respect of the protections accorded to workers on the transfer of an undertaking. Thus, the Directive could be relied upon to ensure that the employee is protected in his relations with the transferee only to the same extent as he or she was in his or her relations with the transferor under the legal rules of the Member State concerned. This meant that if relevant national law allowed the transferor to change terms and conditions in situations other than a transfer of an undertaking, the Directive did not preclude such a change. But this was subject to the rule 'that the transfer of the undertaking itself may never constitute the reason for [the variation]'. The transferee could therefore change terms and conditions for reasons other than the transfer to the extent that the transferor could do likewise under the rules of national law, but the transferee was not entitled to bring about variations to the contract that were prompted by the transfer.

A similar refrain was taken up by the European Court in Rask and anor v ISS Kantineservice A/S 1993 IRLR 133, ECJ, where the European Court again confirmed that terms and conditions may be altered on a transfer only in so far as national law permits variations in contractual terms outside the context of a transfer, and always subject to the rule that the transfer itself cannot be grounds for such a change.

The rationale for the restriction on the transferee's ability to effect changes to a 5.8 transferred employee's terms and conditions was explained in Langeland v Norske Fabricom A/S 1997 2 CMLR 966, EFTA – a decision of the Court set up to deal with European Free Trade Association disputes. The Court explained that: 'The purpose of the [Acquired Rights] Directive is to ensure that the rights arising from a contract of employment or employment relationship of employees affected by the transfer of an undertaking are safeguarded. Since this protection is a matter of public policy, and therefore independent of the will of the parties to the contract of employment, the rules of the Directive must be considered to be mandatory, so that it is not possible to derogate from them in a manner unfavourable to employees. It follows that employees are not entitled to waive the rights conferred on them by the Directive and that those rights cannot be restricted even with their consent. This interpretation is not affected by whether the employee obtains new benefits in compensation for the disadvantages

343

resulting from an amendment to his contract of employment so that, taking the matter as a whole, he is not placed in a worse position than before.'

Until the well-known joined cases of (1) British Fuels v Baxendale and anor (2) Wilson and ors v St Helens Borough Council 1998 ICR 1141, HL, it was presumed that despite these ECJ rulings, employers in the United Kingdom could agree changes with employees on a relevant transfer in accordance with normal principles (see 'Varying terms outside a TUPE context' above). However, the House of Lords in the Wilson/British Fuels cases held that even if employees agreed to new terms and conditions on a transfer, they could subsequently reject these and rely on the previous terms as against the new employer. This did not mean that all variations of contractual terms and conditions – whether made at the time of transfer or afterwards – were void: a variation may be prompted for a reason or reasons entirely unconnected to the transfer, in which case it would be valid and enforceable by the transferee, provided it satisfied the normal principles for effecting a lawful variation of contract. The crucial question was whether the transfer was the sole or principal reason for the variation. If it was, then irrespective of whether it was agreed before, at the time of, or after the transfer, it would be void.

5.9 Lord Slynn, who gave the leading speech in the Wilson/British Fuels cases, acknowledged that it may sometimes be difficult to determine whether a particular variation is due to the transfer or is attributable to some separate cause, particularly in the case where the variation occurs some time after the date of the transfer. Interestingly, in view of changes introduced by the 2006 TUPE Regulations, his Lordship drew an analogy with the provision in what was then Reg 8(2) of the TUPE Regulations 1981. This provided that where the reason for dismissal, although connected to the transfer, comprised an 'economic, technical or organisational reason entailing a change in the workforce', the dismissal would not be automatically unfair, but rather would be judged according to the normal reasonableness test set out in S.98(4) ERA. Lord Slynn implied that where such an ETO reason prompted a variation of contract, tribunals would be justified in holding that the variation was not caused by the transfer and that accordingly it would not be void. This reasoning, as we shall see below, is now expressly incorporated into the 2006 Regulations.

Technically, the observations of the House of Lords in the Wilson/British Fuels cases were obiter because it transpired that the employees had been dismissed prior to the respective transfers for reasons connected with the transfers. It had been argued by the claimants that such dismissals were null and void in so far as they occurred for non-ETO reasons, and that this meant that the diminished terms and conditions on which they were subsequently re-engaged by the respective transferees were also null and void. The claimants argued that, as a result, they continued to be entitled to the terms and conditions they had enjoyed under their contracts with the respective transferors. In rejecting this

344

contention, their Lordships ruled that, although the claimants' dismissals were automatically unfair in that they did not satisfy the 'ETO' exception, it could not be said that they were a nullity. Rather, the dismissals were effective to bring their original contracts of employment to an end. When, following the transfer, the claimants were re-engaged by the transferees, they were re-engaged on valid new contracts the terms and conditions of which were not void even though they were less favourable than those on which the claimants had previously been employed. In these circumstances, no live issue as to the effect of an agreed variation between the employees and the respective transferees fell to be directly considered.

However, two cases decided at virtually the same time as Wilson/British Fuels **5.10** illustrate the principles with regard to transfer-related variations of contract as outlined in the obiter observations of the House of Lords. In neither of these cases was there any question of the employee's contracts having been terminated. They demonstrate that consensual change is not valid where the reason for the change is connected with the transfer and the transferee is unable to establish an ETO reason for the variation. In Crédit Suisse First Boston (Europe) Ltd v Padiachy and ors 1998 IRLR 504, QBD, three employees entered into restrictive covenants with the transferee, including a three-month non-competition clause. However, the employees resigned to join a competitor in breach of the clause. Even though the employees had received substantial financial inducements to agree to the changes, a High Court judge held that the transferee's attempt to enforce the restrictions failed because the change was in connection with the transfer. In so concluding, the judge specifically relied on the ECJ's ruling in the Daddy's Dance Hall case to the effect that the transfer of an undertaking may not constitute the reason for the variation of a transferred employee's contract of employment.

Similarly, in Crédit Suisse First Boston (Europe) Ltd v Lister 1999 ICR 794, CA, an employee entered into a fresh restrictive covenant after the transfer of a business in return for receiving a retention award of £625,000 in the form of phantom shares and a payment of £2,000 in consideration of agreeing to the new terms. However, the employee sought to leave to work for a competitor, whereupon the transferee brought legal proceedings relying on the restrictive covenant in an attempt to prevent him from doing so. A High Court judge refused to grant an interlocutory injunction and, on appeal, the Court of Appeal upheld that decision. In its view the judge had correctly concluded that the covenant was unenforceable in that the variation of the employee's terms and conditions resulting in the inclusion of the covenant occurred solely or principally by reason of the relevant transfer. This was so notwithstanding the fact that, on a fair view of the contract as a whole, the employee was better off by comparison with his terms and conditions under the transferor. Taking all of the rulings discussed above together, the following picture emerges as to what the position was prior to the enactment of the TUPE Regulations 2006. In the

345

absence of a transfer-related dismissal, the ability of transferees to renegotiate terms and conditions of employment was severely restricted. Any such change would be void if it occurred by reason of the transfer. This was so even if the employees had agreed to it and even if they were in a better position when their new terms of employment were considered as a whole. Changes unconnected with the transfer, on the other hand, would be permissible provided they complied with the normal rules governing variation of contract. Tribunals would be required to decide on a case-by-case basis whether any particular variation of contract was connected with a transfer – a task that was not necessarily straightforward, especially where the variation occurred some time after the transfer. Moreover, as a means of ensuring that contractual changes would be enforceable, it was open to a transferee, in the light of the main and binding part of the House of Lords' decision in the Wilson/British Fuels joined cases, to ensure that an employee was dismissed prior to any contractual changes being agreed. Obviously, any such dismissal might well be automatically unfair for being by reason of the transfer or a reason connected to the transfer that is not an ETO reason. But, ultimately, it would be for the transferee to assess whether, in view of the compensation that was likely to be payable, the commercial costs of such a manoeuvre were worthwhile.

5.11 Position under the 2006 Regulations

The 2006 TUPE Regulations now make express provision for the circumstances in which the transferee may effect a variation to a transferred employee's terms and conditions of employment. The position is largely a codification of the case law discussed above, although, as we shall see, a modification has been made to allow variations where the sole or principal reason for the changes is a reason connected to the transfer that is an ETO reason.

The basic principle is set out in Reg 4(4), which provides that: 'Subject to Regulation 9, in respect of a contract of employment that is, or will be, transferred by [Reg 4(1)], any purported variation of the contract shall be void if the sole or principal reason for the variation is – (a) the transfer itself; or (b) a reason connected to the transfer that is not an economic, technical or organisational reason entailing changes in the workforce.'

5.12 **Special rules in insolvency situations.** The first thing to note is that the principles set out in Reg 4(4) are 'subject to regulation 9'. That regulation deals with relevant transfers that take place within an insolvency context and provides for special rules to apply regarding the capacity of the transferor, transferee or insolvency practitioner to make valid changes to employees' contractual terms and conditions in agreement with workforce representatives. The policy behind this was to correct the anomaly under the old TUPE Regulations whereby it was possible, in order to ensure the survival of an insolvent business, for employees to be dismissed for redundancy or another ETO reason whereas it was not possible to preserve jobs by getting employees to consent to changes to their financial terms and conditions. The scope that the 2006 Regulations now afford for effecting variations where the transferred undertaking is insolvent is discussed in detail in Chapter 6.

Prohibited changes – Reg 4(4)   5.13
The basic premise of Reg 4(4) (set out above) is to render void any purported variation of an employee's contract of employment if the sole or principal reason for the variation is:

- the transfer itself, or

- a reason connected to the transfer that is not an economic, technical or organisational reason entailing changes in the workforce ('an ETO reason').

It will be seen that this provision essentially mirrors the principles that determine the lawfulness of transfer-related dismissals, which have been fully discussed in Chapter 4. Such dismissals will be automatically unfair unless it is for an ETO reason, in which case the question of fairness will be judged according to the normal reasonableness test set out in S.98(4) ERA. Analogously, a transfer-related variation will be void unless it is for an ETO reason. It follows that identifying the precise meaning of 'ETO reason' is a crucial matter when determining the scope for permitted variations of contract in a transfer context. This issue is considered in detail under 'Types of variation permitted by TUPE' below.

It should be noted that the prohibitions against transfer-related variations in **5.14** Reg 4(4) apply 'in respect of a contract of employment that is, or will be, transferred by [virtue of the 'automatic transfer of employment' rule in Reg 4(1)]'. Use of the present and future conditional tenses – '*is or will be* transferred' – shows that the prohibitions specified in that provision are intended to cover changes to the employee's contract of employment made either by the transferor prior to the transfer or by the transferee after the transfer, and includes the situation where a transferor purports to change terms and conditions because the transferee has insisted on this or in order to make the business more saleable. The extent to which a pre-transfer variation may be said to be connected to a transfer where a potential purchaser of a business has yet to be identified has not yet been the subject of any case law. However, the matter has arisen in the context of dismissal, and it is submitted that the same type of reasoning would be applied to variations of contract. The relevant case law is discussed in Chapter 4 under 'Automatically unfair dismissals – dismissals for a reason "connected with" the transfers'.

If contractual variations are attempted for either of the reasons falling within Reg 4(4), then they will be void even if the employee has received a payment or benefit as the quid pro quo for consenting to the changes. Depending on the nature of the variation and in the absence of consent, the employee may also be able to resign and claim constructive dismissal or material detriment dismissal (see 'Substantial changes to employee's working conditions' below). Any such dismissal is likely to be automatically unfair given that it will almost certainly be by reason of the transfer or for a non-ETO reason connected to the transfer.

5.15 Scope of employment contract to which prohibitions in Reg 4(4) apply. The scope of the contract that is subject to the restriction on variations stipulated by Reg 4(4) is fairly broad, since, as we have seen in Chapter 2, Reg 2(1) provides for a wide-ranging definition of 'contract of employment'. This extends to 'any agreement between an employee and his employer determining the terms and conditions of his employment'. The words 'any agreement' imply that the contract may be express or implied, written or verbal, and are apt to include any collective agreement from which the terms and conditions of individual contracts of employment derive. Thus, detrimental changes made to such an agreement – even if these have been collectively negotiated and agreed by the recognised union or other workplace representational body – will be void in so far as they are incorporated into individual employment contracts and have been prompted by the transfer itself or a reason connected to it that is not an ETO reason.

5.16 Sole or principal reason for variation. A purported variation is only void under Reg 4(4) if the 'sole or principal reason' for it is one of the prohibited reasons. Prior to the enactment of the 2006 Regulations, there was some confusion as to whether the transfer or a reason connected to it had to be the sole reason for the variation, or merely the main or principal reason. In Ralton and ors v Havering College of Further and Higher Education 2001 IRLR 738, EAT, the Appeal Tribunal concluded that, unless a contractual change is made 'solely because of the transfer', it does not fall foul of the Acquired Rights Directive as interpreted by the ECJ in the Daddy's Dance Hall case (see under 'Case law background' above). Technically, in view of other issues decided by the EAT in that case, its decision on this particular matter was merely obiter and thus not binding.

In any event, in the subsequent decision of Martin and ors v South Bank University 2004 ICR 1234, ECJ, the European Court appeared to accept that where a transfer is one of a number of reasons for a purported detrimental variation to an employee's contract, then it will be void under the Directive provided that the transfer is the main operating cause of the variation. In that case there were several reasons put forward by the transferee as to why it was necessary to harmonise early retirement terms of the transferred workforces with those of its existing employees. The European Court ruled that any consent given by the transferred employees to the unfavourable alteration of their early retirement terms was invalid in so far as the transfer or a reason connected to it was the main reason for the change. Although the Court did not specifically comment on the position where there is a multiplicity of reasons given for making a contractual variation, this was a matter that had been considered by Advocate General Alber when giving his Opinion to the Court. The Advocate General observed that there will seldom be only one reason for a variation of terms and conditions of employment. In order for the variation to be valid, it is necessary to show that the transfer was not the 'key argument in the reasoning, and thus not the main reason for the change'. On the other hand, there could be no objection to the employer making contractual changes that are otherwise permissible under national law where these are dictated by legitimate other reasons – such as economic, technical or organisational considerations – and are merely linked chronologically rather than causally to the transfer of the undertaking.

The wording of the 2006 Regulations now puts the matter beyond doubt by **5.17** providing that a purported variation will be void if the sole or principal reason for it is the transfer or a reason connected to the transfer that is not an ETO reason. This implies that, even if there are other subsidiary, non-transfer connected reasons for a variation, the variation will nonetheless be void provided that the principal reason is the transfer or a non-ETO reason connected to it.

Reason 'connected with the transfer'. As previously mentioned, Reg 4(4) **5.18** stipulates two reasons that render a purported variation void – i.e. the transfer itself and a reason connected to it that is not an ETO reason. In most cases in which this provision is held to render a variation void, the reason prompting the contractual changes is more likely to be one 'connected with the transfer' than simply the transfer *per se*. The DTI's 'Employment rights on the transfer of an undertaking: a guide to the 2006 TUPE Regulations for employees, employers and representatives' (the DTI Guide) states that where an employer changes terms and conditions simply because of the transfer, and there are no extenuating circumstances linked to the reason for that decision, then such a change is prompted by reason of the transfer itself. However, where the reason for the change is prompted by a knock-on effect of the transfer – for example, the need to re-qualify staff to use the different machinery used by the transferee – the reason is 'connected to the transfer'.

In essence, what has to be shown to make a purported variation void is a *causal link* between the transfer and the variation in question. This was made clear by the EAT in Wilson and ors v St Helens Borough Council 1996 IRLR 320, HL – a decision which, it should be stressed, remains valid despite the later judgments of the Court of Appeal and House of Lords in respect of other issues in that case. The Wilson decision was subsequently applied by the EAT in Lansing Linde Severnside Ltd v Spiers EAT 1490/01. This was a case where the transferee purported, as part of a post-transfer harmonisation exercise, to alter enhanced redundancy terms derived from a collective agreement that had been incorporated into the transferred employee's contract of employment. An

349

employment tribunal found the purported variation to be void because the reason that prompted it was intimately linked to the transfer. Upholding this decision on appeal, His Honour Judge McMullen QC observed that: 'As was made clear by the EAT in Wilson, in circumstances such as these there is to be consideration of whether or not there is a causal link between the variation of the terms and conditions and the transfer of the undertaking. If there is such causal link then the employee is entitled to be regarded as being employed on the old terms and conditions.' The EAT went on to point to the proximity of the variation to the date of the transfer as being a relevant factor, noting that, in the light of this, it was not only open to the tribunal to reasonably conclude that the principal reason for the variation was connected to the transfer but that that conclusion was 'inescapable'.

5.19 In Carlton Care Ltd v Rooney and ors EAT 112/00 the EAT speculated that there may not be a causal link between the transfer and a variation of terms and conditions if (i) it can be shown that, prior to the transfer, circumstances existed that would have entitled the transferor to vary the employees' contracts, and (ii) those same circumstances continue to pertain after the transfer. However, on the facts of the case, the employment tribunal had found that no such circumstances existed. The reality of the situation was that the transferee had effected the variation for a reason solely connected with the transfer. This was a decision, in the EAT's view, that fell squarely within the fact-finding responsibility of the lower tribunal.

The above cases all concerned post-transfer variations effected by the transferee, but the same reasoning would apply to pre-transfer variations implemented by the transferor. Cases decided in the context of unfair dismissal rather than contractual variation show that dismissals that are demonstrably linked to a contemplated transfer will be regarded as being automatically unfair under Reg 7(1) unless there is an ETO reason. The case law does not speak with one voice in respect of whether it has to be shown that a prospective transferee has actually been identified at the time of dismissal before it can be said that the dismissal is by reason of, or in connection with, the transfer. The weight of authority, however, suggests that it does not. Rather, the proper approach is to ask whether a transfer to any transferee who might appear, or a reason connected with such a transfer, was the reason, or principal reason, for the employee's dismissal – see Harrison Bowden Ltd v Bowden 1994 ICR 186, EAT; and Morris v John Grose Group Ltd 1998 IRLR 499, EAT. In the latter case, the Appeal Tribunal observed that, in determining whether an employee has been dismissed by reason of 'the transfer' for the purposes of Reg 7(1), no special significance should be attached to the fact that the definite article – 'the' – is used. It is not necessary for the dismissal to relate to the particular transfer that has actually occurred. This approach has most recently been endorsed by the EAT in CAB Automotive Ltd v Blake and ors EAT 0298/07. No doubt similar reasoning would be adopted where the issue is whether the sole or principal reason for a pre-transfer variation was the transfer itself or a non-ETO reason connected with the transfer for the purposes of Reg 4(4).

In Turner-Brady v Prospect Legal Ltd ET Case No.1101350/08 a contractual **5.20** variation that took place before the transfer in respect of T-B's notice period was held to be entirely unconnected with the transfer and was therefore enforceable against the transferee. Here, T-B worked for MBL, whose managing director was her father. Her contract of employment was transferred to the transferee when a third party terminated its agency agreement with MBL and took out a similar agreement with the transferee. T-B's contract originally provided for one month's notice but this was changed to six months' notice by her father to protect her interests in the event of a relevant transfer occurring. Following the transfer, T-B was dismissed by the transferee on one month's notice. An employment tribunal upheld the contractual variation as it was made before a transfer had taken place and before it was explored in any detail by the client company. T-B's father's motive in protecting his daughter did not invalidate the variation of the contract, and the transferee had therefore been obliged to give six months' notice of dismissal.

As a general rule, tribunals are more likely to hold that the provisions of Reg 7(1) dealing with automatic unfair dismissal and of Reg 4(4) dealing with contractual variations will apply where the relevant dismissal or variation occurs after the details of a transfer have been agreed between the commercial parties, or at least where it can be shown that such agreement was imminent. If transfer negotiations start weeks or months after the dismissal or variation has taken place, it is far less likely that the necessary causal link will be established. In Parmar v Ferranti International plc (in administrative receivership) EAT 710/96 (an unfair dismissal case) the EAT dismissed a claim brought by a former Ferranti employee against the eventual transferee of the business. Its reasoning was that because the employee was dismissed in December 1993 and the transfer did not occur until the end of October 1994 the claim against the transferee was 'almost bound to fail'.

It is suggested that, when determining whether a variation is void under Reg **5.21** 4(4), the following factors may be relevant:

- the time gap between the date of the variation and the date of the transfer

- the extent to which the variations were required simply to permit the business to carry on trading from a financial point of view

- whether the putative transferor expected or hoped to be able to dispose of the business by way of transfer

- if so, how long the transferor envisaged it would take before receiving an offer from a potential transferee.

351

5.22 **Relevance of effluxion of time.** In the Lansing Linde case (discussed above), the EAT specifically pointed to the proximity in time of the variation to the date of the transfer as evidence of the fact that the reason for the variation was connected with the transfer. (In that particular case, changes in the terms of a collective redundancy agreement incorporated into the claimant's contract of employment were proposed on 19 May 1999 to come into effect on 1 June 1999; the employee accepted the variation on 21 May; and the transfer occurred on 1 June.) This logically suggests that the greater the time lag between the date of the variation and the date of the transfer, the less likely it is that the requisite causal link will be established. Certainly, this was the view taken by Lord Slynn in the Wilson/British Fuels cases when he said: 'I do not accept the argument that the variation is only invalid if it is agreed on as a part of the transfer itself. The variation may still be due to the transfer and for no other reason even if it comes later. However, it seems that there must, or at least may, come a time when the link with the transfer is broken or can be treated as no longer effective.'

Misconceptions, however, have arisen in some quarters about when, following a transfer, it is 'safe' to start a process of effecting changes to terms and conditions. In truth, there is no specific length of time after which it can be guaranteed that the nexus between the variation and the transfer will be broken. The DTI Guide recognises this when it states: 'There is likely to come a time when the link with the transfer can be treated as no longer effective. However, this must be assessed in the light of all the circumstances of the individual case, and will vary from case to case. There is no "rule of thumb" used by the courts or specified in the Regulations to define a period of time after which it is safe to assume that the transfer did not impact directly or indirectly on the employer's actions.'

5.23 In Taylor v Connex South Eastern Ltd EAT 1243/99 the EAT held that the fact that the claimant's dismissal for refusing to accept contractual variations took place two years after a relevant transfer was not enough to negate the connection between the two events. According to the Appeal Tribunal in that case, 'the mere passage of time without anything happening does not in itself constitute a weakening to the point of dissolution of the chain of causation'. A similar conclusion was reached recently in London Metropolitan University v Sackur and ors EAT 0286/06, in which the EAT upheld an employment tribunal's ruling that employees dismissed two years after a transfer in order to effect harmonisation changes had been dismissed for a reason connected with the original transfer.

5.24 **Substantial changes to employee's working conditions.** Regulation 4(9) provides that where an employer (which means either the transferor or the transferee) makes substantial changes in working conditions to the employee's material detriment, the employee is entitled to resign and will be treated as having been dismissed by the employer. In effect, this provision introduces the concept of 'material detriment dismissal', although that expression is nowhere used in the Regulations. What is clear is that the right under Reg 4(9) is freestanding, in that it is in addition to, and separate from, any right arising, apart from the Regulations, to terminate the contract in acceptance of a repudiatory breach of contract by the employer and to claim constructive dismissal on this basis. To make a claim based on Reg 4(9), the employee has to show that there has been a substantial change in working conditions and that that change is to his or her 'material detriment'. Although this clearly rules out trivial or 'de minimis' detrimental changes, the resignation does not have to be in response to a change to working conditions amounting to a fundamental breach of contract by the employer, and so is not strictly speaking a constructive dismissal. The better view would appear to be that, even though termination occurs by reason of the employee's resignation, the termination is nonetheless to be regarded as a form of express dismissal by the transferor, thus giving rise to a potential claim of unfair dismissal on that basis. Any such dismissal, if shown to be by reason of the transfer or a reason connected to it that is not an ETO reason, will be automatically unfair. Chapter 4 contains a more detailed exploration of 'Material detriment dismissals'.

Types of variation permitted by TUPE 5.25

Regulation 4(5) of the TUPE Regulations 2006 provides that: '[Reg 4(4)] shall not prevent the employer and his employee, whose contract is, or will be, transferred by [Reg 4(1)], from agreeing a variation of that contract if the sole or principal reason for the variation is – (a) a reason connected with the transfer that is an economic, technical or organisational reason entailing changes in the workforce; or (b) a reason unconnected with the transfer.'

Thus, an employer – i.e. transferor or transferee – can agree with a transferred employee to vary his or her employment contract as long as the sole or principal reason for the variation is:

- a reason connected with the transfer that is an ETO reason entailing changes in the workforce (Reg 4(5)(a)), or

- a reason unconnected with the transfer (Reg 4(5)(b)).

If variations are properly agreed with an employee for either reason, there will 5.26 be no breach of contract by the employer and no cause for the employee to resign and claim constructive dismissal or to bring a claim based on material detriment dismissal (see Chapter 4 under 'Material detriment dismissal'.) But to be valid there must be agreement. Although no specific procedural requirements for gaining the consent of employees to changes are laid down in the Regulations themselves, it is vital for the employer to follow a fair procedure (including undertaking individual consultation and, where appropriate, collective consultation with union or elected employee representatives) as well as to

353

ensure that each employee agrees to the change in writing. A failure to do this might result in the employees bringing a claim of unfair constructive dismissal.

The two types of potentially permissible variations are examined in detail below, although in reverse order to that in which they are set out in Reg 4(5).

5.27 Variations unconnected with the transfer – Reg 4(5)(b)

A reason will probably be regarded as being entirely 'unconnected' with the transfer if it is unforeseen, unexpected and out of the control of the transferor and transferee. In Lorimer v Aberdeenshire Council EAT 0055/02 the EAT said that the test was whether there was evidence of a 'wholly separate cause unrelated to' the transfer, rather than whether, 'but for' the transfer, the contractual variation would have taken place. Examples given in the DTI Guide of reasons unconnected with the transfer are:

- the sudden loss of an expected order by a manufacturing company

- an upturn in demand for a particular service

- a change in a key exchange rate.

5.28 It is important to remember that just because the reason for a contractual variation is unconnected with the transfer does not mean that the variation is necessarily lawful. The normal rules relating to variation – as explained under 'Varying terms outside a TUPE context' above – still apply. Accordingly, the consent of the employee(s) in question will be necessary before any such variation is imposed. If, in spite of the employer's best efforts, such consent is not forthcoming, it will be necessary to terminate the contract(s) on proper notice and offer re-engagement on the desired terms (see under 'Alternative strategies for effecting changes' below).

5.29 'ETO reasons' for variation – Reg 4(5)(a)

The original intention of the Government when enacting the revised TUPE Regulations was to make it far easier for the parties involved in a relevant transfer to agree to binding contractual variations of employees' terms and conditions. The Government was mindful of the fact that the decision of the House of Lords in the Wilson and British Fuels joined cases – which confirmed that variations by reason of the transfer were void – had been greeted with dismay by many employers claiming they would be put off buying businesses if they were unable to harmonise or otherwise alter terms and conditions at the time of the transfer or shortly afterwards. In the event, for reasons explained below, the latitude introduced by the new TUPE Regulations for making contractual changes turned out to be a good deal narrower than first contemplated.

The solution settled on by the legislature was to permit variations, in so far as they are connected to a transfer, only if these were shown to be for an 'economic, technical or organisational reason entailing a change in the workforce' (ETO reason). The Government's stated aims in amending TUPE to allow for this were to:

- reduce disputes and thereby save costs for businesses and employees

- allow employers to negotiate changes to terms and conditions

- stop the risks of employers agreeing changes 'by the back door' by dismissing and re-engaging employees

- reduce transaction costs associated with transfers.

Is Reg 4(5) compatible with the Directive? The Government acknowledged in **5.30** its initial Consultation Document on the draft regulations published in March 2005 that the Acquired Rights Directive contains no explicit provisions allowing for variations to be potentially effective where the sole or main reason for them is a transfer-related ETO reason. But it reasoned that, since the Directive permits transfer-related dismissals to take place where the reason for dismissal amounts to an ETO reason, the same should apply with regard to contractual variations. Employers would otherwise have 'a perverse incentive... to dismiss employees and then offer to re-engage them... or recruit new staff on different terms and conditions', contrary to the policy aims of both the Acquired Rights Directive and TUPE.

Contrary to the Government's belief, however, it is by no means clear cut that the Directive contemplates variations of the kind expressly permitted by Reg (4)(5)(a). It is arguable that the Directive – as interpreted by the European Court – in fact precludes *any* changes where the main operating reason behind such variation is the transfer itself or any reason connected to it. The Daddy's Dance Hall case (discussed under 'Varying terms in a TUPE context – case law background' above) specifically established that a transfer of an undertaking itself may *never* constitute the reason for a variation in an employee's terms and conditions to his or her detriment. Nothing in the ECJ's ruling in that case or in any of the subsequent decisions where the Daddy's Dance Hall principle has been endorsed suggests that even a limited exception to this rule is permissible. Accordingly, it may be that the Regulations are, on a strict reading, incompatible with the Directive. But even if this is so, the breach is unlikely to have any significant impact in practice for the reasons explained immediately below.

Scope of ETO-exception very limited. The ETO exception in Reg 4(5)(a) is **5.31** unlikely to provide much scope for detrimental contractual changes to be lawfully effected, having regard to the way in which the expression 'economic, technical or organisational reason entailing a change in the workforce' has been interpreted. In this regard, it should be noted that the 2006 Regulations do not contain any statutory definition of an ETO reason, but it is highly likely that the same test will be applied to Reg 4(5)(a) as has been applied by the courts to ETO dismissals in the context of what is now Reg 7(2). This subject is discussed in detail in Chapter 4 under 'Dismissals potentially fair for an "ETO reason" – "entailing changes in the workforce"'. The crucial point to note for present purposes is that the Court of Appeal in Berriman v Delabole Slate Ltd 1985 ICR 546, CA, established that, for an ETO reason to 'entail changes in the workforce' in the context of dismissals connected with the transfer, there must be a change in the job functions or numbers of the workforce as a whole.

The Court emphasised in Berriman that the reason for the constructive dismissal relied upon by the transferee in that case – namely, to produce standardisation of pay terms – did not involve any change in either the number or the functions of the workforce as a whole. The most that could be said was that such an organisational reason might (not must) lead to the dismissal of any employees who did not fall into line, coupled with the filling of the vacancies thereby caused by new employees prepared to accept the conditions of service. This was not enough to establish a change in numbers or job functions for two reasons. First, the phrase 'economic, technical or organisational reason *entailing changes in the workforce*' (our emphasis) required that the change in the numbers or job functions be an integral part of the economic, technical or organisational reason relied upon by the employer. In other words, the employer must deliberately plan to bring about changes in the workforce rather than that being merely a consequence of, or incidental to, the employer's objective. Secondly, a change in the identity of the individuals who make up the workforce did not constitute a change in the workforce itself where the overall numbers and functions of the employees looked at as a whole remain unchanged. The word 'workforce' connoted in this context the whole body of employees as an entity, and corresponded to phrases such as 'the strength' or 'the establishment'. It followed from this that the dismissal of one employee followed by the engagement of another in his or her place does not bring about a 'change in the workforce' for the purposes of establishing an ETO reason.

5.32 One important aspect of the decision in Berriman was later clarified by the decision in Crawford v Swinton Insurance Brokers Ltd 1990 ICR 85, EAT. In that case, the EAT made clear that 'changes in the workforce' for the purposes of the ETO defence can also encompass changes in the functions of personnel without necessarily involving a reduction in overall numbers. Where the same employees are kept on after a relevant transfer but are required to perform entirely different jobs, the EAT confirmed, such an organisational change will 'entail a change in the workforce'.

Essentially, then, one of two things must be shown in order for any economic, technical or organisational reason for a dismissal or contractual variation to be said to 'entail a change in the workforce'. Either the employer will have to show that the reason 'entailed' (i.e. necessitated) a change in the numbers of the workforce overall, or the employer will have to show that the reason for the dismissal/variation involves a significant change in the job functions or job description of members of the transferred workforce. The upshot is that the exception provided by Reg 4(5)(a) will almost certainly prove to be very narrow in practice, since most variations in terms and conditions do not involve changes in either general job functions or the numbers of the transferred workforce as a whole. Any transfer-connected variation that does not result in one or other of these changes will not satisfy the ETO exception and will therefore be void. So, for example, an employer could not argue that he needed to reduce pay and benefits of transferred employees for an economic reason (e.g. to make the business more profitable or to forestall a financial crisis): altering an employee's financial terms is not a reason that, in and of itself, entails changes in employee numbers or job functions. Equally, while the transferee may reasonably be able to claim that there was an organisational reason for a change when, for example, new working hours or shift arrangements are implemented, it would have to go on to show that the change in working hours or shifts was bound up with a necessary change in job function or numbers. In most cases, this is unlikely. The same would apply to a post-transfer harmonisation process, since the motive to standardise terms and conditions across a merged workforce does not typically entail changes in numbers or job functions and so will not fall within the ETO exception. This point is amplified under 'Harmonising terms and conditions' below.

Changes to job functions. As stated above, the Berriman test requires a **5.33** wholesale change in the numbers or functions of members of the workforce in order for such a change to 'entail changes in the workforce' and thus come within the ETO exception. As we have seen, this hurdle is unlikely to be met in most transfer situations because rarely will the impetus behind effecting transfer-related contractual variations be to reduce the numbers of the workforce or to substantially alter an employee's job functions.

That said, it is possible to envisage situations where, for economic, technical or organisational reasons, the employer may be forced to change the job descriptions of employees who are or will be transferred. If such a reason is the sole or principal reason for the change, then, provided that the employee agrees to it, the variation will be for an ETO reason and therefore valid. Furthermore, if, in these circumstances, the employee were to refuse to consent to the change and be dismissed on notice for so refusing, then provided that he or she is offered re-engagement on new terms, the dismissal will not be automatically unfair under Reg 7(1). The employer will be able to rely on there being an ETO reason for dismissal, and in that case the fairness or otherwise of the dismissal will be judged according to the normal reasonableness test set out in S.98(4) ERA. The same reasoning applies if the employee were to resign and claim constructive dismissal as a result of a transferee's insistence that his or her basic job function change.

5.34 A key question in this regard is how wide-reaching a change to an employee's job description must be in order to amount to a change in his or her 'function', and thus to a 'change in the workforce' for the purposes of the employer's ETO defence. We explored this matter at some length, with reference to a considerable body of case law, in Chapter 4 under 'Dismissals potentially fair for an "ETO reason" – "entailing changes in the workforce"'. Although that discussion concerned when an employer might establish an ETO defence under Reg 7(2) with regard to a transfer-connected dismissal, rather than under Reg 4(5) with regard to a transfer-connected change to terms and conditions, we suggest that the same considerations will apply here.

5.35 Are beneficial changes void?

In Crédit Suisse First Boston (Europe) Ltd v Lister 1999 ICR 794, CA – discussed under 'Varying terms in a TUPE context – case law background' above – the Court of Appeal upheld a High Court judge's decision that a restrictive covenant introduced into the employee's contract by the transferee at the time of the transfer was void because the contractual variation had occurred for a reason connected to the transfer. Lord Justice Clarke, who gave the Court of Appeal's judgment, acknowledged that a number of difficult questions arose from the basic premise that a transfer-related variation cannot be enforced by the transferee. Chief among these was whether an employee would have the right to enforce any terms that were more favourable to him or her where these have been agreed by reason of the transfer. Although his Lordship did not provide the answer to this question as it did not directly arise for decision in that case, the weight of informed legal opinion has always been that there was nothing in the Acquired Rights Directive or TUPE Regulations to prevent the enforcement of varied terms which are to an employee's advantage, even if those terms comprise the quid pro quo for the employee agreeing to other terms that are to his or her detriment and which are therefore unenforceable.

This interpretation has been endorsed by the Court of Appeal in Power v Regent Security Services Ltd 2008 ICR 442, CA, where an employee was held to be entitled to enforce a beneficial contractual variation agreed immediately prior to the transfer. The variation in question concerned the employee's normal retirement age. The transferee had sent the employee a letter shortly before the transfer in July 2005 informing him that his contractual retirement age was to be increased from 60 to 65. However, two months later the transferee told the employee that he would be retired on his 60th birthday in November 2005. The employee brought a claim of unfair dismissal, in response to which the transferee contended that the variation did not apply since the employee had reached his normal retirement age of 60, with the result that he was barred from claiming unfair dismissal by virtue of S.109 ERA. An employment tribunal ruled that the contractual variation of the retirement age to 65 was void and so could not be relied upon by the employee. On appeal, the EAT ruled that the tribunal had erred. It agreed with the employee's submission that nothing in the Acquired Rights Directive was aimed at protecting the interests of the employer; nor was there any public policy reason why the employee should be barred from relying upon the variation. In the EAT's view, 'it would be inconsistent with the aim of protecting the workforce to refuse them benefits conferred by the transferee'. The EAT's decision, and the reasoning on which it was based, was subsequently upheld by the Court of Appeal.

The Court of Appeal in the Power case observed that the decisions in Daddy's **5.36** Dance Hall and Crédit Suisse merely established that, where an employee wishes to rely on a term in his or her contract with the transferor, rather than a term in a varied agreement with the transferee, he or she will be entitled to do so, and there is no need for an objective assessment of whether the original term is more beneficial to the employee. Similarly, where an employee considers a new term to be more favourable, there is no reason why he or she should be prevented from relying on it. In the words of Lord Justice Mummery: 'The safeguarding of an employee's acquired rights on the transfer of an undertaking means that a transferred employee, who wishes to take the benefit of the original retiring age of 60 agreed with the transferor, is entitled to do so as against the transferee. If the retiring age is then varied by agreement with the transferee, the employee must be treated as obtaining an additional right not as waiving an acquired right. His acquired right to retire at the original retiring age of 60 is transferred by the 1981 Regulations. The acquired right cannot be removed by his agreement on the transfer of the undertaking or by reason of it. There is, however, nothing in the European or domestic legislation to prevent the employee from obtaining an additional right. Neither the public policy reflected in the Directive and the Regulations nor the reasoning in the authorities cited by Regent prevent an employee from reaching an agreement with the transferee employer under which he obtains an additional right by reason of the transfer. The transferred employee can then choose between enforcing the transferred acquired right or the newly obtained right.' This meant, in the instant case, that the employee was entitled to rely on the contractual variation increasing his retirement age to 65 and was therefore eligible to pursue his claim of unfair dismissal.

The decision in the Power case was made under the old TUPE Regulations, but there is no good reason to suppose that the same reasoning would not apply to contractual variations governed by the 2006 Regulations. It is true that, taken at face value, Reg 4(4) appears to render void any and all variations – whether beneficial or detrimental – which are by reason of the transfer or a reason connected with it that is not an ETO reason. However, given the purposive interpretation applied to TUPE by the Court of Appeal in the Power case, and the fact that the Court referred expressly to both the Directive and the ECJ case law governing the matter, the overriding principle established in Lord Justice Mummery's judgment – that an employee should not be barred from enforcing more favourable terms – would apply just as much to Reg 4(4). In consequence, only changes that, from the employee's point of view, are detrimental will be void. The DTI's Guide on the TUPE Regulations was amended in March 2007 to reflect the stance adopted by the EAT in the Power case, which the Court of Appeal subsequently resoundingly approved. It asserts that 'the underlying purpose of the Regulations is to ensure that employees are not penalised when a transfer takes place. Changes to terms and conditions agreed by the parties which are entirely positive are not prevented by the Regulations.'

5.37 As a result of the Court of Appeal's interpretation of Daddy's Dance Hall, an employee who has entered into a new or varied contract with the transferee is entitled to choose whichever pre-and post-transfer terms he or she prefers. This pick 'n' mix approach is arguably unfair on employers who have offered benefits in exchange for contractual variations. It certainly seems to allow each contractual change to be looked at in isolation rather than taking account of the package of changes as a whole. What is clear is that it is the employee's and not the employer's preference that is important – i.e. it is entirely up to the employee whether he or she prefers the original term or the new term regardless of the fact that he or she has agreed to the variation.

It is interesting to note that, at EAT level, Mr Justice Elias in the Power case referred (albeit obiter, so the comments are non-binding) to the employee giving up any benefits obtained under the varied contract – reported at 2007 ICR 290, EAT. His Lordship suggested that there are powerful arguments as to why it may be an implied condition for relying on the original terms that he does forgo any advantageous terms accepted as a quid pro quo for other disadvantageous new terms. However, Elias J declined to offer any guidance on this point, since it was not at issue in the case. Nor, when the case was considered on appeal, did Elias J's observations attract any specific comment by the Court of Appeal. It therefore remains unclear whether a transferee could draft an enforceable agreement removing benefits from an employee in the event that he or she seeks to rely on more favourable pre-transfer terms. Until the matter comes directly before an appellate court for consideration, it will remain unclear precisely what the powerful arguments are that Elias J had in mind or the validity of those arguments in a TUPE context.

5.38 # Harmonising terms and conditions

Harmonisation, in the context of TUPE, is a process by which the transferee varies the terms and conditions of transferred employees so as to put them on the same contractual footing as those employed in its existing workforce. It was already clear from the cases decided prior to TUPE 2006 that post-transfer harmonisation does not comprise an 'ETO reason', since the process is invariably effected because of the transfer or a reason connected to it and, even if for an organisational reason, the standardisation of terms will not 'entail changes in the workforce' in terms of numbers or job functions as required by the Berriman v Delabole Slate Ltd test (see under 'Types of variation permitted by TUPE – "ETO reasons" for variation – Reg 4(5)(a)' above).

The facts of the Berriman case eloquently demonstrate how little room for manoeuvre a transferee has to harmonise terms and conditions if this causes disadvantage to the transferred employees. The case concerned B, who was employed as a quarry worker and whose contract of employment guaranteed him a weekly wage of £100. Following the transfer of the undertaking in which he worked, the transferee sought to alter B's pay terms in order to standardise his terms of employment with those of the transferee's existing staff. As a result, he was offered an hourly rate of £1.94 (equating to £77.60 a week) and an anticipated weekly bonus of around £22 in accordance with the transferee's current agreement with the TGWU. B refused the offer, gave notice of termination of his employment and claimed unfair constructive dismissal. An employment tribunal held that although he had been constructively dismissed and the dismissal was connected to the transfer, B's dismissal was not unfair because it was for an ETO reason and satisfied the reasonableness test under S.98(4) ERA. On appeal, the EAT reversed the tribunal's decision, holding that the reason for the dismissal (to produce standardisation of pay) did not entail changes in the workforce, so that the dismissal was automatically unfair under what is now Reg 7(1). In upholding that decision, the Court of Appeal, as has been seen, laid down crucial guidance as to how the phrase 'economic, technical or organisational reason entailing a change in the workforce' should be interpreted.

The Court of Appeal accepted that its narrow interpretation would have **5.39** adverse consequences on transferees' reorganisation programmes. The Court reasoned, however, that although unfair dismissal law outside the transfer context was generally sympathetic to business reorganisations, one of the main aims of TUPE was to safeguard employees' rights over a transfer and that had to prevail in a transfer situation. The same reasoning will no doubt apply to the capacity to effect valid transfer-related variations under Reg 5(4) and (5) of TUPE 2006.

The fact that harmonisation will be difficult to accomplish following a TUPE transfer is also shown by the decision in Martin and ors v South Bank University 2004 ICR 1234, ECJ. The European Court there confirmed that Article 3 of the Acquired Rights Directive – which requires the transfer of all the transferor's rights and liabilities existing on the date of the transfer to be transferred to the transferee – precluded the transferee from offering transferred employees *less favourable terms* in respect of early retirement than those provided by the transferor, and further precluded the transferred employees from accepting inferior terms. The Court ruled that the Directive does not prevent a transferred employee and the new employer making an agreement to amend the employment relationship, provided the transfer of the undertaking does not constitute the reason for the amendment. Where, however, a transferee merely seeks to align the terms on which it offers early retirement to transferred employees with those of its other employees, it is clear that the alteration of terms is connected to the transfer and will therefore be precluded by Article 3. In these circumstances, any consent given by the transferred employees to the unfavourable alteration is invalid.

5.40 These established principles were recently applied by the EAT in London Metropolitan University v Sackur and ors EAT 0286/06. Although that case was decided under the 1981 TUPE Regulations, the outcome would not have been any different under TUPE 2006. In August 2002 the University of North London (UNL) merged with the London Guildhall University (LGU) to form London Metropolitan University (LMU). LMU wished to harmonise terms and conditions by using the UNL standard contract for all staff. In September 2004, following consultation and some dispute with the recognised trade unions, the members of staff originally employed by LGU were dismissed and given offers of re-engagement on the new terms. Some of these brought claims for automatic unfair dismissal. The EAT held that the Berriman decision remained good law and that the tribunal had been correct to conclude that harmonisation of terms and conditions was not an ETO reason because it was related to the transfer and did not 'entail changes in the workforce'. There was no change in the numbers or job functions of employees in this case because LMU intended to retain all transferred staff in their existing roles.

The effect of the above decisions and Reg 4(4) of TUPE 2006 is that the purchaser of a business is denied the freedom of manoeuvre that an ordinary employer may have to alter terms and conditions for sound commercial reasons. If the transferee seeks to standardise terms and conditions as between the old and new workforce to the detriment of either, then any dismissals of employees who refuse to agree to the changes will be automatically unfair because they are connected to the transfer and will not be an ETO reason as defined by the Court of Appeal in Berriman. Given that the maximum compensatory award is (currently) £60,600, this route is potentially very costly. If the employer terminates the employment of all 'refuseniks', having offered to re-engage them on the new terms and conditions immediately after the transfer, then although the employee's loss would be reduced the dismissal would still be automatically unfair.

5.41 Acknowledging these practical difficulties, the Government has made it clear that it would have liked to have gone further in allowing parties to change contracts for the purpose of harmonisation, as long as employees were no worse off overall, and that it would in the future like to see the Acquired Rights Directive amended to allow this. However, the Government reluctantly concluded that, in view of the relevant case law, there was a very serious risk that widening the ability of parties to agree to vary contracts for the express purpose of harmonisation would be incompatible with the Directive as currently drafted. For that reason, it decided not to include a provision in the 2006 Regulations permitting post-transfer harmonisation.

In practice, some transferees delay the process of harmonisation so as to be in a stronger position to risk imposing changes (possibly as part of a wider business reorganisation) and to defend any subsequent claims of constructive dismissal by asserting that the reason for dismissal was 'some other substantial reason' unconnected with the transfer. However, as we have already seen, there is no 'safe' time limit for doing this. The question in every case is always whether the variation of contractual terms was made by reason of or in connection with the transfer.

Alternative strategies for effecting changes 5.42

Some employers have tried alternative methods of changing terms and conditions in an attempt to avoid the restrictions of TUPE, particularly after the decision of the House of Lords in the Wilson/British Fuels joined cases (discussed under 'Varying terms in a TUPE context – case law background' above). The most common of these strategies are outlined below. However, since the courts and tribunals will be wary of allowing any changes that are contrary to the basic premise that detrimental variations connected to the transfer for a non-ETO reason are void, none of the alternative methods are likely to meet with much success. Employers should therefore ensure that they are aware of the legal risks if they agree changes with employees which are not permitted under Reg 4(5).

Offering inducements/incentives 5.43
The transferee might seek to offer transferred employees financial or other inducements (such as a one-off payment, extra holiday or enhancements to fringe benefits) to encourage them to agree to the required changes in their terms and conditions. Harmonisation exercises outside a TUPE context often involve this kind of quid pro quo. The hope, so far as the transferee is concerned, is that such inducements will *reduce* the risk of claims being brought, especially if they result in employees being better off (or at least no worse off) overall.

But reducing the risk is not the same as extinguishing it. It may well be that an employee who accepts both the advantageous and disadvantageous variations will lose the right to treat the contract as terminated and claim unfair dismissal on the basis that he or she has suffered a substantial change in working conditions to his or her material detriment within the meaning of Reg 4(9). This would depend on how that provision is interpreted. There is a possibility that tribunals will be encouraged to adopt a 'swings-and-roundabouts' approach to the question of whether a substantial change to working conditions

363

has occurred. (For a detailed discussion of 'material detriment dismissals', see Chapter 4). But whether or not this particular option is closed off to employees, there is still the prohibition in Reg 4(4) to consider. Any detrimental changes would, in accordance with that provision, be void unless made for an ETO reason for the purposes of Reg 4(5), regardless of whether the employee has accepted an incentive or inducement in return for consenting to the change. In consequence, the transferee may well find that somewhere down the track it ends up in disputes with employees who claim that they can rely on their pre-transfer terms and conditions.

5.44 The abiding hope for employers in this situation is that, for an employee to be entitled to enforce the terms of the original contract, he or she would have to relinquish any advantages he or she received in return for consenting to new detrimental changes. In Power v Regent Security Services Ltd 2007 ICR 970, EAT, the Appeal Tribunal intimated that, if an employee had been given additional benefits in return for any changes to terms and conditions, he or she might have to give up those benefits before being entitled to object to the detrimental changes at a later stage. But these remarks were made only in passing in the context of a judgment whose main thrust was that the transfer-related changes to the benefit of the employee are not void. Nor did the Court of Appeal provide any further elucidation when the Power case was appealed – see report at 2008 ICR 442, CA. It may well be that future case law will develop the EAT's thinking in the Power case. But until then, employers should be cautious in assuming they can enforce terms to which the employee has agreed as part of a suite of transfer-related changes containing both new benefits and new detriments so far as the employee is concerned.

5.45 **'Red-circling' TUPE-protected staff**

The obligation under TUPE is to maintain rather than improve terms and conditions. If the transferee cannot obtain the consent of the transferred employees to contractual changes, he may agree to 'red-circle' their terms. This would entail agreeing to honour their better terms vis-à-vis the inferior terms of the transferee's existing workforce, but freezing the transferred terms by not paying annual increases until such time as the terms of the existing workforce have caught up. This option, however, assumes that the introduction of red circling would not itself constitute a breach of contract. If the transferred employee's contract provides for a guaranteed annual pay increase or uplift of financial benefits – as it might do, either expressly or as a result of custom and practice – then the act of freezing increases or uplifts would itself be a breach of contract. In that case, the imposition of red circling would amount to a unilateral variation of the employee's terms and conditions and would be invalid on normal contractual principles. Even were the employee to consent to the change, the detrimental variation would still be void if the red circle has

364

been implemented for a reason connected with the transfer that is not an ETO reason.

In Buchanan v Skills Development Scotland Co Ltd ET Case No.113105/08, B and her male comparator, S, transferred to Careers Scotland, part of Scottish Enterprise, in 2002. Both were employed as Customer Service Managers. Under the terms of S's contract at the time of the transfer, S was paid approximately £10,000 more than B. S was also entitled to contractual pay increases for the next two years, after which his salary was to be 'reviewed on an annual basis'. In 2004, Scottish Enterprise introduced a performance-related pay scheme (PRP Scheme) for all employees. The PRP Scheme allowed for certain employees' pay to be 'red circled' if their salary exceeded the pay grade for their role. Both B and S continued to receive across-the-board pay increases in line with the PRP Scheme until 2008, when their employment was transferred a second time, to SDS Ltd. B and another employee in the same situation brought equal pay claims against their new employer. An employment tribunal held that the incoming employers had been obliged to honour S's contractual pay and contractual entitlement to pay increases at the time of transfer. However, after 2004, when his entitlement to contractual pay increases ceased, Scottish Enterprise could not rely on the historical pay differential to maintain the inequality of terms. There was no evidence that Scottish Enterprise had given any thought as to whether it was obliged to continue the pay increases after 2004, let alone whether this was due to any continuing obligations under TUPE. Accordingly B's equal pay claim was upheld.

5.46 In any case, there are legal dangers for the employer even if there is no absolute contractual guarantee of pay or benefit increases. It has been established that pay reviews must be carried out in good faith and in a reasonable manner – see Clark v Nomura International plc 2000 IRLR 766, QBD. And in Glendale Managed Services v Graham and ors 2003 IRLR 465, CA, the Court of Appeal held that a transferee who was bound by an implied term concerning wage rises owed the general duty of trust and confidence to employees when exercising that term. A breach of that duty – for example, by acting capriciously in the matter of awarding basic pay increases or discretionary bonuses – would afford the employee grounds for claiming unfair constructive dismissal. In such a case, were the dismissal shown to be for a reason connected to the transfer that is not an ETO reason, then the dismissal would be automatically unfair under Reg 7(1).

Dismissal and re-engagement on new terms   **5.47**
The problem with terminating a transferred employee's existing contract of employment on proper notice and offering the employee re-engagement on revised terms is that, unless there is an ETO reason entailing changes in the workforce, the resulting dismissal will be automatically unfair by virtue of Reg 7(1). This may even so be a relatively attractive option where the difference

365

between the old and new contracts is not very great in financial terms, as this will reduce the level of any compensatory award payable should employees bring a claim of unfair dismissal.

It should be remembered that employees with less than one year's continuous service will not – as the law currently stands – be entitled to bring a complaint of unfair dismissal. This means that a transferee who wishes to effect post-transfer variations in respect of short-service employees may do so with relative impunity by terminating their contracts and offering re-engagement on the revised terms – provided, of course, that the notice necessary to ensure that termination occurs lawfully expires before the employee notches up a year's continuous service. It should be borne in mind that any previous service with the transferor is likely to be added to the employee's service with the transferee when calculating the total period of continuous service.

5.48 In any case, the strategy of dismissal followed by re-engagement is not one that should be embarked upon lightly. An employee in this situation has the option to resign with a view to claiming unfair constructive dismissal while at the same time accepting the new contract under protest. Alternatively, he or she may simply allow the employer to terminate the existing contract on notice, accept the new contract at the end of the notice period and then claim unfair dismissal in respect of the terminated contract – see Hogg v Dover College 1990 ICR 39, EAT (constructive dismissal); and Alcan Extrusions v Yates and ors 1996 IRLR 327, EAT (express dismissal). The employee's requested remedy is likely to be reinstatement on his or her old terms and conditions. Or, if pay or financial benefits have been varied, the employee might seek compensation to the value of the difference between the old and new terms. The fairness of the dismissal will be judged on normal principles – i.e. whether a sufficient business reason has been made out to comprise 'some other substantial reason of a kind such as to justify the dismissal' within the meaning of S.98(1) ERA, and, if so, whether the decision to dismiss the employee for that reason was reasonable in all the circumstances within the meaning of S.98(4). For further details of the law relating to unfair dismissal in this situation, see IDS Employment Law Handbook, 'Unfair Dismissal' (2010), Chapter 8.

It is also possible that if the employer seeks to use a compromise agreement as a mechanism for preventing an employee from commencing or continuing with a tribunal claim, a tribunal might view this as an attempt to exclude the operation of TUPE, contrary to Reg 18 (see below).

5.49 Transferees should always take on board that it is they who are likely to incur any costs associated with a 'termination followed by offer of re-engagement' strategy. This is so even if the dismissals are effected by the transferor prior to the transfer. Unless the dismissals are for an ETO reason, they will almost certainly be automatically unfair for being by reason of the transfer or for a reason connected to it within the meaning of Reg 7(1). As such, the dismissed employees will be 'deemed' to have been employed in the transferred undertaking immediately before the transfer for the purposes of Reg 4(3), which means that Reg 4(2) will apply to transfer any liability arising from their dismissals to the transferee – see Chapter 3 under 'Rights and liabilities relating to the individual'.

Compromise agreements   5.50

Compromise agreements may be used on termination of employment in order to preclude the bringing of tribunal claims by employees arising from that termination. In Solectron Scotland Ltd v Roper and ors 2004 IRLR 4, EAT, the Appeal Tribunal rejected the argument that compromise agreements entered into by employees who had been made redundant within months of their employment being transferred following a relevant transfer and who contended that they remained entitled to an enhanced redundancy package they had enjoyed with their original employer were rendered invalid because the agreements infringed the express restriction on excluding or limiting the operation of the TUPE Regulations in what is now Reg 18. The EAT accepted that an employer cannot, after a transfer, vary the terms of an employee's contract if that variation is by reason of the transfer. In the instant case, however, the effect of the compromise agreements was solely to compromise the financial claims that the employees had on the termination of their employment. The employer was not thereby trying to vary the employees' contracts, but to compromise a dispute as to their value. The fact that the dispute arose because of uncertainty as to the precise nature and scope of the terms transferred did not make the compromise agreements themselves ones which effected a detrimental variation in the terms of the contracts solely or even mainly by reason of the transfer. However, if, in contrast to the Solectron case, employment with the transferee were to continue on revised terms, and the compromise agreement is used to secure the employee's agreement to re-engagement on such terms, there is a high risk that a tribunal would regard this as a strategy to avoid the effect of Reg 4(4). This would go against Reg 18, which prohibits agreements that exclude or limit the operation of TUPE.

Delaying the change   5.51

Waiting for a period following the transfer before making contractual changes may not successfully reduce the risk of claims because the test is whether the change is connected to the transfer, and the effluxion of time does not necessarily break that link – see 'Relevance of effluxion of time' under 'Varying terms in a TUPE context – prohibited changes – Reg 4(4)' above. There does, in all probability, come a point in time when a variation will no longer be regarded as connected with the original transfer, but precisely when that point is will vary from case to case. This makes the matter very difficult to judge with any degree of certainty.

367

5.52 Exploiting the employee's right to object

Some transferees have tried to secure a variation of terms and conditions by the rather counter-intuitive route of getting employees formally to object to the transfer for the purposes of Reg 4(8). Such an objection, as we have seen in Chapter 2 under 'Objecting to the transfer', means that the employee's employment is not transferred to the transferee but rather is terminated in circumstances where the termination is not treated as a dismissal for any purpose. In theory, therefore, the employee could then be taken back on by the transferee on new terms and conditions without the protections of Reg 4 applying. The DTI Guide states that although continuity of employment will be broken, the transferee may 're-engage the employee on whatever terms they agree'.

However, in our view, the Guide may well be erroneous in this regard. In the first place, there is no reason to suppose that a break of continuity would occur unless there is a substantial gap between the date of termination and the date of re-engagement – see further Chapter 7 under 'Relationship between Regulations and ERA'. Secondly, and more importantly for present purposes, the Guide would appear to be contrary to the EAT's decision in Senior Heat Treatment Ltd v Bell and ors 1997 IRLR 614, EAT, in which it was held that any objection must be genuine and not a device to evade the TUPE Regulations. In that case, employees were held not to have 'objected' to becoming employed by the transferee in circumstances where they accepted the transferor's option of 'opting out' of the transfer of the business in return for receiving severance packages. Since the employees had, before the date of the transfer, entered into contracts of employment with the transferee to take effect immediately after the transfer, the EAT held that it was open to the employment tribunal to find that, notwithstanding their agreement to 'opt out' of the transfer, they had not objected to it. In consequence, the employees' contracts of employment were automatically transferred to the transferee and their continuity of employment remained unbroken for the purposes of claiming redundancy payments and compensation for unfair dismissal against the transferee.

5.53 Effecting variations – practical considerations

Even if a proposed variation falls within one of the changes permitted by Reg 4(5), the employer should consider carefully the strategy for effecting the change. Most importantly, it should be remembered that the general legal principles governing changes to terms and conditions will apply – see under 'Varying terms outside a TUPE context' above. A failure to observe these requirements will mean that the employer may become liable for breach of contract and/or unfair constructive dismissal claims.

368

In addition, there are a number of general points that should be kept in mind **5.54** when considering changing terms and conditions in the context of TUPE:

- potential contractors should be wary of pricing tenders for the supply of services on the basis that changes are going to be made to the acquired workforce's terms and conditions (for example, reductions in pay or benefits). If their bid is successful, it may prove impossible to effect the desired changes and/or be too expensive in terms of legal claims

- the transferee should always ensure that proper due diligence is carried out. This will include obtaining information on collective bargaining procedures, terms and conditions, details of all benefits and pension arrangements, pay reviews and other changes that may have been promised to employees. This will ensure that costs and potential liabilities can be quantified

- the reasons for any change should be considered very carefully to establish whether it is permitted under TUPE. Assuming the change is for an ETO reason or for a reason entirely unconnected with the transfer, this should be emphasised in the consultation process. There should be a proper paper trail and evidence of the employer's reasoning in this regard. In Banger v Pall Mall Services EAT 395/97 the transferee's argument that changes in terms and conditions were made for reasons other than the transfer was rejected because there was no documentary evidence of this

- the legal implications of employees not agreeing to a change must be properly considered. Imposed changes of a fundamental nature may constitute a repudiatory breach of contract entitling the employee to resign and claim constructive dismissal. But even changes of a lesser kind that are nonetheless a substantial change to working conditions to the employee's material detriment may result in claims of unfair dismissal

- the transferee should devise a plan of action in the event that employees do not agree to the proposed changes. In the absence of consent, the employer may need to resort to dismissal on notice followed by re-engagement on the proposed new terms (see 'Varying terms outside a TUPE context' above). Other methods of obtaining agreement may also be tried (see 'Alternative strategies for effecting changes' above), but it should always be borne in mind that the courts and tribunals are unlikely to allow an employer to use any method that is in reality a device to avoid the effect of TUPE

- even where a variation of contractual terms has been agreed by an employee, such agreement will not stop the varied terms being rendered void if the change is to the employee's detriment and the sole or principal reason for the variation is the transfer or a reason connected to it that is not an ETO reason. This principle applies even if the employee has received substantial consideration for agreeing to the change. Depending on the nature of the contractual change in question, it may be that the employer will only seek to enforce the varied term a long while after the transfer occurred – for example, a mobility clause. Even so, if the term has been rendered void by Reg 4(4), then it remains incapable of being enforced

- both transferor and transferee have a duty to inform and consult with workplace representatives of affected employees about any 'measures' that either party envisages taking in connection with the transfer, or in relation to any affected employee (Reg 13(2)(c)). The transferor is under the additional duty to inform and consult the representatives about the measures, in connection with the transfer, that he envisages the transferee will take in relation to any affected employees who will become employees of the transferee after the transfer by virtue of Reg 4 (Reg 13(2)(d)). Both these duties would include any planned dismissals or changes in terms and conditions. In the absence of elected workplace representatives, the employer must provide the requisite information to the affected employees themselves. Failure to inform and consult properly could result in a tribunal awarding compensation to employees. It is crucial, therefore, that a realistic timetable be set out for the consultation process. Employees would have to be made aware of any time limits for agreeing to changes and the consequences of declining to agree. For full details of the information and consultation rights and duties in the TUPE Regulations, see Chapter 8.

5.55 If the employer decides to adopt a strategy of dismissing and re-engaging employees on new terms and conditions, then depending on the number of employees to be dismissed, the employer would also need to follow a collective redundancy consultation procedure. Full contractual notice would also have to be given to each employee, and new contracts issued to take effect when that notice expires. Details of the collective consultation procedure can be found in IDS Employment Law Handbook, 'Redundancy' (August 2008), Chapter 11.

6 Transfer of insolvent companies

European law background

Types of insolvency procedures

Outline of insolvency provisions in TUPE

Bankruptcy and liquidation proceedings

'Relevant insolvency proceedings'

Dismissal by insolvency practitioners

Information and consultation

Notification of employee liability information

Hiving down

An insolvency situation arises when a business, or an individual, is unable to **6.1** meet its financial liabilities. This difficulty can arise for many reasons – for example, under-capitalisation, imprudent business judgement or unforeseen circumstances such as loss of a crucial order or client. The type of insolvency proceedings used in each case depends mainly on the level of debt and whether or not the business can be continued as a going concern. However, in most types of proceedings a qualified insolvency practitioner is appointed to maximise the recovery of assets for the benefit of creditors. Depending on the type of procedure, the insolvency practitioner will generally be a liquidator, administrative receiver, receiver or administrator.

At the time the original TUPE Regulations were enacted in 1981, the UK Government clearly intended that the protections contained in them should apply to transfers of undertakings in the context of insolvency just as they applied to any other type of relevant transfer. The only provision that was made to deal specifically with insolvency was Reg 4, which dealt with transfers by receivers, liquidators and administrators in a 'hiving down' situation. This is an insolvency procedure by which employees are retained within the insolvent company while the assets of that company are transferred to the outside purchaser (see under 'Hiving down' at the very end of this chapter).

The position that now obtains under the Transfer of Undertakings (Protection **6.2** of Employment) Regulations 2006 SI 2006/246 (TUPE) has been radically altered. It remains the case that if a business cannot be continued and is wound up, the employment of all employees employed in that business will be terminated and there will be no question of the TUPE Regulations applying.

371

However, where a business, or the underlying profitable part of it, is continued and subsequently sold, the TUPE Regulations may apply. In practice this happens quite often. Although it is rare for the insolvency practitioner to sell the entire company itself because a potential purchaser will be put off by the fact that, as a corporate legal entity, it will remain liable for all the debts owed to its creditors, the viable part of the company is often sold off so that it can continue to trade under new ownership as a going concern.

A detailed analysis of insolvency law and insolvency procedures is beyond the scope of this Handbook and specialist advice should always be sought in respect of these matters. However, an overview of the procedures is given below, since certain of these trigger application of the provisions contained within Regs 8 and 9 of the TUPE Regulations 2006. These in effect modify the normal TUPE rules in the event of a relevant transfer occurring of an insolvent business or part of a business. This chapter therefore discusses the following issues:

- the way in which the TUPE Regulations 1981 applied to insolvency proceedings and the changes introduced by Regs 8 and 9 of the 2006 Regulations

- the main types of insolvency proceedings and the extent to which these have an effect on the employment contracts of those employed in the insolvent business

- the specific limitations contained in Reg 8 regarding the transfer of employee debts and liabilities to the transferee in respect of where the transferor is subject to certain insolvency proceedings, and the disapplication of the automatic transfer of employment rule in Reg 4 and the provisions dealing with unfair dismissal in Reg 7 in respect of certain insolvent liquidations

- the special provision made in Reg 9 for permitting employees' terms and conditions of employment to be varied where the transferor is subject to certain insolvency proceedings

- the extent to which the unfair dismissal provisions of Reg 7 apply in the case of employees who are dismissed by insolvency practitioners

- the practical issues relevant to information and consultation and the notification of employee liability information when the transferor is subject to insolvency proceedings.

6.3 European law background

The EU Acquired Rights Directive 1977 (No.77/187) and its implementation in the United Kingdom through the TUPE Regulations 1981 is outlined in the Introduction to this Handbook. In this section we consider how the Directive applied to the disposition of businesses that were subject to insolvency proceedings. This background is relevant to the way in which the 1977 Directive was amended to deal with transfers of insolvent undertakings, and accordingly to the interpretation of the TUPE Regulations 2006, which give effect to those amendments.

The 1977 Directive initially made no express provision in relation to businesses which were transferred in the context of insolvency proceedings. This led to a substantial amount of case law concerning the scope of the Directive with regard to such transfers. The first major consideration of this issue by the European Court of Justice was in Abels v Administrative Board of the Bedrijfsvereniging voor de Metaalindustrie en de Electrotechnische Industrie 1987 2 CMLR 406, ECJ. According to the ECJ, the Directive did not apply to the transfer of an undertaking where the transferor has been declared insolvent with a view to the realisation and distribution of the undertaking's assets on behalf of its creditors. The Court reasoned that, as the paramount purpose of the Directive was to protect the rights of workers, that aim in the context of insolvency would not be best achieved by applying the provisions to sales of insolvent businesses by liquidators because potential purchasers might be deterred by the prospect of having to take on all the workers employed by the insolvent company. However, the Court qualified this by confirming that the Directive was applicable to a judicially controlled procedure where the primary aim was to protect the assets of the undertaking and to ensure that it continued to trade by means of an agreement to suspend payment of the transferor's debts. This created some confusion about whether it was the degree of control exercised by the judicial or administrative authority over the transfer, or the purpose of the insolvency procedure in question, which determined whether the Directive applied.

6.4 The position was clarified by the ECJ in its subsequent ruling in D'Urso and ors v Ercole Marelli Elettromeccanica Generale SpA (in special administration) and ors 1992 IRLR 136, ECJ. There, the Court held that the Directive did, in fact, apply to the transfer of an insolvent business where the purpose of the insolvency procedure was to enable the undertaking to continue trading. The only circumstances in which it did not apply was in the context of compulsory liquidation proceedings designed to dispose of an insolvent company's assets rather than of the business (or part business) as a going concern. In Jules Dethier Équipement SA v Dassy and anor 1998 ICR 541, ECJ, the European Court reiterated that the 1977 Directive would apply where the substance and form of the insolvency proceeding was to allow the business to trade with the aim of making it commercially viable in the longer term.

New 'rescue culture' options
6.5 Amendments to the 1977 Directive made by EU Directive 98/50 codified the position as confirmed by the case law of the European Court discussed above. In particular, new Article 4A provided that: 'Unless Member States provide

otherwise, Articles 3 and 4 [providing for transfer of employment liabilities on a relevant transfer] shall not apply to any transfer of an undertaking, business or part of an undertaking or business where the transferor is the subject of bankruptcy proceedings or analogous insolvency proceedings which have been instituted with a view to the liquidation of the assets of the transferor and are under the supervision of a competent public authority (which may be an insolvency practitioner authorised by a competent public authority).' This wording was retained when the Acquired Rights Directive was reissued in 2001 (EU Directive 2001/23). The provision – which is now to be found in Article 5.1 of the 2001 Directive – is considered in detail under 'Bankruptcy and liquidation proceedings' below.

In addition to the right in Article 5.1 to exclude application of the normal protections on a transfer in a situation where the transferor is subject to bankruptcy or analogous insolvency proceedings, Article 5.2 of the 2001 Directive confers on EU Member States scope for enacting limitations on the protections otherwise guaranteed by the Directive in cases where insolvent businesses (or parts of businesses) are sold or otherwise disposed of. The policy objective behind these options is to increase the chances that the viable parts of insolvent businesses can be sold as going concerns, and therefore maximise the chance that some employees will be retained in those businesses. In this regard, Member States are given the following two options:

- to legislate to prevent the transferor's pre-existing debts towards affected employees from passing to the transferee – Article 5.2(a); and/or

- to allow the transferor, transferee or insolvency practitioner and employees' representatives to negotiate changes to terms and conditions of employment (in so far as current national law permits) if this is done with a view to ensuring the survival of the business and the preservation of jobs – Article 5.2(b).

6.6 These options were introduced in response to the trend across Europe towards legislating to promote a 'rescue culture' for insolvent businesses. As we shall see, the provisions of Article 5.1 and 5.2 provide the platform for the new regime put into place by the 2006 TUPE Regulations for dealing with relevant transfers of businesses within an insolvency context.

6.7 Implementation of Article 5 options into UK law

In the light of European case law interpreting the Acquired Rights Directive (see above), there is no doubt that the 1981 TUPE Regulations were in harmony with the requirements of the Directive as it applied at that time. The Regulations applied to any transfer of an insolvent business as a going concern and that is what the Directive also required, as confirmed by the ECJ in the D'Urso and Jules Dethier cases.

374

The only issue that remained unclear was the extent to which the TUPE Regulations applied to liquidations designed to dispose of the assets of an insolvent company. Initially, the EAT's view – as expressed in Belhaven Brewery Co Ltd v Berekis and ors EAT 724/92 – was that a relevant transfer occurred when individuals running a business were declared bankrupt and a trustee in bankruptcy was appointed to manage their affairs. A further transfer then occurred when the trustee subsequently transferred the business to new management. However, in the later decision of Perth and Kinross Council v Donaldson and ors 2004 IRLR 121, EAT, the Appeal Tribunal concluded that, since the ECJ had made it clear that the Directive did not apply in a case of irretrievable insolvency and cessation of business, neither could the 1981 TUPE Regulations apply in that situation. The fact that the Directive was implemented into UK law by subsidiary legislation meant that that legislation (i.e. the TUPE Regulations) could not go beyond the scope of the protection provided by the Directive. There was accordingly no relevant transfer when a local council took back work that it had contracted out to a company that had been subject to liquidation proceedings and had ceased to trade.

The EAT's reasoning in the Perth case is open to question in view of later **6.8** decisions confirming that it is permissible for statutory regulations made under the powers conferred by S.2 of the European Communities Act 1972 to confer wider protection than that provided for by the European Directives on which the TUPE Regulations are based – see Numast and anor v P & O Scottish Ferries Ltd and ors EAT 0060/04. But in any event this controversy has now been overtaken by the adoption of the 'rescue culture' options contained in the 2001 Acquired Rights Directive.

When enacting the 2006 TUPE Regulations, the Government chose to take up all of the options available to it under Article 5 of the Acquired Rights Directive as outlined under 'European law background' above. In so doing, it introduced a radically different legislative regime from the one that applied under the predecessor Regulations, which (apart from the specific provision covering hiving-down situations mentioned above) contained no special provisions dealing with insolvency transfers. In its consultation and guidance papers on the 2006 Regulations, the Government stressed that its main objective as regards the insolvency changes was to promote the 'rescue culture'. With more flexibility in the application of TUPE and a reduction of the financial burden on the transferee, insolvent businesses had a better chance of remaining viable, with a resulting saving of jobs. The changes also took into account the leading TUPE cases decided under the 1981 Regulations relating to insolvency proceedings.

375

6.9 Types of insolvency procedures

If a business gets into extreme financial difficulties, an insolvency practitioner can be appointed either to wind up the business or to keep it running with a view to the sale of the whole or part of it as a going concern. Once appointed, the insolvency practitioner will normally want to sell the business as soon as possible to avoid a depletion in its value. As we shall see, the nature of the particular insolvency proceedings is the determining factor in ascertaining whether and to what extent the key protections in the TUPE Regulations apply when an insolvency practitioner disposes of an insolvent business to an outside purchaser.

6.10 Personal bankruptcy

Bankruptcy only applies to insolvent individuals (although individuals in a partnership can be made bankrupt). The TUPE Regulations are not usually relevant to these situations unless a sole trader or other individual is the employer and his or her business is sold to an outside purchaser in the course of bankruptcy proceedings. For this reason, and also because the definition of 'relevant insolvency proceedings' in Reg 8(7) specifically refers to bankruptcy, it is appropriate to consider personal bankruptcy briefly here.

Bankruptcy proceedings commence when a bankruptcy order is made by the court following a petition usually presented by a creditor who is owed more than £750 or the individual himself, on the grounds that he or she cannot pay his or her debts. Once the order is made, control over the bankrupt's assets passes to a trustee in bankruptcy whose function is to collect in those assets and distribute them to creditors. The trustee in bankruptcy has very wide powers, including the power to sell the bankrupt's assets and carry on his or her business as well as wide investigatory powers. The bankrupt loses any rights to that property other than those required to meet his or her basic domestic and business needs. Creditors are paid in the preferential order prescribed by law: the costs of the bankruptcy proceedings first, followed by payment of debts owed to secured and preferential creditors, and then, if there are sufficient funds, payments to unsecured creditors. The bankrupt is normally discharged from bankruptcy automatically after one year, or earlier if appropriate.

6.11 The appointment of a trustee in bankruptcy does not necessarily terminate the contracts of employment of anyone personally employed by the bankrupt – see Thomas v Williams 1834 1 Ad & EL 685, Ct of King's Bench – although this may be the effect if the court appoints a receiver over the bankrupt's affairs – see Reid v Explosives Co Ltd 1887 19 QBD 264, CA. If the trustee opts to carry on the business, this may well constitute a TUPE transfer of the business to the trustee in the sense that the responsibility for operating the business has changed hands. This assumes that what has transferred is an economic entity. In this situation, it might be thought that the usual TUPE protections would apply to any employee employed by the transferor (i.e. the person declared bankrupt) and assigned to the business, and, indeed that is precisely what the position was under the 1981 TUPE Regulations – see Belhaven Brewery Ltd v Berekis and anor EAT 724/92. However, as we shall see, Regs 4 and 7 (which deal with the transfer of employment and special protection against unfair dismissal in a TUPE context) would now be excluded by virtue of Reg 8(7) of the 2006 Regulations – see under 'Bankruptcy and liquidation proceedings' below. This would also be true if the bankrupt's insolvent business is subsequently sold on by the trustee as a going concern.

An individual who is in financial difficulties can also ask his or her creditors to agree to an individual voluntary arrangement, which will provide some protection in relation to those creditors for a specified period of time, normally one to five years – see under 'Voluntary arrangements' below.

Liquidation (winding-up)   6.12
As well as being a stand-alone procedure, liquidation, or winding up, can be used following a receivership or administration. The main tasks of a liquidator are to take over the powers of the directors and management of the business, realise the assets of the business, and use the proceeds to pay the debts of the business in the order prescribed by insolvency legislation. As soon as the winding-up commences, the liquidator is permitted to carry on the business only so far as may be necessary for its 'beneficial winding-up' – para 5, Sch 4 Insolvency Act 1986 (IA). In practice, he or she will generally run the business down while liquidating its assets, with the result that all contracts of employment will eventually be terminated. Once the liquidation process is completed, the company is dissolved and struck off the Companies Register at Companies House.

There are three different types of liquidation. These are:

*   *compulsory liquidation*: this is commenced by a court petition presented by the company itself, its directors or its creditors, normally on the ground that the company is unable to pay its debts (Ss.122 and 123 IA). If the court makes a winding-up order, then the only person who can be appointed to act as a liquidator (unless the compulsory liquidation has followed a company voluntary arrangement or an administration) is the Official Receiver. This person is a civil servant who will rarely (and certainly not without the court's consent) continue to trade the company. Following a creditors' meeting, another person may be appointed to act as liquidator with the consent of the majority of the creditors and contributors voting. The liquidator's main responsibility is to secure the assets of the company and distribute these to the creditors and shareholders. In accordance with Part XII of the Employment Rights Act 1996 (ERA), should employees not

377

be retained in employment by the liquidator, they are eligible to receive specific protected payments (such as wages of up to eight weeks' pay and pay in lieu of untaken holiday entitlement) as well as statutory redundancy payments from out of the National Insurance Fund

- *members' voluntary liquidation*: this type of winding up (also known as a 'solvent voluntary liquidation') is put in train by a special resolution of the members of a company (i.e. its shareholders and any 'contributors') and is appropriate where the company is genuinely able to meet its liabilities with the prospect of a surplus left over for distribution among the members once its debts have been paid. The directors must be in a position to make a statutory declaration stating that the company is solvent and will be able to pay its debts in full within 12 months, in which case the shareholders will appoint the liquidator. A members' voluntary winding up arises for reasons other than insolvency – for example, if there is no further use for the company or shareholders want to extract their capital. Such liquidations often occur in respect of subsidiaries in a group of companies, where the dissolution of the subsidiary is required on account of structural corporate change. The insolvency provisions in Regs 8 and 9 of the 2006 TUPE Regulations are therefore not relevant, but there may be a 'relevant transfer' if the business of the company is transferred by the appointed liquidator to an external purchaser, in which case the normal TUPE provisions would apply

- *creditors' voluntary liquidation*: this form of winding up (also known as an 'insolvent voluntary liquidation') is by far the most common form. It occurs if the directors are not in a position to make a statutory declaration of solvency or the company is unable to pay its debts as they fall due. In that case, the creditors will convene a meeting, appoint the liquidator and be in effective control. They may also appoint a 'liquidation committee', the purpose of which is to ensure that the liquidator complies with his or her duty to act in the interests of the creditors as a whole. The basic purpose of the appointment of a liquidator is always to realise the company's assets and, after the payment of costs, distribute the proceeds among the creditors and shareholders according to their respective rights and interests – S.107 IA. Again, dismissed employees are eligible for redundancy and insolvency payments in accordance with Part XII of the ERA.

6.13 **Effect of appointment on contracts of employment.** A liquidator in either of the two types of voluntary winding up is regarded as an agent of the company so that his or her appointment does not, of itself, automatically terminate existing contracts of employment – see Midland Counties District Bank Ltd v Attwood 1905 1 Ch 357, ChD. The rationale for this is that there is no change in legal identity of the employer when such a liquidator is appointed because the assets remain under the control of the company liquidator, who is an officer of the company. The general rule is that, subject to any contrary specific terms of a contract of employment, the passing of the resolution to wind up in a creditors' voluntary liquidation does not constitute notice of termination of employment of all employees. This is certainly the case if the purpose of the winding up is to reconstitute the business under new management – Barnes and ors v Leavesley and ors 2001 ICR 38, EAT. However, on the authority of Deaway Trading Ltd v Calverley and ors 1973 ICR 546, NIRC, it may be that if the effect of a creditors' voluntary winding up is to bring about the immediate cessation of the company's activities, this could constitute a repudiatory breach that brings employees' contracts to an immediate end. But the accuracy of the Deaway decision is debatable. It would certainly have to be questioned whether the reality in that case was that it was not so much the appointment of the liquidator that brought the contracts of employment to an end as the cessation of the business.

In the specific case of a members' voluntary liquidation, since the company is not, by definition, insolvent, the appointment of a receiver has no discernible effect on employees' contracts unless and until the liquidator chooses to terminate these expressly. In practice, however, the process of corporate restructuring is likely to have begun even prior to the appointment of the receiver, and, as part of this, employees may well already have been transferred to another subsidiary or have had their employment terminated. If this happens, then it is possible that these manoeuvres themselves constitute a 'relevant transfer', in which case the general principles of the TUPE Regulations will apply.

The position as described above in respect of voluntary liquidation is to be **6.14** contrasted with a compulsory liquidation where the winding-up order is issued by the court. The Official Receiver or any subsequently appointed liquidator is an agent of the court, not of the company. Since the effect of his or her appointment is to place the control of the company and its assets in the hands of a court-appointed outside party, this comprises a repudiatory breach that automatically and immediately terminates the contracts of employment of all employees – Re Oriental Bank Corporation 1886 32 Ch 366. This is so even where employment is continued after the order to facilitate the liquidation. However, it is possible that the rule is different where the business continues. In that case, the continued employment of employees may militate against the automatic termination of their contracts – Re English Joint Stock Bank 1867 LR 2 Eq 341. In practice, however, it will be very rare indeed for the Official Receiver or any other liquidator in a compulsory winding up to continue trading. To do so, he or she would need to obtain the permission of the court and show that this is necessary for the beneficial winding up of the company – S.145 IA.

Where employees are dismissed as soon as the liquidator is appointed, they will be entitled to claim damages for wrongful dismissal based on the notice of

379

termination they should have received. In addition, they will be eligible to receive certain guaranteed sums out of the National Insurance Fund in accordance with Part XII of the ERA – for example, up to eight weeks' arrears of pay and up to six weeks' holiday pay (subject to the statutory cap on a week's pay), as well as statutory redundancy payments. Although there is nothing to prevent those with sufficient qualifying service claiming unfair dismissal, their chances of recovering any compensatory award that may be ordered should they succeed in their claims is usually minimal: rarely are there sufficient assets recovered from a liquidation to pay off the claims of unsecured creditors, which is what employees are in respect of the compensatory award of unfair dismissal.

6.15 **Does appointment of liquidator constitute a TUPE transfer?** In the light of the above, it is relevant to consider the situation where a liquidator does choose to carry on trading the business after his or her appointment. To what extent does this, in itself, constitute a 'relevant transfer'? The position appears to be clear cut in relation to a members' or creditors' voluntary liquidation. Since contracts are not automatically terminated, and the appointed receiver acts as an agent of the company, there is no reason to assume that any change in the person responsible for operating the company occurs when the liquidator is appointed. Hence, there is no relevant transfer at that stage. If the business or the commercially viable part of it (as opposed to merely its assets) is subsequently sold to an outside purchaser, then that is likely to constitute a relevant transfer. The test, as always, is whether an economic entity has been transferred – see Chapter 1 for details. If a relevant transfer does occur, it will be important to consider the extent to which employees' rights are affected by the insolvency provisions of the 2006 Regulations – see under '"Relevant insolvency proceedings"' below.

Where, however, the Official Receiver or other liquidator in the course of a compulsory liquidation continues to trade (with the court's consent) after appointment, it is possible that a relevant transfer could be regarded as taking place at that stage. This is because, unlike in a voluntary liquidation, the liquidator acts as an agent not of the company but of the court. As a result, it could be argued that the continued trading by the liquidator in this case represents a change in the legal or natural person responsible for carrying on the economic entity in the capacity of employer. Since that is the test determining whether there has been a relevant transfer of an undertaking to another person of an economic entity within the meaning of Reg 2(1)(a) – see Chapter 1, under 'Standard transfers – transfer "to another person"' – it is conceivable that a TUPE transfer of the insolvent company's business to the liquidator would be regarded as having occurred.

6.16 There does not appear to be any direct case authority confirming the above proposition – which probably testifies to how rare it is for a liquidator to continue the business in a compulsory liquidation context. However, in the context of personal bankruptcy, the EAT in Belhaven Brewery Ltd v Berekis and anor EAT 724/92 held that the appointment of a trustee in bankruptcy in a case where an individual employer was subject to bankruptcy proceedings had the effect of causing a TUPE transfer of the business to the trustee. This was on the basis that, on appointment, legislative provisions (now contained in S.306 IA) applied to vest the bankrupt's estate (property, assets and legal rights) in the trustee and that, since he had continued to operate the bankrupt's public house business and retained the staff, this constituted a change in the person operating the business for the purposes of TUPE. Given the similarities in the status of liquidators in a compulsory winding up and trustees in bankruptcy in personal bankruptcy proceedings, it seems logical to extend the EAT's reasoning in Belhaven to cases where a compulsory liquidator continues to run the business after being appointed.

Even if the TUPE Regulations were to apply, however, it seems reasonably clear that employees would not receive a great deal of benefit from their application. Compulsory liquidation is almost certainly a form of insolvency proceedings 'instituted with a view to the liquidation of the assets of the transferor' within the meaning of Reg 8(7). As such, the protections in relation to transfer of contracts of employment in Reg 4 and unfair dismissal in Reg 7 are disapplied – see '"Relevant insolvency proceedings"' below.

Receivership and administrative receivership 6.17

The purpose of receivership and administrative receivership is to protect the whole or part of the business and assets of a company from the actions of creditors while seeking to realise those assets for the benefit of secured and other creditors. A receiver can be appointed in three ways: by the court; by the holder of a fixed charge attaching to specific property under the Law of Property Act 1925 (LPA), also known as a 'fixed charge receiver' or 'LPA receiver'; or by the holder of a floating charge secured over the whole or substantially the whole of a company's assets under the terms of a debenture or other loan agreement ('administrative receiver'). The main functions of the receiver in the latter case are to realise sufficient assets to pay off the secured creditor by whom the receiver was appointed and the costs of the receivership. In order to achieve this, the receiver normally takes over the day-to-day running of the company with a view to either selling the assets piecemeal or disposing of the business as a going concern.

Administrative receivers. In practice, many receivers are administrative 6.18 receivers appointed by a bank under the terms of a debenture agreement with the company following the company's breach of the terms of its borrowing. However, with the coming into force of S.250 of the Enterprise Act 2002, the appointment of administrative receivers under qualifying floating charges created on or after 15 September 2003 was abolished. This was part of the then

381

Government's drive to encourage the use of administration (see under 'Company administration' below). The power to appoint such administrative receivers continues in respect of capital market arrangements, public-private partnerships, utilities, urban regeneration projects, project finance, financial markets, registered social landlords and protected railway companies. Except in these cases, any power to appoint an administrative receiver under the terms of a floating charge created on or after 15 September 2003 will no longer be exercisable and, instead, the debenture holder will have the right to seek the appointment of an administrator.

In so far as the appointment of administrative receivers continues to occur, such receivers have much wider powers and duties than an LPA/fixed charge receiver. These include not only the contractual powers contained in the relevant security document but also statutory powers set out in Schedule 1 IA (Schedule 2 in Scotland) embracing the power to take possession of the company's property, manage its business, borrow money, hire staff and sell the business.

6.19 An administrative receiver is deemed to be the agent of the company unless and until that company goes into liquidation (S.44 IA). This means that there is no change in employer on his or her appointment because any employees who are not expressly dismissed continue to be employed by the company. Subject to a 14-day grace period, an administrative receiver will be taken to have 'adopted' contracts of employment of any employees he or she continues to retain, in which case he or she will owe a personal liability to the employees in respect of certain 'qualifying liabilities' set out in S.44(2A) IA. The provisions for adoption and the definition of qualifying liabilities are virtually identical to those that apply to administration (again, see under 'Company administration' below).

6.20 **LPA/fixed charge receivers.** If a company defaults on the terms of a fixed charge, such as a mortgage over a property or a charge over fixed assets (such as plant and machinery, intellectual property or interests in equities and securities), the holder of the charge may appoint a receiver to recover its property. Technically a fixed charge receivership is a method of enforcing security, not an insolvency proceeding, and the receiver has a contractual relationship with the company that is determined by the terms of the charge and/or the limited powers set out in S.109 LPA. There is normally no direct effect on employees arising from the appointment of an LPA receiver.

If receivers who are not administrative receivers permit contracts of employment to continue for 14 days or more, they will be deemed to have adopted the contracts and thereby assume personal liability for sums incurred (such as wages) in respect of those contracts from that point onwards. A detailed discussion of this is beyond the scope of this Handbook, although the issues are briefly outlined under 'Company administration' below.

Court-appointed receivers. Most receivers are appointed by debenture holders **6.21**
as described above. The courts do have a discretionary power to appoint a
receiver in limited circumstances – for example, to enforce a judgment – but
this is rarely exercised. A receiver who is the appointee of the court is an officer
of the court and so is not regarded as acting as the company's agent. His or her
appointment therefore automatically terminates the contracts of employment
of all employees working in the business – see Reid v Explosives Co Ltd 1887
19 QBD 264, CA. If the receiver keeps the employees on in order to keep the
business viable, he or she becomes their employer. The same argument can
therefore be made that this constitutes a relevant transfer of the insolvent
business to the receiver as that which applies to personal bankruptcy and
compulsory liquidations (see above).

Company administration
6.22

Administration orders are specifically intended to assist companies that are
insolvent but have a good chance of being rescued. A simpler administration
procedure was introduced by the Enterprise Act 2002 with effect from 15
September 2003, the relevant provisions of which are now contained in
Schedule B1 to the IA. An administrator can be appointed by the court, as was
always the case prior to the coming into force of the Enterprise Act. However,
as part of the simplified procedures that now apply, the administrator can also
be appointed by the holder of a qualifying floating charge over the assets of the
business, or the shareholders/directors of the insolvent company, and in both
cases without the need to apply to the court first (paras 14 and 22 of Schedule
B1). The main limitation on the right of the company or directors to appoint an
administrator is that, before doing so, they must notify the holders of a
qualifying floating charge of their intention to appoint an administrator and
then wait at least five days before doing so (para 28 of Schedule B1). This gives
the holder of the floating charge time to appoint its own administrator should
it so desire. (A qualifying floating charge is one that expressly states that
para 14 of Schedule B1 applies to it or, if made prior to the coming into force
of the provisions of Schedule B1, expressly empowers the holder of the charge
to appoint an administrator or administrative receiver – para 14(2), Sch B1.) It
is a cardinal principle of administration that irrespective of who appoints him
or her, the administrator owes a duty to act in the interests of all the company's
creditors – para 3(2), Sch B1.

Objectives of administration. Paragraph 3(1) of Schedule B1 sets out three **6.23**
potential objectives of an administration. Whereas the administrator was
previously at liberty to choose which of these to prioritise, he or she is now
obliged to observe a strict order of priority. The primary objective is to rescue
the company as a going concern, with as much of its business intact as possible,
if that would provide the best result for the company's creditors as a whole. If
this is not possible, the second objective is to achieve a better return for creditors

383

than would be achieved if the company was simply wound up. This may entail keeping the business trading while seeking a purchaser of a viable part of its business or of its key assets. For example, the saleable assets of a loss-making part of the business may need to be disposed of to enable the rest of the business to continue. Only if the administrator cannot meet the first or second objectives does the third come into play, which is to realise the assets in order to make a distribution to secured and preferential creditors.

During the currency of an administration, a moratorium applies, which means that creditors are prevented from taking steps to have the company wound up or enforce any security they hold over the company's property. Furthermore, legal proceedings against the company cannot be commenced or continued except with the leave of the administrator or the court. This moratorium is crucial as it provides a breathing space during which the possibility of some form of rescue or arrangement with creditors can be explored.

6.24 An administration must normally be concluded within one year, unless extended with the agreement of creditors or the court – para 76, Sch B1. There are several possible outcomes of the administration. The company may be returned to the control of its directors and management; it may be dissolved if there are insufficient funds for distribution to unsecured creditors; a voluntary arrangement agreed during the administration may be continued; or it may be wound up.

6.25 **Status of administrator.** The formal status of the administrator is that of an officer of the court, regardless of whether it was the court that appointed him or her – para 5, Sch B1. But, crucially, in exercising his or her principal functions, the administrator acts as the company's agent – para 69, Sch B1. On being appointed, he or she takes custody and control of all the property to which he or she believes the company is entitled, and is empowered to do anything necessary or expedient for the management of its affairs, property or business – paras 59 and 67, Sch B1. The administrator's specific powers (as set out in Schedule 1 to the IA) include taking possession of, collecting or getting in the property of the company and selling or otherwise disposing of it; raising or borrowing money and granting securities over the property of the company; employing and dismissing employees; bringing or defending legal proceedings in the name of the company; establishing subsidiaries and transferring the business or property of the company (in whole or in part) to subsidiaries; removing and appointing directors; and carrying on the business – paras 1, 2, 3, 5, 11, 14, 15, and 16, Sch 1.

6.26 **Effect of appointment on contracts of employment.** Since the administrator is an agent of the company, no question arises of employees' contracts of employment being automatically terminated on his or her appointment. If, subsequently, the administrator does terminate the employment of employees, then the resulting act of dismissal will be regarded as having been done on behalf of the company.

Special provision is made under the IA for administrators to 'adopt' contracts of employment. This is seen as a necessary facility given that the usual aim of an administration is to keep the insolvent business trading until the whole (or any viable part of it) can be sold as a going concern, as distinct from breaking up the company's assets. Normally, to achieve this goal, it is essential that administrators can call upon the continued service of all or most of the employees employed in the business.

The adoption of contracts by administrators is governed by para 99 of Schedule B1 – a provision concerned with whether debts and liabilities arising out of contracts entered into by the administrator in the course of the administration receive special priority in respect of the proceeds of sale. Para 99(4) and (5) stipulates that liability in respect of 'wages or salary' arising under a contract of employment that has been 'adopted' by the administrator is chargeable on and payable out of the property of which the administrator has custody and control in priority to the administrator's own remuneration and expenses. 'Wages or salary' in this context is defined in para 99(6) as including holiday entitlement, sums paid in lieu of holiday, sickness pay, sums in respect of any period that would be treated as earnings during that period for the purposes of social security, and contributions to an occupational pension scheme. **6.27**

Although the IA contains no definition of 'adoption', para 99(5)(a) of Schedule B1 expressly stipulates that any action taken by the administrator within the period of 14 days after his or her appointment shall not be taken to amount to the adoption of a contract. Thus, any wages or salary payable during this grace period do not attract priority over the administrator's remuneration and expenses. In Powdrill and anor v Watson and anor and other cases 1995 ICR 1100, HL, the House of Lords considered what might demonstrate that 'adoption' has occurred after the expiry of the 14-day grace period and whether it was possible for an administrator to expressly contract out of adoption in respect of employees who are retained by the insolvent company. The relevant provisions at the time of that decision were contained in S.19 of the IA, but have since been transferred in slightly amended form to Schedule B1. Their Lordships concluded that if employment is continued for more than 14 days after the administrator's appointment, it inevitably follows that the whole of the employee's contract is to be regarded as having been adopted. In Lord Browne-Wilkinson's words: '[The word "adoption"] can only connote some conduct by the administrator or receiver which amounts to an election to treat the continued contract of employment with the company as giving rise to a separate liability in the administration or receivership.' Thus, adoption in essence denotes nothing more than a decision to allow a pre-existing contract of employment to continue. The House of Lords went on to confirm that it was

385

not possible for the administrator to avoid this result or alter the consequences that the IA specifies where a contract of employment has been adopted by informing employees that he or she is not adopting their contracts or is only doing so on specific terms.

6.28 It is clear from Lord Browne-Wilkinson's definition of 'adoption' that even where the administrator retains the services of employees after 14 days he or she does not personally become their employer. Their contracts of employment continue to be with the company. As a result, no TUPE transfer occurs at that point. If the administration eventually results in the disposal of the business or part of it as a going concern, then a relevant transfer will occur at that stage, and this will trigger the special provisions in Regs 8 and 9 of TUPE modifying the application of the normal protections guaranteed under the Regulations – see under '"Relevant insolvency proceedings"' below.

6.29 Voluntary arrangements

A debtor (whether an individual or a company) in financial difficulties can enter into a voluntary arrangement with his or its creditors. If a company, such arrangement may well enable it to continue as a going concern – for example, by arranging reduced or delayed debt repayment terms (Ss.1–7 IA). The arrangement will normally last from two to four years. Usually the directors of the company appoint an insolvency practitioner to consider and report on the proposals they have made for the voluntary arrangement. Shareholders and creditors then vote on whether to approve it. If at least 75 per cent in value of creditors approve the arrangement, it is binding on all the company's creditors. The function of the insolvency practitioner is simply to supervise the arrangement. Since the business normally continues to trade while subject to the voluntary arrangement, there is no automatic termination of contracts of employment, and the TUPE Regulations will not normally be relevant. A voluntary arrangement can be run at the same time as an administration.

6.30 Outline of insolvency provisions in TUPE

The way in which the TUPE Regulations 2006 apply to the sale of an insolvent business or part thereof is set out in Regs 8 and 9. In places these provisions are difficult to interpret, often because they require familiarity with concepts that are not contained in the Regulations themselves, including insolvency procedures and the statutory payment provisions relevant to employees of insolvent companies. There has been much criticism of the complexity and drafting of the insolvency provisions, in particular by insolvency specialists such as R3 (the Association of Business Recovery Professionals), who were concerned that the provisions may not work well in practice. On 3 May 2006 an application to revoke the new TUPE Regulations was made in the House of Lords by Lord Hunt of Wirral on behalf of R3, defended by Lord Sainsbury of

Turville for the Department of Trade and Industry. The motion was defeated by just two votes. Key points of the debate are considered below in the context of the relevant insolvency provisions. In his conclusion, Lord Sainsbury said that the Government would monitor closely how the 2006 Regulations operate in practice, and if problems emerge it will consider the case for amending them.

In broad outline, the key changes introduced by Regs 8 and 9 of the TUPE Regulations 2006 are:

- the wholesale disapplication of Regs 4 and 7 where the transferor is subject to bankruptcy or analogous insolvency proceedings instituted with a view to liquidating the transferor's assets under the supervision of an insolvency practitioner. In such cases, employees will not be accorded the normal protections in respect of the automatic transfer of their employment and attendant rights, duties, powers and liabilities on a relevant transfer, nor the protections against detrimental variation of contracts or unfair dismissal by reason of the transfer – Reg 8(7)

- the non-transfer of liability by the transferor for certain core debts (such as statutory redundancy payments, payments in lieu of notice and unpaid holiday pay of up to six weeks) where the transferor is the subject of 'relevant insolvency proceedings'. Rather than debts being 'inherited' by the transferee in the usual way by virtue of Reg 4, they will become payable by the Secretary of State for Trade and Industry out of the National Insurance Fund – Reg 8(5)

- the legal right – subject to certain procedural safeguards – for the transferor, transferee or insolvency practitioner to negotiate variations to terms and conditions with employee representatives where the transferor is subject to 'relevant insolvency proceedings' even if the reason for the changes is connected with the transfer and is not an economic, technical or organisational reason entailing changes in the workforce – Reg 9.

6.31 The second and third of these provisions – which are specifically drawn from the 'rescue culture' options conferred on Member States by Article 5.2 of the Acquired Rights Directive – involve a significant modification to the application of Reg 4. Both only apply in a case where the transferor is subject to 'relevant insolvency proceedings', defined in Reg 4(6) as being 'insolvency proceedings which have been opened in relation to the transferor not with a view to the liquidation of the assets of the transferor and which are under the supervision of an insolvency practitioner'. This is to be contrasted with the first of the provisions outlined above – drawn from Article 5.1 of the Directive – which provides for the wholesale disapplication of Regs 4 and 7 where the particular insolvency proceedings to which the transferor is subject has the aim of liquidating the transferor's assets.

387

Although there has been a considerable amount of confusion and debate about the wording of these different sets of provisions, it seems to be reasonably clear that the types of proceedings to which Reg 8(7) is intended to apply are mutually exclusive to those that are intended to come within the definition of 'relevant insolvency proceedings' to which the remainder of Reg 8 and the whole of Reg 9 apply. In other words, each of the different types of insolvency procedure discussed under 'Types of insolvency procedure' above will be caught either by Reg 8(7) or by Regs 8(1)–(6) and 9, unless the procedure is not a genuine 'insolvency' procedure, in which case it will be caught by neither. The key criterion for determining into which category a particular procedure falls is whether or not the insolvency proceedings in question were instituted with a view to liquidating the assets of the transferor's business. The wording of the Regulations leaves plenty of scope for argument as to whether the aim of one or another particular proceeding is to liquidate the transferor's assets. However, as we shall see when we examine Regs 8 and 9 in detail – starting with Reg 8(7) below – it is possible to reach a commonsensical view about this, particularly if it is accepted that the point at which the aim of the proceedings has to be determined is their commencement rather than at any later date.

6.32 Bankruptcy and liquidation proceedings

Reg 8(7) stipulates that: 'Regs 4 and 7 do not apply to any relevant transfer where the transferor is the subject of bankruptcy proceedings or any analogous insolvency proceedings which have been instituted with a view to the liquidation of the assets of the transferor and are under the supervision of an insolvency practitioner.' Where it applies, this provision has a much more dramatic effect on the rights of employees than the provision in Reg 8(5) limiting the transfer or specific liabilities payable to relevant employees under a relevant statutory scheme (see under '"Relevant insolvency proceedings"' below). However, the reach of Reg 8(7) is much narrower because its application is limited to where the transferor is subject to insolvency proceedings that aim to liquidate the business rather than keep it trading with a view to its sale or disposition as a going concern. As we shall see, this means that in practice Reg (7) only applies to compulsory and creditors' voluntary liquidations.

6.33 Proceedings 'under the supervision of' insolvency practitioner
Before considering Reg 8(7) in detail, it should be noted that the insolvency proceedings have to be under the supervision of an 'insolvency practitioner'. Such a person is defined in Reg 2 of TUPE in terms of the meaning given by S.388 IA, which states that, in relation to a company, a person acts as an insolvency practitioner when he or she acts as its liquidator, administrator, administrative receiver, or supervisor of a voluntary arrangement. Subsequent sections set out various requirements that must be met for an insolvency practitioner to be validly appointed. For example, all insolvency practitioners

388

must be members of a recognised professional body or otherwise properly authorised. This means that they must be appointed by one of the chartered accountancy bodies, the Law Society, the Insolvency Practitioners Association, or the Department of Trade. Note that the definition of insolvency practitioner does not cover court-appointed receiverships or LPA receiverships, as these are not true insolvency proceedings.

Transferor 'the subject of bankruptcy proceedings or any analogous insolvency proceedings...' 6.34

The language of Reg 8(7) is imported word-for-word from Article 5.1 of the Acquired Rights Directive. Both provisions speak of the disapplication of the rules dealing with transfer of contractual rights and protection against unfair dismissal by reason of the transfer 'where the transferor is the subject of bankruptcy proceedings or any analogous insolvency proceedings which have been instituted with a view to the liquidation of the assets of the transferor'. The problem is that 'bankruptcy' in UK insolvency law has a special and very narrow meaning whereas, in the context of the Directive, there is a sense that it is intended to carry a wider and less specific meaning. This was recognised by Advocate General Sir Gordon Slynn in Abels v Administrative Board of the Bedrijfsvereniging voor de Metaalindustrie en de Electrotechnische Industrie 1987 2 CMLR 406, ECJ, when explaining his choice of terminology in the written Opinion he gave to the European Court: 'Since in English "bankruptcy" and "liquidation" have technical meanings, one referring to the insolvency of individuals or partnerships, the other to the winding up of companies... I use the words "liquidator" and "liquidation" as covering also "a trustee in bankruptcy" and "bankruptcy".'

In view of this, it would seem fairly clear that, in the context of corporate insolvency, the type of proceedings that comes closest to personal bankruptcy is liquidation – certainly compulsory liquidation and probably creditors' voluntary liquidation. Although there is no question of the legal interest in the debtor's assets becoming vested in the liquidator (unless the court specifically so orders) – as happens when a trustee in bankruptcy is appointed – the insolvent company's assets nevertheless become entirely controlled by the liquidator. The notion that this brings liquidations into the scope of Reg 4(7) is further strengthened by the next clause of that regulation, considered below.

'... which have been instituted with a view to the liquidation of the assets' 6.35

In order to determine which of the insolvency procedures discussed under 'Types of insolvency procedures' above are caught by Reg 8(7), it is necessary to dissect the meaning of 'proceedings which have been instituted with a view to the liquidation of the assets'.

389

The first thing to note is the words 'which have been instituted'. The proceedings that are covered by Reg 8(7) have to have been instituted with a view to the liquidation of the assets. Rather oddly, the word is not used in the Reg 8(6) definition of 'relevant insolvency proceedings', which refers to 'proceedings which have been *opened* in relation to the transferor'. Why the difference? Unfortunately, none of the official guidance on the TUPE Regulations offers an explanation. But there is no apparent reason why the words should be interpreted differently. Therefore, unless and until the courts discover a nuance of practical or legal import that is not immediately obvious, it seems safe to assume that 'instituted' in Reg 8(7) and 'opened' in Reg 8(6) simply mean 'commenced' – that being the word usually applied by insolvency practitioners when insolvency proceedings are begun.

6.36 Recent case law suggests that, in order for the consequences set out in Reg 8(7) to apply, it is necessary that bankruptcy or analogous proceedings have already commenced by the time the transfer takes place. If this is not the case, then Reg 4 will apply unabated, which means that the transferee will acquire the contract of employment and all liabilities thereunder of any employee employed immediately before the transfer. The transferee will also be subject to the full rigour of Reg 7 should any such employee be dismissed for a reason connected to the transfer. This is made clear in the following decision.

In Secretary of State for Trade and Industry v Slater 2008 ICR 54, EAT, the Appeal Tribunal had to consider whether Reg 8(7) applied in circumstances where the appointment of a liquidator was imminent at the time a relevant transfer occurred. Faced with financial difficulties, the directors of C Ltd decided on 25 July 2006 to put the company into voluntary liquidation. Since it was insolvent, a creditors' voluntary winding up was the appropriate type of insolvency proceedings, and the directors appointed a firm of accountants to assist in preparing for this. The following day, R (an employee of the accountants), gave the staff notice of redundancy. C Ltd's assets and goodwill were then purchased by a new company, CFGN Ltd, on 27 July in circumstances that were found to amount to a TUPE transfer. C Ltd was formally put into liquidation on 16 August at a meeting of the shareholders, who passed a resolution to wind up the company. The creditors then appointed R and another person as joint liquidators. C Ltd's employees, who were taken on by CFGN, sought payment of back pay and holiday pay from their new employer on the basis that it had acquired those liabilities following the transfer. CFGN, however, denied liability, relying on Reg 8(6), or alternatively Reg 8(7). An employment tribunal agreed with the transferee that the insolvency procedure in this case fell under Reg 8(6) and went on to find that the insolvency proceedings had been opened on 25 July – two days before the transfer – when the directors had resolved to call the shareholders' meeting to wind up the company. Since those proceedings had been opened before the transfer, liability did not pass to the transferee and, instead, the Secretary of State was liable to make the payments out of the National Insurance Fund.

On appeal to the EAT by the Secretary of State, certain concessions were made **6.37** by the parties, which meant that the question of whether the case fell within Reg 8(6) or Reg 8(7) was no longer specifically relevant. The sole remaining issue was whether the insolvency proceedings in question had commenced prior to the transfer. In this regard, the EAT held that neither Reg 8(6) nor 8(7) applied given that, as a consequence of the creditors' voluntary winding up, the resulting insolvency proceedings – whether these were taken to commence at the time of the resolution of the members or with the subsequent decision reached at a creditors' meeting – were begun only after the transfer had occurred. But even if those proceedings had been in place when the business was transferred, those proceedings were not – as at the date of the transfer – under the supervision of an insolvency practitioner, as required by both Reg 8(6) and 8(7). This was despite the fact that it was apparently assumed that the accountant appointed by the transferor was an insolvency practitioner from the moment he was first asked to assist the company. The definition of an insolvency practitioner in S.388 of the Insolvency Act 1986 made it plain that it was not until he was appointed liquidator that he could be so described. He was of course qualified to act as an insolvency practitioner, but he was not acting in that capacity with respect to the transferor. As a result, since neither Reg 8(7) nor Reg 8(6) applied to limit the operation of the automatic transfer of contractual liability rule in Reg 4, the transferee, CFGN, was responsible for the payment of the debts owed to the transferred employees.

The EAT's decision makes it clear that preparatory steps for a winding up – there, the appointment of accountants – do not mean that insolvency proceedings have been formally commenced. Similar reasoning has been adopted in subsequent cases, as the following tribunal decisions make clear:

- **Darlington v Martin Group Ltd (In Administration) and anor** ET Case No.2401949/09: D was employed by MG Ltd as a senior art worker, dealing with off-the-page advertising for a major client, P. MG Ltd suffered the loss of a number of contracts in 2008, and, in particular, lost P's contract at the end of September 2008. At that point, D was informed that he was to be made redundant with effect from 21 November. On 23 November, MG Ltd was advised that the company could not be saved and administration should be considered. Some two weeks before this, a new company, MDI Ltd, was set up and incorporated on 6 November 2008 and a senior employee of MG Ltd (W) was appointed director of that company on 26 November. On 28 November W met MG Ltd's liquidator and agreed to purchase that company's outstanding debts and goodwill, together with its equipment. Following a break of one week, MDI Ltd commenced operation of a slightly different service, and approached various clients of MG Ltd who

391

had been acquired as part of its purchase by MDI Ltd. The question arose whether the dismissal of D (who was not taken on following the transfer) was caught by Reg 8(7) of TUPE. MDI Ltd contended that it was, with the consequence that neither Regs 4 nor 7 applied. In rejecting this contention, an employment tribunal ruled that in this case the insolvency proceedings instituted by MG Ltd had not commenced prior to the date of the transfer. It followed that Reg 8(7) had no application, so that the unfair dismissal provisions of Reg 7 applied. As D was dismissed for a reason connected with the transfer that was not for an ETO reason, Reg 7 operated to render his dismissal automatically unfair

- **Dearing v Pentagon Glass Tech Ltd (in liquidation) and ors** ET Case No.3302313/08: D was employed by PGT Ltd as a workshop manager and controller. The company encountered financial difficulties and decided these could not be resolved. Even so, some employees, including D, were told that their jobs were secure, whereas others were made redundant. D's employment continued until 31 May 2008, when PGT Ltd ceased trading. He had been told he would be given a new contract to do the same job in a new location but with a 10 per cent reduction in salary. One of PGT Ltd's directors had been looking for alternative premises from which the business could be run. When these were found, they had to be fitted out and a newly incorporated company, PG Ltd, set up. This did not begin trading until 20 July 2008. Eight days later, PGT Ltd went into voluntary liquidation and the final transfer of assets from it to PG Ltd was made by invoice dated 22 September. In the meantime, D had refused the offer of the new contract because of the proposed pay cut and claimed he was entitled to be paid a redundancy payment by PGT Ltd (the liability for which had been transferred to PG Ltd). An employment tribunal held that the relevant date of the transfer was 31 May – the date that PGT Ltd ceased to trade. As at that date, no insolvency process had been instituted, which meant that Reg 8(7) did not apply. It followed that PG Ltd was the only appropriate respondent to the tribunal proceedings and D was entitled to proceed with his claim.

6.38 Assuming, then, that liquidation or analogous proceedings have been commenced by the time the transfer occurs, the next – and very significant – issue concerns the question of the point in time at which the aim of the proceedings in question has to be assessed. The proceedings have to have been instituted '*with a view*' to the liquidation of the assets. As mentioned above, it would seem that the determining factor as to whether a particular insolvency procedure falls within Reg 8(7) as opposed to the definition of 'relevant insolvency proceedings' in Reg 8(6) is the extent to which, at the time it is commenced, its object is the liquidation of the transferor's assets. The difficulty here is that all of the insolvency procedures available under UK law to a greater or lesser extent entail realising the value of the transferor's assets and all can end up in the disposal of the insolvent business as a going concern (or the viable parts of the business). Clearly, a distinction is intended to be drawn between those types of proceedings which, by their nature, drive towards the disposal of the business or part of it as a going concern (or at least see this as ensuring the best realisation of the assets) and those that have as their usual goal merely the realisation of the assets and the beneficial distribution of the proceeds to creditors. For reasons explained under '"Relevant insolvency proceedings"' below, it would seem that the point at which to judge the nature of the insolvency proceedings is at the outset of those proceedings. So, on this basis, proceedings that have as their usual aim the liquidation of the transferor's assets would be caught by Reg 4(7) even if, in a particular case, the insolvency practitioner happened to end up selling the viable part of the insolvent business as a going concern.

In determining whether a particular insolvency procedure is to be regarded as instituted with a view to liquidation of the transferor's assets as distinct from keeping the business operating with a view to its sale as a concern, it is useful to remember that the language of Article 5.1 of the Directive (which Reg 8(7) replicates) was drawn from the decisions of the European Court in Abels and in D'Urso and ors v Ercole Marelli Elettromeccanica Generale SpA (in special administration) and ors 1992 IRLR 136, ECJ (discussed under 'European law background' above). An examination of those cases is accordingly instructive in elucidating the wording of Reg 8(7). In D'Urso the ECJ noted that Abels was concerned with whether the transfer of a business arising out of a Dutch insolvency procedure known as a 'surséance van betaling' was covered by the Directive. This procedure entails the national court giving leave to insolvent companies to suspend payments to their creditors while options for rescue are investigated. The ECJ summarised the ruling in Abels as follows: 'The Court held that the Directive did not apply to transfers effected in bankruptcy proceedings designed to liquidate the transferor's assets under the supervision of the competent judicial authority... [However], the Directive was applicable to a procedure like a "surséance van betaling" (suspension of payments), although that procedure did have some features in common with liquidation proceedings.' The Court considered that the reasons which justified not applying the Directive in the case of liquidation proceedings were not valid when the procedure in question involved court supervision more limited than in liquidation proceedings and when its purpose was primarily to safeguard the assets and, where possible, to continue the business of the undertaking by means of a collective suspension of the payment of debts with a view to reaching a settlement which would ensure that the undertaking was able to continue operating in the future. The ECJ in D'Urso then went on to point out that the extent of court supervision of the insolvency procedure in question was not itself determinative of whether the Directive applies. Rather, 'the decisive test is... the purpose of the procedure in question'.

6.39 The particular insolvency procedure under scrutiny in the D'Urso case was an Italian one called 'amministrazione straordinaria delle grandi imprese in crisi' ('special administration procedure for large undertakings in critical difficulties'). The characteristics of this procedure differed according to whether the national court decreed that the insolvent undertaking should be compulsorily liquidated or should continue trading. If the former, then in the ECJ's view the aim of the special administration procedure would be comparable to that which had led the Court to conclude in Abels that the Directive did not apply to transfers of an undertaking (or part transfers). That was because it would be primarily designed to liquidate the debtor's assets in order to satisfy the body of creditors. On the other hand, as was apparent from the relevant Italian national law, when the court authorised the undertaking to continue trading under the supervision of an insolvency practitioner, the primary purpose of the special administration procedure would then be to give the undertaking some stability, allowing its future activity to be safeguarded. In that case, the ECJ concluded, the Directive would apply to any transfer effected in the course of the procedure in question.

Returning to the position under UK domestic law, the following employment tribunal decision specifically focused on whether the insolvency proceedings in question attracted the application of Reg 8(7):

*   **Bowater and ors v NIS Signs Ltd (in liquidation)** ET Case No.1901191/09 and others: in 2009 the group of which NS Ltd was a part encountered serious financial difficulties. A management buyout was proposed, and a new company – NS(L) Ltd – was incorporated for this purpose on 8 April 2009. At the same time the entire group of companies was about to be put into insolvency administration. NS(L) Ltd took legal advice, as a result of which it was advised that it should purchase NS Ltd from a liquidator rather than an administrator so that Reg 8(7) of TUPE would be engaged. This would have the beneficial effect, so far as NS(L) Ltd was concerned, of disapplying the entirety of Regs 4 and 7 with regard to the former employees of NS Ltd. On 22 April NS Ltd passed a resolution voluntarily winding up the company and on the same day the liquidator sold that company to another subsidiary, LS Ltd. Following claims brought by B and others, an employment tribunal was called upon to consider whether Reg 8(7) applied – and, in particular whether a creditors' voluntary liquidation (CVL) was analogous to bankruptcy or analogous proceedings and whether the CVL in this case was a mere sham. It held that, under UK domestic insolvency law, the liquidation of assets is the only possible outcome of a CVL. The tribunal accepted that, in this case, the liquidation was undertaken solely with a view to precluding the operation of TUPE. However, on closer inspection of the facts, the tribunal discovered that this objective was primarily aimed at securing the commercial interests of NS Ltd's principal creditor – namely, its bank, which had advanced the money to enable the purchase of NS Ltd's

business by LS Ltd. By engineering the situation to avoid liabilities that would otherwise have been transferred under TUPE, the bank was thus able to transfer its investment to an independent viable concern away from a financially fragile group of companies. The CVL was therefore not a sham, and the fact that the CVL was not the only option available did not mean that the tribunal could mitigate the clear effect of Reg 8(7).

A more controversial finding was reached by the EAT in Oakland v Wellswood **6.40** (Yorkshire) Ltd 2009 IRLR 250, EAT. In that case, joint administrators were appointed by a company facing severe financial difficulties. Prior to their appointment, the managing director of the company had discussions about the possibility of a major supplier purchasing the company. Reluctant to take on the company's debts, the supplier decided to set up a subsidiary for the purposes of purchasing purely the company's assets and premises and employing several of its staff, including the claimant. The joint administrators were appointed on the same day as the sale of assets to the new subsidiary. Just short of a year later, the claimant was dismissed and sought to claim unfair dismissal. Before the tribunal, the question arose as to whether Reg 4(7) applied to exclude the normal protections afforded by Regs 4 and 7. This depended on whether the joint administration comprised 'bankruptcy or analogous proceedings' within the meaning of Reg 4(7) or 'relevant insolvency proceedings which have been opened in relation to the transferor not with a view to the liquidation of the assets of the transferor' within the meaning of Reg 8(6). If the latter, then the operation of Regs 4 and 7 would not be excluded. The employment judge found that, in this case, the appointment of joint administrators was made with a view to the eventual liquidation of the assets of the transferor company, within the meaning of Reg 8(7), and that Reg 4 was therefore disapplied, with the consequence that the claimant's employment was not transferred to the transferee.

On appeal, the EAT upheld the employment judge's decision. His Honour Judge Peter Clarke (sitting alone) reasoned that the question of whether particular insolvency proceedings are to be characterised as having been instituted with a view to the liquidation of the transferor company's assets, within the meaning of Reg 8(7), is a question of fact for the employment tribunal; it is not purely a question of domestic insolvency law. Where joint administrators continue to trade the business with a view to its sale as a going concern, any relevant transfer in those circumstances will attract the Reg 4 protection for employees (apart from the specific exception in Reg 8(5) carved out in respect of debts that are payable under the National Insurance Fund - see 'Relevant insolvency proceedings - liability for sums payable under statutory scheme'). However, that is not what happened in the instant case. The administrators of the company had concluded that the first objective of rescuing the company as a going concern was not achievable and had taken immediate steps to sell the assets. This was seen as the best course for realising the optimum

395

return for creditors in the final liquidation of the company. On those facts the tribunal had been entitled to conclude that the appointment of joint administrators was with a view to the eventual liquidation of the assets of the company.

6.41 It is fair to say that the EAT's decision in Oakland has received a good deal of criticism – not least because so-called corporate administration was presumed, at the time the 2006 Regulations came into force, to be a clear-cut example of an insolvency procedure that leans towards the rescue of insolvent businesses as going concerns rather than aiming simply to realise failed companies' assets in order to pay their principal creditors. Indeed, this was the view taken by the Insolvency Service in its detailed guidance, 'The Transfer of Undertakings (Protection of Employment) Regulations 2006 (TUPE): redundancy and insolvency payments' (URN 06/1368) ('the insolvency guidance'), which states: 'Regulations 4 and 7 will always apply in relation to a relevant transfer that is made in the context of an administration.' According to the Insolvency Service, administration is not analogous to bankruptcy proceedings, since its main purpose is not to realise assets. However, that guidance does not appear to consider the kind of situation that arose in the Oakland case, where the administrator considered there to be no prospect of rescuing the business and moved straight away to securing a better deal for the creditors. Nor does it take on board the complex nature of administration as governed by the Insolvency Act 1986, or the fact that, when appointed, administrators are expected to identify one out of a number of strictly ranked principal objectives, which, while usually entailing an attempt to rescue the company as a going concern, may, if this is not viable, comprise simply the realisation of assets in order to make a distribution to the company's secure and preferred creditors – see under 'Types of insolvency procedure – company administration' above. These arguments give considerable support to HHJ Clarke's nuanced approach when determining whether administration falls within the scope of Reg 8(7) or Reg 8(6). The judge himself was surely right when pointing to the Government's failure, when enacting the revised TUPE Regulations in 2006, to specify which types of insolvency procedures fell into which category, as the root cause of the confusion and complexity that surrounds the operation of Reg 8.

It should further be pointed out that the EAT's decision in Oakwood was, in fact, successfully appealed to the Court of Appeal, but on the basis of reasoning that was entirely unrelated to the Reg 8(6)/8(7) issue – see Oakland v Wellswood (Yorkshire) Ltd 2010 ICR 902, CA. The Court of Appeal ruled that the courts below had overlooked the fact that the claimant was, in fact, able to establish the necessary continuity of employment to claim unfair dismissal against the transferee without needing to resort to the TUPE Regulations at all – see Chapter 7, 'Continuity of Employment', under 'Residual application of the ERA – insolvency'.

396

Notwithstanding that the TUPE issues were out-of-scope on the appeal in **6.42** Oakland, certain obiter remarks made by Lord Justice Moses regarding those issues are of interest. He observed: 'It would seem to me most unwise for us to give a binding pronouncement on the correctness or otherwise of the contention that administration necessarily excludes the application of Reg 8(7). I would only, for my part, wish to emphasise that that is a strongly arguable point, and the only reason I agree that it should not be resolved today is that the Secretary of State is not here and, since [the respondent] is in the process of being liquidated almost as we speak, and therefore has no representation here today, it would be unwise to reach and pronounce upon any definitive conclusion.' A further opportunity to revisit the issue of whether administration falls within Reg 8(6) or Reg 8(7) will be accorded to the EAT when it gives judgment in the joined cases of Olds v Late Editions Ltd and Otford Tool Ltd v Barker EAT 0321/09. A judgment is expected imminently.

In the light of the above, the following types of insolvency proceedings would appear to come within the scope of Reg 8(7):

- *bankruptcy*. This is expressly excluded by Article 5.1 and Reg 8(7). Therefore if a trustee in bankruptcy sells a business that was run by the bankrupt the employees' contracts of employment do not automatically pass to the purchaser and the employees will be redundant. They would be eligible for redundancy and insolvency payments payable by the Secretary of State in accordance with Parts XI and XII of the ERA

- *compulsory liquidation*. Clearly, an order by a court for the compulsory winding up of an insolvent company would be 'analogous' to bankruptcy and is instituted with a view to the liquidation of the assets of the transferor. Reg 8(7) would therefore apply

- *creditors' voluntary liquidation*. Such proceedings are commenced with a view to winding up the company and are also 'analogous' to bankruptcy. This view concurs with the stance taken by the DTI in its guidance on the insolvency provisions contained in Regs 8 and 9, which states that: 'Where a liquidator sells a business run by a company that is in creditors' voluntary liquidation Reg 4 and Reg 7 will not apply. These provisions are disapplied by Reg 8(7) by virtue of the fact that creditors' voluntary liquidations are liquidation proceedings under the supervision of an insolvency practitioner that are analogous to bankruptcy proceedings' (see the insolvency guidance)

- *administration (when commenced with a view to liquidation of assets)*. Although, as outlined above and further discussed under '"Relevant insolvency proceedings" – meaning of "relevant insolvency proceedings"' below, it was widely assumed that administration falls within Reg 8(6) rather than Reg 8(7), the EAT's decision in Oakland v Wellswood (Yorkshire) Ltd 2009 IRLR 250, EAT, undermines this generalised assumption. While it

397

remains true that administration will often be used as part of the 'rescue culture' in so far as an administrator will normally strive from the outset to keep the business running while taking steps to restructure it or sell off the viable parts as a going concern, in some cases the principal objective is simply to realise and distribute the assets, eventually leading to a dissolution of the failed business. In this scenario, the EAT's decision suggests that it is open to an employment tribunal to regard the administration as being akin to liquidation, which will mean, in the words of Reg 8(7), that the 'transferor is subject to bankruptcy proceedings or... analogous insolvency proceedings which have been instituted with a view to the liquidation of the transferor'.

6.43 As has previously been noted, the appointment of the Official Receiver in a compulsory winding up automatically terminates the contracts of employees employed in the insolvent business – see under 'Types of insolvency procedures – liquidation (winding-up)' above. Although the same is not necessarily true in a creditors' voluntary winding up, in practice liquidators will often take immediate steps to terminate employees' contracts of employment because their continued employment will not be in the best interests of creditors. Since the special protection against unfair dismissal in Reg 7 is disapplied as a consequence of Reg 8(7) applying, such dismissals would not be automatically unfair but may be unfair on normal principles. Employees would be eligible to receive redundancy and insolvency payments from the National Insurance Fund in accordance with the provisions of Parts XI and XII of the ERA. In the comparatively rare event of the liquidator retaining the services of employees and subsequently selling the viable parts of the insolvent business as a going concern, these would be a relevant transfer to which the TUPE Regulations would apply. However, Reg 8(7) would operate to prevent the automatic transfer of the employees' employment to the transferee (see immediately below).

6.44 Consequences of disapplication of Regs 4 and 7
When it applies, the effect of Reg 8(7) is to disapply the whole of Regs 4 and 7 in respect of employees who are employed by the transferor at the time of the relevant transfer. So far as Reg 4 is concerned, this means that such employees will not be entitled to the automatic transfer of their employment to the new employer; nor will the new employer acquire the rights, duties, powers and liabilities under or in connection with the employees' contracts. If the employees are taken on by the new owner, they will not be entitled to the protection against detrimental variation of their terms and conditions by reason of the transfer, which would normally be guaranteed by Reg 4(4).

As for the disapplication of Reg 7, the consequence of this is that employees will be deprived of the special protections against unfair dismissal normally applicable to dismissals by reason of a relevant transfer. Thus, employees who are dismissed by the liquidator or trustee in bankruptcy prior to the relevant

398

transfer will not be able to claim that they have been automatically unfairly dismissed for a reason connected to the transfer that is not an economic, technical or organisational reason entailing changes in the workforce. The same applies if they are taken on by the new employer but subsequently dismissed for a transfer-connected reason. However, it is important to note that this is not to say that unfair dismissal rights are entirely excluded. There is nothing to prevent an employee who qualifies for the right to claim unfair dismissal from bringing a claim against the transferor and/or insolvency practitioner personally prior to the transfer, or, if taken on, the new employer after the transfer. In such a case, the unfairness of any such dismissal would be judged according to normal principles of unfair dismissal law.

6.45 Although the disapplication of Regs 4 and 7 means that the key provisions of the TUPE Regulations do not apply, it is also important to note that the Regulations' other key substantive provisions do so. Thus, employees will be entitled to the protection in respect of the transfer of collective agreements in Reg 5 and the transfer of union recognition in Reg 6 (see Chapter 3). The provisions dealing with employee liability information in Reg 11 and information and collective consultation in Regs 13–16 will also apply (see Chapter 8).

Finally, it should be noted that an employee who is taken on by the transferee is likely to retain his or her continuity of employment notwithstanding the operation of Reg 8(7). By virtue of S.218(2) ERA, where a business or undertaking 'is transferred from one person to another' an employee's period of employment in the trade, business or undertaking at the time of the transfer is deemed to count as a period of employment with the transferee, and the transfer will not break the continuity of the period of employment. This provision – which is discussed in detail in Chapter 7 – sits entirely outside of the TUPE Regulations, which means that the disapplication of Reg 4 has no effect on an employee's continuity.

'Relevant insolvency proceedings' 6.46

Reg 8(1) provides that the provisions of Reg 8(2)–(6) will apply 'if at the time of a relevant transfer the transferor is subject to relevant insolvency proceedings'. Reg 8(5) stipulates: 'Reg 4 shall not operate to transfer liability for the sums payable to the relevant employee under the relevant statutory schemes.' The phrases 'relevant employee' and 'relevant statutory schemes' in this context are defined by Reg 8(2) and (4). The overall effect of Reg 8(5) can be summarised as providing that, in a case where the transferor is subject to relevant insolvency proceedings, its liability to employees for some types of statutory payment will be excluded from the liabilities that pass to the transferee on a relevant transfer, and instead that liability will be paid to the employee out of the National Insurance Fund.

399

Regulation 9(1) provides: 'If at the time of a relevant transfer the transferor is subject to relevant insolvency proceedings these Regulations shall not prevent the transferor or transferee (or an insolvency practitioner) and appropriate representatives of assigned employees agreeing to permitted variations.' Sub-paragraphs (2)–(7) flesh out what is meant by 'appropriate representatives', 'assigned employees' and 'permitted variations' in this regard.

6.47   It will be noted that both of these provisions are only triggered where the transferor is subject to 'relevant insolvency provisions' as defined in Reg 8(6). This raises the question: which types of insolvency procedure outlined earlier in this chapter fall within the scope of this definition? This is a crucial matter to which we shall now turn.

6.48   **Meaning of 'relevant insolvency proceedings'**
The starting point in considering the application of Reg 8(5) and Reg 9 is the meaning given to 'relevant insolvency proceedings'. Reg 8(6) defines these as being 'insolvency proceedings *which have been opened* in relation to the transferor not with a view to the liquidation of the assets of the transferor and which are under the supervision of an insolvency practitioner'. It should be noted that the insolvency proceedings have to be under the supervision of an 'insolvency practitioner'. This point has also been made in respect of Reg 8(7) – see under 'Bankruptcy and liquidation proceedings' above.

Attention has also already been drawn to the slight difference in wording between Reg 8(6) and Reg 8(7), in that the former speaks of 'proceedings which have been *opened*', whereas the latter speaks of 'proceedings which have been *instituted*'. As outlined previously, we can find no clear explanation for this difference in wording, but do not believe that it has any significance in practice – see discussion under 'Bankruptcy and liquidation proceedings' above. What is identical between the two provisions is that both use the words 'which have been', denoting the past tense. As was made clear by the EAT in Secretary of State for Trade and Industry v Slater 2008 ICR 54, EAT, in order for either Reg 8(6) or Reg 8(7) to be engaged, it is necessary for the insolvency proceedings in question to have actually been opened/instituted *prior* to the date of the relevant transfer. If the proceedings commence after the transfer has occurred, then the TUPE Regulations will apply in full, not just the reduced protections provided for in Reg 8(6) or Reg 8(7). For a fuller discussion of the Slater decision, see under 'Bankruptcy and liquidation proceedings' above.

6.49   **Criticism of drafting of Reg 8(6).** Turning to the types of proceedings that will qualify as 'relevant insolvency proceedings' under Reg 8(6), it is immediately apparent that a straightforward list is not provided. This lack has been criticised in some quarters. However, the DTI in its Public Consultation Document on the draft regulations in March 2005 gave a number of reasons for not simply listing the proceedings to which Reg 8(5) (and, for that matter, Reg 9) was intended to apply. These included that the lack of a list made the provision much simpler, given that there are different (albeit largely equivalent) procedures in England and Wales, Scotland and Northern Ireland, and that this ensured beyond doubt that the United Kingdom has not extended the coverage of the exclusionary provision more widely than the Acquired Rights Directive allows.

Many insolvency practitioners were unconvinced by these arguments. In the Parliamentary challenge to the Regulations in May 2006 previously discussed under 'Bankruptcy and liquidation proceedings' above, Lord Hunt of Wirral observed that the definition of relevant insolvency proceedings seeks to draw a distinction between two types of insolvency proceedings: those opened with a view to the liquidation of the assets of the transferor, and those opened not with a view to the liquidation of the assets. This, in his view, was a rather simplistic view of the United Kingdom's very complex insolvency laws. Assets can be sold in every type of insolvency procedure, whether administration, administrative receivership, voluntary arrangement or liquidation, and also where the whole or part of the business is preserved and sold as a going concern. Lord Hunt was concerned that any uncertainty in assessing whether the specific limitations in Regs 8 and 9 applied would cause delays in the administration of the insolvency, thereby reducing the chances of successful rescue and preservation of jobs. He also pointed out that the definition of 'relevant insolvency proceedings' refers to liquidation of 'the' assets, when in fact many transfers of insolvent businesses involve the liquidation of only some assets. Use of the words 'some', 'all' or 'any' would have provided greater clarity.

Identifying main purpose of the insolvency proceedings. Whatever may be 6.50 the drafting ambiguities, it seems reasonably clear that in assessing whether the limitation provided for by Reg 8(5) applies, the most important factor to consider is the purpose of the proceedings – in particular, whether they have been opened with a view to the liquidation of the assets of the transferor. In its 'Employment rights on the transfer of an undertaking: a guide to the 2006 TUPE Regulations for employees, employers and their representatives', the DTI asserts that '"relevant insolvency proceedings" means any collective insolvency proceedings in which the whole or part of the business or undertaking is transferred to another entity as a going concern'. In this context, the DTI makes clear that a 'collective' insolvency proceeding means 'a proceeding in which all creditors of the debtor may participate, and in relation to which the insolvency office-holder owes a duty to all creditors'. The Guide expressly states that this would exclude a situation where the insolvent company is wound up as a result of a members' or creditors' voluntary liquidation.

It has to be said that this interpretation is not immediately apparent from the language of the Regulations. In any event, in order to clarify the Government's approach, more specific guidance was given in June 2006 by the Insolvency Service. This insolvency guidance states that the determining factor is the main

401

or sole purpose of the procedure rather than its outcome in a specific instance. This fits in with the words 'opened with a view to' in the definition of 'relevant insolvency proceedings' in Reg 8(6), which implies that the key factor is the aim at the outset of the proceedings. Although this insolvency guidance is sufficient to enable insolvency practitioners to understand how Regs 8 and 9 apply to most straightforward types of insolvency proceedings, problems of interpretation may still arise in more complex scenarios – particularly where different types of insolvency proceedings overlap, or where the purpose of the insolvency proceedings changes.

6.51 **Which insolvency procedures comprise 'relevant insolvency proceedings'?** Neither guide published by the DTI comprises definitive legal advice, and it will therefore be for courts and tribunals to establish the precise definition of 'relevant insolvency proceedings' through case law. It is nonetheless possible to be fairly confident that certain of the kinds of insolvency proceedings discussed under 'Types of insolvency procedures' will be found to come within the definition of 'relevant insolvency proceedings' in Reg 8(6). This is because they are opened for a purpose other than the liquidation of the assets, and are under the supervision of an insolvency practitioner. The proceedings in question are:

- a company voluntary arrangement: the objective of this type of insolvency arrangement is to enable the company to continue as a going concern under the supervision of an insolvency practitioner. As the insolvency guidance points out, in a voluntary arrangement the debtor is left in control of the assets and the function of the insolvency practitioner is merely to supervise the arrangement

- administrative receivership: since an administrative receiver is appointed to realise assets to pay off secured creditors but not to liquidate all the company's assets, it would seem that this form of insolvency proceeding comes within Reg 8(6) as it would 'have been opened... not with a view to the liquidation of the assets of the transferor'.

6.52 A much bigger question mark, however, hovers over administration, one of the most commonly used forms of insolvency procedure. As has already been seen, the provisions in the IA governing administration require the objective of the administration to be identified according to a strictly prioritised order – see under 'Types of insolvency procedures – company administration' above. The first two objectives seek to avoid a winding up, and it is only if these are unachievable that an administrator is entitled to select the third option; namely, the realisation of the assets in order to make a beneficial distribution to secured and preferred creditors. Since the administrator is required to identify his or her aim at the outset of the administration, it is arguable that if he or she chooses the third option the administration might fall outside the definition of 'relevant insolvency proceedings' and instead become 'proceedings that are "analogous" to bankruptcy' and which are 'instituted with a view to the liquidation of the assets' within the meaning of Reg 8(7). However, the stance taken by the Insolvency Service in its insolvency guidance does not draw any distinction between these various possible objectives. It simply states: 'Administration is not in the view of the Secretary of State analogous to bankruptcy proceedings. The correct approach is to look at the main or sole purpose of the procedure rather than its outcome in a specific instance. The main purpose of bankruptcy proceedings is to realise the free assets of an insolvent debtor and share the proceeds after deduction of costs and expenses amongst all the debtor's creditors. This is not the main purpose of administration. It follows that Reg 8(7) will not apply to administration. It is also the view of the Secretary of State that Regs 8(2) to (6) will apply to administration so that liabilities owed to transferring employees at the transfer date of the kinds described in Part XII of the Employment Rights Act 1996 would fall to be paid out of the National Insurance Fund by the Secretary of State and not by the transferee.' Although even administrations that start off aiming to preserve the business can end up becoming a creditors' voluntary liquidation, it is arguable that this would not disqualify it from falling within the definition in Reg 8(6) as the proceedings would not have been 'opened with a view to' the liquidation of the insolvent company's assets.

Administration. The EAT's decision in Oakland v Wellswood (Yorkshire) Ltd 2009 IRLR 250, EAT, has certainly caused some consternation in the context of Reg 8(6). On the basis of the guidance described above, it was widely assumed that when a company is placed under the supervision of an administrator the main or sole purpose of the procedure is to rescue the business rather than to realise the assets with a view to distribution among creditors. However, the EAT in Oakland allowed for the possibility that the main objective may not be to rescue the insolvent company but to realise and distribute the proceeds of the assets in circumstances where there is little or no hope of the company surviving as a going concern. In these circumstances, it is apparently open to an employment tribunal to find that the administration does not fall within Reg 8(6), but rather is an insolvency procedure analogous to bankruptcy proceedings, so that the more draconian effect of Reg 8(7) applies. This means that instead of the transferee simply being freed of a limited number of the transferor's debts (such as holiday pay and outstanding wages), it will not be bound at all by the entirety of Regs 4 and 7. Thus, the transferee will not inherit the contracts of employment of any transferred employees or acquire liabilities under those contracts; and nor will it be subject to the specific provisions dealing with unfair dismissal in the context of a TUPE transfer. **6.53**

The Oakland decision has been discussed in detail in the context of Reg 8(7) – see under 'Bankruptcy and liquidation proceedings' above. We pointed out there that the EAT's decision was in fact overturned on appeal, but that the grounds on which the Court of Appeal reached its decision were entirely new and unrelated to the Reg 8(6)/8(7) controversy that had been the sole focus of

403

the EAT's decision. This means that the EAT's reasoning in that case survives unless and until it is reassessed or overturned. In this regard, the EAT will soon have an opportunity to revisit the question of whether administration necessarily falls within the scope of Reg 8(6) in the joined cases of Olds v Late Editions Ltd and Otford Tool Ltd v Barker EAT 0321/09.

6.54 In the meantime, it seems fairly safe to assume that in the majority of cases the main purpose of an administration – at least at the point of commencement – will be to undertake the necessary restructuring and/or selling off of an insolvent company's viable parts to effect its survival. The following employment tribunal decision shows that, in these circumstances, it will be Reg 8(6) rather than Reg 8(7) that applies:

- **De'antiquis v Drummond Kirkwood LLP and ors** ET Case No.2329822/08: in June 2008 DK LLP was in serious financial difficulty and took advice with a view to placing the partnership into a formal insolvency process. An application for an Administration Order was made on 14 July, following which the partnership was advertised in the *Financial Times* with a request for offers. This produced a strong response from a number of potential purchasers. On 21 July, some of DK LLP's employees were informed that they were redundant. An Administration Order was granted and joint administrators appointed, who immediately contacted a practice that had submitted an offer for the business with a view to finalising negotiations for its sale. However, those negotiations broke down and the administrators offered management contracts to a number of firms in order to keep DK LLP's business afloat. At this point K plc entered into a management contract in respect of two of DK LLP's offices and proceeded to trade from those premises, retaining a number of DK LLP's solicitors. In February 2009 the Administration Order was discharged and DK LLP was formally wound up. Following claims brought by one of DK LLP's employees, the question arose whether there had been a TUPE transfer to K plc and, if so, whether the provisions of Reg 8(6) or Reg 8(7) applied. At a pre-hearing review to consider this matter, an employment tribunal judge held that the administration proceedings in this case were not opened with a view to the liquidation of the assets and that accordingly Reg 8(6) applied. This meant that Reg 4 did not operate to transfer liability to K plc for sums that were in fact payable under the National Insurance Fund by virtue of Reg 8(5) – see under 'Liability for sums payable under statutory scheme' below.

6.55 *Members' voluntary liquidation.* With regard to members' voluntary liquidations, the point has already been made that these operate to wind up companies that are solvent and are therefore not an insolvency proceeding. The DTI takes the view that fixed-charge receiverships and court-appointed receiverships similarly do not come within the definition of 'relevant insolvency proceedings'. Any relevant transfer that occurs in the course of such a proceeding would therefore be subject to the normal TUPE rules rather than the modified rules discussed in this chapter.

Foreign insolvency proceedings. In the rare event of a relevant transfer **6.56** occurring in Great Britain where the business or undertaking is subject to foreign insolvency proceedings, it would be necessary to consider whether those proceedings come within the definition of 'relevant insolvency proceedings'. If they do, then the provisions of Regs 8(5) and 9 as described below would apply.

Liability for sums payable under statutory scheme **6.57**
Under the 1981 Regulations, the liabilities in respect of employees transferring from an insolvent business passed to the transferee in accordance with the same principles as those applicable to any other type of TUPE transfer. However, under the 2006 Regulations, Reg 8(5) now provides that certain liabilities in respect of transferring employees that would ordinarily attach to the transferee will instead be met by the payments out of the National Insurance Fund where the transferor is subject to 'relevant insolvency proceedings' as described above. This is in keeping with the Government's desire to encourage the rescue of more insolvent businesses.

As previously mentioned, Reg 8(5) reflects the option given in Article 5.2(a) of the Acquired Rights Directive. This allows EU Member States to provide that the transferor's debts arising from any contracts of employment or employment relationships and payable before the transfer or the opening of the insolvency proceedings need not be transferred to the transferee, provided that employees' rights in this regard are protected by payments from state guarantee institutions that are at least equivalent to those required by the EU Insolvency Directive (No.80/89). The categories of debt guaranteed under the relevant UK provisions satisfy this condition, since they are more extensive than those required under the Directive itself.

Regulation 8(5) stipulates that 'Reg 4 shall not operate to transfer liability for **6.58** the sums payable to a relevant employee under the relevant statutory schemes'. As we shall see below, Reg 8(2) and (4) define 'relevant employee' and 'relevant statutory schemes' for this purpose. Taken together, these provisions essentially aim to ensure that where a relevant transfer takes place in the context of 'relevant insolvency proceedings', liabilities in respect of certain debts and payments payable to employees do not transfer – as they normally would – but remain with the transferor. However, in view of the transferor's insolvency, responsibility for payment is taken on by the Secretary of State for Trade and Industry out of the National Insurance Fund. Whenever such a payment is made, all rights and remedies of the employee with respect to that payment are transferred to the Secretary of State. Under insolvency law, such payments will usually attract preferential status, and so the Secretary of State will often seek

405

to recover sums paid from the proceeds of sale or other realisation of the insolvent business's assets.

6.59 **'Relevant employee'.** Regulation 8(5) only applies in respect of a 'relevant employee'. Such a person is defined as an employee of the transferor whose contract of employment transfers to the transferee by virtue of the operation of the TUPE Regulations (Reg 8(2)(a)); or whose employment with the transferor is terminated before the time of the relevant transfer in circumstances where he or she has been automatically unfairly dismissed by reason of the transfer or for a reason connected to it within the meaning of Reg 7(1).

6.60 **'Relevant statutory schemes'.** The liabilities that are not transferred by virtue of Reg 8(5) are specifically those sums payable under 'the relevant statutory schemes'. These are defined in Reg 8(4) as the statutory insolvency payments provisions in Part XII of the ERA and the statutory redundancy payments provisions in Chapter VI of Part XI of the ERA (and their equivalent under the statutory provisions applicable to Northern Ireland).

Part XII of the ERA (or Part XIV of the Employment Rights (Northern Ireland) Order 1996) covers 'Insolvency of Employers' and provides that an employee can apply to the Secretary of State for payment of certain debts out of the National Insurance Fund if the employee can demonstrate that the employer is insolvent, that his or her employment has been terminated, and that he or she was entitled to the whole or part of the debt in question on the 'appropriate date' (S.182 ERA). However, these requirements are modified by Reg 8(3) of the TUPE Regulations, which provides that the normal qualifying condition for payment of these debts – namely that the employee's employment has actually been terminated by the insolvent employer or insolvency practitioner – does not apply to a relevant employee as defined in Reg 5(2). Thus, such employees do not have to show that their employment has been terminated to be eligible for payments out of the Fund in respect of the debts in question. Reg 8(3) also deems that the date of the transfer is to be treated as the date of termination and the transferor is to be treated as the employer. Of course, the employee needs actually to be entitled to the debt. In this regard, the specific debts and payments covered by the statutory schemes are listed below.

6.61 Chapter VI of Part XI of the ERA (Ss.166–170) (and the equivalent Chapter VI of Part XII of the Employment Rights (Northern Ireland) Order 1996) deals with 'Payments by Secretary of State'. In summary, it provides that, where an employee has not been paid a redundancy payment that is due to him or her from an insolvent employer, he or she can apply to the Secretary of State for payment of it out of the National Insurance Fund (S.166 ERA). It should be noted that the provision in Reg 8(3) deeming a 'relevant employee' to have been dismissed for the purposes of payment of debts under the statutory scheme in Part XII of the ERA does not apply in respect of payments of statutory redundancy pay. Relevant employees will not therefore be deemed to have been dismissed if they have not actually been so in order to enable them to claim redundancy payments.

Under both statutory schemes, it is the insolvency of the employer that triggers entitlement to claim for the respective debts or payments from out of the National Insurance Fund. An employer is regarded as being 'insolvent' under either scheme if: (a) a winding up order has been made or a resolution for winding up has been passed; (b) an administration order has been made; (c) a receiver or manager of the company's undertaking has been appointed; (d) possession has been taken by or on behalf of the holders of any debentures secured by a floating charge, of any property of the company comprised in or subject to the charge; or (e) a voluntary arrangement has been approved under Part 1 IA (Ss.166(7) and 183(3) ERA). For the reasons mentioned under 'Meaning of "relevant insolvency proceedings"' above, it would seem likely that (b)–(e) would come within the definition of 'relevant insolvency proceedings' and so would trigger the application of Reg 8(5), but that a winding up order or resolution for winding up would not. Instead, Reg 8(7) – providing for the disapplication of Reg 4 in its entirety – would apply (see 'Bankruptcy and liquidation proceedings' above).

Which liabilities for debts and payments do not transfer? The payments **6.62** included in the relevant statutory schemes are set out below (note that all of these are subject to the statutory cap on a week's pay – currently (as at January 2011) £380. This is uprated annually):

- up to eight weeks' arrears of pay, owed as at the date the employer became insolvent (subject to a current maximum (as at January 2011) of £3,040). 'Arrears of pay' includes a guarantee payment, payment for time off for carrying out trade union duties or the duties of a public office, payment when an employee is suspended on medical or maternity grounds, and a protective award made under S.189 of the Trade Union and Labour Relations (Consolidation) Act 1992 (TULR(C)A)

- pay in lieu of notice up to the statutory minimum notice periods (up to a current maximum (as at January 2011) of £4,560)

- up to six weeks' accrued but unpaid holiday pay (to a current maximum (as at January 2011) of £2,280). The holiday must have accrued in the last 12 months

- the basic award of compensation for unfair dismissal (up to a current maximum (as at January 2011) of £11,400), due on the later of the date the employer became insolvent, the date of termination of employment or the date the award was made

407

- a reasonable sum as reimbursement for any fee or premium paid by an apprentice or articled clerk (which is not subject to the current limit on a week's pay)

(all payable by virtue of S.174 ERA); and

- a statutory redundancy payment (up to a current maximum (as at January 2011) of £11,400) – S166 ERA.

6.63 It must be borne in mind that, in order for any of the above payments to be payable, the employee has to be entitled to it. Generally, so far as redundancy is concerned, if the transferor or insolvency practitioner dismisses an employee for a transfer-connected reason comprising an economic, technical or organisational reason entailing changes in the workforce within the meaning of Reg 7(2), the dismissal will be regarded as being for redundancy and will thus trigger entitlement to a statutory redundancy payment (provided the employee has at least two years' continuous service) – see Chapter 4, 'Unfair dismissal', under 'Dismissals potentially fair for an "ETO" reason – ETO reasons will be redundancy or SOSR'. In such a case, if the employee is a relevant employee as defined by Reg 8(2) – see above – then his or her statutory redundancy payment will be met by the Secretary of State via a payment out of the National Insurance Fund. If, however, the employee is dismissed solely or mainly because of the transfer or for a reason that is not an ETO reason, the reason for the dismissal will not be 'redundancy', and no entitlement for a payment out of the Fund will arise. Of course, as the dismissal is unfair and the employee is likely to be entitled to compensation, he or she would be entitled to a basic award, which is calculated according to the same formula as used for statutory redundancy payments. However, the Fund would not pay out the compensatory award. This is made clear in para 12 of the guidance issued by the Insolvency Service entitled 'Redundancy and Insolvency – A Guide for Insolvency Practitioners to employees' rights on the insolvency of their employer' (URN 08/550). That said, it may be that, following a finding of unfair dismissal, a tribunal's decision to award sums in respect of unpaid holiday and the statutory minimum notice period as elements of the compensatory award would provide evidence that these debts, which as we have seen are recoverable from the Fund, were owed by the insolvent transferor to the employee. Any payment already made by the Secretary of State in respect of these particular matters by the time of the remedies hearing would fall to be offset against the compensatory award.

Similar reasoning would apply if an employee is taken on by the transferee. In that case, he or she will not be entitled to a redundancy payment, as such a payment is only payable if (a) the employee had been dismissed, and (b) the reason for dismissal satisfies the definition of redundancy in S.139 ERA. If such a payment is made despite the fact that the employee does not meet the above conditions, then the rule in S.214(2) ERA, that the payment of a statutory redundancy payment serves to break the employee's continuity of employment for redundancy pay purposes, will not apply – Senior Heat Treatment Ltd v Bell and ors 1997 IRLR 614, EAT. This view is supported in the Insolvency Service's insolvency guidance on Regs 8 and 9, which states: 'Where an employee's contract of employment is transferred pursuant to Reg 4 and his employment continues with the transferee, no redundancy payment will be payable as the employee has not been dismissed.' (It is worth reiterating that the provision in Reg 8(3) deeming employees to have been dismissed, which is discussed under '"Relevant statutory schemes"' above, does not apply to redundancy payments paid by the Secretary of State out of the National Insurance Fund under Chapter VI of Part XI of the ERA.)

Other debts that do transfer. Regulation 8 will result in fewer liabilities **6.64** transferring to a transferee, and should in theory make the business more attractive to a potential purchaser. However, there are still liabilities over and above those included in the 'relevant statutory schemes' which will transfer to the transferee in the usual way. These include:

- debts and liabilities that fall outside the categories payable under the relevant statutory schemes (see Chapter 3)

- sums owed to employees which exceed the statutory upper limits on the statutory payments (since these payments are subject to the statutory cap on a week's pay, currently (as at January 2011) £380). This would include, for example, arrears of pay in excess of eight weeks. In Connor and anor v Secretary of State for Trade and Industry EAT 0589–90/05 the EAT held that the eight-week limit in this regard was not contrary to the requirements of either the Insolvency Directive or the EU Collective Redundancies Directive (No.80/987).

Changing terms and conditions   6.65
Under the TUPE Regulations 1981 there was some confusion over whether an employee's terms and conditions could be varied by agreement where the reason for the variation was a TUPE transfer. This confusion stemmed partly from the decisions of the House of Lords in (1) British Fuels Ltd v Baxendale and anor (2) Wilson and ors v St Helens Borough Council 1998 ICR 1141, HL. The position is clarified in the 2006 Regs in relation to a non-insolvency TUPE transfer by Reg 4 and in relation to transfers that take place in the course of relevant insolvency proceedings by Reg 9. For a detailed discussion of the normal TUPE rules regarding the ability to vary contracts of employment, see Chapter 5, 'Changing terms and conditions'. This section looks at the special rules on changing terms and conditions of employment in 'relevant insolvency proceedings'.

Summarising the position as it applies outside an insolvency context, Reg 4(5) stipulates that contracts of employment can only be varied by agreement between the transferee and transferred employees if the sole or principal reason

409

for the change is (a) a reason connected with the transfer that is an economic, technical or organisational reason entailing changes in the workforce ('ETO reason'); or (b) a reason altogether unconnected with the transfer. It follows that if the reason for a change is the transfer itself or is a reason connected to the transfer that is not an ETO reason, that change will be void (and so cannot be accepted by conduct) – see Reg 4(4).

6.66 Regulation 9 reflects the Government's policy to promote the 'rescue culture' that underlies the insolvency provisions of the Regulations. In accordance with this policy, the Government took advantage of the option given to Member States in Article 5.2 of the Acquired Rights Directive designed to promote the sale of insolvent businesses as going concerns. This allowed Member States to permit employers and employee representatives to agree alterations to employees' terms and conditions of employment provided those alterations were designed to safeguard jobs by ensuring the survival of the undertaking or part of the undertaking. Reg 9 enacts this option, with the additional requirement that the changes must be agreed with appropriate employee representatives and in writing. Changes to terms and conditions can therefore now be agreed even in the absence of an ETO reason subject to compliance with these procedural safeguards. In theory Reg 9 should make it easier for insolvency practitioners to achieve a sale of a going concern by allowing employees to transfer on inferior terms and conditions, and by enabling transferees to harmonise terms and conditions. Under the 1981 Regulations this would not have been possible. However, it may be that the procedural steps required to effect the changes are so time-consuming that Reg 9 will not assist insolvency practitioners in securing the sale of insolvent businesses as much as was hoped.

6.67 **Procedural requirements.** Regulation 9(1) stipulates that: 'If at the time of a relevant transfer the transferor is subject to relevant insolvency proceedings these Regulations shall not prevent the transferor or transferee (or an insolvency practitioner) and appropriate representatives of assigned employees agreeing to permitted variations.' The remainder of Reg 9 sets out the criteria that must be met for the changes to terms and conditions to be valid:

- the transferor must be subject to 'relevant insolvency proceedings' at the time of the relevant transfer (Reg 9(1)) (see '"Relevant insolvency proceedings"' above)

- the change must be a 'permitted variation' as defined in Reg 9(7)

- the permitted variations must be agreed between the transferor, the transferee or an insolvency practitioner and 'appropriate representatives' of assigned employees as defined in Reg 9(2) – see below. In essence, these are union representatives if there is a recognised independent trade union or, if there is no recognised trade union, employee representatives who have been elected either specifically for the purposes of Reg 9 or for other purposes provided they have authority to agree changes to contracts of employment on behalf of employees (Reg 9(2) and (3))

- the permitted variations must be agreed with representatives of 'assigned employees' – defined in Reg 9(7) as those employees assigned to the organised grouping of resources or employees that is the subject of the relevant transfer. The overarching requirement for employees to be assigned to the business or undertaking being transferred in order for Reg 4 to apply is discussed in detail in Chapter 2

- if employees are represented by non-trade union representatives, the permitted variations must be in writing and signed by each representative. In addition, before the agreement is signed, the employer must provide all employees to whom it is going to apply with a copy of the agreement and any guidance that they may need in order to understand it fully (Reg 9(5)).

'Permitted variations'. Regulation 9 applies only if the variation comprises a **6.68** 'permitted variation'. This is defined in Reg 9(7) as 'a variation to the contract of employment of an assigned employee where – (a) the sole or principal reason for it is the transfer itself or a reason connected with the transfer that is not an economic, technical or organisational reason entailing changes in the workforce; and (b) it is designed to safeguard employment opportunities by ensuring the survival of the undertaking, business or part of the undertaking or business that is the subject of the relevant transfer'.

The first thing to note is that, in the light of the first limb of Reg 9(7), the variation in question must not be one where the sole or principal reason for it is an ETO reason. This is in order to distinguish 'permitted variations' that may arise in the course of relevant insolvency proceedings from the kind of variation of contract that is permissible outside of an insolvency context as governed by Reg 4(5). An ETO reason for a variation is valid provided that the normal non-TUPE rules governing variation of contract are adhered to – see Chapter 5 under 'Types of variation permitted by TUPE'. A Reg 9 'permitted variation', on the other hand, attracts the special rules and procedures discussed in this section, and can only arise in an insolvency context. So, for example, a variation to which Reg 9 might apply but Reg 4(5) would not would be changes entailing employees accepting lower pay or holiday entitlement, giving up a company car or other benefit, or changes made in order to harmonise terms and conditions. None of these are likely to comprise an ETO reason since, as we have seen in Chapter 5, they do not 'entail changes in the workforce'. That said, any new terms and conditions agreed by way of a permitted variation must not breach any other statutory entitlements – for example, a change in contractual pay terms must not be set below the national minimum wage.

—— **411**

6.69 The second limb of Reg 9(7) makes it clear that the objective of agreeing the permitted variation must be to safeguard employment opportunities by ensuring the survival of the undertaking or business. The wording of this requirement may cause difficulties in practice, as the transferee will need to be able to show that the business could not survive without those particular changes. In reality, the effect of the change may not be as clear cut as envisaged by this definition.

Once agreed, a permitted variation takes effect as a term or condition of the assigned employee's contract of employment in place (where relevant) of any term or condition which it varies – Reg 9(6). This raises the question of whether the contractual terms of individual employees who decline to give their consent to the proposed variation are overridden so long as all the procedural requirements, including the reaching of agreement with appropriate representatives, have been honoured. This matter is discussed under 'What if the employee does not agree?' below.

6.70 **'Appropriate representatives'.** The requirements to appoint and elect employee representatives for the purposes of Reg 9 closely mirror those required to appoint and elect employee representatives for information and consultation purposes which are set out in Reg 14. This procedure is discussed in detail in Chapter 8. But the two sets of requirements are not identical, as we shall see below.

As defined in Reg 9(2), 'appropriate representatives' are:

- if the employees are of a description in respect of which an independent trade union is recognised by their employer, representatives of the trade union. It seems likely that union representatives must have the right to agree changes to terms and conditions on behalf of their members, a right which will usually be found in collective agreements or will arise out of custom and practice; or

- in any other case, whichever of the following employee representatives the employer chooses: (i) employee representatives appointed or elected by the assigned employees other than for the purposes of Reg 9, who nevertheless have authority to agree variations to contracts of employment on their behalf; (ii) employee representatives elected by assigned employees for the purposes of Reg 9, in an election satisfying the requirements set out in Reg 14 in respect of information and consultation.

6.71 There are two significant differences between these provisions and those that apply in respect of the employer's duty to inform and consult. First, in respect of non-trade union representatives, the employee representatives under Reg 9 can only be elected by 'assigned employees' (in other words, employees who are assigned to the undertaking or business or part that is the subject of the relevant transfer). This is in contrast to the position in respect of electing employee representatives to deal with the information and consultation duties. Such representatives are electable by all 'affected employees' – i.e. employees of either the transferor or transferee who may be affected by the transfer or measures connected with it, whether or not they are assigned to the undertaking or part transferred. Secondly, in the case of Reg 9 representatives, a specific term of office does not need to be determined by the employer, in contrast to the position of Reg 14 representatives, in respect of whom the employer must determine a period of office sufficient to ensure that the representatives are properly informed and consulted – Reg 9(2)(b)(ii).

The remaining requirements are identical for both sets of representatives. Indeed, the same individual may be an appropriate representative for the purposes of both agreeing permitted variations under Reg 9 and participating in the information and consultation process under Regs 13–15. All representatives are entitled to the same protections so far as dismissal and detriment for carrying out their respective duties are concerned – Ss.47(1)(a) and 103(2) ERA. And all such employees (including candidates for an election, not just those who are actually elected) have the right to a reasonable amount of paid time off to enable them to carry out their duties – S.61(1) ERA and, in the case of union representatives, S.168(1)(c) TULR(C)A.

Additional procedural requirements for non-trade union representatives. 6.72
Where assigned employees are represented by non-trade union representatives there are additional requirements designed to give the employees greater protection with regard to permitted variations of their terms and conditions. In its Public Consultation Document on the Regulations published in March 2005, the Government stated that the additional safeguards included in Reg 9 are based on similar provisions relating to working time agreements under the Working Time Regulations 1998 (see IDS Employment Law Handbook, 'Working Time' (2009), Chapter 1 for details). They are designed to take into account the fact that non-union representatives are not normally involved in negotiating changes to employees' terms and conditions, and are likely to be less experienced and knowledgeable than union representatives. Reg 9(5) accordingly stipulates that:

- the agreement recording a permitted variation must be in writing, and

- must be signed by each of the representatives who have made it or, where that is not reasonably practicable, by a duly authorised agent of that representative, and

- the employer must, before the agreement is made available for signature, provide all employees to whom it is intended to apply on the date on which it is to come into effect with (i) copies of the text of the agreement and (ii) such guidance as those employees might reasonably require in order to understand it fully.

413

6.73 It is not yet clear how tribunals will interpret the requirement for guidance – for example, how wide its scope needs to be and whether employees should be advised on what to do if they do not agree to the proposed variation. Clearly these additional requirements will add another procedural hurdle for an insolvency practitioner, taking up time and resources in the quest to sell the viable parts of the insolvent business as a going concern. On the other hand, given the potential significance of the changes for an individual employee, the additional procedural requirements may help to reduce the risk of the insolvency practitioner (on behalf of the transferor) or the transferee having to face legal challenges from members of a disenchanted workforce. Although not strictly a requirement within the scope of Reg 9, it may be advisable to obtain from employees their individual written consent for permitted variations that are negotiated and agreed with their representatives. This could be achieved by issuing new contracts containing the amended terms and asking employees to sign these.

6.74 **What if the employee does not agree?** Even if an agreement to vary contracts of employment is negotiated with employee representatives, there may be problems if individual employees do not agree to those changes. The circumstances of insolvency proceedings are such that the negotiated changes will normally involve employees taking a pay cut or a reduction in benefits. While ultimately such changes, in order to be valid, have to be shown to be designed to save jobs, obviously there may be some employees who are unhappy about them. Assuming the procedure has been followed correctly, in theory the permitted variation takes effect nonetheless as a term or condition of their contracts of employment.

It should also be borne in mind that the TUPE Regulations now accord employees the right to resign where a relevant transfer involves or would involve a substantial change in working conditions to their material detriment – Reg 4(9). This right – which has been extensively analysed in Chapter 4 under 'Material detriment dismissals' – appears to allow the employees to regard themselves as having been dismissed if they resign on the basis of a change that need not amount to a fundamental breach of contract or even to a breach of contract at all. It is, as yet, far from clear how Reg 4(9) will be interpreted by employment tribunals, and even less clear how (if at all) this provision ties in with the ability to agree permitted variations in the course of insolvency proceedings under Reg 9. However, there is a risk that individual employees who are disgruntled with the outcome agreed on their behalf by their representatives might utilise the right in Reg 4(9) to challenge permitted variations. Presumably, the hope is that employees will weigh up the risk of losing their employment altogether – which is a considerable risk if the prospects for sale of the business are reduced owing to concern about legal challenges to the validity of agreed contractual changes.

414

Practical issues. There may be situations where negotiating permitted variations 6.75 does safeguard employment opportunities and ensure the survival of the company. However, the business of complying with the procedure may not be straightforward in practice. This is because:

- it can take time to appoint appropriate representatives, particularly if all employees are not covered by recognised trade unions and elections need to be arranged

- the negotiations to seek agreement to changes in terms and conditions may take some time and even then may not result in an agreement. In particular, it will be hard for insolvency practitioners to manage this process if there are ongoing negotiations with several potential purchasers, each with different ideas about the changes which need to be made to safeguard the business

- the second limb of the definition of a 'permitted variation' (Reg 9(7)(b)) may in practice limit its scope, since it will have to be demonstrated that the change directly ensures the survival of the business. Although there is no prescribed time limit for the change to take place, it therefore seems likely that in order to come within the definition of 'permitted variations', a change should be effected as close to the transfer as possible

- it is possible to agree permitted changes after the transfer has taken place. However, due to the uncertain financial position of the insolvent company, a prospective purchaser may not be willing to take on the business without knowing that the changes it requires can be effected. A conditional sale agreement may solve the problem, but this may not be acceptable to the insolvency practitioner.

Dismissal by insolvency practitioners 6.76

Except in the case of a compulsory liquidation, the appointment of an insolvency practitioner will not, in itself, have any effect upon contracts of employment. This means that employees will continue to be employed by the insolvent company unless and until their employment is terminated – for example, because the insolvency practitioner forms the view that the dismissal of some or all of the workforce is necessary in order to achieve an optimum realisation of the insolvent company's assets.

Dismissals of employees in the context of a TUPE transfer are governed by Reg 7, which is discussed in Chapter 4. These general principles also apply where dismissals occur during the course of relevant insolvency proceedings. In summary, Reg 7(1) provides that where the sole or main reason for dismissal is the transfer itself, or a reason connected with the transfer that is not an economic, technical or organisational reason entailing changes in the workforce ('ETO reason'), the dismissal is automatically unfair. Reg 7(2) provides that

415

where the sole or main reason for the dismissal is a reason connected with the transfer that is an ETO reason entailing changes in the workforce of the transferor or the transferee, before or after a relevant transfer, the dismissal could be for the potentially fair reason of redundancy or 'some other substantial reason' of a kind such as to justify the dismissal. TUPE has no impact on dismissals that are unconnected with the transfer.

6.77 Under Reg 4(3), transferring employees include any employees who would have been employed immediately before the transfer had they not been automatically unfairly dismissed under Reg 7(1). This provision reflects the House of Lords' judgment in Litster and ors v Forth Dry Dock and Engineering Co Ltd (in receivership) and anor 1989 ICR 341, HL (see Chapter 2 under 'Employed "immediately before" transfer').

6.78 Is the dismissal 'connected with' the transfer?

Any dismissal that is connected with a relevant transfer which is not for an ETO reason will be automatically unfair by virtue of Reg 7(1). If an insolvency practitioner dismisses employees immediately prior to selling the viable parts of an insolvent business, those dismissals will invariably be 'connected with' the transfer. The purchaser will inherit the contracts of the employees and all related liabilities, including liability for those dismissals, subject to the provisions of Reg 8 (see under '"Relevant insolvency proceedings" – non-transfer of liability for sums payable under statutory scheme' above).

It may be that the insolvency practitioner decides shortly after his or her appointment that the dismissal of some or all of the workforce is unavoidable because no potential sale of the business seems likely and its continuation would merely serve to deplete the realisable assets available for distribution to creditors. Dismissals may also be necessary because certain parts of the business entirely lack commercial viability. In either case, the dismissals will be for redundancy in that there will be a cessation of the business or a diminution in the requirements of the business for employees. If it should later transpire that, against expectations, the insolvency practitioner does manage to sell some or all of the business in circumstances constituting a 'relevant transfer', employees who were dismissed previously would not be entitled to rely on Reg 7(1) because their dismissals will be regarded as having been for a valid ETO reason.

6.79 It can be much more difficult where dismissals are effected at a time when tentative plans to sell the business exist, but the sale does not actually happen until a much later date. It is often hard to say whether such dismissals are connected with the subsequent transfer. Each case will be decided on its own distinct facts and circumstances. However, the cases below (which were decided under the 1981 Regulations) illustrate the problems which can arise:

- **Harrison Bowden Ltd v Bowden** 1994 ICR 186, EAT: the receivers had received enquiries about the sale of the company when they decided to dismiss the majority of the staff employed in the business, including the complainant. Eight days later the receivers completed the sale to a third party. The EAT held that the employment tribunal had not erred in holding that the dismissal by the receiver was for a reason connected with the transfer that was not an ETO reason (and therefore automatically unfair) even though no actual or prospective transferee had been identified at the time of the dismissal. The reason for the dismissal was to facilitate a transfer and, in that sense, was connected with the transfer that took place at a later date. This case was followed in Michael Peters Ltd v (1) Farnfield (2) Michael Peters Group plc 1995 IRLR 190, EAT, and Morris v John Grose Group Ltd 1998 ICR 655, EAT

- **Ibex Trading Co Ltd (in administration) v Walton and ors** 1994 ICR 907, EAT: the administrators dismissed employees in mid-October 1991 with the aim of making the insolvent business more saleable. In November the administrators received an offer for the business and this eventually led to a sale being completed in February 1992. The employment tribunal rejected the argument of the complainants that they had been dismissed in connection with the transfer. On appeal the EAT ruled that, while it could be said of the employees that they were dismissed for a reason connected with 'a' possible transfer, they had not been dismissed for a reason connected with 'the' transfer. The EAT considered that the use of the definite article in the language of old Reg 8 was significant. At the time that the employees were dismissed, no offer had been made for the business and a transfer might well never happen. Moreover, in view of the time gap (nearly four months) between the dismissals and the date the business was in fact sold, it was difficult to say that, but for their dismissals, the employees would have continued to be employed up to the date of the completed transfer. Since the employees were not dismissed because of the transfer or a reason connected with it, they could not be said to have been employed 'immediately before the transfer' so that liability for their dismissals did not transfer to the transferee.

The linguistic argument relied upon in the Ibex Trading case was expressly **6.80** considered and rejected by the EAT in the Harrison Bowden case. Subsequent decisions of the EAT have favoured the stance that dismissals in the context of insolvency, which are designed to slim down a business in preparation for its eventual sale and which take place before a specific transferee has been identified, should be regarded as being in connection with the transfer once it takes place – see Morris v John Grose Group Ltd 1998 ICR 655, EAT, and CAB Automotive Ltd v Blake and ors EAT 0298/07. In the latter case, Mr Justice Beatson, giving the judgment of the EAT, observed: '[Counsel for the appellant company] accepted that there does not have to be a concluded contract to buy the assets for [Reg 7(1) of the TUPE Regulations] to apply. He, however, suggested that where, at the time of the dismissal, no offer has been made to

417

buy the assets of the transferor company and the transferee is not on the scene, [Reg 7(1)] can only apply where there had previously been a potential transferee who had dropped out. We reject this suggestion. We consider [Reg 7(1)] can apply, for example, where a number of potential transferees are interested but, at the time of the dismissal, matters were at a very early stage.'

European case law lends tacit support to the position described above. In P Bork International A/S (in liquidation) v Foreningen af Arbejdsledere i Danmark and ors 1989 IRLR 41, ECJ, the European Court ruled that the proper approach to the issue of whether dismissals are made in connection with a transfer is to consider what happened in retrospect. Applying that approach, the fact that no transferee could be identified at the moment of the dismissal would not necessarily prevent an employee's rights from being protected by the Directive.

6.81 Is the dismissal for an 'ETO' reason?

Dismissals that are for an ETO reason are potentially fair under Reg 7(2) and (3). The scope of this defence is considered fully in Chapter 4. In the specific context of insolvency, it can be very difficult to determine whether dismissals by insolvency practitioners prior to a transfer are for an economic, technical or organisational reason 'entailing changes in the workforce'. It has to be shown that the ETO reason *necessitated* a reduction in the numbers of the workforce or a change in the job functions of those employed – Berriman v Delabole Slate Ltd 1985 ICR 546, CA. For example, harmonising terms and conditions would not normally involve a change in numbers or job functions.

In Wheeler v Patel and anor 1987 ICR 631, EAT, the Appeal Tribunal held that the dismissal of employees for the purpose of enhancing the sale price of an insolvent business did not constitute an 'economic... reason... entailing changes in the workforce' because the reason did not relate, as the EAT held it must, to the conduct of the business. This decision was approved in Gateway Hotels Ltd v Stewart and ors 1988 IRLR 287, EAT, where another division of the EAT ruled that the dismissal of a workforce at the behest of the transferee as a condition for agreeing to the sale of the business was not for an ETO reason.

6.82 In Longden and anor v Ferrari Ltd and anor 1994 ICR 443, EAT, the Appeal Tribunal held that employees had not been dismissed by receivers in connection with the transfer of the insolvent business where there was evidence that, despite the original intention of the receivers to keep all employees on and to sell the business as a going concern, it became necessary to effect some dismissals and to rationalise costs in order to minimise trading losses and to meet the pressure being applied from the bank to close the business down. This was treated as a genuine redundancy situation.

Where dismissals occur at an early stage of the insolvency at a time when a future sale is neither contemplated nor expected, it is generally easier to demonstrate that this is a genuine redundancy situation. The nearer the

418

dismissals are made to a subsequent relevant transfer, the more difficult it will be for the insolvency practitioner to argue that the dismissals were for an ETO reason that necessitated reductions in the workforce as part of the conduct of the insolvent business.

Information and consultation   6.83

Chapter 8 outlines the requirements to inform and consult appropriate employee representatives in connection with an actual or proposed TUPE transfer. These requirements apply equally in any insolvency situation to which TUPE applies, whatever the nature of the insolvency proceedings. In this section, we consider the practical issues which can arise in this context.

Briefly, Reg 13(2) requires that the representatives of employees who are affected by a transfer be informed of specified information about the transfer, and consulted about any measures which are envisaged by the employer in relation to those employees. The prescribed information must be provided long enough before a relevant transfer to enable consultation to take place, and consultation must take place with a view to seeking the agreement of employee representatives to the intended measures (Reg 13(6)). The Regulations themselves do not give further guidance on these timescales. In many cases it will also be necessary to factor in time for the election of employee representatives.

The main problem for insolvency practitioners is the very tight timescale 6.84 normally involved in the transfer of an insolvent business, which means that in practice it is often impossible to comply fully with the information and consultation requirements. In addition, an insolvency practitioner may not have sufficient information to inform and consult employees properly in any event. However, the cases decided under the 1981 TUPE Regulations (which are still relevant) have consistently held that these obligations apply even in insolvency situations unless there are very sudden unforeseen circumstances. The best course of action for an insolvency practitioner, and the potential purchaser, is to make every effort to comply with the information and consultation requirements, and to bear in mind that the steps they have taken may come under the scrutiny of a tribunal.

The risks inherent in failing to take steps to comply with the Regulations are considerable. Potential liability for failure to inform and consult is an award of up to 13 weeks' pay per employee (with no limit on the amount of a week's pay). In the context of insolvency proceedings, particularly where there are large numbers of employees, this could amount to a liability significant enough to influence whether the transfer actually goes ahead. It seems clear that if no attempt is made to comply with the requirements, in many cases maximum compensation will be awarded by the tribunal. In the case of Sweetin v Coral Racing 2006 IRLR 252, EAT, the Appeal Tribunal reiterated that compensation

419

for failure to inform and consult on a TUPE transfer is intended to punish the employer for default, so non-compliance is taken very seriously. However, in Baxter and ors v Marks and Spencer plc and ors EAT 0612/05, the EAT did not award compensation for a minor technical breach where employees suffered no detriment.

6.85 The 2006 Regulations provide for joint and several liability between transferor and transferee (Reg 15(9)). This means that employees have a greater chance of recovering any compensation. Although liability for failure to inform and consult may be covered in sale documentation, the transferor and transferee are best advised to cooperate to minimise the likelihood of expensive tribunal claims.

6.86 Notification of employee liability information

Under Reg 11 the transferor is obliged to notify the transferee of certain employee liability information of any employee who is assigned to the transferring business. This obligation applies to any relevant transfer, including relevant insolvency proceedings. The meaning of employee liability information and the notification procedure are considered in Chapter 8. In brief, these are:

- 'employee liability information' means the following information relating to each employee: his or her identity and age; statutory particulars of employment; details of disciplinary procedures taken against him or her and grievance procedures taken by him or her in the previous two years, in either case, where the statutory dispute resolution procedures apply; employment claims or actions brought against the transferor in the last two years or which the transferor has reasonable grounds to believe may be brought against the transferee, arising out of the employee's employment with the transferor; and information on transferring collective agreements (Reg 11(2))

- the information must be supplied in writing or made available to the transferee in a 'readily accessible form' (Reg 11(1))

- the information must be provided at least 14 days before the transfer or, if special circumstances make this not reasonably practicable, as soon as reasonably practicable thereafter (Reg 11(6))

- notification can be given in instalments and indirectly, through a third party (Reg 11(7)). However, the transferor remains liable if the third party does not pass the information on

- information must be correct as at a specified date which must be not more than 14 days before the date on which the information is notified to the transferee (Reg 11(3))

- the information also has to be provided in respect of any employee who would have been employed by the transferor had he or she not been unfairly dismissed under Reg 7(1) (Reg 11(4))

- the transferor must notify the transferee of any changes in the employee liability information (Reg 11(5))

- it is not possible to contract out of the notification obligations although Regs 11 and 12 can be covered in any relevant sale indemnities

- failure to comply with Reg 11 will normally lead to minimum compensation for the transferee of £500 per employee (Reg 12). This can be reduced if it is just and equitable in all the circumstances, having particular regard to any loss sustained by the transferee and to the terms of any relevant indemnities in the sale documentation. However, there is no upper limit.

These obligations appear to be fairly onerous for insolvency practitioners, who **6.87** are normally trying to conclude a sale as quickly as possible and may not have a detailed knowledge of the business, its employees or its internal information systems. The Government has argued that, in most cases, the information will be available from payroll and personnel records. However, in an insolvency context, even simply collating the information may be more time-consuming than usual, making it harder to comply with the time limits. The requirement to provide information about claims which the transferor has reasonable grounds to believe an employee may bring against the transferee, arising out of his or her employment with the transferor, may also be harder to comply with in the context of insolvency proceedings, not only because of the practical difficulties, but also because there may be more potential claims.

There is some flexibility in Regs 11 and 12 which may assist insolvency practitioners. The DTI's 'Employment rights on the transfer of an undertaking: a guide to the 2006 TUPE Regulations for employees, employers and representatives' notes that it may not be practicable to comply with the time limit if the transferor does not know the identity of the transferee until very late in the process, which might be relevant where there are competing bids to buy the business, or where the transfer takes place at very short notice because it is the only option for saving the business and therefore jobs. These examples would be relevant to many insolvencies, but the Guide is not binding on tribunals, and all cases will be decided on their particular facts. In any event, the insolvency practitioner will need to be able to demonstrate to the satisfaction of a tribunal that he or she notified the transferee of the employee liability information as soon as was reasonably practicable.

Insolvency practitioners may also be able to persuade the tribunal that lower **6.88** compensation should be awarded because it is 'just and equitable in all the circumstances'. Although the facts of each insolvency are different, the special circumstances involved in the transfer of an insolvent company may well discourage large awards. This is likely to depend on whether the transferor is able to demonstrate that he has in fact made every reasonable effort to comply with TUPE. Doing nothing to comply is likely to be expensive unless there are very exceptional circumstances.

6.89 Hiving down

'Hiving down' was a procedure in which an insolvency practitioner could retain employees in an insolvent company while transferring the other assets of the business to a wholly-owned subsidiary of that company. Employees could then be dismissed without passing on the cost of those dismissals to either the subsidiary or an eventual purchaser of the subsidiary, thereby making the business a much more attractive proposition. The purchaser could re-engage some or all of the employees if required on new terms and conditions and with no continuity of employment. Reg 3(4) of the 1981 TUPE Regulations restricted the use of hiving down by deeming that TUPE applied at every stage of the hiving down process, but Reg 4 sought to allow it in some insolvency situations.

The commercial usefulness of Reg 4 was almost totally undermined by the House of Lords' decision in Litster and ors v Forth Dry Dock and Engineering Co Ltd (in receivership) and anor 1989 ICR 341, HL. In that case their Lordships held that where employees are dismissed solely or principally because of a relevant transfer, they must be regarded as employed immediately before the transfer, with the consequence that liability for their dismissals passes to the transferee – see Chapter 4 under 'Automatically unfair dismissals'.

6.90 In its Public Consultation Document published in September 2001 the Government indicated that Reg 4 had in its view ceased to serve any useful purpose. There is therefore no provision in the 2006 Regulations equivalent to the old Reg 4.

7 Continuity of employment

Parallel provisions

Continuity under the Regulations

Relationship between Regulations and ERA

Residual application of ERA

An employee's entitlement to many statutory employment rights is dependent **7.1** upon his or her having been engaged for a particular period of continuous employment. For example, the right to claim unfair dismissal (other than in cases of 'automatically' unfair dismissal) and the right to claim a redundancy payment under the Employment Rights Act 1996 (ERA) apply only to employees with one year's continuous employment when dismissed. Moreover, even where an employee has sufficient continuous service to bring a claim, his or her period of continuous employment will often affect the value of the right claimed; for example, the amount of statutory redundancy pay or statutory notice entitlement will increase in proportion to length of service. For these reasons, establishing the length of an employee's period of continuous employment can be crucial. The rules governing the computation of continuous employment are set out in detail in IDS Employment Law Handbook, 'Continuity of Employment' (2001). In this chapter, we focus on the application of those rules where a business or undertaking is transferred from one employer to another.

Parallel provisions
7.2

In the absence of statutory provision to the contrary, continuity of employment would be broken on any change of employer. At common law, following the principle established in Nokes v Doncaster Amalgamated Collieries Ltd 1940 AC 1014, HL – that an employee must be free to choose his or her employer – there is no automatic transfer of an employment contract from one employer to another and no transfer at all without the employee's consent. A change of employer would therefore have the effect of terminating the employee's contract with the transferor and any employment with the transferee would involve a fresh contract. However, the TUPE Regulations effectively reverse this common law position in specified circumstances. Furthermore, S.218(2) ERA applies to preserve continuity of employment where 'a trade or business, or an undertaking… is transferred from one person to another'.

Difficulties have arisen in this area since the introduction of the original TUPE Regulations in 1981, which have now been replaced with the Transfer of Undertakings (Protection of Employment) Regulations 2006 SI 2006/246 in

423

respect of relevant transfers taking place on or after 6 April 2006 (or relevant service provision changes taking place on or after 4 May 2006). The central difficulty is that, while the cornerstone of the Regulations (in both their 1981 and 2006 guises) is the automatic transfer of employees' contracts from the transferor to the transferee, the Regulations do not expressly mention continuity of employment or alter or amend S.218(2) in any way. However, the Acquired Rights Directive (No.2001/23) (the Directive), which the Regulations implement in this country, is arguably intended to cover employees' rights based on continuity of service in the same way as any other rights. Indeed, if employees' rights on transfers were prejudiced by the statutory concept of continuity in the ERA, the Regulations would almost certainly be in breach of the Directive.

7.3 Much of the debate has centred on whether the Regulations themselves are effective in preserving continuity or whether S.218(2) is to be applied. The matter has been resolved to the extent that there is now little doubt that continuity of employment will be preserved on the transfer of an undertaking in the vast majority of cases. What remains to be definitively clarified is the means by which this is achieved, which may be an important question in determining whether or not continuity is preserved in certain situations.

While some courts and tribunals have proceeded on the basis that the Regulations themselves preserve continuity, others have chosen to apply S.218(2). This may well be because S.218(2) clearly states that its purpose is to preserve continuity, while the Regulations are silent on the point (although the reasons given vary from one judgment to the next). A difficulty could arise for an employee relying solely on S.218(2) if the concept of a 'transfer' were to be more restrictively defined under that section than under the Regulations: this would leave a residual category of relevant transfers under the Regulations to which S.218(2) would not apply. Employees transferring by virtue of such transfers would not, therefore, enjoy the benefit of preserved continuity of employment.

7.4 However, in light of the scope and aims of the Directive, it would be surprising if a tribunal were to deny continuity in a case where the Regulations applied, given that the Regulations must be interpreted purposively in a manner consistent with the Directive (see Litster and ors v Forth Dry Dock and Engineering Co Ltd (in receivership) and anor 1989 ICR 341, HL). Therefore, in the majority of cases it is unlikely to matter whether the tribunal applies S.218(2) or the Regulations (although it should be noted that the Regulations apply to the whole of the United Kingdom while the ERA only applies to Great Britain). The basic position is that continuity of employment on a transfer is very likely to be preserved, if not by one regime, then by the other (or by both). Indeed, there is authority from the EAT in D36 Ltd v Castro EAT 0853/03; 0113/04 (discussed under 'Relationship between Regulations and ERA' below) to the effect that the two sets of provisions must be interpreted consistently

424

with one another, at least as far as each defines a 'transfer'. However, there is conflicting EAT authority on the point so until the issue is resolved at Court of Appeal level both regimes need to be considered. Below, we address how the two schemes have been applied in practice, first focusing on the Regulations and then considering the relationship between the Regulations and S.218(2). We then discuss the residual application of S.218.

Continuity under the Regulations   7.5

Regulation 4(1), which provides for the automatic transfer of contracts to the transferee, states that 'a relevant transfer shall not operate so as to terminate the contract of employment of any person employed by the transferor and assigned to the organised grouping of resources or employees that is subject to the relevant transfer, which would otherwise be terminated by the transfer, but any such contract shall have effect after the transfer as if originally made between the person so employed and the transferee'.

The first thing to note about this provision is that it does not mention continuity of employment. Nor does it expressly provide that an employee's accrued period of employment is transferred along with his or her contract. However, the fact that it provides that the transferred contract shall have effect 'as if originally made between the [employee] and the transferee' would appear to support the view that the employee's continuity of employment will not be broken by the transfer and, consequently, it may well be that the Regulations alone preserve continuity. This argument appeared to be accepted by the Court of Appeal in Royal Ordnance plc v Pilkington 1989 ICR 737, CA, where Lord Justice Neill observed that the effect of Reg 4(1) was 'to require a person whose employment has been transferred to be treated as though employed throughout by the transferee company'. However, this opinion was obiter – i.e. not strictly necessary to decide the case and therefore not binding on other courts.

The Department for Business, Innovation and Skills' 'Employment rights on   7.6
the transfer of an undertaking: a guide to the 2006 TUPE Regulations for employees, employers and representatives' (2009) (the BIS Guide) states that: 'An employee's period of continuous employment is not broken by a transfer and, for the purposes of calculating entitlement to statutory employment rights, the date on which the period of continuous employment started would usually be the date on which the employee started work with the old employer.' However, it does not make it clear whether it is the Regulations themselves that preserve continuity. Thus, the question as to which set of provisions has the desired effect remains unanswered. This question is discussed further under 'Relationship between Regulations and ERA' below. However, it would not arise at all if continuity of service could be shown to form part of the 'rights, powers, duties and liabilities' that transfer with the employee under the Regulations and so we turn to this issue first.

425

7.7 Continuity as a 'right, duty or liability'

Regulation 4(2)(a) fleshes out the novation principle enunciated in Reg 4(1) by specifying what exactly is 'transferred' in respect of the employment contract. It states that 'without prejudice to [Reg 4(1)]… on the completion of a relevant transfer… all the transferor's rights, powers, duties and liabilities under or in connection with any such contract shall be transferred by virtue of this regulation to the transferee'. In Green-Wheeler v Onyx (UK) Ltd EAT 925/92 (discussed further under 'Relationship between Regulations and ERA' below) the transferor's 'liabilities' were held by the EAT to include an employee's right not to be unfairly dismissed where that right had already accrued before the date of the transfer. Since, by virtue of S.108(1) ERA, qualification for that right is (generally speaking) dependent upon an employee having one year's continuous employment, it would seem that the EAT was implying that continuous employment could be regarded as a 'liability' under the contract of employment which is transferred on a relevant transfer.

However, it is difficult to see how a statutory right such as the right not to be unfairly dismissed can be conflated with the period of continuous employment necessary to qualify for such a right. Continuity of employment is merely a calculation of the length of an employee's service. The statutory rights that may flow from a period of continuous service can, of course, comprise liabilities that are transferred to the transferee under Reg 4(1). But that is not, in our view, the same as saying that the period of continuous service itself is a liability. It is not possible to maintain that statutory continuity in a general sense will be transferred by virtue of Reg 4(2) as a liability under or in connection with a transferred contract without undue straining of the statutory language.

7.8

This view is enforced by the EAT's subsequent decision in Nicholas v Grant (t/a Sandancers Café) EAT 0198/06. In that case the EAT stated in clear terms that continuity is 'not aptly described as a right or an obligation and so does not fit within [Reg 4]'. The EAT held further that it is S.218(2) ERA that is effective in preserving continuity in the event of a transfer, which has the added implication that the calculation of an employee's continuity of employment following a transfer will be in accordance with the detailed rules contained in Ss.210–219 ERA. However, the EAT's reasoning does not mean that the Regulations prevent, or are irrelevant to, the preservation of an employee's accrued service post-transfer: it merely rules out one mechanism by which it might occur. The other means by which the Regulations and S.218(2) may be effective in preserving continuity are considered below.

7.9 Relationship between Regulations and ERA

There have been remarkably few cases where both S.218(2) and the Regulations have been at issue and those that have considered the relationship between them show marked inconsistencies in approach:

426

- **Green-Wheeler v Onyx (UK) Ltd** EAT 925/92: G-W, who had been employed since 1975, was dismissed for redundancy from his job as driver of a council refuse-collection vehicle on Friday 6 December 1991. He was re- employed by O (UK) Ltd on the following Monday, the day on which O (UK) Ltd took over the refuse collection service. He was dismissed shortly thereafter and the question for the tribunal was whether G-W had the necessary qualifying service to proceed with his unfair dismissal claim. The tribunal dismissed G-W's claim and he appealed to the EAT. The EAT addressed the question of whether, if there had been a relevant transfer under the Regulations, G-W's past service with the council could be carried forward to establish the necessary continuity of employment. Having found that the breadth of the word 'transfer' in the Regulations is wider than in S.218(2), the EAT held that where there is a transfer situation to which the latter does not apply, an employee who has accrued the necessary continuous service prior to the transfer may rely on the alternative route provided by the Regulations in order to transfer his or her right not to be unfairly dismissed. In the EAT's view, the statutory right not to be unfairly dismissed fell within the scope of the word 'liabilities' contained in Reg 4(2), which states that 'all the transferor's rights, powers, duties and liabilities under or in connection with any [employment] contract shall be transferred by virtue of this Regulation to the transferee'. In reaching this conclusion, the EAT relied on a speech given by Lord Lyle in the House of Lords when the Regulations were passing through Parliament (Hansard, 10 December 1981, paras 1482–1500) to find that it had been the intention of the legislature to include continuity of employment in the rights and liabilities that transferred under the Regulations.

In the Green-Wheeler case the EAT also had to consider G-W's contention that **7.10** S.218(2) should be construed in accordance with the Acquired Rights Directive. In support of this argument, he cited the ECJ's decision in Marleasing SA v La Comercial Internacional de Alimentacion SA 1992 1 CMLR 305, ECJ, as interpreted by the House of Lords in Webb v EMO Air Cargo (UK) Ltd 1993 IRLR 27, HL. In that case their Lordships stated that the principle established in Marleasing meant that 'a national court must construe a domestic law to accord with the terms of a Directive in the same field only if it is possible to do so. That means that the domestic law must be open to an interpretation consistent with the Directive whether or not it is also open to an interpretation inconsistent with it.' However, the EAT thought that it was inappropriate to construe S.218(2) in line with the ECJ decisions on the Acquired Rights Directive on three grounds: (i) the rights provided by the ERA did not have any parallels in any EU Directives; (ii) the provisions of Part XVI ERA (which include S.218) were only relevant to determining the jurisdiction of a UK court; and (iii) the EAT considered itself bound by a long succession of Court of Appeal cases giving clear guidance on the meaning of that section.

While it is perhaps understandable that the EAT chose not to apply the ECJ's rulings on the meaning of a transfer under the Directive to the definition of a transfer for the purposes of the continuity provisions (as these were not introduced specifically to implement the Directive), we would nonetheless argue that the law should operate consistently. To allow for one definition of a transfer in the context of continuity of employment and another in the more general context of the Regulations is likely to lead to inconsistencies, in that it could create situations in which there is a relevant transfer but continuity is not preserved. For example, it may transpire after judicial elucidation that the definition of a transfer is wider under the 2006 Regulations than it was under the 1981 Regulations by virtue of their specific inclusion of 'service provision changes' (see Chapter 1). If that is the case, then unless the courts and tribunals take the view that the meaning of 'transfer' under S.218(2) is to be read consistently with the Directive and the Regulations and has evolved accordingly (or at least is no narrower), there will be cases where there is a relevant transfer under the Regulations but where the transferring employees' continuity of employment is not preserved, because there will not have been a transfer for the purposes of S.218(2).

7.11 Further, while the EAT in Green-Wheeler may have avoided the problem in that case by finding that the employee's right not to be unfairly dismissed (which he had gained by accruing the then requisite two years' continuous employment with the council) was a 'duty or liability under or in connection with' the transferring employee's contract, the same reasoning would not apply to an employee seeking to establish continuity for other purposes, such as the calculation of a redundancy payment or basic award. Nor would it apply to an employee who has not accrued the required period of continuous service for claiming unfair dismissal by the time of the transfer. In this situation, the reasoning in Green-Wheeler would leave such an employee vulnerable to losing any continuity built up with the transferor and having to start again with the transferee, simply by virtue of not having accrued enough continuity to claim unfair dismissal at the date of the transfer.

A different division of the EAT took a more holistic view in the case below, holding that the Regulations go further than merely transferring the right not to be unfairly dismissed by establishing a presumption that continuity is preserved for all purposes:

* **Harrison Bowden Ltd v Bowden** 1994 ICR 186, EAT: B had been employed by NGS Bowden for over two years when he was dismissed for redundancy by the company's receivers. The dismissal took place at a time when the receivers had advertised the sale of the business as a going concern and had received a positive response from HB Ltd. Three days after his dismissal, B went to work for HB Ltd to 'help them get into the saddle' and formally commenced employment with them one week later. One month later, he

was dismissed. The main issue for the tribunal was whether B's dismissal for redundancy by the receivers was a dismissal in connection with the transfer to HB Ltd for the purposes of the Regulations. The tribunal took the firm view that if this was a dismissal in connection with a transfer, the legal significance was that B's employment continued and HB Ltd would have responsibility for his contract as though it had employed him since 1988, when he was originally taken on by NGS Bowden. The tribunal went on to find that the dismissal was in connection with the transfer and HB Ltd appealed to the EAT. Before the EAT, HB Ltd argued that the tribunal's approach was wrong on the basis that the reference in Reg 7(1) to dismissals in connection with 'the' transfer meant that there must be a transfer in existence, or at least a prospective transferee, at the time of the dismissal. The EAT rejected this argument on the basis that such an interpretation would 'open a loophole in this legislation [the Regulations] which *presumes continuity of employment* and attempts to ensure the protection of workers when undertakings are transferred' (our emphasis).

7.12 In the course of its judgment the EAT noted that there was another route by which the tribunal could have reached the same conclusion on continuity of employment, namely under S.218(2), as interpreted by the EAT in Macer v Abafast Ltd (see 'Breaks in employment' below). However, as the tribunal had not considered this route, the EAT said no more on this issue.

This route was taken by the EAT in the case below, however, where it expressly applied S.218(2), although it also relied heavily on the ECJ's definition of a 'transfer' under the EU Acquired Rights Directive, thereby implicitly finding that the definition of a 'transfer' under S.218(2) was the same as under the Regulations:

- **Farmer v Danzas (UK) Ltd** EAT 858/93: F was employed by his own transport business, F Ltd, which he set up in 1988. In essence, his business was to supply D Ltd with lorries and drivers so that D Ltd could provide a transport service called Eurapid to its customers. F leased and maintained the lorries and had office accommodation on D Ltd's premises. In 1991 D Ltd decided to move the Eurapid service to its main site and offered F the position of manager of the Eurapid service on condition that F ceased to operate his own business. F agreed but was dismissed just over five months later. The preliminary issue for the tribunal was whether F had the necessary continuity of service to bring an unfair dismissal claim. This depended on whether there had been a transfer of F's business within the meaning of S.218(2). The tribunal decided that there had been no such transfer on the ground that F's business had been integrated into that of D Ltd and had not, therefore, retained its identity after the transfer. The EAT disagreed and decided to adopt the ECJ guidelines as to the proper interpretation of what constitutes a transfer of an undertaking. In the EAT's view, there was

429

nothing in the ECJ's decisions to suggest that a business ceased to retain its identity merely because its activities had been absorbed into the transferee's business. Accordingly, the EAT held that, as there had been a relevant transfer, F had the necessary continuity to bring a claim.

7.13 What is particularly interesting about the Farmer case is that, while the EAT expressly stated at the beginning of the judgment that it was concerned with S.218(2), it had substantial regard to the decisions of the ECJ on the scope of the Acquired Rights Directive and concluded by finding that the transfer in question was covered by the Regulations. This analysis runs directly counter to that adopted in the Green-Wheeler case (above), where the EAT was of the view that the interpretation of the Directive was irrelevant for the purposes of construing S.218(2). The Appeal Tribunal in that case did go on to find, however, that the right not to be unfairly dismissed could be transferred by the Regulations, which must themselves be interpreted in line with the Directive. It should be noted that the EAT in the Farmer case did not appear to have been referred to Green-Wheeler, but the underlying proposition in Farmer is clearly that S.218(2), the Regulations and the Directive are to be interpreted consistently with one another.

Indeed, more recently, the EAT has upheld an employment tribunal's view that the provisions of S.218(2), the Regulations and the Acquired Rights Directive should be treated as part of a 'single scheme'. In D36 Ltd v Castro EAT 0853/03; 0113/04 C began working at the Windsor office of McCann Erickson ('McCann'), an advertising agency, as senior art worker on 2 April 2001. In December the Windsor office was closed and C was transferred to D36 Ltd, which was solely engaged in conducting work for McCann on a sub-contract basis. C received a letter from D36 Ltd dated 18 December 2001 confirming that from 1 January 2002 his employment would be with D36 Ltd and stating that his continuity of employment would be protected from 2 April 2001. A draft contract was also supplied, which gave the date of commencement of his employment as 2 April 2001. C was subsequently dismissed for redundancy by D36 Ltd in September 2002 and at a preliminary hearing a tribunal found that C had sufficient continuity of employment to bring a claim. In rejecting the employer's appeal, the EAT agreed with the tribunal that S.218(2) and the Regulations should be seen as a single scheme for preserving continuity in the event of a business transfer. The EAT noted that neither S.218(2) nor S.235 ERA (the definition section) offers any explanation of the meaning of the word 'transfer' used in S.218(2). Reg 2(1), on the other hand, defines a 'relevant transfer' as 'a transfer... to which these Regulations apply' and Regs 3 and 4 provide further guidance on what constitutes a transfer and what rights are transferred. The EAT observed that there was no further definition of 'transfer' in the Regulations themselves, and that there was no reference anywhere in them to the concept of continuity of employment. The question the EAT posed for itself was whether there was anything in the domestic case law militating

430

against applying the definition of 'transfer' in the Regulations to S.218(2), and found that there was not. It held that such an approach was consistent with judgments of the Court of Appeal in Celtec Ltd v Astley and ors 2002 ICR 1289, CA, and the European Court in Sànchez Hidalgo and ors v Asociación de Servicios Aser and Sociedad Cooperativa Minerva and another case 1999 IRLR 136, ECJ, and Collino and anor v Telecom Italia SpA 2002 ICR 38, ECJ, to the effect that the Acquired Rights Directive preserves continuity of employment upon a relevant transfer.

Thus case law shows a head of steam developing in favour of the view that the **7.14** separate regimes for preserving continuity under the Regulations and S.218(2) should be construed consistently as a single scheme. However, the matter cannot be regarded as conclusively resolved, since a differently constituted EAT appeared to reject that proposition in the following case:

- **Nicholas v Grant (t/a Sandancers Café)** EAT 0198/06: N started work for F as a griddle cook at the Sandancers Café in April 2004. On 14 February 2005 the café was taken over by a new concessionaire, Mrs Grant. Prior to the transfer N had a meeting with Mrs Grant to agree new terms of employment and she then tendered her resignation to F on 7 February 2005, giving one week's notice. N was later dismissed by Mrs Grant in May 2005 and she presented a claim for unfair dismissal. Rejecting her claim, the tribunal found that, because of her resignation, N had not been employed in the undertaking immediately before the transfer and that as a result she had taken up new employment with Mrs Grant under new terms. That employment had commenced on 14 February, meaning that N had not accrued the requisite period of continuous employment to enable her to bring an unfair dismissal claim. On appeal, the EAT held that the tribunal had made an error of law in failing to have regard to the test laid down by the ECJ in Botzen and ors v Rotterdamsche Droogdok Maatschappij BV 1986 2 CMLR 50, ECJ, requiring it to consider whether N had been assigned to the undertaking transferred. The EAT found on applying that test that she was employed by the café at the time the transfer took place. For the EAT, the essential issue was whether N had sufficient continuity of employment, and that was a matter to be determined by reference to S.218(2) and not the Regulations. It accepted that unless there had been a relevant transfer, N had insufficient service to present a claim. However, it emphasised that 'the resolution of whether there was a transfer for the purposes of the Regulations can only be described as an aid to what was the essential task of determining whether there was continuity of employment for the purposes of the 1996 Act'.

If the EAT had only had to consider this one point, the position following **7.15** Nicholas would have been clear and could have been reconciled with the decision in D36 Ltd v Castro (above), despite the latter case not having been referred to in Nicholas. The position would be that, applying Castro, the definition of a 'transfer' would be the same under both the Regulations and S.218(2) (or at least no *narrower* under the latter). Indeed, the EAT in Nicholas said that the case 'was correctly decided to be a relevant transfer for the purposes of TUPE. The claimant was employed at the relevant time and her contract of employment went over. We would have made the same decision if it were necessary for us to do so under S.218.' This would mean that in the event of a relevant transfer for the purposes of the Regulations, there would always be a transfer for the purposes of S.218(2), but it would be S.218(2) that would actually have the effect of preserving continuity. This would also appear to be the approach implicitly taken by the EAT in Farmer. However, there is a further hurdle which must be overcome before continuity will be preserved under S.218(2), even if the definition of a transfer is the same for both sets of provisions: whether the employee was employed in the transferring entity at the time of the transfer.

7.16 **'At the time of' or 'immediately before' the transfer**

It is on this issue that Nicholas differs from Castro. The point did not need to be addressed in Castro, which can be treated as authority only for the proposition that the definition of a transfer must be applied consistently across the two sets of provisions. The difficulty is that the ERA and the Regulations use slightly different wording in respect of the point at which the employee must have been employed in the entity transferred. S.218(2) applies to employees employed in the trade or business or undertaking 'at the *time* of the transfer' (our stress), whereas the Regulations require employees to be employed in the entity transferred '*immediately before* the transfer' – Reg 4(3) (our stress). Although the EAT did not cite these phrases in Nicholas, it clearly considered them to be distinct concepts, noting that there 'will rarely be cases that do not satisfy both but, in any event, we hold that using the language of TUPE Reg [4] and of S.218, the claimant was in the employment of the café at the time that the transfer came about'.

On the facts, the claimant in Nicholas was employed both immediately before *and* at the time of the transfer. N had given seven days' notice, which (applying West v Kneels Ltd 1987 ICR 146, EAT) ended on 14 February, the date of the transfer. But, continued the EAT, even if West v Kneels had been wrongly decided, '[N] would still have been employed on the day immediately before the transfer, 13 February'. Albeit obiter, the clear implication here is that had N been unable to rely on West v Kneels, she would *not* have been employed 'at the time of the transfer' for the purposes of S.218(2).

7.17 Thus, it appears that there may in theory still be cases where there is a relevant transfer under both the Regulations and S.218(2) and where the employee was employed in the entity transferred 'immediately before' the transfer (so that his or her contract will have transferred under the Regulations), but was *not* so employed 'at the time of the transfer' for the purposes of S.218(2). Had N handed in her notice a day earlier, for example, (so that it would have expired on 13 February, the day before the transfer), she would have fallen into this category. She would have been employed on the day immediately before the transfer and would have transferred under TUPE, but her continuity of employment would have been at risk for the purposes of any subsequent claim in respect of dismissal by the transferee. On its face, this formulation ignores the effect of Macer v Abafast Ltd 1990 ICR 234, EAT, in which the Appeal Tribunal held that S.218(2) should not have a restrictive meaning and that since a transfer can take place over a period of time, any gap will be inconsequential if it can be said to be part of the 'machinery of the transfer'. However, this case must now be treated with some caution following Celtec Ltd v Astley and ors 2006 ICR 992, HL, where the House of Lords held that transfers under the Directive (and therefore, by implication, the Regulations) occur at a fixed point in time (see further below under 'Breaks in employment').

The situation would be different if the end of the first employment came about by *dismissal*, with the employee then taking up subsequent employment with the transferee and being dismissed a second time by the transferee. The House of Lords in Litster and ors v Forth Dry Dock and Engineering Co Ltd (in receivership) and anor 1989 ICR 341, HL, held that old Reg 5(3) deemed an employee to have been employed immediately before a transfer where he or she was unfairly dismissed close to the transfer for a reason connected with it. This statement of law has now been codified in new Reg 4(3). It does not mean, however, that the employee is deemed to have transferred, only that he or she is able to claim unfair dismissal against the transferee – see (1) British Fuels Ltd v Baxendale and anor (2) Wilson and ors v St Helens Borough Council 1998 ICR 1141, HL, where the House of Lords clarified that such dismissals cannot be a nullity. In other words, liability for the dismissal passes to the transferee under Reg 4. The question of continuity would not normally arise in these circumstances, as the claim would be one of automatically unfair dismissal under what is now Reg 7(1), for which no continuity of service is required. Continuity up to the point of dismissal would not be affected in any event, but there would be a serious question mark over its preservation in respect of any subsequent employment under a new contract.

7.18 On one view, it would not be preserved, because employment with one employer will have ceased and employment with a completely different employer will have commenced and the employee will not have transferred. Continuity would only begin to run from the date of employment with the transferee, thereby preventing the employee from bringing a claim for non-automatic unfair dismissal in respect of any subsequent dismissal taking place within a year of that date. However, it could be argued that this is a somewhat simplistic view. For S.218(2) to operate to prevent the transfer breaking continuity it requires there to have been a transfer; for there to be employment with the transferee;

433

and for there to have been employment in the transferor's business at the time of the transfer. It does not require the individual employee to have actually transferred, provided the transfer has occurred. It could therefore be argued that an employee who does not transfer under Reg 4 because he or she was dismissed shortly before the transfer may still have continuity of employment preserved by S.218 if he or she subsequently takes up employment with the transferee under a new contract. Whether continuity is in fact broken would then depend on the existence of any non-counting week and whether Macer remains good law – see 'Breaks in employment' below.

The scenario discussed above is fairly common in transfer situations: the employees of the transferor are dismissed before the transfer and then re-employed by the transferee, perhaps on a selective basis, after the transfer. Another common scenario involves the dismissal of employees by the transferor and re-engagement by the transferee before the transfer takes place. In other cases, there is no express dismissal and the employee is simply transferred by agreement over to the transferee ahead of the actual time when the transfer is completed (with or without a gap in employment). In all these situations, continuity has to be determined.

7.19 Breaks in employment

Two questions arise here. Will an employee who resigns, is dismissed or is transferred before the transfer be regarded as not being employed 'at the time of the transfer' under S.218(2), so that his or her continuity is broken because of the change of employer? And even if the answer to that question is 'no', does the gap between employments break continuity if it lasts for more than one 'non-counting week' under the rules governing the computation of continuity in Ss.210–219 ERA? (Note that a 'non-counting week' is one that ends on a Saturday and, unless it is covered by one of the exceptions in S.212, e.g. sickness or temporary cessation of work, breaks continuity of service – see IDS Employment Law Handbook, 'Continuity of Employment' (2001), Chapters 2 and 3.)

7.20 Employment 'at the time of the transfer'.
In Brook Lane Finance Co Ltd v Bradley 1988 ICR 423, EAT, the EAT held that in order for continuity to be preserved under S.218(2), it was necessary for the employee to be employed by the transferor at the moment of the transfer. As a result, B, who had left the employment of the transferor prior to the date of the transfer and began working for the transferee two days after the transfer, did not have continuity of employment preserved. The EAT thought that the phrase 'at the time of the transfer' in S.218(2) should be read strictly, in the same way that 'immediately before the transfer' in Reg 4 had been read by the Court of Appeal in Secretary of State for Employment v Spence and ors 1986 ICR 651, CA (which was not overruled by the decision of the House of Lords in Litster – see '"At the time of" or "immediately before" the transfer' above – on that point).

There had previously been some divergence of opinion on the issue in the Court of Appeal in Teesside Times Ltd v Drury 1980 ICR 338, CA. In that case, Lord Justice Goff thought that 'at the time of the transfer' did in fact mean at the moment of transfer. But Lord Justice Stephenson felt that it referred to the period of the transfer, and that a gap between dismissal and transfer followed by re-employment after the transfer would be acceptable as long as it did not fall foul of the general continuity provisions in the ERA (i.e. that there be no non-counting weeks). More radically, Lord Justice Eveleigh stated that, where 'the dismissal was a step towards the re-engagement', any break in employment was immaterial and that the two periods of employment could simply be added together. However, these views were obiter (i.e. not binding) as the case was decided on different grounds.

A couple of years after the Brook Lane Finance case, a differently constituted **7.21** EAT, in a judgment which attracted some criticism, disposed of both the non-counting week problem and the narrow interpretation of 'at the time of the transfer' in the following case:

- **Macer v Abafast Ltd** 1990 ICR 234, EAT: M had been employed by CTR Ltd for four years when its business was transferred to a subsidiary of A Ltd called CTR (Recruitment) Ltd ('Recruitment'). M and the other employees of CTR Ltd were dismissed by CTR Ltd and offered re-engagement with Recruitment but A Ltd managed to engineer a gap of 12 days between M leaving CTR Ltd and joining Recruitment. Exchange of contracts on the transfer took place about a month *after* M joined Recruitment and completion was finally achieved a year after that. However, M was dismissed prior to the date of completion and he brought an unfair dismissal claim against A Ltd. The EAT held that Reg 4 did not apply to M's employment contract, but that S.218(2) preserved continuity nonetheless. Mr Justice Wood stated that a broad interpretation of S.218(2) had to be applied and that there was no reason that the phrase 'at the time of the transfer' should be read to mean the same as 'immediately before the transfer'. Furthermore, he took a similar view to that taken by Eveleigh LJ in the Teesside Times case – holding that an interval between employments, however long, did not matter for continuity purposes as long as it related to the 'machinery' of the transfer. Wood J concluded, therefore, that the Brook Lane case was wrongly decided and should not be followed. In reaching this conclusion, he was influenced by the reasoning behind the Litster decision (above), where the House of Lords extended the meaning of employees 'employed immediately before the transfer' in the old Reg 5(3) (now rewritten in Reg 4(3)) to include, for the purposes of claiming unfair dismissal, employees who would have been so employed had they not been dismissed for a reason connected with the transfer. The EAT's decision in Macer abandons entirely the restrictive construction of S.218(2) adopted in Brook Lane Finance. Wood J, who examined the various analyses of that provision by the Court

435

of Appeal in the Teesside Times case (above), concluded that the reasoning of Eveleigh LJ was the most persuasive since he properly focused on the fact that the wording of S.218(2) requires 'the period of employment... at the time of the transfer' to be counted as a period of employment with the transferor rather than requiring the employee actually to be employed at the time of the transfer. Eveleigh LJ rationalised his construction by pointing out that Ss.210–219 ERA are primarily concerned with the computation of periods of employment, not with the circumstances in which rights or benefits may arise. He also showed himself to be alive to the policy behind S.218(2), i.e. the protection of employees' rights on the transfer of the business in which they are employed. He therefore eschewed any restrictive interpretation of the relevant provision that would enable employers easily to defeat that policy by causing a break in continuity to occur simply by dismissing employees prior to completion and re-engaging them after the transfer.

7.22 The EAT's endorsement in the Macer case of Eveleigh LJ's interpretation of S.218(2) gives effect to the presumed legislative intention behind that provision. If correct, then the questions of whether a transfer occurs on completion or on exchange, and whether it necessarily occurs at a specific point in time or can extend over a period, become, strictly speaking, irrelevant for the purposes of the ERA. Instead, what matters is that the period of employment vested in the employee at the time of the transfer falls to be included in the total period of reckonable service with the transferee. And, as Wood J pointed out, any gap between these two periods of employment will, in most cases, be kept within reasonable proportions given that commercial interests usually dictate that employees be re-engaged as soon after a transfer as possible in order for the business to continue normally.

7.23 **Non-counting weeks.** There is, however, one major problem with the decision in Macer that was not covered at all by the EAT in that case. In order to deal with the non-counting week, Wood J relied on S.218(1). However, this is an ambiguous provision that can be interpreted in diametrically opposed ways. It actually states: 'Subject to the provisions of this section, this Chapter relates only to employment by the one employer.' This can mean either that S.218(2) is subject to the rule on non-counting weeks in the same way as employment with only one employer is subject to the rule or that, since S.218(2) applies to more than one employer, it takes effect without any reference at all to the other provisions of the Chapter (i.e. Ss.210–219). Wood J preferred the latter interpretation. However, in order for this argument to stand up it would have to apply to Ss.218(3)–(9) as well – all of which cover situations involving more than one employer. Unfortunately, the decision of the Court of Appeal in Minetti v DVK Executive Hotels Ltd, unreported 22.11.88, CA, is authority to the contrary, at least in relation to S.218(6), which covers the transfer of employees between associated employers.

436

The EAT's generously purposive approach to the interpretation of S.218(2) in Macer was followed by another division of the EAT in Justfern Ltd v D'Ingerthorpe and ors 1994 IRLR 164, EAT, where it held that S.218(2) can bridge gaps in employment of longer than one week, provided the gap relates to the 'machinery' of the transfer. The EAT also rejected any suggestion that the decision in Macer be limited to situations in which there was evidence of collusion between the transferor and the transferee to avoid the operation of the Regulations. In the Justfern case, D was employed by EM as a college lecturer until the business was closed on 10 October 1988 due to financial difficulties. D was paid until 7 October and sent home. The following day he applied for unemployment benefit. Shortly after the closure, J Ltd bought the college and it was reopened on 24 October. D was re-employed by J Ltd but resigned and claimed constructive dismissal seven months later. The tribunal had to decide whether D had the requisite continuous service to proceed with his claim when there had been a two-week gap between his employment and re-employment. On the basis that the sale of the college was a transfer within S.218(2), the tribunal held that D's employment with EM had been preserved over that transfer. J Ltd appealed unsuccessfully to the EAT.

The EAT rejected the contention that D's employment with EM should not be **7.24** carried over because he was not employed by EM 'at the time of the transfer'. The EAT noted that Wood J in Macer said that the words 'at the time of the transfer' did not mean that there had to be one identifiable point in time when the transfer took place – a transfer of a business is something which takes time and 'the time' of the transfer means a period of time rather than a specific moment. The EAT found further support for this wide interpretation in S.210(5), which provides that: 'A person's employment during any period shall, unless the contrary is shown, be presumed to have been continuous' (but see under 'Residual application of the ERA – presumption of continuity' below).

J Ltd tried to distinguish Macer by contending that the termination of D's employment with EM was for commercial reasons of insolvency rather than as a step in a transfer of the business. The EAT rejected this line of argument on the ground that the issue is whether there is a transfer of a business in relation to which an employee's employment can be regarded as also transferred. EM's motive for terminating D's employment was, in its opinion, irrelevant. All S.218(2) required was that the business and the employment of the relevant employee should survive sufficiently to be capable of transfer to the transferee, i.e. that there should be enough of the original business left to transfer. Thus, if the first employer closed down the business so completely that the new employer was effectively starting a new business, S.218(2) would not apply. However, the tribunal did not consider that that had happened here and the EAT saw no reason to challenge that view.

437

7.25 The most difficult aspect of the case for the EAT was D's application for, and receipt of, unemployment benefit for more than one week during the gap in his employment. Claiming unemployment benefit may indicate that the employee has severed the link with the former employer, thus breaking continuity. However, the EAT saw a major distinction between taking on a new job on the one hand and applying for benefit when wages are no longer being paid on the other. In D's particular case, his claim did not mean that he was unavailable for work in the college. Furthermore, re-employment was still a possibility. While acknowledging that there was uncertainty in the situation, the EAT saw no reason why S.218(2), which was capable of bridging a period of more than one week, could not also bridge a period of uncertainty. It concluded that D's receipt of benefit did not break his continuity.

What is the position if an employee remains in the employment of the transferor after the transfer but then goes to work for the transferee, who subsequently dismisses him or her? Will the fact that the employee is retained by the transferor (albeit for only a short period) mean that when he or she begins work with the transferee this will be regarded as new employment, with the consequence that continuity of employment is broken? The answer depends on whether the employee is considered to have been employed 'at the time of the transfer' for the purposes of S.218(2). The case below sought to tackle this thorny issue:

- **A and G Tuck Ltd v Bartlett and A and G Tuck (Slough) Ltd** 1994 IRLR 162, EAT: B had worked for two associated companies, S and H, since 1989, although he remained an employee of S throughout. On 10 August 1992, he discovered that S had been sold to C (trading under the name of A&GT Ltd) while he was on holiday. B was not transferred to C but on 12 August C invited B to go and work for him. B started work for C two weeks later but was subsequently dismissed. C maintained that B's continuity had been broken when he remained in his previous employment for two weeks after the transfer. The main question for the EAT was whether B was employed 'at the time of the transfer'. The EAT rejected C's argument that the Macer case did not apply because it was concerned with a gap in employment before the transfer, not after. The issue, following Macer, was whether the gap in B's employment related to the 'machinery' of the transfer and whether that could extend beyond the date of legal completion of the sale. The EAT decided that the tribunal had taken the right course when refusing to limit the transfer to that moment in time when the legal documentation was completed. The members of the tribunal were also correct in taking into account their experience of industrial life and the fact that the normal problems associated with business takeovers could extend the actual machinery of the transfer beyond the actual date of transfer. Moreover, the way the tribunal had interpreted S.218(2) was consistent with the intention of Parliament and with the requirements of justice.

438

It would appear, therefore, that unless and until a higher authority overrules **7.26** Macer, the problem of the 'non-counting' week has ceased to be an issue, provided the gap in employment can be considered to be part of the machinery of the transfer. This will be a question of fact in each case, although obviously the longer the gap the less likely it will be considered a part of that machinery.

(Note that if Macer is wrong on the question of non-counting weeks, S.212(3) ERA may nonetheless apply to protect continuity of employment in certain circumstances – see 'Residual application of the ERA – breaks in employment covered by S.212(3) ERA' below.)

Effect of Celtec. The approach in Macer v Abafast Ltd 1990 ICR 234, EAT, **7.27** has been applied in a number of subsequent cases and was adopted by the Court of Appeal in Clark and Tokeley Ltd t/a Spellbrook Ltd v Oakes 1999 ICR 276, CA. However, a potential difficulty has arisen since the decisions of the ECJ and the House of Lords in Celtec Ltd v Astley and ors 2006 ICR 992, HL, which effectively confirmed the view taken by the Court of Appeal in Secretary of State for Employment v Spence and ors 1986 ICR 651, CA (although without referring to it), that – for the purposes of the Regulations at least – a transfer can only take place at a specific point in time. It could be argued, of course, that the same does not necessarily apply under the ERA and that courts and tribunals are perfectly entitled to continue to apply the Macer line of cases for the purposes of S.218(2). But this would lead to a rather unsatisfactory situation in which 'at the time of the transfer' under the ERA would have to be given a wider meaning than 'immediately before' the transfer in the Regulations. Moreover, it is difficult to see how this could be consistent with D36 Ltd v Castro EAT 0853/03; 0113/04 (above), where it was held that the same definition of a 'transfer' applies across both sets of provisions. The two positions could be reconciled if the view is taken that Castro only requires a definition of 'transfer' under the ERA that is *no narrower* than that under the Regulations, but this may be to strain the words of the EAT in that case.

It would seem, therefore, that there is a very serious issue to be determined by the courts in the light of Celtec. If Celtec and a strict view of Nicholas v Grant (t/a Sandancers Café) EAT 0198/06 (that continuity is a matter to be determined by reference to S.218(2), not the Regulations – see above) are applied rather than the Macer line of cases, the result could potentially be catastrophic for employees, particularly those with long service with the transferor. It would mean that if an employee was not employed at the exact moment of the transfer, S.218(2) simply would not apply to preserve continuity, regardless of the nature and/or duration of any gap between employments (but see 'Residual application of the ERA – breaks in employment covered by S.212(3) ERA' below). It is equally arguable, however, that in order for S.218(2) to preserve continuity, the individual employee does not actually need to transfer so long as a transfer occurs and he or she takes up employment with the transferee. If Macer prevails,

439

employees employed at the time of the transfer in its wider sense will be protected by S.218(2), provided the interval between employments related to the machinery of the transfer.

7.28 Employee objection to transfer

Regulation 4(1) and (2) of the 2006 Regulations provide that the contract of employment of anyone employed by the transferor will be automatically transferred to the transferee. However, this is subject to the employee's right to object to being transferred. This right is provided for in Reg 4(7), which states that paras (1) and (2) will not operate to transfer the contract of employment of an employee who informs the transferor or transferee that he or she objects to becoming employed by the transferee. Reg 4(8) goes on to provide that where there is an objection under Reg 4(7), the transfer will have the effect of terminating the employee's contract but he or she will not, for any purpose, be considered to have been dismissed by the transferor.

Regulation 4(7) and (8) should be read in conjunction with Reg 4(9) and (11), however. Reg 4(9) states that where a transfer involves or would involve a substantial change in the employee's working conditions that is to his or her material detriment, the employee may treat the contract as having been terminated and he or she will be treated for any purpose as having been dismissed by the employer. Furthermore, nothing in paras (1), (7), (8) or (9) prejudices an employee's right to terminate his or her contract without notice in acceptance of a repudiatory breach by the employer and to claim constructive dismissal – Reg 4(11).

7.29 In Humphreys v University of Oxford and anor 2000 ICR 405, CA, the Court of Appeal held that an objection under Reg 4(7) (which, according to the Court, must relate to the actual identity of the transferee to be valid) and a claim under Reg 4(11) can be made together in advance of the transfer. The same is likely to be true of claims under Reg 4(9), although this provision was only introduced in the 2006 Regulations. This means that an employee may treat him or herself as dismissed prior to the transfer and claim constructive dismissal (or 'material detriment dismissal') against the transferor, with the dismissal taking effect at the date of the transfer (as per Reg 4(8)). Alternatively – although Humphreys did not decide the point – if an employee does not object under Reg 4(7) but simply waits until after the transfer to bring a claim under Reg 4(9) or 4(11), Reg 4(8) will not operate so as to make the transfer date the point at which the contract is terminated: the employee will transfer and the date on which he or she treats the contract as having terminated will be the date of dismissal.

It seems clear, based on the well-reasoned decision of the High Court in New ISG Ltd v Vernon 2008 ICR 319, ChD, that if an employee is kept in the dark about a transfer and is therefore given no opportunity to object to the new employer's identity before the transfer takes place, he or she can make an objection at a later stage once he or she becomes aware of the transfer. This means that the objecting employee's employment will not be regarded as having transferred to the transferee, and he or she will be left with those rights under Reg 4(9) and (11) enforceable against the transferor. Thus the normal rule is that any objection to a transfer has to be made *before* the transfer occurs – see Capita Health Solutions Ltd v McLean and anor 2008 IRLR 595, EAT (discussed in detail under 'Secondments and employees who go to work for the transferee' below). However, according to the High Court in the New ISG case, there is an exception to this rule where the employee does not know the identity of the transferee before the date of the transfer. To hold that such an employee had lost his or her right to object to the transfer would be to 'undermine the fundamental freedom of the employee to chose his employer'. It was therefore necessary to adopt a purposive construction of Reg 4(7) to permit an objection to be made once the identity of the transferee had become known.

An employee's right to object to a transfer, and the interrelationship between **7.30** Reg 4(7) and (8) and Reg 4(9) and (11), is discussed in detail in Chapter 2 under 'Objecting to the transfer'. In this chapter, we consider the effect of those provisions on an employee's continuity of employment.

What is an objection? It is not precisely clear what sort of conduct will be **7.31** sufficient to constitute a Reg 4(7) 'objection', although in Hay v George Hanson (Building Contractors) Ltd 1996 IRLR 427, EAT, the EAT stated that the word in this context effectively means 'a refusal to accept the transfer', and that this state of mind 'must be conveyed to either the transferor or transferee'. Logically, it would seem that an objection in these circumstances cannot consist simply of the act of resigning from employment or the giving of notice of resignation. This is because, under basic contractual principles, the resignation itself would terminate the contract on the date of its occurrence, whereas Reg 4(8) stipulates that where there is a Reg 4(7) objection it is the date of the transfer that constitutes the date of the termination. The effect of Reg 4(7) and (8) is that after the employee has manifested an objection, he or she continues in employment until the date of the transfer, at which point he or she is deemed to have been dismissed by the transferor. Of course, it may be that in the context of transfers, a resignation in such circumstances will not have the usual contractual effect, meaning that if the resignation is in opposition to the identity of the transferee, the transfer itself will terminate the contract (rather than the resignation). But up to now no case has specifically held this to be so.

A resignation on other grounds *would* have the usual effect, with the proviso that if notice is given and the notice period extends up to or beyond the date of the transfer, the employee will transfer to the transferee (see Nicholas v Grant (t/a Sandancers Café) EAT 0198/06). In these circumstances, the employee's continuity would not be affected because, if he or she transfers, there can be no issue as to whether or not he or she was employed 'at the time of the transfer'.

441

Continuity problems arise where the notice period expires *before* the transfer occurs and the employee then takes up employment under a new contract with the transferee. Continuity in these circumstances will depend on two things: first, that the EAT's reasoning in Macer v Abafast Ltd 1990 ICR 234, EAT, continues to be applicable (post-Celtec) and that any gap between the two employments is seen as part of the 'machinery of the transfer'; and, secondly, that it is accepted that, for the purposes of S.218(2), the individual employee does not need to transfer so long as there is a transfer and the employee can be said (pursuant to Macer) to have been employed in the transferor's business at the time of the transfer (see under 'Breaks in employment' above).

7.32 Judicial clarification is needed as to the true effect of a resignation on the date of termination where the resignation is based on an objection to the identity of the transferee. This is especially so since the BIS Guide to the 2006 Regulations appears to take the orthodox contractual position, stating that: 'The objection terminates the contract of employment and the employee is not treated for any purpose as having been dismissed by either the transferor or the [transferee]'. However, this is inconsistent with the actual words used in the Regulations, which state at Reg 4(8) that: 'Subject to paragraphs (9) and (11), where an employee... objects, the *relevant transfer* shall operate so as to terminate his contract of employment with the transferor but he shall not be treated, for any purpose, as having been dismissed by the transferor' (our emphasis). There is therefore a divergence between the Regulations and the Guide, and it is submitted that the Guide is unreliable in this regard.

The distinction is crucially important for continuity purposes. If the *objection* terminates the employment, this will generally be in advance of the transfer. This means that there would be a serious risk of the employee being found not to have been employed 'at the time of the transfer', so that even if employment is subsequently taken up with the transferee (on a new contract), continuity would not be preserved. This could well be so even if the Macer line of cases is followed, since the reasoning in those cases applies where the employee is *dismissed* prior to the transfer and re-engaged by the transferee. A Reg 4(7) objection means there is no dismissal 'for any purpose', despite the contract having been terminated by the transfer – Reg 4(8).

7.33 If, however, as Reg 4(8) suggests, the *transfer* terminates the contract, this means that the employee would be employed 'at the time of the transfer', since it would be the event of the transfer itself that would bring about the end of the employment contract. The fact that the individual does not transfer does not mean that the transfer itself does not occur. In these circumstances, an employee making a Reg 4(7) objection in advance of the transfer could have continuity of employment preserved by S.218(2) if subsequently employed by the transferee under a new contract. (This would be subject to the proviso that any gap between the employments did not break continuity, although even this proviso may not apply if Macer remains good law – see 'Breaks in employment' above.)

Secondments and employees who go to work for the transferee 7.34
There are situations in which – far from objecting to the transfer – the employee may be unaware that a transfer has even taken place. The decision of the House of Lords in Celtec Ltd v Astley and ors 2006 ICR 992, HL (implementing that of the ECJ reported at 2005 IRLR 647), has implications for the preservation of continuity of employment in circumstances where the transferor purports to second employees to another entity in an attempt to avoid them being transferred:

• **Celtec Ltd v Astley and ors** 2006 ICR 992, HL: civil servants employed by the Department of Employment were seconded in 1990 to a Training and Enterprise Council (TEC), that later became Celtec. It was common ground that Celtec was an emanation of the state. In 1993, the civil servants opted to become employees of Celtec and resigned from the Department. In their letters of engagement, they were told that their periods of continuous employment would re-start from that point and that their periods of service with the Department would no longer count. When a redundancy situation later arose, the claimants sought a declaration from an employment tribunal that their continuous service included service in the Department. The tribunal upheld the claims under both S.218 and the Directive. After appeals to the EAT, the Court of Appeal, the House of Lords and a referral to the ECJ, the House of Lords concluded that the tribunal had reached the correct decision, albeit via different reasoning. Their Lordships held by a majority (Lord Mance dissenting) that the claimants were deemed to have transferred in 1990 when they were initially seconded, despite the fact that none of the parties was aware of this at the time or intended that to be the legal effect of the arrangement. The claimants' contracts therefore passed to the transferee on the date they were seconded and their continuity of employment was preserved by Article 3(1) of the Directive. The claimants had also relied on S.218, but the majority of their Lordships took the view that in this case it was only necessary to consider the Directive.

The fact that the House of Lords in the Celtec case did not address S.218 does 7.35 not mean, however, that that section is no longer effective to preserve continuity within the context of a transfer of undertaking. The events in Celtec occurred before the 1981 Regulations were amended in 1993 to extend the definition of an undertaking to non-commercial entities by S.33 of the Trade Union Reform and Employment Rights Act 1993. Thus, the claims, while clearly analogous to claims under the Regulations, were technically claims brought directly under the Acquired Rights Directive. What the case means is that, even outside the context of pre-1993 transfers between state entities, the Directive requires domestic legislation to preserve the continuity of employment of employees

443

when they are deemed to have transferred at the point of their initial secondment. Although the TUPE Regulations were passed in order to transpose the Directive, UK law will not be in breach of its requirements if continuity is preserved by other means, i.e. by S.218(2).

On the face of it, the Celtec case would seem to suggest that employees are saddled with the consequences of their employment having automatically transferred simply because they remained in employment until the date of the transfer, even where they knew nothing about the change in the identity of their employer and would have exercised their right to object had they been in a position to do so. In most cases, of course, employees in this situation would prefer their continuity to be preserved since, sometime down the track, they may well wish to maximise their period of continuous service with their 'new' employer. For example, if they are made redundant, their entitlement to and scale of statutory redundancy payments will be depend on the amount of continuous employment they have accrued. In such cases, S.218 operates to preserve continuity notwithstanding the lack of any objection or even the opportunity to object. But what is the position if the employee genuinely would not have wished his or her employment to transfer had he or she been informed of the imminent change of employer?

7.36   This was the situation in New ISG Ltd v Vernon 2008 ICR 319, ChD, discussed under 'Relationship between Regulations and ERA – employee objection to transfer' above. There, the employee was kept in the dark about the identity of his new employer following the sale of the transferor's business by joint administrators. When, two days after the transfer, he learned of the identity of the transferee, he resigned and subsequently went to work for a competitor. The new transferee immediately sought to enforce restrictive covenants in the employee's contract, contending that this had been transferred automatically in accordance with Reg 4 of TUPE. Initially, the transferee was successful in obtaining a temporary injunction restraining the employee from working for the competitor. However, on review, a High Court judge lifted the injunction on the basis that the employee, by resigning as soon as he found out about the transfer, had in effect objected to the transfer within the meaning of Reg 4(7). This had the consequence that his contract of employment had not transferred, so the transferee was not in a position to enforce the restrictive covenants contained within it. The judge rejected the transferee's argument that the employee's objection was ineffective because it was made after the transfer had occurred. The employee had not known of the identity of the transferee before the date of the transfer and had submitted a letter of resignation within two working days of the transfer. In those circumstances, while the wording of Reg 4(7) envisaged that an employee must object before or at the time of the transfer of the undertaking for the objection to be valid, the judge reasoned that a purposive approach was necessary to give force to the principle behind the right to object.

444

There are limits, however, to the extent to which the courts will allow an employee to object after a transfer has occurred. In Capita Health Solutions Ltd v McLean and anor 2008 IRLR 595, EAT, an employee employed by the BBC had deep reservations about the imminent transfer of her employment as an occupational nurse to CHS Ltd, which was due to take over the entirety of the BBC's HR department, including its occupational health service. These reservations were expressed by way of a grievance alleging that the change of employer entailed a significant change to the employee's role and pension benefits. However, in subsequent dealings, the employee and the BBC agreed that she would go to work for CHS Ltd for the six-week period during which she was working out her notice of resignation, and that she would continue to be paid by the BBC during this period. At the end of the six weeks, the employee duly resigned and claimed unfair dismissal against both CHS Ltd and the BBC and the issue arose as to whether the transferor – i.e. the BBC – should be regarded as a proper respondent to the proceedings. This depended on whether the employee had validly objected to the transfer: if not, her employment would have transferred to CHS Ltd, making it the sole respondent potentially liable for the unfair dismissal.

The EAT ruled that the act of going to work for the transferee under a temporary **7.37** secondment arrangement in circumstances where the employee was fully aware of the change in the identity of the employer was wholly inconsistent with having evinced an objection to the transfer. What, in fact, the employee's approach showed was that she was agreeable to working for CHS Ltd, albeit for only six weeks: this was wholly inconsistent with her claim that she had objected to the transfer. In the EAT's view, the intention of the parties, while a relevant consideration, was not determinative of the question whether an objection within the meaning of Reg 4(7) had been made. This was wholly an objective matter to be decided not by the intention of the parties but by the facts and circumstances of the case at issue. Furthermore, the fact that the BBC had continued to pay the employee during the secondment period was irrelevant, as was the fact that the employee was working out notice given prior to the transfer. In Lady Smith's judgment, 'if… it had been intended that objecting employees be required or able to work out notice periods that ran on after the date of the transfer, it is more than reasonable to have expected that to be provided for in the Regulations… That is not to say that an objecting employee cannot be employed by the transferor employer after the transfer date, but the transferor is not obliged to retain such an employee in his employment. Any such employment would be under a new contract.'

Residual application of ERA

7.38

Section 218(2) ERA provides that: 'If a trade or business, or an undertaking… is transferred from one person to another – (a) the period of employment of an employee in the trade or business or undertaking at the time of the transfer

445

counts as a period of employment with the transferee, and (b) the transfer does not break the continuity of the period of employment.' 'Except in so far as the context otherwise requires', the term 'business' includes 'a trade or profession and... any activity carried on by a body of persons (whether corporate or unincorporated)' – S.235(1).

Prior to the amendment of the TUPE Regulations in 1993, this provision was much wider than the corresponding provision in those Regulations, which originally applied only to transfers of undertakings that were 'in the nature of a commercial venture'. This meant that S.218(2) was the only available mechanism for preserving continuity on non-commercial takeovers. However, with the removal of the 'commercial venture' requirement from the Regulations, one of the major distinctions between the two schemes has disappeared and both now apply to commercial and non-commercial ventures. Furthermore, the EAT made it clear in D36 Ltd v Castro EAT 0853/03; 0113/04 that the Regulations and S.218(2) should be interpreted consistently as part of a 'single scheme' for preserving continuity in the event of a transfer. This view is arguably supported indirectly by the ERA itself, in that it provides that the definition of 'business' under S.235 can adapt according to the context; for example, according to the definition applied for the purposes of the Regulations.

7.39 It may even be the case that a wider definition of 'transfer' applies under S.218(2) than it does under the Regulations. In Dabell v Vale Industrial Services (Nottingham) Ltd and ors 1988 IRLR 439, CA, the Court of Appeal found that a transfer under the ERA had occurred despite the fact that only an informal agreement to a transfer had ever been reached. The decision in Castro (above) is not necessarily inconsistent with this as it can be interpreted as simply requiring that the definition of 'transfer' under the ERA should be no narrower than that under the Regulations. This leaves open the possibility that there may be situations that would constitute a transfer for the purposes of S.218(2) but not amount to a relevant transfer under the Regulations. In other words, falling within the definition of a 'relevant transfer' would be a sufficient, but not a necessary, requirement for a transfer to exist under S.218(2).

Thus, it seems that S.218(2) will apply to preserve continuity in all cases where there has been a relevant transfer under the Regulations (subject to the question of whether the employee was employed in the entity transferred 'at the time of' the transfer – see 'Relationship between Regulations and ERA – "at the time of" or "immediately before" the transfer' above). However, there are a number of situations in which the ERA applies entirely independently of the Regulations to preserve continuity of employment and these are now considered.

7.40 Redundancy pay and continuity

It is not uncommon for employees to receive a statutory redundancy payment from the transferor, despite taking up employment with the transferee. S.214

ERA states that continuity of employment is broken by receipt of a redundancy payment but only for the purposes of the statutory redundancy scheme. This means that employees start counting again as far as future entitlement to redundancy payments is concerned – but not for other purposes (as long as continuity has otherwise been preserved). S.214 applies where the employee's contract was renewed or the employee was re-engaged under a new contract, whether by the same or by another employer.

However, it is crucial to note that, in order for S.214 to apply, the transferor must have been liable to pay a redundancy payment under the legislation. If an employee is paid a redundancy payment by the transferor where there is a relevant transfer, his or her dismissal, if connected with the transfer within the meaning of Reg 7(1), will be automatically unfair unless the reason for the dismissal constitutes an ETO reason under Reg 7(2). In such circumstances, the payment made by the transferor will not have been in respect of a true liability because there will not have been a true redundancy situation. Therefore, S.214 would not apply and continuity for the purposes of calculating a future redundancy payment could be preserved.

7.41 There is an exception to the rule that S.214 will not apply if a payment is made in respect of a dismissal that is not a genuine redundancy. S.167 ERA essentially provides that where an employee is dismissed by an insolvent company by reason of redundancy, the Secretary of State will make a redundancy payment out of the National Insurance Fund. The Court of Appeal has examined a situation where the Secretary of State made redundancy payments to employees dismissed by an insolvent company where the dismissals were later found to have been by reason of a relevant transfer and automatically unfair under Reg 7(1) rather than by reason of redundancy:

* **Lassman and ors v Secretary of State for Trade and Industry and anor** 2000 ICR 1109, CA: L and others were employed by R Ltd, which became insolvent in 1988. On 29 March 1988 T Ltd signed an option agreement with R Ltd's receivers to purchase R Ltd. Two days later the employees were dismissed. However, they subsequently accepted jobs with T Ltd to commence on the next working day. They later received redundancy payments in respect of their dismissals by R Ltd from the Secretary of State, who was unaware that TUPE applied. Some years later, when T Ltd also became insolvent, the employees were again dismissed. They claimed that they were entitled to redundancy payments calculated by reference to their periods of employment with both employers. They argued that, since TUPE applied to the 1988 transaction, the Secretary of State should not have made redundancy payments at the time and that, accordingly, S.214 had not operated to break their continuity of employment for redundancy purposes. The Court of Appeal stated that the case turned on whether the payments made by the Secretary of State in 1988 were valid in the sense

that they were payments which, under the relevant legislation, the Secretary of State was empowered to make. S.214(5) provides: 'For the purposes of this section a redundancy payment shall be treated as having been paid if... (c) the Secretary of State has paid a sum to the employee in respect of the redundancy payment under S.167.' S.167(1) provides that the Secretary of State must make a payment where he or she 'is satisfied that the requirements specified in subsection (2) are met'. One requirement set out in S.167(2) is that the employee is entitled to the employer's payment. The Court pointed out that S.167 does not require an employee to be entitled to a redundancy payment for that payment to be valid. Rather, it requires the Secretary of State to be satisfied that the employee is so entitled. This is a subjective test, not an objective one. The Court believed that the Secretary of State could have properly concluded (on the basis of the decision in Secretary of State for Employment v Spence and ors 1986 ICR 651, CA, which was the leading authority at the time) that the employees concerned were not employed immediately before the transfer and, therefore, were not affected by the Regulations. Accordingly, the Secretary of State could properly have concluded that the employees were entitled to a redundancy payment. Therefore, the Court held that S.214 had operated in 1988 to break the employees' continuity of employment for redundancy purposes.

7.42 Insolvency

Regulation 4 of the 2006 Regulations (automatic novation of contracts) does not apply where the transferor is the subject of bankruptcy proceedings or other insolvency proceedings commenced under the supervision of an insolvency practitioner *with a view* to the liquidation of the transferor's assets – Reg 8(7). If, however, despite the initial aims of the insolvency proceedings, the trustee in bankruptcy or liquidator ends up selling the business as a going concern, this may well be a relevant transfer under the Regulations but the employee's employment will not automatically transfer under Reg 4. This does not necessarily mean that the employees will not be taken on voluntarily by the transferee but it does mean that their terms and conditions of employment will not be protected by the Regulations. However, for the purposes of continuity of employment this is unlikely to matter since, applying Nicholas v Grant (t/a Sandancers Café) EAT 0198/06 (see 'Relationship between Regulations and ERA' above), it is S.218(2) that actually preserves continuity where there has been a business transfer (provided continuity has otherwise been preserved). An example:

• **Belhaven Brewery Co Ltd v Berekis and ors** EAT 724/92: BB Co Ltd owned the pub in which B and his fellow claimants worked. It went into bankruptcy and the pub, as one of its assets, became vested in the trustee in bankruptcy. The pub remained open, but management responsibility was transferred to a new management company. As well as holding that there

448

had been a relevant transfer for the purposes of the 1981 Regulations (both when the trustee in bankruptcy had been appointed and again when the new managers had taken over), the EAT held that the employees' continuity of employment had been preserved by S.218(2).

Note that if the same facts were to be considered under the 2006 Regulations, **7.43** the tribunal would first have to decide whether BB Co Ltd had entered into bankruptcy and appointed trustees in bankruptcy with a view to liquidating the assets (and therefore whether Reg 8(7) would apply to prevent Reg 4 from having effect). However, this issue would arguably have no impact on that part of the EAT's decision concerned with the preservation of the employees' continuity of employment and it is submitted that Berekis remains good law on that particular point.

This has recently been reinforced by the Court of Appeal in Oakland v Wellswood (Yorkshire) Ltd 2010 ICR 902, CA. Both the employment tribunal and the EAT in that case concentrated on the issue of whether Reg 8(7) applied to exclude the operation of the automatic transfer of employment rules in Reg 4 and the automatic unfair dismissal provisions of Reg 7 in the context of a transfer that took place following a so-called 'pre-pack' administration. The specific issue in the case was whether the employee had the requisite one year's continuous service to claim unfair dismissal against the transferee. When the matter reached the Court of Appeal, it cut through all the complex issues surrounding Reg 8(7) to point out that continuity was simply dependent on whether there had been a transfer of a trade, business or undertaking from one person to another within the meaning of S.218(2). On that basis, it had little difficulty in concluding that there had been such a transfer. Accordingly, the employee's period of continuous employment with the transferor was added to his period of employment with the transferee, with the result that he had sufficient continuous service to bring an unfair dismissal claim.

For a detailed discussion of transfers in an insolvency context, see Chapter 6, 'Transfer of insolvent companies'.

Breaks in employment covered by S.212(3) ERA

7.44

In Macer v Abafast Ltd 1990 ICR 234, EAT, Mr Justice Wood stated that a broad interpretation of S.218(2) had to be applied and that an interval between employments, however long, did not matter for continuity purposes provided it related to the 'machinery' of the transfer (see 'Relationship between Regulations and ERA – breaks in employment' above). This meant that the normal continuity rules governing 'non-counting' weeks in Chapter I of Part XIV of the ERA were not relevant to transfer situations provided the gap in employment could be considered a part of the machinery of the transfer.

However, as discussed above, the Macer decision must now be treated with some caution following Celtec Ltd v Astley and ors 2006 ICR 992, HL, where

449

the House of Lords held that transfers under the Acquired Rights Directive (and therefore, by implication, the Regulations) occur at a fixed point in time. If, as a result of that decision, the broad approach adopted in Macer is no longer good law, then the non-counting week rules in the ERA must still apply in transfer situations. These would potentially deprive employees of continuity under S.218(2) where there is a gap of more than a week between the ending of the employee's employment with the transferor and the beginning of his or her employment with the transferee.

7.45 However, S.212(3) ERA may be of help here. This provision lists the circumstances in which an otherwise non-counting week counts as a period of employment, notwithstanding the absence of an employment contract. It provides, inter alia, that any week during the whole or part of which an employee is absent from work

- on account of a temporary cessation of work, or
- in circumstances such that, by arrangement or custom, he or she is regarded as continuing in the employment of his or her employer

counts in computing the employee's period of employment.

7.46 In Robert Elliot Ltd v Edgar EAT 581/85 it was suggested that a temporary cessation of work might preserve continuity during an interval on a transfer. This could be where there is no work available for employees to do while the business is being transferred. Similarly, it is possible that an agreement whereby employees were asked to keep themselves available for employment by the transferee could qualify as an 'arrangement' for the purposes of S.212(3).

Even if Macer remains good law it is arguable that these provisions are still relevant in respect of gaps in employment that fall outside the machinery of the transfer. However, it may be difficult to convince a tribunal that such gaps nevertheless amount to a temporary cessation of work or an arrangement or custom.

The general effect of S.212(3) is discussed in detail in IDS Employment Law Handbook, 'Continuity of Employment' (2001), Chapter 2.

7.47 Changes in employer where no business transfer occurs
It is important to note that specific statutory provisions apply in respect of preserving continuity of employment where an employee's employment transfers between two 'associated' employers – see S.218(6) ERA. Such a transfer does not usually constitute a transfer of a business or undertaking and therefore application of the provisions of S.218(2) is inappropriate.

There are similar provisions in S.218 which provide for preservation of continuity in other non-transfer situations where there has for some reason been a change of employer. These cover:

- statutory changes of employer – S.218(3)

- the death of an employer – S.218(4)

- a change in the partners making up an employing partnership – S.218(5)

- transfers of employees between local education authorities and governing bodies of local authority-run schools – S.218(7)

- transfers of relevant employment between Health Service employers – S.218(8). 'Relevant employment' for these purposes means employment where the individual is undergoing professional training which involves him or her being employed successively by a number of different health service employers and which is specified in an order made by the Secretary of State – S.218(9).

These provisions are considered in greater depth in IDS Employment Law Handbook, 'Continuity of Employment' (2001), Chapter 5.

Note that there are also specific provisions contained in other legislation **7.48** preserving continuity in particular circumstances or for particular professions. For example, continuity of employment for employees of NHS hospitals which become NHS trusts is governed by S.6 of the National Health Service and Community Care Act 1990. This provides that continuity will be preserved for an employee who 'immediately before an NHS trust's operational date... is employed by a health authority to work solely at... a hospital... which is to become the responsibility of the trust'.

Presumption of continuity **7.49**
Section 210(5) lays down a presumption that continuity is preserved 'unless the contrary is shown'. However, S.218(1) states that: 'Subject to the provisions of this section, this Chapter [i.e. Ss.210–219] relates only to employment by the one employer'. According to the EAT in Secretary of State for Employment v Cohen and anor 1987 ICR 570, EAT, this means that the presumption applies only to employment by the one employer unless the case can be brought within one of the exceptions in S.218 (e.g. S.218(2)). However, it is sometimes unclear from the facts what exactly has taken place, as the Cohen case illustrates:

- **Secretary of State for Employment v Cohen and anor** (above): C worked for F Ltd until it became insolvent. F Ltd was succeeded by W Ltd as C's employer. When W Ltd in turn became insolvent, B Ltd became C's employer. B Ltd then went into liquidation and C was made redundant. C's entitlement to a redundancy payment depended on whether there had been transfers of businesses between successive employers so as to preserve his continuity of employment through his successive employments by F Ltd, W Ltd and B Ltd. There was scant evidence on the nature of the transactions that had taken place between the three companies. A tribunal decided to apply the presumption of continuity and to hold that C was entitled to a redundancy payment, which was payable by the Department of Employment because of the insolvency of C's last employer. The Secretary of State appealed. The EAT held that the statutory presumption of continuity applies only to employment with one employer unless the case can be brought within one of the statutory exceptions. It follows that the existence of a statutory exception must be demonstrated before the presumption of continuity can be applied.

7.50 This ruling means that in cases of transfers between employers the employee must show that the provisions on transfers and continuity contained in S.218(2) are applicable without resort to the presumption of continuity. It is only after it has been shown that there has been a transfer of a business that the presumption may be applied in the employee's favour. This may operate to the disadvantage of employees, who will often not have access to the information which could help to establish the nature of the transfer.

8 Information and consultation

In this chapter we turn our attention to the specific rules in the Transfer of **8.1** Undertakings (Protection of Employment) Regulations 2006 SI 2006/246 (TUPE) that govern information and consultation. We divide these into two categories. The first concerns the duty on the transferor, introduced by the 2006 Regulations, to provide information to the transferee about the employees who are to transfer under TUPE. The second concerns the established duty on both the transferor and the transferee to inform and consult appropriate representatives of employees who may be affected by a relevant transfer.

The Government has issued guidance on the issues raised by the provisions considered in this chapter. A document entitled 'Employment rights on the transfer of an undertaking: a guide to the 2006 TUPE Regulations for employees, employers and representatives' was published by the Department for Trade and Industry (DTI) at around the time the 2006 Regulations came into force. That document was updated in 2009 and republished by the Department for Business, Innovation and Skills (BIS), which has since replaced the DTI. We shall refer to this updated guide as 'the BIS Guide' in this chapter.

Employee liability information   8.2

In Chapters 2 and 3 we saw that, when a relevant transfer occurs, the contracts of employment of certain members of the transferor's workforce, together with all the transferor's rights, powers, duties and liabilities under or in connection with such contracts, will (if the employees in question do not object) transfer automatically to the transferee owing to Reg 4 of the 2006 Regulations.

It is clear that a transferee will want to be aware, prior to a relevant transfer, of the employees and the liabilities that he is about to take on. To this end, he will usually expect the transferor to provide the relevant information and to sign up to warranties in respect of it (see Chapter 10 for further details). However, some smaller firms might have insufficient bargaining power to negotiate the appropriate contractual safeguards. Moreover, where TUPE applies to a service provision change following a re-tendering exercise, the incoming contractor (the transferee) does not normally have a contractual relationship with the outgoing contractor (the transferor), and thus, historically, has had no simple means of ascertaining the extent of the liabilities that are about to transfer. As we shall see, however, the new TUPE regime has ameliorated transferees' difficulties in this regard.

453

8.3 Article 3.2 of the new EU Acquired Rights Directive (No.2001/23) gives Member States the option to introduce provisions 'to ensure that the transferor notifies the transferee of all the rights and obligations which will be transferred to the transferee... so far as those rights and obligations are or ought to have been known to the transferor at the time of the transfer'. This option, which was not available under the previous version of the Directive, was taken up by the United Kingdom Government in the 2006 Regulations, which oblige transferors to notify transferees about so-called 'employee liability information'. As we discuss below, Regs 11 and 12 of the 2006 Regulations lay down rules as to the manner, extent and timing of the notification that the transferor must give to the transferee, and the remedy for failure to observe the requirements.

In the 2005 Consultation Document the Government expressed the view that 'the introduction of these new provisions will ensure that transferees are entitled to full, accurate information about the employees, and the associated rights, obligations etc, that they are taking on in a relevant transfer, and so are well placed to honour those rights, obligations etc'. Furthermore, it continued, 'it will help to ensure transparency in the transfer process and to prevent instances of sharp practice – such as where, shortly before a transfer is completed, the transferor changes the terms and conditions and/or the composition of the workforce assigned to the undertaking in question, to the disadvantage of the transferee'.

Note that, although for the most part the 2006 Regulations came into force on 6 April 2006, the duty to notify under Reg 11 applies only to relevant transfers taking place on or before 19 April 2006 – Reg 21(4).

8.4 Information in respect of transferring employees
Regulation 11(1) specifies that 'the transferor shall notify to the transferee the employee liability information of any person employed by him who is assigned to the organised grouping of resources or employees that is the subject of a relevant transfer'. Reg 11(4) then clarifies that the Reg 11(1) duty 'shall include a duty to provide employee liability information of any person who would have been employed by the transferor and assigned to the organised grouping of resources or employees that is the subject of a relevant transfer immediately before the transfer if he had not been dismissed in the circumstances described in regulation 7(1)'.

Put more simply, then, the transferor must supply the transferee with 'employee liability information' – for which, see below – in respect of the following two categories of employees:

- those whose contracts of employment will, subject to the employees' right to object, transfer to the transferee under Reg 4(2) – see Chapter 2

- those whose contracts would have transferred under Reg 4(2) had they not been automatically unfairly dismissed under Reg 7(1) by reason of the relevant transfer, or for a reason in connection with the relevant transfer that was not 'an economic, technical or organisational reason entailing changes in the workforce' – see Chapter 4.

Definition of 'employee liability information'   8.5
The list of information that must be provided in respect of the transferring employees is set out in Reg 11(2), which defines 'employee liability information' as:

- the identity and age of an employee

- the particulars of employment that an employer is obliged to give to an employee pursuant to S.1 of the Employment Rights Act 1996 (ERA)

- 'information of any (i) disciplinary procedure taken against an employee; (ii) grievance procedure taken by an employee, within the previous two years, in circumstances where a Code of Practice issued under Part IV of the Trade Union and Labour Relations (Consolidation) Act 1992 which relates exclusively or primarily to the resolution of disputes applies'

- 'information of any court or tribunal case, claim or action brought by an employee against the transferor, within the previous two years' and of any court or tribunal case, claim or action 'that the transferor has reasonable grounds to believe that an employee may bring against the transferee, arising out of the employee's employment with the transferor'

- 'information of any collective agreement which will have effect after the transfer, in its application in relation to the employee, pursuant to Reg 5(a)'.

Identity and age. In WGC Ltd v Resource (UK) ET Case No.2302094/09 an   8.6
employment tribunal decided that there is no material difference between providing employees' dates of birth and providing ages. Accordingly, where the transferee requested dates of birth, it should have been provided with them. As to employees' identities, a tribunal in Kentklean Ltd v Southern Cleaning ET Case No.1100807/08 held that this does not include a requirement to provide employees' addresses. The tribunal thought addresses could to some extent be regarded as sensitive, private information, and that if such information were required to be given, the Regulations would have said so expressly.

Particulars of employment. As stated above, under Reg 11(2) the transferor   8.7
must provide the transferee with the transferring employees' S.1 ERA particulars of employment. These will include reasonably extensive information about the employees' terms and conditions, dealing with job title, remuneration, hours, holidays, sickness absence, when employment began, length of notice, place of work, relevant collective agreements and overseas working. For more details,

455

see IDS Employment Law Handbook, 'Contracts of Employment' (2009). In WGC Ltd v Resource (UK) (above) the employment tribunal held that information such as the employee's marital status, nationality, attendance record and right to work in the United Kingdom is not required under Reg 11(2). However, information about sickness absence was necessary to enable the transferee to calculate accurately the employees' entitlement to contractual or statutory sick pay.

8.8 **Disciplinary and grievance procedures.** The transferor must also provide information about any disciplinary procedure instituted in respect of a transferring employee, and about any grievance procedure instituted by a transferring employee, within the previous two years, and to which a Code issued under Part IV of the TULR(C)A applies. The only relevant Code currently in force is the Acas Code of Practice on Disciplinary and Grievance Procedures (2009) – see IDS Employment Law Supplement, 'Disciplinary and Grievance Procedures' (2009) for details. Given that the transferor will be required to provide details on any disciplinary action it has taken in the previous two years, disciplinary policies providing for a shorter retention period for expunged disciplinary sanctions will need to be reviewed to ensure that adequate records are kept in the employee's personnel file for the relevant two-year period.

8.9 The following points ought also to be considered:

- the transferor is only obliged to provide details of occasions when a disciplinary or grievance procedure has actually been instituted – not about occasions on which a procedure should have been instituted but was not

- there is no indication in the Regulations or in the BIS Guide of how much detail the transferor is obliged to provide in respect of the disciplinary or grievance proceedings in question. This might, in time, be ironed out by case law. In the meantime, we suggest that a transferor should, at the very least, state when and why the procedure was followed, and what the outcome of it was

- it would seem from the wording of Reg 11(2) that the transferor is obliged to provide information about any disciplinary or grievance procedure instituted by or in respect of a transferring employee within the previous two years, *whether such procedure involved the transferor himself or a previous employer*. Where the employee in question transferred to the transferor from a previous employer under TUPE – meaning that any liabilities arising from such previous employment passed to the transferor and will, in turn, pass to the transferee – it makes sense that the transferee should be made aware of this information. It makes less sense, however, if the employee's employment with the previous employer did not transfer to the transferor under TUPE and was not otherwise continuous. In such circumstances, anything that happened in the employee's previous employment could not, via the transferor, lead to liability on the part of the transferee; and thus the provision of information about the employee's previous employment would seem to be beyond the scope of Article 3.2 of the Directive and outside the purpose of Reg 11

- information need only be provided in respect of proceedings taken 'within the previous two years'. The date on which the two-year period starts is clear: it is the date on which the disciplinary or grievance procedure was instituted – that is, the date on which the employer or employee respectively complied with the first step of the relevant procedure. But on which date the two-year period ends is less clear. Is it the date of the relevant transfer? Is it the date on which the employee liability information is provided? Or is it the specified date in respect of which the employee liability information is accurate? In the absence of any guidance on this issue, and in order to ensure compliance, transferors should probably assume that the third alternative is correct, as it would involve the earliest of the three possible 'end dates' – see 'When and how should the information be provided?' below for further details.

Claims and prospective claims. Regulation 11(2) states that a transferor must **8.10** provide information about any legal action that a transferring employee has brought against it within the previous two years, and about any legal action that the transferor has reasonable grounds to believe that a transferring employee may bring against the transferee arising out of the employee's employment with the transferor.

Again, this raises questions about how much detail the transferor is obliged to provide, and what might amount to 'the previous two years'. In this regard, the points made above in relation to the requirement to provide information about disciplinary and grievance procedures apply equally here. On other matters, the following issues are pertinent:

- under Reg 11(2) the transferor must provide information of any court or tribunal case, claim or action brought by an employee *against the transferor*, within the previous two years, as opposed to against the transferor or a previous employer. This is to be contrasted with the wording with regard to information about disciplinary and grievance procedures, which we discussed above. The logic behind this difference is unclear

- the transferor must provide information about any legal action that it has 'reasonable grounds' to believe that a transferring employee may bring against the transferee, arising out of the employee's employment with the transferor. This raises the question of what might amount to 'reasonable grounds'. The first point to make is that it is irrelevant whether the prospective claim is itself 'reasonable'. It might be utterly hopeless. The key question is whether the *transferor* has reasonable grounds to believe that a claim might be brought. In this regard, the BIS Guide states: 'This is a matter

457

of judgment and depends on the characteristics of each case. So, where an incident seems trifling – say, where an employee slipped at work but did not take any time off as a result – then there is little reason to suppose that a claim for personal injury damages would result. In contrast, if a fall at work led to hospitalisation over a long period or where a union representative raised the incident as a health and safety concern, then the transferor should inform the transferee accordingly.'

8.11 **Collective agreements.** The final aspect of the 'employee liability information' under Reg 11(2) is 'information of any collective agreement which will have effect after the transfer, in its application in relation to the employee, pursuant to Regulation 5(a)'.

We shall not discuss the intricacies of Reg 5(a) here, as it is dealt with at length in Chapter 3 under 'Collective rights and liabilities'. Essentially, it provides that where at the time of a relevant transfer the transferor recognises a collective agreement with a trade union, which covers a transferring employee, that agreement shall, in respect of that employee, have effect after the transfer as if made between the trade union and the transferee.

8.12 **Additional information.** Note that although the above employee liability information will clearly be useful, the transferee will usually wish to receive information that is far more extensive than that referred to in Reg 11(2). In Chapter 10, under 'Due diligence', we discuss what additional information the transferee might consider requesting.

8.13 **How and when should the information be provided?**
Having discussed what 'employee liability information' is, we now consider the manner in which the transferor should provide it to the transferee. In this regard, Reg 11 provides:

- the transferor shall notify to the transferee the employee liability information 'in writing' or shall make it available to the transferee 'in a readily accessible form' – Reg 11(1)

- the notification under Reg 11(1) shall contain employee liability information 'as at a specified date not more than fourteen days before the date on which the information is notified to the transferee' – Reg 11(3)

- once the information has been provided, the transferor shall notify the transferee of any changes to it – Reg 11(5)

- a notification under Reg 11 'shall be given not less than fourteen days before the relevant transfer or, if special circumstances make this not reasonably practicable, as soon as reasonably practicable thereafter' – Reg 11(6)

- a notification may be given in more than one instalment, and may be given indirectly, through a third party – Reg 11(7).

458

In writing or in a 'readily accessible form'. Under Reg 11(1), then, the **8.14** employee liability information must be notified in writing or made available in readily accessible form. In this regard, the BIS Guide states: 'The information must be provided in writing or in other forms which are accessible to the [transferee]. So, it may be possible for the transferor to send the information as computer data files as long as the [transferee] can access that information, or provide access to the transferor's data storage. Likewise, in cases where a very small number of employees are transferring and small amounts of information may be involved, it might be acceptable to provide the information by telephone. However, it would be a good practice for the transferor to consult the [transferee] first to discuss the methods which he can use.' The Guide goes on to point out that it is open to the transferor to supply some information in the form of staff handbooks, sample contracts or the texts of collective agreements 'if it would assist'.

Timing of the notification. Whereas the original draft of the Regulations **8.15** proposed that notification should be given 'in good time' before the transfer, the final draft is more specific, requiring that the information be given at least 14 days before the transfer or, if this is not reasonably practicable owing to special circumstances, as soon as is reasonably practicable (Reg 11(6)). The BIS Guide is vague as to what might qualify as 'special circumstances', saying that 'these would be various depending on circumstances'. It does, however, go on to give a specific example, saying 'clearly, it would not be reasonably practicable to provide the information in time, if the transferor did not know the identity of the [transferee] until very late in the process, as might occur where service contracts are re-assigned from one contractor to another by a client, or, more generally, when the transfer takes place at very short notice'.

When the Reg 11(2) notification is given, it should specify the date as at which the information in question was accurate. This date does not have to be the same as the date of notification, but must not be more than 14 days before it – Reg 11(3). Reading Reg 11(3) and (6) together, then, the employee liability information provided by the transferor can be specified as accurate as at any date within 28 days of the relevant transfer. There is thus considerable scope for the information becoming out of date. This is recognised by Reg 11(5), which states that following notification 'the transferor shall notify the transferee in writing of any change in the employee liability information'. Two points about Reg 11(5):

- unlike the rules with regard to the initial notification, it requires changes to the information to be notified *in writing*

- at first glance, it gives no indication of the timescale within which notification of changes has to be provided. However, since such a notification is, presumably, 'a notification under this regulation', it would seem that the rule set out in Reg 11(6), which we discussed above, applies. In other words,

459

notification of the changes shall be given not less than 14 days before the relevant transfer or, if special circumstances make this not reasonably practicable (e.g. where the change itself takes place after that deadline), as soon as reasonably practicable thereafter.

8.16 **Provided via a third party.** The specified information may, according to Reg 11(7), be given by the transferor indirectly through a third party to the transferee as well as directly to the transferee. The BIS Guide states: 'For example, where a client is re-assigning a contract from an existing contractor to a new contractor, that client organisation may act as the third party in passing the information to the new contractor.'

8.17 **Data protection.** Several respondents to consultation on the draft 2006 Regulations were concerned about a potential conflict between the provision of employee liability information and the Data Protection Act 1998 (DPA), which places limits on the disclosure of personal information. The Government suggested, in its response to consultation, that the disclosure of employee liability information would be fully compliant with the DPA. The Government's logic would seem to be as follows. S.35 of the DPA states that the Act's provisions with regard to the non-disclosure of 'personal data' will not apply 'where the disclosure is required by or under any enactment'. Thus, where transferors provide the information required by Reg 11 of the 2006 Regulations, they will not, owing to S.35, be in breach of the DPA's provisions.

This analysis, on its face, seems to make sense. However, the reality is more complicated. If, when providing employee liability information, the transferor provides slightly more than is 'required' by Reg 11, the provision of this additional information will fall outside the S.35 exception to the DPA provisions. As we have seen, Reg 11(2) does not go into great detail as to how much information need be provided. Thus, a transferor wishing to ensure compliance with Reg 11 is almost certainly going to end up providing more information than is strictly necessary, and therefore might bring the DPA into play.

8.18 Owing to this, transferors providing notification under Reg 11 should take note of the Information Commissioner's *Employment Practices Code*, which provides guidance for employers on data protection compliance. In particular, paras 2.11 and 2.12 of the Code provide the following advice about publishing information about workers in the context of a transfer or merger situation:

- ensure that there is a legal obligation to publish the information, that the information is clearly not intrusive, that the worker has consented to disclosure, or that the information is in a form that does not identify individual workers

- ensure, wherever practicable, that information handed over to another organisation in connection with a prospective acquisition, merger or business reorganisation is anonymised

- only hand over personal information prior to a final merger or acquisition decision after securing assurances that it will be used solely for the evaluation of assets and liabilities, will be treated in confidence and not be disclosed to other parties, and will be destroyed or returned after use

- unless it is impracticable to do so, tell workers if their employment records are to be disclosed to another organisation before an acquisition, merger or reorganisation takes place. If the acquisition, merger or reorganisation proceeds, make sure workers are aware of the extent to which their records are to be transferred to the new employer

- where a merger, acquisition or reorganisation involves a transfer of information about a worker to a country outside the European Economic Area (EEA), ensure that there is a proper basis for making the transfer.

Contracting out   8.19
Regulation 18 of the 2006 Regulations, which restricts contracting out of the Regulations' provisions, applies to the transferor's obligation to provide employee liability information. This is reflected in the BIS Guide, which notes that the transferor and the transferee cannot agree between themselves that the Reg 11 employee liability information should not be provided since 'that would disadvantage the employees involved'. We discuss Reg 18 and its implications in Chapter 10 under 'Avoidance of TUPE provisions'.

Remedy for failure to notify   8.20
Regulation 12(1) gives the transferee the right to complain to an employment tribunal, 'on or after a relevant transfer', that the transferor has failed to comply in whole or in part with any of the notification requirements set out above. The complaint has to be made to the tribunal before the end of the period of three months beginning with the date of the relevant transfer, or within such further period as the tribunal considers reasonable in a case where it is satisfied that it was not reasonably practicable for the complaint to be presented before the end of that period.

Where the tribunal finds that the complaint is well founded, it *shall* make a declaration to that effect and *may* make an award of compensation to be paid by the transferor to the transferee – Reg 12(3). Under Reg 12(4), 'the amount of the compensation shall be such as the tribunal considers just and equitable in all the circumstances... having particular regard to (a) any loss sustained by the transferee which is attributable to the matters complained of; and (b) the terms of any contract between the transferor and the transferee relating to the transfer under which the transferor may be liable to pay any sum to the

461

transferee in respect of a failure to notify the transferee of employee liability information'. Reg 12(5) provides that, subject to the transferee's duty to mitigate its loss (for which, see IDS Employment Law Handbook, 'Contracts of Employment' (2009)), the sum awarded shall be at least £500 per employee in respect of whom the duty to inform arose – although the tribunal has the discretion to award a lesser sum if it considers it just and equitable to do so. The BIS Guide suggests that 'trivial or unwitting' breaches may lead the tribunal to depart from the minimum award.

8.21 Finally, Reg 12(7) provides that S.18 of the Employment Tribunals Act 1996, which concerns Acas conciliation, applies to claims under Reg 12 as it applies to the rights conferred by and to proceedings under that Act. See IDS Employment Law Handbook, 'Employment Tribunal Practice and Procedure' (2006) for details.

8.22 Informing and consulting representatives

It is one of the central pillars of the EU Acquired Rights Directive, and hence of TUPE, that transferor and transferee employers must inform, and usually also consult with, appropriate representatives of employees who might be affected by a proposed transfer.

At European level, the relevant provisions are found in Article 7 of the Directive (previously Article 6). Article 7.1 provides that the transferor and transferee 'shall be required to inform the representatives of their respective employees affected by the transfer' of the date or proposed date of the transfer, the reasons for it, the 'legal, economic and social implications' for the employees, and 'any measures envisaged in relation to the employees'. In this regard, Article 7.1 continues, the transferor shall be required to give the information to appropriate representatives in good time before the transfer is carried out. Similarly, the transferee shall be under a duty to provide the information to appropriate representatives in good time and, in any event, before his employees 'are directly affected by the transfer as regards their conditions of work and employment'. Article 7.2 goes on to state that 'where the transferor or the transferee envisages measures in relation to his employees, he shall consult the representatives of [his] employees in good time on such measures with a view to reaching an agreement'.

8.23 Article 7 is given effect by Regs 13, 14, 15 and 16 of the 2006 Regulations, which we discuss at length below. These are in largely the same form as the TUPE information and consultation regime's previous incarnation, which was found in Regs 10 – 11A of the 1981 Regulations.

Note that Reg 21, which provides for transitional arrangements between the old and new TUPE regimes, makes special provision with regard to informing and consulting employees in relation to service provision changes – i.e.

insourcing, outsourcing and re-tendering processes. Reg 21(5) disapplies the duty in relation to a 'service provision change' that is not also a business transfer (see Chapter 1) taking place on or before 4 May 2006.

Affected employees

8.24

Regulation 13 only obliges transferors and transferees to inform and consult in respect of 'affected employees'. This term is defined by Reg 13(1), which states: 'In this regulation and regulations 14 and 15 references to affected employees, in relation to a relevant transfer, are to any employees of the transferor or the transferee (whether or not assigned to the organised grouping of resources or employees that is the subject of a relevant transfer) who may be affected by the transfer or may be affected by measures taken in connection with it.'

This means that, in order to be an 'affected employee' within the meaning of Reg 13(1), an individual must be:

- an 'employee' for the purposes of the 2006 Regulations. 'Employee' is defined by Reg 2(1) as meaning 'any individual who works for another person whether under a contract of service or apprenticeship or otherwise but does not include anyone who provides services under a contract for services'. For a full discussion of the implications of this definition, see Chapter 2 under 'Who is an "employee" for TUPE purposes?'

- an employee of either the transferor or the transferee (not a third party), and

- someone who may be affected by the transfer or by measures taken in connection with it. It is important to note that the word 'may' is included, as opposed to the word 'will' – meaning that an employer does not have to be sure that an employee *will* be affected in order for Reg 13 to be triggered in respect of that employee. We consider the meaning of 'measures taken in connection with a transfer' below under 'The duty to consult'.

It is clear from the above that it is not only the employees scheduled to transfer **8.25** from the transferor to the transferee under TUPE who can be 'affected employees' for the purposes of Reg 13. A relevant transfer may also have repercussions for the employees of parts of the transferor's undertaking that are not transferred, and for the transferee's existing workforce. So, as is reflected in the BIS Guide, there are three possible categories of 'affected employees'. They are, '(a) those individuals who are to be transferred; (b) their colleagues in the transferor employer who will not transfer but whose jobs might be affected by the transfer; or (c) their new colleagues in employment with the [transferee] whose jobs might be affected by the transfer'.

The EAT considered this guidance in Unison v Somerset County Council and ors 2010 ICR 498, EAT. There, two Councils decided to transfer the bulk of the work of their resources directorates to a joint venture company, SWO Ltd. Employees 'in scope' were given the option of either transferring to SWO Ltd

463

or remaining as employees of the relevant Council and being seconded to SWO Ltd. A dispute arose over the Councils' compliance with Reg 13 in relation to SWO Ltd's proposed recruitment policy following the transfer. The union initially hoped to secure agreement that in-scope employees would receive preferential treatment for any future vacancies that might arise with SWO Ltd; that existing employees of the Councils would be second in order of preference; and only then, if that failed to fill the post, would vacancies be advertised externally. SWO Ltd could not accept this arrangement. It agreed to give preference to in-scope employees but reserved the right to advertise posts to the world at large if that produced no successful applicant. The union asserted that this meant non-transferring employees of the Councils were 'affected employees' for the purposes of Reg 13(1), since their prospects of securing future employment with SWO Ltd, if vacancies became available, were adversely affected.

8.26 The EAT rejected that argument. It held that the 'affected employees' on these facts were:

- employees who will or may be transferred

- employees whose jobs are in jeopardy by reason of the proposed transfer; and

- employees who have job applications within the undertaking subject to the transfer pending at the time of the transfer.

The EAT could not accept that 'affected employees' included everyone in the transferor's workforce who may apply for a vacancy at some point in the future with the transferred part of the organisation. We would suggest that, where the BIS Guide states that affected employees include non-transferring employees whose jobs might be affected by the transfer, it should be read with the EAT's qualification in mind.

8.27 Appropriate representatives

In attempting to give effect to the mandatory provisions of what was then Article 6 (and is now Article 7) of the Directive, the 1981 Regulations, as originally enacted, imposed a duty on transferors and transferees to inform and consult with representatives of any independent trade union recognised in respect of affected employees. However, in Commission of the European Communities v United Kingdom 1994 ICR 664, ECJ, the European Court of Justice decided that, in limiting the scope of those whom employers had to inform and consult to trade union representatives, the 1981 Regulations were defective.

The United Kingdom Government responded to the ECJ's ruling by introducing the Collective Redundancies and Transfer of Undertakings (Protection of Employment) (Amendment) Regulations 1995 SI 1995/2587, which gave employers a choice whether to consult representatives of a recognised trade union or other employee representatives. This, however, proved exceedingly unpopular with trade unions, as it gave employers the opportunity to bypass them with regard to information and consultation under TUPE even where they were recognised in the workplace. This situation was rectified by further amendments, activated by the Collective Redundancies and Transfer of Undertakings (Protection of Employment) (Amendment) Regulations 1999 SI 1999/1925. These produced the current state of affairs, whereby an employer must consult with trade union representatives where the union is recognised with regard to affected employees, and with 'employee representatives' in other circumstances.

8.28 This position is set out in Reg 13(3) of the 2006 Regulations, which provides that, for the purposes of the TUPE information and consultation rules, 'appropriate representatives' of affected employees are:

- 'if the employees are of a description in respect of which an independent trade union is recognised by their employer, representatives of the trade union, or

- in any other case, whichever of the following employee representatives the employer chooses – (i) employee representatives appointed or elected by the affected employees otherwise than for the purposes of this regulation, who (having regard to the purposes for, and the method by which they were appointed or elected) have authority from those employees to receive information and to be consulted about the transfer on their behalf; (ii) employee representatives elected by any affected employees, for the purposes of this regulation, in an election satisfying the requirements of regulation 14(1)'.

We now turn to consider in more detail who these union/employee representatives might be, and look at what other rules in the 2006 Regulations and elsewhere apply in respect of them.

8.29 **Independent and recognised trade union.** As we saw directly above, Reg 13(3) states that where affected employees are represented by a recognised, independent trade union, the employer must inform and consult representatives of that trade union, as opposed to other employee representatives. This is reflected and expanded upon in the BIS Guide, which states that 'where employees who may be affected by the transfer are represented by an independent trade union for collective bargaining purposes, the employer must inform and consult an authorised official of that union. This may be a shop steward or a district union official or, if appropriate, a national or regional official. The employer is not required to inform or consult any other employee representatives in such circumstances, but may do so if the trade union is recognised for one group of employees, but not for another.'

465

This raises the questions of when a trade union is independent, and when such a union is recognised. These questions are dealt with in IDS Employment Law Handbook, 'Trade Unions' (2000), and shall not be examined at length here. The basics, however are set out below.

8.30 *Independence.* The law acknowledges that, for trade unions to carry out their functions properly, they must be truly independent of employers. For example, house unions or staff associations to which management may belong or to whom they may provide funds might not, owing to management's apparent control, robustly defend the interests of their members.

There is a statutory definition of independence, found in S.5(1) of the Trade Union and Labour Relations (Consolidation) Act 1992 (TULR(C)A), which provides that a union is independent if it is:

- not under the domination or control of an employer, and

- not liable to interference by an employer (arising out of the provision of financial or material support or by other means) tending towards such control.

Note that a listed trade union – that is, one found on the list of unions maintained by the Certification Officer – may apply to the Certification Officer under S.6(1) TULR(C)A for a certificate stating that it satisfies the statutory definition of independence.

8.31 *Recognition.* Put simply, 'recognition' is the process by which an employer accepts a trade union as being entitled to act on behalf of a particular group (or groups) of workers for some purpose.

Regulation 2(1) of the 2006 Regulations provides that 'recognised' has the meaning given to it by S.178(3) TULR(C)A. Thus, a recognised trade union for the purposes of the Reg 13 information and consultation rules is one that is recognised 'by an employer, or two or more associated employers, to any extent, for the purposes of collective bargaining'. 'Collective bargaining', also defined by S.178 TULR(C)A, means negotiations relating to or connected with one or more of the following:

- terms and conditions of employment, or the physical conditions in which any workers are required to work

- engagement or non-engagement, termination or suspension of employment

- allocation of work between workers or groups of workers

- disciplinary matters

- a worker's membership or non-membership of a trade union

- facilities for trade union officials

- machinery for negotiation or consultation, and other procedures, relating to any of the above matters, including the recognition by employers or employers' associations of the right of a trade union to represent workers in such negotiation or consultation or in the carrying out of such procedures.

Recognition can be either voluntary on the part of the employer or compulsory under the complex scheme contained in Schedule A1 to the TULR(C)A, which is discussed at great length in the 'Trade Unions' Handbook referred to above.

Is union recognised in respect of all affected employees? Where there is an **8.32** independent trade union that is recognised in the workplace, it will be important for the transferor or transferee in question to determine whether that union is recognised in respect of all the employer's 'affected employees'. If the union is not so recognised, then the employer will be obliged to inform/consult 'employee representatives' of the employees who are not represented by the union.

Employee representatives. Where employees who may be affected by the **8.33** transfer are not represented by a recognised independent trade union, the employer must inform and consult employee representatives of these employees. As we saw above, under Reg 13(3) the employer has a choice between informing and consulting existing employee representatives or new ones especially elected for TUPE purposes.

Existing employee representatives. One option, then, is for the employer to **8.34** inform and consult 'employee representatives appointed or elected by the affected employees otherwise than for the purposes of this regulation, who (having regard to the purposes for, and the method by which they were appointed or elected) have authority from those employees to receive information and to be consulted about the transfer on their behalf' – Reg 13(3).

If existing employee representatives are to be informed and consulted, then it is obviously important that they meet the above description. As the BIS Guide puts it, 'their remit and method of election or appointment must give them suitable authority from the employees concerned'. As set out above, Reg 13(3) provides that the question of whether the existing representatives have such authority is to be answered with 'regard to the purposes for, and the method by which they were appointed or elected'. With this in mind, the BIS Guide states: 'It would not, for example, be appropriate to inform and consult a committee specially established to consider the operation of a staff canteen about a transfer affecting, say, sales staff; but it may well be appropriate to inform and consult a fairly elected or appointed committee of employees, such as a works council, that is regularly informed and consulted more generally about the business's financial position and personnel matters.' In our view, this suggests that a committee established under the Information and Consultation of Employees Regulations 2004 SI 2004/3426 would suffice (for details, see IDS Employment Law Supplement, 'Information and Consultation Regulations 2004' (2005)).

467

8.35 Note that Reg 15(3) provides that if tribunal proceedings are brought in relation to an employer's alleged failure to inform or consult under Reg 13, and if in the course of those proceedings a question arises as to whether an employee representative was an appropriate representative for the purposes of Reg 13, it shall be for the employer to show that the employee representative had the necessary authority to represent the affected employees.

8.36 *Inviting elections for new employee representatives.* In the absence of a recognised trade union, and whether or not there are appropriate existing employee representatives, an employer caught up in a relevant transfer might choose to invite the affected employees to elect new employee representatives specifically for Reg 13. Any such election must be conducted in accordance with Reg 14, which we discuss below.

Before turning to the method of election itself, however, there is a significant issue surrounding an employer's 'inviting' affected employees to elect employee representatives that should be considered here. That is, where there is neither a recognised trade union nor existing employee representatives in place with regard to 'affected employees', need the employer concerned invite the affected employees to elect employee representatives for the purposes of Reg 13 information and consultation, or can he simply sit back and do nothing?

8.37 Perhaps unsurprisingly, the majority of EAT case law suggests that the employer does need to take action of some sort. We shall explore this case law in due course, but first it is necessary to set out a number of Reg 13 provisions that we have not yet touched upon in this chapter, and which have been central to the EAT's reasoning on this issue:

- Regulation 13(9) provides that 'if in any case there are special circumstances which render it not reasonably practicable for an employer to perform a duty imposed on him by [Reg 13(2)--(7)], he shall take all such steps towards performing that duty as are reasonably practicable in the circumstances'

- then, Reg 13(10) provides that 'where (a) the employer has invited any of the affected employees to elect employee representatives; and (b) the invitation was issued long enough before the time when the employer is required to give information under [Reg 13(2)] to allow them to elect representatives by that time, the employer shall be treated as complying with the requirements of this regulation in relation to those employees if he complies with those requirements as soon as is reasonably practicable after the election of the representatives'

- under Reg 13(11), 'if, after the employer has invited any affected employees to elect representatives, they fail to do so within a reasonable time, he shall give to any affected employees the information set out in [Reg 13(2)]'.

In Russell v Bacon's College and anor EAT 98/99 a transferor employer **8.38** informed neither R (an affected employee) nor any representative of R about an imminent TUPE transfer. R brought a claim in respect of this failure before an employment tribunal. At the hearing, the transferor made the point that its obligations under Reg 13 were to inform and consult appropriate representatives. In its view, it followed that where, as in this case, there were no appropriate representatives in place, no obligation under TUPE to inform and consult had arisen. The employment tribunal accepted the transferor's argument, noting that 'there appears to be no duty to inform and consult individual employees when no representative has been elected'. R appealed to the EAT.

R referred the Appeal Tribunal to R v Secretary of State for Trade and Industry ex parte Unison 1996 ICR 1003, QBD, a case in which the High Court had considered whether the EU Acquired Rights Directive was properly implemented in the United Kingdom. There, expressing satisfaction with the way in which the Regulations were structured, Lord Justice Otton stated that compliance with the Directive was achieved by the Regulations' imposing a primary duty on the employer to inform and consult appropriate representatives. If there are no such representatives in place, he continued, the employer is bound to be in breach of this primary duty unless he can show that he is within one of the specified exceptions in the Regulations.

Mr Justice Burton, giving judgment in the instant case, affirmed the above **8.39** comments of Otton LJ and, in light of what is now Reg 13 of TUPE, made the following comments:

- there is a 'primary' duty on employers to inform employee representatives under Reg 13(2) – see 'The duty to inform' below

- if employers do not inform appropriate representatives they are, on the face of it, in breach, whether or not such representatives exist

- this is not imposing a statutory obligation to do the impossible. In Reg 13(10), provision is made that where an employer has invited any employees to elect employee representatives, the employer's duty is fulfilled if he informs and consults those representatives

- furthermore, Reg 13(9) provides that where special circumstances render it not reasonably practicable to comply with TUPE's information and consultation duties, the employer shall take all such steps towards performing that duty as are reasonably practicable in the circumstances.

In the instant case, the transferor employer had not informed appropriate **8.40** representatives and thus, on the face of it, was in breach of the Regulations. The question for Burton J was whether the employer could rely on the 'special circumstances' defence set out in Reg 13(9). Turning to this, Burton J acknowledged that 'it is quite plain that one special circumstance which renders

469

it not reasonably practicable for an employer to perform a duty to consult an employee representative is if there are no employee representatives'.

However, he continued, 'it is equally clear that the step which is reasonably practicable to resolve that problem is for the employer to invite an employee to appoint a representative under [Reg 13(10)]'. If an employer does invite affected employees to elect representatives under Reg 13(10) then, if no representatives are in fact appointed, 'the employer is entitled to perform its duty... by informing the employee himself or herself, and thus avoid what would otherwise be a breach of the [absolute] duty to inform a representative'. In the circumstances, then, where the respondent transferor did not invite the affected employees to elect representatives, it had not taken all reasonably practicable steps towards complying with its information and consultation duties, and was thus in breach of them.

8.41 In Howard v Millrise Ltd (in liquidation) and anor 2005 ICR 435, EAT, the EAT went even further. There, contrary to the previous decision of the EAT in Ashford School and anor v Nixon and ors EAT 666/00, the EAT held that, where no appropriate representatives already exist, the employer in question is actually under a statutory obligation to invite the affected employees to elect such representatives. The Howard case involved H, who brought a claim in respect of M Ltd's failure to inform and consult prior to the transfer. An employment tribunal rejected his complaint, taking the view that the information and consultation provisions 'appear to apply only to appropriate representatives, as defined by the Regulations'. Since H had at no time been an appropriate representative, his claim could not succeed. He appealed to the EAT, which overturned the tribunal's decision.

The EAT stated that where there are no recognised trade union or other employee representatives in place for information and consultation purposes, Reg 13 provides for the election of representatives for the purpose of the required consultation. Furthermore, Reg 13(11) provides that where an employer has invited affected employees to elect representatives but they fail to do so, the employer must give the required information about the transfer (see 'The duty to inform' below) to each individual affected employee. This provision would be rendered pointless, the EAT continued, if the employer (assuming there were no recognised trade union or other appropriate representatives in place) were not obliged to set the ball rolling by inviting affected employees to elect representatives. The EAT concluded that in this case it was unnecessary to determine whether H's claim related to the employer's failure to take any steps to invite the election of representatives, the failure to give information to such representatives, or, in default of election, the failure to give information to the claimant himself. It was clear that H's complaint was well founded, and his case was remitted to the employment tribunal for his compensation to be determined.

So, it seems that an employer will be in breach of Reg 13 where, in the absence **8.42** of existing appropriate representatives, he fails to invite affected employees to elect representatives for the purposes of information and consultation. The next question, then, is when such an invitation should be issued.

The simple answer is that the invitation to elect employee representatives should be issued in accordance with the timescale suggested by Reg 13(10). That is, long enough prior to the time when the employer is required to provide information under Reg 13(2) for the representatives to be elected. Since, as we discuss in 'The duty to inform' below, the relevant information must itself be provided to the representatives long enough before the transfer to enable consultation to take place, the invitation to elect would ideally be issued some time before the transfer. There will, of course, be times when this is not reasonably practicable to achieve – at which times the employer might be able to throw himself upon the mercy of the Reg 13(9) 'special circumstances' defence.

Note that we discuss Reg 13(9), (10) and (11) further under 'Employer's defences' below.

Election of employee representatives. If there are no existing appropriate **8.43** representatives who can be consulted about a relevant transfer, or if there are existing employee representatives that the employer does not wish to use, then – as explained immediately above – the employer should invite the election of employee representatives. Any election that ensues should be conducted in accordance with the requirements set out in Reg 14, which are as follows:

- the employer shall make such arrangements as are reasonably practicable to ensure the election is fair – Reg 14(1)(a)

- the employer shall determine the number of representatives to be elected so that there are sufficient representatives to represent the interests of all the affected employees, having regard to the number and classes of those employees – Reg 14(1)(b)

- the employer shall determine whether the affected employees should be represented either by representatives of all the affected employees or by representatives of particular classes of those employees – Reg 14(1)(c)

- before the election, the employer shall determine the term of office of an employee representative so that it is of sufficient length to enable information to be given and consultations to be completed – Reg 14(1)(d)

- the candidates for election as employee representatives shall be affected employees on the date of the election – Reg 14(1)(e)

- no affected employee shall unreasonably be excluded from standing for election – Reg 14(1)(f)

471

- all affected employees on the date of the election are entitled to vote – Reg 14(1)(g)

- the employees entitled to vote may vote for as many candidates as there are representatives to be elected to represent them or, if there are to be representatives for particular classes of employees, may vote for as many candidates as there are representatives to be elected to represent their particular class of employee – Reg 14(1)(h)

- the election itself must be conducted so as to ensure that (i) so far as reasonably practicable, those voting do so in secret, and (ii) the votes are accurately counted – Reg 14(1)(i).

8.44 Furthermore, according to Reg 14(2), where an employee representative is elected in accordance with these rules but ceases to act as such and as a result any affected employees are no longer represented, then another election shall be held – in accordance with Reg 14(1)(a), (e), (f) and (i) – to elect a new employee representative.

While the above requirements are detailed, they do not answer all the questions that employers will have about organising elections. As the BIS Guide explains, 'the legislation does not specify how many representatives must be elected or the process by which they are to be chosen. An employment tribunal may wish to consider, in determining a claim that the employer has not informed and consulted in accordance with the requirements, whether the arrangements were such that the purpose of the legislation could not be met. An employer will therefore need to consider such matters as whether:

- the arrangements adequately cover all the categories of employees who may be affected by the transfer and provide a reasonable balance between the interests of the different groups;

- the employees have sufficient time to nominate and consider candidates;

- the employees (including any who are absent from work for any reason) can freely choose who to vote for;

- there is any normal company custom and practice for similar elections and, if so, whether there are good reasons for departing from it.'

8.45 Further assistance as to the number of representatives that are required, and how 'constituencies' of different categories of employee should be decided upon, might be gleaned from the guidance provided by Acas with regard to the Information and Consultation of Employees Regulations 2004. Although these Regulations are unconnected with TUPE, similar considerations with regard to the issues highlighted would seem to apply. The Acas good practice guide to the ICE Regulations is available on the Acas website (www.acas.org.uk).

In Games-Thomas v UBS and anor ET Case No.2201962/09, an employment tribunal held that the representative appointed was appropriate in respect of a particular employee, even though that employee had not taken part in the election process as he was working abroad at the relevant time. It held that while the Regulations grant all affected employees an entitlement to vote, they do not impose a requirement that they do so.

8.46 Note that Reg 15(4) provides that where a tribunal claim is brought in respect of an employer's alleged failure relating to the election of employee representatives, it shall be for the employer to show that the requirements of Reg 14 have been satisfied.

8.47 **Rights of appropriate representatives.** Under Reg 13(8), an employer must allow 'the appropriate representatives' (who, as we have seen, might include elected representatives and/or trade union representatives) access to any 'affected employees' and to 'such accommodation and other facilities as may be appropriate'. Undeniably, as the BIS Guide states, 'what is "appropriate" will vary according to circumstances'. These circumstances, presumably, will include the size and complexity of the transfer. We suggest that appropriate 'accommodation and other facilities' should generally include access to a room, photocopier, telephone and IT equipment. Furthermore, an employer might consider whether, in certain circumstances, inexperienced representatives need to be afforded facilities for training. The Acas guidance to the ICE Regulations, mentioned above – which does not apply directly to TUPE – makes the sensible point that 'employee representatives will need training to make sense of the business information disclosed to them'.

In addition, most employee representatives and candidates for election will have certain statutory rights and protections to enable them to carry out their functions properly. We say 'most' rather than 'all' because such protections are provided by the ERA only to 'employees' within the meaning of S.230 of that Act. As we have discussed at length in this Handbook, particularly in Chapter 2, 'employees' for ERA purposes comprises a narrower grouping than 'employees' for TUPE purposes. It follows that some 'affected employees' under Reg 13 who become 'employee representatives' under Reg 14 might not be 'employees' capable of attracting the ERA protections set out below.

8.48 The rights and protections in question are essentially the same as those granted to trade union representatives under the TULR(C)A (for which, see IDS Employment Law Handbook, 'Trade Unions' (2000)), and are as follows:

- an employee has the right not to be subjected to any detriment by any act or deliberate failure to act by his or her employer done on the ground that, being an employee representative for the purposes of TUPE, or a candidate in an election in which any person elected will become such an employee representative, he or she performed or proposed to perform any functions

473

or activities as such an employee representative or candidate – S.47(1) ERA. He or she has the right to complain to an employment tribunal that he or she has been subjected to such a detriment – S.48(1) ERA. The complaint must be presented (a) before the end of the period of three months beginning with the date of the act or failure to act or, where that act or failure is part of a series, the date of the last of them, or (b) within such further period as the tribunal considers reasonable where it is satisfied that it was not reasonably practicable for the complaint to be presented in time – S.48(3) ERA

- an employee who is dismissed shall be regarded as unfairly dismissed if the reason or principal reason for dismissal is that the employee, being an employee representative (or a candidate for election as an employee representative) for the purposes of TUPE performed or proposed to perform any functions or activities as such an employee representative or candidate – S.103 ERA. The qualifying period of service usually required by the ERA unfair dismissal regime does not apply to this type of automatically unfair dismissal – S.108 ERA. Any such claim should be brought (a) before the end of the period of three months beginning with the effective date of termination, or (b) within such further period as the tribunal considers reasonable where it is satisfied that it was not reasonably practicable for the complaint to be presented in time – S.111(2) ERA

- an employee who is an employee representative (or candidate for election as an employee representative) is entitled to reasonable, paid time off during working hours in order to perform his functions as an employee representative or candidate or in order to undergo training to perform such functions – Ss.61 and 62 ERA. Where this right has been breached, the employee can bring a tribunal claim under S.63 ERA. The claim must be brought (a) before the end of the period of three months beginning with the day on which the time off was taken or should have been permitted, or (b) within such further period as the tribunal considers reasonable where it is satisfied that it was not reasonably practicable for the complaint to be presented in time – S.63(2).

8.49 Note that similar protection with regard to detriment (S.47(1A) ERA) and dismissal (S.103(2) ERA) is afforded to any 'employee' for ERA purposes, where such detriment is done or dismissal carried out on the ground of his or her participation in an employee representative election.

8.50 ## The duty to inform
Having examined who 'affected employees' and 'appropriate representatives' might be, we now turn to the substance of the duty to inform under TUPE. This is contained in Reg 13(2), which provides that 'long enough before a relevant transfer to enable the employer of any affected employees to consult the

appropriate representatives of any affected employees, the employer shall inform those representatives' of the following:

- the fact that the transfer is to take place, the date or proposed date of the transfer and the reason for the transfer

- the 'legal, economic and social implications' of the transfer for any affected employees

- the 'measures which he envisages he will, in connection with the transfer, take in relation to any affected employees or, if he envisages that no measures will be so taken, that fact'

- if the employer in question is the transferor, 'the measures, in connection with the transfer, which he envisages the transferee will take in relation to any affected employees who will become employees of the transferee after the transfer by virtue of regulation 4 or, if he envisages that no measures will be so taken, that fact'.

The wording of Reg 13(2) carries the strong implication that the duty to inform **8.51** and the duty to consult are interlinked – information is provided 'to enable the employer of any affected employees to consult'. As we shall see below, under Reg 13(6), the statutory duty to consult only arises if the employer of an affected employee envisages that he will take 'measures' in relation to the transfer. However, this does not mean that the duty to provide information depends on the statutory duty to consult applying. This was established by the EAT in Cable Realisations Ltd v GMB Northern 2010 IRLR 42, EAT. In that case, CR Ltd proposed to sell off its cable business and was informed by the prospective purchaser that it did not envisage taking any 'measures' in connection with the transfer. CR Ltd provided that information, along with the other information required by Reg 13(2), to the recognised trade union but thereafter undertook little consultation. The GMB complained to a tribunal that CR Ltd had not met its obligations under Reg 13(2). The tribunal upheld the complaint. On appeal to the EAT, CR Ltd argued for the first time that, since no consultation was prescribed under Reg 13(6), there was no requirement to provide information at all. The EAT rejected that contention. While the EAT recognised that such a submission may seem logical as a matter of construction, it was plainly wrong in light of the industrial relations rationale behind TUPE. Reg 13(2) is designed to allow the representatives of affected employees to engage in informed consultation about a wide range of matters relating to a TUPE transfer, whether that consultation is entered into voluntarily or as a result of Reg 13(6).

Legal, economic and social implications. The phrase 'legal, economic and **8.52** social implications', which is copied verbatim from the Directive, is clarified by neither the 2006 Regulations themselves nor the BIS Guide. We imagine that 'legal' implications will cover the impact of the transfer on employment contracts, statutory rights and collective agreements. 'Economic' implications may refer to any effect on employees' remuneration, benefits and future prospects. And, according to an employment tribunal in NALGO v British Waterways Board COET 2034/124, the 'economic implications' requirement also means that sufficient information should be given about the new employer to enable the employees to assess its 'worth'.

Another tribunal subsequently went further. In Grindrod v Excel Europe Ltd and anor ET Case Number 2702651/06 the transferor operated a frozen food facility at Heathrow Airport and until 2004 its sole customer was Safeway. The second respondent took over Safeway in 2004 and in due course decided that its own employees would carry out frozen food distribution from a purpose-built facility in Corby. It gave notice to the transferor to terminate the contract in March 2006. Only one employee transferred from Heathrow and G was made redundant in October 2006. The tribunal held that the transferor had failed to provide information on the economic and social implications of the transfer. In its view, the obligation extended to providing the affected employee with information on the housing market in Corby, the nature and availability of schools and education, the job market, comparability of wage rates and the future of the second respondent's business and its investment in the Corby area.

8.53 Note that there is no duty on the employer to warrant the legal accuracy of the information he provides as to the legal implications of a transfer. In Royal Mail Group Ltd v Communication Workers Union 2010 ICR 83, CA, RMG Ltd transferred certain Post Office businesses to WHS. RMG Ltd genuinely believed that, although TUPE would apply, no contracts would automatically transfer since the affected employees would all either take voluntary redundancy or be redeployed. It therefore informed and consulted on that basis under Reg 13. The issue that eventually came before the Court of Appeal was whether information and consultation on the basis of a mistaken but genuine belief as to the legal implications of a transfer was an automatic breach of Reg 13. The Court held that it was not. Lord Justice Waller noted that 'the language of Reg 13(2) was not the language of strict liability or warranty'. Although an employer must inform employees' representatives of its 'considered view' as to the legal implications for employees prior to a transfer of its business to another, the employer is not required in effect to warrant the accuracy of the law in this regard.

8.54 **Envisaged measures.** The employer – whether transferor or transferee – must inform representatives of whether or not he 'envisages' that he will take 'measures' in relation to any of his affected employees, and if so, what those measures are. Neither 'measures' nor 'envisages' is defined in the Regulations, but the following cases cast some light on what these words might mean in the context of Reg 13:

• **Institution of Professional Civil Servants and ors v Secretary of State for Defence** 1987 IRLR 373, ChD: two dockyards at Rosyth and Devonport were privatised by transfer to commercial management in April 1987. This was achieved by the Dockyard Services Act 1986, which re-enacted the TUPE information and consultation provisions almost word for word. IPCS brought a High Court action claiming that the duty to inform and consult under the Dockyard Services Act had not been fulfilled. In the course of giving judgment, Mr Justice Millett discussed the meaning of 'measures' and 'envisages' in the relevant provisions. In his opinion, 'measures' is a word of the widest import and includes any action, step or arrangement. 'Envisages' simply means 'visualises' or 'foresees'. He went on to state that the phrase 'measures which he envisages he will... take' is apt to exclude mere hopes and possibilities. So, 'it is not enough that there should be some possibility in contemplation; the company must have formulated some definite plan or proposal which it has in mind to implement'. Turning to the facts, he concluded that manpower projections were not 'measures', but that positive steps to achieve planned reductions in manpower levels would be

- **Baxter and ors v Marks and Spencer** EAT 0162/05: M&S decided to outsource its 'profit protection operation', which was concerned with preventing theft, to Securicor. This outsourcing amounted to a TUPE transfer. A group of employees brought tribunal claims, some of which related to the Regulations' information and consultation provisions. These claims were largely unsuccessful, and the employees appealed on a number of points. Before the EAT, the employees argued that the refocusing of their work from 'internal theft' to 'external theft' was a 'measure' for the purposes of the information and consultation rules. The EAT disagreed. The change in question was simply a change of emphasis within the employees' agreed job description. Furthermore, the detail of the different procedural steps that employees would have to take as a result of their being employed by Securicor rather than by M&S 'was not something which could be regarded as a "measure in connection with the transfer" but simply an inevitable administrative consequence of the transfer'

- **Todd v Strain and ors** EATS 0057/09: an employment tribunal upheld a complaint of breach of Reg 13 on the basis that the transferor, T, had failed to inform employees affected by the sale of a care home of certain proposed administrative changes. These included arrangements for payment for work done in the three days prior to the transfer and for untaken holiday, and information that some staff would receive a tax rebate that was to be reclaimed by the transferee the following month. On appeal, T argued that these were not 'measures', being merely administrative consequences of the transfer. The EAT rejected that argument. It held that at least two of the proposals – changing the normal payment date and the payment for untaken holiday – represented a departure from what would otherwise have occurred. They were not, therefore, an inevitable consequence of the transfer itself, but measures taken by the transferor. Furthermore, the fact that the

477

change envisaged with regard to pay dates was not to the disadvantage of the employees in question was irrelevant to the issue of whether it constituted a measure for TUPE purposes. Nothing in the legislation requires a measure to be disadvantageous (or indeed of a particular level of materiality) for it to be 'envisaged' by either transferor or transferee and so trigger the information and consultation obligations of TUPE.

8.55 We saw above that the EAT in the Baxter case held that a change was not a 'measure' for the purposes of Reg 13 where it was simply a change of emphasis falling within the employees' job descriptions. We should point out, however, that it is universally accepted that the duty to inform (and consult) under Reg 13 applies not only to measures resulting in changes to contractual terms and conditions of employment. Other measures covered could include those relating to non-contractual benefits, collective issues and occupational pensions (notwithstanding that pension rights do not transfer under TUPE – see Chapter 3).

As set out above, if the employer who is doing the informing is the transferor, he must inform the appropriate representatives of the measures which the transferee envisages taking in relation to the affected employees in connection with the transfer; and if the transferee does not envisage taking any measures, the transferor must inform the representatives of that fact – Reg 13(2)(d). In order that the transferee will be in a position to comply with this requirement, Reg 13(4) provides that 'the transferee shall give the transferor such information at such a time as will enable the transferor to perform the duty imposed on him by virtue of paragraph (2)(d)'.

8.56 **When should the information be provided?** In contrast with the TULR(C)A, which lays down a clear timetable as to when information with regard to collective redundancies should be passed on, the 2006 Regulations are vague as to when information about a TUPE transfer should be provided. Reg 13(2) simply states that the employer must provide the information long enough before the relevant transfer to enable consultation with the representatives of affected employees. Common sense suggests that information concerning larger and more complex transfers will need to be provided earlier in the process than information about smaller transfers.

The issue did arise in Cable Realisations Ltd v GMB Northern 2010 IRLR 42, EAT. There, CR Ltd had been making a loss since late 2006 and in May 2007 made a decision to either close or sell off its cable business. It received a non-binding purchase offer from an India-based company on 31 May 2007, which CR Ltd's holding company decided to pursue on 28 June 2007. CR Ltd first met with the GMB union, representing the affected employees, on 3 July. However, at that stage, it felt that it was not in a position to reveal the identity of the purchasing company. By 15 August, the purchasing company was happy to reveal itself and had informed CR Ltd that it did not envisage taking any 'measures' in connection with the transfer. CR Ltd provided that information, along with the other information required by Reg 13(2), to the GMB that same day and held a meeting. It held a further meeting on 17 August but then, on 20 August, the company's annual two-week shutdown began. The transfer eventually took place on 3 September. The EAT upheld a tribunal's decision that, while providing the required information over two weeks before the transfer looked, on the face of it, 'long enough', the company shutdown changed matters. In order to engage in meaningful consultation it is essential that union representatives are available to speak with management and that those representatives can communicate with the members whom they represent. This was not possible when around 90 per cent of the affected employees were on holiday.

It might be thought that, when the transfer has minimal or no implications for affected employees, required information may not have to be given so long before the transfer. However, a tribunal in Spencer and ors v Somerset Crane and anor ET Case No.1701703/08 decided that information given the day before a transfer cannot be given 'long enough before' the transfer even when no measures are proposed. **8.57**

Note that, under Reg 13(9), if there are special circumstances which make it not reasonably practicable for an employer to provide the requisite information in time, the employer shall take all such steps towards performing that duty as are reasonably practicable in the circumstances – see 'Employers' defences' below.

How should the information be provided? According to Reg 13(5), the Reg 13(2) information shall be delivered to the appropriate representatives or sent by post to an address notified by them to the employer, or, in the case of trade union representatives, sent by post to the trade union at the address of its headquarters or main office. This wording suggests that the information must always be provided in writing. **8.58**

Note that in Institution of Professional Civil Servants and ors v Secretary of State for Defence 1987 IRLR 373, ChD (above), the High Court held (about an identical provision in the Dockyards Services Act 1986) that the unions were not entitled to the particular documents from which the information was extracted, but only to the information itself.

The importance of the information disclosed being accurate and not misleading is illustrated by the High Court case Hagen and ors v ICI Chemicals and Polymers Ltd and ors 2002 IRLR 31, QBD. That concerned the transfer of the central engineering resource section of ICI. Prior to the transfer, the parties to the proposed sale realised that the transfer could not take place successfully if the relevant group of staff could be persuaded to accept it. Various promises were given and representations made by the transferor and transferee to the **8.59**

479

employees, especially about occupational pension arrangements after the transfer. After the transfer, employees believed that the promises had not been honoured and that they had been misled, and so sued. The High Court held that a transferor is under a duty in contract in tort to take reasonable care to ensure that information provided in accordance with TUPE is accurate, and that statements of intent are capable of being fulfilled. The Court decided that the transferor had been guilty of negligent misstatement in respect of pension arrangements and so was in breach of its duty of care. The employees had reasonably relied on the transferor's representations and, in this unusual case, where the transfer depended on employee approval, damages could be recovered for negligent misstatement on the basis of what would have happened if the correct information had been given.

8.60 **Decision resulting in transfer taken by third party.** Note that Reg 13(12) provides that the duty on employers to inform under Reg 13(2) will apply whether or not the decision resulting in the transfer is taken by the employer or a person controlling the employer.

8.61 **The duty to consult**
The employers' duty to consult with appropriate representatives of affected employees (for the meaning of 'appropriate representatives' and 'affected employees', see above) is contained in Reg 13(6) and (7) of the 2006 Regulations. Reg 13(6) states that 'an employer of an affected employee who envisages that he will take measures in relation to an affected employee, in connection with the relevant transfer, shall consult the appropriate representatives of that employee with a view to seeking agreement to the intended measures'. And Reg 13(7) adds that 'in the course of those consultations the employer shall (a) consider any representations made by the appropriate representatives; and (b) reply to those representations and, if he rejects any of those representations, state his reasons'.

8.62 **Envisaged measures.** So, unlike the duty to inform, the duty to consult under Reg 13(6) does not arise in every transfer situation. Rather, it does so only where a transferor or transferee 'envisages that he will take measures' in respect of one or more affected employees. The meaning of the words 'envisages' and 'measures' in the context of Reg 13 was discussed in 'The duty to inform', above.

We should emphasise that the duty to consult arises only where the employer in question envisages that *he* will take measures in respect of affected employees. Thus, where a *transferor* envisages that the *transferee* will take measures in respect of the transferring employees, the transferor will not be obliged to consult in respect of such measures. As we saw under 'The duty to inform' above, however, he will be required to *inform* the appropriate representatives of any measures he envisages that the transferee will take – Reg 13(2)(d).

Need the transferee consult in respect of the transferring employees? We 8.63
have explained that Reg 13(6) does not place the *transferor* under a duty to
consult the transferring employees about measures that will be taken, post-
transfer, by the *transferee*. But will the *transferee* be under a duty to consult
about such measures, either before or after the transfer takes place?

It was generally accepted that, under the 1981 Regulations, the transferee was
not obliged to consult representatives of the transferor's employees prior to the
transfer. The relevant rule, old Reg 10(5), stated that the consultation duty only
arose 'where an employer of any affected employees envisages that he will, in
connection with the transfer, be taking measures in relation to any such
employees'. The only employees referred to in this rule, it was thought, were
the relevant employer's employees, and not anybody else's.

However, owing to a slight change in wording, the position under Reg 13(6) of 8.64
the 2006 Regulations appears rather more complicated. As we have seen, Reg
13(6) provides that the consultation duty arises where 'an employer of an
affected employee... envisages that he will take measures in relation to an
affected employee, in connection with the relevant transfer'. On the face of it,
this wording would seem to cover some situations where transferees envisage
taking measures in respect of transferors' employees. Consider the following: a
transferee has an existing workforce, some of whom are to be affected by the
relevant transfer and are thus 'affected employees' for the purposes of Reg 13
(see 'Affected employees' above). In such circumstances, the transferee is clearly
'an employer of an affected employee' within the meaning of Reg 13(6). Prior
to the transfer, the transferee envisages that he will take measures in respect of
one of the employees who is to transfer from the transferor under TUPE. That
employee is also, clearly, 'an affected employee'. Thus, again within the meaning
of Reg 13(6), the transferee 'envisages that he will take measures in relation to
an affected employee'. It does not appear to matter that the affected employee
of whom the transferee is the employer, and the affected employee in respect of
whom measures are envisaged, are not the same person. Arguably, then, the
effect of Reg 13(6) in this situation would be to place the transferee under a
duty to consult in respect of the transferor's employee.

It remains to be seen whether the courts agree with this analysis. Since the
wording of Reg 13(6) is unclear, one pertinent question they might ask is
whether the Government intended the position under the 2006 Regulations to
be different to that under the 1981 Regulations. In this regard, the fact that the
new wording was not referred to specifically in the BIS Guide or in the 2005
consultation document suggests that any substantive change to TUPE's
consultation requirements was inadvertent. Moreover, the Directive itself only
requires the transferee to consult representatives of his own employees, and not
representatives of the transferor's employees; Article 7.2 of the Directive, which
Reg 13(6) is intended to implement, states that 'where the transferor or the

481

transferee envisages measures in relation to *his employees*, he shall consult the representatives of [those] employees' (our emphasis). With this in mind, the courts might be disinclined to conclude that transferees' consultation duties have been extended.

8.65 On balance, then, it seems that the transferee is not obliged to consult representatives of the transferor's employees prior to the transfer. But when the transfer occurs, the transferring employees will no longer be the transferor's employees, but will be the transferee's own. This raises the question of whether, at the point of the transfer or thereafter, the transferee becomes obliged to consult representatives of the transferred employees in respect of measures he envisages taking in respect of those employees.

Such post-transfer consultation does not generally happen. And case law suggests it need not. In Sweetin v Coral Racing 2006 IRLR 252, EAT, for example, the EAT stated categorically that 'the obligation is to consult in advance of the transfer'. However, there is nothing obvious in Reg 13, or indeed in the Directive, that suggests that the duty to consult cannot arise upon or after the date of the transfer. Indeed, there seems no reason at all why post-transfer measures that the transferee envisages taking in respect of a transferred employee could not amount to 'measures in relation to an affected employee, in connection with the transfer' within the meaning of Reg 13(6), triggering the duty to consult; in fact, as we saw in Chapters 4 and 5, 'transfer-connected' events have been held to take place some years after the transfer date.

8.66 However, the EAT has considered this issue and decided that the Directive does – at least implicitly – bring the duty to consult to a halt at the date of the transfer. Lady Smith, presiding over the Scottish EAT in UCATT v Amicus and ors and another case 2009 ICR 852, EAT, held that the Directive does not oblige a transferee employer to consult, after the transfer, about measures that it envisages taking in respect of transferred employees. Several factors supported this conclusion. In particular, Lady Smith noted that the obligation in Article 7.1 to provide information clearly looked forward to the date of the transfer, and that any post-transfer duty to consult would not be supported by any corresponding duty to inform. Furthermore, if the Directive did impose a post-transfer duty to consult, which would have to be read into Reg 13, this would create an entirely open-ended consultation duty, since it is well established that measures taken by a transferee years after a transfer can still be 'transfer-connected', and so potentially within the duty to consult.

Lady Smith also endorsed the view given in the 2007 edition of this Handbook that the Reg 15(12) time limit for claims relating to a failure to consult points away from a duty on the transferee to consult post-transfer. Reg 15(2) states that any claim in relation to a failure to consult must be brought within three months of *the relevant transfer* (or, where not reasonably practicable, within such further period as the tribunal considers reasonable). Unlike Reg 13(6), then, Reg 15(12) seems to suggest that the date of the transfer is significant with regard to the duty to consult, perhaps forming some kind of cut-off point. In other words, it implies that all consultation has to take place prior to the transfer, meaning that the transferee will be under no obligation, post-transfer, to consult representatives of his newly acquired workforce. Lady Smith thought that this indicated that the drafter of the Regulations clearly read the Directive as envisaging no post-transfer duty on the transferee to consult. She considered that the drafter was right to read the Directive in that way.

Consultation with a view to seeking agreement. As initially drafted, the 1981 **8.67** Regulations omitted to require that consultation under TUPE needed to take place *with a view to reaching agreement*. As this requirement was specified in Article 6.2 (now Article 7.2) of the Directive, the ECJ, in Commission of the European Communities v United Kingdom 1994 ICR 664, ECJ, concluded that the 1981 Regulations were defective in this regard. This deficiency was rectified by the Trade Union Reform and Employment Rights Act 1993, which introduced the phrase 'with a view to seeking agreement' into what eventually became Reg 13(6).

The European Court of Justice considered the meaning of the phrase 'with a view to reaching agreement' in Junk v Kühnel 2005 IRLR 310, ECJ, stating that it imposes an obligation to negotiate to try to reach an agreed solution. Although this case was concerned with the Collective Redundancies Directive, it is likely that the same words in the Acquired Rights Directive (and the similar words in the 2006 Regulations) should be given the same meaning. In essence, then, it would seem that an employer should discuss the proposed measures with an open mind and negotiate with the appropriate representatives about them. This is backed up by Reg 13(7)(a), which states that in the course of consultations the employer shall consider any representations made by the appropriate representatives. It is not the case, however, that the employer is necessarily obliged to change his position. In fact, Reg 13(7)(b) acknowledges that an employer might reject representations, provided that, if the employer does so, he states his reasons why.

Timing of consultation. The Regulations do not lay down a timetable for **8.68** consultation under Reg 13. At first glance, it would seem that consultation must begin long enough before the *measures* are to be taken to allow a meaningful consultation process to be carried out. However, as stated above, Reg 15(12) states that any claim in relation to a failure to consult must be brought within three months of *the relevant transfer* (or, where that is not reasonably practicable, within such further period as the tribunal considers reasonable). This, together with the not particularly extensive case law in this area, seems to suggest that all consultation under Reg 13(6) should be completed before the transfer takes place, regardless of when the measures are scheduled to be taken.

483

If 'measures' are not 'envisaged' until the last minute, meaningful consultation within the appropriate timeframe might not be possible. Here, the employer has two choices: delay until consultation has taken place, or rely on the Reg 13(9) 'special circumstances' defence – see 'Employers' defences' below.

8.69 **Decision resulting in transfer taken by third party.** As with the rules with regard to information set out above, Reg 13(12) provides that the duty on employers to consult under Reg 13(6) will apply whether the decision resulting in the transfer is taken by the employer or a person controlling the employer.

8.70 **Employers' defences**

Before looking at the appropriate remedies in relation to a failure to inform or consult, we shall examine two ways in which employers who have not followed Reg 13(2) (information) or Reg 13(6) (consultation) to the letter might be able to avoid liability.

8.71 **The 'special circumstances' defence.** As we saw under 'Appropriate representatives' above, under Reg 13(9) employers have an excuse for not complying with the duties to inform or consult if there are 'special circumstances which render it not reasonably practicable' to do so. They must, however, take all such steps to fulfil the duty as are reasonably practicable in the circumstances. If the question of reasonable practicability reaches a tribunal, the onus is on the employer to show that the special circumstances defence should apply – Reg 15(2).

We should note here that this 'special circumstances' defence is not provided for in the EU Acquired Rights Directive, a fact that has led to speculation that the Regulations do not implement that Directive properly. But it is perhaps significant that when the European Commission commenced infraction proceedings against the UK Government with regard to aspects of the Regulations that it believed were in breach of the Directive, which led to the ruling in Commission of the European Communities v United Kingdom 1994 ICR 664, ECJ, the 'special circumstances' defence was not one of the objections taken by the Commission. It may be, therefore, that the defence is accepted as being a reasonable proviso to the duty to inform and consult so long as it is narrowly construed.

8.72 And in fact, case law suggests that the defence *will* be narrowly construed. The wording of Reg 13(9) is similar to that of S.188(7) TULR(C)A, which sets up a 'special circumstances' defence when an employer has failed to carry out the statutory duty to consult trade union representatives about proposed redundancies. Case law on the meaning of 'special circumstances' in the context of redundancy consultation is therefore likely to be applicable in the context of information and consultation about proposed transfers. The basic principle is that circumstances are only 'special' if they are 'exceptional or out of the ordinary' – Clarks of Hove Ltd v Bakers' Union 1978 ICR 1076, CA. Appellate courts have applied this strictly, as illustrated by the fact that neither insolvency (if it was reasonably foreseeable) nor the need for confidentiality will normally be viewed as special circumstances in this regard – see IDS Employment Law Handbook, 'Redundancy' (2008) for further details.

Below we set out some examples, from case law and the Regulations, of situations which may or may not amount to 'special circumstances' for the purposes of Reg 13(9):

- in Reg 15(6), it is provided that a failure by a person controlling the employer, whether directly or indirectly, to provide information necessary for the employer to fulfil its duties to inform and consult shall not constitute special circumstances rendering it not reasonably practicable for the employer to comply with the statutory requirements. Thus, for example, the possible defence of a subsidiary company that its parent company kept it in the dark about the transfer will not succeed

- in NATTKE v Rank Leisure Ltd COET 1388/134 an employer attempted to rely upon the defence of 'special circumstances' where the need to speed through the transfer was a pertinent factor influencing the employer's failure properly to inform and consult. In September 1982 negotiations for the sale of a West End cinema owned by R Ltd took place with a view to ensuring that its transfer as a going concern was achieved within a month. NATTKE, representing a transferred employee, complained to a tribunal that R Ltd had failed to consult and inform it adequately before the transfer. The tribunal held that the speed with which the transaction had to be completed was a 'special circumstance', but that R Ltd had not taken all reasonable steps in trying to inform the union. It could have written to the union a day earlier and delivered the letter by hand instead of posting it

- in Unison v Somerset County Council and ors 2010 ICR 498, EAT, the Appeal Tribunal endorsed a tribunal's finding that 'fast moving events and [an] approaching deadline' were special circumstances, where the transferee sought to unpick an agreement in principle it had reached with the transferor over future staffing policy. However, the EAT appeared to have been influenced by the fact that the consultation up to that point on other matters had been 'lengthy and exemplary', the proposed transfer having been known about and consulted on for two years.

8.73 Another 'special circumstance' that might well be alleged in transfer situations is that information cannot be provided and consultation cannot take place because of the need to keep the transfer process secret. This may be so particularly where, for example, it is claimed by a company in financial difficulties that the transfer would not take place without strict maintenance of confidentiality. However, if tribunals are too ready to accept such arguments, the whole purpose of Reg 13 will be defeated. In NALGO v British Waterways Board COET 2034/124 the tribunal saw no reason why commercially sensitive

485

information could not be omitted from an agreement to transfer with only the remaining parts being disclosed to the union. European law may be of particular relevance on this point. One of the basic principles on which the Acquired Rights Directive is based is that the rights of employees must generally prevail over commercial considerations.

Note that Reg 15(5) suggests that the Reg 13(9) 'special circumstances' defence, or at least a variant of it, is available to the transferor where it was not reasonably practicable for him to provide the Reg 13(2) information to representatives because the transferee had failed to provide him with the information specified by Reg 13(4) (see 'The duty to inform' above). Reg 15(5) provides that, in these circumstances, the transferor must notify the transferee that he intends to give this reason for non-compliance with Reg 13(2) to an employment tribunal. The effect of giving the notification is to add the transferee as a party to the tribunal proceedings, which, if the transferor's argument is successful, may lead to the transferee paying compensation to affected employees under Reg 15(8).

8.74 **The 'invitation to elect' defence.** If an employer fails to inform or consult appropriate representatives in accordance with Reg 13(2) and (6) this is, generally, a breach of the Regulations. But if there are no appropriate representatives, what is an employer to do? As we saw in 'Appropriate representatives' above, he can invite his 'affected employees' to elect such representatives, but what if the employees decline to do so or fail to do so in good time?

Regulation 13(10) and (11) provide comfort for employers in such circumstances. Reg 13(10) provides that 'where (a) the employer has invited any of the affected employee[s] to elect employee representatives; and (b) the invitation was issued long enough before the time when the employer is required to give information under [Reg 13(2) – see 'The duty to inform' above] to allow them to elect representatives by that time, the employer shall be treated as complying with the requirements of this regulation in relation to those employees if he complies with those requirements as soon as is reasonably practicable after the election of the representatives'. Reg 13(11) then states that 'if, after the employer has invited any affected employees to elect representatives, they fail to do so within a reasonable time, he shall give to any affected employees the information set out in [Reg 13(2)]'.

8.75 In the light of these provisions, we should make the following points concerning the situation where there are no appropriate representatives in the workplace:

- if the employer invites the affected employees to elect employee representatives in accordance with the time limit set down in Reg 13(10), it will not be in breach of Reg 13 if it complies with its information and consultation duties as soon as is reasonably practicable after the representatives are elected.

486

Although Reg 13(10) does not expressly state that the consultation process can be curtailed in such circumstances owing to the election taking longer than expected, this might well be the provision's intention

- if the affected employees fail to elect representatives within a reasonable time, having been invited to do so by the employer, under Reg 13(11) the employer must give the information required by Reg 13(2) to the affected employees themselves. Again, this is worded as an obligation on the part of the employer, rather than as a defence, but we suggest that the purpose of Reg 13(11) is to relieve the employer from its consultation obligations in such circumstances.

We have dealt, then, with the situation where there are no existing appropriate **8.76** representatives in place. What, then, of the situation where there *are* such representatives? As discussed in 'Appropriate representatives' above, if the existing appropriate representatives are recognised trade union representatives, the employer will be obliged to inform and consult them. But if they are employee representatives elected or appointed for some other purpose, the employer is entitled to choose, under Reg 13(3), to ignore them and instead inform and consult new representatives elected for TUPE purposes. If the employer chooses to consult new representatives to be elected in such circumstances, the following propositions with regard to Reg 13(10) and (11) seem to make sense:

- if the employer is to invite affected employees to elect new representatives, he must give them sufficient time to do so. If he does not (where the transfer is imminent, a timely invitation might not be possible) the invitation to elect will not fall within Reg 13(10). In such circumstances, the Reg 13(10)/(11) defence will not be available, and the employer will be obliged to inform and consult the existing representatives

- if the employer invites in accordance with Reg 13(10) – that is, invites all affected employees, in time, to elect employee representatives for TUPE purposes – Reg 13(10) and Reg 13(11) would seem to apply regardless of whether there are already employee representatives in existence. So, for example, if the employees fail to elect new employee representatives within a reasonable time, the employer will be able to provide the information required by Reg 13(2) to the individual affected employees under Reg 13(11), and will not, it seems, be obliged to inform or consult the existing employee representatives at all.

Claims for failure to inform or consult   **8.77**
Regulation 15 contains the provisions concerning complaints to an employment tribunal where an employer – whether the transferor or the transferee – is alleged to have failed to comply with Reg 13 (the duty to inform and consult) or Reg 14 (the election of employee representatives). The sanctions imposed by

487

the Regulations are similar to those prescribed by the TULR(C)A in respect of a failure to inform and consult about collective redundancies (see IDS Employment Law Handbook, 'Redundancy' (2008)).

8.78 **Who can bring claims?** Where it is alleged that an employer has failed to comply with any requirement of Regs 13 or 14, then only certain persons can bring a complaint to the employment tribunal. These, as specified in Reg 15(1), are:

- in the case of a failure relating to the election of employee representatives, by any of the employer's employees who are affected employees – Reg 15(1)(a)

- in the case of any other failure relating to employee representatives, by any of the employee representatives to whom the failure related – Reg 15(1)(b)

- in the case of failure relating to representatives of a trade union, by that trade union – Reg 15(1)(c), and

- in any other case, by any of the employer's employees who are affected employees – Reg 15(1)(d).

8.79 The issue of whether employees can directly enforce breaches of Reg 13, when no appropriate representatives are already in place or have been elected, was discussed in Howard v Millrise Ltd (in liquidation) and anor 2005 ICR 435, EAT. In that case, it was held that an affected employee had standing to bring a claim for breach of Reg 13 where an employer had failed to invite affected employees to elect representatives or, in the absence of any election, to provide the requisite statutory information to the employee himself. Further, it was unnecessary to decide under which particular section of Reg 15 the complaint should be made. This decision was followed by a later EAT in Hickling (t/a Imperial Day Nursery) and ors v Marshall EAT 0217/10. The EAT there acknowledged that individual entitlement to claim is not obvious under Reg 13, since only Reg 13(11) imposes obligations on an employer in respect of individual employees. However, the EAT held that the case was 'on all fours' with Howard and upheld the tribunal's decision that Ms Marshall could bring a claim for breach of the employer's obligations under Reg 13.

Note that both Howard and Hickling considered the entitlement of individual employees to bring claims where no appropriate representatives were in place. By contrast, the EAT in Nationwide Building Society v Benn and ors 2010 IRLR 922, EAT, took the view that where appropriate representatives are in place, only they may seek remedies for breaches of Regs 13 and 14 on behalf of the affected employees. In reaching this conclusion, the EAT relied on the Court of Appeal's decision in Mercy v Northgate HR Ltd 2008 ICR 410, CA, which set down the same rule in relation to failures under the information and

488

consultation regime for collective redundancies under Ss.188 and 189 of the Trade Union and Labour Relations (Consolidation) Act 1992.

Time limit. As discussed in 'The duty to consult' above, Reg 15(12) provides **8.80** that any claim under Reg 15(1) must be brought before the end of the period of three months beginning with the date on which the relevant transfer is completed, or within such further period as the tribunal considers reasonable where it is satisfied that it was not reasonably practicable for the complaint to be presented within this timeframe.

In South Durham Health Authority v Unison 1995 IRLR 407, EAT, the Appeal Tribunal considered an appeal by an employer that a claim for lack of information and consultation had been premature, and thus that it should not be heard, in that it was brought before the transfer was completed. The EAT rejected the appeal, noting that TUPE only specified an end date – the end of the period of three months beginning with the date on which the transfer is completed – and did not prohibit a tribunal from considering a claim *before* any particular date. The EAT concluded that the claim in this case was not premature, as it had not been made before there was something to complain about. Thus, a tribunal had jurisdiction to hear the claim.

Compensation. Where a tribunal finds a complaint under Reg 15(1) (see **8.81** above) to be well founded, it *shall* make a declaration to that effect, and *may* order the relevant employer to pay 'appropriate compensation to such descriptions of affected employees as may be specified in the award' – Reg 15(7) and (8).

'Appropriate compensation' is defined by Reg 16(3) as 'such sum not exceeding thirteen weeks' pay for the employee in question as the tribunal considers just and equitable having regard to the seriousness of the failure of the employer to comply with his duty'. Under Reg 16(4), a 'week's pay' for this purpose is to be determined by reference to Ss.220–228 ERA (see IDS Employment Law Handbook, 'Wages' (2003)). Note that a week's pay for this type of award is not subject to the limit (currently, as at January 2011, £380) imposed by the ERA.

The nature of the compensation to be awarded under Reg 15 was considered **8.82** by the EAT in Sweetin v Coral Racing 2006 IRLR 252, EAT. There, mirroring the approach taken in the collective redundancy regime (see Susie Radin Ltd v GMB and ors 2004 ICR 893, CA), the EAT held that the amount of the award should reflect the nature and extent of the employer's default. In the EAT's view, a tribunal is entitled to have regard to any loss caused to the employee by the failure to consult, but only so long as it is recognised that the focus of the award must be its penal nature, and that proof of loss is neither necessary nor determinative of the level at which to fix the award. In the case in question, continued the EAT, the employment tribunal had erred in awarding affected

489

employees the equivalent of six weeks' pay calculated on the basis that this was what they had lost as a consequence of the employer's failure to consult. Given that the employer's failure to consult had been complete, and given the absence of any mitigating circumstances, a maximum award of 13 weeks' pay was appropriate.

8.83 Three illustrations of circumstances that have been taken into account in determining the appropriate award:

- **Cable Realisations Ltd v GMB Northern** 2010 IRLR 42, EAT: CR Ltd provided the appropriate representative GMB union with the information required by Reg 13(2) and met with Union representatives two days before the company's annual two-week shutdown began. The transfer took place a few days after the return to work. A tribunal upheld the GMB's complaint of failure to give information long enough before the transfer. In the light of the annual shutdown, during which around 90 per cent of the union members were not at work, there had been insufficient time for proper consultation. The tribunal awarded three weeks' pay to each of the union's affected members, an amount that the EAT agreed on appeal was 'just right'

- **Todd v Strain and ors** EAT 0057/09: the EAT reduced the employment tribunal's award from 13 to seven weeks' pay per employee on the basis that the failure was not at the most 'extreme end of the scale so as to justify a maximum award'. The transferor had not arranged the election of employee representatives, but had informed a group of approximately one third of the affected employees of the impending sale and confirmed that their jobs were safe, the intention being that they would inform their colleagues of the position. The transferor had also made clear that the transferee would not be reducing staff numbers or changing terms and conditions

- **GMB v Eastleigh Borough Council and anor** ET Case No.3102915/08: the transferor had provided all the information to the employees, albeit in instalments and not all of it in writing. The tribunal found that oral discussions with the employees, forewarning them of the inevitability of a transfer, was sufficient to satisfy Reg 13. However, the transferor had not provided information in writing of the measures that the transferee proposed to take, namely to change the depot from which the employees worked. As that failure was not deliberate, and deemed to be a technical failure only, each employee was awarded £200.

8.84 **Which employer is liable?** It has always been clear – and this remains the case – that where the *transferee* fails to inform or consult in accordance with Reg 13, he, and not the transferor, will be liable in respect of his default. However, the situation is more complicated where it is the *transferor* who fails to inform or consult.

490

Joint and several liability. Under the 1981 Regulations it was unclear whether **8.85** the transferor or the transferee should be liable where the transferor failed to inform or consult, prior to the transfer, in respect of transferring employees. The debate in this regard focused on Reg 5(2) of the 1981 Regulations (now, with minor changes, Reg 4(2) of the 2006 Regulations), which provided that 'on the completion of a relevant transfer (a) all the transferor's rights, powers, duties and liabilities under or in connection with [a contract of a transferring employee] shall be transferred by virtue of this Regulation to the transferee; and (b) anything done before the transfer is completed by or in relation to the transferor in respect of that contract or a person employed in that undertaking or part shall be deemed to have been done by or in relation to the transferee'. The key question was whether liability for the transferor's failure to inform or consult was capable of transferring to the transferee under this provision. In the following two cases, the EAT reached different conclusions:

- **Transport and General Workers' Union v James McKinnon, JR (Haulage) Ltd and ors** 2001 ICR 1281, EAT: the EAT held that the transferor's liability to pay compensation for his failure to inform and consult representatives prior to a relevant transfer did not pass to the transferee under old Reg 5(2). TUPE would be construed in a way that ensures that a transferor has an incentive to comply with the information and consultation obligations imposed upon him during the transfer process. This required the conclusion that the transferor would retain the liability to pay compensation for his own failure to consult

- **Alamo Group (Europe) Ltd v Tucker and anor** 2003 ICR 829, EAT: the EAT held that where a transferor fails to comply with his duty to inform or consult under TUPE, liability for that failure *will* pass to the transferee by virtue of old Reg 5(2). Had the legislature intended to exclude liability in respect of the obligation to inform and consult from the scope of Reg 5, then it would have expressly done so.

Recognising that there was conflicting case law on this point, the Government **8.86** wished to make the position clear when drafting the 2006 Regulations. Its chosen solution, found in Reg 15(9), was to make the transferor and transferee *jointly and severally liable* – that is, both collectively and individually liable – where a *transferor* has failed to inform or consult in respect of affected employees. In deciding upon this course of action, the Government, in the 2005 consultation document, reiterated the EAT's concern in the TGWU case that if liability were to pass wholly to the transferee, there would be little or no statutory incentive for the transferor to comply with the information and consultation requirements.

The BIS Guide explains how the new system of joint and several liability will work. It notes that it will be for the appropriate representatives or individual employees seeking redress to choose whether to take action against the

491

transferor, the transferee or both. Furthermore, a party who is a sole respondent in such an action will have the possibility of joining others who are jointly liable in respect of the same liability. When this occurs, it will be for the tribunal to apportion the compensation between the two respondents fairly. Alternatively, the Guide continues, if judgment is given against a sole respondent, that respondent might be able to recover a contribution from others who are jointly liable in respect of the same liability by suing them in the civil courts. There, liability would then be apportioned fairly, in line with the provisions of the Civil Liability (Contribution) Act 1978.

8.87 Where a court or tribunal is obliged to consider how liability should be apportioned, it will focus on the extent of each respondent's responsibility for the damage in question. Since joint and several liability only arises in respect of the transferor's failure to inform and consult, and not the transferee's, one would imagine that the transferor will usually be required to pay most if not all of the compensation awarded.

Note that, however liability is to be apportioned by the tribunal, the transferor and transferee might have agreed between themselves, by way of indemnities, who will actually bear the cost for any failure on the part of the transferor to inform or consult – see Chapter 10 for details.

8.88 *Problem with the new rule.* Before moving away from Reg 15(9) we should point out one rather odd aspect of it. As we have seen, the debate under the 1981 Regulations centred on whether liability for the transferor's failure to inform or consult passed to the transferee under Reg 5(2). Whatever the right answer to that question was, it is abundantly clear that such a transfer of liability could only be possible where the transferor's failure was in respect of the employees who transferred to the transferee.

But, as stated earlier in this chapter under 'Affected employees', it is not necessarily only the transferring workforce in respect of which the transferor is obliged to inform/consult. The transferor may well be under a duty to inform/consult in respect of members of its workforce who will *not* transfer to the transferee, but will nevertheless be affected in some way by the transfer situation.

8.89 It was clear under the 1981 Regulations that the transferor would himself be liable if he failed to inform/consult in respect of his non-transferring employees. And this clearly makes sense. However, Reg 15(9), which provides for the joint and several liability of the transferor and transferee, does not distinguish between the transferor's failure to inform/consult in respect of the transferring employees and his failure to inform/consult in respect of the employees whom he is to retain. In other words, Reg 15(9) provides that whenever a transferor fails to comply with his TUPE information and consultation obligations, he and the transferee will be jointly and severally liable for the compensation awarded. So, in theory, the transferee can be liable for the transferor's failure to inform/consult employees in respect of whom the transferee will never have an employment relationship. This, we imagine, cannot have been the Government's intention, and presents tribunals with a tricky problem: do they apply Reg 15(9) as it *is* written, or as it *was supposed to be* written? Hopefully, common sense will prevail here over legal form.

Transferee's failure to provide information. Note that there is one situation in **8.90** which the transferee will be solely liable for the transferor's failure to inform transferring employees. Reg 15(8)(b) states that where the transferor (after giving notice to the transferee in accordance with Reg 15(5) – see 'Employers' defences' above) shows that his failure to inform was due to the transferee's failure to provide him with the information specified in Reg 13(4) (see 'The duty to inform' above), the tribunal may order the *transferee* to pay appropriate compensation to such descriptions of affected employees as may be specified in the award.

Failure to comply with compensation order. If a tribunal makes an award of **8.91** compensation under Reg 15 and the employer in question fails to pay it, either wholly or in part, the affected employee concerned (as opposed to an appropriate representative) may complain to a tribunal – Reg 15(10). If the tribunal upholds such a complaint, it shall order the employer to pay the complainant(s) the amount owed – Reg 15(11). The time limit with regard to bringing a Reg 15(10) claim is three months after the date of the tribunal's initial compensation order, or within such further period as the tribunal considers reasonable where it is satisfied that it was not reasonably practicable for the complaint to be presented within this timeframe.

It should be noted that even this simple scheme is infiltrated by the bizarre. Reg 15(9), aspects of which were discussed immediately above, states that 'the transferee shall be jointly and severally liable with the transferor in respect of compensation payable under sub-paragraph 8(a) [the transferor's failure to inform or consult] *or paragraph 11*' (our emphasis). Paragraph 11 – that is, Reg 15(11) – is the provision under which the tribunal shall order the transferor or transferee, as applicable, to pay the sum owed where the employer in question has failed to comply with a tribunal's order for compensation.

Why is this bizarre? Consider, for example, the following situation: The **8.92** transferee recognises, prior to a relevant transfer, that members of his existing workforce (as opposed to the transferring workforce) may be affected by that transfer, rendering them 'affected employees' for the purposes of the TUPE information and consultation rules. It fails miserably to inform and consult in respect of those employees, whose representatives bring a tribunal claim seeking compensation. The tribunal upholds the claim and makes a compensatory award, which the transferee fails to pay. The employees themselves then bring a claim under Reg 15(10), pointing out that the transferee has failed to pay, and

493

the tribunal rules in their favour. Accordingly, in line with Reg 15(11), the tribunal orders the transferee to pay what is due. At this point – that is, at the point where compensation becomes payable under Reg 15(11) – according to Reg 15(9) the transferee *and the transferor* become jointly and severally liable for the amount due. This is so even though the transferor has at no point had any relationship with the employees in question, and was not liable for the original award that the transferee failed to pay. This, again, is surely not what the Government intended. And, again, we should hope (and indeed imagine) that tribunals will not apply the letter of the law strictly in this regard.

9 Transnational issues

Transfers from and to United Kingdom
Employees working outside United Kingdom

There is an increasing trend for business acquisitions and outsourcing exercises **9.1** to span more than one country. It is not unusual, for example, to read that a call-centre function is being outsourced to India, where there is a surfeit of highly qualified English-speakers available for a fraction of the cost of their UK counterparts. Of course, a 'global outsourcing' exercise such as this is extremely unlikely to result in the transfer of the relevant UK workforce to India. The companies involved in such exercises tend to proceed on the basis that the 2006 Regulations do not apply, and simply treat the UK-based workforce as redundant.

It is not necessarily the case, however, that the TUPE regime has no part to play with regard to cross-border transfers. Thus, an employer's simple assumption that the 2006 Regulations do not apply in such circumstances could potentially lead to legal difficulties. This might particularly be so where the transfer in question takes place from the United Kingdom to another European Union Member State. After all, employees might well be willing to move from one Member State to another, and free movement of workers is a fundamental aspect of the function of the EU.

Despite the fact that cross-border transfers are becoming more common, **9.2** however, neither the EU Acquired Rights Directive (No.2001/23) nor the Transfer of Undertakings (Protection of Employment) Regulations 2006 SI 2006/246 are clear as to whether their provisions apply to such transfers or, if they do apply, what exactly this might mean. In this chapter, we examine the wording of the Directive and the Regulations (so far as there is any) in this regard, and provide a brief analysis of some of the issues involved. We should point out, however, that this is simply an overview. A detailed exposition of the principles of private international law that might come into play if the Directive/ Regulations do apply to cross-border transfers is beyond the scope of this Handbook. For further details, see the document prepared for the European Commission by the CMS Employment Practice Area Group, entitled 'Study on the application of Directive 2001/23/EC to cross-border transfers of undertakings' (the 2006 Study), available on the European Commission Website (www.ec.europa.eu).

Also in this chapter, turning to an issue that can arise with regard to transfers taking place within the United Kingdom, we consider the extent of the protection bestowed by the 2006 Regulations upon employees who spend some or all of their time working overseas.

495

9.3 Transfers from and to United Kingdom

As stated above, neither the Acquired Rights Directive nor the 2006 Regulations contain much information as to their application to cross-border transfers. And, perhaps owing to many employers and employees being wary of taking the transfer rules into account where a cross-border relocation takes place (a wariness presumably fuelled partly by uncertainty), there has been virtually no case law on the subject until the EAT's decision in Holis Metal Industries Ltd v GMB and anor 2008 ICR 464, EAT, which is helpful to some degree but unfortunately of persuasive authority only. This case is discussed in detail under 'Application of the 2006 Regulations' below.

Below, we examine what the Directive and TUPE do manage to say on the matter, consider briefly some instruments of private international law (the Brussels I Regulation and the Rome Convention) that might have a part to play, and attempt to draw some sensible conclusions.

9.4 Application of the Directive

Each EU Member State and member of the EEA is required to implement the Acquired Rights Directive. But the Directive says little as to whether or how its rules apply to transfers between Member States, or to transfers from a Member State to a country not covered by the Directive.

9.5 **Theoretically Directive can cover cross-border transfers.** The fact that the Directive is unclear about its impact upon cross-border transfers has not gone unnoticed at EU-level. In 1998 Sir Bob Hepple QC produced a report for the European Commission entitled 'The Legal Consequences of Cross Border Transfers of Undertakings within the European Union'. In it, Hepple QC noted that the original 1974 draft of the Acquired Rights Directive made it clear that the rules would apply irrespective of whether the transfer occurred between two companies of one or more Member States or between a company in a Member State and another in a third country. However, the current Directive (No.2001/23) states simply that it applies 'where and in so far as the undertaking, business or part of the undertaking or business to be transferred is situated within the territorial scope of the Treaty [of Rome]' – Article 1.2.

Despite the paucity of detail contained in Article 1.2, on its face the current wording has the same effect as that contained in the 1974 draft. That is, it seems to apply the Directive whenever the business to be transferred is, prior to the transfer, located within the territorial scope of the EU Treaty; its application does not depend upon where that business is to be transferred to.

This is the view taken by the CMS Employment Practice Area Group in the 2006 Study, which we referred to in the introduction to this chapter. As to the Directive's scope, the Study states that 'the provisions of the Directive cover

496

each transfer in the boundaries of the Member States having signed or acceded to the Treaty establishing the European Community, i.e., cross-border transfers from one Member State to another... are subject to the Directive. Moreover, since the Directive only refers to the place of origin of the business unit "to be transferred" and gives no regard to the destination of the transfer, the Directive is – according to its wording – also applicable to transfers outside the territory of the European Union (EU).' The Directive does not apply, however, 'where the undertaking is situated outside the EU originally, even if the transferor, transferee or both of them are domiciled in the EU'.

But transferring entity must retain its identity. So, it seems that the Acquired **9.6** Rights Directive is capable of applying to cross-border transfers. But before highlighting some of the practical difficulties its application might cause, there is another important matter to consider. That is, regardless of the *theoretical* scope of the Directive to apply to such transfers, its provisions will only apply *in practice* where there is a transfer of an 'economic entity which retains its identity' (Article 1.1(b)) – see Chapter 1.

It is therefore pertinent to ask whether it is possible for an entity to retain its identity, and thus to be covered by the Directive, where the entity moves from one country to another. If this is not possible, then the debate with regard to the application of the Directive to cross-border transfers will be nipped in the bud. Unfortunately, there is not as yet any ECJ case law on this point. The case of Merckx and anor v Ford Motors Co (Belgium) SA 1997 ICR 352, ECJ, is helpful to an extent, in so far as the ECJ confirmed that the fact that an economic entity operates at a different location post-transfer does not necessarily mean that its identity has not been retained. But this case was concerned not with a cross-border transfer, but with a transfer taking place within Belgium.

So, can an entity retain its identity when it transfers to a different country? In **9.7** order to answer this question we must first return briefly to the seminal ECJ case of Spijkers v Gebroeders Benedik Abattoir CV and anor 1986 2 CMLR 296, ECJ, which we discussed at length in Chapter 1. In Spijkers the European Court set out a number of factors (none of which was to be decisive) that a court or tribunal should consider in order to determine whether an economic entity has retained its identity. These factors included, for example, the type of business or undertaking, the transfer or otherwise of tangible assets such as buildings and stocks, whether the majority of the staff are taken over by the new employer, the transfer or otherwise of customers and the degree of similarity of activities before and after the transfer.

In many cross-border relocation situations, we imagine that certain key factors of the Spijkers 'retention of identity' test will not be present. Often, neither tangible assets nor the transferor's workforce will relocate. In such circumstances, the Directive is unlikely to apply, and the relocation will be viewed as a business

497

closure rather than as a transfer of an undertaking. In the United Kingdom, this would result in a redundancy situation.

9.8 Nevertheless, there will be some cross-border transfer situations in which, in essence, the Spijkers 'retention of identity' test will be fulfilled. Where this is so, the 2006 Study takes the view that the fact that the entity in question is transferred to a different country will not preclude the Directive's application. It states that where, aside from the fact that the transfer has an international aspect, the transferring entity retains its identity, 'the relocation of a business to another country constitutes a transfer of business within the meaning of the Directive. To this [extent] the question of distance of the relocation is of minor importance.' This view is backed up by one of the few decided cases concerning cross-border transfers, the 'Englischer Dienst' case (Hamburg Labour Appeal Court, 22.05.03). There, the Court held that the transfer of a German news agency to Ireland *did* constitute a relevant transfer under German business transfer law. The Court had particular regard to the distance between the transferor and the transferee, but stated: 'Although great geographical distance generally militates against the preservation of economic entity, this is not the case here because the activities of news editing and news dissemination are determined much more by the information systems used than by the location of the establishment.' In the event, the claimants were able to succeed with their claims in respect of their dismissals by the transferor employer.

The 2006 Study does acknowledge, however, an alternative proposition that the application of the Directive to cross-border transfers 'might be doubtful because of the radical changes that would necessarily result from a cross-border transfer (change of country and general language, change in the legal, economic and social context), threaten *per se* the identity of the transferred economic entity'. This, the Study notes, was the view taken by the French Supreme Court in respect of a relocation from France to Brazil.

9.9 On balance, we suggest, in line with the Englischer Dienst decision, that there will be at least some cross-border transfers with regard to which the 'retention of identity' test will be satisfied. We now turn to some of the difficulties that the application of the Directive to such a transfer might pose.

9.10 **Difficulties arising from the Directive's application.** Although it might well be the case that the Directive is capable of applying to a cross-border transfer, its application in practice would lead to many difficult legal and practical conundrums.

As the 2006 Study notes, the Directive simply provides a framework with regard to the law on the transfer of undertakings, meaning that Member States have a wide margin of discretion regarding implementation. It follows that the transfer rules applicable in different countries vary quite considerably, and that there are no uniform rules that apply throughout the EU. Moreover, the transfers law of some countries (such as Spain) expressly covers EU transfers *into* those countries, whereas the law of others (such as the United Kingdom, as we shall see below) does not. All this raises complex questions as to which country's law might apply to one or more of the parties at the various stages of the transfer process, and, indeed, how parties in different locations might go about bringing and enforcing claims. These are questions that, in the absence of any assistance from the Directive, can only be answered with reference to the complex rules of private international law.

Furthermore, the purpose of the Directive is, in a nutshell, to preserve acquired **9.11** employment rights. However, just as the laws of the Member States differ with regard to the application of the Directive, they differ – and even more so – with regard to employment rights generally. So how, in reality, will employment rights be preserved following a cross-border transfer? For example, the 2006 Regulations preserve and augment the transferring employees' right not to be unfairly dismissed under the Employment Rights Act 1996 (ERA). But how will such rights conceivably be maintained where employees of a UK operation transfer to a country whose dismissal law is completely different?

And consider the situation where employees who transfer have their pay adjusted to reflect the cost of living in the country to which they have been relocated. Would a reduction in pay in such circumstances be contrary to the transfer rules and thus void? As the 2006 Study states: 'A remuneration calculated as adequate for a work assignment in the City of London will certainly not mirror the adequate remuneration for an assignment in Naples and vice versa. A rule of law that does not consider this and does compel employers to maintain the remuneration agreed upon in the employee's contract concluded at the employee's place of origin, does not foster mobility and is unfair, because it treats different matters the same.'

The 2006 Study proposals. Owing to the Directive's silence with regard to **9.12** cross-border transfers, and to the numerous difficulties this silence gives rise to, the 2006 Study was prepared for the European Commission by the CMS Employment Practice Area Group. It begins by examining the different ways in which Member States have implemented the Directive. It then considers how 'existing legal instruments of international private law' (such as the Brussels I Regulation and the Rome Convention, which we touch upon under 'Claims arising from cross-border transfers' below) might provide solutions to some of the jurisdictional and conflict of laws problems arising. The Study concludes by setting out proposals as to how the Directive might be amended in order 'to establish a seamless legal framework for cross-border transfers', which might well form the basis of any amendment to the Directive ultimately proposed by the Commission.

We do not intend to go into any great depth about the Study's proposals. However, some of the main ones suggest that the Directive should:

- provide either that it can apply to transfers from one Member State to another or that it only applies to transfers within a Member State. If the latter option is taken, specific rules relating to cross-border situations could be drawn up

- set out whether or not a Member State's national law should cover transfers into that State

- provide that the law of the Member State applicable to the transferor will apply to define the central concepts of 'employee' and 'representative', determine what will transfer, and determine the extent to which the transferor must provide information to the transferee

- determine that employees are not deprived of their rights and remedies in connection with a termination of/substantial change to their contracts where they either object to or opt in to a cross-border transfer

- provide that the place of work where the employee has effectively and regularly rendered his services shall determine the jurisdiction in which he or she can sue the transferee – that is, the jurisdiction in which he or she worked for the transferor, unless the employee has started to work at the transferee's site

- introduce rules aimed at determining the law applicable to employment contracts where there is a conflict of laws between Member States

- determine whether a change of place of work can, in fact, be changed automatically in connection with the transfer of the business.

9.13 Following the 2006 Study Proposals, the European Commission implemented the first phase consultation of social partners under Article 138(2) of the EU Treaty concerning cross-border transfers of undertakings. The question posed by the Commission was whether the Directive should be modified to clarify its application to such cross-border transfers. The communication stated that if the Commission considered Community action advisable, it would consult the social partners on any proposals it might make. No further action has so far been taken.

9.14 Application of the 2006 Regulations

With regard to their potential to apply to cross-border transfers, the 2006 Regulations take a similar approach to that of the Directive they are designed to implement. That is, they expressly apply where, prior to the transfer, the entity or group of employees to transfer *is situated in the United Kingdom*. They seem ambivalent as to where that entity or group is to be transferred to.

500

The relevant provisions in this regard are contained in Reg 3(1). Reg 3(1)(a) stipulates that 'these Regulations apply to a transfer of an undertaking, business or part of an undertaking or business situated immediately before the transfer in the United Kingdom to another person where there is a transfer of an economic entity which retains its identity'. Then, Reg 3(1)(b) and 3(3) extends the application of the Regulations (beyond the scope of the Directive) to service provision changes where, among other things, 'immediately before the service provision change there is an organised grouping of employees situated in Great Britain'. Note that Reg 3(1)(b) has now been extended to Northern Ireland by separate Regulations (SI 2006/177).

Regulation 3(4)(b) then goes on to emphasise the mandatory nature of TUPE in respect of transfers falling within Reg 3(1), providing that the rules will apply 'notwithstanding (i) that the transfer... is governed... by the law of a country or territory outside the United Kingdom... (ii) that the employment of persons employed in the undertaking... is governed by any such law'.

Transfers from the United Kingdom. There has been much discussion, but **9.15** precious little agreement, as to whether all this means that the 2006 Regulations are capable of applying to a transaction resulting in a business/service moving overseas. One argument against TUPE applying to such a transfer is based on the presumption that UK legislation does not have extra-territorial effect unless it expressly provides otherwise. Some believe that the 2006 Regulations do not do enough to rebut this presumption, in that they do not expressly refer to their application to cross-border situations.

In addition, those opposed to the application of transfer rules in such circumstances point out that this would not be practical, post-transfer. For example, Reg 4(2) provides that upon a relevant transfer 'all the transferor's rights, powers, duties and liabilities' in connection with transferring employees' contracts (and this includes UK statutory employment rights) shall be taken on by the transferee employer. However, the transferee's country might well have a very different statutory employment regime, meaning that the transferring employees' statutory rights would almost certainly change. Moreover, it might prove difficult for jurisdictional reasons, which we discuss below, for any employees who have transferred abroad to succeed with claims against their foreign employer under the 2006 Regulations.

On the other hand, those who argue that TUPE can apply to cross-border **9.16** transfers point out, as we did above, that Reg 3(1) of the 2006 Regulations requires only that the transferring entity or group of employees be situated in the United Kingdom prior to the transfer. Since the rule stipulates no requirement as to where that entity or group is to be transferred, the argument goes, the clearly stated intention of the 2006 Regulations is that they can apply to cross-border transfers. Proponents of this argument tend also to point to the similar wording of the Directive itself, contending that the Directive is intended to

501

apply to at least those cross-border transfers involving Member States. They accept that there are practical difficulties with bringing claims post-transfer, but argue that it would be wrong to consider these in conjunction with the question of whether the 2006 Regulations are capable of applying. The fact of TUPE's application to the transfer situation itself should be sorted out first, and the practical difficulties of such application examined afterwards.

Moreover, those who believe that TUPE applies in such circumstances argue that, in reality, such a transfer does not even require the extra-territorial application of the Regulations. This argument proceeds thus: under TUPE, the transferee inherits the transferring workforce under their pre-transfer terms and conditions. Generally, those terms will involve the workers performing their jobs in the United Kingdom. So, the transfer, in essence, takes place within the United Kingdom (and is thus covered by TUPE), and the employees only move abroad *as a result* of the transfer.

9.17 It now appears that the 2006 Regulations can potentially apply to standard transfers from the United Kingdom to another Member State or to another country not covered by the Directive. The position was considered by the EAT in Holis Metal Industries Ltd v GMB and anor 2008 ICR 464, EAT. N Ltd ran a track, pole and blind manufacturing business from a factory in Tamworth. In February 2006 the company informed its staff that the track and pole part of the business was to be purchased by H Ltd, an Israeli company, on 9 April of that year. The track and pole employees were told that, unless they agreed to relocate to Israel, they would be made redundant following the sale. In the event, none of the employees wished to relocate so they were dismissed. For administrative reasons, the redundancy payments were made through N Ltd rather than through the Israeli purchaser. The GMB, a union recognised by N Ltd for collective bargaining purposes, brought a claim before an employment tribunal alleging that both N Ltd and H Ltd had breached the duty under Reg 13 of the TUPE Regulations to consult employee representatives about a relevant transfer. In response, H Ltd applied to have the claim struck out on the basis that the TUPE Regulations did not apply to what it termed an 'off-shoring situation'.

An employment judge refused the strike-out application – a decision subsequently upheld on appeal. The EAT (His Honour Judge Ansell sitting alone) decided that, in this particular case, both the business transfer and the redundancy dismissals took place within the United Kingdom. As such, the question of the application of TUPE to employees of a business transferred outside the United Kingdom was, strictly speaking, not a matter that needed to be determined for the purposes of this particular case. However, HHJ Ansell did address the extra-territorial issue. He held that 'the wording of both the ARD and Regulation 3 is precise in setting the application of the regulation to transfers of undertakings situated immediately before the transfer in the UK.

Set against the purpose of protecting the rights of workers in the event of change of employer... a purposeful approach requires that those employees should be protected even if the transfer is to be across borders outside the EU. It is not a case of either the UK or the EU seeking to legislate outside their jurisdictions without good reason.' He went on to say that 'the service provision changes brought into the 2006 regulations, where again the only limitation is that there should have been an organised group of employees situated in Great Britain immediately before the service provision change, is clearly aimed at the modern outsourcing of service provision, particularly call centres, whether inside or outside the EU'.

Given the Holis case, there is now some judicial guidance, albeit of persuasive **9.18** authority only, that TUPE can potentially apply to a transfer from the United Kingdom to a non-EU entity in the event that, upon transfer, the undertaking does not remain in the United Kingdom. The impact of the Holis decision may be limited in practice, as a key component in determining whether TUPE applies in a standard transfer is whether the entity transferred retains its identity. In many cross-border transactions the identity of the undertaking will not be retained on the transfer to another country given the accompanying changes in language and in the legal, economic and social context. This is particularly likely to be the case where personnel or tangible assets do not transfer. However in relation to service provision changes, Reg 3(1)(b) can apply regardless of whether the group of employees and activities retains its identity post transfer. Arguably, then, the increasingly common practice of 'off-shoring' jobs – for example, where a business shuts down its in-house call centre and buys in cheaper services from India – is likely to fall within this provision.

Transfers to the United Kingdom. As we have seen, in order for a relevant **9.19** transfer to occur for the purposes of the 2006 Regulations, the business or group of employees to transfer must be situated in the United Kingdom immediately before the transfer – Reg 3(1). Thus, it is clear that the Regulations do not apply (regardless of whether the Directive wishes them to) to transfers into the United Kingdom from elsewhere, whether or not the business in question is transferred from a fellow Member State.

It is possible that employees moving to the United Kingdom might glean protection from the transfers law of their own country, but their bringing and enforcing claims against the UK employer in that regard will depend on the nature of the law in question, and on some of the principles touched on below under 'Claims arising from cross-border transfers'.

Difficulties arising from TUPE's application. Even if one concludes that the **9.20** 2006 Regulations can apply to a cross-border transfer, in practical terms, a 'place of work' redundancy situation will normally arise in this type of scenario. Employees are often paid redundancy payments on this basis and any further complications in respect of TUPE are ignored or overlooked. But while the lack of a body of case law on cross-border transfers suggests that parties are often happy to assume that TUPE does not apply when an undertaking, or part of one, moves abroad, employers would be unwise simply to put their heads in the sand and ignore the Regulations in such situations. If TUPE does apply, the common practice of the transferor making the affected employees redundant becomes risky, as any dismissals effected in connection with the transfer are likely to be automatically unfair under Reg 7. Also, employers might fall foul of the additional information and consultation obligations that TUPE imposes.

As for transferring employees, they will rarely want to follow their jobs abroad and will be likely to take redundancy or a similar settlement where offered. However, if negotiations are not going well – perhaps because their current employer insists that TUPE applies – the employees might find themselves in a tricky situation. They are not, however, without options. If the Regulations do apply, as a last resort they could 'object' to the transfer under Reg 4(7) and argue that the forthcoming move abroad would amount to a fundamental breach of contract entitling them to resign and claim constructive dismissal, or to a substantial change in terms and conditions to their material detriment, entitling them to resign and claim unfair dismissal under Reg 4(9). Case law suggests that, in such circumstances, employees can claim against the UK-based transferor, thus avoiding the tricky problem of enforcing UK law against the foreign transferee.

9.21 Employees who wish to bring claims against the foreign transferee in another Member State of the European Union will need to consider international laws. We now turn to look, briefly, at how some of these matters might be sorted out.

9.22 **Enforcing claims arising from cross-border transfers within the EU**
Below, we touch on some of the principles that might apply where an employee involved in a cross-border transfer wishes to bring claims against the transferor or, perhaps more problematically, the transferee. At the outset we should point out that we do not seek to provide a through exposition of what is an extremely complicated area of law, but intend simply to give a flavour of the types of issue that might crop up. We shall focus our attention on transfers from the United Kingdom to other European Union Member States, in that, as discussed above, such transfers are arguably capable of attracting the application of the 2006 Regulations.

Before attempting to reach some conclusions, we shall provide some information about:

• the Brussels I Regulation, which deals with matters of international jurisdiction within the EU

• the Rome Convention, the terms of which determine which Member State's law applies to an employment contract

- the fact that, in order to rely upon the special unfair dismissal rules contained in the 2006 Regulations, an employee is likely to have to be 'employed in the United Kingdom' in line with the test elucidated by the House of Lords in Lawson v Serco Ltd and other cases 2006 ICR 250, HL.

The Brussels I Regulation. The Brussels I Regulation (Council Regulation **9.23** No.44/2001), which took effect on 1 March 2002, sets out mandatory rules as to jurisdiction and the enforcement of judgments within the EU (other than Denmark, with regard to which the similar rules of the 1988 Brussels Convention still apply).

Articles 18–21 of the Brussels I Regulation are concerned with employment disputes involving employers domiciled in an EU Member State. Article 19.1 provides for a default position whereby a claim must be brought in the courts of the country where the respondent employer is domiciled. The domicile of the employer will be where its 'statutory seat', 'central administration' or 'principal place of business' is located – Article 60. Article 60.2 further provides specifically for the United Kingdom and Ireland that 'statutory seat' means 'the registered office or, where there is no such office anywhere, the place of incorporation or, where there is no such place anywhere, the place under the law of which the formation took place'. If the employer is domiciled outside the EU but has a 'branch, agency or establishment' in a Member State, that Member State will be deemed to be the employer's domicile by virtue of Article 18.2.

Article 19.2 provides, however, that the employee can choose instead to institute **9.24** proceedings against the employer in the courts of the Member State where the employee 'habitually carries out his work' or where he or she 'last did so'. If the employee does not or did not carry out his or her work habitually in any one country, he or she may commence proceedings in the State where the business that engaged him or her is or was situated.

The Brussels I Regulation goes on (in Articles 32–56) to set out formalities which, if complied with by the claimant, will result in a judgment against an employer being recognised and enforced in another Member State.

The Rome Convention. With regard to disputes within the EU, the question of **9.25** which country's law will cover an employment relationship (as opposed to the question of which country a claim should be brought in) will be determined with reference to the 1980 Rome Convention on the law applicable to contractual obligation. This was implemented into UK law by the Contracts (Applicable Law) Act 1990.

The basic rule of the Convention is that the parties can choose (a choice that must be expressed on the face of the contract or otherwise demonstrated with reasonable certainty) which law should govern the contract – Article 3. However, the parties' choice of law cannot have the effect of depriving the employee of the protection afforded by the 'mandatory rules' of the country

505

with which the contract is otherwise most closely connected. So, for example, an employee working in Germany will not be deprived of certain German employment rights simply because the parties have decided that UK law will apply to his or her employment contract.

9.26 In the absence of a choice of law, Article 6 of the Convention provides that a contract is to be governed by the law of the country in which the employee habitually carries out his or her work, even though he or she may be temporarily employed in another country. If the employee does not habitually work in any one country, the contract is governed by the law of the country in which the place of business that employs him or her is situated, or the law of another country if, in the circumstances of the case, the contract is more closely connected with that other country.

9.27 **TUPE and employees working abroad.** Regardless of whether an employee's claim satisfies the terms of the Brussels I Convention, and regardless of whether the employee's contract is governed by UK law, it is not necessarily the case that the employee, if working outside the United Kingdom, can rely upon the full spectrum of rights conferred by the 2006 Regulations. In fact, it is unlikely that employees who have transferred to a foreign state will be able to rely upon the automatically unfair dismissal rules set out in Reg 7, which were discussed in Chapter 4 of this Handbook.

That is because it is assumed that, in order to rely on these rules, the employee in question must satisfy a test of 'employment in the United Kingdom' analogous with the 'employment in Great Britain' test laid down in respect of ordinary unfair dismissal law by the House of Lords in Lawson v Serco Ltd and other cases 2006 ICR 250, HL. In essence, the upshot is that an employee will only be protected if at the time of dismissal he or she was:

- working in the United Kingdom

- a peripatetic employee based in the United Kingdom, or

- an expatriate employee, who (i) worked for a UK employer who can be regarded as an extra-territorial political or social British enclave, (ii) worked for a UK employer for the purposes of a business carried on in the United Kingdom, or (iii) had a close connection with the United Kingdom and UK employment law.

9.28 The Lawson v Serco test might well have an impact on employees working abroad following a cross-border transfer. But it will also affect employees working abroad but assigned to a UK business that transfers within the United Kingdom under the 2006 Regulations. Owing to this, we consider the test separately, and at much greater length, under 'Employees working outside United Kingdom' below.

Conclusions. We shall now attempt to bring all this together, by considering **9.29** how the above rules might affect some of the claims that could arise as a result of a cross-border transfer from the United Kingdom to another EU Member State.

Information and consultation. If a UK-based 'transferor' suspects/fears that **9.30** the 2006 Regulations might apply to a cross-border transfer from the United Kingdom, he should do the best that he can in the circumstances to inform and consult representatives of 'affected employees' in accordance with Reg 13 (see Chapter 8). A transferor's failure to do so can result in his being liable to pay compensation of up to 13 weeks' pay in respect of each affected employee. If the transferor alone is pursued by the employees' representatives for a failure to inform or consult, no cross-border jurisdictional issues will arise.

Dismissal by transferor prior to or upon the transfer. The usual ploy adopted **9.31** in cross-border transfers is for the transferor to proceed as if the employment of the relevant workforce is terminated upon the transfer by reason of redundancy. This will work perfectly well until somewhere along the line one of the parties to the transfer decides that there is no redundancy situation and that it is more advantageous to argue that TUPE applies. For example, the transferor might decline to make redundancy payments on the basis that the workforce should transfer to the transferee; or an employee might wish to pursue an unfair dismissal claim in the hope of obtaining compensation.

We now consider whether an employee involved in a cross-border transfer situation from the United Kingdom to another EU Member State might claim unfair dismissal where (i) he or she is treated as redundant by the UK transferor upon the transfer, (ii) the transferor does not treat the employee as redundant and the transferee refuses to take the employee on, and/or (iii) the employee is not treated as redundant by the transferor and the transferee does wish to take him or her on.

In situation (i) – where the transferor purports to make the employee redundant **9.32** – the employee might seek to bring unfair dismissal claims in a UK employment tribunal against both the transferor and the transferee. In this regard, we should make the following points:

- presuming that the 2006 Regulations applied to the cross-border transaction in question, the redundancy dismissal would be automatically unfair owing to Reg 7 (see Chapter 4 under 'Automatically unfair dismissals') unless the transferor carried it out for an 'economic, technical or organisational reason entailing changes in the workforce' (see Chapter 4 under 'Dismissals potentially fair for an "ETO reason"')

- if the transferor can establish such an 'ETO reason' then, as long as the redundancy was carried out fairly, there would be no unfair dismissal. If the transferor can establish an ETO reason but the redundancy dismissal was

507

carried out unfairly, then the dismissal would be unfair for the purposes of the ERA, and liability for that dismissal would lie with the transferor

- as discussed in Chapter 4 under 'Dismissals potentially fair for an "ETO reason" – transferor cannot dismiss for transferee's ETO reason', however, it is extremely unlikely that the transferor could establish an ETO reason in these circumstances. That is because the supposed ETO reason for dismissal would not relate to the transferor's (as opposed to the transferee's) future conduct of the business in question. Thus, the purported redundancy dismissal would most likely be automatically unfair owing to Reg 7

- under Reg 4(2) (see Chapter 3 under 'Rights and liabilities relating to the individual – unfair and wrongful dismissal'), liability for the automatically unfair dismissal would pass to the transferee. This is why the employee would wish to claim against the transferee as well as the transferor, and this is where the Brussels I Regulation would come into play

- if the transferee employer, although running an overseas business, is domiciled in the United Kingdom within the meaning of Article 19.1 of the Brussels I Regulation, the employee's claim in the employment tribunal against that employer could proceed

- we suggest, in any event, that since the employee's last habitual place of work was the United Kingdom, he or she would be entitled to rely upon Article 19.2 of the Brussels I Regulation to bring a claim in the United Kingdom against a foreign transferee. The transferee, however, might dispute that this conclusion is correct. He might point out that since the transferor dismissed the employee, and since the dismissal was effective, the transferee did not at any point have an employment relationship with the employee. As a result, he might contend, the 'habitual place of work' provision of Article 19.2 is not available to the employee, meaning that the tribunal should not accept jurisdiction

- if the employee is successful with his or her unfair dismissal claim against the transferee, the tribunal's judgment will be capable of being enforced in the courts of the transferee's Member State, in accordance with Articles 32–56 of the Brussels I Regulation.

9.33 As with situation (i) above, in situation (ii) – where the transferor declines to make a redundancy payment in the belief that the employee will pass to the transferee under the 2006 Regulations, but where the transferee refuses to take the employee on – the employee might wish to bring claims in the employment tribunal against both the transferor and the transferee. Some of the considerations with regard to situation (ii) are the same as those in situation (i), but note the following:

- the employee would argue that if the 2006 Regulations did not apply, he or she was unfairly dismissed by the transferor under the normal provisions of the ERA (in which case the transferor would retain liability). In the alternative, the employee would contend that the Regulations did apply, and that he or she was unfairly dismissed by the transferee contrary to Reg 7

- if there was a relevant transfer in this situation, the employee would, we suggest, be able to proceed with an unfair dismissal claim in the United Kingdom against the transferee. The employee's contract, under which he or she last habitually performed work in the United Kingdom, would be deemed by the Regulations to have transferred from the transferor to the transferee. Since the transferee became the employee's employer, and since the employee habitually worked in the United Kingdom, the employment tribunal would, owing to Article 19.2 of the Brussels I Regulation, more than likely have jurisdiction to hear the claim. Furthermore, the employee, who never actually worked abroad, would be able to satisfy the 'employment in the United Kingdom' test for bringing an unfair dismissal claim (see 'Employees working outside United Kingdom' below).

If the employee in situation (iii) does not wish to transfer to the transferee, yet **9.34** both employers insist that the 2006 Regulations will apply to transfer his or her employment, he or she does have some options, as the following demonstrates:

- the employee could refuse to transfer and bring a tribunal claim against the transferor, arguing that the 2006 Regulations did not apply. Thus, the argument would go, he or she will have been unfairly dismissed by the transferor, who would be liable for the dismissal

- alternatively, if the employee accepts that the 2006 Regulations do apply, he or she could resign prior to the transfer and claim constructive dismissal (envisaged by Reg 4(11)) or material detriment dismissal (within the meaning of Reg 4(9)). These types of claim are discussed at length in Chapter 4 under 'Constructive dismissals' and 'Material detriment dismissals'. Put simply, in many cases a transferee's requirement that an employee move abroad to continue with his or her job would leave the way open for the employee to bring one of these claims, if not both

- as also explained in Chapter 4, the question of which employer (transferor or transferee) will be liable for a constructive or material detriment dismissal might depend on whether the employee has (in addition to resigning) made a formal objection to the transfer within the meaning of Reg 4(7) – for further details about objection see Chapter 2 under 'Objecting to the transfer'. Cases including Humphreys v University of Oxford and anor 2000 ICR 405, CA, suggest that where an employee has objected to the transfer, liability for a constructive or material detriment dismissal will remain with the transferor;

509

but where the employee has not so objected, any such liability will pass to the transferee

- so, in most cases, an employee who wishes to resign when faced with a cross-border transfer situation would be best served by objecting to the transfer as well as claiming constructive or material detriment dismissal. That is because liability might well remain with the transferor, meaning that no complicated matters of international jurisdiction will arise

- if the employee has not objected to the transfer – perhaps the employee actually wants liability to pass to the transferee owing to the fact that the transferor is insolvent – similar considerations with regard to the Brussels I Regulation will arise to those set out with regard to situation (i) above.

9.35 *Dismissal or contractual variation by transferee on or after the transfer.* We now consider the situation where the employee has transferred under the 2006 Regulations, and as a result has gone to work for the transferee in another Member State. What can the employee do if, some time after the transfer, he or she is dismissed by the transferee or subjected to post-transfer contractual variations? The following points are relevant in this regard:

- unless the transferee is domiciled in the United Kingdom, a UK employment tribunal will not be able to accept jurisdiction to hear any claim arising from the employee's post-transfer employment. This is because, for the purposes of Article 19.2 of the Brussels I Regulation, the employee's habitual place of work will no longer be the United Kingdom

- we assume, in any event, that the employee would not be protected, with regard to a post-transfer dismissal, by the unfair dismissal rules contained in Reg 7 of the 2006 Regulations. This is because the employee would (other than in peculiar circumstances) presumably fail the 'employment in the United Kingdom' test (see 'Employees working outside United Kingdom' below)

- in the absence of a choice of law, the law of the country in which the employee habitually works will apply to his or her employment contract (Article 6.2 of the Rome Convention). So, generally, the contract of an employee who transfers to another Member State on a permanent basis would attract the law of that Member State as soon as the employee moves there.

9.36 In conclusion, this means that in most cases an employee who has transferred to another Member State under the 2006 Regulations will, in respect of the post-transfer conduct of the transferee employer, need to seek recourse in the Member State in which he or she is working. Furthermore, the protection that he or she is afforded will depend to a large extent on the law of the Member State in question.

Employees working outside United Kingdom 9.37

The question we pose in this section is whether, and to what extent, the 2006 Regulations can afford protection to employees working abroad. As we saw earlier in this chapter, this question is relevant to cross-border transfers, in that it might impact upon the ability of an employee who has transferred from the United Kingdom to another jurisdiction to bring a claim against his or her new employer. In addition, the question is relevant to a TUPE transfer taking place within the United Kingdom, where some of the workforce assigned to the business or service to be transferred spend some or all of their time working in another country. We shall focus on the latter situation here.

The first thing to note is that the 2006 Regulations can apply to a transfer of a business or service whether or not there are employees assigned to that business or service who work outside the United Kingdom. This is made clear by Reg 3(4)(c), which provides that, as long as the transferring business or service can be said to be situated in the United Kingdom immediately prior to the transfer, the Regulations will apply to 'a transfer of an undertaking, business or part of an undertaking or business (which may also be a service provision change) where persons employed in the undertaking, business or part transferred ordinarily work outside the United Kingdom'. With regard to Reg 3(4)(c), the DTI's 'Employment rights on the transfer of an undertaking: a guide to the 2006 TUPE Regulations for employees, employers and representatives' (the DTI Guide) gives an example of a transfer of a UK exporting business, whose sales force spends the majority of its working week outside the United Kingdom. The Guide states that the fact that the sales force essentially works abroad will not prevent the Regulations applying to the transaction in question.

So, the Regulations can apply where some members of the transferring 9.38 workforce perform their duties overseas. But what protection is bestowed on such employees? Under the 1981 Regulations, it was clear that this protection was somewhat limited. Reg 13(1) stated that TUPE's provisions with regard to unfair dismissal and information and consultation 'do not apply to employment where under his contract of employment the employee ordinarily works outside the United Kingdom'.

The 'ordinarily working in the United Kingdom' test contained in Reg 13 of the 1981 Regulations mirrored the 'ordinarily working in Great Britain' test found in S.196 ERA, which used to determine the territorial scope of the right to claim unfair dismissal. However, S.196 was repealed by the Employment Relations Act 1999, leaving the ERA silent as to whether it affords protection to overseas workers. In drafting the 2006 Regulations, the Government noted this change and decided to bring the TUPE regime into line with the ERA once more. It therefore removed the old Reg 13 exclusion in its entirety. In this regard, the Government stated in the 2005 consultation document: 'Consultees

511

may wish to note that the draft revised Regulations contain no provision equivalent to Reg 13 of the existing Regulations, excluding employees working abroad. Similar provisions were removed from other employment rights legislation by the Employment Relations Act 1999, so this is simply a "tidying up" exercise to bring the TUPE Regulations into line with the general position established some five years ago. Whether or not an employee working abroad is able to bring a claim under the Regulations will in future depend on the normal principles of international law.'

9.39   Where does this leave us now? Helpfully, the matter of the application of the ERA (post-S.196) to overseas workers has now been determined by the House of Lords in Lawson v Serco Ltd and other cases 2006 ICR 250, HL. In essence, the House of Lords constructed a new test based on the concept of 'employment in Great Britain'. As we assume that the reasoning adopted by their Lordships in this regard is applicable to at least some aspects of the TUPE regime, we shall examine the Lawson decision in some depth below.

9.40   **The 'employment in the United Kingdom' test**
We now turn to examine Lawson v Serco Ltd and other cases 2006 ICR 250, HL. To recap, the background to the case was as follows. Prior to 1999, S.196 of the ERA expressly excluded employees who ordinarily worked outside Great Britain from the right to claim unfair dismissal under S.94 of that Act. When S.196 was repealed, and nothing was put in its place, there was widespread confusion with regard to the ERA's territorial scope. Following a number of conflicting decisions of the lower courts, it fell to the House of Lords in Lawson v Serco to determine whether employees working outside Great Britain are entitled to bring unfair dismissal claims. Their Lordships formulated a new 'employment in Great Britain' test, which we examine below.

As stated above, it is widely assumed that a similar test now applies with regard to aspects of the 2006 Regulations, albeit with regard to 'employment in the United Kingdom' rather than simply to 'employment in Great Britain'. In other words, a test analogous with that set out in Lawson v Serco will determine whether employees working outside the United Kingdom, but assigned to a transferring UK business, receive the unfair dismissal (and probably the information and consultation) rights normally bestowed upon affected UK employees by the TUPE regime.

9.41   In order to understand the nuances of the Lawson v Serco decision, it is necessary to examine it in some depth. We start by setting out the facts of the three appeals involved, before moving on to look at the principles elucidated by Lord Hoffmann and at how those principles were applied to the facts in question.

9.42   **The facts of the three appeals in Lawson v Serco.** In Lawson v Serco Ltd and other cases 2006 ICR 250, HL, the House of Lords considered three appeals

512 ───────────────────────────────

with regard to whether overseas employees were entitled to bring unfair dismissal claims under the ERA. The relevant facts were as follows:

- *Lawson v Serco Ltd:* L, of British nationality and domiciled in England, worked as security supervisor for S Ltd, a company registered in the United Kingdom and based in England. The job required L to carry out all his work on Ascension Island in the South Atlantic, where the company was contracted to provide security services to the Royal Air Force. L was paid in pounds sterling into his UK bank account, but paid no UK taxes because he worked abroad. When L resigned, he brought a claim under the ERA for unfair constructive dismissal. The matter progressed to the Court of Appeal, which decided that the tribunal had no jurisdiction to hear it as L had been employed wholly outside Great Britain. L appealed to the House of Lords

- *Botham v Ministry of Defence:* B, a British national, was employed by the MoD in Germany. He was considered part of the 'civil component' of the British Forces in Germany, he paid UK tax on his earnings, and his contract of employment was expressly stated to be governed by the law of England and Wales. Furthermore, his statement of employment particulars described him as a 'UK-based Youth Worker'. Following the termination of his employment, B brought unfair dismissal proceedings before an employment tribunal. Applying the 'employment in Great Britain' test advocated by the Court of Appeal in Lawson (above), the tribunal held that it had no jurisdiction to hear his claim. The EAT upheld the tribunal's decision, as did the Court of Appeal. B appealed to the House of Lords

- *Crofts v Veta Ltd:* C was employed as a pilot by V Ltd, a wholly-owned subsidiary of CPA Ltd. Both V Ltd and CPA Ltd were registered in Hong Kong. C's contract was governed by Hong Kong law and his flight instructions were issued from Hong Kong. However, his 'permanent home base' – where his flight cycle would start and end – was Heathrow Airport. C was dismissed and submitted an unfair dismissal claim to an employment tribunal in London. When the matter reached the Court of Appeal, the Court noted that in Todd v British Midland Airways Ltd 1978 IRLR 370, CA – a case decided under the now repealed 'ordinarily working in Great Britain' test of S.196 ERA – an airline pilot 'based' in England had been allowed to proceed with an unfair dismissal claim. Lord Justice Waller found it 'difficult to believe' that an employee such as Mr Todd, who had managed to comply with the 'ordinarily working' test, would now be precluded from claiming unfair dismissal following that test's repeal. Lord Justice Maurice Kay agreed. In his view, the location of an employee's base is likely to be of particular relevance to the question of jurisdiction when the employment is 'inherently mobile and international'. The majority of the Court concluded that C was entitled to pursue his unfair dismissal claim. V Ltd appealed to the House of Lords.

513

9.43 **Unfair dismissal law covers 'employment in Great Britain'.** When the appeals came before the House of Lords, Lord Hoffmann, with whom the other members of the House agreed, began by stating that it would be 'a mistake to try to formulate an ancillary rule of territorial scope, in the sense of a verbal formula such as S.196 used to provide'. His Lordship agreed with the Court of Appeal in Lawson that Parliament must have intended the standard or normal application of the unfair dismissal rules to be to 'the employee who was working in Great Britain'. He believed, however, that the 'employment in Great Britain' test should be treated as a general principle rather than as a firm rule to be interpreted and applied.

His Lordship then turned to the question of how, in a 'standard' case, a tribunal should determine whether there is 'employment in Great Britain'. He noted that under the now-repealed S.196, the question of where an employee 'ordinarily worked' was determined by reference to the contract of employment. This could produce 'arbitrary and counter-intuitive results', such as in the case of Carver v Saudi Arabian Airlines 1999 ICR 991, CA, where a flight attendant in reality based at Heathrow was denied unfair dismissal protection because her contract of employment contemplated that she would be based in Jeddah. In Lord Hoffmann's view, the application of the unfair dismissal rules should now depend upon whether the employee in question was actually working in Great Britain at the time of dismissal, rather than upon what was contemplated, perhaps many years earlier, when the contract of employment was entered into. He stated: 'The terms of the contract and the prior history of the contractual relationship may be relevant to whether the employee is really working in Great Britain or whether he is merely on a casual visit... but ordinarily the question should simply be whether he is working in Great Britain at the time when he is dismissed.'

9.44 **'Base' of peripatetic employees is key.** Next, Lord Hoffmann focused on peripatetic employees, such as C, who, owing to the nature of their work, did not perform services in one particular territory. He held that the common sense of treating the base of such an employee as his or her place of employment for ERA purposes, as applied by the Court of Appeal in Todd v British Midland Airways Ltd (above), remained valid. In order to determine the peripatetic employee's base, he continued, it was necessary to 'go by the conduct of the parties and the way they have been operating the contract', as opposed to just looking at the terms of the contract.

Turning to the facts of C's case, Lord Hoffmann noted that the tribunal had concluded that the centre of C's operations was quite manifestly London. In the circumstances, the tribunal had been right to conclude that C was protected by the ERA, and V Ltd's appeal was therefore dismissed.

9.45 **Some expatriate employees might be covered.** Turning to the position of expatriate employees, Lord Hoffmann stated that 'the circumstances would have to be unusual for an employee who works and is based abroad to come within the scope' of S.94. He thought, however, that expatriate employees can be protected in certain circumstances. Nevertheless, it would be very unlikely that someone working abroad would be protected by S.94 unless he or she was working for an employer based in Great Britain. And even then, something more would be required to remove the case from the general principle that the place of employment is the deciding jurisdictional factor.

Lord Hoffmann moved on to set out two examples of circumstances in which an employee working abroad might be able to pursue an unfair dismissal claim. The first was of an employee posted abroad by a British employer for the purposes of a business carried on in Great Britain – for example, a foreign correspondent on the staff of a British newspaper. The second was of an expatriate employee of a British employer 'who is operating within what amounts for practical purposes to an extra-territorial British enclave in a foreign country'. His Lordship accepted that there may be other qualifying situations, but stated that in order to come within the scope of S.94 ERA employees would need to show 'equally strong connections with Great Britain and British employment law'.

Turning to the facts of the Lawson and Botham cases, Lord Hoffmann concluded **9.46** that both L and B fell within the second example set out directly above. B was a UK civil servant who worked on a military base in Germany, which clearly amounted to an extra-territorial British enclave. L's case was not as strong, but there was no local community on Ascension Island and 'it would be unrealistic to regard him as having taken up employment in a foreign community in the same way as if Serco Ltd were providing security services… in Berlin'. Ascension was in practice a British outpost in the South Atlantic. Furthermore, although there was a local system of law, 'the connection between the employment relationship and the United Kingdom [was] overwhelmingly stronger'. Both L and B, therefore, would be entitled to pursue their unfair dismissal claims.

More recent cases such as Bleuse v MBT Transport Ltd 2008 ICR 488, EAT, and Kücükdeveci v Swedex GmbH and Co KG 2010 IRLR 346, ECJ, suggest that national laws must be set aside if they conflict with European Community laws in order to give effect to the directly effective rights under EU law. This, it seems clear, would include the Acquired Rights Directive and therefore protect employees whose 'base' is not in Great Britain applying the Lawson and Serco test to the ERA.

Conclusion. To reiterate, then, the above reasoning would seem to apply with **9.47** regard to claims brought with reference to the 2006 Regulations for automatically unfair dismissal and an employer's failure to inform or consult – albeit with the new ERA 'employment in Great Britain' test expanded slightly for TUPE purposes to cover 'employment in the United Kingdom'.

515

In our view, the majority of the employees of a UK business who could be said to be 'assigned' to such a business for the purposes of the automatic transfer of employment rule contained in Reg 4 of the 2006 Regulations (see Chapter 2 under '"Assigned" to the undertaking transferred'), will be able to satisfy the 'employment in the United Kingdom test' explained above. Take, for instance, the example given in the DTI Guide of a UK exporting business whose sales force spends the majority of its working week outside the United Kingdom. Those sales staff, it would seem, would be peripatetic employees, whose base would be in the United Kingdom. Thus, just like the employee in the Crofts v Veta Ltd case, they would be protected by the relevant legislation.

9.48 Even if the sales staff were based *permanently* outside the United Kingdom, if they were performing their roles for the UK business, and were assigned to that business for the purposes of Reg 4 of the 2006 Regulations, it would seem that they would fulfil the Lawson v Serco 'employment in Great Britain' test. Their position would seem to be analogous with that of the foreign correspondent on the staff of a British newspaper, given as an example by Lord Hoffmann of someone who would be protected by the relevant law.

The final port of call for employees who are working for a British employer in another Member State is to use the Bleuse line of argument to found an unfair dismissal claim in the United Kingdom.

10 Practical aspects of transfers

Avoidance of TUPE provisions

The course of a sale and purchase transfer

Due diligence

Common practical transfer issues

Conditions precedent

Warranties

Restrictive covenants

Indemnities

Although many of the changes introduced by the Transfer of Undertakings **10.1** (Protection of Employment) Regulations 2006 SI 2006/246 (TUPE) were fairly modest or simply sought to codify the developed case law on particular aspects of the predecessor Regulations, nobody would suggest that the new Regulations have made transfer of undertakings law much simpler than it was before. Indeed, as discussed in the previous chapters of this Handbook, many problems (both of a practical and of a legal nature) remain. The Government's declared aims when enacting the 2006 Regulations were to:

- assist with the smooth management of necessary business restructuring and public sector modernisation by securing the interests and commitment of the employees affected

- promote a cooperative partnership approach towards change; and

- help create a level playing field and reduce transaction risks and costs in business acquisitions and in contracting operations in the business services sector.

Many had hoped that the review of the law in this area would lead to substantial **10.2** improvements in the operation of the Regulations, but unfortunately that has not entirely been the case. For example, the problem of the validity of agreed variations to terms and conditions of employment when there is a transfer remains, and the 2006 Regulations do little more than restate the case law position for fear that anything more ambitious would be outwith the scope of the EU Acquired Rights Directive (No.2001/23) as currently drafted. However, there are changes that are welcome, such as the notification of employee liability information provision (Reg 11) and the new rules relating to service provision changes (Reg 3(1)(b)).

517

It is clear from the foregoing chapters that the Regulations, even in the 2006 version, still represent a minefield to those involved in the sale or purchase of a business, or to those involved in a service provision change. That minefield may inevitably catch out the parties to small-scale transfers who innocently believe their transaction to be a simple one. The same mistake would be inexcusable on the part of professionals, such as lawyers, receivers and accountants, who may be engaged by the parties to effect the sound transfer of a larger business. There may, of course, be other ways of structuring the transfer so that it is not covered by the Regulations, the most common method being by way of a share acquisition. However, a share transfer is not always practical for a variety of reasons and, in any case, recent case law has blurred the distinction between a TUPE transfer and a pure share acquisition – see Print Factory (London) 1991 Ltd v Millam 2007 ICR 1331, CA, discussed in detail in Chapter 1, under 'Standard transfers – transfers "to another person"'). It is also sometimes the case that, in order to prepare a large business for a share acquisition, elements of it have to be restructured in a way that attracts the TUPE Regulations.

10.3   Much of the lawyer's task will be the drafting of an agreement that protects the party by whom he or she is instructed from unexpected liabilities. These may arise as a direct consequence of the Regulations, or they may be inherent in the nature of a business transfer itself. The commercial parties will also need to know whether and to what extent they may contract as between themselves or with employees who are assigned to the undertaking or grouping of resources to be transferred to contract out of the key protections guaranteed by the Regulations. In this chapter we first examine the scope for contracting out of the Regulations, and then will outline some practical tips as to the kinds of matters which will need to be considered during the negotiations leading to the transfer of an undertaking.

Careful planning will ensure that significant issues are not overlooked, and will ensure that a timescale for the transfer is considered at an early stage. In all transfers the vital factors are likely to be the time and knowledge available – knowledge not just about the Regulations but also about the undertaking or activities to be transferred. This Handbook focuses mainly on the employment aspects of relevant transfers. While employment law issues are just one among many of the matters that need to be considered, their proper handling of the employment relations issues will reduce legal claims and can address some of the natural concerns of affected employees so that the new employer has a more committed workforce. This process takes time, and time is often in short supply.

10.4   ## Avoidance of TUPE provisions

As one would expect, the TUPE Regulations 2006 contain an express provision restricting the capacity of any party to a transfer – transferor, transferee or employee – to contract out of the employment protection provisions contained within the Regulations. These provisions are mandatory in that they operate irrespective of the parties' wishes in the matter. So, for example, in MRS Environmental Services Ltd v Dyke and anor EAT 93/96 the EAT ruled that the automatic transfer of employment rule in what is now Reg 4 of TUPE 2006 imported a statutory novation that has effect regardless of whether the parties consented or had knowledge of each other's identity. This meant that a relevant transfer occurred and the consequences which TUPE provides on such a transfer followed irrespective of the fact that employees had not agreed to the transfer and had not been informed of the identity of the transferee.

Similarly, in relation to variation of terms and conditions, the European Court of Justice has also made it clear that it is not open to employees to waive rights conferred on them by the Acquired Rights Directive to be protected against such variations. In Foreningen af Arbejdsledere i Danmark v Daddy's Dance Hall A/S 1988 IRLR 315, ECJ, a question was referred to the ECJ as to whether a worker may waive these rights even if the disadvantages to him of agreeing to detrimental changes to contractual terms as a result of the transfer were offset by the offer of more advantageous terms, so that he was not left in a worse position overall. In answer to that question, the Court ruled that: 'The workers concerned do not have the option to waive the rights conferred on them by the Directive and... it is not permissible to diminish these rights, even with their consent. This interpretation is notwithstanding the fact that, as in the instant case, the worker, to offset disadvantages arising for him from a change in his employment relationship, obtains new advantages so that he is not, overall, left in a worse position than he was before.'

10.5 Regulation 18 of the 2006 Regulations reflects the mandatory nature of the Directive's provisions by stipulating that: 'Section 203 of the [Employment Rights Act 1996 (ERA)] (restrictions on contracting out) shall apply in relation to these Regulations as if they were contained in that Act, save for that section shall not apply in so far as these Regulations provide for an agreement (whether a contract of employment or not) to exclude or limit the operation of these Regulations.' In essence, what this does is apply the same restrictions on contracting out as apply to substantive claims contained within the ERA (such as unfair dismissal and unlawful deductions of wages), with the exception of where the TUPE Regulations expressly provide for a right to contract out of, or limit the application of, specific provisions of the Regulations.

It follows that, in order to determine the precise ambit of Reg 18, it is necessary to understand two things: (i) what is the scope for contracting out (or waiver) of the provisions of the ERA as set out in S.203 of that Act? And (ii) what specific exceptions are made in the Regulations to allow for their protections to be disapplied or limited?

519

10.6 Waiver of rights

Section 203 ERA – to which Reg 18 of the 2006 Regulations refers – contains a wide-ranging restriction on the capacity of employers to enforce agreements entered into by employees to compromise or waive their substantive rights conferred by or under that Act. In particular, S.203(1) provides that: 'Any provision in an agreement (whether a contract of employment or not) is void in so far as it purports – (a) to exclude or limit the operation of any provision of this Act, or (b) to preclude a person from bringing any proceedings under this Act before an employment tribunal.' S.203(2) then goes on to qualify the general position set out in S.203(1) by providing for specific exceptions in which any agreement to preclude a person from bringing or continuing tribunal proceedings is allowed. Two of these exceptions are relevant for present purposes. These are:

- where the agreement in question is one in respect of which an Acas conciliation officer has taken action under S.18 of the Employment Tribunals Act 1996 (ETA) – S.203(2)(e); or

- where the agreement is a compromise agreement that (a) satisfies the conditions for validity set out in the ERA, and (b) which relates to the compromise of proceedings in respect of contravention or alleged contravention of one of the specific statutory provisions in the ERA listed in S.18 of the ETA – S.203(2)(f)(i).

10.7 Acas-conciliated settlements.

Thus, the first way in which an agreement to refrain from continuing or bringing proceedings may be effective is where it has been reached through Acas conciliation. S.18 ETA sets out a comprehensive list of the types of claim or proceedings in respect of which a conciliation officer may 'take action' to help parties to settle such claims or proceedings. Included in that list are claims or proceedings brought under provisions of the ERA relating to unlawful deductions from wages or unfair dismissal (S.18(1)(d)) and breach of contract claims arising on, or outstanding at, the termination of employment (S.18(1)(e)).

The claims most relevant in S.18 in a TUPE context are claims for unfair dismissal and unlawful deduction from wages. Thus, where a conciliated settlement settles claims relating to the employee's unfair dismissal rights in Reg 7 or provides for compromise of a wages claim against the transferor or transferee, this will be both effective and binding on all parties.

10.8

The same is true in respect of settlement of claims of breach of the employee liability notification obligations in Reg 11 and the duty to inform and consult appropriate representatives of employees affected by the relevant transfer under Regs 13–16 of TUPE 2006. Although neither of these claims are specifically mentioned in Reg 18 as being claims over which an Acas conciliation officer is entitled to take action, express provision is made in the Regulations themselves for S.18 to apply. Accordingly, Reg 12(7) in respect of a claim of failure to comply with the employee liability obligations provides that 'S.18 of the [ETA] (conciliation) shall apply to the right conferred by this regulation and to proceedings under this regulation as it applies to the rights conferred by that Act and the employment tribunal proceedings mentioned in that Act'. Reg 16(1) provides likewise in respect of claims concerned with breaches of the duty to inform and consult.

Compromise agreements. The second means by which it may be possible to **10.9** refrain from continuing or bringing proceedings concerned with rights provided by the TUPE Regulations is through a valid compromise agreement. As mentioned above, S.203(2)(f) ERA exempts the general prohibition against contracting out of the ERA's provisions in S.203(1) where a compromise agreement relates to claims/proceedings of the kind listed in S.18(2)(d) ETA, provided that the agreement also complies with the validity conditions specified in the ERA. The list in S.18(2)(d) refers to a large number of statutory provisions within the ERA, but the only ones of relevance so far as TUPE is concerned are S.13 (the right not to suffer unlawful deductions from wages) and Part X (unfair dismissal).

It is important to note that, unlike the position in respect of *conciliated* agreements, it is not possible to compromise TUPE claims relating to employee liability information or the duty to inform and consult. This is because the provisions dealing with these matters in regulations are not mentioned in S.18(2)(d) ETA. The fact that Regs 12(7) and 16(1), as we have seen, specifically state that S.18 shall apply to the rights conferred by relevant regulations and to proceedings brought to enforce those rights is not sufficient to enable these matters to be compromised. S.18(2)(d) itself restricts the scope for use of compromise agreements specifically to tribunal proceedings and claims under or arising out of the particular ERA provisions that it lists. Any claim that is not listed cannot therefore be the subject of a valid compromise agreement.

In respect of the TUPE claims that can be settled by compromise agreements, it **10.10** is necessary, in order to be valid, that any such agreement also complies with the stringent conditions specified in S.203(3)–(4) ERA. These are discussed in detail in IDS Employment Law Handbook, 'Employment Tribunal Practice and Procedure' (2006), Chapter 9 under 'Compromise agreements – statutory requirements'. Essentially, they require the agreement to be in writing, relate to 'particular proceedings' and to have been made only after the employee has received advice from a relevant independent adviser as to the terms and effect of the proposed agreement. In University of East London v Hinton 2005 ICR 1260, CA, the Court of Appeal interpreted the requirement for the agreement to 'relate to particular proceedings' to mean that the relevant proceedings had to be specifically identified. Thus, there had to be either a reference to the relevant statutory provisions or a phrase generically describing each type of

521

claim (e.g. 'unfair dismissal' or 'unlawful deductions from wages') that the parties intended to compromise. What was not acceptable was to use a rolled-up expression such as 'all statutory rights'.

10.11 **Waiver of contractual claims.** We have seen above that statutory claims such as unfair dismissal or deduction from wages can be settled by an Acas-conciliated settlement or a compromise agreement, and that, in addition to these, claims relating to breach of Reg 11 and 13 duties can also be settled, but only via an Acas-conciliated settlement. But what of breach of contract claims? Owing to the constraints that the TUPE Regulations themselves impose with regard to varying contractual terms and conditions, the capacity of the parties to reach valid compromises of breach of contract actions and claims is severely limited. Such claims do not fall within the categories of claim or proceeding capable of being settled by way of a compromise agreement, since they are not listed in S.18(2)(d) ETA, which is the provision that establishes the scope for making potentially valid compromise agreements (see above).

By way of contrast, breach of contract claims arising on termination of employment do come within the remit of an Acas conciliation officer's powers to take action to help the parties reach a conciliated settlement. This is because S.203(2)(e) ERA empowers a conciliation officer to take such action in respect of all the types of claim set out in S.18 rather than – as is the case in respect of compromise agreements – merely those set out in S.18(2)(d). S.18(2)(e) specifically extends the powers of the conciliation officer to 'proceedings in respect of which an employment tribunal has jurisdiction by virtue of S.3 of this Act', and S.3 is the provision that entitles the appropriate Minister to issue an Order conferring jurisdiction on employment tribunals to hear breach of contract claims. Such an Order – the Employment Tribunals Extension of Jurisdiction (England and Wales) Order 1994 SI 1994/1693 – was passed pursuant to the precursor of S.3 ETA. Article 4 of that Order makes it clear that a claim can be brought before a tribunal relating to damages for breach of contract provided that the sum claimed arises or is outstanding on the termination of the employee's employment.

10.12 However, there are two important factors that, in practice, limit the scope of parties to use the services of a conciliation officer to settle a breach of contract of claim in a TUPE context. First, only claims for breach of contract arising or outstanding on termination of employment up to the value of £25,000 fall within the jurisdiction of the employment tribunal. It would have to be questioned, therefore, whether a conciliation officer would be acting within his or her powers (or in any case would be willing to take action) in respect of claims that exceeded such an amount. Secondly, and more importantly, the scope for making valid and binding agreements to compromise claims based on changes to contractual terms and conditions brought about by a relevant transfer is very limited. The general rule, as we shall see below, is that a TUPE-

522

related variation will be void even if the employee agrees to the variation or enters into a conciliated settlement or compromise agreement restricting his or her right to bring action based on breach of contract to enforce his or her original terms.

Express exceptions enabling waiver of rights. Chapter 5, 'Changing terms **10.13** and conditions', was concerned with explaining the limited ability of the parties to negotiate valid changes to terms and conditions where it is the relevant transfer that prompts such changes. As we saw in that chapter, Reg 4(4) – which applies, along with the entirety of Reg 4, to employees who are employed by the transferor and assigned to the undertaking or organised grouping of resources being transferred immediately before the transfer – renders void any purported variation if either of the following applies:

- the sole or principal reason for the variation is the transfer itself

- the sole or principal reason is a transfer-connected reason that is not 'an economic, technical or organisational reason entailing a change in the workforce' (ETO reason).

As Reg 4(5) makes clear, only variations that are entirely unconnected to the transfer or which, if connected, are for an ETO reason, will be valid.

One significant exception to the rule that purported variations for transfer- **10.14** related reasons are void is where such variations are made in the course of insolvency proceedings. In this regard, Reg 8(7) provides for the entirety of Reg 4 to be disapplied where the relevant transfer occurs while the transferor is the subject of bankruptcy proceedings or any analogous insolvency proceedings that have been instituted with a view to the liquidation of its assets – see Chapter 6, under 'Bankruptcy and liquidation proceedings'. Furthermore, Reg 9 provides that, in the case of 'relevant insolvency proceedings' – i.e. proceedings that have been opened in relation to the transferor but not with a view to the liquidation of its assets – the transferor, transferee or insolvency practitioner can agree 'permitted variations' with appropriate representatives of employees assigned to the transferred undertaking that would otherwise be rendered void by Reg 4(4) – see Chapter 6, under '"Relevant insolvency proceedings" – changing terms and conditions'.

The only other way in which an employer may effectively bring about transfer-related variations is to dismiss employees and re-engage them on new terms. Obviously, an employer risks such dismissals being automatically unfair under Reg 7(1) for being principally by reason of the transfer or for a reason connected to the transfer that is not an ETO reason, but even if the dismissals are unfair, they will be effective to bring the old contract to an end. Any re-engagement will be on the new terms and will be valid, subject to the power of the employment tribunal subsequently ordering reinstatement on the previous terms as one of the remedies available for unfair dismissal – see Chapter 5

523

under 'Alternative strategies for effecting changes – dismissal and re-engagement on new terms'.

10.15 Putting all these 'strands' together, the position can be summarised as follows: the employer (whether it be the transferor pre-transfer or the transferee post-transfer) can implement binding contractual terms and conditions only if one of the following sets of circumstances obtain:

- there is a TUPE transfer but any variation to contractual terms and conditions is not transfer-related

- the variation to contractual terms is for an ETO reason

- the variation occurs while the transferor is subject to bankruptcy or analogous insolvency proceedings opened with a view to liquidation of its assets, or, in respect of other insolvency proceedings, comprises a 'permitted variation' negotiated with appropriate representatives

- a new contract of employment based on new terms is entered into following the termination of the previous contract. However, the employer is likely to be liable for unfair dismissal under Reg 7(1) unless the reason for dismissal can be shown not to relate to the transfer at all or, if it was so related, comprised an ETO reason within the meaning of Reg 7(2)

- the transferring employee has not expressly objected to the changes and has affirmed the contract such that any actionable claim for breach of contract in the courts while the employee remains employed is arguably lost at common law.

In the absence of one of these legitimate bases for effecting variations, any Acas agreement to settle a claim in relation to a non-ETO transfer related variation in terms would be void under Reg 18(1) of TUPE and S.203 ERA.

10.16 The difficulty in securing a valid settlement of a breach of contract claim in relation to a subsisting contract was underlined in Solectron Scotland Ltd v Roper and ors 2004 IRLR 4, EAT. The Appeal Tribunal in that case ruled that the precursor of Reg 18 – Reg 12 of the TUPE Regulations 1981 – would apply to exclude an agreement where employees formally retained their rights under TUPE but simply gave up their right to enforce those rights in the courts or tribunals. In the EAT's view, the retained rights would be of no value at all if they could not be enforced in a court of law. Thus, a compromise agreement could not be used as a back door route to effect a transfer-related variation by purporting to compromise a claim for breach of contract in relation to the transferor's or transferee's failure to comply with the original terms.

However, the EAT did accept that if the compromise agreement related to the re-engagement of employees on new terms following the prior termination of their employment, the agreement would be valid. On the facts of the Solectron case, the EAT ruled that compromise agreements signed by employees who were made redundant within months of their employment being transferred under TUPE were not rendered invalid by what is now Reg 18. It was true that, under TUPE, an employer cannot, after a transfer, vary the terms of an employee's contract if that variation is solely by reason of the transfer. However, in this case the effect of the compromise agreements was solely to compromise the financial claims that the employees had on the termination of their employment. The employer was not thereby trying to vary the employees' contracts, but to compromise a dispute as to their value. The dispute arose as to the sums due on termination of employment because there was disagreement as to whether the enhanced redundancy payments were still part of the employees' contracts. The fact that the dispute arose because of uncertainty as to the precise nature and scope of the terms transferred did not make the compromise agreements ones that had given rise to a variation in the terms of the contracts solely or even mainly by reason of the transfer.

It has been argued that the Solectron decision opens up the possibility of an **10.17** employer securing valid and consensual variations in terms and conditions by a process of terminating the employment to bring the contract to an end, and then entering a compromise of claims upon dismissal. But we would sound a note of caution about this. There remains a high risk that in a case where employment with the transferee continues on the revised terms after the compromise agreement has been signed (which is *not* what happened in the Solectron case), a tribunal would regard this as a strategy to avoid the effect of Reg 4(4). In that case, it could be contended that this strategy was in breach of Reg 18, with the result that the compromise agreement would be void so far as the breach of contract claims are concerned. There is also the point – not considered by the EAT in Solectron – that a compromise agreement cannot in any event be used to compromise an employee's right to bring a breach of contract claim over which an employment tribunal has jurisdiction under S.3 of the ETA. If this is so, then even if the 'termination followed by re-engagement strategy' were possible, the parties would need to compromise any breach of contract claims through an Acas-conciliated settlement.

Validity of contracting-out clauses in the transfer agreement **10.18**

The scope of Reg 18 extends to the commercial transaction between transferor and transferee. Thus, the non-contracting out rule will apply to the obligation on the transferor to notify the transferee of employee liability information under Reg 11. If the transferor fails to do so, the transferee can make a claim in the employment tribunal.

One consequence of the non-contracting out provision is that even if commercial agreement expressly stipulates that the transferee will waive its right to require this information, such waiver will not be capable of being relied upon should the transferee subsequently seek to bring a complaint to the

525

employment tribunal regarding a failure to supply the relevant information. That said, Reg 12(4)(b) provides that, in assessing compensation payable for failure under Reg 11, a tribunal shall have a particular regard to 'the terms of any contract between the transferor and the transferee'. In the light of this, the tribunal would no doubt take on board what the parties had previously agreed between themselves in assessing what was just and equitable to award by way of compensation.

10.19 Regulation 15 of the 2006 Regulations also contains provisions concerning complaints to an employment tribunal where an employer – whether the transferor or the transferee – is alleged to have failed to comply with Reg 13 (the duty to inform and consult) or Reg 14 (the election of employee representatives) – see Chapter 8 under 'Informing and consulting representatives'. Reg 15(9) makes the transferor and transferee jointly and severally liable whenever a transferor has failed to inform or consult in respect of affected employees or where the transferee has failed to comply with its duty relating to the election of employee representatives. Although the commercial parties will often apportion liability in respect of such failures as between themselves in the form of indemnities in the transfer agreement, Reg 18 operates to preclude them avoiding joint and several liability to pay any compensation due to employees.

As always, transferors and transferees should ensure that, in relation to the provisions where contracting out is prohibited, appropriate mutual warranties and indemnities are drafted in their commercial agreements. This will clarify upon whom the financial burden falls if there is any failure to comply with mandatory provisions of the Regulations.

10.20 # The course of a sale and purchase transfer

Purchasers, incoming contractors and other transferees will need to learn as much as possible about what precisely they are acquiring before being able to anticipate accurately the various liabilities that may arise. Once the risks are assessed, the precautions (in the form of conditions, warranties, restrictive covenants and indemnities) can then be taken. The old maxim 'caveat emptor' remains true, as one of the basic thrusts of the Regulations is to pass employee liabilities on a TUPE transfer from the transferor to the transferee.

As we have seen in Chapter 1, the TUPE Regulations 2006 cover three different types of transaction. These are:

- a group reorganisation where the businesses in a group are restructured and come under the ownership of different legal entities but are all ultimately controlled by the same parent

- the sale or disposal of a business to a third party, including the creation of joint ventures, company takeovers and privatisations

- outsourcing (service provision change) where an activity previously performed in house is contracted out to a third party (outsourcing), or where such a contract is re-let, or where it is taken back in house (insourcing).

These are very different transactions where different considerations will apply **10.21** in practice, but in any commercial transaction based on a sale and purchase of a business the three principal variables are price, warranties and indemnities. In relation to outsourcing agreements, a further significant variable is the duration of the service contract. If the potential liability for employment claims can be identified precisely and quantified, then the simple way to deal with such liability is through a variation in the price of the business. However, things are seldom so clear cut. For example, the commercial negotiations may not be straightforward and the relative bargaining strength of the parties may not allow for significant price negotiation. Furthermore, even if the liabilities can be identified and precisely quantified, there is no guarantee that all the potential employment claims will actually be brought, let alone succeed. Thus a reduction in the price of the maximum amount of the potential claims may be unrealistic. It might, however, be possible to hold back part of the purchase price until an agreed date (e.g. until the expiration of the statutory time limits for claims) and/or to deal with this through indemnities and warranties.

Typical stages of a transfer
10.22

The degree of complexity involved in a transfer will principally depend, of course, upon the size of the undertaking being transferred. It will also depend on the corporate or organisational structure into which the newly acquired business is to be fitted. Typically, however, a more involved transfer in the form of the sale and purchase of a business will have the following stages:

- *pre-contractual negotiations.* The intending transferee will attempt to determine, in general terms, whether the undertaking has the trading position and reputation which the transferor claims for it. The transferee may involve his solicitors and accountants in examining published accounts and other statutory information as well as making company searches. The negotiations at this stage will usually determine the form that the transfer will take; the price to be paid; preparation of the commercial sale agreement; disclosure of information by the transferor; and then exchange of contract

- *post-contract investigation and approval.* The transferee will probably instruct his accountants to investigate the accounting and financial aspects of the business to a greater depth than previously, with a view to their verifying the warranties, representations and disclosures made by the transferor prior to exchange. The transferee's solicitors will further investigate the business's freehold and leasehold properties and may ask the transferor's solicitors to compose a report as to title and vouch for the accuracy of that report. In a case where prior shareholders' approval is necessary, a condition precedent will be drawn up which will make purchase of the business conditional upon such approval being obtained. Usually, the approval of shareholders to the transaction is required where the value of the assets being acquired by the transferee equals or exceeds 25 per cent of the value of the assets of the acquiring company

- *completion.* This will usually include a special meeting of the transferor's board of directors; delivery of statutory books, title deeds and other completion documents; and payment of any cash consideration. The transferee and his accountants will usually meet after the transfer in order to determine whether there is any need to bring claims for breach of warranty by the transferor. Human Resources will normally issue TUPE transfer letters to the transferring employees and ensure that any relevant TUPE objection letters have been provided by the transferor

- *post-completion integration.* On completion, the transferee will need to ensure the successful integration of the new business into its existing activities. This will entail communication with the transferring employees, managing cultural differences and implementing changes to the target company after completion. Human Resources may need to deal with any post-transfer redundancy dismissals and manage the tricky process of harmonising the terms and conditions of employment of the transferring employees with the rest of the workforce. A post-acquisition audit may also be carried out to monitor the success of the business transfer.

10.23 It is a common experience that transfers do not fully follow this pattern because negotiations and investigations become greatly protracted. Sometimes this causes the date for exchange of contracts to be postponed so that the exchange occurs at the same time as completion. The danger of this is that both parties are left free to pull out of the negotiations. On the one hand, the transferee may find that he has been gazumped after having incurred substantial and irrecoverable costs during the process of the negotiation and investigation by his solicitors and accountants. On the other, the transferor may find that it has put all its eggs in one basket and has let other opportunities for a lucrative sale slip by. Also, the exposure for a protective award is high as there would be no opportunity to carry out TUPE information and consultation. One way to avoid the expense and inconvenience of such disappointments is for the transferee to exchange contracts at the earliest possible stage on the basis of the transferor's representations and warranties. A deferred completion date can then be arranged to allow for full pre-completion investigations to take place in order to verify the transferor's claims. The sale agreement, in such circumstances, usually preserves the transferee's right to bring claims for breach of warranty after completion even where his investigations before completion had not disclosed any breach.

Due diligence

Due diligence is the process by which formal investigations are carried out in relation to the company or undertaking that is subject to the TUPE transfer prior to its transfer. The essential purpose is for the transferee to obtain as much information as possible about the target business. If carried out thoroughly, the process will help the transferee to identify any potential problems and avoid any unexpected costs and liabilities following completion of the sale or other disposition. Whether the transfer is the sale and purchase of a business or a service provision change, the disclosure of information that forms a key part of due diligence is essential.

Regulation 11 lists the employee liability information that has to be notified by the transferor to the transferee (see Chapter 8 under 'Employee liability information'). This provision – new to the 2006 Regulations – is particularly designed to reduce uncertainty in second generation outsourcing arrangements, where the lack of a direct connection between outgoing and incoming contractor can make it difficult for a transferee to obtain information about the employee liabilities for which it will become responsible. However, the obligation will apply to all transfers and is not limited to outsourcing situations.

In some simple small-scale cases, this employee liability information may be **10.25** sufficient, and in some service provision changes, this may be all the information that is received. However, in most cases a transferee would want more information at an earlier date than merely that which is required by Reg 11.

The many decisions that have to be taken by the transferee in the course of negotiations leading to the purchase of a business can only be effectively made once it has acquired accurate information about the target undertaking or activities. Also, the transferee will only be in a position to assess the prospects of the business and the risks and costs involved once such information has been fully disclosed. It is important that the information is not just collated but is analysed to assess risks. The analysis can identify 'hidden' costs and problems for the transferee. For example, specific deal-breaker issues that can arise from disclosure are: occupational pension problems; enhanced redundancy pay arrangements that are very expensive where rationalisation is essential; and health and safety issues and discrimination issues, where there are serious and extensive problems that may not only prove very expensive but may adversely impact on the reputation of the transferee if the deal proceeds.

Subject to Reg 11, how much information is disclosed is clearly a matter of **10.26** balance depending on each particular transaction: too much, and the transferee may feel flooded with information that it cannot properly assess; too little, and the transferee may miss vital data that has serious commercial implications.

529

As a general rule, the transferee should, through its lawyers and accountants, seek the kinds of information set out below.

10.27 Employee details

- names and addresses
- ages
- sex, race, disability
- dates from which continuous employment began
- identification of which employees are key personnel
- details of employees who are in active service and those who are on leave of absence (e.g. maternity leave, sabbatical leave and secondment)
- resignation letters
- amounts of salaries/wages
- other remunerative benefits (e.g. commissions, bonuses)
- normal working hours and overtime arrangements
- notice entitlements
- holidays and holiday pay
- job grades
- sickness absence, sick pay and permanent health insurance entitlements
- membership of or participation in other benefit schemes (e.g. private health plans, life assurance, pension, company car provision or car allowance)
- restrictive covenants, confidentiality agreements and intellectual property agreements
- details of any grievance raised by employees or any disciplinary action taken over the last 2 years.

The purpose of these details is to determine the entitlements of each employee (both financially and in terms of employment rights), and to assess the extent to which variation or harmonisation of contractual terms may have to be considered following the transfer. These details, combined with the employment data set out below, can also be used to build up a picture of how flexible the terms and conditions of employment are, and whether there are any particular problems.

10.28 Non-employee details
This would include details – including their terms of engagement – of any atypical workers such as consultants, workers and agency workers, so that the transferee can determine their employment status and termination arrangements.

Demographics

10.29

- numbers of weekly and monthly paid employees

- salary bands and total employment costs

- number of temporary and part-time staff

- number of consultants, trainees, apprentices, casual workers and self-employed

- number and identity of employees on maternity, paternity and dependant leave or off work due to long-term sickness

- absence records

- ethnic breakdown of workforce

- sex breakdown of workforce

- age breakdown of workforce

- job evaluation structures in force.

The purpose of these enquiries is to identify any latent discrimination or equal pay problems, to ascertain potential problems of incompatibility with the transferee's existing business(es) and to establish who is working in the business and in what capacity, and whether there are any significant absenteeism problems. The process of due diligence should be used to enable the transferee to identify which employees are assigned to the undertaking or grouping of workers at the time of the transfer, and an accurate list of the names of such employees should be linked to an appropriate indemnity protecting the transferee in respect of costs or liabilities arising from the transfer of employees who are not on the list.

Contractual documentation

10.30

The written contracts of all employees (including directors) will be valuable, especially where the transferee intends to implement job changes or changes to other terms and conditions after the transfer. If this would be too onerous in terms of the sheer number of employees who are liable to be transferred, then sample contracts should be asked for and supplied. The following documents might contain contractual provisions or evidence of them in the absence of a comprehensive written contract of employment:

- S.1 ERA written statement of terms and conditions

- sample offer letters

- job descriptions

- company rules and policies (e.g. whistleblowing, computer misuse, family-friendly policies, drugs and alcohol, data protection)

531

- disciplinary and grievance procedures
- staff handbooks.

10.31 Pay and benefits

- basic pay
- pension schemes
- employee share schemes
- company cars/petrol or other travel allowances (including loans)
- bonus/profit-sharing/commissions/long-term incentive plans
- insurance-based benefits, such as permanent health insurance and private health plans (e.g. BUPA)
- mortgage subsidies and relocation packages
- redundancy schemes
- contractual sick pay arrangements.

Many of the above arrangements will be contractual, with the consequence that entitlement to the benefits of such schemes will continue if employees' contracts of employment are transferred. The financial implications of this therefore ought to be considered. Even if the benefits are non-contractual (e.g. discretionary), any discontinuation or change in the basis on which, or level at which, they are paid may provide grounds for an employee to resign and claim that he or she has suffered a substantial change to working conditions to his or her material detriment within the meaning of Reg 4(9). In that case, the employee will be regarded as having been dismissed and will, it seems, be entitled to bring a claim of unfair dismissal on that basis – see Chapter 4 under 'Material detriment dismissals'. In the case of pension schemes, although Reg 10 excludes such schemes from the operation of automatic transfer of contracts provided for by Reg 4, the problems about occupational pensions when there are to be transfers remain, and there are now minimum statutory legal requirements that have to be met – see Chapter 3 under 'Rights and liabilities that do not transfer – terms relating to pensions'). While occupational pension issues can involve substantial sums of money, there are often other contentious issues, such as company car arrangements.

10.32 Directors and senior executives

- names of all executives and non-executive directors
- details of directors' fees paid within a prescribed period and due to be paid in the current year

- details of all directors' other interests

- copies of senior executives' service agreements

- copies of confidentiality agreements, restrictive covenants and intellectual property agreements

- details of special benefits (e.g. company apartments and special bonus or share option schemes).

The employment contracts will need to be examined in detail with a view to assessing employment costs, potential termination costs and how such contracts will operate in the context of the transferee's business.

Collective issues 10.33

- details of trade union presence within the undertaking and union recognition

- any applications for statutory trade union recognition

- industrial dispute history

- arbitration awards

- wages and salary review dates

- current state of employer-union negotiations

- details of any consultation committees

- health and safety policies and related matters, such as health and safety representatives and committees, with a record of any prohibition or improvement notices

- collective and workplace agreements, including working time opt outs

- requests made under the Information and Consultation of Employees Regulations 2004 SI 2004/3426.

Miscellaneous matters 10.34

- tied accommodation commitments

- loans to employees

- lay-off and guarantee payment provisions

- actual and potential employment-related litigation, as well as investigations and inquiries by the Equal Opportunities Commission, the Commission for Racial Equality and the Disability Rights Commission (or, from 1 October 2007, the Commission for Equality and Human Rights); this information should include personal injury as well as employment law claims

533

- policies on equal opportunities, data protection, redundancy, and family-friendly policies

- disabled staff and details of reasonable adjustments that have been made or requested

- normal retirement age and details of any justification for relying on a retirement age of below 65

- flexible working arrangements (including part-time, job-sharing and homeworking).

The ways in which this type of information is disclosed vary. The main methods are for all the information to be put into a data room by the transferor for inspection by potential transferees, or for the transferor to respond to the transferee's questions in open correspondence. Alternatively, the transferor may give the transferee an open letter that makes all the general and specific disclosures of information.

10.35 Confidentiality and data protection

Given the specific requirements in the Regulations to provide employee liability information under Reg 11, all potential transferors, but most particularly contractors, should ensure that their data protection policies allow for the necessary retention of personal data so that they are in a position to retrieve the requisite information.

Previously, there has been uncertainty as to whether the Data Protection Act 1998 required information relating to employees to be disclosed on an anonymous basis, and the general practice has been to disclose it in anonymised form. However, the UK Information Commissioner has confirmed that the DPA does allow employers to disclose personal employee data on a named basis as required by TUPE 2006 – see 'Employment Practices Code – Supplementary Guidance' (June 2005), p.72.

Notwithstanding the Information Commissioner's guidance, it remains advisable for transferors to ensure that explicit consent for the transfer of data in the event of a sale of the business (within Great Britain and, where appropriate, outside of the European Union) has been obtained from the employees in their contracts of employment. This is particularly so in situations where the information disclosed is wider than that prescribed under statutory due diligence. In addition, transferors might consider imposing confidentiality obligations in the sales agreement and/or during negotiations which extend to requiring the return of personalised information if the sales transaction falls through.

Common practical transfer issues 10.36

The transferor and transferee need to consider how to handle the employment aspects of the transfer. The key to successful TUPE transfers lies in good planning, including identifying key risks at an early stage and holding a genuine dialogue with employees about the sale of the business and the impact this is likely to have on the workforce. Fear of change is a natural human instinct and frank communication from the management is essential to ensure the business transfer proceeds smoothly. For example, what will be the attitude of affected employees and their representatives to the transfer? Have they the power to disrupt the deal, and what concessions or promises may have to be made to them?

Issues to be managed on transfer 10.37
Set out below are the common practical challenges that need to be managed by transferors and transferees:

Representations to affected employees. The decision in Hagen and ors v ICI 10.38 Chemicals and Polymers Ltd and ors 2002 IRLR 31, QBD, is an excellent example of the dangers of making promises to ease the deal which are then not kept. That case concerned occupational pensions, which, along with redundancies, is the area usually of most concern to employees who may be affected by the transfer. While the decision in the Hagen case was about misrepresentation, the decision in Gill and ors v Cape Contracts Ltd 1985 IRLR 499, QBD, is about breach of warranty when the prospective employer does not deliver on promises made. In this non-TUPE case, the employees were induced to give up their employment at Harland and Wolff in Northern Ireland on the basis of a representation that they would be employed at Sullom Voe in the Shetland Islands by Cape Contracts on much higher wages. However, after they had left Harland and Wolff but before they started work at Sullom Voe, Cape Contracts cancelled the offers of employment due to threat of industrial action by employees at Sullom Voe. The High Court held that the representation was a warranty in the collateral contract between Cape Contracts and the employees to give up their existing work and go to work at Sullom Voe, and this warranty had been broken, entitling the employees to damages.

Employees or their representatives sometimes ask for guarantees of no compulsory redundancies within specified periods of time after a transfer, and for guarantees by the transferor to pay redundancy payments if the transferee becomes insolvent. If such concessions are made, then they can be included in the commercial agreement, but often the best way of the transferor guaranteeing redundancy payments in the event of transferee insolvency is to make the promise directly with the employees through their representatives as part of the collective consultation process.

535

10.39 **Identifying the employees who are 'in scope'.** Although it may seem obvious and easy to resolve, there are often problems surrounding exactly who are the transferred employees. The supply of a provisional list of transferring employees prior to exchange of contract and the provision of a finalised list prior to completion are therefore indispensable. This requires the transferor to plan and organise in advance exactly who is and who is not going to transfer, but the transferee should also take steps to ensure that it is clear about the individual identity of the transferred workforce and to clear up discrepancies in this regard. So, for example, in some transfer situations – particularly where an integrated large business is being broken up – there will be those who do some work for the undertaking or activity being transferred but do other work for other parts of the transferor organisation. There will also be situations where an employee is employed by the company due to be sold but is seconded to another subsidiary within the group structure. Some employees (especially managers) may provide key services to different parts of the organisation. This raises the question of which employees are assigned to the undertaking or part of it that is being transferred – see Chapter 2, under '"Assigned" to the undertaking transferred'. In such cases, it must be decided what will happen to these employees when there is a transfer, and if some are to transfer, which ones will do so and which will remain with the transferor. Obviously the views of the transferee may be important, but it is common in larger transfers for employees providing common services to be allocated to a specific business in advance of any transfer. Therefore if that specific business is transferred then the employees allocated to it will transfer. This process of allocation is not without risks of breach of employment contract, and the process itself will alert employees and their representatives as to what is being planned and precipitate the need for information and consultation. In practice, it is usually the employees who believe they will be transferred who will be the most concerned, as employees normally prefer to stay with their existing employer rather than transfer to the unknown.

Another common problem about which employees are to transfer arises with larger and more complex organisations. This is that there are employees working full time in the business to be transferred who should transfer except that they are not employed by the transferor but by some associated organisation or company. In these cases, the employees may need to be moved from employment with the associated company into the employment of the transferor prior to the transfer.

10.40 **Insurance-based benefits, such as permanent health insurance.** If, for example, employees who are to be transferred are away on long-term sickness leave and in receipt of benefits under insurance-based sickness or disability policies, then the transferee will inherit the duty to make equivalent payments, but the benefit of the policy to fund such payments will not pass to the transferee – see Chapter 3 under 'Rights and liabilities that do not transfer – tortious and other civil liabilities'. Furthermore, even if the transferee has existing similar insurance arrangements, it cannot be expected that the insurer will automatically cover the transferred long-term sick employees. Therefore there will often be issues to be resolved prior to the transfer about these insurance-based benefits.

Restrictive covenants. The restrictive covenants in employees' contracts of employment will have been drafted to be appropriate to the circumstances of the transferor prior to the transferee. They may, however, be inappropriate and unenforceable in the circumstances of the transferee after the transfer (see Chapter 3, under 'Rights and liabilities relating to the individual – restrictive covenants'). If such covenants are of real importance to the transferee, and there is a real risk that the existing covenants will be unenforceable or inappropriate, then the issue needs to be resolved either at the time of the transfer or soon afterwards with the individuals concerned. Difficulties can arise, however, with variations to contractual terms and conditions made after a relevant transfer for a reason connected to the transfer, since, if these are made for a reason related to the transfer and are to the detriment of the employee, they may well be rendered void – see Chapter 5, under 'Varying terms in a TUPE context'. **10.41**

Redundancy. If the transferee plans redundancies soon after the transfer and the deal only makes commercial sense if there is major rationalisation, then disclosed information that shows that the redundancy exercise will be very expensive will be a problem. For example, the disclosed information may show that there is an enhanced redundancy payments scheme that has become incorporated into individuals' contracts of employment and/or that there is an agreement about redundancy procedures or redundancy selection criteria that the transferee does not wish to follow. It is of course very difficult to negotiate successfully to reduce such benefits, or to change redundancy procedures or redundancy criteria, and so there will often be a discussion about how the transferor may help the transferee with the cost of the redundancies. This could be by varying the price or by sharing the cost of redundancies when they arise. The transferor would need to take care as to the precise basis on which it makes any promise to contribute to redundancy costs. The amount of a redundancy payment is dynamic in the sense that it is based on wages and service at the time of dismissal over which the transferor will have no control once the transfer has been completed. **10.42**

'Piggy backing' on the transferor's redundancy consultation. Where the transferee operates from a different geographical location, a 'place of work redundancy' may well arise in relation to the transferring employees. Many transferees in such a situation will need to effect the redundancy dismissals on the day of the transfer and so will not be in a position to consult with the affected employees for 30 or 90 days as the case may be prior to the first dismissal. The commercial solution is for the transferee to ask the transferor to **10.43**

537

effect collective consultation on its behalf to avoid the risks of protective awards. As the legality of such 'piggy back' arrangements has yet to be tested in the tribunals, appropriate indemnities should be negotiated by the transferor.

10.44 **Pensions.** Although occupational pensions are excluded by Reg 10 from automatic transfer, this does not resolve the problem about what will happen with regard to employees' pension rights following the transfer. This will always be an issue of great concern to affected employees and their representatives and the sums of money involved can often have a major impact on the deal. The current law about occupational pension protection on transfer, if explained clearly, can help address employees' concerns (see Chapter 3 under 'Rights and liabilities that do not transfer – terms relating to pensions').

10.45 **Bonus and share option schemes.** It is likely that there will be problems about the automatic transfer of these arrangements from the transferor to the transferee (see Chapter 3 under 'Rights and liabilities relating to the individual'). The practical issues are likely to be how to replicate comparable benefits that make sense in the circumstances of the transferee's business or whether to buy out such arrangements.

10.46 **Harmonisation.** Transferees for a variety of reasons often wish to harmonise the terms and conditions of employment of the transferred employees with their existing workforces. The information disclosed by the due diligence exercise will show how different the terms and conditions of employment are between the transferred employees and the existing employees of the transferor and thus reveal the scale of the problem. All methods of achieving harmonisation, including 'red circling', agreed variation of employment contracts and dismissal and re-engagement with a compromise agreement, involve significant risks (see Chapter 5, under 'Harmonising terms and conditions' and 'Alternative strategies for effecting changes').

10.47 **Accrued holiday pay and loans.** At the time of transfer, there will probably be transferring employees who have accrued holiday pay that they have not taken. There may also be outstanding loans made by the transferor to some employees. Unless specific apportionment arrangements are made, the transferee is likely to benefit from the repayment of employee loans rather than the transferor, but the transferee will have to grant holiday and holiday pay for holidays accrued while the employees were working for the transferor. The importance of these issues will depend on the circumstances of each proposed transfer but in the case of TUPE transfers comprising service provision changes, the size of the sums involved can often be substantial.

10.48 **Transferee's access to the transferring employees before the transfer date.** It is not uncommon for the transferee to request access to the transferor's workforce prior to the transfer date in order to discuss the business transfer. A transferor who is willing to agree to such arrangements will need to ensure that measures are put in place to protect itself from any pre-transfer dismissals by vetting the proposed communications and contents of any corporate presentations and by negotiating appropriate indemnities.

Service provision changes (outsourcing)

10.49

There are a number of important differences between the sale and purchase of a business and outsourcing, even though both are covered by the TUPE Regulations. Particular issues tend to arise in an outsourcing context, and these are highlighted below.

When there is a sale and purchase of a business there will be a contract between the transferor and transferee, but there is no such contractual link between one contractor and a successor contractor where there is a service provision change. The contractors are likely to be rivals and may be reluctant to cooperate where one may be losing the contract and the other winning it. It is for this reason that the introduction of the employee liability information provision in Reg 11 is important, as it should ensure the flow of basic employee information where there is a service provision change. In any event, the client remains in the central position. The client will have the contractual and financial links when granting and administering the commercial contract to control the relationship between the outgoing and incoming contractors. Thus the commercial contracts between the client and respective contractors often contain 'employment entry provisions' at the start of the contract and 'employment exit provisions' when the contract is terminated so as to better regulate the handover procedure to be observed when a change of contractor is imminent.

Unlike a sale and purchase, the client often wishes to provide in the commercial contract that the contractor cannot sub-contract or assign, but must do the work itself. Further, the client will often want to control through the commercial contract the terms and conditions of employment of the contractor's employees who are employed on the client's contract. This is frequently to help the client control costs, maintain standards and prevent manipulation of the contract, particularly where there may be a change of contractor. **10.50**

Another difference between a sale and purchase agreement and an outsourcing agreement is that the client may wish through the commercial contract to have some degree of control over the quality and number of personnel employed to service the particular contractual activity and over changes to such personnel. The reasons for this are that the client will want to maintain service standards and retain staff who might have special knowledge of the client's work, as well as preventing contractors about to lose contracts from removing good staff from the contract and replacing them with poor staff. Also, in sensitive working environments such as the financial services industry, governmental bodies, prisons and schools, the client might wish to retain a veto over who is allowed access to its premises. On the other hand, contractors themselves will usually

539

look for some degree of flexibility over the issue of who they assign to work on a particular contract to enable them to move employees from one contract to another as business needs demand.

10.51 The client in outsourcing arrangements will often have the contractor's staff working on the client's premises and this raises a number of special issues that can be covered in the commercial contract. For example, the client may wish to specify that the contractor's staff comply with the client's policies such as discrimination while working on the client's premises, data protection, professional code of conduct and any compliance issues imposed by a regulator (e.g. the Financial Services Authority). The client may also require the contractor's staff to comply with the health and safety and security arrangements established by the client when the contractor's staff are on the client's premises. In some cases the client may want to have the right to require the contractor to remove any of its staff who are in breach of these policies, and replace them with staff who will comply with the client's policies.

Finally, 'standstill' provisions are normally found in the outsourcing agreement restricting the outgoing contractor's ability to effect changes between the period when notice for termination of the contract has been given by the client and the expiry of the contract. Typical restrictions include:

- increasing the total number of the contractor's personnel save for the purposes of fulfilling certain projects or assignments previously agreed with the client

- changing the terms and conditions of employment of the contractor's personnel

- increasing the proportion of working time spent by the contractor's personnel without the consent of the client

- replacing any of the contractor's personnel with other persons engaged to provide the services

- terminating the employment of the contractor's personnel

- introducing any new contractual or customary practice concerning the making of lump sum payments on the termination of employment of the contractor's personnel.

10.52 Conditions precedent

The transferee (and occasionally the transferor) may well wish to make the purchase of the business conditional upon certain events happening. To this end, conditions precedent can be inserted into the sale agreement which will have to be satisfied before completion takes place. Where such conditions are not met, the sale or disposition of the business will fall through, and the transferee will be entitled to claim damages (unless agreement to the contrary has been made). Such conditions may include the following:

- that the transferor continue to conduct the business in the ordinary way until completion

- that the transferor will not, prior to completion, do anything which may materially prejudice the business or any of the assets to be transferred

- that a full opportunity be afforded by the transferor to the transferee and its advisers to investigate and verify the business and assets to be transferred

- that the sale agreement be submitted for approval by an ordinary resolution of shareholders of the transferee at a duly convened general meeting of the transferee to be held by a specified date

- that the transferee reimburse all of the transferor's reasonable expenses in the event that the transferee's shareholders fail to approve the transfer; and further, that the transferor reimburse all the transferee's reasonable costs in the event that the latter rescinds the agreement on account of breach of condition by the transferor.

10.53 Sometimes the transferee will want the transferor to make changes to the business being transferred before it is transferred. These types of changes may be sufficiently important to be made conditions precedent in the commercial agreement. If these changes involve pre-transfer dismissals of employees and/or variations of employment contracts by the transferor to suit the transferee, then it will be important to bear in mind that the dismissal may well be unfair under Reg 7 and the attempted variations of employment contracts may be rendered void by virtue of Reg 4(4) (see Chapters 4 and 5 respectively).

Warranties

10.54

The transferee, and to a lesser extent the transferor, will need to feel confident that the representations made by the other side are true and accurate. Disclosure of information and due diligence will, if thorough, go a long way towards establishing this. But there is always the danger of an item being overlooked, undiscovered, and even sometimes deliberately disguised. For this reason, the parties will often make express written warranties that vouchsafe the statements each has made to the other concerning the important aspects of the transaction.

A warranty is a contractual assurance from the transferor to the transferee. It is a subsidiary or collateral provision to the main purpose of the transfer agreement. Thus, in the event that the representations made prove false or inaccurate, the innocent party will be entitled to sue to recover damages as a result. However, the transferor is only responsible for the loss and damage that is foreseeable as a result of the breach. Furthermore, breach of a warranty does

541

not afford the transferee the right to rescind the contract as in the case of a breach of condition.

10.55 The use of warranties is common but obviously much depends on the nature of the deal, the bargaining strengths of the parties and the disclosure process. Whereas transferees, if they can, will seek extensive warranties to back up disclosure, transferors will be pulling in the opposite direction to limit their warranties, for example by words that qualify the warranty. Often, a minimum liability floor is agreed whereby only sums in excess of the specified minimum will trigger indemnity payments. It is also common to agree if the transferor's liability for breach of warranty should be capped on a 'per claim' or 'aggregate claim' basis.

Usually warranties are given by the transferor to the transferee rather than vice versa. Warranties can be general – for example, about the state of the business – or specific, and can cover both acts and omissions. Warranties can relate to facts or to compliance with legislation.

10.56 The kinds of warranty which typically may be made are:

- that all the employees listed in [specify letter or document] will transfer but no other employees

- that the appropriate representatives have been informed and consulted in accordance with Reg 13 by the transferor

- that the disclosed data (including the employee liability information under Reg 11) is full and accurate

- that there is no threatened or impending industrial dispute

- that there is no recognised trade union except that which has been disclosed and that there are no outstanding applications for recognition

- that there are no outstanding claims to tribunals or other courts or facts which could give rise to such claims

- that no contract or service agreement exists which cannot be lawfully terminated on less than [three] months' notice

- that no profit share or bonus agreements are in force other than those already disclosed

- that the transferee warrants that it has informed the transferor of all measures the transferee will take in respect of transferred employees

- that all PAYE, national insurance, pension contributions, remuneration and expenses are paid up to the transfer date

- that there have been no resignations or dismissals in connection with the relevant transfer (other than those which may have already been disclosed)

- that all details of formal and informal agreements have been disclosed

- that the transferor has complied with all recommendations made by Acas in relation to the transferring employees and with all awards and declarations made by the Central Arbitration Committee in relation to the transferring employees

- that employee liability information has been provided by the transferor in a readily accessible form and is true and accurate in all material respects

- that the transferor has obtained all necessary proofs of legal status for the purposes of the Immigration, Asylum and Nationality Act 2006

- that there is not at present a claim, occurrence or state of affairs which may give rise to a claim against the transferee arising out of the employment or termination of employment of the transferring employees for compensation for loss of office or employment.

Short form of warranty   10.57

In more simple cases, a short and general warranty might be appropriate. If, however, it is used to cover a multitude of sins, then the transferor may put himself at risk of incurring substantial liabilities. The short form of warranty may approximate to the following: 'The Vendor warrants to the Purchaser: (1) that the accounts have been correctly prepared in accordance with good accounting practice and make full provision and reserve for all accruing and accrued liabilities and commitments of the Vendor in relation to the business at the balance sheet date, and show a true and fair view of the profitability and assets and liabilities of the Vendor employed in the business; and (2) that there are no adverse matters apparent from the accounts and which have not been disclosed in a disclosure letter dated [insert date] from the Vendor's solicitors to the Purchaser.'

Duration of warranties   10.58

From the transferor's point of view, the warranty clauses may prove (or at least threaten) to be a millstone round his neck. In order to place some limit upon the period for which he remains liable for the representations made in the sale agreement, the transferor will usually insist upon a clause providing for a period (e.g. 12 months from the date of completion) in which he must be notified of any claim(s) for breach of warranty intended to be brought by the transferee. It is not uncommon for a term to be inserted on the transferee's part, waiving any claim or claims which do not in aggregate amount to or exceed a specified sum.

Restrictive covenants   10.59

Restraint of trade clauses are important means, especially for smaller businesses providing services, by which the transferee of a business may seek to prevent the transferor (or the transferor's former employees) from setting up in direct

543

competition against him. The presence of such restrictive covenants is a good indication that the transferee has acquired the goodwill of the transferor's business. However, such covenants are notoriously difficult to enforce, and the practicability of their enforcement depends greatly upon the extent to which they are drawn circumspectly in order to meet the legitimate and reasonable needs of the business and no more. Breach of any covenant can be remedied by way of injunction and/or damages to the extent that the terms of the covenant are reasonable in the circumstances.

A typical covenant may impose the following kinds of restraints:

'(1) The Vendor shall observe (and shall procure its officers and use bona fide endeavours to procure the employees to observe) strict confidence in relation to the Business and the Assets Transferred to the extent that and for so long as information relating to the Business and Assets Transferred is confidential and not in the public domain.

(2) For a period of [X] months following completion the Vendor shall not, either alone or jointly with others or directly or indirectly and whether as principal, agent, or employee, invest or otherwise be directly or indirectly engaged or concerned or interested within the area specified in (3) below in any business which competes directly or indirectly with the Purchaser's continuance of the Business in succession to the Vendor.

(3) The area referred to in (2) above is: (a) [X] miles radius of the premises; and (b) any other part of the United Kingdom in which any director or employee of the Vendor has had a territorial responsibility for sales or customer service within the [X] months prior to completion; and (c) any other part of the [European Union] in which the Vendor has had an active trading interest with which any director or employee of the Vendor was actively and personally engaged within the [X] months prior to completion.'

10.60 It will also be usual to insert clauses that require the transferor to procure that the directors and certain named key employees enter into new restrictive covenants with the transferee so that the terms of the covenant are contemporary and of particular relevance to the business of the transferee, so increasing the chances of being enforceable in the courts (see Chapter 3, 'What transfers?', under 'Rights and liabilities relating to the individual – restrictive covenants').

10.61 # Indemnities

Very often contingencies arise that may cause loss to the transferor or transferee. In order to protect against such eventualities, the parties to a transfer deal will usually deploy contractual indemnities. Unlike a warranty, an indemnity is a promise to reimburse the other party in respect of a particular type of liability, should it arise. The purpose of an indemnity is to provide guaranteed compensation to the other party in circumstances in which a breach of warranty would not necessarily give rise to a claim for damages or to provide a specific remedy that might not otherwise be legally available.

Typical liabilities (depending on the nature of the event indemnified) include claims for damages, legal costs, compensation, expenses, fines, court awards and penalties. The basic aim is to apportion the financial liability between the parties for employment costs associated with the transfer. Frequently, the indemnity will be in respect of a particular risk disclosed by the transferor either during due diligence or in a disclosure letter, e.g. where information reveals the risks of certain employee grievances leading to discrimination claims. The indemnity will give the transferee in this instance an ability to get recompense without necessarily having to sue in the civil courts. It may be, for example, that the parties agree to hold a specified sum of money in the joint names of their solicitors for a fixed period of time out of which any indemnity can be made. There is also a role for indemnities in a service provision change, but as explained earlier, these have been arranged through the client's contracts with the outgoing and incoming contractors, as no contract will exist between the outgoing contractor (transferor) and incoming contractor (transferee).

The range and scope of indemnities largely depend on the relative bargaining **10.62** strength of the respective parties. The nature of the indemnities will also reflect decisions which the parties have had to make in the course of negotiations concerning on whose shoulders the burden lies in respect of compensating for events that cause loss. When indemnities are used, the parties will have to agree between themselves whether full recompense is to be made or merely a percentage of the loss actually incurred. In some cases, a maximum (or cap) is agreed either on a per-employee basis or as a total covering liabilities in respect of all the employees transferred. Sometimes, instead of indemnities being used, the purchase price will be adjusted in accordance with decisions about, for example, who is to pay redundancy payments or monies in lieu of notice. But the complexity and uncertainties of many business transfer situations and the ever-present danger of nasty surprises more often than not make the process of detailed indemnification an essential commercial exercise.

There is usually a consensus among the parties to the transfer that the transferor will indemnify the transferee for all acts and omissions prior to the transfer date, and that the transferee will likewise indemnify the transferor for all acts and omissions after the transfer date – so called 'mirror indemnities'. The same arrangement is perfectly possible as between a client and contractor in a first generation change of service provider. However, difficulties arise in the case of a second generation change of service provider as there will be no commercial contract between the outgoing and incoming contractors. A solution is for the client to impose on both contractors mutual 'own watch' indemnities whereby each contractor agrees to hold the client and any predecessor or successor

545

contractor indemnified against all employment liabilities relating to the period for which it is or was responsible for operating the service contract. In other words, the 'mirror indemnities' agreed between the client and the contractor are replicated and cascade downwards in the event of a subsequent service provision change. In practice, the preponderance of the liability risk tends to be with the transferee because of the automatic transfer of employment provisions in Reg 4, which means that it will usually be the transferee who is the most assiduous in ensuring that appropriate indemnities are agreed.

10.63 Indemnities can cover a very wide variety of matters. For example, an indemnity might specifically deal with the legal expenses incurred as a result of, or in connection with, the transfer, and both commercial parties will have an interest in securing their position in this regard. This is because it is common in employment litigation relating to transfers for employees to bring proceedings against both parties, and even if a party is wrongly joined it may prove costly to establish this. Furthermore, if legal expenses are to be indemnified, these should be precisely defined, as with the other liabilities covered by the indemnity. A party granting an indemnity against legal expenses needs to consider whether to set some financial limit on the amount indemnified, or whether to have some right to control the legal proceedings in order to ensure that legal claims are dealt with as economically as possible.

10.64 Typical indemnities

While indemnities are not a panacea and are only as good as the financial position of the party giving them, the following are the kinds of events for which indemnities may prove a wise precaution:

- *late completion:* it is common for late completion to be one contingency covered by some kind of indemnity. This may, for example, take the following form: 'In the event that completion is delayed beyond the completion date for any reason not attributable to default or delay of the Vendor in performing its obligations under this agreement, interest shall be payable to the Vendor in respect of the consideration due under Clause [X] of this Agreement at the rate of [X] per centum over [X] Bank plc's base rate current from time to time, such interest to be calculated on a daily basis and to be compounded at monthly intervals'

- *uncompleted contracts:* the transferee may agree to indemnify the transferor in respect of losses, costs and claims arising from uncompleted contracts, but usually with exemption for such losses, etc which are attributable to acts or omissions of the transferor prior to the completion date

- *general indemnity against acts or omissions:* the sale agreement may include a general indemnity clause which purports to indemnify against losses, costs and claims arising from acts or omissions of the parties. So far as the transferor's indemnity is concerned, the transferee will usually insist that the period covered includes the completion date, although an exemption may be made if the transferor has acted on the express written request of the transferee. In his turn, the transferee will probably undertake to indemnity the transferor against losses which the latter incurs as a result of the former's acts or omissions after the completion date

- *general indemnity about any inaccuracies in the disclosed information:* this clause will indemnify the transferee and be given by the transferor supplying the information

- *specific indemnity for employee liability information:* this clause will indemnify the transferee where no statutory information has been disclosed by the transferor at all prior to completion

- *specific indemnity for redundancy and unfair dismissal claims:* the indemnity clause will deal with who will pay for these claims. In particular, it will be important to stipulate whether the indemnity covers pre- and post-transfer dismissals and for how long; what level of severance pay will be covered by the indemnity clause, e.g. statutory redundancy pay only or enhanced redundancy pay; what types of unfair dismissal claims will be covered, e.g. express and constructive dismissal claims, including claims based on a substantial change to working conditions based on Reg 4(9); the termination procedure that will need to be adopted; and what levels of unfair dismissal compensation will be covered by the indemnity. With specific regard to Reg 4(9), transferors might seek a specific indemnity from transferees to protect against liability arising from the dismissal that is deemed to occur where an employee resigns prior to the transfer as a result of a proposal by the transferee to make substantial changes to working conditions

- *specific indemnity for protective awards under Reg 13:* the penalty for failure to comply with the duty in Reg 13 to inform and consult employees affected by a relevant transfer is up to 13 weeks' pay per affected employee (which is not subject to any cap on weekly pay) – see Chapter 8 under 'Informing and consulting representatives'. In light of this, the parties may wish to address and apportion financial liability for any failure to inform and consult through an appropriately worded indemnity depending on any timescales imposed and by whom

- *specific indemnity for failure to elect 'appropriate representatives' under Reg 14:* the penalty for this failure is set out in Reg 15 – see Chapter 8, under 'Claims for failure to inform or consult'

- *specific indemnity for payment of emoluments:* this will address who is responsible for salaries, expenses, NI contributions, pensions and other benefits up to the completion date. This is a particularly important question where the transferee begins to assume de facto control over the business before completion of the transfer takes place

547

- *'wrong pocket' indemnity:* this will deal with who is to indemnify whom if some employees who should have been on the list of transferring employees are left off the list, or if some personnel (e.g. atypical workers) are on the list of transferring employees but should not be

- *indemnity for specific employment claims:* this clause will deal with who will pay for any identifiable and potential claims such as discrimination, wrongful dismissal and breach of contract before and after the transfer, and for how long.

Case list

(Note that employment tribunal cases are not included in this list.)

A

ADI (UK) Ltd v Willer and ors 2001 IRLR 542, CA   1.72

AEEU and ors v Lyndon Scaffolding plc EAT 1242/99   1.57, 1.120

A and G Tuck Ltd v Bartlett and A and G Tuck (Slough) Ltd 1994 IRLR
   162, EAT   2.148, 7.25

Abbey National plc v Holmes EAT 406/91   3.13

Abels v Administrative Board of the Bedrijfsvereniging voor de Metaalindustrie
   en de Electrotechnische Industrie 1987 2 CMLR 406, ECJ   1.121, 3.66, 6.3, 6.38, 6.34

Abler and ors v Sodexho MM Catering GmbH and anor 2004 IRLR 168, ECJ   1.61, 1.78

Ackinclose and ors v Gateshead Metropolitan Borough Council 2005 IRLR 79, EAT   3.94

Adams and ors v Lancashire County Council and anor 1996 ICR 935, ChD   3.137

Addison and ors v Denholm Ship Management (UK) Ltd and ors 1997 IRLR
   389, CA   1.82

Air Foyle Ltd v Crosby-Clarke   4.104

Alamo Group (Europe) Ltd v Tucker and anor 2003 ICR 829, EAT
                  3.38, 3.118, 3.156, 8.85

Alcan Extrusions v Yates and ors 1996 IRLR 327, EAT   5.48

Alemo-Herron v Parkwood Leisure Ltd 2010 ICR 793, CA   3.89

Alexander and ors v Standard Telephones and Cables Ltd (No.2) 1991 IRLR
   286, QBD   3.12, 3.89

Allen and ors v Amalgamated Construction Co Ltd 2000 ICR 436, ECJ   1.19

Anderson v Pringle of Scotland Ltd 1998 IRLR 64, Ct Sess (Outer House)   3.12

Angus Jowett and Co Ltd v National Union of Tailors and Garment Workers
   1985 ICR 646, EAT   3.127, 3.128

Argyll Training Ltd v Sinclair and anor 2000 IRLR 630, EAT   1.36

Armstrong and ors v Newcastle upon Tyne NHS Hospital Trust EAT 0158 59/04   3.36

Ashford School and anor v Nixon and ors EAT 666/00   8.41

Askew v Governing Body of Clifton Middle School and ors 2000 ICR 286, CA   2.15, 2.81

(1) Associated Newspapers Ltd v Wilson (2) Associated British Ports v Palmer 1995
   ICR 406, HL   3.105

Astle and ors v Cheshire County Council and anor 2005 IRLR 12, EAT   1.59, 1.73, 1.120

B

BET Catering Services Ltd v Ball and ors EAT 637/96   3.95

BSG Property Services v Tuck and ors 1996 IRLR 134, EAT   1.36

Bacica v Muir 2006 IRLR 35, EAT   2.23

Balfour Beatty Power Networks Ltd and anor v Wilcox and ors 2007 IRLR
   63, CA   1.36, 1.79

Banger v Pall Mall Services EAT 395/97   5.54

Banking Insurance and Finance Union v Barclays Bank plc and ors 1987 ICR
   495, EAT   2.84

Barclays Bank plc v O'Brien and ors 1994 ICR 865, CA   3.42

Barnes and ors v Leavesley and ors 2001 ICR 38, EAT   6.13

Baxter and ors v Marks and Spencer EAT 0162/05   8.54

551

G

H

I

J

555

Thomas v Williams 1834 1 Ad & EL 685, Ct of King's Bench 6.11
Thompson and ors v Walon Car Delivery and anor 1997 IRLR 343, EAT 3.72
Thompson v SCS Consulting Ltd and ors EAT 0034/00 3.27, 4.55, 4.131
(1) Tibbitt v Wagon plc and ors; (2) McNabb v Wagon plc and ors EAT 0121–2/02 2.90
Todd v British Midland Airways Ltd 1978 IRLR 370, CA 9.42, 9.44
Todd v Strain and ors EAT 0057/09 8.54, 8.83
Torith Ltd v Flynn EAT 0017/02 2.23
Transport and General Workers' Union v James McKinnon, JR (Haulage) Ltd
  and ors 2001 ICR 1281, EAT 3.118, 8.85
Triton Oliver (Special Products) Ltd v Bromage EAT 709/91 4.78

U

UCATT v Amicus and ors and another case 2009 ICR 852, EAT 8.66
Unicorn Consultancy Services Ltd v Westbrook and ors 2000 IRLR 80, EAT 3.64
Unison v Somerset County Council and ors 2010 ICR 498, EAT 8.25, 8.72
United Guarding Services Ltd v St James Security Group Ltd and anor EAT
  0770/03 2.98, 2.104
University of East London v Hinton 2005 ICR 1260, CA 3.72, 10.10

V

Viggósdóttir v Íslandspóstur HF 2002 IRLR 425, ECJ 2.24, 3.4, 4.26
Visionhire Consumer Electronics Ltd t/a Visionhire v Easton EAT 20/87 2.40, 2.148

W

Walden Engineering Co Ltd v Warrener 1993 IRLR 420, EAT 3.140
Ward Hadaway Solicitors v Love and ors EAT 0471/09 1.114, 1.117
Warner v Adnet Ltd 1998 ICR 1056, CA 4.21
Webb v EMO Air Cargo (UK) Ltd 1993 IRLR 27, HL 7.10
Werhof v Freeway Traffic Systems GmbH and Co KG 2006 IRLR 400, ECJ
  3.4, 3.89, 3.93
Western Excavating (ECC) Ltd v Sharp 1978 ICR 221, CA 2.138, 4.77, 4.104, 5.5
West v Kneels Ltd 1987 ICR 146, EAT 7.16
Wheeler v Patel and anor 1987 ICR 631, EAT 1.134, 2.48, 4.54, 4.71, 6.81
Whent and ors v T Cartledge Ltd 1997 IRLR 153, EAT 3.95
Whitehouse v Chas A Blatchford and Sons Ltd 1999 IRLR 492, CA 4.56, 4.71
Whitewater Leisure Management Ltd v Barnes and ors 2000 IRLR 456, EAT 1.25, 1.29
Whitney v Monster Worldwide Ltd 2010 EWCA Civ 1312, CA 3.75
Williams v Advance Cleaning Services Ltd and anor EAT 0838/04 2.79
Williams v Executive Committee of the North Wales Society for the Blind 1.94
Williams v Lockhart Security Services Ltd EAT 1395/01 1.74, 1.120
Wilson and ors v St Helens Borough Council 1996 IRLR 320, HL 5.18
Worrall v Wilmott Dixon Partnerships Ltd EAT 0521/09 3.90
Wynnwith Engineering Co Ltd v Bennett and ors 2002 IRLR 170, EAT 1.29

Z

Zabaxe Ltd v Nicklin and ors EAT 123/89 2.88

Index

561

564

577

579

583

585